GERMANTOWN

A Military History of the
Battle for Philadelphia, October 4, 1777

Michael C. Harris

Savas Beatie
California

Library of Congress Cataloging-in-Publication Data
Title: Germantown: A Military History of the Battle for Philadelphia, October 4, 1777 / Michael C. Harris.
Other titles: Military history of the Battle for Philadelphia, October 4, 1777
Description: El Dorado Hills, CA : Savas Beatie, LLC, [2020] | Includes bibliographical references and index. | Summary: "On October 4, 1777, the Battle of Germantown represented George Washington's attempt to recapture Philadelphia. Obscured by darkness and a morning fog, Washington launched a surprise attack on the British garrison at Germantown. His attack found initial success and drove the British legions before him. The recapture of the colonial capital seemed within Washington's grasp until poor decisions by the American high command brought about a reversal of fortune and a British victory"— Provided by publisher.
Identifiers: LCCN 2020007690 | ISBN 9781611215199 (hardcover) | ISBN 9781611215205 (ebook)
Subjects: LCSH: Germantown, Battle of, Philadelphia, Pa., 1777.
Classification: LCC E241.G3 H27 2020 | DDC 974.8/03—dc23
LC record available at https://lccn.loc.gov/2020007690

First edition, first printing

Savas Beatie LLC
989 Governor Drive, Suite 102
El Dorado Hills, CA 95762
Phone: 916-941-6896 / (E-mail) sales@savasbeatie.com

Savas Beatie titles are available at special discounts for bulk purchases in the United States. Contact us for more details.

Proudly published, printed, and warehoused in the United States of America.

Jacket: The Attack upon the Chew House, 1898. Illustration for *The Story of the Revolution*, by Henry Cabot Lodge, in *Scribner's Magazine*, June 1898, NY Howard Pyle (1853–1911). Oil on canvas. 24 × 36 1/4 inches. Delaware Art Museum, Museum Purchase, 1912.

To my grandfather CSM Wilbert "Lum" Harris,
who introduced me to military history.

Table of Contents

Table of Contents (continued)

Maps have been placed throughout the book for the convenience of the reader.

Preface

My first book, *Brandywine: A Military History of the Battle that Lost Philadelphia but Saved America, September 11, 1777*, appeared six years ago. Once it was finished I was certain I would not embark on the adventure of writing another.

I was deeply invested in the Brandywine story and believed it was my mission to dispel the many myths surrounding the battle. Speaking with people at events and book signings confirmed that there was a deep desire for well-documented military studies on American Revolution topics. Many gracious enough to come and hear a presentation, get a book signed, or join me on a battlefield tour expressed a desire for a follow-up work. I politely declined. When the urge hit, however, I would dig into my research files now and again and discover that I had collected a substantial body of research on the phase of the war that picked up where the Brandywine story ended. The months passed, I proposed the idea to my publisher, and the result is now in your hands: *Germantown: A Military History of the Battle for Philadelphia, October 4, 1777.*

Like Brandywine, there were more than enough firsthand accounts to write a solid monograph on Germantown, which erupted just three weeks later on October 4, 1777. Germantown was one of the war's largest battles and another in a string of American losses, but there was less written about Germantown than there had been for Brandywine. As I came to discover, this is often true for American losses—especially those fought on battlefields not under the care and protection of the National Park Service—including, but not limited to, Long Island, White Plains, Brandywine, Germantown, and Camden.

Despite the defeat, the American army remained in high spirits in the days and weeks following the battle, and many of its members believed the war was nearly won. Some referenced the hand of God in the outcome. "Unfortunate as was the issue of the battle at Germantown, it manifested the unsubdued, though broken spirit, of the American army; and taught the enemy to expect renewal of combat, whenever adequacy of force or fitness of opportunity should authorize repetition of battle," explained Henry "Light-Horse Harry" Lee, one of Washington's cavalry officers. "It gave, too, animation to the country at large, exciting in congress, and in the people, invigorated zeal in the great cause in which they were engaged." Major Henry Miller agreed. "Our army is in higher spirits than ever . . . being convinced from the first officer to the soldier, that our quitting the field must be ascribed to other causes than the force of the enemy: for even they acknowledged that we fled from victory. . . . We hope to meet them soon again," Miller continued, "and, with the assistance of Providence, to restore to our suffering citizens their possessions and homes."[1]

Germantown was overshadowed not only by Brandywine but by the stunning American victory at Saratoga just days later. Most works relegate it to a few paragraphs. William Gordon's 1788 history of America's establishment covered one of the largest attacks of the war in just four pages. "The British officers acknowledged soon after this affair, that it was the severest blow they had met with; that it was planned with judgment and executed with spirit; and that they were at a loss for its not being followed up, unless it was for want of ammunition," wrote the author. At the end of the basic battle summary Gordon succinctly concluded, "General Washington is of opinion that the Americans retreated at an instant when victory was declaring in their favor. The royal army was indeed completely surprised; and appearances in the beginning were evidently on the side of the former."[2]

More than 40 years would elapse before another book offered anything significant on Germantown. Most writers focused on the morning fog and the fight at Cliveden. "The principal causes of the failure of this well concerted enterprise," wrote Charles Botta in his 1845 history of the Revolution, "were the extreme haziness of the weather; which was so thick, that the Americans could neither discover the situation nor movements of the British army, nor yet those of their own . . . and, finally, the unexpected resistance of Musgrave, who found means, in a critical moment, to transform a mere house into an impregnable fortress." That

1 Henry Lee, *Memoirs of the War in the Southern Department of the United States*, 2 vols. (Philadelphia, 1812), vol. 1, 28-29. "A Memoir of General Henry Miller," Henry Miller Watts, ed., in *The Pennsylvania Magazine of History and Biography* (Philadelphia, 1888), vol. 12, 427, hereafter cited as PMHB.

2 William Gordon, *The History of the Rise, Progress, and Establishment of the Independence of the United States of America*, 4 vols. (London, 1788), vol. 2, 526.

same year Jacob Neff published a history of armed forces in North America and regurgitated Botta's summary word-for-word.[3]

Two years later in 1847 George Lippard poetically described the fighting at Cliveden by assigning a part in the action to Washington himself that never occurred:

> 'Follow me who will!' he cried, and in a moment, his steed of iron grey was careering over the sod, littered with ghastly corpses, while the air overhead was alive with the music of bullets, and earth beneath was flung against the war steed's flanks by the cannon ball. . . . At every step, a dead man with a livid face turned upward; little pools of blood crimsoning the lawn, torn fragments of attire scattered over the sod; on every side hurrying bodies of the foemen, while terrible and unremitting, the fire flashing from the windows of Chew's House, flung a lurid glare over the battle-field. . . . Washington dashed over the lawn; he approached the house, and every man of his train held his breath. Bullets were whistling over their heads, cannon balls playing round their horses' feet, yet their leader kept on his way of terror. A single glance at the house, with its volleys of flame flashing from every window, and he turned to the north to regain the American lines, but the fog and smoke gathered round him, and he found his horse entangled amid the enclosures of the cattle-pen to the north of the mansion.[4]

Lippard continued his exaggerated account of Washington:

> 'Leap your horses—' cried Washington to the brave men around him—'Leap your horses and save yourselves!' And in a moment, amid the mist and gloom his officers leaped the northern enclosure of the cattle-pen, and rode forward to the American line, scarcely able to discover their path in the dense gloom that gathered around them. They reached the American lines, and to their horror, discovered that Washington was not among their band. He had not leaped the fence of the cattle-pen; with the feeling of a true warrior, he was afraid of injuring his gallant steed, by this leap in the dark. . . . He rose proudly in the stirrups, he placed his hand gently on the neck of his steed, he glanced proudly round him, and then the noble horse sprang forward with a sudden

3 Charles Botta, *History of the War of the Independence of the United States of America*, George Alexander Otis, trans. (Cooperstown, NY, 1845), 47. Jacob Neff, *The Army and Navy of America: Containing a View of the Heroic Adventures, Battles, Naval Engagements, Remarkable Incidents, and Glorious Achievements in the Cause of Freedom* (Philadelphia, 1845), 348-353.

4 Edward G. Lengel, *Inventing George Washington: America's Founder, in Myth & Memory* (New York, 2011), 39.

leap, and the mist rising for a moment disclosed the form of Washington, to the vision of the opposing armies.[5]

In the 1850s, as the country tore itself apart over the issue of slavery, Republicans and Democrats conjured up Revolutionary heroes to support their cause. In October 1856, members of the recently formed Republican Party held a "grand gathering . . . on the ground where the Revolutionary Battle of Germantown was fought" and invoked "a time hallowed in our country's history, [when] patriots poured out their blood in a struggle for freedom." As these Republicans urged their followers to fight for freedom again, they hoped the grounds of Germantown "will ring with the crys of freedom for [Bleeding] Kansas."[6]

In 1858, Lord Mahon praised the effort of the Continentals in his *History of England*: "Yet defeat though it was, this battle brought no discredit, but the contrary, to the American troops, and the American commander. It showed that neither their spirit, nor their strength, had been broken by the reverses they had sustained . . . It proved them to want only that discipline and self-confidence which longer warfare was certain to produce."[7]

During the Civil War the country looked toward Revolutionary heroes as a source of patriotism. Very few veterans of the Revolution were still alive, and Reverend Elias Hillard set out to interview those he could find before they died. Hillard, wrote one modern historian, "was from a school of thought that strove not to chronicle events explicitly, but instead to personalize them and derive allegory from them. The nation, divided by civil war, needed heroes to instill a sense of unity and national pride. It also needed to stimulate the heroism that would be required to heal the still-bleeding nation." Men like Washington, Jefferson, Adams, Madison, Franklin, and many other famous "demigods of the nation's founding were gone," and the contemporaries of Hillard's time, including Abraham Lincoln and Ulysses S. Grant, "had yet to transcend the controversies and contempt that befall living men of accomplishment." The few remaining men who had lived and fought through the Revolution were "true symbols of a bygone glorious cause. No

5 Ibid., 40.

6 Thomas A. Chambers, *Memories of War: Visiting Battlegrounds and Bonefields in the Early American Republic* (Ithaca, NY, 2012), 178.

7 Lord Mahon, *History of England from the Peace of Utrecht to the Peace of Versailles, 1713-1783*, 7 vols. (London, 1858), vol. 6, 163.

matter how modest their contributions, and no matter how divisive the actual revolution had been, veterans of that conflict were ideal candidates to be made perfect in the eyes of a public hungry for heroes." In search of his allegory, Hillard stretched the truth when chronicling the stories of these living heroes.[8]

George Bancroft's 1866 history of the United States is one of the earliest accounts to tie the importance of Germantown to the French alliance that followed. "The renewal of an attack so soon after the defeat at the Brandywine, and its partial success, inspirited congress and the army. In Europe," stressed Bancroft, "it convinced the cabinet of the king of France that the independence of America was assured."[9]

By the end of the 19th century, changes affecting America influenced how the story of the Revolution was told. The transformation from a collection of rural economies into an industrialized nation after the Civil War tarnished the idealistic view many Americans had about their country. The earlier period glorified war and emphasized the greatness of heroes like Washington and Lafayette. The carnage wrought by the Civil War, however, went a long way toward eliminating that mindset. Postwar industrialization, coupled with the massive influx of European immigrants, brought class struggles to the forefront of American consciousness. The writing of history started emphasizing the role of the common man rather than heroes or the upper class.[10]

On the centennial of the battle, newspaper editor Alfred Lambdin delivered an address that doubled as an early account of the battle. Lambdin was one of the first to acknowledge the battle was more extensive than just the fighting that swirled around Cliveden. "The Battle of Germantown . . . was very much more than a contest with a half dozen companies for the possession of a country house," he insisted. "It was a contest for the possession of a widely-extended and strongly posted line, between two armies; not large, indeed, according to our modern ideas, but such as not often met face to face in the war for independence."[11]

8 Don N. Hagist, *The Revolution's Last Men: The Soldiers Behind the Photographs* (Yardley, PA, 2015), xviii-xix.

9 George Bancroft, *History of the United States, from the Discovery of the American Continent*, 8 vols. (Boston, MA, 1866), vol. 9, 428.

10 Michael C. Harris, *Brandywine: A Military History of the Battle that Lost Philadelphia but Saved America, September 11, 1777* (El Dorado Hills, CA, 2014), xi.

11 Alfred C. Lambdin, "Battle of Germantown," in *PMHB* (Philadelphia, PA, 1877), vol. 1, 369.

More than three decades passed before Francis Heyl's *The Battle of Germantown* in 1908. "Splendid was the material which made up the rank and file of the American army at Germantown, the flower of the young manhood of New England, Pennsylvania, New Jersey, Maryland, Virginia and North Carolina," he penned. "All honor to the brave and patriot soldiers who periled their lives at Germantown to maintain the liberties of their country. . . ."[12]

Four years later British statesman and author Sir George Otto Trevelyan continued the theme that Germantown had influenced the French court. "That the battle had been fought unsuccessfully was of small importance when weighed against the fact that it had been fought at all," stressed Trevelyan. "Eminent generals, and statesmen of sagacity, in every European Court were profoundly impressed by learning that a new army, raised within the year, and undaunted by a series of recent disasters, had assailed a victorious enemy in his own quarters, and had only been repulsed after a sharp and dubious conflict." A handbook published in 1927 for the 150th anniversary of the battle also mentioned the influence on France: "The military results of the battle were a disappointment to Washington and others, still they did not dishearten the rank and file of the army, who, in a day or two, were hoping for another brush with the enemy. The political effect was decidedly favorable to the American cause, eventually bringing France into the war as an ally of the struggling republic."[13]

Christopher Ward's outstanding *The War of the Revolution*, a two-volume history published in 1952, devoted nine pages to Germantown and summarized the fighting as "unquestionably a defeat for the Americans; but, as has happened more than once in warfare, that fact was of small consequence in comparison with its ulterior effects"—yet another reference to the coming French alliance.[14]

John Reed's *Campaign to Valley Forge: July 1, 1777-December 19, 1777* made its appearance in 1965. The study is now considered a classic and stands up against many later monographs. Germantown has its own 24-page chapter. While Reed gets some basic facts incorrect his sources are mostly documented—unlike some newer works on the campaign. Like others, Reed connects Germantown to Saratoga: "Most wars have a single node, or turning point. The American

12 Francis Heyl, *The Battle of Germantown* (Philadelphia, PA, 1908), 63.

13 George Otto Trevelyan, *The American Revolution*, 4 vols. (New York, NY, 1912), vol. 4, 249; Edward B. Phillips, essay in *150th Anniversary of the Battle of Germantown: October 1st to 4th* (Germantown, PA, 1927), n.p.

14 Christopher Ward, *The War of the Revolution*, 2 vols. (New York, 1952), vol. 1, 371.

Revolution had several. Each time the cause seemed lost, some magnificent event lifted the cause into being again. The combination of Germantown and Saratoga was one of these events."[15]

The war's bicentennial saw a resurgence in the publication of books and articles on the American Revolution. Only two dealt in any meaningful way with Germantown. John Pancake's *1777: The Year of the Hangman* covered Germantown in just six pages, provided few details, and offered no new conclusions. Historian John Jackson researched and wrote on the British occupation of Philadelphia and the fighting along the Delaware River and provided a 22-page chapter on Germantown in his *The British Army in Philadelphia: 1778-1778*. Jackson's study covered most aspects of the battle, but lacked eyewitness accounts. "Much has been written about the rashness of Washington's strategy, the elaborate plan, and the impossibility of coordinating attacks by the various columns," wrote Jackson. "Washington's plan undoubtedly would have taxed the abilities of the most veteran soldiers; in spite of the reverses, it did not depress the average American soldier."[16]

Despite the size and scale of the engagement, W. J. Wood's well-received and reviewed *Battles of the Revolutionary War, 1775-1781* (1990) does not even mention Germantown. Wood believed Brandywine and Saratoga overshadowed it into insignificance. David Martin's 1993 *The Philadelphia Campaign: June 1777-July 1778* includes an 18-page chapter on the battle but lacks documentation and misrepresents several aspects of the contending forces. *Angel in the Whirlwind: The Triumph of the American Revolution*, a 1997 book by Benson Bobrick, briefly mentions Germantown though it does connect the battle to the French alliance. "In Europe, the battle was taken as proof of the Americans' ability to win the war," explained Bobrick. "As a result, there began an inexorable shift in the policy and attitude of the European states." Finally, Gregory Edgar's 1998 *The Philadelphia Campaign: 1777-1778* relied on undocumented block quotes of battle participants in its 15-page chapter on the engagement. None of these works did anything to further the understanding and history of the Battle of Germantown.[17]

15 John F. Reed, *Campaign to Valley Forge: July 1, 1777-December 19, 1777* (Philadelphia, PA, 1965), 239.

16 John S. Pancake, *1777: The Year of the Hangman* (Tuscaloosa, AL, 1977), 192-198; John W. Jackson, *With the British Army in Philadelphia* (San Rafael, CA, 1979), 49-50.

17 W. J. Wood, *Battles of the Revolutionary War, 1775-1781* (Chapel Hill, NC, 1990), 92-114. David G. Martin, *The Philadelphia Campaign: June 1777-July 1778* (Conshohocken, PA, 1993), 99-120. Benson Bobrick, *Angel in the Whirlwind: The Triumph of the American Revolution* (New York,

Germantown has been the subject of just two previous book-length treatments. Of those, Donald Brownlow's 1955 study *A Documentary History of the Battle of Germantown* is by far the best. It is also a rare book. The only copy I have ever seen was given to me as a gift by an admirer of my Brandywine book. Brownlow's work is well-researched and evenhanded for its age and provides both British and American accounts. His conclusion includes this summary: "The bright stars of Trenton and Princeton were dulled by the gloomy atmosphere rendered by the succession of defeats, Brandywine, Paoli, and Germantown. However, the victory at Saratoga boosted the morale in the colonies."[18]

The only other book on the battle appeared 39 years later than Brownlow's. Thomas McGuire's 1994 *The Surprise at Germantown: October 4th, 1777*, a short study that focuses mainly on the fighting around Cliveden to the detriment of other important aspects of the battle.[19]

McGuire improved upon his earlier work in the second installment of his two-volume set on the Philadelphia Campaign, which appeared in 2007. In *The Philadelphia Campaign: Germantown and the Roads to Valley Forge*, McGuire went a long way toward rectifying the aspects of the battle he had neglected in his first installment by devoting 82 pages to Germantown. He is an impeccable researcher, but a lack of quality maps make it more than difficult to understand the ebb and flow of his narrative and the complex action it attempts to describe.[20]

A New Study

An evenhanded in-depth study of Germantown is long overdue. In addition to being one of the largest battles of the war, it is also significant because it was the first time George Washington launched an assault against the main British army in North America. But the once rolling fields over which Continental and British soldiers struggled have been mostly destroyed by urban blight. Now engulfed by Philadelphia, Germantown is no longer the small village surrounded by fields and

NY, 1997), 269. Gregory T. Edgar, *The Philadelphia Campaign: 1777-1778* (Bowie, MD, 1998), 55-70.

18 Donald Grey Brownlow, *A Documentary History of the Battle of Germantown* (Germantown, PA, 1955), 67-68.

19 Thomas J. McGuire, *The Surprise of Germantown October 4th, 1777* (Gettysburg, PA, 1994), 37-84.

20 Thomas J. McGuire, *The Philadelphia Campaign: Germantown and the Roads to Valley Forge*, 2 vols. (Mechanicsburg, PA, 2007), vol. 2, 43-124.

woodlots that it was in 1777. Researching on the ground to analyze the terrain is almost impossible and one more reason why the battle has been mostly neglected.

My hope is that this study satisfies those looking for the most recent research coupled with good maps, insightful footnotes, and a complete order of battle. While the focus of this book is the Battle of Germantown, it is impossible to fully understand that engagement without knowing what transpired between Brandywine and Germantown. As a result, the first section of the books introduces readers to the main cast of characters and the movements and clashes of the armies, including the Battle of the Clouds, the Battle of Paoli, and several other skirmishes including the early fighting along the Delaware River (including Billingsport and Fort Mifflin). All of this is a prelude to Germantown. This period is also when Washington's men became battle-hardened troops on their way to the army's great awakening at Valley Forge that winter. Without this understanding, a complete picture of what happened at Germantown and why would be impossible.

Acknowledgments

An undertaking of this magnitude requires the help of many people around the world. If I fail to include your name, please know I appreciate deeply your help in making this book a reality.

I would like to collectively thank the staffs at the following repositories: the Historical Society of Pennsylvania, the Library of Congress, the National Archives, the Massachusetts Historical Society, the Chicago Historical Society, the British Library, the Historical Society of Delaware, Durham University in England, the Princeton University Library, the Maryland Historical Society, the Historical Society of Montgomery County Pennsylvania, the Virginia Historical Society, the New York Public Library, the National Library of Scotland, Morristown National Historical Park, the William Clements Library, the North Carolina Department of Archives and History, the University of Delaware Library, the archives at Windsor Castle, the First City Troop Archives, the University of Virginia Library, the Harlan Crow Library, the Duke University Library, the New York Historical Society, the American Philosophical Society, the Canadian Archives, and Alnwick Castle.

While many people have assisted over the years with tracking down sources, a personal thank you needs to go out to Kathie Ludwig—the faithful librarian of the David Library of the American Revolution in Washington Crossing, Pennsylvania.

Likewise, Carl Klase, curator at Pennypacker Mills Historic Site in Montgomery County, Pennsylvania, took the time out of a busy day to pull sources from archives for my perusal and use. Bruce Knapp and Jim Christ of the Paoli

Battlefield Historical Park spent more than one occasion discussing their site with me. Historian Robert Selig was kind enough to help me track down Hessian sources on the campaign. Researcher John Rees helped with sources on the New Jersey militia. Berle Schiller kindly gifted me copies of Donald Brownlow's rare books on Paoli and Germantown. The staffs of Wyck, Grumblethorpe, Cliveden, and Rittenhouse Town (all historic properties in Germantown) are thanked for providing my family and I access during the closed season. Lastly, a big thank you goes to Chris Reardon for showing me the locations for the Battle of the Clouds and for providing invaluable resources on that action.

While I have met many people because of my Brandywine work, I want to specifically acknowledge two of them: Bruce Venter for his support and encouragement, and Rob Ayer, who invited me along on a kayaking trip down the Brandywine, which has since become an annual event for us.

Several people were kind enough to read the manuscript in part or whole, including Bill Welsch of the American Revolutionary Round Table of Richmond, Virginia. Also, Eric Wittenberg, a renowned author and historian in his own right, took time to read an early version, as did Jim Christ of the Paoli Battlefield. Edward Alexander deserves high praise and thanks for producing the fine maps, and Lee Merideth for the index.

I would like to thank everyone at Savas Beatie for their often overlooked efforts. SB's marketing and promotions team, including Sarah Keeney, Lisa Murphy, Sarah Closson, and Donna Endacott, is unparalleled, and Joel Manuel did a wonderful job helping me find mistakes while proofreading. Managing Director Theodore P. Savas was amazingly supportive throughout the process of my first book and has equally supportive with me every step of the way on this one. To think I have finished two books seems like a dream, and that is all because of Ted.

Lastly, I would be remiss if I did not thank my family. My son Nate was just a toddler when my Brandywine book was released. He gamely traveled with us to places like King's Mountain, Guilford Courthouse, and Fort Ticonderoga as I journeyed around the country promoting my work. He has had the chance to see parts of America many have not by the age of seven. Many hours have been taken from him as I sat at the computer writing. Many times he came down and asked, "Are you working on your book?" And a special thanks to my wife Michelle who endures more than should be asked to bear. She too has come along on many of the promotional trips, helped find resources, traipsed many of these long-lost sites of fighting with me, and helped read and edit this work. All you have done over the years to help keep the house running and my sanity intact is appreciated more than you know, and I love you.

Note on Sources and Methods

This work relies heavily on primary source material. Spelling and grammar acceptable in the 18th century would not pass muster in any classroom today. However, to preserve and distill the flavor of the period, I have refrained from correcting sentence structure and misspellings when directly quoting them. I also have avoided the use of "sic," which interrupts the flow of the narrative. Though a united Germany did not exist in 1777, both "German" and "Hessian" are used interchangeably to identify the various Germanic troops who served with Howe's army. While most of those troops were true Hessians, there was one company of Anspachers as well.

Dramatis Personae

William Alexander, Lord Stirling

Lord Stirling was one of Washington's senior commanders. He was born in 1726 in New York. An accomplished mathematician and astronomer, Alexander served during the French and Indian War as an aide-de-camp to Governor Shirley of Massachusetts. Later, while in London, he attempted to claim the vacant title of Earl of Stirling. Although only partially successful in his effort, he was known to most thereafter as Lord Stirling. Once back in the colonies he became the surveyor-general for East Jersey and helped found Columbia University.

Library of Congress

He began the war as a colonel in the New Jersey militia, and in 1776 was appointed brigadier general. After he was captured in the fighting on Long Island, an exchange was worked out for Montfort Browne, the governor of Nassau in the Bahamas, who had been captured in a naval action. Stirling rejoined the colonial effort and served with Washington at Trenton. Stirling had a mixed record thus far in the Philadelphia Campaign. His division was caught off guard at Short Hills in northern New Jersey, but performed admirably under difficult circumstances at Brandywine. He commanded the army's reserve division, part of John Sullivan's column, at Germantown.

John Armstrong

Armstrong was born in 1717 in Ireland, was educated as a civil engineer, and emigrated to Pennsylvania to work as a surveyor for the Penn family. He laid out the town of Carlisle and became the surveyor of Cumberland County. During the French and Indian War, he commanded the Pennsylvania contingent on the 1758 Forbes Expedition to capture Fort Duquesne in western Pennsylvania. When the Revolution broke out, he was sent to Charleston to help lay out the defensive works there. However, he returned home to take command of the Pennsylvania militia. His command failed the army at Brandywine, but he and his men were looking forward to redeeming themselves at Germantown.

Yale University Art Gallery

Charles Cornwallis

Lord Cornwallis played a major part in the Germantown campaign. He was born in London in 1738 and educated at Eton and Cambridge University, joined the Grenadier Guards in 1756, and attended the military academy at Turin, Italy. Cornwallis served in Germany during the Seven Years' War and later, like William Howe, became a member of the House of Lords. Although he voted against the Stamp Act and had some sympathy for the colonists, Cornwallis volunteered to serve in America. He took part in the battles of Long Island, the second battle of Trenton, and Princeton. One teenage Philadelphia resident described Cornwallis as "of the ordinary height, square built, one of his eyes was habitually closed, vulgarly termed cock-eyed." Cornwallis performed well at Brandywine and the Battle of the Clouds. He was in Philadelphia, seven miles from Germantown, when Washington attacked.[1]

1 Jacob Mordecai, "Addenda to Watson's Annals of Philadelphia," in *The Pennsylvania Magazine of History and Biography* (Philadelphia, PA, 1974), vol. 98, 165.

Johann Ewald

Ewald, a jaeger captain, played a major role at Brandywine and was in action again at Germantown. Born in 1744 in the Hessian city of Cassel, Johann was the son of a postal employee and a merchant's daughter. He entered the military at age 16 during the Seven Years' War and fought across modern-day Germany, sustaining a wound in the leg in 1761. A drunken argument in 1770 led to a duel with a friend and the loss of his left eye, which he covered with an eye patch. Ewald was promoted to captain in the Hessian Jaeger Corps in 1774. He arrived in America during late summer in 1776, and established himself as a good and dependable officer. His jaeger company had been engaged in the fighting around New York in late 1776. In May 1777 Ewald suffered an injury in a skirmish near Bound Brook, and for the ensuing six months was forced to perform his duty from the back of a horse. In keeping with his service thus far, Ewald would see his share of combat on October 4, 1777. His Diary of the American War offers valuable insight into British operations during the war.[2]

Wikipedia

Joseph Galloway

Prior to the war, Philadelphia aristocrat Joseph Galloway was one of the most powerful politicians in Pennsylvania and a member of the First Continental Congress. Galloway was born to Quaker parents in Maryland in 1731, and married Grace Growden at Christ Church in 1753. During the years between the French and Indian War and the American Revolution, Galloway, along with Benjamin Franklin, was a prime mover in creating the Assembly Party in Pennsylvania. Galloway eventually rose to become the speaker of the Pennsylvania Provincial Assembly.

Tensions with Britain, meanwhile, continued to escalate. When Galloway took his seat in the First Continental Congress in 1775, most members hoped for reconciliation with the

2 Johann Ewald, *Diary of the American War: A Hessian Journal: Captain Johann Ewald,* translated and edited by Joseph P. Tustin (New Haven, CT, 1979).

Wikipedia

crown. To that end, Galloway offered a "Plan of Union." The proposal was vetoed and stricken from the record, an embarrassment that did not sit well with a man of his ambition and standing.

Once Congress pushed for independence, Galloway fled Philadelphia to New York City, where the main British Army was located. Using his social standing, he worked through Ambrose Serle, secretary to Admiral Richard Howe, and gained an audience with Gen. William Howe, who consulted with Galloway during the planning stages of his campaign to capture Philadelphia. When the British troops began that operation in the late spring of 1777, Galloway was with them. He recruited local guides who helped Howe at Brandywine and eventually at the Battle of the Clouds and Paoli. Galloway was rewarded with a position in the provisional government of Philadelphia when the British took the city. One Philadelphia resident described Galloway as "of the ordinary size, rather dark complexioned, a busy, restless politician."[3]

James Grant

Author

Widely disliked by the Americans for advocating the use of draconian measures against them, British Gen. James Grant was a veteran of the French and Indian War, and a former governor of Florida. Grant, born in 1720 in northern Scotland, began his military career in 1744 by purchasing a commission in 1744 in the Royal Scots. He fought with that regiment at the Battle of Fontenoy in present-day Belgium in 1745. After serving in the colonies before the Revolution, he rose to command the 55th Regiment of Foot. In 1776, he served under General Howe as a division

3 Mordecai, "Addenda," 144.

commander during the New York Campaign, and played a key role in the fighting on Long Island. Grant played a minor role at Brandywine (though his writings imply otherwise), but would command one-half of the army at Germantown.

Nathanael Greene

Nathanael Greene was not a healthy man. Born in 1742 into a Rhode Island Quaker family, a childhood accident left him with a life-long limp. He also suffered from asthma and endured a painful spot in his right eye from a smallpox inoculation. None of these issues slowed him down. Greene sold toys to earn money to buy books and was the owner of an iron fabrication business before the war. After serving with a Rhode Island militia company, he was commissioned a brigadier general in 1775 and given command of all of the state's troops.

Yale University Art Gallery

His first field test was the successful defensive action at Harlem Heights in September 1776, one of the few bright spots of the New York Campaign. Greene offered bad advice and was responsible for the disaster at Fort Washington, but redeemed himself by leading a wing of the army well at both Trenton and Princeton. Greene also performed admirably at Brandywine by covering the army's retreat. Washington trusted him implicitly and gave him command of nearly half the army for the assault on Germantown.

Alexander Hamilton

The young and opinionated Hamilton was born an illegitimate child (likely in 1755) in the Caribbean. He commanded a New York militia artillery battery throughout the 1776 campaign. His capabilities caught Washington's attention, and the commander added Hamilton to his staff as an aide-de-camp in March 1777. Hamilton's fluency in French helped Washington translate important documents. Still a member of Washington's staff at Germantown, he would play a leading role in a skirmish at a place called Valley Forge in the coming weeks.

Moses Hazen

A native of Haverhill, Massachusetts, Hazen had a great deal of combat experience by the time his regiment deployed north of Philadelphia. He had fought in the French and Indian War as the commander of a ranger company at Crown Point, Louisburg, and Sainte-Foy before settling in Canada. From 1771 to 1773, Hazen served as a lieutenant in the British 44th Regiment of Foot and married a Catholic woman. He was a prominent Canadian landowner when the Revolution broke out in 1775, and the British seized his land and imprisoned him. Hazen joined Richard Montgomery's advance into Canada in 1775, and was commissioned a colonel in January 1776 to raise a regiment of Canadians. The regiment, which became known as "Congress's Own," was involved in the retreat from Montreal in the spring of 1776. It later joined Washington on Long Island and wintered at Morristown with the rest of the army. Despite his warnings of the British flank march at Brandywine, his regiment was routed with the rest of John Sullivan's division. The lack of general officers elevated Hazen to the command of John Sullivan's division at Germantown.

Richard Howe

Royal Museums Greenwich

Admiral Richard Howe, Gen. William Howe's older brother, was in command of the British fleet in North America. Howe joined the navy at 13 and served throughout the War of the Austrian Succession and the Seven Years' War. Like his brother, the admiral was not unsympathetic to the American cause, which may have influenced how he employed his naval power. His blockade of the American coast proved ineffective. It was mostly his responsibility to open the Delaware River to British shipping after disembarking his brother's army in northeastern Maryland.

William Howe

General William Howe, Washington's chief antagonist in the 1777 campaign, was born in England in 1729 and entered the army in 1746 as an officer in a dragoon regiment. He fought in the War of the Austrian Succession, leading the light infantry under James Wolfe during the latter's Canadian operations during the Seven Years' War, and later served in Havana. Howe was elected to Parliament in 1761 and went on to train the army's light infantry companies. In June 1775, Howe commanded the unimaginative yet determined assaults against Bunker (Breed's) Hill near Boston, and was elevated to overall command in North America that October. His 1776 New York Campaign nearly (and likely could have) destroyed the Continental Army and ended the war at that time. Howe's offensive plan at Brandywine held Washington in place while flanking his right and worked to perfection. He failed to immediately follow up on the victory and lost another opportunity to seriously cripple his opponent. The capture of Philadelphia may have lulled Howe into a sense of false security.

Library of Congress

Henry Knox

Born in 1750, Knox lost two fingers in a musket accident early in life. The native Bostonian later opened a bookstore and became well-read on military issues in general, and ordnance in particular. During the winter of 1775-1776 he orchestrated a daring removal of artillery from Fort Ticonderoga, New York, and oversaw its transfer to Boston—a bold success that earned him Washington's gratitude and a promotion to head the Continental artillery. Knox helped improve the defenses of Connecticut and Rhode Island, and after Trenton was promoted to brigadier general. During the winter of 1776-1777, Washington commissioned Knox to raise a brigade of artillery. By 1777 he had been in command of the Continental artillery for more than a year. He only played a minor role at

Library of Congress

Brandywine, but he had Washington's ear. He would speak into it at the most inopportune time, with the Chew house in sight, at Germantown.

Wilhelm Knyphausen

National Archives

Baron Wilhelm Reichsfreiherr zu Inn-und Knyphausen was born in 1716 in Luxembourg. He became a general in Hesse, but traditionally served the Prussian kings. In 1776, he was sent to North America as second in command of the hired German troops, and the following year, at age 61, became their overall commander. Knyphausen was instrumental in the assault on Fort Washington on upper Manhattan Island (near the current site of the George Washington Bridge), and performed admirably at Brandywine and the Battle of the Clouds. He and his men were camped west of Germantown when the Americans poured out of the fog.

John Laurens

National Archives

Laurens was born in 1754 in Charleston, South Carolina, the son of Henry Laurens, who would become president of the Continental Congress during the Revolution. Money gave the younger Laurens access to a private tutor as a child. After being educated in Geneva, Switzerland, Laurens spent six years in England as a law student and entered the profession in London. He returned to Charleston in early 1777 and traveled north to offer his services to the army. That August, Washington invited him to join his staff as a volunteer aide. Laurens proved quite useful to

Washington. Like Hamilton, he was fluent in French. He would prove his reckless disregard for his own safety at Germantown.

William Maxwell

Maxwell allegedly was born in Ireland about 1733, but was living with his family in New Jersey by 1747. The Scotch-Irish immigrant with a thick accent played a prominent role during the mid-century Indian wars and later became an ardent supporter of colonial rights. Maxwell served as a militia officer during the French and Indian War and took command of the 2nd New Jersey Battalion when the Revolution erupted. He served as a member of the New Jersey Provincial Congress in 1775-1776, and accompanied the Canadian Expedition in 1776. In October of that year he was appointed brigadier general and took part in Washington's successful late December campaign.

Maxwell made a reputation for himself during the various skirmishes in northern New Jersey during the winter and spring of 1777. Washington gave him the command of the light infantry in August 1777, and he led them at Cooch's Bridge and Brandywine. He fought well at the latter battle despite later criticism. The light infantry brigade was disbanded shortly thereafter, and Maxwell lost his independent command. He would lead a New Jersey brigade in Lord Stirling's reserve division at Germantown.

Alexander McDougall

McDougall was born in Scotland in 1732 and moved to New York six years later. Following a stint as a privateer during the French and Indian War, McDougall became a merchant and importer. By the eve of the Revolution he was an ardent patriot in the protest movement, and began the war as colonel of the 1st New York Regiment. After taking part in the New York campaign in 1776, McDougall's brigade formed part of the force holding the Hudson Highlands early in the 1777 campaign. His brigade joined Washington in time for Germantown and was assigned to Nathanael Greene's column.

Wikipedia

Thomas Mifflin

Wikipedia

The 33-year-old Mifflin had been appointed quartermaster general of the Continental Army in August 1775. He broke with Washington in late 1776 and helped lead the movement to replace the Virginian as commander of the army. Mifflin's lackadaisical effort in 1777 led to many of Washington's supply problems. The position of quartermaster general necessarily entailed that Mifflin be fully informed of the army's movements, but by 1777 he was often absent from head- quarters. As a result, both the army's mobility and its health were hampered.

John Montresor

Montresor was born in 1736 in Gibraltar and spent his early life there and on Minorca. During the late 1740s, Montresor attended Westminster School in England and learned the principles of engineering from his father, who was a military engineer. During the French and Indian War, he came to North America with his father and served as an ensign in the 48th Regiment of Foot. After the war, Montresor helped prepare maps of Acadia (a region that today includes parts of Quebec and Maine), the St. Lawrence River, and the Kennebec River in northern New England. The capable engineer designed and built Fort Niagara and Fort Erie. He was in Boston when the Revolution began and took part in the New York Campaign before accompanying Howe on the 1777 Philadelphia Campaign. Prior to the war, Montresor helped design and build Fort Mifflin on Mud Island, an experience that

Wikipedia

would prove valuable to Howe later in the campaign. He left behind his memoirs, which were published in the late 1800s as "The Montresor Journals."[4]

Peter Muhlenberg

John Peter Gabriel Muhlenberg, born in Philadelphia, was the son of Henry Muhlenberg, the founder of Lutheranism in America. He graduated from the College of Philadelphia, settled in the Shenandoah Valley in 1772, served as chair of the House of Burgess's Committee of Safety in 1775, and was a member of Virginia's Provincial Convention in 1776. Muhlenberg entered the Continental Army as colonel of the 8th Virginia Regiment. He was part of Nathanael Greene's large column at Germantown, and commanded Greene's division that day.

Wikipedia

Francis Nash

Nash was born in Virginia in 1742. He moved to North Carolina at an early age, and rose to prominence there as a merchant and attorney. When war broke out in 1775, he was elected lieutenant colonel of the 1st North Carolina Regiment; he was promoted to colonel in 1776, and to brigadier general in February 1777. Nash was sent south to raise troops in western North Carolina and afterward joined Washington in the Philadelphia area. He played but a minor role at Brandywine. Nash was assigned to Lord Stirling's reserve division for the advance on Germantown, where a gruesome fate during the battle's waning hour awaited him.

Timothy Pickering

Pickering was the senior staff officer traveling with Washington's Continental Army. Born in Massachusetts in 1745 and graduated from Harvard in 1763, he was employed in

4 John Montresor, "The Montresor Journals," edited by G. D. Delaplaine, in *Collections of the New York Historical Society for the Year 1881* (1882), 452.

Library of Congress

the office of the registrar of deeds in Salem until the eve of the war. He rose to the rank of colonel in 1774. Pickering's "Plan of Discipline" was widely used in the army until Baron von Steuben's manual was adopted in 1778. Pickering took part in the Lexington alert in 1775 and in the New York and New Jersey campaigns from late 1776 to early 1777. His service and abilities brought the 32-year-old to the attention of Washington, who appointed Pickering to his top staff position, adjutant general, on June 18, 1777. Pickering's postwar writings provide valuable insight into the events at headquarters and flesh out the confusion that unfolded during the Battle of Germantown, especially at the climax of the fighting.

Casimir Pulaski

Pulaski was born on March 6, 1745, on a family estate near Warsaw, Poland. In the late 1760s he led a partisan force against the Russian army during a series of revolts in his native land. By the age of 23 he was in command of the military arm of the Confederation of Bar, a patriotic movement that sought to evict the Russians from Poland and restore sovereignty to the country. Pulaski was captured by the Russians but managed to flee Poland. He briefly aided the Turks against Russia, did time in a French debtors' prison, and finally emigrated to America. Pulaski landed at Marblehead, Massachusetts, on July 23, 1777, and caught up with Washington's army on August 21. In the aftermath of Brandywine, Washington appointed Pulaski commander of the light dragoon brigade on September 15. It was Pulaski's responsibility to keep communications open between the four advancing American columns on the long march to Germantown.

Library of Congress

William Smallwood

Smallwood was educated at Eton College in England and returned to the colonies to serve in the French and Indian War. In 1776, he commanded the Maryland battalion and suffered heavy casualties on Long Island. After being wounded twice at White Plains in October 1776, he was promoted to brigadier general and given command of the 1st Maryland Brigade. Washington detached Smallwood early in the campaign to help raise Maryland militia. His command played a small part in the Battle of Paoli. Washington assigned him to lead a column of his own militia and the New Jersey militiamen in the surprise attack against Germantown.

Library of Congress

Adam Stephen

The well-educated Adam Stephen walked an interesting road on the way to his everlasting embarrassment at Germantown. He was born in Scotland around 1718, graduated from King's College in Aberdeen, studied medicine in Edinburgh, and became a surgeon in the Royal Navy. Stephen moved to Virginia, practiced medicine in Fredericksburg, joined the militia in 1754, and served as an officer in George Washington's Virginia regiment. During the French and Indian War, Stephen saw service at the Battle of Fort Necessity, and was involved in the disastrous Braddock Expedition in 1755.

He served with the Continental Army in New York and New Jersey in 1776-77, and, as a major general, was given command of a division. Some suspected he wasn't up to the task, but he performed well at Brandywine. His two brigades were assigned to Nathanael Greene's column for the Germantown operation. Lingering suspicions about his competency and his familiarity with intoxicants followed him there.

John Sullivan

The son of Irish indentured servants, John Sullivan was born in 1740 in Berwick in what is now the state of Maine. He studied law and served as a major of militia before the war. In June 1775 he was appointed brigadier general in the army and took part in the Canadian operations. Sullivan was promoted to major general in August 1776.

The British captured Sullivan during the Battle of Long Island, and General Howe used him as a pawn in the contemplated peace negotiation by sending him as an errand boy

Library of Congress

under parole to speak with Congress. In September, Sullivan was exchanged for Brig. Gen. Richard Prescott, who had been captured in November 1775. When Gen. Charles Lee was taken prisoner in northern New Jersey, Washington put Sullivan in command of Lee's division, and he performed well at Trenton. Sullivan's conduct was under question after actions at Staten Island and Brandywine, but he fully intended to redeem himself at the head of one of Washington's four columns in the attack against Germantown.

George Washington

Washington was born in Virginia on February 22, 1732. In 1749, he was appointed the official surveyor for Culpeper County, and in that capacity helped lay out the town of Alexandria. Washington was commissioned a major in the Virginia militia in 1752.

The following year the governor, under orders from King George II, sent him to deliver an ultimatum to the French in the Ohio Valley. It was Washington who ordered the shots fired that opened the global Seven Years' War in the colonies. He was promoted to lieutenant colonel, fought in the battle at Fort Necessity in the Pennsylvania back country in July 1754, and was an aide-de-camp to Gen. Edward Braddock during the catastrophic expedition to the forks of the Ohio River. Washington was elected to the Virginia House of Burgesses in 1758 and married widow Martha Custis the following year.

Library of Congress

After Lexington and Concord Congress named Washington commander-in-chief of the Continental Army. He was 45 years old during the 1777 campaign. Modern perception imagines Washington as a gray-haired old man leading troops into battle.

In fact, he pulled back his dark reddish-brown hair into a queue and powdered it white (he never wore a wig) during the Revolution. He was a formidable man—tall, strong, and robust. His poor generalship early in the war nearly trapped the army on Long Island, but his bold, unexpected strikes at Trenton and Princeton demonstrated his ability in the field. He was in desperate need of a decisive battlefield victory in the 1777 campaign, but was defeated by General Howe at Brandywine, where he nearly lost his army once again.

When Washington realized that Howe's advance force at Germantown was ripe for a surprise attack, he formulated a rather complex four-pronged assault strike force that would march all night and destroy it at daybreak.

Anthony Wayne

The bombastic Wayne was born in Chester County, Pennsylvania, in 1745. He attended an academy for two years, became a prosperous tanner, and spent a year as a surveyor. He later became a colonel of the 4th Pennsylvania Battalion, which he commanded at Fort Washington during the New York-area campaigns in 1776. Wayne took part in the Canadian expedition and was put in command of Fort Ticonderoga. In February 1777, he was promoted to brigadier general while commanding a portion of the Pennsylvania Line at Ticonderoga, and then joined the army at Morristown. Wayne was placed in command of the First Pennsylvania Brigade of Benjamin Lincoln's division. When Lincoln was detached to serve under Horatio Gates during the Saratoga Campaign, the 32-year-old Wayne assumed temporary command of the division. He performed well at Brandywine but was surprised and embarrassed at Paoli. The stain of that slaughter hung over him as he marched his division toward Germantown as part of John Sullivan's column.

Library of Congress

Introduction

The Origins of the 1777 Campaign

By the spring of 1777, the American Revolution was entering its third year. Most of 1776 was one disaster after another for American hopes. The fledgling Continental Congress declared independence from Great Britain that summer, but the rest of the year witnessed the failed attempt to make Canada the fourteenth colony, the defeat of Gen. George Washington's army on Long Island and loss of New York City to British occupation, and the retreat (and rapid disintegration) of the Continental army across New Jersey that autumn. With Christmas approaching, Gen. William Howe and the British army settled snugly in winter quarters believing that victory would arrive quickly the following spring.

General Washington, the commander of the nascent American army, had different plans. In a daring raid the day after Christmas Washington's troops defeated the Hessian garrison at Trenton, New Jersey. A bit more than a week later, Washington stunned the British high command a second time with a successful maneuver at Trenton, followed by a second victory at Princeton. The patriot successes forced Howe to withdraw his scattered (and now vulnerable) outposts into the New York City area, leaving Washington to move the remnant of his army into the mountains around Morristown, New Jersey, for the winter. While Washington began rebuilding his command, a perplexed Howe pondered his course of operations for 1777.

British Planning

As early as 1775, British strategy revolved around isolating New England, viewed as the core of the rebellion, from the other colonies. If the Hudson River-Lake Champlain corridor was seized, the New England region would lose its physical connections to, and support from, the rest of the country. Seizing New York City the next year was a part of this plan. If successful, Howe could then move north along the Hudson River, join forces with a command marching south from Canada and together strike east into Massachusetts. Lord George Germain, the Secretary of State for the American Department, was an advocate for this move, which was called the "Hudson River plan." A memorandum later found in his papers outlined this British strategy:

> By our having the entire Command of the Communication between Canada and New York, which is both convenient and easy, being almost altogether by Water, the Troops from both these Provinces will have it in their power to act in Conjunction, as occasion or necessity may require. In consequence whereof, the Provinces of New England will be surrounded on all Sides, whether by His Majesty's Troops or Navy, and liable to be attacked from every Quarter, which will oblige them to divide their Force for the protection of their frontier settlements, while at the same time all intercourse between them and the Colonies to the southward of the Hudson's River will be entirely cut off.[1]

Following the relatively easy capture of New York City, Howe proposed moving up the Hudson—which was in line with Great Britain's original strategic thinking.

Howe sent his proposal to Germain in late November 1776. He would need a 10,000-man force to penetrate Massachusetts from Rhode Island, and an additional 10,000 men to move north along the Hudson. Finally, Howe urged that 8,000 troops remain in New Jersey to block the remnant of Washington's army. Howe planned to use that smaller force to keep Washington busy while the two stronger columns implemented the New England strategy. Howe hoped his bold plan would bring an end to the war by the end of 1777. With the Americans reeling on all fronts by November 1776, Howe's plan appeared feasible.[2]

1 "Observations on the War in America [1776]," Germain Papers, William Clements Library, Ann Arbor, MI. This memorandum was probably not written by Germain.

2 John Stockdale, ed., *The Parliamentary Register; or, History of the Proceedings and Debates of the House of Commons: Containing an Account of the most interesting Speeches and Motions; accurate Copies of the most*

Lord Germain believed the destruction of the Continental armed forces in the field was the key to victory. Howe, on the other hand, advocated that the occupation of colonial territory was the ticket to success. The more colonial territory under British control, he argued, the more Loyalists would have the opportunity to regain control of provincial affairs and restore the Crown's authority. To achieve victory, Howe intended to move through the countryside with "impressive strength through centers of rebellion, relying upon overawing the disaffected, animating the loyal, and demonstrating to the wavering the futility of resistance." Howe's thoughts on how to conduct the war contrasted with Washington's; the American general was more than willing to lose territory and cities if it meant preserving his fighting strength.[3]

By late December 1776 Howe's thinking changed. Washington was beaten, likely despondent, and fleeing west across New Jersey. Instead of shifting his units into the Hudson River valley, Howe pursued the beaten Americans, who by December 20 had crossed the Delaware River into Pennsylvania. The ease with which New Jersey was occupied convinced Howe to change his strategy. Rather than move up the Hudson as he had earlier advocated, Howe now believed he could capture the colonial capital of Philadelphia with similar ease. Washington would be forced to defend the American capital with a beaten and demoralized army. He could be lured into battle on Howe's terms and crushed. An American defeat, followed by the occupation of the capital, would bring about ultimate victory. To capture the enemy's capital city, according to sound European strategy, was to all-but win the war.

Throughout the Revolution British leadership remained convinced that the Loyalists of North America would rise and support the British government if given the opportunity to do so. Philadelphia was believed to be a hotbed of Loyalism. Joseph Galloway, former speaker of the Pennsylvania Assembly, convinced Howe the Loyalists there would rush to his support. In what would prove a gross exaggeration, Galloway told Howe that as much as 90 percent of Pennsylvanians were loyal to the Crown, and they would openly support Great Britain if given the chance. Howe, in turn, wrote that the citizens of the Middle Colonies were

remarkable Letters and Papers; of the most material Evidence, Petitions, &c laid before and offered to the House, During the Fifth Session of the Fourteenth Parliament of Great Britain (London, 1802), vol. 10, 362.

3 John F. Luzader, *Saratoga: A Military History of the Decisive Campaign of the American Revolution* (New York, 2008), xxii, 2-3.

"disposed to peace, in which sentiment they would be confirmed, by our getting possession of Philadelphia, I am, from this consideration, fully persuaded, the principal army should act offensively on that side, where the enemy's chief strength will certainly be collected."[4]

William Howe was abandoning the Hudson River plan—at least in part—before it had even begun. The Northern army under Gen. Guy Carleton would continue moving south out of Canada as planned, but Howe had his eyes firmly set on taking Philadelphia. To his way of thinking, Carleton's army could not reach Albany, New York, before September, which left Howe plenty of time to march toward Philadelphia, achieve a victory over Washington, capture the city, and transfer to the Hudson River to join forces with Carleton before fall. In Howe's mind the capture of Philadelphia trumped all else. This strategy, observed historian Richard Ketchum, demonstrated an "unwillingness to recognize that the capture of Philadelphia, beyond its potential psychological impact on rebels and loyalists, could not in itself determine the outcome of the war." Such a capture, Ketchum continued, "in strategic as well as geographic terms . . . led nowhere." For Howe to win in 1777 he "must destroy Washington's army, and seizing a piece of real estate—no matter how valuable—was no way to achieve that."[5]

Howe had barely adjusted his strategic thinking when the double defeats at Trenton and Princeton rocked him. Those setbacks notwithstanding, Howe remained convinced that moving on Philadelphia was still the right plan and the key to the final campaign and ultimate victory. "The . . . suggestion is, that I ought to have gone up Hudson's River, in order to facilitate the approach of the northern army to Albany," he wrote in 1779 in an effort to explain the reasoning that helped bring about the catastrophic defeat at Saratoga. "What would have been the consequences of such an expedition?" asked Howe, who went on to answer his own question:

> Before the object of it would have been attained, the forts in the Highlands must have been carried, which would probably have cost a considerable number of men, defended, as they would have been, by Washington's whole force. But these forts being carried, how would the enemy have acted? In one of these two ways: He would either have put himself between me and New-York, or between me and the northern

4 Jackson, *British Army*, 3. Stockdale, *Register*, vol. 10, 371.

5 Richard M. Ketchum, *Saratoga: Turning Point of America's Revolutionary War* (New York, 1997), 59.

> army. In either case I am of opinion, that the success of our efforts upon Hudson's-River, could not, from the many difficulties in penetrating though so very strong a country, have been accomplished in time to have possession of Philadelphia that campaign.
>
> But admitting I had at length reached Albany, what should I have gained, after having expended the campaign upon that object alone, that I had not a right to expect by drawing off General Washington, with the principal American army, from any operations on this side? When it is considered how invidious and how minute a scrutiny has been made into my conduct, I shall not be thought to speak absurdly if I say, that had I adopted the plan of going up Hudson's-River, it would have been alleged, that I had wasted the campaign with a considerable army under my command, merely to ensure the progress of the northern army which could have taken care of itself, provided I had made a diversion in its favour, by drawing off to the southward the main army under General Washington.[6]

Unbeknownst to Howe, however, John Burgoyne returned to London during the winter with orders from his commander, Guy Carleton, to report on the needs and intent of the Northern army. During the voyage across the Atlantic Burgoyne jotted down notes and took the liberty to elaborate upon Carleton's plans for 1777. Once in London, Burgoyne met with Lord Germain and King George III to share his plan. The primary objective of his army, he began, would be the capture of Fort Ticonderoga. Thereafter, argued Burgoyne, the "sole purpose of the Canada army [was] to effect a junction with General Howe, or after co-operating so far as to get possession of Albany and open communication to New York, to remain upon the Hudson's river, and thereby enable that general to act with his whole force to the southward." Throughout the planning process Burgoyne assumed he would eventually form a juncture with Howe. George III agreed with Burgoyne's plans, stating that his "force [should move] down to Albany & Join at that [with Howe's army]." Therefore, in March 1777, Burgoyne received orders to lead the Canadian army south along the Lake Champlain-Hudson River corridor and form a junction with Howe. These orders fell in line with the original plan to isolate New England. Once Burgoyne reached Albany, he was to "put himself under the command of Sir William Howe." No matter what complications Burgoyne may encounter along the

6 *The Narrative of Lieut. Gen. Sir William Howe, in a Committee of the House of Commons, on the 29th of April, 1779, Relative to His Conduct, During His Late Command of the King's Troops in North America: to Which are Added, Some Observations Upon a Pamphlet, Entitled, Letters to a Nobleman* (London, 1780), 19-20.

way, he was never to lose sight of the "intended junction with Sir William Howe as their [Burgoyne's army's] principal objective." Germain promised Howe that he would keep him informed of Burgoyne's orders, but no such communication ever took place. Burgoyne went into the campaign assuming Howe would stick to the original plan and clear the lower Hudson River Valley. Although a copy of Burgoyne's orders was not sent to Howe, the long-standing Hudson River operation was more than familiar to him.[7]

Howe, meanwhile, sent dispatches to Lord Germain informing him that his objective had changed. Burgoyne never learned of Howe's change of plan, and Germain was left to reconcile the vexing issue. "It is clear that Lord George expected the armies to join, that he assumed Howe understood the general plan, and that he believed Howe could take Philadelphia and join Burgoyne in a single campaign." Most historians lay blame for the failures of 1777 at the feet of Lord Germain, but they fail to properly consider the limitations of 18th century communication. Germain had no choice but to rely on face-to-face contact with his subordinates or dispatches sent back and forth across the Atlantic Ocean. Sending an inquiry by ship and getting a response could take up to two months. By the time a letter or order arrived it was already outdated. Germain had no personal contact with Howe during this period. Both Burgoyne and Henry Clinton (a subordinate from Howe's army) returned to London that winter, and Germain had to carefully weigh the information and opinions offered up by these self-serving officers. When George III approved Burgoyne's revision of the Hudson River plan and Howe's Philadelphia thrust, it was Germain's duty to point out the contradictory orders to the King, or at least to inform the two principal generals of the coming campaign of the differences in their orders. Burgoyne's advance was undertaken with the full understanding that Howe would indeed support him—but not until Burgoyne had reached Albany.[8]

Part of the problem plaguing British commanders in the field was that neither Germain nor the King had ever led troops in battle and were thus unfamiliar with the difficulties of moving armies through the enemy countryside. What little they knew pertained to European warfare, where well-developed roads and farms could better transport and support large field armies. The relative wilderness of North America, however, lacked a quality road network and in most areas remained heavily wooded and undeveloped. British planners seem never to have considered

7 Piers Mackesy, *The War for America: 1775-1783* (Lincoln, NE, 1964), 115.

8 Ira D. Gruber, *The Howe Brothers & the American Revolution* (New York, 1972), 187-188.

the ability of American militia to disrupt their movements. Germain's and King George III's misunderstanding of these conditions led them to believe that Howe, within just a few months, could not only capture Philadelphia but return to the Hudson River and assist Burgoyne.

Howe's blind ambition to capture the colonial capital played a major part in the disaster that befell Burgoyne in the fall of 1777 at Saratoga. However, argued one historian, "it would be mistaken to assume that Howe sacrificed Burgoyne either through indifference or stupidity." Howe had no enthusiasm for the New England plan, but "a lack of enthusiasm for it . . . leaves the impression that the failure of the government to send Howe reinforcements as numerous as he wished put him in a mood prejudicial to a sympathetic handling of the problem presented by Burgoyne's advance." Despite his obsession with the city, Howe took an inordinate amount of time to achieve his goal, and by that late hour Burgoyne's fate was already sealed.[9]

By the spring of 1777, the British high command knew of Howe's intentions and approved his plans. In a long letter to Germain, Howe explained that Washington would be forced to move south and defend his capital. If he was wrong and Washington moved up the Hudson River Valley, Howe would turn and follow. Several weeks later events in the field proved that Howe's basic assumption was correct: Washington moved to block Howe from taking Philadelphia, which meant the American army could not play a role in the Hudson River operations.[10]

The 1776 campaign had demonstrated many things and one in particular: William Howe lacked a killer's instinct. He chased, pushed, attacked, and pressured his opponent, but somehow he was never able to commit to a final mortal blow against even a weakened enemy. Lord Germain preferred a scorched-earth policy and reasoned that the rebellion would not end until the main Rebel army was eliminated. That policy made little sense to Howe, who believed such brutality would further alienate the Americans and set the stage for future civil wars even if Britain achieved victory. Winning the hearts and minds of the people was more important than military annihilation. Howe intended to "use persuasion in conjunction with demonstrated military might, employing their martial resources

9 Troyer Steele Anderson, *The Command of the Howe Brothers During the American Revolution* (New York and London, 1936), 272-273.

10 Stockdale, *Register*, vol. 10, 414-415. For more information and details on William Howe and British strategy in 1777, as well as the options facing George Washington that year, refer to my first book on the Philadelphia campaign, *Brandywine: A Military History of the Battle that Lost Philadelphia but Saved America, September 11, 1777* (El Dorado Hills, CA, 2014).

to prod the rebels into renewing their allegiance to the Crown." Capturing the capital would achieve this with no change to his personal strategy.[11]

Washington's Strategy

Congress's choice of George Washington to lead the first American army was in many ways a curious one. The Virginia planter had exercised limited departmental command during the French and Indian War and had never led more than a regiment or two in combat. Despite a personal desire to have done so, Washington never served as a British regular, nor had he attended any of the military schools in Europe. Confronted by some of the best military professionals of the 18th century, Washington faced a steep learning curve. Despite his victories at Trenton and Princeton, he and his army had been battered, beaten, and outgeneraled throughout 1776. The overarching lesson of 1776 was simple: The fledgling American army was not yet capable of waging traditional warfare. Washington learned that lesson and would spend 1777 relying on defensive warfare, daybreak assaults, sneak attacks, and trickery—a strategy of guerilla or partisan warfare (petite guerre).

The planter-turned-general realized it would take time to mold the Continental army into a force that could stand toe-to-toe with British regulars. That fact became more than clear after his near-annihilation on Long Island and other defeats. In order to buy that time Washington changed his strategy and spent most of the rest of the war avoiding pitched battles—especially offensive combat. This approach would keep his army intact for the long haul, but Washington still needed to settle on a strategy to defeat the British. He could have waged a guerilla-style war with smaller forces to slowly drain British strength, but the members of Congress, who had to answer to their constituents, wanted to defend every colony and every major city. The public in general supported such a policy. Its implementation, however, would have required Washington to spread his limited manpower too thin to achieve anything and all-but guaranteed an American defeat. Washington needed a strategy that would be effective with the sparse resources he had under his control or within his reach.[12]

11 James Kirby Martin & Mark Edward Lender, *"A Respectable Army": The Military Origins of the Republic, 1763-1789* (West Sussex, United Kingdom, 2015), 51-52.

12 David Hackett Fischer, *Washington's Crossing* (Oxford, 2004), 79-80.

Washington became best known for implementing a Fabian style of warfare. While he preferred a large professional army and constantly begged Congress for one, he was also a realist. The relatively small army he had was easier to supply and could move more rapidly than could its British and Hessian counterparts. When not acting on the defensive Washington could attack rapidly and retreat even more quickly. His tactics prevented heavy casualties, maintained his army, and allowed him to live to fight another day. By avoiding major battles and using the wilds of North America, Washington hoped to frustrate the British by making the war too long and too expensive to maintain.

Despite the realities under which he labored, Washington harbored a strong desire to wage a classic battle against the British army on something approaching equal terms. As historian Ron Chernow observed, Washington "nursed fantasies throughout the war about fighting a grand climatic battle that would end the conflict with a single stroke." The only way he could ever have such an opportunity was to maintain and train his Continentals until his men were ready for the challenge. Washington described his strategy as "time, caution, and worrying the enemy until we could be better provided with arms and other means, and had better disciplined troops to carry on."[13]

The longer the war continued the more unpopular it became in Parliament—especially as the cost of conducting the war skyrocketed. Washington firmly believed the British government would grow weary of losing men and materiel, despise the rising costs of the war, and weaken in the face of increasing criticism from the opposition party. Time was on Washington's side.

When the spring campaign season dawned Washington was in something of a quandary, for he had no idea what strategy William Howe would implement. The British general had several options and the proximity of a Royal fleet commanded by his brother, Admiral Richard Howe. The lack of a credible Continental Navy limited Washington's options. Howe could use his fleet to move north up the Hudson River, jump to any number of ports along the American coastline, or move directly overland to Philadelphia, picking up where the previous campaign had ended.

Washington, who was in no position to assume the initiative, would have to wait and react. His position around Morristown would allow him to block the

13 Ibid., 79. Fabian strategy was named for Fabius Cunctator, a Roman general who had fought a delaying campaign against Hannibal's Carthaginians during the Second Punic War (218-201 B.C.); Ron Chernow, *Washington: A Life* (New York, 2010), 208; James Thomas Flexner, *Washington: The Indispensable Man* (Boston, 1969), 131.

overland route to Philadelphia. If Howe pushed north along the Hudson to meet the British force from Canada, Washington would follow and harass his rear. If Howe completely changed the field of operations by using the British fleet, Washington would have no choice but to wait and see where the British army appeared and then act accordingly.

Chapter 1

The Philadelphia Campaign

June – September 1777

"Our people behaved well but Heaven frowned upon us in a degree. We were obliged to retire after a very considerable slaughter of the enemy."[1]

— Henry Knox, Chief of Artillery, Continental Army, September 1777

George Washington spent the six months after his victories at Trenton and Princeton in late December 1776 and early January 1777 around Morristown, New Jersey, building a new army nearly from scratch. His one-year enlistments—which comprised most of his army in 1776—had expired. During the long and arduous process, Washington harassed British outposts scattered across northern New Jersey in a series of raids and skirmishes. Fortunately for him, British Gen. William Howe was more concerned with strategic planning and writing letters to London than with what he considered the minor doings of the Continental Army.[2]

Between January and June 1777, these small-scale raids and skirmishes were the only military operations that took place in northern New Jersey. The American

1 Noah Brooks, *Henry Knox: A Soldier of the Revolution* (New York, 1900), 104.

2 For more information on the opening months of the campaign, as well as the Battle of Brandywine, refer to my first book on the Philadelphia Campaign, *Brandywine: A Military History of the Battle that Lost Philadelphia but Saved America, September 11, 1777* (El Dorado Hills, CA, 2014).

Revolution had devolved into something more closely resembling a guerilla war than the more traditional European-style of combat. Washington described this form of war in a letter that February. "There have been and almost daily are, some small Skirmishes," he explained, "but without much loss on either side." Happily for Washington and the American cause, this form of warfare continued for the next four months, giving the general the precious time and space he needed to rebuild his weakened army. The stress built up during the extended off-tempo, low-intensity war simmered through the spring of 1777 until it boiled over into the savageness exhibited later in the campaign—especially at Paoli. The rains of April ended in early May and Washington, his army still in flux, shifted his command from the winter encampment at Morristown to a position at Middlebrook, New Jersey.[3]

General Howe mostly ignored Washington's change of base and made little effort to open the 1777 campaign season. He intended to capture Philadelphia as rapidly as possible and return to New York to join forces with Gen. John Burgoyne and the northern army, yet he showed no sign of urgency to actually do so. Nicholas Cresswell, an Englishman soon to return to England, noted in his journal, "I am as ignorant of the Motions or designs of our Army as if I had been in Virginia." The British soldiers, added Cresswell, "seem very healthy and long to be in action."[4]

June 1777

William Howe finally lurched into action in June by ordering an expedition to Middlebush, New Jersey. The British commander decided his best bet was to attempt the overland route to Philadelphia in the hope of luring Washington down from his mountain stronghold. Defeating Washington in New Jersey and then marching to Philadelphia offered Howe the best chance to take the colonial capital and leave in time to aid Burgoyne in New York. Howe's delay in opening the campaign triggered some dissatisfaction within the British officer corps. Timing was crucial to the British plan, and the army could have moved weeks earlier when

3 John D. Fitzpatrick, ed., *The Writings of George Washington from the Original Manuscript Sources, 1745-1799*, 39 vols. (Washington, D.C., 1933), vol. 7, 196.

4 Nicholas Cresswell, *The Journal of Nicholas Cresswell, 1774-1777* (New York, 1928), 229.

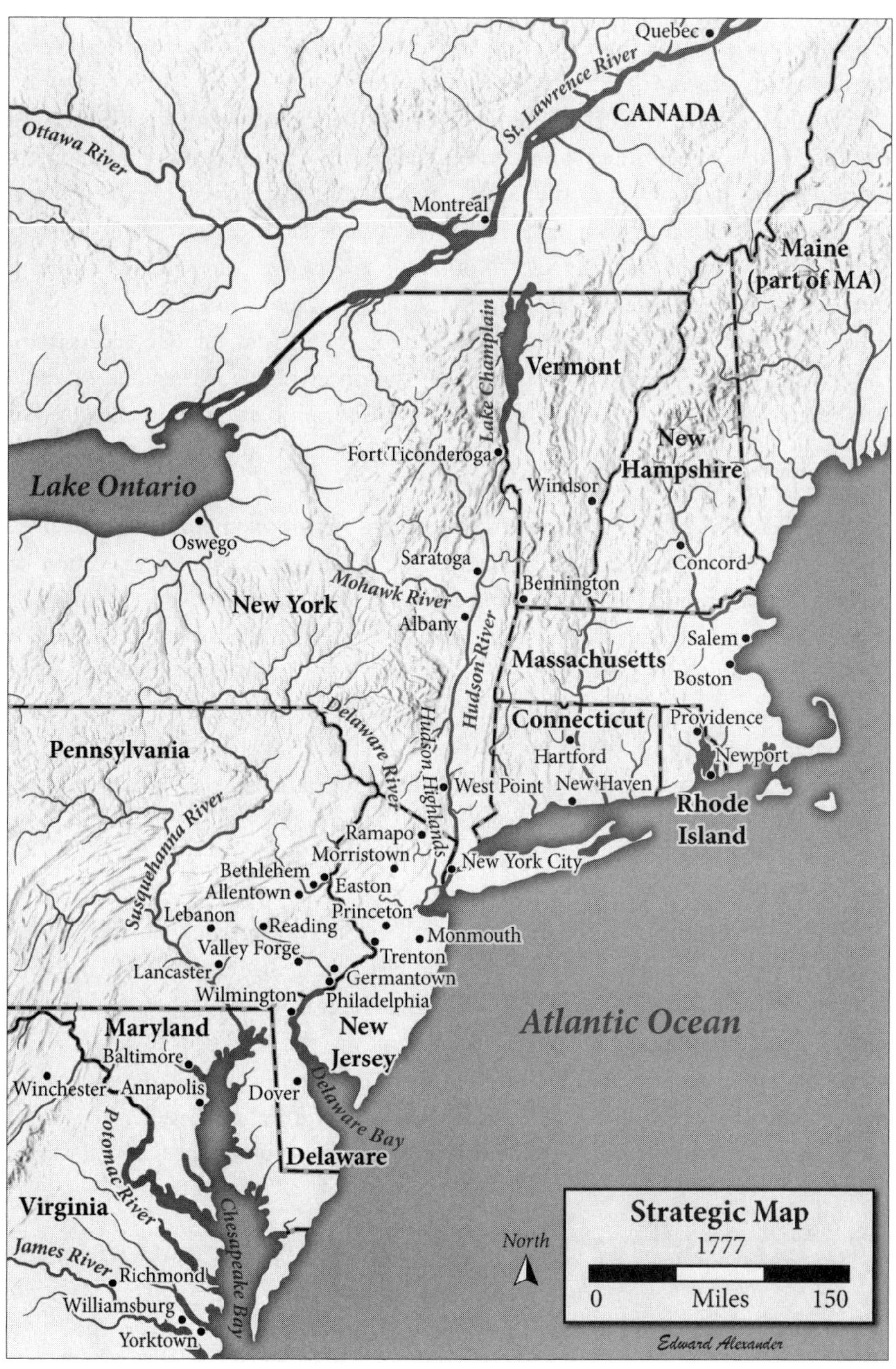
Quebec
St. Lawrence River
CANADA
Ottawa River
Montreal
Maine
(part of MA)
Lake Champlain
Vermont
New
Hampshire
Fort Ticonderoga
Windsor
Lake Ontario
Oswego
Saratoga
Concord
Mohawk River
Bennington
New York
Albany
Hudson River
Salem
Massachusetts
Boston
Delaware River
Hudson Highlands
Connecticut
Providence
Pennsylvania
Hartford
Newport
West Point
New Haven
Susquehanna River
Rhode
Island
Ramapo
Morristown
New York City
Bethlehem
Allentown
Easton
Lebanon
Princeton
Reading
Monmouth
Valley Forge
Trenton
Lancaster
Germantown
Wilmington
Philadelphia
Maryland
New
Jersey
Atlantic Ocean
Baltimore
Winchester
Annapolis
Dover
Delaware Bay
Potomac River
Delaware
Chesapeake Bay
Virginia
Strategic Map
1777
North
James River
Richmond
0
Miles
150
Williamsburg
Yorktown
Edward Alexander

the winter rains stopped and the warmer weather dried the roads. However, Howe did not move into northern New Jersey until June 13.[5]

To the disbelief of officers on both sides, the British army stopped after a march of about ten miles and established camp the day after reaching its destination. Not only did the army stop its advance, but Howe ordered fortifications erected; he apparently no longer intended to move any farther toward Philadelphia through New Jersey. "Nobody in the world could be more careful than he is," wrote Howe's Hessian aide, Capt. Levin Friedrich Ernst von Muenchhausen, in defense of his chief's actions. "This is absolutely necessary in this cursed hilly country." By remaining stationary, Howe intended to draw Washington down from the high ground and offer him battle in the relatively flat country east of the mountain range. To Howe's dismay, Washington refused to take the bait.[6]

The failure to lure the Americans into a fight flummoxed Howe, whose army of professional soldiers was being stymied by Washington's ragtag collection of militia, frontiersmen, and Continental Regulars. No one believed Washington's force was formidable, including Washington himself. His was not the army of veterans that would become hardened and molded in the grueling campaign still ahead of them, followed by the reckoning that would take place at Valley Forge the following winter. Four days ticked past as Howe waited in frustration for Washington to move. Other than light skirmishing and the launching of small raiding parties to plunder the countryside, Howe accomplished nothing. By remaining idle during perfectly good weather, Howe had effectively removed his army from the war effort.

Howe gave up the game and returned to New Brunswick on June 19 as elements of the Continental Army followed, skirmishing fitfully with his rear guard. Howe's actions dumbfounded British Maj. Charles Stuart. "These retrograde movements appear just as incomprehensible to us as they can possibly to you," he wrote his father in England. Howe's half-hearted attempt in New Jersey was as baffling then as it is today. Even though he was on a tight schedule, he moved thousands of troops ten miles, went into camp and constructed earthworks, waited

5 For a complete discussion of the campaign, its strategy, and the relationship between Howe and Burgoyne, see John F. Luzader, *Saratoga: A Military History of the Decisive Campaign of the American Revolution* (Savas Beatie, 2008).

6 Friedrich von Muenchhausen, *At General Howe's Side: 1776-1778: The Diary of General William Howe's aide de camp, Captain Friedrich von Muenchhausen*, trans. Ernst Kipping, ed. Samuel Steele Smith (Monmouth Beach, NJ, 1974), 16.

four days, and returned to his starting point a week later. Most historians attribute Howe's actions to a failed effort to pull Washington from the mountains for an open-field fight. However, Washington had never so obliged his enemy, and in fact rarely fought a battle under his enemy's terms. The more logical explanation is that Howe never intended to assault Philadelphia by marching through New Jersey. He would reach his objective by using the British fleet to transport his army.[7]

On June 22, Howe retired farther to Amboy, New Jersey, to load his army and its baggage for the voyage to the Delaware River. The Americans pressed Howe's rear guard, harassing the tail of his column. Washington remained cautiously optimistic about the state of affairs. "I cannot say that the move I am about to make towards Amboy accords altogether with my opinion," wrote the army commander, "not that I am under any other apprehension than that of being obliged to loose Ground again, which would indeed be no small misfortune as the Spirits of our Troops, and the Country, is greatly reviv'd (and I presume) the Enemys not a little depress'd, by their late retrograde motions."[8]

Washington's willingness to come down off the high ground and pursue Howe's retreating army, however, provided the British general with the opportunity he had been seeking. The Continental Army was on more engageable terrain, and Howe had his chance to attack. He did just that on June 25 by turning and assaulting Maj. Gen. Lord Stirling's isolated and heavily outnumbered American division of some 2,500 men. Stirling waged a well-crafted fighting withdrawal and took up a strong defensive position in the area of Ash Swamp and Scotch Plains. The British pushed hard and forced Stirling's command back once more toward Westfield. Suffering under an intense sun, Howe called off the pursuit and the day's fighting ended. The defensive action cost Stirling perhaps as many as 100 killed and wounded, in addition to 70 men and three cannons captured, while British losses totaled just five killed and 30 wounded. "The Battle of Short Hills," as it became known, bought precious time for Washington to move the balance of his army into the hill country to deny Howe the opportunity of the larger pitched battle he so craved. The affair also demonstrated that Washington's vaunted spy network had been surprised and thus had failed him. The British army, camped a mere eight miles away, had stolen a march on Washington and defeated a portion of the Continental Army. Howe had been unable to bring Washington to battle, but his

7 Mrs. E. Stuart Wortley, ed. *A Prime Minister and His Son: From the Correspondence of the Third Earl of Bute and Lt. General The Honourable Sir Charles Stuart, K.B.* (London, 1925), 110-113.

8 Fitzpatrick, *Writings*, vol. 8, 295-296.

short-lived romp across the Jersey countryside had made one thing clear: the large and often lumbering British army could move about the countryside, plundering as it went, and there was little Washington could or would do about it.[9]

By June 28 Howe was back in Amboy, his attempt to defeat Washington in northern New Jersey at an end. Washington fully expected Howe to use the British fleet to change the field of operations—but where would the ships carry his army? "By means of their Shipping and the easy transportation that Shipping affords, they have it much in their power to lead us [in] a very disagreeable dance," Washington wrote in a letter to his brother, John Augustine Washington.[10]

On the last day of June, Howe removed the last of his troops from New Jersey and returned to Staten Island, New York. He and his command were back where they had started before their attack on New York City nearly a year earlier. The city and its environs, together with Newport, Rhode Island, remained under British control, but Howe's withdrawal allowed Washington and his Continental Army to assume complete control of New Jersey. The strategic situation disgusted Loyalist Nicholas Cresswell: "General Howe, a man brought up to War from his youth, to be puzzled and plagued for two years together, with a Virginia Tobacco planter. O! Britain, how thy Laurels tarnish in the hands of such a Lubber!"[11]

While Howe pondered his next move, Washington redeployed his command, shifting three brigades into the Hudson River Valley in case Howe headed in that direction. "Their Fleet," he explained in a letter to Congress, "give them the most signal advantages, and opportunity of practicing a thousand feints."[12]

July 1777

Early July found most of the Continental Army back in the mountains around Morristown. The position provided Washington with the option of shifting north to block the Hudson River, or south to protect the capital. The next move was up to Howe. Determined to use his fleet to reach Philadelphia, on July 8 the British general began the arduous process of loading his army onto transport ships. Howe believed he could ascend the Delaware River, capture Philadelphia, and still aid

9 Fitzpatrick, *Writings*, vol. 8, 315.

10 Ibid.

11 Cresswell, *Journal*, 252.

12 Fitzpatrick, *Writings*, vol. 8, 329-331.

Burgoyne in a timely fashion. He also believed that moving by sea would freeze the Americans in place until Washington realized where Howe was going. On the second point, he was correct.

By the time Howe finished the loading process on July 9, he had filled some 260 ships with 20,000 soldiers, support personnel, artillery, horses, and everything else he needed to launch a major campaign. Rather than depart immediately, however, Howe left his men and animals bobbing in the harbor for several days, confined in tight overheated quarters aboard stuffy transports. "God knows whether we shall go south or north," wrote a perplexed Col. Carl von Donop, the commander of the Hessian grenadiers, "but the heat which is beginning to make itself felt with the approach of the dog-days makes one wish that the general would choose north rather than south." The delay also confused Howe's Hessian aide, Capt. Friedrich von Muenchhausen, who observed, "No one seems to be able to figure out why we are waiting here so long, considering the fact that everyone, except Howe and a few officers, are aboard ship."[13]

Washington, aware Howe was loading ships for a campaign, decided to get a jump on him by moving the army north on July 12 to the New Jersey-New York border in anticipation of a push up the Hudson River. Leaving New Jersey wide open for Howe to make an overland forced march for Philadelphia was a bold and risky decision that Howe failed to recognize or exploit. The deliberate British general was finally ready to move on July 20. He ordered the large British armada to sail out of New York Harbor, leaving behind Gen. Henry Clinton and the city's garrison of 7,400 troops. American observers along the New Jersey coast speculated that the fleet was turning south, but at this point Howe's target was still an open question. The lack of a Continental Navy hampered Washington, who was forced to rely upon spotters scattered along the coastline to locate the ships and relay information. Until reliable intelligence arrived, Washington had no choice but to mark time in northern New Jersey.

Howe's voyage promised to be long and slow, for the prevailing summer winds along the Atlantic coast tend to blow north—and Howe was heading south. The

13 Carl von Donop, "Letters from a Hessian Mercenary (Colonel von Donop to the Prince of Prussia)," ed. Hans Huth, in *PMHB* (Philadelphia, 1938), vol. 62, 498; Von Muenchhausen, *At Howe's Side*, 21. Thirty-seven-year-old Carl von Donop was the son of one of the great noble families of Hesse-Cassel. He served during the Seven Years' War and when the Revolution began, was the personal adjutant of the Landgraf of Hesse-Cassel. He would take command of the Jaeger Corps in 1776. His men fought throughout the New York Campaign, and by the start of the Philadelphia Campaign, von Donop was in command of the Hessian grenadier brigade.

journey was a miserable experience for man and beast alike. The heat and humidity were stifling and brisk winds buffeted the ships. Frequent late afternoon thunderstorms added to the general misery of the voyage. The weather proved so uncooperative that it took the fleet a week to travel only 150 miles to Cape May, New Jersey. Washington, meanwhile, concentrated near Ramapo, New Jersey, a position from which he could either march to the Hudson Highlands or move rapidly to Philadelphia.

On July 26, shore-based spotters sighted a large portion of the British fleet heading south near Little Egg Harbor, New Jersey. Washington was beginning to hedge his bets and had been slowly moving south, inching toward Morristown with four of the army's five divisions. The Continental Army headed for three separate crossings of the Delaware River to expedite its passage into Pennsylvania, if warranted. When news of the fleet found its way to Washington, there was little doubt Howe was heading for Philadelphia. On July 28 the leading elements of Washington's legions reached the Delaware.

The final days of July saw the British fleet tacking into the Delaware Bay to assess current conditions and intelligence about Washington's army. When this news reached Washington about 24 hours later, he ordered the army to cross into Pennsylvania to block a move against Philadelphia. Almost simultaneously, the Howe brothers made what was perhaps the most critical decision of 1777 aboard bobbing ships in Delaware Bay.

The British general and admiral acted upon incorrect information that Washington's entire army was across the Delaware and approaching Wilmington, Delaware. They were also told that fortifications had been constructed along the shores of the Delaware and various obstructions had been placed in the river to halt the fleet. The "news" should have elated the British high command. The river defenses and a small naval militia were of trifling concern when the most important city in North America was essentially undefended. The Schuylkill and Brandywine rivers that stood between the army and the colonial capital would have to be crossed, but they could be forded at numerous locations. Although William Howe was informed that Washington's army was west of the Delaware River, little if any of the Continental Army had yet to arrive in Philadelphia. The British had a clear and open path to the American capital.[14]

14 At 10:00 a.m. on July 30, Capt. Andrew Hamond reported to Admiral Howe's flagship HMS *Eagle* to meet with the Howe brothers. Hamond was shocked to find the general still asleep. A short time later the two Howes and Hamond met in the admiral's cabin. One of the first questions posed

Despite easy access to Philadelphia, which was approximately 90 miles away by ship, Howe decided to sail south to Chesapeake Bay, where he could put his troops "ashore without molestation, have time to recover the Horses after the fatigue of the Voyage before they entered Service, and where the Transports could remain in perfect security." The move, he also stressed, would threaten backcountry settlements. On July 31, the fleet headed back to sea. Howe later claimed the shift farther south benefited John Burgoyne by drawing Washington away from the Hudson River Valley. In reality, the moment William Howe gave the order to steer toward the Chesapeake, he eliminated any possibility of aiding Burgoyne.[15]

The sailing of the British fleet removed the immediate threat to Philadelphia, but it did not stop panic from erupting inside the capital. City officials ordered that all wagons be detained for the removal of anything that might aid the enemy. Congress passed a resolution recommending "to make prisoners such of the late crown & proprietary officers and other persons in and near this city as are disaffected or may be dangerous to the publick liberty and send them back into the country, there to be confined or enlarged upon parole as their characters & behavior may require." Two of the most prominent arrestees included Gov. John Penn, grandson of founder William Penn, and Chief Justice Benjamin Chew, a prominent Philadelphia lawyer and owner of a large stone home in the village of Germantown.[16]

---

was whether Hamond knew Washington's location. The army, he replied, was across the Delaware heading for Wilmington. His intelligence source is not known, but Hamond's assessment was incorrect. Perhaps one brigade was across the river, but the rest of Washington's army was strung out across northern New Jersey. Howe's most recent dispatch to Germain, however, stated that he would ascend the Delaware River only if Washington remained in northern New Jersey. If Washington entered Pennsylvania instead, Howe was going to revert to the plan to ascend Chesapeake Bay. Hamond's incorrect report made Howe's decision for him. Harris, *Brandywine*, 83-84. At the time there were unfinished earthworks at Billingsport and Red Bank, New Jersey. On the Pennsylvania side could be found incomplete redoubts on Bush Island and on Darby Creek. Fort Mifflin, on Mud Island, was virtually unmanned.

15 Denys Hay, "The Denouement of General Howe's Campaign of 1777," in *English Historical Review*, vol. 74 (1964), 504.

16 Samuel Hazard, ed., *Pennsylvania Archives: Selected and Arranged from Original Documents in the Office of the Secretary of the Commonwealth*, Series 1, 12 vols. (Philadelphia, 1853), vol. 5, 469.

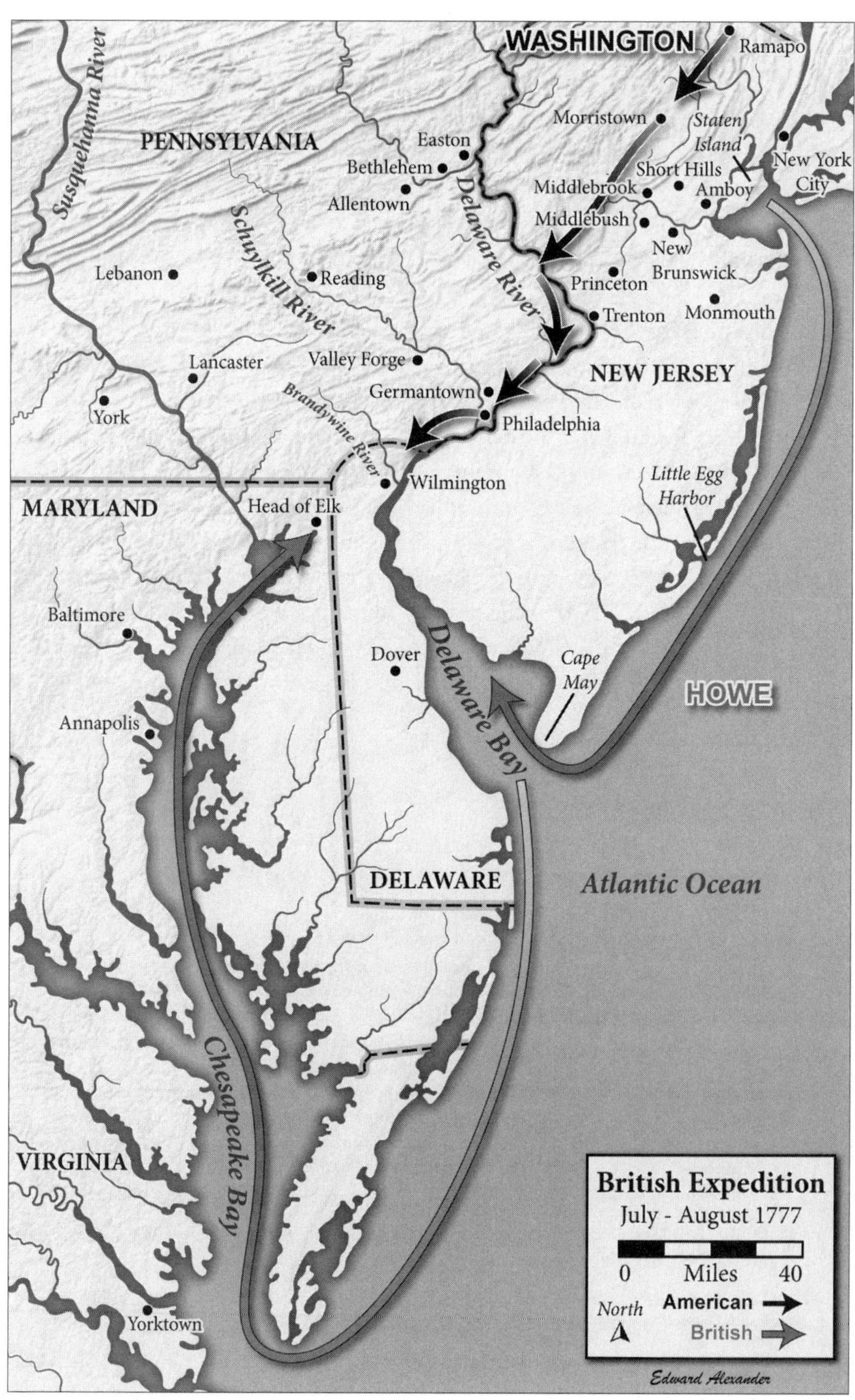
WASHINGTON
Ramapo
Susquehanna River
PENNSYLVANIA
Easton
Morristown
Staten Island
Bethlehem
Allentown
Delaware River
Short Hills
New York City
Middlebrook
Amboy
Middlebush
Schuylkill River
New Brunswick
Lebanon
Reading
Princeton
Trenton
Monmouth
Lancaster
Valley Forge
NEW JERSEY
Germantown
York
Brandywine River
Philadelphia
Wilmington
Little Egg Harbor
MARYLAND
Head of Elk
Baltimore
Dover
Delaware Bay
Cape May
HOWE
Annapolis
DELAWARE
Atlantic Ocean
Chesapeake Bay
VIRGINIA
Yorktown
British Expedition
July - August 1777
0 Miles 40
North
American
British
Edward Alexander

August 1777

By the beginning of August, the British fleet was moving south along the Delaware coast. The move left Washington with a conundrum. Was Howe making for the Hudson River or was his objective one of the port cities farther south? Washington concentrated his command just north of Philadelphia, with four of his divisions camped in and around the village of Germantown on the outskirts of the city. The British strategy also perplexed members of Congress, including John Adams. "What this Man [Howe] is after," he wrote, "no Wisdom can discover."[17]

By August 10, Washington had shifted the army to the banks of Neshaminy Creek, north of Philadelphia and closer to the Delaware River, in case he needed to rush back to the Hudson Highlands. There was little more he could do until definitive intelligence arrived confirming the location of Howe's fleet. Washington may well have smiled had he known that the fleet had reached the entrance to Chesapeake Bay after suffering through terrible storms. Fresh food and water had run out on many transports, and horses were dying by the score and being tossed overboard. When news of Howe's location, if not his army's condition, arrived on August 21, Washington scrambled to move the scattered elements of his army into a position to confront the British south of Philadelphia. Washington started inching towards northern Delaware to block Howe.

With the British fleet anchored near the mouth of the Elk River in the upper reaches of Chesapeake Bay, Washington shifted the Continental Army back into the Germantown area. Howe was going for Philadelphia and would approach from the southwest. The terrain there was cut with several creeks and rivers that would slow, but not stop, Howe's access to the city, including the Red and White Clay creeks, the Brandywine, and the Schuylkill. Washington also was concerned that Howe would march into the interior and threaten the major American supply depots at Lancaster or Reading. There was no real choice: he would have to advance toward Howe.

On August 24, Washington paraded his troops from their Germantown camps through Philadelphia en route to Delaware. It was time to block Howe's approaches to Philadelphia. The next morning, Washington crossed into Delaware with two divisions and camped along Naaman's Creek. About the same time, Howe began offloading troops into northeastern Maryland. Other than some local militia that Howe brushed aside, his landing was unmolested.

17 Paul H. Smith, et al., eds., *Letters of Delegates to Congress*, 26 vols. (Washington, 1981), vol. 7, 403.

Now that Howe had landed, making a connection with the Delaware River was imperative. Throughout the war the British were in short supply of land transportation. Howe's logistical concerns were compounded by the fact that many of his horses had died during the voyage. It was vitally important for British armies to operate in the field near navigable rivers so the Royal Navy could resupply them. In fact, points out one recent historian, "The insecurity of overland communications restricted an army's maximum operational range to about fifteen to twenty miles from navigable water." This operational conundrum affected Howe's decision-making throughout the campaign. Had he landed in northern Delaware at the end of July, he would have had his connection with the Delaware River. Now, Howe was barely back on land and he had no choice but to operate along the Delaware River—ignoring the reason he initially provided for delaying the campaign for another month by shifting his army farther south.[18]

On August 28, the British advanced from their landing site, brushing aside American militia and plundering the countryside. The initial move overran the commercial trading village at Head of Elk, Maryland. By August 31, Howe was devastating the countryside in northeastern Maryland in search of badly needed supplies, including reinforcements and fresh horses. Contrary to Howe's belief, Loyalists had little interest in flocking to his standard. "The prevailing disposition of the inhabitants, who, I am sorry to observe, seem[s] to be, excepting a few individuals, strongly in enmity against us," Howe complained to Lord Germain. "[M]any having taken up arms, and, by far the greater number, deserted their dwellings, driving off, at the same time, their stock of cattle and horses." Howe later claimed that the real reason he could not support Burgoyne's army was the failure to recruit Loyalist support. Excuses for abandoning Burgoyne were growing larger with each telling.[19]

Three factors worked against British recruitment efforts. First, Loyalists in the region were conservative, cautious, and against violence. Because of this, Quakers were viewed as Loyalists. Second, the British Army treated Loyalists poorly. Rather than grant British Army commissions and the permanence that came with them, they gave Loyalists temporary provincial commissions. Even though these people remained loyal to King George III, the British viewed them as inferior second-class citizens, and provincial units were often relegated to non-combat roles like wagon

18 Matthew H. Spring, *With Zeal and With Bayonets Only: The British Army on Campaign in North America, 1775-1783* (Norman, OK, 2008), 35.

19 Stockdale, ed., *Register*, vol. 10, 418.

guards and garrison duty. Finally, Loyalists who came forward when the British occupied a region were often abandoned when the invaders eventually left—leaving them open to abuse by rebel forces.

By late August Washington, who had gathered an army outside Wilmington, nearly equal in size to Howe's, was fully aware of the British supply problems, especially their dire lack of healthy horses. "All accounts agree that [the enemy] are very much distressed for want of horses, numbers of which it is said died on the passage, and the rest are in exceeding bad order," wrote the American commander. "[T]his will probably occasion some delay and give time for the militia, who seem to be collecting pretty fast, to join us." Unfortunately for Washington, the British equine shortage prompted Howe to offer high prices for mounts, and many American dragoons deserted to collect the inducement.[20]

September 1777

By the beginning of September, Howe's soldiers were itching for action. They had spent several weeks cooped up on ships and the last several days conducting a fitful and frustrating advance into northeastern Maryland. Howe was as ready as he would ever be to risk a battle. He had been avoiding a pitched confrontation, but the campaign season was rapidly winding down and there was precious little to show for it.

Washington had an outpost in northern Delaware at Cooch's Bridge on the Christiana River, which Howe would have to deal with in order to reach the main colonial army. He did just that on September 3, sending 450 jaegers and 1,300 light infantrymen on a series of flanking movements against 1,000 Americans under William Maxwell. The fighting lasted some seven hours before Maxwell's men ran out of ammunition and fled across the bridge and eventually back toward Wilmington, leaving the British in command of the banks of the Christiana River. The battle, which carried Howe one step closer to Philadelphia, was the largest land engagement in the history of Delaware. Once he achieved this success, however, Howe settled down for another five days to pillage the countryside. Feeding his army was imperative; providing for it in a hostile land was a constant problem.

Following Cooch's Bridge, Washington convinced himself that Howe would take the main road into Wilmington. He deployed his army behind the Red Clay

20 Philander D. Chase & Edward G. Lengel, eds., *The Papers of George Washington*, 25 vols. (Charlottesville & London, 2001), vol. 11, 112.

Creek with a defense in depth. Since Howe never resorted to frontal assaults, Washington's thinking is a mystery. At Long Island, White Plains, Short Hills, and Cooch's Bridge, Howe utilized flanking movements to avoid a bloody attack. Given his history, Howe's next move was predictable. On September 8, he resorted to what he did best, and gained the Pennsylvania border ahead of Washington. By late morning, the bulk of Howe's army was camped on the hills around Hockessin, Delaware, well above Washington's right flank.[21]

Outgeneraled yet again, Washington scrambled to get his army in motion and into a blocking position to protect Philadelphia. After months of confusion and outright misery, Howe's latest moves impressed his officers and men alike. "All marched in one column, and to our great surprise," wrote Howe's aide von Muenchhausen, "instead of taking the road by way of Christiana Bridge to Wilmington as expected, we went to our left by way of White Clay Creek and Newark. . . . [E]veryone is pleased with the good march and the fact that it was kept a secret, thus cutting off Washington from Lancaster." In the middle of the night, Washington pulled the Continental Army from northern Delaware, marched north, and by the next day began moving into positions on the east side of the Brandywine River near Chads's Ford in Pennsylvania.[22]

Between the evening of September 9 and the morning of September 10, Howe's army moved north parallel to Washington's position and camped at Kennett Square, about six miles west of the American army. Washington had spent the long summer months attempting to hinder British movements with militia and other troops while seeking a favorable opportunity to make a stand should one become necessary. The terrain along the Brandywine River provided him with exactly that.[23]

The Battle of Brandywine

The Battle of Brandywine was the longest and largest single-day engagement of the war. The fighting on September 11, 1777, is also a study of contradictions. George Washington hoped a stout defense along the rolling terrain hugging the Brandywine River would bar British access to Philadelphia. His goal was to defend

21 Harris, *Brandywine*, 140-145.

22 Von Muenchhausen, *At Howe's Side*, 30.

23 Edward G. Lengel, *General George Washington: A Military Life* (New York, 2005), 223.

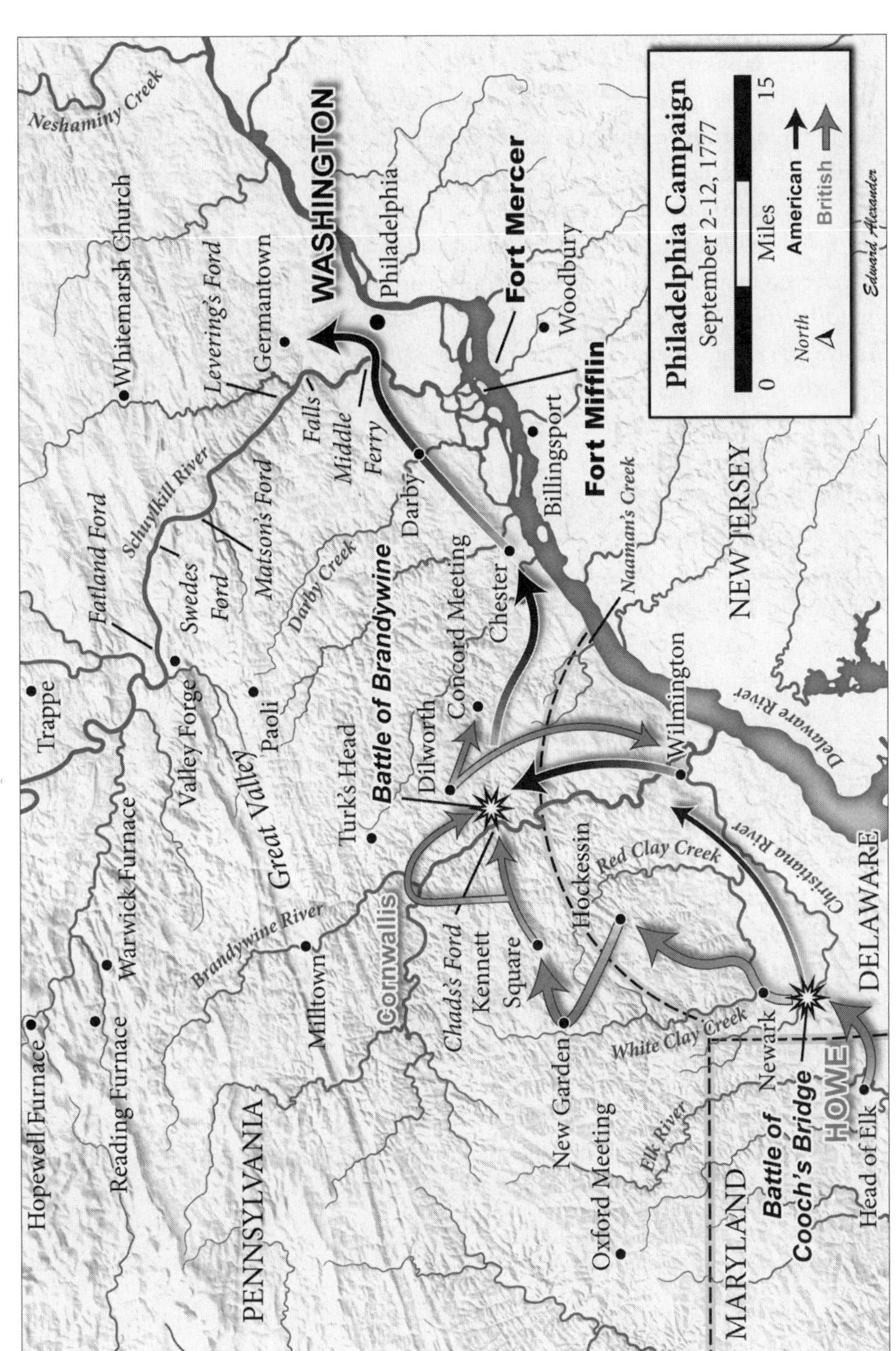
Philadelphia Campaign
September 2-12, 1777
0
Miles
15
American
British
North
Edward Alexander
WASHINGTON
HOWE
Cornwallis
Battle of Brandywine
Battle of Cooch's Bridge
Fort Mercer
Fort Mifflin
PENNSYLVANIA
NEW JERSEY
DELAWARE
MARYLAND
Neshaminy Creek
Whitemarsh Church
Germantown
Levering's Ford
Philadelphia
Woodbury
Falls
Middle Ferry
Darby
Billingsport
Schuylkill River
Fatland Ford
Swedes Ford
Matson's Ford
Darby Creek
Concord Meeting
Chester
Naaman's Creek
Trappe
Valley Forge
Paoli
Great Valley
Turk's Head
Dilworth
Wilmington
Delaware River
Christiana River
Red Clay Creek
Hockessin
Chads's Ford
Kennett Square
Brandywine River
Milltown
Warwick Furnace
Reading Furnace
Hopewell Furnace
New Garden
White Clay Creek
Newark
Oxford Meeting
Elk River
Head of Elk

its various crossings and prevent Howe from gaining access to the east bank. Although Washington had his troops in position east of the Brandywine a full day before the fighting began, he failed to gather all the intelligence needed to execute his defensive battle plan. He intended to use the river to block Howe's advance, yet remained almost completely ignorant of the surrounding terrain and road network, and failed to identify and guard all the fords available to the British. There was a lack of reconnaissance patrols. Even more alarming was that no one in a position of authority thought to speak to the many local residents serving in the Continental Army. The result, argued one writer, was an "American army even more uncertain of the immediate nature of the country than were the British." Washington did not know the region, and did not take the "precaution of having at hand someone who knew the countryside."[24]

Earlier in the war, Washington reasoned that "we should on all Occassions avoid a general Action, or put anything to the Risque, unless compelled by a necessity, into which we ought never to be drawn." By early September 1777, Washington's Continental Army had been maneuvered into a position that warranted and necessitated a pitched battle. Giving up Philadelphia without a fight was not an option.[25]

While Washington prepared for battle with little terrain knowledge and even less help from the locals, William Howe made his plans with the advantage of both. Pennsylvania Loyalist Joseph Galloway and others provided Howe with everything he needed to know about local terrain conditions and the road network. Washington's position east of the Brandywine limited Howe's options. A frontal assault against the American positions would be too costly and the men hard to replace. Howe, who strove to avoid direct assaults, preferred sending a diversionary force forward against the center of an enemy's main position to pin him in place, and a strong column on a flanking march to turn the enemy out of his position.

Howe had used this same tactic repeatedly, and recently, against Washington, but the Virginian had not yet taken the lesson to heart and was consistently unprepared for Howe's predictable maneuver. Brandywine was merely a repeat of Howe's performance on other fields. He sent Wilhelm von Knyphausen's division ahead to pin Washington in place, then executed a wide left hook under the command of Gen. Cornwallis that surprised the Americans by appearing beyond

24 Reed, *Campaign*, 114; Pancake, *1777*, 169.

25 Fitzpatrick, ed., *Writings*, vol. 6, 28.

their vulnerable right flank. Washington discovered the move too late to prevent it—a glaring failure of intelligence gathering. To his credit, he shifted the bulk of his army to oppose it and conducted a dogged defensive action that cost Howe dearly. Howe's success that day can be evenly credited to both his good generalship and to Washington's failures.[26]

Although the Continental Army had suffered a tactical defeat along the Brandywine, Washington's men fought remarkably well. William Maxwell's light infantry brigade conducted the morning's delaying action in splendid fashion, and the divisions of Adam Stephen, Lord Stirling, and John Sullivan found good defensive ground and fought hard upon it when ordered to confront Howe's flanking column. They were ultimately defeated through no fault of their own. Nathanael Greene's men turned in a solid performance and kept the roads open for the American retreat. They suffered some 1,300 casualties, with 300 killed, 600 wounded, and 400 missing or captured. Given the trying circumstances, the Continentals had done their job as well or better than anyone could have reasonably expected. Washington's poor use of scouts and the intelligence they produced haunted him throughout that long day.[27]

Howe, on the other hand, gathered accurate information about local terrain conditions despite operating in hostile territory. His flanking maneuver, which was based on that intelligence, worked almost to perfection. His veteran British and Hessian troops performed well and did all that was asked of them. Knyphausen's division played its diversionary role exceedingly well, deceiving Washington through most of the day as to Howe's true intentions. Cornwallis's division executed a grueling flank march, deployed, and broke the American lines in a frontal assault. British losses approached 600, with 93 killed and nearly 500 wounded. Fortunately for the Americans, Howe was hampered by a lack of mounted troops, which prevented him from pursuing his defeated enemy.[28]

Though they lost the battle, many Americans found reasons for optimism. "Notwithstanding we gave the Enemy the ground, the purchase has been at much blood," explained Gen. Nathanael Greene, "this being by far the greatest loss they have met with since the commencement of the War." Gen. George Weedon, one of Greene's brigade commanders, agreed. "Fake Intelligence saved his [Howe's]

26 For a full discussion of the battle and its results see Harris, *Brandywine*, 202-404.

27 Ibid., 368.

28 Ibid.

Bacon that day, or in all probability America would have had just cause to adore the name of Brandywine to the latest posterity."[29] Continental artillery chief Henry Knox concurred, writing to his wife, "Our people behaved well but Heaven frowned upon us is a degree. We were obliged to retire after a very considerable slaughter of the enemy." Washington knew serious mistakes had been made, though he was not yet ready to admit that he had been the one who had made them. "Unfortunately the intelligence received of the enemy's advancing up the Brandywine, and crossing at a ford about six miles above us, was uncertain and contradictory," he reported immediately after the battle, "notwithstanding all my pains to get the best."[30]

Many British and Hessian officers channeled these thoughts and heaped praise on the Continental Army. "As far as I can tell," admitted Howe's Hessian aide, Capt. von Muenchhausen, "Washington executed a masterpiece of strategy today by sending columns from his right to his left wing in the beginning…Soon after this Washington withdrew from his left wing…All this was done with great speed and especially good order." Rather than praise his enemy Cornwallis applauded Howe by writing, "The manoeuvre that brought on the action of Brandywine certainly reflects the highest honour on the General [Howe]." Hessian Capt. Johann Ewald was pleased by the victory but realized the British had missed a rare opportunity. "Had General Howe set out two hours earlier, or marched faster Washington's army would have been caught between two fires . . . several good friends from headquarters assured me that this mistake was caused by the guides, who had declared the route shorter than we found it to be." The frustrated von Muenchhausen summarized that Washington's escape that night happened because the patriots "could not be pursued by us because of the darkness, and . . . his still fresh men, who knew the terrain very well, could have the same advantage they would have in daylight."[31]

29 Richard K. Showman, Robert M. McCarthy, and Margaret Cobb, eds., *The Papers of General Nathanael Greene*, 13 vols. (Chapel Hill, NC, 1980), vol. 2, *1 January 1777-16 October 1778*, 162; Letter, George Weedon to John Page, 8 October 1777, original in Weedon Letters, Chicago Historical Society, Chicago, IL. Weedon was a native Virginian, a veteran of the French and Indian War, and an innkeeper in Fredericksburg before the war.

30 Harry M. Ward, *Major General Adam Stephen and the Cause of American Liberty* (Charlottesville, VA, 1989), 197. Brooks, *Henry Knox*, 104. Fitzpatrick, ed., *Writings*, vol. 9, 207-8.

31 Von Muenchhausen, *At Howe's Side*, 31-2; *Narrative of Howe*, 95-96. Von Muenchhausen's description reverses Washington's right and left wings; Johann Ewald, *Diary of the American War: A Hessian Journal: Captain Johann Ewald*, ed. and trans. Joseph P. Tustin (New Haven, CT, 1979), 87.

Washington's retreat from the Brandywine didn't end the fighting for Philadelphia, but it was the seminal engagement of the 1777 Philadelphia Campaign. The next several weeks would witness several small skirmishes and other encounters, including the Battle of Germantown, Washington's bold attempt to recapture the lost capital city.

Brandywine's Aftermath

Late on the evening of September 11, Washington and his army were retreating in haste from the battlefield at Brandywine toward Chester, Pennsylvania, reaching the port town along the Delaware River about midnight. While some of the troops had arrived ahead of the commander-in-chief, much of the army was strung out on several roads and paths stretching all the way back to the battlefield, about 14 miles to the northwest. The exhausted Washington desperately needed a few hours of rest, but took several minutes to pen a quick report to John Hancock, the president of the Congress. "I am sorry to inform you," he began, "that in this day's engagement, we have been obliged to leave the enemy masters of the field." After blaming faulty intelligence, Washington concluded on an optimistic note: "[O]ur loss of men is not, I am persuaded, very considerable, I believe much less than the enemy's."[32]

The general civilian population of Chester County spent the next several days dealing with the repercussions of the battle while the politicians in Philadelphia debated whether the defeat meant that the capital was lost. Washington, who needed to reorganize his army, was pleased when early reports demonstrated that nearly 11,000 troops were again present for duty just a few days after Brandywine. This was just 1,000 fewer Continentals than he had taken into battle. Not surprisingly, few of the 3,000 militiamen present at Brandywine reappeared within the army's ranks. More time was needed to gather the Pennsylvania militia and get them back into the fold.[33]

Thus far in the campaign, the militia from Delaware, Maryland, and Pennsylvania had not earned much respect from the Continentals. The militias had done precious little to interfere with Howe's plunderous march through northeastern Maryland and northern Delaware. The sizable division of

32 Fitzpatrick, *Writings*, vol. 9, 207-208.

33 Harris, *Brandywine*, 374.

Pennsylvania militia that had joined the army along the Brandywine had been wisely relegated to a minor role in the battle because Washington knew he could not rely on them when most needed. John Armstrong, who commanded the Pennsylvania militia at Brandywine, agreed with this assessment. "[M]any, too many" of the militia were a "Scandle to the military profession, a nuisance in service & a dead weight on the publick," he declared. Still, Armstrong did not think it fair to compare the militia with the Continental Line, and he also believed the part-time soldiers had many men in the ranks who would stand and fight. Many judged the militia "from a single action, [and] still worse . . . brand the whole with the infamous conduct of only a part."[34]

Gen. Howe did little to interfere with Washington's efforts to regroup in the immediate aftermath of the battle. For four days, Howe kept most of his army on the battlefield instead of launching a vigorous pursuit. In truth, Howe's army was exhausted. The soldiers had endured a long tedious voyage, followed by hard marching and prolonged combat with sustained casualties. They were in no condition to drive ahead, and had earned a much-needed rest. "The fatigues of this Day were excessive," confirmed Lt. Loftus Cliffe of the 46th Regiment of Foot. "If you knew the weight a poor soldier carried, the length of time he is obliged to be on foot for a train of Artillery to move 17 Miles, the Duties he goes thro when near an Enemy & that the whole night of the 9th we were marching, you would say we had done our duty on the 11th." While men on both sides claimed the Americans had dealt Howe a severe blow, Capt. Richard Fitzpatrick of the British Brigade of Guards thought such talk was without foundation. "Some foolish people were much elated with this event [Brandywine] and an insufferable torrent of nonsense was talked for some time afterwards, such as that the whole army must disperse, that it was impossible they should ever recover [from] so severe a blow, &c &c but these silly fellows were soon convinced that they had no foundation for their opinions, Washington still continued to talk high language."[35]

Besides resting his army, Howe had other matters to handle. Hundreds of wounded men needed medical care, and the dead had to be buried. The army needed to establish a bridgehead at Wilmington, to evacuate the injured, the

34 Hazard, et al, eds., *Archives*, Series 1, vol. 6, 100-101.

35 Letter, Loftus Cliffe to brother Jack, October 24, 1777, Loftus Cliffe Papers, William L. Clements Library, University of Michigan, Ann Arbor, MI. Letter, Richard Fitzpatrick to his Brother, the Earl of Upper Ossory, October 28, 1777, Richard Fitzpatrick Papers, Miscellaneous Manuscripts 622, Library of Congress, Washington, DC.

seriously ill, and the collected provisions to a safe garrison town. Insufficient wagons and the paucity of healthy horses hampered Howe's operational ability, and it took several days to accomplish these tasks.[36]

With the dawn of September 12 came an order from Washington for the army to move out, while also doing everything possible to round up stragglers and put them back in the ranks. "The commanding officer of each brigade," he ordered, "is immediately to send off as many officers as he shall think necessary on the roads leading to the places of action yesterday, and on any other roads where stragglers may be found; particularly to Wilmington, where 'tis said, many have retired, to pick up all the stragglers from the army, and bring them on. In doing this, they will proceed as far, towards the enemy, as shall be consistent with their own safety, and examine every house."

Washington also had to carefully assess his losses and the army's fighting condition:

> [Each] Brigadier, or officer commanding a brigade will immediately make the most exact returns of their killed, wounded and missing. The officers are, without loss of time to see that their men are completed with ammunition; that their arms are in the best order, the inside of them washed clean and well dried; the touch-holes picked, and a good flint in each gun. . . . The commanding officer of each regiment is to endeavour to procure such necessaries as are wanting, for his men.[37]

With his own army back in organized motion, Washington needed to find fresh defensive ground to protect Philadelphia from Howe's victorious army. The only remaining natural barrier was the Schuylkill River. The Continentals left Chester, marched through Darby, crossed the floating bridge at the Middle Ferry on the Schuylkill (modern-day Market Street Bridge), and entered the outskirts of Philadelphia. The bridge, explained one modern historian, "an unstable affair, was fashioned of pontoons roughly laid over with planking." The Pennsylvania militia was left on the near side of the river to help screen the army, which bypassed the capital by turning left and marching out to East Falls, about five miles from the crossing near Germantown. The long and exhausting march consumed 19 miles.

36 Spring, *With Zeal*, 269.

37 Fitzpatrick, *Writings*, vol. 9, 209-210.

Washington made his headquarters in the home of Henry Hill on the outskirts of Germantown.[38]

While passing through Darby, Washington sent a letter to Brig. Gen. William Smallwood. The brigadier had been detached from the army to help raise militia in his native Maryland and was organizing them around Oxford Meeting in southern Chester County. "[The] forces under your command," began Washington, "cannot be employed to so much advantage in any way, as by falling on the Enemy's Rear and attacking them as often as possible. I am persuaded many advantages will result from this measure." Such a tactic, he continued, "will greatly retard their march and give us time, and will also oblige them, either to keep a string guard with their Sick and Wounded, with which they must now be much incumbered, or to send them back to their Shipping under an escort, which you will have an opportunity of attacking with a good prospect of Success." The Virginia general had fought a traditional battle along the Brandywine; now it was time to return to a strategy of harassment.[39]

Moving the army north of the Schuylkill River put Washington behind the last natural barrier between the British and Philadelphia. The river was swift-flowing but shallow in many spots. The Falls of the Schuylkill (near modern East Falls), or rapids, splashed through large boulders where the river dropped some 30 feet. Except for the floating bridge Washington's army used to cross, there were no permanent bridges spanning the river. Philadelphia was accessible at the Upper, Middle, and Lower ferries, and many fords farther upriver. As a defensive barrier, the Schuylkill was less than ideal.[40]

If defending the numerous fords across the Brandywine had been difficult for Washington, then defending those crossing the Schuylkill, which were more spread out, would prove a Herculean task. Most of the fords were winding, narrow affairs that snaked across a gravelly river bottom, dependent upon small islands or mud

38 Thomas J. McGuire, *The Philadelphia Campaign: Brandywine and the Fall of Philadelphia*, 2 vols. (Mechanicsburg, PA, 2006), vol. 1, 273. The Hill House was located at the intersection of Midvale Avenue and Stokeley Street in the East Falls section of Philadelphia.

39 Fitzpatrick, *Writings*, vol. 9, 210.

40 The rapids no longer exist because dams were built that raised the water level. The Lower Ferry, also known as Gray's Ferry, was located where Gray's Ferry Avenue Bridge crosses the river today, between south Philadelphia and southwest Philadelphia. The Middle Ferry was located between the modern Market Street and Chestnut Street Bridges, near 30th Street. The Upper Ferry was located within the bounds of modern-day Fairmount Park, near the Philadelphia Art Museum and the Spring Garden Street Bridge.

flats to complete the crossing. Hilly terrain lined the Schuylkill along much of its course, and many of the ford roads meandered down steep inclines. Any force crossing the river at such places as Fatland and Levering's fords would find itself vulnerable to attack. The hills around Swedes Ford tapered more gently to the crossing in a wide and shallow valley, to a point where the river bottom was hard and stony. A body of troops had more room to maneuver and protect itself there. Somehow Washington would have to protect every ford and potential crossing point if he was going to defend the Schuylkill River line.[41]

Moving into the Germantown area left Washington with a vexing conundrum. The Delaware and Schuylkill rivers form a peninsula, at the tip of which sat Philadelphia. Washington felt duty-bound to defend the capital, but he could not leave the critical supply depots at Reading and other places in the backcountry unprotected. Moving northwest to cover the depots would expose Philadelphia. Moving into position to defend Philadelphia exposed the supply centers upon which his army depended. It was now readily obvious that the loss at Brandywine made protecting the American capital nearly impossible. The security of his storehouses had to take precedence over that of the most important city in North America.[42]

Some panic set in once the residents of Philadelphia realized Washington had reached that conclusion. Many had already fled or were soon to do so. Those who remained prepared for the worst or rejoiced in secret because they backed the British cause. "Numbers of the Inhabitants are removing from the City, but the Confusion and Tumult, is much less than I could have supposed, considering the very Critical Situation of Affairs," explained James Hutchinson, a surgeon in the city.[43]

Earlier in the campaign, several prominent Quakers had been imprisoned under suspicion of aiding the British and were housed in the city's Masonic Lodge. While they never filed formal charges, Congress and the Pennsylvania Supreme Executive Council decided to release the Quakers and banish them from

41 McGuire, *Campaign*, vol. 1, 274. Levering's Ford is in modern-day Manayunk, just below the big concrete arch bridge for Green Lane. The ford took its name from the Levering family which lived nearby. Matson's Ford is in modern-day Conshohocken, just north of the Fayette Street Bridge. Fatland Ford is in modern-day Valley Forge National Historic Park, behind where the chapel stands today. Swedes Ford is in what is today Norristown, just below the Route 202 bridge.

42 Pancake, *1777*, 174.

43 Letter, James Hutchinson to James Pemberton, 15 September 1777, James Hutchinson Papers, American Philosophical Society, Philadelphia, PA.

Philadelphia. "We have been obliged to attempt to humble the Pride of some Jesuits who call themselves Quakers, but who love Money and Land better than Liberty or Religion," wrote hawkish Congressman John Adams to his wife Abigail. "The Hypocrites are endeavouring to raise the Cry of Persecution, and to give this Matter a religious Turn, but they cant succeed. The World knows them and their Communications," continued the future president. "American Independence had disappointed them, which makes them hate it. Yet the Dastards dare not avow their Hatred to it, it seems." Reverend Henry Muhlenberg watched as "six wagons with guards passed by," in Trappe, Pennsylvania, some 25 miles northeast of the capital. "[T]hey are to take the most prominent Quakers of Philadelphia, who have been arrested, to Augusta County, in Virginia." The wagons and their human cargo eventually ended up in Winchester, Virginia.[44]

While Washington wrestled with his options, and while most of Howe's troops cleared the Brandywine battlefield and rested, elements of the British army probed ahead in search of the Americans. Gen. James Grant with the 1st and 2nd British Brigades, a squadron of dragoons, and the Queen's Rangers led a scouting expedition east of the Brandywine on the day after the battle. Two miles east they reached Concord Meeting and rounded up American stragglers. Howe sent the 71st Highlanders and elements of the light dragoons south ten miles to Wilmington, Delaware, to secure the town, rendezvous with the fleet, and establish a hospital. The small body of militia defending the city fled when the Highlanders approached. Members of the 71st arrested John McKinley, the president of Delaware. According to McKinley, he remained behind because it was "more solicitous to perform my Duty, than for my own personal Safety." The Highlanders also seized seven artillery pieces. With the port of Wilmington secured, Admiral Howe assured his brother the general "that he would have several ships at Wilmington on September 15th at the latest."[45]

44 Among those exiled from the city were Elizabeth Drinker's husband Henry, Sarah Logan Fisher's husband Thomas, James Pemberton, and Israel Pemberton, who were rounded up on September 2. None of those exiled would ever be charged with a crime or given a trial. Aaron Sullivan, *The Disaffected: Britain's Occupation of Philadelphia During the American Revolution* (Philadelphia, 2019), 1, 4; Smith el. al., *Letters*, vol. 7, 627; Henry Melchior Muhlenberg, *The Journals of Henry Melchior Muhlenberg*, trans. Theodore G. Tappert and John W. Doberstein, 3 vols. (Philadelphia, 1958), vol. 3, 74. The Reverend Henry Muhlenberg was the head of the Lutheran Church in North America and was the father of Peter Muhlenberg, a brigade commander in Washington's Army.

45 Delaware Archives: *Revolutionary War*, 3 vols. (Wilmington, DE, 1919), vol. 3, 1,416. Carl von Baurmeister, "Letters of Major Baurmeister During the Philadelphia Campaign, 1777-1778," in *PMHB* (Philadelphia, 1935), vol. 59, 409.

Most of Howe's men, meanwhile, remained idle. An aggressive pursuit of Washington's defeated army would have maintained the initiative, forced additional fighting on his terms, and likely crushed or further dispersed the Americans. Howe could have crossed the upper fords on the Schuylkill River with ease, cutting Washington off from his crucial supply depots. Earlier in the campaign, Howe told Lord Germain that he took the long route up Chesapeake Bay so he could threaten those American storehouses, but his continued lethargy gave Washington the time he required to block access to them. Like his propensity for flanking operations, Howe had a history of unenthusiastic follow through after successful battles. Brandywine's aftermath was no different.[46]

Free from having to mount another vigorous defense, Washington took the time to congratulate his army, thanking "those gallant officers and soldiers, who, on the 11th. instant, bravely fought in their country and its cause." He had "full confidence that in another Appeal to Heaven (with the blessing of providence, which it becomes every officer and soldier humbly to supplicate), we shall prove successful." Praying for the "blessing of providence" only went so far, however, and Washington issued orders for the Pennsylvania militia to build redoubts above the Schuylkill River fords.[47]

While Washington praised his army and the militia prepared defensive positions, the Pennsylvania Assembly worried. What was to become of Philadelphia? Washington expressed his views to Thomas Wharton, Jr., president of the Assembly. "As I am well apprized of the importance of Philadelphia you may rest assured that I shall take every measure in my power to defend it," he explained, "and I hope you will agree with me that the only effectual Method will be to oppose General Howe with our whole united Force." Local forces, he added, must be pressed into action. Washington also offered his thoughts on the state of the Delaware River defenses. "In my opinion, the River would be sufficiently secured against any sudden attacks by Water only, if the City Artillery Companies [militia] were thrown into Fort Mifflin, and all the Vessels of War of different kinds drawn up behind the Chevaux de Frize. I have given orders to Colo. [Joseph] Penrose [of the Pennsylvania Militia] to overflow the Grounds upon Province Island, which

46 Reed, *Campaign*, 143.

47 Fitzpatrick, *Writings*, vol. 9, 211.

will render it impossible for the Enemy to approach the Fort in the Rear and raise Batteries against it."[48]

As far as Washington was concerned, it was impossible to defeat Howe, prevent the British occupation of Philadelphia, and defend the river line simultaneously. The direct defense of the city would have to be handled by the State Assembly, at least for now. With the Continental Army seeking reinforcements, and Congress and the Assembly scrambling to get out of Philadelphia, it was, explained historian John Jackson, "little wonder the State forces were having difficulty in obtaining recruits for the State fleet or to work on the river defenses."[49]

While Washington agonized over how to counter Howe, Thomas Wharton worried about the precarious state of the river defenses, which had been stripped of nearly every available Continental soldier and militiaman to reinforce the main army. By September 5, there were only 80 men at Billingsport, New Jersey, 45 men manning Fort Mifflin, and none at all at Fort Mercer, the Bush Island redoubt, or the Darby Creek redoubt. The three rows of chevaux-de-frise jamming the river between Forts Mifflin and Mercer were next to useless without soldiers and guns to protect them.[50]

With the Continental Army once more camped around Germantown, the local civilian population cast a wary eye on their property. James Hutchinson mounted his horse to ride out and examine his uncle's home, which doubled as "General Sullivans Head Quarters." Thankfully, he reported to James Pemberton, his uncle, "Thy House, Garden, and Orchard, have not sustained any damage, but above 150 Pannels of thy Fence is destroyed, and burnt, most of the Neighbours shared the same (and many of them a much worse) fate, particularly Dr. Bensel, several Cornfields are entirely destroyed."

Unfortunately for the civilians, the armies would return to Germantown on a scale they could not yet imagine.[51]

48 Chase and Lengel, eds., *Papers*, vol 11, 222.

49 John W. Jackson, *The Pennsylvania Navy, 1775-1781: The Defense of the Delaware* (New Brunswick, NJ, 1974), 119-21.

50 Jackson, *Navy*, 118-119.

51 Letter, Hutchinson to Pemberton, 15 September 1777.

Chapter 2

The Battle of the Clouds

September 13-16, 1777

"The Blow could not be followed on account of the badness of the weather."[1]

— British Gen. James Grant, October 20, 1777

Two days after the Battle of Brandywine, William Howe was busy shifting elements of his army to better control the surrounding area. Lord Cornwallis led the British light infantry and grenadiers to join James Grant at Concord Meeting before marching to the heights at Aston within five miles of Chester. Patrols probed to the outskirts of Chester, and Cornwallis soon discovered that Washington had left. The British had allowed Washington nearly two full days to regroup and move, Cornwallis's march to Aston being the extent of the British pursuit of the defeated rebels.

1 James Grant to Harvey October 20, 1777, in James Grant Papers, National Archives of Scotland, Edinburgh, microfilm copy in the David Library of the American Revolution, Washington Crossing, PA, microfilm 687, reel 28.

Washington Crosses the Schuylkill River

On September 14 Washington's army left the Germantown area, marched down Ridge Road, crossed the Schuylkill River at Levering's Ford (modern-day Manayunk), and moved to the Old Lancaster or Conestoga Road.[2] The light dragoons led the way, followed by the divisions of John Sullivan, Lord Stirling, Anthony Wayne, Adam Stephen, and Nathanael Greene, with Francis Nash's brigade sandwiched between Wayne and Stephen. The end of the march found the army stretched out from near Radnor Meeting House back six miles to Merion Meeting House. Washington established his headquarters at Mary Miller's Buck Tavern, 11 miles from Philadelphia. The sight Mrs. Miller beheld was surely something she never forgot. Soldiers had passed by during the French and Indian War, but not in numbers exceeding Washington's 10,000. The tavern stood on the line between Chester and Philadelphia counties. Those returning from Sunday worship would have had great difficulty getting home with the road clogged with tramping soldiers the entire day, spread out along the Lancaster Road and approaching the Great Valley in northern Chester County. By moving into the valley toward Milltown (modern Downingtown), the army blocked the roads leading to Swedes' Ford. Milltown, Chester County's largest inland town, was a depot for flour and other supplies for the Continental Army. It was halfway between Philadelphia and Lancaster, some 30 miles from each.[3]

The Great Valley was the area of Chester County called the Welsh Tract. The 40,000-acre area stretching from the Schuylkill River through the Great Valley to Uwchlan had been settled by William Penn. Most of the residents were first or

2 Levering's Ford was about half way between Swedes' Ford (Norristown) and Philadelphia. The Lancaster Road (roughly parallel to modern-day U.S. Route 30), was the direct route between Lancaster, Pennsylvania, and Philadelphia. Lancaster, America's largest inland city at the time, was 60 miles west of the colonial capital, surrounded by rolling acres of rich farmland and dozens of mills, ironworks, and rifle shops. A 1778 traveler described the town: "There are some few good houses, and exclusive of those, it appears neither handsome, nor agreeable; however the markets are plentifully supplied with all sorts of provision, and the cyder is very excellent, the nearest to English of any I met with in America." Thomas Anburey, *Travels Through the Interior Parts of America* (North Charleston, SC, 2017), 216.

3 Radnor Meeting House was located at the modern intersection of Conestoga Road, Sproul Road, Newtown Road, and South Radnor Chester Road. The Buck Tavern, which was demolished in 1965, stood near where Delaware and Montgomery Counties meet today. The site is denoted by a historical marker on U.S. Route 30 between Old Buck Lane and Martin's Lane in Haverford. Thomas J. McGuire, *Battle of Paoli* (Mechanicsburg, PA, 2000), 13 & 227; *McGuire*, Campaign, vol. 1, 291.

second generation Americans, but many of the older inhabitants still spoke their native Welsh. The area included a few English, some Scotch-Irish Presbyterians, German and Swiss Mennonites, Amish, and a few Africans. The region was a microcosm of Pennsylvania.[4]

The Setting

With Washington moving back across the Schuylkill River, the operations of the two combatants would continue to impact Chester County for most of the next two weeks. Chester was one of the three original counties established by William Penn, and the village of the same name was the earliest settlement in the state. There were no significant towns in the starkly rural county, which was thick with forests of chestnut, hickory, and oak growing out of rolling hills. The well-watered limestone topsoil was some of the best on the continent, which explains why most of the residents were farmers. "This region of Pennsylvania is extremely mountainous and traversed by thick forests; nevertheless it is very well cultivated and very fertile," observed impressed Hessian Johann Ewald.[5]

Loyalist Thomas Anburey travelled through Pennsylvania in 1778 and left a detailed description of the countryside, which was "Extremely well cultivated and inhabited." The roads, he continued,

> are lined with farm houses, some of which are near the road, and some at a little distance, and the space between the road and houses is taken up with fields and meadows. . . . The farmers in Pennsylvania . . . pay more attention to the construction of their barns than their dwelling-houses. . . . The Pennsylvanians are an industriou . . . s and hardy peoplethey are well lodged, fed, and clad . . . having but few blacks among them. . . . In travelling through Pennsylvania, you meet with people of almost every different persuasion of religion that exists; in short, the diversity of religions, nations, and languages here is astonishing, at the same time, the harmony they live in no less edifying.[6]

Local families grew, made, or traded for much of what they needed, supplementing supplies or purchasing goods during trips to Wilmington or Philadelphia. The buckwheat fields were in full bloom by the middle of September,

4 McGuire, *Campaign*, vol. 1, 294-5.

5 Ewald, *Diary*, 80.

6 Anburey, *Travels*, 210-217.

and ready to be harvested the following month, but the tall corn needed for animal fodder was still green. Apple and peach orchards were ripe for picking. Farmers plowed their fields to prepare for winter wheat and rye. Except for some iron manufacturing along the Schuylkill River, Chester County had no large-scale industry. It was not unusual for a farmer to practice a trade like blacksmithing, and they supplied gristmills with grains to grind for flour. Weaving was a cottage industry, and itinerant butchers, tailors, and cordwainers traveled the county seeking work.[7]

Chester County boasted a population of 21,000 people, about 500 of whom were slaves. Most of the residents lived in tiny hamlets at crossroads centered on taverns, mills, and ferries. Blacksmith shops, tanneries, and other establishments provided natural meeting places. Shopkeepers or affluent farmers provided local banking services and distilled liquor for their neighbors.[8]

Although the area was almost exclusively rural, the major road linking Philadelphia with other cities farther south passed through Chester County. Philadelphia was within a day's journey of most of the county and drew most of its trade, including as much as half of the wheat produced there. The American capital provided professional services and was the county's religious, political, social, and cultural center. Besides the farmers and millers, Chester County was home to a variety of cabinetmakers, clockmakers, doctors, self-taught mathematicians, and scientists, with several members of the American Philosophical Society among them. While the region had ties to Philadelphia, the county was far enough away from the commercial center to be self-reliant and able to live separately from the city. The restrictive trade laws that fueled the Revolution had little effect on Chester County. Only a small portion of the populace supported the war. Most remained neutral for religious reasons or leaned toward supporting the British. Quakers comprised about 40 percent of the population, and their neutrality garnered contempt from American soldiers, who viewed Quakers as little more than Loyalists.[9]

Loyalists were so prevalent that Howe's quartermasters would often find the supplies they needed from among the inhabitants, much to Washington's chagrin. The Board of War later claimed that "a great Number of the Inhabitants of the

7 McGuire, *Campaign*, vol. 1, 166.

8 Ibid., 164; John B. Frantz and William Pencak, eds., *Beyond Philadelphia: The American Revolution in the Pennsylvania Hinterland* (University Park, PA, 1998), 1-2.

9 McGuire, *Campaign*, vol. 1, 165.

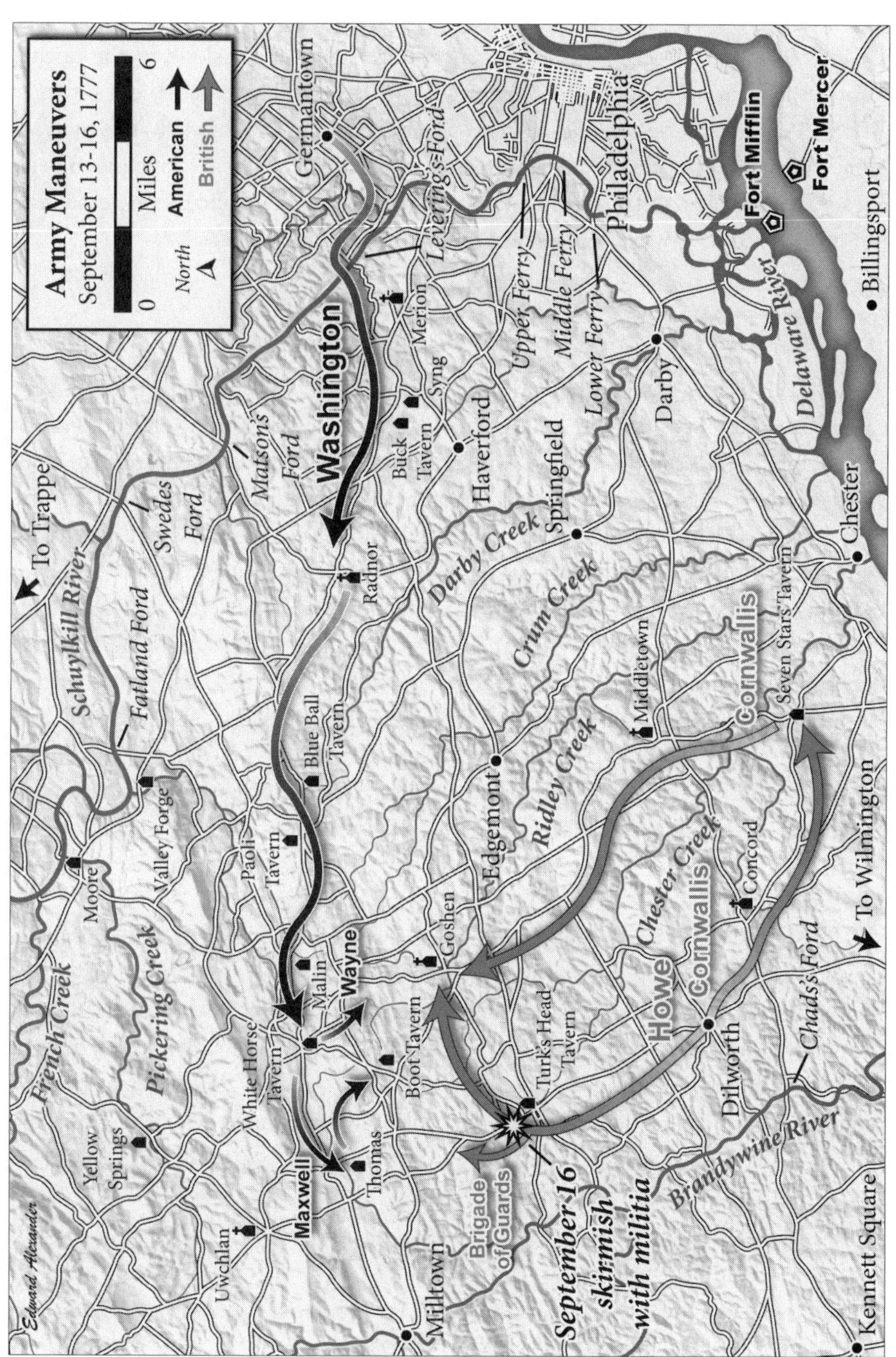
Army Maneuvers
September 13-16, 1777
North
0
Miles
6
American
British
Edward Alexander
Washington
Maxwell
Wayne
Howe
Cornwallis
Cornwallis
Cornwallis
Brigade of Guards
September 16 skirmish with militia
To Trappe
To Wilmington
Schuylkill River
French Creek
Pickering Creek
Darby Creek
Crum Creek
Ridley Creek
Chester Creek
Brandywine River
Delaware River
Fatland Ford
Swedes Ford
Matson's Ford
Levering's Ford
Upper Ferry
Middle Ferry
Lower Ferry
Chads's Ford
Germantown
Philadelphia
Fort Mifflin
Fort Mercer
Billingsport
Chester
Darby
Haverford
Springfield
Radnor
Merion
Buck Tavern
Syng
Blue Ball Tavern
Paoli Tavern
Valley Forge
Moore
Yellow Springs
Uwchlan
White Horse Tavern
Malin
Goshen
Boot Tavern
Thomas
Turk's Head Tavern
Edgemont
Middletown
Seven Stars Tavern
Concord
Dilworth
Milltown
Kennett Square

County of Chester, conveyed Intelligence, & supplied Provisions to the enemy during their Progress thro' that County." The report disavowed these citizens. "These Persons can be considered in no other Light than as Traitors to this State, & avowed enemies to the United States, & therefore the great principle of self Preservation requires that the most effectual means should be forthwith pursued to put it out of their Power to persist in their former Mal-Practices."[10]

Washington's Problems

Although the army had moved south of the Schuylkill River again, leaving the capital exposed, Washington continued to issue orders regarding the defense of Philadelphia. The Middle Bridge, which the army used during the retreat from Chester, was to be removed "as the Enemy (being now advanced near Chester) will probably Detach a party of light Troops to take possession of it." Washington sent a French engineer and military officer, Col. Louis Le Begue de Presle DuPortail, to General Armstrong of the militia to fortify Swedes' Ford with a redoubt and heavy cannon. "As it is not expected that these Works will have occasion to stand a long defence," explained Washington, "they should be as such as can with the least labour & in the shortest time be completed, only that part of them which is opposed to cannon, need be of any considerable thickness & the whole of them should be rather calculated for Dispatch than any unnecessary Decorations or Regularity which Engineers are frequently too fond of." As it turned out, the earthwork would be the only defensive fortification constructed west of Philadelphia.[11]

As Washington moved his army, Congress voted to recall John Sullivan, pending an inquiry into his conduct at Brandywine. In a fortunate turn regarding manpower, Philippe Hubert, Chevalier de Preudhomme de Borre, resigned from the army. De Borre had led John Sullivan's division to its disastrous fate at Brandywine, and the army was happy to see him go. If Washington suspended Sullivan, however, no general officers would have remained with the Maryland

10 Hazard, et al, eds., *Archives*, Series 1, vol. 5, 686. This same report claims that the British capture of Philadelphia "would in all Probability not have succeeded" if not for Chester County's residents.

11 Chase and Lengel, eds., *Papers*, vol. 11, 224.

division. Washington informed Congress that he was delaying the investigation, but promised to deal with the Sullivan issue later.[12]

Congressional meddling with his officer corps continued to plague Washington. For example, Congress granted high rank to foreign volunteers, which in turn created animosity between American officers and the newly arrived foreign generals. Back in July, several of Washington's officers threatened to resign when French officer Phillipe Charles Jean Baptiste, Tronson du Coudray, was named head of the Continental artillery—a position already held by Henry Knox. Knox, Nathanael Greene, and John Sullivan all threatened to leave over du Coudray's appointment. "Coudray," wrote one historian, "was a bombastic elitist who valued his own knowledge above all else." Members of Congress mistook his "haughty attitude" for military aptitude, which in turn "alienated him from America's military commanders." Washington, who knew losing Knox, Greene, and Sullivan would cripple his high command, appeased his officers by naming du Coudray Inspector General of Ordnances and Military Manufactories. That role put du Coudray in position to prepare the defenses of the Delaware River. Considering the dire condition of those defenses, Washington's choice of du Coudray was about to come back to haunt him.[13]

Not only did the English-speaking American officers dislike "these Frenchmen," but the French engineers disliked one another. Duportail, the engineer with orders to construct a redoubt at Swedes' Ford, did not get along with du Coudray. Discussions on how to improve Forts Mifflin and Mercer, for example, resulted in heated discussions between the Frenchmen. Duportail had arrived in America from France that summer with an entourage of 18 officers and ten sergeants—the type of European pageantry guaranteed to trigger American scorn. Du Coudray also was rather pompous. One French officer described him as a man "with the airs of a lord, and let on that he was one . . . he reviles all the Frenchmen, even the Marquis de Lafayette, to whom he wrote a very rude letter." The defense of the Delaware River would be critical in the coming weeks and

12 Congress largely blamed Sullivan for the defeat at Brandywine for not having his own division in place to blunt the British flank attack, and for being in overall command of the force sent to stop that attack. He would face a court of inquiry later in the campaign. For more details, see Harris, *Brandywine*, 415-427.

13 Robert F. Smith, *Manufacturing Independence: Industrial Innovation in the American Revolution* (Yardley, PA, 2016), 65; Robert K. Wright, Jr., *The Continental Army* (Washington, D.C., 1983), 129.

months, and infighting between arrogant foreign engineers was the last thing Washington needed.[14]

While the engineers squabbled, stragglers from the fight at Brandywine trickled back to the army. John Hawkins of the 2nd Canadian Regiment (also called "Congress's Own Regiment") was happy to see some of his lost comrades, recalling how "This Night several of our Men came up with us whom we thought had been taken." Their arrival pleased Washington, who was desperate to replace his Brandywine losses. It had only been three days since the bloodletting at Brandywine, but Washington had already dispatched orders to the Hudson River Highlands for the two regiments of the Rhode Island Brigade and Alexander McDougall's 2nd Connecticut Brigade to move south and join him. He had high hopes that others who were not with the main army could still help him. The Maryland militia under William Smallwood was gathering at Oxford Meeting nearly 50 miles distant. Washington issued orders for Smallwood to "push on as expeditiously as possible with what Troops you now have, leaving those in your rear to follow, and that you will either annoy or harass the Enemy on their Flank or Rear." Washington added at the end of the dispatch that the best service Smallwood could render was "perpetually hanging on and annoying [the British] Rear."[15]

To his disappointment, Washington soon learned that Smallwood had 1,400 poorly armed and barely trained men with no artillery, little ammunition, and almost no supplies. If they joined the main army, they would be a more of a burden than a blessing. "The Condition of my Troops, their Number, the State of their Arms, Discipline and Military Stores," Smallwood wrote Washington, "I am Apprehensive will not enable me to render that essential Service." In response to Washington's hope that the Marylanders could harass Howe's rear, Smallwood feared that Howe might "detach a Body of Infantry with their light Horse to Attack and disperse the Militia. . . . Your Excelly. is too well acquainted with Militia to place much Dependence in them when opposed to regular and veteran Troops, without Regular Forces to support them." These Marylanders would be of little or no help. Still, Washington maintained a positive outlook. He had been tactically

14 Memoir of Chevalier Dubuysson, Stanley J. Idzerda, et al, eds., *Lafayette in the Age of the American Revolution: Selected Letters and Papers*, 5 vols (Ithaca, NY, 1977), vol. 1, 79.

15 John H. Hawkins Journal 1779-1782 [sic], MS Am. 0765, Historical Society of Pennsylvania, Philadelphia, PA; Fitzpatrick. *Writings*, vol. 9, 222-23; Wright, *Army*, 227-238. The 2nd Connecticut Brigade seems to have contained just three regiments at the time.

defeated at Brandywine and chaos enveloped the army, but "Our troops have not lost their spirits," he wrote General William Heath, "and I am in hopes we shall soon have it in our power to compensate for the disaster we have sustained."[16]

While Washington regrouped and formulated a plan to protect Philadelphia, William Howe ordered more troops to Wilmington. Hessians under Col. Johann von Loos escorted the sick and wounded from Brandywine down into Delaware along with the army's invalids and American prisoners.

Just after dawn on September 15, Washington rode toward the rear of his army near Merion Meeting, where he breakfasted with Philip Syng, Jr., a 74-year-old master silversmith from Philadelphia who had retired in 1772, at Syng's home east of Buck Tavern.[17] Later that morning the American army was on the move again, this time going down the Lancaster Road another 12 miles (to what are today modern Malvern and Frazer). The armies spent the day under threatening skies that foreshadowed the storm that would arrive the next day. Washington made his headquarters at the Randall Malin House at the intersection of the Swedes' Ford Road and Lancaster Road.[18] Advance elements of the army ranged farther west to the vicinity of the White Horse Tavern (modern East Whiteland Township), two miles away.[19] The rear of the army stretched back to the General Paoli Tavern in Tredyffrin Township. Beyond the White Horse Tavern, William Maxwell's light infantry brigade camped near the home of Col. Richard Thomas (modern Exton near the intersection of Route 100 and Lancaster Road).[20]

When the army finally halted, the Continentals were strung out along three miles of the Lancaster Road. The White Horse Tavern overlooked the intersection of six key roads. Heading west down the Lancaster Road would take Washington to

16 McGuire, *Campaign*, vol. 1, 284; Chase and Lengel, eds., *Papers*, vol. 11, 241.

17 Syng's home was once the Prince of Wales Tavern. It stood on Montgomery Avenue in Ardmore near Anderson Avenue. McGuire, *Paoli*, 17 & 228.

18 The Randall Malin house is no longer standing.

19 The White Horse Tavern was operated by John Kerlin and was one of the earliest taverns established in Pennsylvania. Interestingly, it stood on the watershed between the Brandywine and Schuylkill rivers. As of 2000, the tavern was a private dwelling standing at the intersection of Planebrook and Swedesford Roads in Frazer, just south of the modern Battle of the Clouds Park.

20 The Paoli Tavern was named in honor of Gen. Pasquale Paoli, a Corsican patriot who had fought for Corsica's independence and who was a hero of the Whigs, both in England and America. Destroyed by fire in 1892, the Paoli Tavern stood on the northwest corner of the U.S. Route 30 and Valley Road intersection in Paoli. McGuire, *Paoli*, 28 & 232. Thomas commanded the 5th Battalion of Chester County militia at the time.

Milltown (modern Downingtown) seven miles away, or to Lancaster, which was another 33 miles down the road. East along the Lancaster Road was Philadelphia, 26 miles behind them. The junction at Malin's House led to Swedes' Ford, 12 miles to the northeast. Running southeast from the tavern over the South Valley Hill was the road to Goshen, Edgemont, and Chester, where Charles Cornwallis was camped. Another road led southwest to Boot Tavern, Turk's Head Tavern, and ultimately to Wilmington, beyond where Howe had made his camp. The Paxton Road ran northwest over the North Valley Hill to Yellow Springs and the French Creek iron region. Furnaces that turned out cannon, ammunition, and iron implements for the army were scattered along the creek. Finally, a road ran northeast to Judge William Moore's on Pickering Creek near the Schuylkill River, not far from another ironworks known as Valley Forge. From Moore's house, other roads led to the French Creek region and Reading, another major supply depot.[21]

Washington's army was strategically positioned to block a British advance to the Schuylkill River. Although the Americans had taken a roundabout route to get there, they were just ten miles from where they had fought at Brandywine four days ago. While the Great Valley could cover the approaches to the Schuylkill, it did not protect Philadelphia, along the Delaware River. The Delaware was still vulnerable to British warships that were even then making their way toward the river after backtracking from Chesapeake Bay. Captain Charles Alexander of the Continental frigate *Delaware*, anchored off Billingsport, New Jersey, believed 100 men could capture the fortification located there. Washington wanted to improve the various redoubts and forts along the Delaware but believed "if we should be able to oppose Genl Howe with success in the Field, the Works will be unnecessary."[22]

Eve of Battle

Determined to prevent a repeat of Brandywine, where large numbers of men had fled the field and mounted troops were inefficiently utilized, Washington

21 Boot Tavern stood at the intersection of Ship Road and Boot Road. It would become British army headquarters following the Battle of the Clouds. McGuire, *Paoli*, 28-29, 232. In addition to being a supply center, a major hospital facility was established in September in Reading. Mary C. Gillett, *The Army Medical Department, 1775-1818* (Honolulu, HI, 2002), 91.

22 Jackson, *Navy*, 121; Chase and Lengel, eds., *Papers*, vol. 11, 213.

issued a brutal order that authorized summary execution in the field. "The Brigadiers or Officers commanding regiments," he began,

> are also to post some good officers in the rear, to keep the men in order; and if in time of action, any man, who is not wounded, whether he has arms or not, turns his back on the enemy, and attempts to run away, or to retreat before orders are given for it, those officers are instantly to put him to death—The man does not deserve to live, who basely flies, breaks his solemn engagements, and betrays his country.

To remedy the poor performance of his cavalry, Washington appointed Casimir Pulaski, an officer on par with artillery commander Henry Knox, to lead the army's mounted arm. The Warsaw-born Polish nobleman would perform his task so well that he would one day be known as "the father of the American cavalry."[23]

Sometime on September 15, Washington sent a detachment from Sullivan's division, comprised of the German Regiment and a mixture of Delaware and Maryland troops under Capt. Enoch Anderson, to observe the British army around Chester. Colonel Henry Arendt of the German Regiment, who commanded the operation, reported to Washington just before noon that he had skirmished with a British outpost likely placed there by Cornwallis. Arendt had planned to move up the Edgemont Road back to the army, but Cornwallis's camp at Aston blocked that route. "[W]e were certainly in a dangerous situation—on the bank of the Delaware—the enemy close by—and we were in the land of the Tories," concluded Captain Anderson. Little did Anderson and his men know that their ordeal was only just beginning.[24]

In an attempt to keep supplies and weapons caches out of British hands, Washington ordered the Continental Army to strip the numerous iron furnaces, forges, powder magazines, and other places of items of military value. In the village of Trappe, observed Henry Muhlenberg, "a large number of freight wagons crossed the Schulkiel and passed by our place. They had loaded ammunition from a

23 Chase and Lengel, eds., *Papers*, vol. 11, 233. Savannah, Georgia's Fort Pulaski, which is best known for its role during the American Civil War, was named in honor of Casimir Pulaski.

24 Ibid., 238; Enoch Anderson, *Personal Recollections of Captain Enoch Anderson, an officer of the Delaware Regiments in the Revolutionary War*, ed. Henry Hobart, *Historical and Biographical Papers of the Historical Society of Delaware*, vol. 2, No.16 (1896), 39.

magazine in order to take it safely in the direction of Bethlehem because the British division has approached the magazine last night."[25]

While this careful chess match continued, the issue of why Howe was moving so slowly permeated the ranks of the British army. Captain Friedrich von Muenchhausen, Howe's aide-de-camp, took umbrage at the idea and noted as much in his diary. "Some stupid people are dwelling on the fact that our General does not quickly follow Washington with his whole force," he began. "Of course this would be a good thing if it were possible, but it is definitely not, because the General first has to send away the sick and wounded on the wagons, which carry our provisions and baggage. It is not possible to procure enough wagons here to do both at the same time," he added, "and neither of the two could be left behind."[26]

While Washington contemplated how best to defend Philadelphia and weaken the British, information reached Howe that would prompt action sufficient to quell any more talk of a dilatory pursuit: Washington was south of the Schuylkill River. "At 4 o'clock P.M. learnt that the rebel army which had crossed the Schuylkill at Philadelphia had repassed it to this side of Levering's Ford and were pursuing the road to Lancaster," recorded engineer officer John Montresor. The American army was within reach, and Howe intended to move on that intelligence. On the night of September 15, he issued orders for the army to move into the Great Valley the following day. The Hessian von Mirbach battalion, still on the Brandywine battlefield, was to march for Wilmington to reinforce that garrison. Howe ordered Cornwallis to take two British brigades, the grenadiers, and the light infantry with him toward a junction with the main army, while Howe would move out from Dilworth. Cornwallis put his column in motion up Edgemont Road that night. After passing Seven Stars Tavern, he halted to wait for daybreak. When dawn arrived, he would make for Goshen Meeting, unite with Howe, and proceed toward the White Horse Tavern. Rain had already moved into the area, turning the rutted dirt roads of Chester County into a dense paste through which thousands of soldiers tramped. What Howe seems not to have known is that on the morning of September 16, Washington's army was moving from the Lancaster Road and ascending the South Valley Hill to block the British from the Schuylkill River. The

25 Muhlenberg, *Journals*, vol. 3, 74-75.

26 Von Muenchhausen, *At Howe's Side*, 32.

armies were once more on a collision course, only five days after the conclusion of the largest battle of the American Revolution.[27]

Battle of the Clouds

The heavy rain continued into and through September 16. Around midday, under cascading sheets of rain, the headache that was General du Coudray ended in abrupt fashion. The French officer was crossing the Schuylkill River to ride to Washington's camp at the Lower Ferry when his horse jumped off the ferry into the river, taking the general with him. Although he managed to wriggle free from his stirrups, his aides were unable to save him. "About eleven o'clock, General Coudray, with nine French officers, set out for camp over Schuylkill," recalled a civilian named Jacob Hiltzheimer. "The General being mounted in the boat, his horse became restive and jumped overboard with him, and the General was drowned. I was present when his body was recovered, toward evening." John Hancock, president of Congress, would later inform Washington that they interred the Frenchman the next afternoon "at the public Expence."[28]

The issue of what to do about the squabbling French engineering officers was but a minor matter compared to the complex and weighty issue facing Washington: the British army was on the move. So were American scouting parties. Three Pennsylvanians out on the Edgemont Road, Lt. Col. Persifor Frazer, Maj. John Harper, and Jacob Vernon, stopped in the Blue Ball Tavern for refreshment on their way back to the army. "Major Harper looking from the window saw a number of horsemen coming up the road who from their uniform he supposed were part of a company of Virginia light horse," recalled American officer Persifor Frazer. The assumption was logical, for some troopers from the 4th Continental Light Dragoons had donned captured uniforms of the 8th and 24th Regiments of Foot—red coats with blue facings, much like those worn by the 16th Light Dragoons of Howe's army. Unfortunately for the three Pennsylvanians, the men trotting up the road that morning were not Americans, but British dragoons. One they realized their mistake, Jacob Vernon made his exit by jumping out a window.

27 John Montresor, "The Montresor Journals," ed. G. D. Delaplaine, *Collections of the New York Historical Society for the Year 1881* (1882), 452. The modern route that Cornwallis took from Aston had him marching up Route 452 to Lima, then north on Route 352 to Goshen Meeting House.

28 Jacob Hiltzheimer, *Extracts from the Diary of Jacob Hiltzheimer, of Philadelphia. 1765-1798*, ed. Jacob Cox Parson (Philadelphia, 1893), 35; Chase and Lengel, eds., *Papers*, vol. 11, 254. Du Coudray was buried in the yard of St. Mary's Church in Philadelphia.

"The others in attempting to do so," continued Frazer, "were fired upon, the house surrounded and they captured, their swords and horses taken from them and themselves compelled to proceed with their captors." Light Infantryman Lt. Henry Stirke confirmed their capture. "This morning a party of Light Dragoons, with us, surpris'd at a house a Rebel Colonel and a Major of Brigade; 3 Light Dragoons was with them but made their escape out of a backdoor, leaving their Horses behind them."[29]

Other American scouting parties were less careless and thus more fortunate, though their situations were still precarious. The mixed command from Sullivan's division (the German Regiment and some Delaware and Maryland troops under Capt. Enoch Anderson) had spent the previous night in Chester hovering in the rear of Cornwallis's column, and would continue doing so throughout the long rainy day. "The British were on the march, bearing northwardly," recorded Captain Anderson. "We marched on all this day, keeping near the British army. When they marched—we marched; when they stopped—we stopped. Our guide was the beating of their drums." Everyone, he continued, was "wet to the skin but we walked, say marched, ourselves dry!"[30]

Howe, with the main body of the British army, left Dilworth and passed by the Turk's Head Tavern (modern West Chester) en route to Goshen Friends Meeting House to join forces with Cornwallis's column. The rain showers, which had been heavy but intermittent, were now turning into a nearly continuous downpour. Howe's column was passing by Turk's Head Tavern when American militia hidden off the road fired into the British ranks, killing a soldier of the 33rd Regiment, wounding another, and injuring an officer.[31] The militia fled the scene of their ambush for the main American lines before the British could muster a response. The British buried their lone casualty and Howe, before moving on to Goshen

29 Persifor Frazer, *General Frazer: A Memoir Compiled Principally from his Own Papers by his Great-Grandson* (Philadelphia, 1907), 161. Henry Stirke, "A British Officer's Revolutionary War Journal, 1776-1778," S. Sydney Bradford, ed., *Maryland Historical Magazine* (1961), vol. 56, 170-171.

30 Anderson, *Recollections*, 39-40. According to Anderson's account, the detachment spent several more days stuck behind British lines and did not rejoin the American army until September 26 on the north side of the Schuylkill River.

31 Jacob James, the operator of the Turk's Head Tavern, joined the British army as a guide after Brandywine. He spent several months aiding Howe and Joseph Galloway by spying, recruiting, and participating in kidnapping operations, and later was commissioned a captain of the Goshen Troop of Light Horse, a Loyalist unit. McGuire, *Campaign*, vol. 1, 287; John Andre, *Major Andre's Journal: Operations of the British Army under Lieutenant Generals Sir William Howe and Sir Henry Clinton June 1777 to November, 1778 Recorded by Major John Andre, Adjutant General* (Tarrytown, NY, 1930), 48.

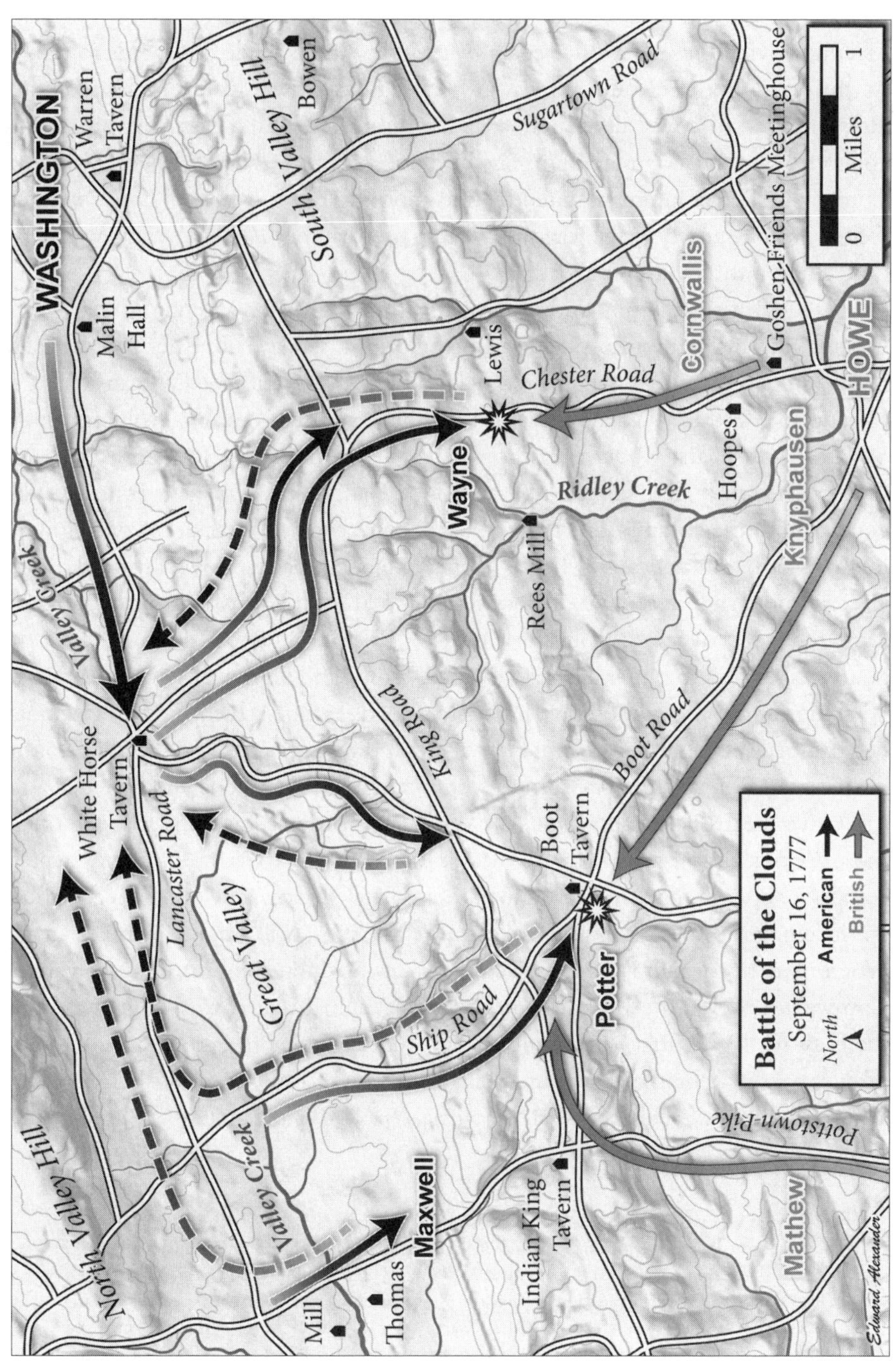
Battle of the Clouds
September 16, 1777
North
American
British
0
Miles
1
WASHINGTON
Warren Tavern
South Valley Hill
Bowen
Sugartown Road
Malin Hall
Lewis
Chester Road
Goshen-Friends Meetinghouse
Cornwallis
HOWE
Hoopes
Knyphausen
Ridley Creek
Wayne
Rees Mill
Valley Creek
White Horse Tavern
King Road
Boot Road
Boot Tavern
Lancaster Road
Great Valley
Ship Road
Potter
Pottstown-Pike
North Valley Hill
Valley Creek
Maxwell
Indian King Tavern
Mathew
Mill
Thomas
Edward Alexander

Meeting, divided his army once again by ordering the Brigade of Guards to move north (along modern Route 100 towards Pottstown) toward Indian King Tavern. Howe needed to cover all the roads leading into the Great Valley. Knyphausen's column, with the commanding general along, continued forward to join with Cornwallis. The columns reunited by mid-morning but lost several hours waiting for the artillery and baggage wagons to catch up with them. Howe's army was now operating on three different roads.[32]

As the British columns were coming together at Goshen Meeting, Washington was moving his army into position on the South Valley Hill. The Continentals moved in two columns. A Pennsylvania militia detachment from William Irvine's brigade and Anthony Wayne's division led the left, or easternmost, column south out of White Horse Tavern on the Chester Road (modern Route 352) toward Goshen Meeting, and moved up the South Valley Hill. Wayne was in overall command of the column. The right column, composed of William Maxwell's light infantry and James Potter's Pennsylvania militia brigade, moved toward Boot Tavern (modern intersection of Boot Road and Ship Road). Washington intended to march his army south from the Lancaster Road and deploy along the crest of South Valley Hill to block Howe's advance. Howe and Cornwallis hoped to catch Washington moving west along Lancaster Road, astride which the Continentals had camped the night before, not knowing that the Americans were heading south of that road. Instead, the two armies were marching toward one another.

Once the artillery and wagons arrived, Howe ordered his army forward once more. Cornwallis moved north up Chester Road heading toward Anthony Wayne's southbound column, which unbeknownst to Cornwallis was even then approaching the slope of South Valley Hill near Rees' Mill, about 1½ miles away. When American militia were discovered in position blocking the advance, Cornwallis ordered the 1st Battalion of British Light Infantry to assault and drive them away. "[We] attack'd a body of 500 rebels, under the command of Genl Waine, posted behind a fence, on a hill, about a half mile from Goshen meeting House," wrote Lt. Henry Stirke in his journal. "[O]n our advancing very briskly [the

32 This grave was dug up in 1827 when cellars were being prepared for a row of brick buildings. The modern route that Howe took had him moving north up the Old Wilmington Pike from Dilworth, and then north on portions of US. Route 202 to South High Street in West Chester. The Turk's Head Tavern was at the intersection of High and Market Streets. From there, the Brigade of Guards marched north on the Reading Road (modern Route 100). Howe, with the rest of the army, marched east on Goshen Road, which roughly paralleled the modern Paoli Pike, to unite with Cornwallis's column.

PA militia] gave us one fire and run away; leaving 10 men kill'd and Wounded on the field." "A few muskets were fired in advance of us," recalled Isaac Anderson, a member of the Chester County militia. "It was not late in the morning when it began to rain, and soon poured down a most copious shower. It was said that the ammunition had been much damaged in consequence." The sputtering American fire wounded one man in the light infantry, but the British musketry struck down a dozen militiamen. Wayne's Continental Regulars did not have time to deploy and were swept away with the retreating militia.[33]

Cornwallis's brief fight on the Chester Road was dying down when Wilhelm von Knyphausen's advance unit of Hessian jaegers made contact with part of Maxwell's column on Boot Road, a little more than two miles west of Cornwallis. The American light infantry brigade remained near the Thomas House watching the Pottstown Pike, but Potter's Militia Brigade had moved down Ship Road to the vicinity of Boot Tavern. Hessians screening the front of Knyphausen's column encountered the militia there. "The advance guard had hardly arrived at the Boot Tavern when they learned that an enemy corps of two to three thousand men had appeared on the left flank of the army," explained 33-year-old jaeger officer Johann Ewald. Colonel Carl von Donop had been seeking an opportunity to avenge the honor of the Hessians since the humiliating disaster at Trenton on December 26, 1776. His chance had now arrived, and he made the decision to lead the jaegers into the fight. The attack did not unfold as the revenge-seeking colonel intended.

"The colonel pursued them too far, through which mistake an enemy party passed between him and the army and cut off his retreat," concluded Captain Ewald. "Captain [Richard] Lorey, fearing an enemy trick, urged the colonel to go back, because he believed this enemy party was sent out to lure him into a trap. The colonel agreed and drew back, but found his return route occupied by the enemy. Captain Lorey," continued Ewald, "decided to break through with the horsemen [mounted jaegers] to relieve the foot jagers, notwithstanding that the enemy had posted himself very favorably behind walls and fences and kept up a sustained rifle fire." Ewald found von Donop's effort humorous. "The colonel got off with his skin—That is not a trade for one to follow who has no knowledge of it—We all

33 Stirke, "Journal," 171; McGuire, *Campaign*, vol. 1, 289; Isaac Anderson, "Historical Sketch of Charlestown Township," *Potter's American Monthly: Illustrated Magazine of History, Literature, Science and Art*, Vols. 4-5 (Philadelphia, 1875), 30. Many histories of the campaign credit Wayne's fight with the British light infantry as occurring near the Three Tuns Tavern. However, that establishment was not constructed until 1811. The fighting took place near the intersection of Alcott Circle with Route 352.

laughed secretly over this partisan trick." Two Hessian units, the grenadiers and the Leib Regiment, were deployed to support the jaegers, but never got into the fight.[34]

Hessian Ensign Wilhelm Freyenhagen, a member of the von Donop Regiment, recorded a more detailed version of the fighting in his personal journal:

> We came upon a corps of 1700 Rebels, who had positioned themselves on a hill in a very thick woods. We received the Minnigerode Batl. [Battalion] for support and Col. v. Wurmb had two amusettes [field pieces] brought up. Under their fire we attacked them with the exception of Capt. Ewald who was marching more to the left; he fell on their [right] flank. We were fortunate to drive them off with minimal losses. Pursuit was not possible because of a heavy rain. We took 8 prisoners including a wounded officer and three wounded privates. We had five Jägers wounded.[35]

Ensign Stephen Giffen of the York County Militia provided a detailed account of the fight when he applied for a pension many years later. "As we were dividing our rations we were attacked by the enemy at our encampment," he began. "Our quarter guard was driven in. Our Regt was in disorder & before we could get the men paraded we received a fire." Giffen was not impressed with the performance of his colonel. "At the second fire [of the enemy] our Col. (Walker) received a shot in the arm and in a cowardly manner ordered a retreat & fled about the same time my Capt. [Samuel Ferguson] and our Corporal (Geo Cress) fell, the first mortally wounded the latter very dangerously. At my instance," he continued, "about 20 of us made an effort to carry away our wounded Capt but we desisted at the remonstrance of the dying man. We then changed our position and after getting into a situation near a fence that favored us, we (the above remnant of about 20) turned upon a body of the enemies cavalry [mounted jaegers] & fired as we thought with considerable effect. About this time the force of the enemy were brought to bear upon us so powerfully that we followed the rest of our Regt in its retreat." After falling back, Giffen spotted his colonel. "I there saw our wounded and as I thought cowardly Col. for the last time. His wound I saw & understood was but a slight one. Eight of our men were killed and two taken prisoners in this skirmish

34 Ewald, *Diary*, 88-89.

35 "The Journal of Ensign/Lt. Wilhelm Johann Ernst Freyenhagen Jr - 1776-78. Part 2 – 1777-1778," Henry J. Retzer trans., Donald M. Londahl-Smidt, ed. *The Hessians: Journal of the Johannes Schwalm Historical Association* Vol. 14, (2011), 66.

(Corporal Cress who was supposed to have been killed followed & joined us the next day evening)."[36]

Late in the afternoon, Ewald led some jaegers forward as the Americans withdrew. "I believe it was about five o'clock in the afternoon, an extraordinary thunderstorm occurred, combined with the heaviest downpour in the world," recalled Ewald with some exaggeration. "General Knyphausen, who arrived at my company on horseback, ordered me to attack the people in the wood." The heavy rain made the muskets and rifles of both armies inoperable, so Ewald ordered his men into action with their "hunting swords [knives]. I reached the wood at top speed and came to close quarters with the enemy," reported Ewald, "who during the furious attack forgot that he had bayonets and quit the field, whereby the jagers captured four officers and some thirty men. The entire loss of the Jager Corps in this fight consisted of five killed, seven wounded, and three missing." Another dozen Americans fell in this part of the action. Among the militiamen battling the jaegers was Dunlap's Partisans, a unit largely armed with rifles of their own. Private James Patten remembered long after the fact that, "Owing to a tremendous rain that fell that day, the small armes were out of order and but little execution was done on either side."[37]

Twenty-six-year-old Lt. Heinrich von Feilitzsch of the Anspach Jaegers took part in this last round of combat. "The enemy had positioned himself in a forest, had kept his guns dry, while our men's powder was like mush in the tin pan, the enemy fire was therefore very lively, while ours was very weak," he explained, "and because it had lasted almost an hour, we decided to run an assault, guns hung over our shoulder and hunting knife [swords] in hand; right away we were among the enemy, but most of them fled; the enemy left the field to us." Lieutenant von Feilitzsch "had to deal with an old American, who attacked me about 5 times unsuccessfully, and tried to throw me to the ground with his gun, I could not get at him with my short bowie knife and only warded off his blows, his bayonet was hanging on his side; 2 Jägers came to my assistance, one of them bashed his head in."[38]

36 Revolutionary War Pension and Bounty-Land-Warrant Application Files (M804), Record Group 15, Records of the Veterans Administration, National Archives, Washington, D.C., file W7584., hereafter cited as RWPF.

37 Ewald, *Diary*, 89; RWPF, file S30629.

38 Heinrich von Feilitzsch, *Journal of several Campaigns in America by Heinrich Earl Philipp von Feilitzsch Prussian Lieutenant of the Ansbach Feldjager*, manuscript journal located in the Harlan Crow Library,

The tactical defeat put Washington in a bad position. His two advance militia elements had been driven off the crest of South Valley Hill, and the rest of the army was stacked up along the Lancaster Road, with muddy roads leading back into the Great Valley up the formidable North Valley Hill behind them. Howe's third column, the Brigade of Guards under Edward Mathew, had reached Indian King Tavern and was turning east on the King Road heading for Washington's right flank. With Mathew approaching from the west and Cornwallis on the road from the east, Washington had no easy way to exit the Great Valley. If the British drove over the top of South Valley Hill into the Great Valley, they would likely catch and destroy the Americans.

Timothy Pickering, the army's adjutant general, knew the army was not in position for sustained combat and pressed his horse close to Washington to drive that point home. "It was a question whether we should receive the British on the ground then occupied by our troops, or retire beyond a valley in their rear." He informed Washington that "the advancing of the British is manifest by the reports of the musketry. The order of battle is not completed. If we are to fight the enemy on this ground," continued Pickering, "the troops ought to be immediately arranged. If we are to take the high grounds on the other side of the valley, we ought to march immediately, or the enemy may fall upon us in the midst of our movement." Washington understood the tactical situation and the good advice. "Let us move," came the general's reply.[39]

Washington deployed the Continentals north of the White Horse Tavern "where they had a most favourable position being a prevailing gradual height in the valley." Because the majority of the army never began marching up the South Valley Hill, Washington was able to quickly form a line on the southern slope of the North Valley Hill, about three miles north from where the two earlier actions involving the American militia had occurred. The ammunition in American cartridge boxes, however, was being rendered useless by wind-whipped rain. If they were attacked, they would have no choice but to rely on bayonets, an unpalatable option that would have given the British a huge advantage. The army was repositioned, "choosing to avoid an action in which the discipline of the enemy

---

Dallas, Texas, 85. This manuscript version of the journal contains considerably more information and detail than the published version.

39 Timothy Pickering, "Col. Timothy Pickering's Account of the Battles of Brandywine and Germantown," *The Historical Magazine and Notes and Queries Concerning the Antiquities, History and Biography of America*, vol. 7 (New York, 1863), 219.

in the use of their bayonets (the only weapon that could then be of any service, and which we were by no means generally supplied with) would give them too great a superiority."[40]

Other than some skirmishing and muddy maneuvering, the "Battle of the Clouds" ground to a halt without a major clash of arms. To the dismay of Howe and his subordinates, the driving rain of a nor'easter prevented the general from exploiting his initial success. "The Blow could not be followed on account of the badness of the weather," explained British Gen. James Grant. "[I]t was the heaviest Gale of Rain I ever saw in any Country, during which Washington, astonished at our unexpected move from Chester, fled in the utmost confusion & by that means according to intercepted Letters, He lost all his ammunition." Virginia Loyalist James Parker, traveling with the British army as a volunteer guide, was in full agreement with Grant's assessment and recalled the effect the weather had on the dirt roads. "It had threatened rain all day, & now it fell, a Mud deluge, the Roads so deep there was no bringing on the Artillery, the Wind was at south East & every thing look'd like the Equinoctial storm, which it realy was." Artillery certainly could not move forward, and the men had much the same problem. Knyphausen's top aide "wish[ed] I could give a description of the downpour which began during the engagement and continued until the next morning. It came down so hard that in a few moments we were drenched and sank in mud up to our calves."[41]

It was, writes one historian of the campaign, "perhaps the best storm in American history, for it saved an American army." The claim is not without merit, and the men of both armies understood its significance. Ensign John Kinney of the 3rd New Jersey Regiment agreed, noting that the fighting ended thanks to the "occation of a tremendous storm of rain, which continued 48 hours." "All our

40 Reed, *Campaign*, 155; Montresor, "Journals," 454. Some of the fighting took place near the grounds of modern Immaculata College. The college's campus has a historical marker memorializing the engagement, as well as a gravesite that is believed to contain casualties from the fighting. The position the Americans moved to near White Horse Tavern was close to the grounds of the modern Philadelphia Memorial Park Cemetery. Samuel Shaw, *The Journals of Major Samuel Shaw: The First American Consul at Canton, ed. Josiah Quincy* (Boston, 1847), 37.

41 Grant to Harvey October 20, 1777, Grant Papers; James Parker Journal, September 16, 1777 entry, Parker Family Papers, originals in Liverpool, England, microfilm copies at the David Library of the American Revolution, Washington's Crossing, PA, film 45, reel 2. James Parker was born in Scotland in 1729 and emigrated to America in 1750, and he later became a wealthy merchant in Norfolk, Virginia. During the Philadelphia campaign, Parker linked up with Howe's army in Maryland and accompanied the British into Philadelphia. John A. Nagy, *Spies in the Continental Capital: Espionage Across Pennsylvania During the American Revolution* (Yardely, PA, 2011), 87; von Baurmeister, "Letters," 410-11.

Cartridges was wet and I much feared the ruen of the whole Army would have been the consequence, & indeed it must have been the case had G. Howe Advanced upon us in this situation," confessed New Jersey Continental Elias Dayton. "But fortunately for us he never moved towerds us." Captain Charles Porterfield, a Virginian attached to the Light Infantry Brigade, later described the army's precarious situation. "[I]t began to rain," he observed during the court martial of William Maxwell, "but Certain I am had the Enemy come on in our confusion, Posted at the [foot] of a hill, whilst they the Enemy Possessed the advantageous high Ground, & woods, we must have fallen to sacrifice." Hessian Johann Ewald admitted Maxwell's men had held them up, "but it would not have provided much advantage for Washington's army had not the severe downpour occurred."[42]

Major John Howard of the 4th Maryland Regiment offered an insightful summation of the situation faced by Washington's army that day, and why the engagement ended in the manner it did. "The advanced parties had met, and were beginning to skirmish, when they were separated by a heavy rain, which becoming more and more violent, soon rendered the retreat of the Americans a matter of absolute necessity." American weaponry and accoutrements, continued the major, were decidedly inferior. "The vast inferiority of [our] arms, which imposed on [us] at all times the cruel task of engaging the enemy on unequal terms, never brought [us] into such imminent peril as on this occasion," complained Howard. "[Our] gun locks not being well secured, many of [our] muskets were soon unfit for use. [Our] cartridge boxes [had] been so inartistically constructed as not sufficiently to protect [our] ammunition from the severity of the tempest. [Our] cartridges were consequently soon damaged; and this mischief was the more serious as very many of the soldiers were without bayonets." The disgruntled army officer concluded that the "army being rendered thus totally unfit for action, the design of giving the enemy battle, was necessarily, though reluctantly, abandoned, and a retreat commenced."[43]

42 RWPF, file S33357; Reed, *Campaign*, 156; Dennis P. Ryan, ed., *A Salute to Courage: The American Revolution as Seen through Wartime Writings of Officers of the Continental Army and Navy* (New York, 1979), 100; William Maxwell court martial papers, located in the Nathanael Greene papers, University of Delaware, Microfilm 667, reel 1: General Correspondence volume 1, 1775-April 1781; Ewald, *Diary*, 89.

43 John Eager Howard was the son of a prosperous farmer and had no military background when made a captain in 1776. Letter, John Howard to Colonel Bentalou, 4 March 1826, Bayard Papers, Maryland Historical Society, Baltimore, Maryland.

American Retreat

Rather than retreat to the commissary depot at Downingtown, Washington gave orders to move to Yellow Springs (modern Chester Springs), ten miles distant on the other side of the North Valley Hill. "We began to March towards the Yallow springs where we Arrived About 2 o'Clock the next Morning," wrote Lt. William Beatty of the 7th Maryland Regiment in his journal. "All the small Branches that we were obliged to Cross on this march were so rais'd by the Hard rain that they took us to the waists and under the Arms when we Waded them, None of our men preserv'd a single round of Ammunition that did not get thoroughly wet." The soggy tramp consumed fourteen long hours and, as Lt. James McMichael recalled, resulted in "excessive fatigue [that] surpassed all I ever experienced." The 4th Maryland's Major Howard remembered marching "through a cold, and most distressing night, and very deep roads."[44]

Artillery commander Henry Knox explained in a letter to his wife why so much ammunition was lost to the rain. "This was a most terrible stroke to us and owing entirely to the badness of the cartridge-boxes which had been provided for the army," he penned, echoing Major Howard's complaint. "This unfortunate event obliged us to retire, in order to get supplied with so essential an article as cartridges." The "badness" of the American cartridge boxes—Howard described them as "inartistically constructed"—referenced the flaps that folded over the tops of the boxes. Simply put, they were too narrow, allowing the driving rain to pour in and soak the paper-wrapped ammunition cartridges common to both armies. As Washington later informed Congress, "we had the mortification to find that our Ammunition which had been completed to Forty Rounds a Man was intirely ruined." Pickering, Washington's aide, confirmed the ammunition problem. "The cartridge boxes were bad, and nearly all the ammunition in them was spoiled.

44 Yellow Springs, a mineral water source Pennsylvanians had visited for years, also boasted the only hospital built for that purpose during the Revolution. Later, it played an important role as the closest general hospital to the Valley Forge encampment. Unfortunately, the structure burned down in 1902. Reed, *Campaign*, 407; William Beatty, "Journal of Capt. William Beatty, 1776-1781," *Maryland Historical Magazine* (Baltimore, 1906), vol. 3, 110; James McMichael, "Diary of Lieutenant James McMichael, of the Pennsylvania Line, 1776-1778," *PMHB*, William P. McMichael, ed (Philadelphia, 1892), vol. 16, 151. The route the army took to Yellow Springs is unclear. The most direct route would have been over the North Valley Hill to Yellow Springs Road. Another road that might have been used was the Paxton Road, the main route to Harris's Ferry (Harrisburg). It roughly followed Valley Hill Road west through Exton County Park to Ship Road, and then north to Lionville, where the Red Lion Tavern was located at the time. From there, Kimberton Road (Route 113) led directly to Yellow Springs. Letter, Howard to Bentalou, 4 March 1826, Bayard Papers.

Hence it became necessary to keep aloof from the enemy till fresh ammunition could be made up and distributed."[45]

The same rain that prevented the British from bringing up their artillery hindered the Americans from removing theirs. Sixteen-year-old Jacob Nagle described the difficulties of moving the guns over the North Valley Hill. "We came to a regular decented hill, the ground being so soft that they had to onhich the horses from one piece of artillery and hitch them to another till they got them all up," he penned in his diary. "The nights was so dark you could not tell the man next to you. I being a horseback, I kept close behind one of the ammunition waggons but dripping wet and shivering with cold." Another teenager, just 14 years old, named Hugh McDonald of the North Carolina Line remembered the exhaustion of the retreat. "After marching all day in the rain, we came late at night to a creek at the foot of a mountain, or very high hill," he told his journal. "The front making a halt, I very well remember that the platoon in which I was, halted in the creek. Resting my head on the butt end of my musket, I fell asleep. The first thing I knew, I was punched by some one behind me, and my file leader had gone a hundred yards. This caused a trot in the whole line to fill the gap which my weariness had occasioned."[46]

When the army stopped to rest at Yellow Springs, the Americans dropped onto the soggy ground with little or no shelter to protect them from the cold, driving rain. Most had thrown away their blankets during the retreat from Brandywine and so lacked even that meager cover. The miserable conditions were not confined to the men in the ranks. One of Washington's senior aides, Lt. Col. John Laurens, was as drenched and as tired as everyone else. "My old [green aide's] sash [was] rather disfigur'd by the heavy Rain which half drown'd us on our march to the Yellow Springs, (and which by the bye spolit me a waistcoat and breeches of white Cloth and my uniform Coat, clouding them with the dye wash'd out of my hat)." The men were already soaked before they made camp. "The brooks were swollen with the heavy rain, and Pickering's Creek up to the horses' bellies," recalled Thomas Pickering, "so that the passage of the artillery and wagons was difficult. The foot passed over, in a single file, on a log laid across as a bridge for

45 Letter, Henry Knox to Lucy Knox, 23 September 1777, Brooks, *Henry Knox*, 104; Edgar, *Campaign*, 46; Chase and Lengel, eds., *Papers*, vol. 11, 301; Pickering, "Account," 219.

46 Jacob Nagle, *The Nagle Journal—A Diary of the Life of Jacob Nagle, Sailor, From the Year 1775 to 1841*, John C. Dann, ed. (New York, 1988), 10; Hugh McDonald, *A Teen-ager in the Revolution: Being the Recollections of a High-Spirited Boy who Left his Tory Family at the Age of Fourteen and Joined the Continental Army* (Harrisburg, PA, 1966), 12.

foot passengers. To add to the difficulties, the night was dark." The lessons of the near-disaster were already being learned. "The great destruction of ammunition by the battle and heavy rain . . . shows the necessity of having very large stocks ready made up," observed Washington's adjutant, "otherwise you become defenceless, or are rendered incapable of any enterprise for a long time. This very circumstance obliged us to keep aloof from the enemy…for a considerable time, not being able fully to supply the men with a complement of cartridges till they had made some up themselves." Major Howard agreed, writing, "Scarcely a musket in a regiment could be discharged, and scarcely one cartridge in a box, of which forty rounds per man had just been drawn, was capable of being used."[47]

As the army slogged into Yellow Springs, a messenger was riding to Washington as fast as the sloppy roads allowed with an update on the Schuylkill River. "The River was rising fast & scarcely fordable the heavy Rains since have swelled it so much that it is now impassable," he explained, and "it will be 24 Hours before it will be fordable for the Footmen. . . . The Militia are collecting at this Place & the fords lower down. . . . The [Middle] Bridge is fully removed." Crossing north of the Schuylkill would have to wait.[48]

Just as he was after the victory at Brandywine, Hessian jaeger Johann Ewald was furious because Howe did not vigorously pursue the retreating Americans—despite the driving rain storm. "I firmly believe that we still could have caught up with the greater part of the enemy army, at least the baggage . . . if it had been the will of General Howe," wrote the frustrated officer in his diary. "But the three-day delay on the battlefield [Brandywine] after the battle convinced me that we certainly would have halted even if no rain had fallen, because we surely knew that we were hard on Washington's heels."[49]

While the American army trudged through that miserable night, the British took up camp wherever they happened to be when the action stopped. Howe made his headquarters in Boot Tavern, while Cornwallis took up residence in the home of George Hoopes along the Chester Road (modern Route 352). Other officers found shelter in local farmhouses. The British were also without tents, which had

47 Letter, John Laurens to Henry Laurens, 6 November 1777, "Correspondence Between Hon. Henry Laurens and His Son John, 1777-80," *The South Carolina Historical and Genealogical Magazine*, vol. 6, no. 1 (January 1905), 8-9; Octavius Pickering, *The Life of Timothy Pickering* (Boston, 1867), vol. 1, 159-160; Letter, Howard to Bentalou, 4 March 1826, Bayard Papers.

48 Chase and Lengel, eds., *Papers*, vol. 11, 251.

49 Ewald, *Diary*, 89.

been left with the fleet when they offloaded in upper Chesapeake Bay. Most of the enlisted men sought out barns or built wigwams, which one modern historian describes as "lean-to shelters that were easily and quickly constructed out of tree branches, fence rails, saplings, cornstalks, straw, sod, and other such materials. They served well in lieu of tents to shelter men from the blazing sun and light rain, but did little in the case of heavy downpours." Not everyone found protection from the elements. "The Troops ordered to pile their arms & make fires, but no shelter for a wieried soldier wet to the skin & under a heavy rain all night," complained a grenadier officer. Little dry firewood was at hand, and nature found a way to laugh at the soldiers who put that meager amount to good use. "We stayed here and camped, and during the night the rain changed to an actual cloud burst," wrote Jaeger officer von Feilitzsch, "and all our fires were washed down the mountain at the same time; It is hard without an overcoat or baggage."[50]

Once in camp, the British Guards and the 1st Light Infantry Battalion were deployed as pickets to protect the army. The Guards were pushed out on the left about half a mile in front of Boot Tavern, while the light infantrymen were posted on the right on a hill overlooking White Horse Tavern, where they confiscated crops to eat and fence rails for campfires.[51]

When the storm clouds cleared the next morning, the path was clear to the Schuylkill River fords and an easy occupation of Philadelphia. If Howe delayed his advance, as he had after Brandywine, Washington might have enough time to move his troops into a blocking position north of the river. The initiative rested with Howe.

50 McGuire, *Campaign*, vol. 1, 135; *John Peebles, John Peebles' American War: The Diary of a Scottish Grenadier, 1776-1782*, ed. Ira D. Gruber (Mechanicsburg, PA, 1998), 135; von Feilitzsch, *Journal*, 85-6.

51 McGuire, *Campaign*, vol. 1, 292.

Chapter 3

After the Storm

September 17-20, 1777

"To get wet up to one's chest and then to march in the cold, foggy night while enduring hunger and thirst, etc. is hard for the poor men. It takes courage."[1]

— Rev. Henry Muhlenberg, September 19, 1777

The early hours of September 17 found Washington's waterlogged army trudging into Yellow Springs, with most of its ammunition supply ruined by defective cartridge boxes. The Continental Army was essentially defenseless that morning, its members exhausted by their recent travails and in a foul mood. "Shortages of materials of all types, rampant inflation, and the sort of shoddy materials and incompetence too often associated with hasty government contracts and unscrupulous contractors plagued the army," noted historian Thomas McGuire. Washington had no choice but to distance his army from the British and find new sources of ammunition and other badly needed supplies. He decided upon Warwick Furnace in the French Creek Valley in northwestern Chester County, where he could rest his army and obtain what was needed to fight again. "[T]he enemy seem now to be straining every nerve to

1 Muhlenberg, *Journals*, vol. 3, 78.

accomplish their purpose," he wrote John Hancock, "but I trust, whatever present success they may have, they will ere long experience a reverse of fortune."[2]

Finding Supplies

If the soldiers were expecting to rest and dry out their belongings at Yellow Springs, they were deeply disappointed. No sooner had they arrived than Washington put their wet and weary bodies back in motion to Warwick Furnace. Anthony Wayne's Pennsylvania Division stayed behind near the Red Lion Tavern in Uwchlan Township to screen the rear of the army and to keep a close watch on Howe, who was only five miles away at Goshen. The balance of the army departed by the Kimberton Road and, because French Creek was flooded, moved six miles east by country roads to the bridge on Reading Road (modern Route 23). It was another nine miles to Warwick Furnace. Even though the rain had stopped, the roads were still a quagmire. The army was now within reach of its supply depots at Reading, and was in a position to observe British movements and move into blocking positions along the Schuylkill River, whose nearest ford was just nine miles away.[3]

While the main army moved toward Warwick Furnace, the baggage train rolled through the Valley Forge area. The slow-moving wagons could barely keep up with the army under perfect conditions, and the deep mud made movement agonizingly slow. Since the wagons didn't carry any dry munitions, it was not worth the rest of the army's time to wait for them; they would arrive as soon as they could. William Maxwell's light infantry brigade and James Potter's brigade of Pennsylvania militia stayed near Valley Forge to screen the wagon train. "I would have you remain where you are untill that part of the Baggage & stores at the Valley can be got away," Washington directed Maxwell, "which I wish to be effected as expeditiously as possible."[4]

Washington's worsening supply situation was not lost on Congress, which authorized him to impress from civilians whatever provisions he needed for the

2 McGuire, *Philadelphia Campaign*, vol. 1, 293; Chase and Lengel, eds., *Papers*, vol. 11, 253.

3 The likely route the army took was up Kimberton Road to Route 113 and then left onto Township Line Road, then another left onto Route 23, where the bridge across French Creek was located. The Red Lion Tavern still stands at the intersection Whitford Road and South Village Avenue in Lionville. Wayne's actual camp was about three miles away at Chester Springs.

4 Chase and Lengel, eds., *Papers*, vol. 11, 258.

army within a 70-mile radius of his headquarters. Ephraim Blaine, a merchant from Carlisle, Pennsylvania, and the deputy commissary general for the Middle Department, worked around the clock to obtain enough food to sustain the soldiers. He contracted coopers to make barrels to store meat, bakers in Lancaster, Reading, and Lebanon to make hard bread, and tallow chandlers to supply soap and candles. "The constant movement of Washington's army made supply very difficult, however, and despite his efforts the army on occasion lacked provisions," explained Erna Risch, historian of the Continental Army's supply problems.[5]

The grave difficulties encountered by Washington in moving his army, obtaining supplies, and bringing up his wagon train were duly noted in a journal kept by Robert Morton, a civilian traveling on the road to Reading on the morning of September 17. "In the morning we crossed Skippack [Creek] though very rapid, and proceeded on to Perkioming [Creek], where we found it dangerous to pass owing to the rapidity of the stream and the inconvenience attending the swimming of our horses," penned Morton. "We thought it most advisable to proceed to Pawling's Ferry upon Schuylkill, which having raised above 8 feet perpendicularly, and great numbers of trees and other rubbish coming down so fast, the Boatman would not go over." Rowland Evans, who operated a mill near the confluence of Perkiomen Creek and the Schuylkill just over the river from Valley Forge, described in a letter to a friend how the rising waters had carried away a "great part of the Fences along the [Perkiomen] Creek." The rains had triggered flooding "which was the highest known for a great many years past."[6]

While the weather forced the Americans to undertake yet another defensive movement, the British remained mostly in place while quartermaster parties spent the morning plundering the countryside. Most of Howe's soldiers spent the day trying to minimize the effects of the previous day's storm that had flooded the lowlands. Only part of the army under Cornwallis inched forward to White Horse Tavern, where the Americans had camped the night before the Battle of the Clouds. After waiting out the rain, Howe had his army in motion on September 18. The various columns linked up at White Horse Tavern and marched together to the Malin Farm, where Washington had made his headquarters three nights earlier.

5 Worthington Chauncey Ford, ed., *Journals of the Continental Congress 1774-1789*, 34 vols. (Washington, D.C., 1907), vol. 8, 752; Risch, *Washington's Army*, 173-174, 209.

6 Robert Morton, "The Diary of Robert Morton," *PMHB* (Philadelphia, 1877), vol. 1, 3; Letter, Rowland Evans to Edward Physick, March 2, 1778, Penn Family Papers, Collection 0485A, Additional Miscellaneous, Volume 2, Folder NB-004, Historical Society of Pennsylvania, Philadelphia, PA.

Howe divided his army at the road fork there; Cornwallis took his command east down Lancaster Road past the Admiral Warren and General Paoli Taverns while Howe, with General von Knyphausen's men, moved east along Swedes Ford Road to Tredyffrin Township. "The roads were extremely bad, partly because of the heavy rains and partly because Washington, with the large part of his army, artillery, and all his baggage, had passed this way last night," explained British engineer John Montresor.[7]

Howe's new position stretched for three miles along Swedesford Road facing Valley Forge. "They call this region Great Valley because there are chains of high hills covered with woods on both sides of the valley," explained von Muenchhausen once his part of the army arrived in Tredyffrin Township. "The Valley Creek, part of which flows through our camp, has the best water I have tasted here in America." A variety of mills and small manufactories dotted the landscape along the numerous streams of the bountiful landscape. Valley Creek meandered between Mount Joy and Mount Misery before emptying into the Schuylkill River, where an iron production facility known as Valley Forge was located three miles from the British camp.[8]

Howe intended to cross the Schuylkill River, but like every waterway in the region it was above flood stage. Washington knew his opponent wanted to move north of the Schuylkill and hoped to use the barrier to his advantage and make Howe pay for the effort. "[F]rom the present State of the River," he wrote to John Hancock on September 19, "I shall be down in time to give them a meeting, and if unfortunately they should gain Philadelphia, that it will not be without loss."[9]

The Americans also were moving on September 18. By that morning, the last elements of Washington's army were tramping into the vicinity of Warwick Furnace. Washington established headquarters at Reading Furnace, two miles

7 Montresor, "Journals," 453. The Admiral Warren Tavern was named for British naval hero Sir Peter Warren. The tavern's name was changed after the war to the General Warren Tavern in honor of Dr. Joseph Warren, who had been killed at Breed's Hill in 1775. The structure still stands today just north of Malvern near U.S. Route 30, but retains little of its 18th Century appearance. McGuire, *Campaign*, vol. 1, 294-295.

8 The right flank of the British encampment was located at the crossing of the Baptist Road in present day Centerville. The left flank was positioned at Howell's Tavern in present day Howellville. No longer standing, the tavern stood at the intersection of Howellville Road and Route 252. Howe established his headquarters at the home of Samuel Jones, which still stands on Old State Road near Contention Lane. McGuire, *Paoli*, 51; Von Muenchhausen, *At Howe's Side*, 34.

9 Chase and Lengel, eds., *Papers*, vol. 11, 269.

beyond the Warwick Furnace.[10] He needed to buy time for the army to recover before taking up a position to block Howe. William Smallwood and his Maryland militia had disappointed Washington, who had put faith in the prospect that they could successfully harass Howe's rear. To compensate for that deficiency, Washington ordered General Wayne to march his division into the British rear. The four light cannon of Randall's Independent Artillery, together with some light dragoons, were to accompany Wayne, whose operational column totaled 2,200 men.[11] "I must call your utmost Exertion in fitting yourselves in the best manner you can for following & Harasssing their Rear," directed the commanding general. "Genl Maxwell will have a Similar Order & will Assist you with the Corps under his command." Further time to contemplate the dangerous move prompted Washington to add a plea for timely information, coupled with an admonition. "Give me the earliest Information of every thing Interesting & of your moves that I may know how to govern mine by them," he instructed later that afternoon. "[T]ake care of Ambuscades."[12]

A change of orders was dispatched to the Maryland militia. During the day, 700 additional Marylanders and three iron cannon under the command of Col. Mordecai Gist joined Smallwood. Now in command of nearly 2,100 militiamen and three guns, Washington thought better of wasting the militia behind Howe, where they were doing nothing of substance, and sent an order to Smallwood to join the main army. For reasons that remain unclear, the order never reached Smallwood. "I proceeded on my march to fall on the Rear of the Enemy," he later

10 Both the Reading and Warwick Furnaces had been established in the 1730s and were busy making cannon and cannon shot for the Continental Army at the time. Arthur Cecil Bining, *Pennsylvania Iron Manufacture in the Eighteenth Century* (Harrisburg, PA, 1938), 41.

11 While no secondary sources and very few primary sources mention it, at least some Pennsylvania militiamen from Chester County voluntarily showed up at Wayne's encampment and took part in the Battle of Paoli. John Hair of West Nantmeal Township claimed in his pension application to have been at Paoli. "We joined Gen. Wayne at the Paoli, and participated in the bloody affair of the Paoli which took place the same night--In the morning after coming out of the woods to which we had fled, our Captain marched us home and it ended our expedition." Nathaniel Irwin made a similar claim in his pension deposition. "He with about 30 of his neighbors volunteered under Captain [John] Gardner & marched to old Chester on the Delaware where we joined Genl Wayne's command; that they marched with Genl Wayne from Chester & encamped at the Paoli Battle ground; & after lying there some days we was attacked by Genl Gray on the night of the 20th of September 1777 where many of the Americans were bayoneted & Genl Wayne and his command defeated & driven off the field, that your declarant immediately left the battle went home." McGuire, *Campaign*, vol. 1, 300; RWPF, files S2593 & S5599.

12 Chase and Lengel, eds., *Papers*, vol. 11, 265-266.

reported, "in order to harass and obstruct their march, to give time to our main Army to recover."[13]

Philadelphia was being evacuated during this period, and supplies for the army were stripped from warehouses and sent to Trenton, New Jersey. Washington did not think Trenton was secure as a supply depot. "That place, in the first instance, was fixed on through necessity, and conveying 'em there was better than to leave them where they were; But I am clear in Opinion, that they should not be suffered to remain there a Moment longer than can be avoided, and I would beg leave to recommend that the earliest & most vigorous measures should be adopted for removing 'em to Allen Town."[14]

With two large armies operating across the Pennsylvania countryside, farmers feared the loss of their livestock. Many residents attempted to drive their cattle away from the armies. One unfortunate blacksmith, John Hang, took cows to Warwick Furnace, hoping they would be safe there. Unfortunately for Hang, he drove his livestock right into the arms of the Continentals. His cows were appraised at "1350 weight of Beef which was Receipted for by some Compy or other officer of the Army I Was told belonging to the Maryland Line whose Name I have forgot."[15]

Skirmish at Valley Forge

The heavy rains turned the Schuylkill River into a rushing torrent, so it would be a while before the British could cross. Howe instead set his sights on Continental supply depots south of the river. Three miles down Valley Creek from the British camp sat Valley Forge, an ironworks and the site of an American storehouse. Built in 1742, the forge was owned by the partnership of David Potts and Col. William Dewees of the Pennsylvania Militia. "Whether military items were actually fabricated at the forge is uncertain, but the state government began storing large quantities of iron goods there, such as axes, shovels, tomahawks, and camp kettles, in the spring of 1777." West of Valley Forge, several ironworks, such as Warwick and Hopewell Furnaces, were casting cannons and ammunition. The

13 McGuire, *Campaign*, vol. 1, 300. Letter, William Smallwood to Governor Johnson, September 23, 1777, Maryland Historical Society, Baltimore, MD.

14 Chase and Lengel, eds., *Papers*, vol. 11, 262.

15 Letter, John Hang to unknown recipient, March 17, 1789, original manuscript in private family collection, scanned copy in author's possession.

government established the Continental Powder Mill on French Creek six miles from Valley Forge, together with the "public Gun Manufactory" and "Public Gunlock Factory" under the supervision of scientist David Rittenhouse. The Valley Forge storehouses were convenient depots for finished goods and flour ground at local mills.[16]

Dewees was less than excited about military supplies being stored at his facility and operated under the fear that the approaching British would burn down his complex. Now that the enemy were but a short march away, he wanted the supplies ferried north of the Schuylkill. All his workers had been called up for militia duty, however, and were thus unavailable, and William Maxwell's command departed the area without helping. General Henry "Lighthorse Harry" Lee and Washington's aide, Alexander Hamilton, were sent with a handful of dragoons to Valley Forge to assist Dewees on the afternoon of September 18. Lee approached from the west via Nutt Road (modern Route 23), while Hamilton crossed the Schuylkill aboard a commandeered barge. The task proved impossible. A mere eight men and two rafts were available to move 4,000 barrels of flour, each weighing around 200 pounds, plus tons of iron goods. Not only would they need to make many trips across the river, but they would have to move all the materials 400 yards just to reach the Schuylkill.[17]

Dewees was right to be worried about the safety of his facility. That evening, Howe sent a column to seize the storehouse at Valley Forge. Lieutenant-Colonel William Harcourt, with two mounted squadrons of the 16th Light Dragoons, 200 dismounted dragoons, and three companies of light infantry, pushed up Baptist Road to Gulph Road to gain access to the forge. There was no road between the hills at Valley Forge and therefore no direct access to it. The only way to reach it was from the north. Once the British reached Gulph Road, they moved

16 The ironworks at Valley Forge were established to convert pig iron into bar iron. David Potts's brother, Isaac, operated a sawmill and gristmill not far from the forge operation. Within the narrow valley between Mount Joy and Mount Misery, the intersection of present-day Gulph Road and Nutt Road was not far from the industrial complex. Mere yards from the mills sat Isaac Potts's modest home, which would become Washington's headquarters during the Valley Forge encampment later in the year. McGuire, *Paoli*, 55-56, 70, 236; McGuire, *Campaign*, vol. 1, 296.

17 Lighthorse Harry Lee was the father of famed Civil War General Robert E. Lee. McGuire, *Campaign*, vol. 1, 297.

cross-country over the hill to their left to get to Valley Creek, along which sat the forge complex.[18]

Captain Henry Lee had posted sentinels atop Mount Joy overlooking the complex to warn of any British approach. "The fire of the vedettes announced the enemy's appearance. The dragoons were ordered instantly to embark," recalled Lee. "Of the small party, four with the lieutenant-colonel [Hamilton] jumped into the boat, the van of the enemy's horse in full view, pressing down the hill in pursuit of the two vedettes. Captain Lee, with the remaining two, took the decision to regain the bridge, rather than detain the boat." Lee made it to safety even though the leading element of British cavalry "emptied their carbines and pistols at the distance of ten or twelve paces." The cavalryman escaped back up Nutt Road, but could hear in the distance "volleys of carbines discharged upon the boat, which were returned by guns singly and occasionally." One of the British shots killed Alexander Hamilton's horse in the boat, while an American round accounted for the only British casualty—the horse of Maj. Peter Craig, commander of the light infantry detachment. Lee and Hamilton escaped without injury, but two men in the boat were hit, one killed and one wounded. Without any serious opposition the British easily seized the 4,000 barrels of flour and other items, such as soap, candles, kettles, tools, and axes. More important than seizing the complex, the British now controlled a critical road junction, explained Lee, "with roads leading to Reading, the French Creek iron region, Lancaster, and several Schuylkill River fords."[19]

Panic in Philadelphia

Once across the river, Alexander Hamilton dashed off a letter to John Hancock, president of the Congress. "If Congress have not yet left Philadelphia, they ought to do it immediately without fail," urged Hamilton, "for the enemy have the means of throwing a party this night into the city." He continued:

> The enemy are on the road to Swedes ford, the main body about four miles from it. . . . They came on so suddenly that one boat was left adrift on the other side, which will of

18 Reed, *Campaign*, 162. The 16th Light Dragoons were designed to be highly mobile and heavily armed; every trooper carried two pistols, a short-barreled carbine, and a long cavalry sword. Fischer, *Crossing*, 36.

19 Lee, *Memoirs*, vol. 1, 91.

> course fall into their hands and by the help of that they will get possession of another, which was abandoned by those who had the direction of it and left afloat, in spite of every thing that I could do to the contrary. These two boats will convey 50 men across at a time so that in a few hours they may throw over a large party, perhaps sufficient to overmatch the militia who may be between them and the city.[20]

Hancock acted on Hamilton's news as soon as he received it, packing up and departing the city. "About one oClock (& I was not in bed, nor had my Cloaths off for three Nights before) I Rec'd an Express from the General's aid De Camp recommending the immediate Removal of Congress," he explained, "as the Enemy had it in their power to throw a party that Night into the City. I instantly gave the alarm, Rous'd the Members, collected my Waggons, Horses, Carriage &c and after having fix'd my Packages, Papers &c in the Waggons and Sent them off, about 3 oClock in the morning I Set off myself for Bristol."[21]

Philadelphia had been in a panic before, but reports of the approach of the British escalated tensions in the capital city. Washington learned of the news though a note from Joseph Reed. "I cannot help acquainting you, my dear General that the Distance of the Army from the City & its March so remote has given great Alarm & very much discourages the Militia, if any real Service is expected [of them]," wrote the prominent Philadelphia attorney. "I do not doubt you have sufficient Reasons for a Measure which seems so mysterious—but if you could consistently with your Plan disclose them it would have a happy Effect on the Minds of the People."[22]

Henry Laurens, a member of the Continental Congress who had grown skeptical of the news that the city was in dire straits, described the growing panic. "The Scene was equally droll & melancholy," he began,

> Thousands of all Sorts in all appearances past by in such haste that very few could be prevailed on to answer to the Simple question what News? I however would not fly, I stayed Breakfast & did not proceed till 8 oClock or past nor would I have gone then but returned once more into the City if I had not been under an engagement to take charge of the Marquis delafayette who lay wounded by a ball through his Leg at Bristol. My bravery

20 Harold C. Syrett & Jacob E. Cooke, eds., *The Papers of Alexander Hamilton*, Vol. 1, *1768-1778* (New York, 1961), 326-328.

21 Paul H. Smith, et al., eds., *Letters of Delegates to Congress*, 26 vols. (Washington, 1981), vol. 8, 38.

22 Chase and Lengel, eds., *Papers*, vol. 11, 264.

however was the effect of assurance for could I have believed the current report, I should have fled as fast as any Man, no Man can possibly have a greater reluctance to an intimacy with Sir William Howe than my Self.

"Fright sometimes works Lunacy," Laurens had penned just one day earlier. "This does not imply that Congress is frightened or Lunatic but there may be some Men between this & Schuylkill who may be much one & a little of the other." Unlike Laurens, John Adams believed the news and fled. "The Congress were alarmed, in their Beds, by a letter from Mr. Hamilton that the Enemy were in Possession of the Ford over the Schuylkill, and the Boats, so that they had it in their Power to be in Philadelphia, before morning. The Papers of Congress, belonging to the Secretary's [Charles Thomason's] Office, the Treasury Office, &c., were before sent to Bristol. The President, and all the other Gentlemen were gone that road, so I followed . . . to Trenton."[23]

"The city was alarmed about two o'clock [a.m.] with a great knocking at peoples doors & desiring them to get up," wrote Sarah Logan Fisher, the wife of a prominent Philadelphia Quaker merchant, in her diary about the panic gripping the city. "Wagons rattling, horses galloping, women running, children crying, delegates flying & all together the greatest consternation, fright & terror that can be imagined." Pamphleteer Thomas Paine, author of the influential *Common Sense*, described the confusion in a letter for Benjamin Franklin, who was overseas negotiating an alliance in France. "The confusion, as you may suppose, was very great. It was a beautiful, still, moonlight morning, and the streets as full of men, women, and children as on a market day." Within a short time refugees had clogged the ferries to New Jersey and the roads leading to Allentown, Easton, and Bethlehem. The next day, Congress found itself in Trenton, New Jersey. The decision to leave, wrote North Carolina Congressman Thomas Burke, "was made not by vote but by universal Consent, for every Member Consulted his own particular safety."[24]

23 Smith, et al., eds., *Letters*, vol. 7, 695; Smith, et al., eds., *Letters*, vol. 8, 27, 80. Adams was awakened at 3:00 a.m. on September 19 by Congressman James Lovell and told that Congress had already started to leave town. Adams and his roommate Henry Marchant gathered their things and headed for Trenton with Benjamin Harrison, John Witherspoon, and other delegates from New York and New England. William L. Kidder, *Crossroads of the Revolution: Trenton 1774-1783* (Lawrence Township, NJ, 2017), 191.

24 Sarah Logan Fisher, "A Diary of Trifling Occurrences," *PMHB*, Nicholas B. Wainwright, ed. (Philadelphia, 1958), vol. 82, 448; "Military Operations near Philadelphia in the Campaign of

Bethlehem was a German community perched above the Lehigh River. Founded by the Moravians in the 1740s, the population numbered about 600 by 1777. Massive stone buildings dominated a "community dedicated to work and worship." Attractive houses, each with its own carefully cultivated garden, dotted the countryside outside the village. The army had used the community as a general hospital after the Battle of Long Island, and it would soon be called into service again. "It gives me great pain to be obliged . . . to send my sick and wounded soldiers to your peaceable village," Dr. William Shippen informed the community. "Your large buildings must be appropriated to their use. We will want room for two thousand at Bethlehem, Easton, Northampton, etc.," he continued, adding, "These are dreadful times, consequences of unnatural wars. I am truly concerned for your society and wish sincerely this stroke could be averted, but 'tis impossible."[25]

Jockeying for Advantage

On September 19, Smallwood's Maryland militia reached James McClellan's Tavern in Sadsbury Township (modern Parkesburg) on their march to link up with Wayne's division; they were now just 15 miles west of Downingtown. That morning, General Wayne began his new assignment by marching his 2,200-man column out of Yellow Springs back into the Great Valley onto Lancaster Road. After passing the Admiral Warren Tavern, Wayne halted at the Paoli Tavern, 10 miles east of Yellow Springs and just two miles behind the British camp at Tredyffrin. In front of Howe's army, which was on the hills on the south side of the Great Valley, were overflowing creeks and rivers, and his flanks were exposed to various highways between Lancaster and Philadelphia. Wooded terrain clogged his rear. Wayne's division lurking behind him would make Howes's ability to conduct a speedy retreat difficult, and perhaps impossible. Washington's choice of using Wayne to move behind the British made good sense. Wayne's 500-acre plantation

---

1777-8," *PMHB* (Philadelphia, 1878), vol. 2, 284; Jackson, *British Army*, 13-14; Smith, et al., eds., *Letters*, vol. 8, 6.

25 McGuire, *Campaign*, vol. 2, 22; John W. Jordan, ed., "Bethlehem During the Revolution: Extracts from the Diaries in the Moravian Archives at Bethlehem, Pennsylvania," *PMHB* (Philadelphia, 1888), vol. 12, 405.

(Waynesborough) was less than a mile from Paoli Tavern, and he knew every road, hill, and cart path intimately, having personally surveyed many of them.[26]

Once in position the optimistic Wayne sent a situation report to Washington. The British were in their camp and did not seem to be aware of his arrival. "There never was, nor never will be a finer Opportunity of giving the Enemy a fatal Blow than the Present," Wayne urged Washington, adding, "for Gods sake push on as fast as possible." Unbeknownst to Wayne, his position was more precarious than he believed. Later that morning, he sent another update to Washington. "I expect Genl. Maxwell on their left flank every Moment and as I lay on their Right, we only want you in their Rear—to Complete Mr Hows business," Wayne informed the army command. "I believe he knows nothing of my Situation—as I have taken every precaution to prevent any Intelligence getting to him. . . . I have not heard from you since last Night." What neither man knew was that their communications had broken down with the capture of at least one American courier. "A Dragoon deserter came in. . . . Couriers constantly going towards and returning from the Enemy's Camp," recorded British staffer John Montresor in his September 19 journal entry.[27]

Chester County was littered with pockets of Loyalists who now served the British. Wayne should have known this. In 1776, the army mustered in Wayne's regiment, the 4th Pennsylvania Battalion, at Turk's Head Tavern. Jacob James, the tavern keeper, now worked as a guide for the British. The sheriff of the county, Nathaniel Vernon, and his son Nathaniel, Jr., were serving Howe as guides. Job, Nathaniel's other son, was a captain in the 5th Pennsylvania Regiment under Wayne. Joseph Galloway and William Allen, Jr., were with Howe. Allen had been lieutenant colonel of the 2nd Pennsylvania Battalion under Wayne in 1776. Congressman James Lovell summed up the situation: "Consider that Galloway, the Allens, &c are conducting the enemy thro the most torified tracts assisted by Sheriffs of counties who know all the paths accurately, while our worthy Chief is intirely among foes, who will not or friends who dare not act the part of spies for him." Wayne had not even taken up his position at Paoli Tavern, and Howe already was aware of his presence—despite Wayne's belief to the contrary.[28]

26 Waynesborough was two miles southeast of the eventual American encampment. Wayne's wife and two children were living in the home at the time. McGuire, *Campaign*, vol. 1, 300.

27 Chase and Lengel, eds., *Papers*, vol. 11, 273; Montresor, "Journals," 455.

28 McGuire, *Campaign*, vol. 1, 301; Smith, et al., eds., *Letters*, vol. 8, 15.

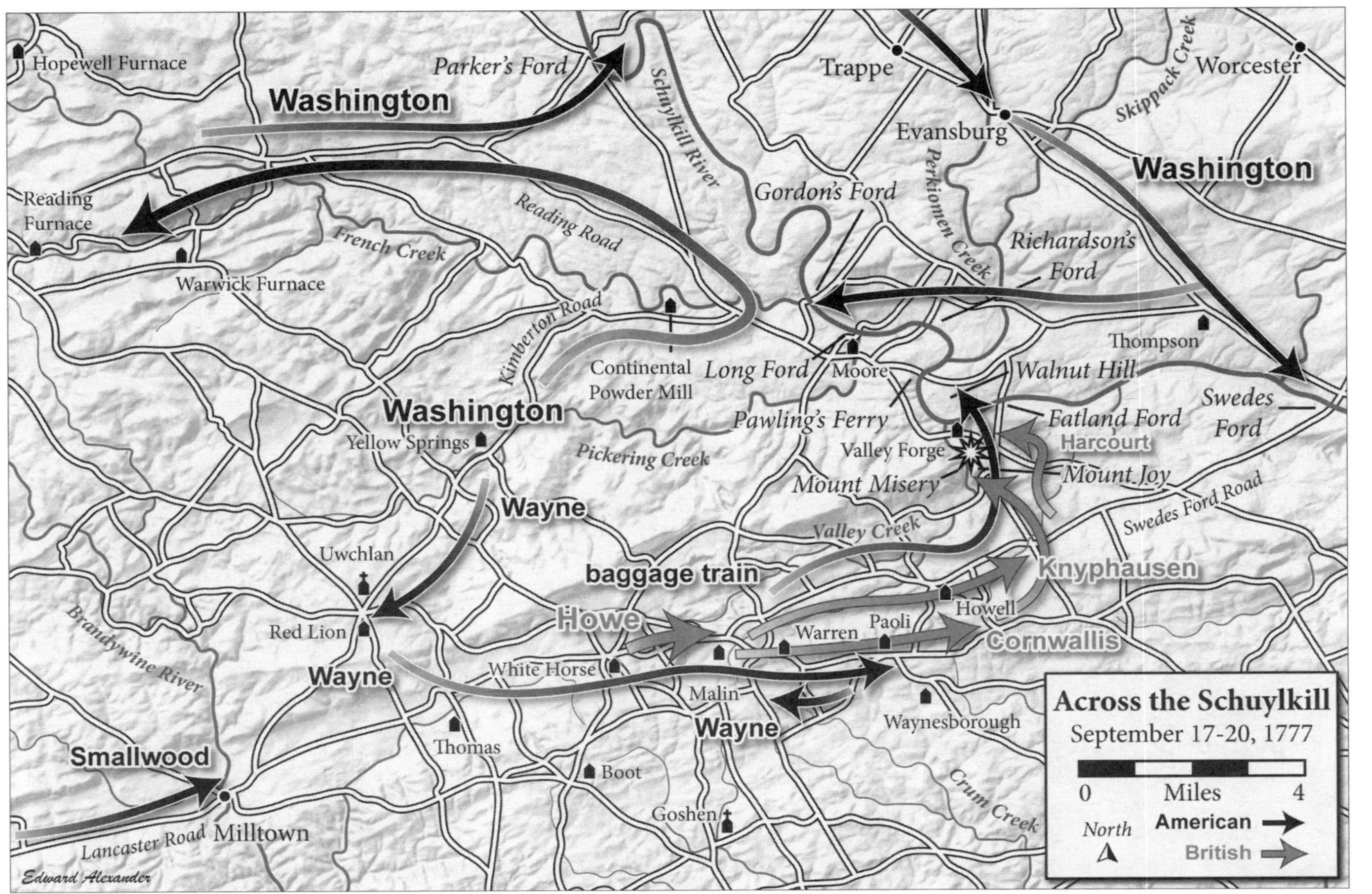
Across the Schuylkill
September 17-20, 1777
0 Miles 4
North
American
British
Hopewell Furnace
Parker's Ford
Washington
Schuylkill River
Trappe
Evansburg
Skippack Creek
Worcester
Washington
Reading Furnace
Reading Road
French Creek
Warwick Furnace
Gordon's Ford
Perkiomen Creek
Richardson's Ford
Kimberton Road
Thompson
Continental Powder Mill
Long Ford
Moore
Walnut Hill
Swedes Ford
Washington
Pawling's Ferry
Fatland Ford
Harcourt
Yellow Springs
Valley Forge
Pickering Creek
Mount Misery
Mount Joy
Wayne
Swedes Ford Road
Valley Creek
Uwchlan
baggage train
Knyphausen
Howe
Howell
Red Lion
Warren
Paoli
Cornwallis
White Horse
Wayne
Malin
Brandywine River
Waynesborough
Wayne
Thomas
Smallwood
Boot
Crum Creek
Goshen
Lancaster Road
Milltown
Edward Alexander

About noon a messenger informed Howe that William Harcourt's detachment at Valley Forge was under attack. In all likelihood, the Americans under Maxwell and Potter hovering in the area were taking potshots at Harcourt's men. The British had a spectacular view of the region from Mount Joy ("a fine Prospect from this Hill," confirmed grenadier Lt. John Peebles) and likely spotted these American forces. Sources are unclear as to whether any actual shooting took place or if there was just an appearance by a large body of Americans. Regardless of what had occurred, Howe rushed reinforcements into the area by ordering Cornwallis to take both British grenadier battalions and the 1st Light Infantry Battalion to Valley Forge to support Harcourt. When these units started gearing up from their camp along the South Valley Hill, Wayne—who had scouts out watching the main British camp—feared they had spotted him and were coming for his command.[29]

Wayne moved his Pennsylvania division back up the road toward Admiral Warren Tavern, then turned left "and took Post on some high Ground above the Warren Tavern on the Lancaster Road." After ascending the thickly wooded hills of Willistown Township, Pennsylvanians debouched into farm fields surrounded by stands of trees and fences owned by Ezekiel Bowen and Cromwell Pearce. Pulling these troops back to the high ground at the Warren Tavern was a wise move. When Cornwallis headed in the opposite direction to Valley Forge rather than toward him, Wayne probably thought his position was still a secret. "The Ground we lay on was the Strongest and best suited for our Purpose, that could be found for many Miles," Wayne reported. "The Disposition was prefect for Defence." The only approach by which the British could reach Wayne's new position was a path winding up from the Warren Tavern. Wayne had a good line of retreat and supply over a well-travelled road leading southwest to White Horse Tavern, two miles behind the Continental camp. The new campsite was in an open field surrounded by woods, with roads passing on both flanks of the division. "Genl. Wayne," explained Col. Thomas Hartley, "being acquainted with the Country chose the Ground himself." The local landowner-turned-general only intended to remain in his new position until Smallwood's Maryland militia joined him.[30]

29 Peebles, *Diary*, 136.

30 Colonel Thomas Hartley's testimony at Wayne's Court of Inquiry, original documents in Library of Congress, transcription in McGuire, *Paoli*, 203; McGuire, *Paoli*, 69, 76; Undated manuscript detailing Wayne's defense at his Court of Inquiry, Wayne Papers, Historical Society of Pennsylvania, vol. 4. The camp took up the ground between the present Sugartown Road on the west to modern

The British were aware that Wayne was in the general vicinity of their camp, but they did not know his precise whereabouts. "In the evening it was reported that General Wayne had been detached by General Washington . . . to make the region behind us insecure," wrote Howe's aide von Muenchhausen in his journal. Having already detached Cornwallis to Valley Forge, Howe now ordered the 2nd Battalion of Light Infantry and Ferguson's Riflemen to search for Wayne. This movement quickly fizzled out when two drunken British soldiers fired at one of Wayne's pickets. Any surprise assault on Wayne would have to wait.[31]

Although the British knew about Wayne, they had been misinformed about what was going on at Valley Forge. Cornwallis arrived at Harcourt's position at Valley Forge that evening to see Americans dotting the hills on the far side of the Schuylkill River. Although Cornwallis did not know it, these included William Maxwell's Continental light infantry and Pennsylvania militia under James Potter. Scouts sent out on the roads to the west, however, did not spot any enemy troops. With Cornwallis's arrival, Harcourt returned to the British camp with the 16th Light Dragoons. The army was experiencing such a shortage of horses that Harcourt immediately rode east on the Conestoga Road as far as Radnor and Marple Townships looking to acquire livestock. He swung back to camp through Newtown Square and Easttown Township.[32]

Channing Avenue on the east. The present Paoli Battlefield Park occupies the eastern half of the original campsite. Wayne's new position was two miles southwest of the Paoli Tavern, one mile south of the Admiral Warren Tavern, and about three miles southwest of the British camp in Tredyffrin. Donald Grey Brownlow, *A Documentary History of the Paoli "Massacre,"* (West Chester, PA, 1952), 5; McGuire, *Paoli*, 74; Hartley's testimony at Wayne's Court of Inquiry, original documents in Library of Congress, transcription in *McGuire*, Paoli, 204.

31 On the evening of September 19th, Wayne put his division back in motion. They moved out the left side of the camp and began heading down the road toward the White Horse Tavern. It is possible this movement was in response to the threatened British attack mentioned by von Muenchhausen in his journal. However, there is no solid evidence to explain Wayne's mysterious movement that night. Regardless of the movement's purpose, the division returned to the evacuated campsite later that night. Von Muenchhausen, *At Howe's Side*, 34; Brownlow, *Paoli*, 5.

32 The lengthy sea voyage the army had undertaken during the hot summer months to get to northeastern Maryland had taken a devastating toll on its animals. While enough horses had recovered or been procured to move the artillery and wagons, many of the light dragoons remained dismounted. The limited mobility of Howe's cavalry plagued him for much of the campaign. Pancake, *1777*, 168.

Blocking the Schuylkill

On September 19, the same day these British movements took place and Wayne shifted to a new camp, Washington had his main army on the move. Howe knew of this thanks to an intercepted message between Washington and Wayne. Washington wanted to cross north of the Schuylkill River at Parker's Ford, and move into a blocking position above its many crossings. With Wayne behind the British, Washington hoped to catch the enemy in a pincer movement and force him into battle on his own terms. Sometime that evening, William Smallwood with the Maryland militia arrived at Downingtown, just twelve miles from Wayne and close enough to potentially work with him. Though he was expecting Smallwood to make for the main army, Washington was moving away from Wayne and the Maryland militia, leaving them without close support.[33]

With its supplies replenished, the Continental Army headed east down the Reading Road (modern Route 23). Just beyond present Bucktown, Washington turned the army left onto the road to Parker's Ford, crossed at that ford (modern Linfield), and moved along Linfield Road to Reading Road (modern Ridge Pike) in Trappe. The Schuylkill River was still running high from the recent rains, so Delaware officer Enoch Anderson "gave orders to link arm in arm—to keep close and in a compact form, and to go slow—keeping their ranks. We moved on—we found the river breast deep."[34]

The army marched past the Trappe home and the church of Rev. Henry Muhlenberg. "The American troops marched through the Schulkiel, four miles from us, and came out on the road to Philadelphia at Augustus Church. They had to wade through the river up to their chests," wrote Muhlenberg in his journal. "His Excellency General W was himself with the troops who marched passed here to the Perkiome," continued the Reverend. "The passage of the troops lasted through the night and we had all kinds of visitors, officers, etc. To get wet up to one's chest and then to march in the cold, foggy night while enduring hunger and thirst, etc. is hard for the poor men. It takes courage, health, etc." Not everything he witnessed pleased Muhlenberg. "Instead of prayers, what one hears from many of them is the horrible national vice: cursing," he complained. "At midnight a regiment camped

33 The fords Washington wished to block included: Fatland Ford, Pawling's Ferry, Richardson's Ford, Long Ford, Gordon's Ford, and Swedes Ford.

34 Reed, *Campaign*, 164-165; Anderson, *Recollections*, 40.

on the street in front of my house. Some vegetables and chickens were taken, and a man with a flint came to my chamber, demanded bread, etc."[35]

Muhlenberg was not the only one complaining about the American army. Its deputy quartermaster general, Henry Lutterloh, was outraged by the conduct of some of the teamsters. "There is a great Complain[t], That where ever our Baggage marches—they Soldiers & Waggoners plunder all houses & destroy every thing. It is the Waggon Masters Genl or his deputys duty."[36]

Most of the army camped along the east side of Perkiomen Creek after a grueling 29- mile march. Once in place, Washington dashed off a dispatch to Alexander McDougall, the commander of a Connecticut brigade marching to the army from the Hudson Highlands. Washington needed to replace his Brandywine losses and looked forward to the veteran Connecticut troops joining him. "The exigency of our affairs makes it necessary, you should use all the diligence and dispatch in your power to join this army, with the troops under your command," urged the Virginian on September 19. No one in Washington's Continental Army knew that an American force under Gen. Horatio Gates had won a decisive victory against General Burgoyne at Freeman's Farm the same day. The consequences of Howe's decision to campaign for possession of Philadelphia instead of moving north to join forces with Burgoyne were coming to fruition.[37]

Washington's movement left Wayne in a terrible position. The main body of the Continental Army had increased its distance from Wayne, leaving him without immediate support and with Howe's main army between him and Washington. Wayne was operating under the impression that Washington would march back into the Great Valley once the army had been resupplied. Washington had sent a dispatch to Wayne informing him of the new plans, but neither general was aware that a British patrol had intercepted it, leaving both in the dark as to the true nature of the danger.[38]

35 Muhlenberg, *Journals*, vol. 3, 77-78.

36 Chase and Lengel, eds., *Papers*, vol. 11, 270. Lutterloh was appointed deputy quartermaster general for the main Continental Army on July 1, 1777.

37 Washington established his headquarters at the Castleberry house near the Episcopal Church in Evansburg. Reed, *Campaign*, 165; Chase and Lengel, eds., *Papers*, vol. 11, 271. Freeman's Farm was part of the Saratoga Campaign (June 14 to October 17, 1777), which is widely recognized as a major turning point of the Revolutionary War. For more on this campaign and its leadership, see, generally, Luzader, *Saratoga*.

38 McGuire, *Paoli*, 68.

Also on the busy day of September 19, William Shippen, director-general of the Continental Hospitals, informed the officials in Bethlehem, Easton, and Allentown that Congress wanted each of those communities to set aside its largest buildings to house a total of 2,000 sick and wounded, and to expect their arrival in a few days. Easton officials put the Reformed Church into service, while the Zion Reformed Church was utilized in Allentown. Bethlehem received many hundreds of wounded from Brandywine—the largest number to reach any of the communities. More than 700 were housed in the Single Brethren's House, while others bedded down in tents nearby. Officers filled the Sun Inn and the Germein Haus, and when those places overflowed the additional injured were sent across the Lehigh River to the Crown Inn and other buildings. The wounded Marquis de Lafayette stayed at the home of George Frederick Boeckel, superintendent of the Bethlehem farm. Though members of the Continental Congress were impressed by the outpouring of help from the citizens of Bethlehem, they also were concerned about the effect the influx of soldiers might have on the community. "Having here observed a diligent attention to the sick and wounded, and a benevolent desire to make the necessary provision for the relief of the distressed," announced Congress, "as far as the powers of the Brethren enable them, we desire that all Continental officers may refrain from disturbing the persons or property of the Moravians in Bethlehem, and particularly, that they do not disturb or molest the houses where the women are assembled."[39]

When the British did not pour into Philadelphia, John Adams came to the realization that the evacuation had been both hasty and premature. "It was a false alarm which occasioned our Flight from Philadelphia. Not a Soldier of Howes has crossed the Schuylkill," he recorded in his diary on September 21. Washington had again crossed the river, he continued,

> which I think is a very injudicious Maneuvre. . . . If he had sent one Brigade of his regular Troops to have heald the Militia it would have been enough. With such a Disposition, he might have cutt to Pieces, Hows Army, in attempting to cross at any of the Fords.... Oh, Heaven! grant Us one great Soul! One leading Mind would extricate the best Cause, from that Ruin which seems to await it, for the Want of it. We have as good a Cause, as ever was

39 The Sun Inn still stands at the intersection of Main and Broad Streets in Bethlehem but is much altered in appearance. Frantz & Pencak, eds., *Beyond Philadelphia*, 57-58; Gillett, *Medical Department*, 70; John W. Jordan, ed., "Bethlehem During the Revolution: Extracts from the Diaries in the Moravian Archives at Bethlehem, Pennsylvania," *PMHB* (Philadelphia, 1889), vol. 13, 71-72.

> fought for. We have great Resources. The People are well tempered. One active masterly Capacity would bring order out of this Confusion and save this country.[40]

Howe, concerned that Cornwallis's detachment at Valley Forge was exposed to possible attack, sent the Brigade of Guards to reinforce him on the morning of Saturday, September 20. The reinforcements marched up the Valley Forge Road to the Gulph Road and deployed on the northern slope of Mount Joy, adjacent to Cornwallis's command. The Guards skirmished lightly with Americans on the opposite side of the river and sustained a few casualties, including Capt. Charles Horneck, who was wounded.[41]

While Howe was reinforcing his lieutenant, Washington was marching his main army. The Continentals moved from their camp along Perkiomen Creek between 10 to 15 miles and took up positions along the Schuylkill, forming a nine-mile front stretching from Gordon's Ford to Swedes' Ford. Just as he had done at Brandywine, Washington spread his army thin along a wide front to keep the British from crossing a natural barrier. As his troops took up their positions, Washington established his headquarters at Thompson's Tavern in Norriton Township.[42] None of this was done in secret. The British atop Mount Joy, who were visible to the Americans, spent the day watching the Continental forces deploy along the hills skirting the north side of the Schuylkill. Lieutenant James McMichael, who belonged to Nathanael Greene's command, observed the enemy from Walnut Hill north of the river. The American officer "had a fair view of the enemy's encampment, being only separated from us by the Schuylkill and a small hill."[43]

40 Smith, et al., eds., *Letters*, vol. 8, 7-8.

41 McGuire, *Campaign*, vol. 1, 305. The British position was on the hill over which Inner Line Drive now passes.

42 Washington's new front covered several fords. The right flank was at Gordon's Ford in modern Phoenixville. The line then bent past Long Ford and Richardson's Ford. Next, the Americans stood around the mouth of Perkiomen Creek in Audubon, and along the river at Valley Forge. The left flank was at Swedes' Ford in Norristown. Thompson's Tavern was located at the intersection of Egypt Road and Ridge Road. The British burned the tavern when they passed through the area a few days later.

43 Walnut Hill was located on the large farm of Henry Pawling, directly across the Schuylkill River from the Valley Forge mill complex. McMichael, "Diary," 152. It is unclear which troops in Washington's army guarded what ford.

Howe and Cornwallis were not the only problems Washington faced. "It is with the utmost concern, that the General observes, a continual straggling of soldiers on a march, who rob orchards and commit other disorders," complained the commander in general orders, "and that many officers pay little or no attention to prevent a practice attended with such mischievous consequences, notwithstanding the orders relative thereto." Washington saw fit to remind his officers that it was their duty to do so, and that he expected that, in the future, "they know precisely, the number of men in their division or platoon; and where the time will admit of it, take a list of their names, previous to their marching; and that on a march they frequently look at their division to see if it be in order, and no man missing."[44]

Washington's latest maneuver to block the fords impressed British headquarters. "Washington, having achieved his aim by his forced marches . . . has now gained our left flank," confessed Von Muenchhausen. "He has uncontested access to supplies as well as a route of retreat to the lower provinces. He himself is positioned behind the Schuylkill with a strong force. . . . It is said he intends to prevent our crossing of the Schuylkill, which is wider and deeper than the Brandywine." Howe now had American forces of varying strength on multiple sides. Despite his defeat at Brandywine and the near-disaster at the Battle of the Clouds, Washington once more had managed to seize the initiative. Temporarily at a loss as to how to proceed but hellbent on taking Philadelphia, Howe pondered how to cross the Schuylkill.[45]

General Wayne and British patrols from Howe's main camp spent most of September 20 scouting one another. Wayne intended to follow Howe when he moved and reconnoitered the British camp with that purpose in mind, but he did not want to begin his march before linking up with Smallwood's militia. Wayne was still operating under the original set of orders for Smallwood to join forces with him. "I had sent Col. [James] Chambers As a Guide to Genl. Smallwood to Conduct him into my Rear—he was expected to Arrive every hour from 2 in the Afternoon," reported Wayne. When clouds began to build late in the afternoon, Wayne ordered his division to "build Booths to secure [their] Arms &

44 Chase and Lengel, eds., *Papers*, vol. 11, 274.

45 Von Muenchhausen, *At Howe's Side*, 34.

Ammunition." The precaution was judicious, considering the damage the army had sustained to its ammunition supplies just four days before.[46]

On the other side of the field, Howe reached a decision on how to extricate his command from this predicament while still achieving his objective. Before moving the main army to the Valley Forge area, he would deal with General Wayne.

46 Undated manuscript detailing Wayne's defense at his Court of Inquiry, Wayne Papers, vol. 4. Smallwood was marching to join Wayne, as Wayne expected, because neither officer knew that the order Washington had dispatched for Smallwood to join the main army had been intercepted by the British or had gone astray. It seems odd, at first glance, that Wayne would select Col. James Chambers, one of his regimental commanders, to act as a guide for Smallwood. Chambers, however, had suffered a severe wound nine days earlier at Brandywine. It is possible that he had not yet recovered sufficiently to reassume active command of his regiment. Broadhead's evidence at Wayne's Court of Inquiry, original documents in Library of Congress, transcription in McGuire, *Paoli*, 206.

Chapter 4

The Battle of Paoli

September 20-21, 1777

"I don't think that our battalion slept very soundly after that night for a long time."[1]

— Lt. Martin Hunter, 52nd Regiment of Foot, September 21, 1777

General Howe made his decision by the early evening of Saturday, September 20. The problem behind him had to be eliminated so he could focus on Washington's troops north of the Schuylkill River and achieve his objective of capturing Philadelphia: Anthony Wayne's Pennsylvania division had to be destroyed.

Howe tapped Maj. Gen. Charles Grey to command the operation. As the fourth son of Sir 1st Baronet Henry Grey, born in 1729, Grey had no hope of inheriting his father's estates or titles and, though born just a mile from the North Sea, embarked on a career in the army. By the time of the American Revolution he had three decades of extensive military experience and was considered one of Britain's best commanders. Grey's attack column consisted of the 2nd Light Infantry Battalion, the 42nd Highlanders, the 44th Regiment of Foot, Ferguson's riflemen, and a dozen troopers from the 16th Light Dragoons, all told about 1,200 men. They had assembled and marched out Swedes Ford Road toward the Admiral

1 Martin Hunter, *The Journal of Gen. Sir Martin Hunter and Some Letters of his Wife, Lady Hunter*, ed. A. Hunter (Edinburgh, 1894), 32.

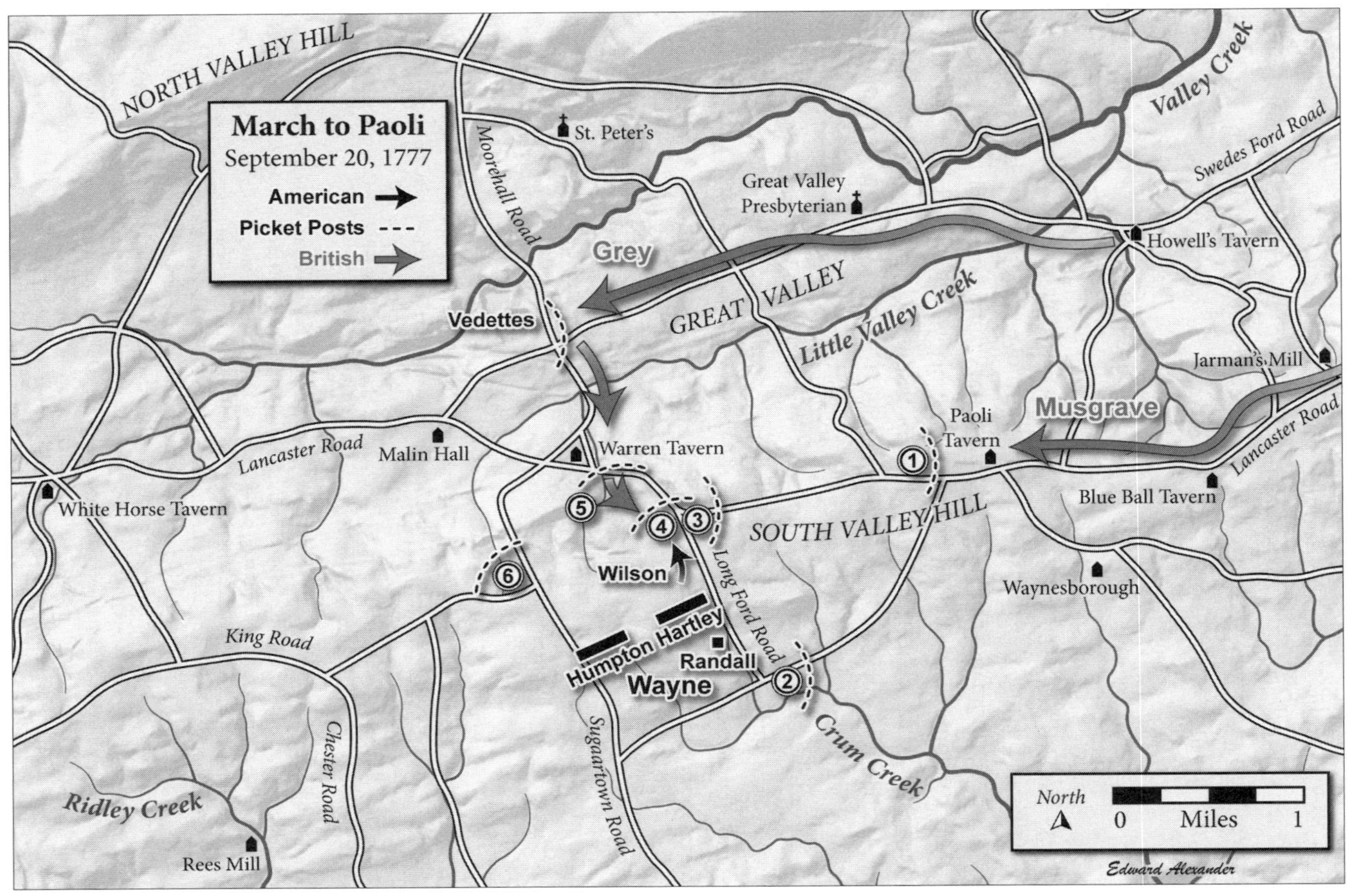
March to Paoli
September 20, 1777
American
Picket Posts
British
NORTH VALLEY HILL
St. Peter's
Moorehall Road
Great Valley
Presbyterian
Valley Creek
Swedes Ford Road
Howell's Tavern
Grey
Vedettes
GREAT VALLEY
Little Valley Creek
Jarman's Mill
Musgrave
Paoli
Tavern
Lancaster Road
Blue Ball Tavern
Malin Hall
Warren Tavern
White Horse Tavern
SOUTH VALLEY HILL
Waynesborough
Long Ford Road
Wilson
Hartley
Humpton
Randall
Wayne
King Road
Sugaartown Road
Chester Road
Crum Creek
Ridley Creek
Rees Mill
North
0
Miles
1
Edward Alexander
1
2
3
4
5
6

Warren Tavern by 10:00 p.m. Another column under Lt. Col. Thomas Musgrave, 500 men consisting of the 40th and 55th Regiments of Foot, moved in support on a different road. It was Musgrave's task to deploy at the Paoli Tavern and block Wayne's escape route.[2]

Early Warning Signs

According to later testimony, at least two people carried information into Wayne's camp that the British were on the move. Lieutenant-Colonel Morgan Connor, the commander of Hartley's Additional Continental Regiment, recalled "a Mr. Bartholomew of Chester County in Company Who Sayed he believed the Enemy wou'd attack us that night—the reasons he gave for Such an opinion I do not recollect." Connor's brigade commander, Col. Thomas Hartley, supported Connor's account: "In the Evening Mr. Batholamew came up, and spoke of the vicinity of the Enemy and their Numbers—an Old Man by the Name of Jones also visited us . . . he had been down at the Paoli [Tavern] where he had seen a Servant or some other Person who had been with the Enemy, where the Soldiers had told him, that they would attack Genl. Wayne's Party that Night. That they would have done it the Night before had he not changed his Ground." Though Wayne, convinced the British were gearing up to head for the Schuylkill River, discounted these warnings, he established additional picket posts and sent out mounted vedettes to further protect his encampment.[3]

2 Following the wounding of Capt. Patrick Ferguson at Brandywine, his specially equipped company of riflemen was assigned to the British light infantry brigade by Howe. Several pieces of circumstantial evidence indicate that the men took their Ferguson rifles with them when reassigned. The road taken by Musgrave's column led to Jarman's Mill (present Howellville & Cassatt Roads), then on to the Paoli Tavern. McGuire, *Campaign*, vol. 1, 308.

3 John Bartholomew was a 30-year-old Pennsylvania militia officer who lived on the Swedes Ford Road just down the hill from Wayne's camp. Connor's testimony at Wayne's Court of Inquiry, original documents in the Library of Congress, transcription in McGuire, *Paoli*, 200; McGuire, *Campaign*, vol. 1, 308-309. The precise identity of "an Old Man by the Name of Jones" remains uncertain. One source claims it was a Robert Jones who lived near the Paoli Tavern, while another believes it was Thomas Jones of Easttown Township. Hartley's testimony at Wayne's Court of Inquiry, original documents in the Library of Congress, transcription in McGuire, *Paoli*, 203, 240. Wayne established six picket posts, each consisting of a junior officer, one sergeant, one corporal, and 16 privates. The modern locations of these pickets are as follows: Picket 1 was on U.S. Route 30 near Cedar Hollow Road; Picket 2 on Paoli Pike just east of Warren Avenue; Picket 3 near the intersection of Channing Avenue and First Avenue (near St. Patrick's Church); Picket 4 at the intersection of Old Lincoln Highway and Longford Avenue; Picket 5 at the Admiral Warren Tavern;

Despite the proximity of the British and credible warnings, Wayne failed to disseminate this information to his brigade commanders. Colonel Richard Humpton, commander of the 2nd Pennsylvania Brigade and Wayne's second in command, later claimed that it was not until four days after the battle that he learned "Wayne had notice of the Enemies Intention, which I scarcely could believe as I never before then had heard any thing of the Matter. As Second in Command," he added in frank frustration, "I think the Genl. ought to have acquainted Me with it." While Howe planned his destruction and Grey prepared his attack column, Wayne marked time waiting for Smallwood's Marylanders, who would not arrive in time to help him.[4]

Hoping to achieve complete surprise, General Grey ordered his men to remove their flints to prevent their muskets from accidently discharging, and to perform their dirty work with bayonets. Grey's aide, Capt. John Andre, later explained the advantage of Grey's order. "It was represented to the men that firing discovered us to the Enemy, hid them from us, killed our friends and produced a confusion favorable to the escape of the Rebels and perhaps productive of disgrace to ourselves," he wrote. "On the other hand, by not firing we knew the foe to be wherever fire appeared and a charge ensured his destruction; that amongst the Enemy those in the rear would direct their fire against whoever fired in front, and they would destroy each other." Once the column stepped off down Swedes Ford Road, Grey took additional security measures by taking "every inhabitant with them as they passed along."[5]

The American vedettes posted at the intersection of Swedes Ford Road and Moorehall Road (modern Route 29) were the first to spot the approaching British. When they did not respond to the American challenge, the vedettes opened fire and galloped south on Moorehall Road to warn other picket posts and the main

---

and Picket 6 on Sugartown Road just north of King Road. A vedette post was established at Swedes Ford Road and Moorehall Road (Route 29). McGuire, *Paoli*, 240-241.

4 Humpton's testimony at Wayne's Court of Inquiry, original documents in Library of Congress, transcription in McGuire, *Paoli*, 212. The 44-year-old Humpton was a native of Yorkshire, England and had served as a captain in the British Army.

5 Although it is not entirely clear, it appears that two men guided Grey's column that night. One was Curtis Lewis, a blacksmith from East Caln Township who also had guided the British flanking column during the Battle of Brandywine. The other may have been Pvt. John Farndon, a deserter from Hartley's Additional Continental Regiment. Farndon was captured by the Americans either that night or soon after and was hanged "on a Gallows, erected for that Purpose; he hung from Noon until Sunset for an Example to deter others from the like or Similar Crimes." Hawkins Journal; Andre, *Journal*, 49-50; McGuire, *Paoli*, 94.

camp. Grey pushed his men after the retreating sentinels, though he had no knowledge of Wayne's precise location or the layout of his camp. "We knew nearly the spot where the Rebel Corps lay," explained Andre, "but nothing of the disposition of their Camp."[6]

The videttes rode into Wayne's camp and spread word of the British advance. Wayne sent one of the dragoons back to confirm the news and moved to alert his Pennsylvanians. "The Genl. Rose up and ordered the Troops under arms immediately," confirmed Colonel Hartley, commander of the 1st Pennsylvania Brigade. Major Francis Mentges of the 11th Pennsylvania recalled that "at about 12 o'clock Genl. Wayne came Riding along in the Rear of the 2d Brigade Calling out turn out my Boys, the Lads are Comeing. . . . The Troops turned out as quick as Could be Expected, and Formed by Platoons, in less than five Minutes."[7]

The division formed on the parade ground in front of camp facing north, with Humpton's brigade (4th, 8th, 11th, and 5th Pennsylvania regiments, left to right) on the western end, and Hartley's brigade (10th, 2nd, Hartley's Additional, 7th, and 1st Pennsylvania regiments, left to right) on the eastern side. The artillery was in position on the division's right flank. About 50 yards from the artillery was a thin strip of woods, and just beyond that lay the Long Ford Road (present Channing Avenue), where a picket post was stationed. Thick woods masked the front and rear of the division. On the left, or western side, the only viable means of retreat were strongly fenced fields running about 500 yards to the Sugartown Road. Wayne intended to move his division across the fields and get his men on the road to the White Horse Tavern before the British could strike his camp. "The division wheeled accordingly," remembered Wayne after the battle, and "the artillery moved off, but owing to some neglect or misapprehension . . . the Troops did not move until a Second and third order, were sent, altho they were wheeled and faced for the purpose. At the very time this order for the Retreat was first given (and which I presumed was obeyed)," he continued, "I took the light infantry and the

6 Andre, *Journal*, 49. Moorehall Road was the road leading to Moore Hall (the home of Judge Moore).

7 Hartley's evidence at Wayne's Court of Inquiry, original documents in the Library of Congress, transcription in McGuire, *Paoli*, 203; Mentges's testimony at Wayne's Court of Inquiry, original documents in Library of Congress, transcription in McGuire, *Paoli*, 208.

first Regiment, and formed them on the Right—and remained there with them and the horse in order to cover the retreat."[8]

Taking out the Pickets

The British were unsure which way to turn once the head of the column reached the Admiral Warren Tavern. A blacksmith was roused out of bed to help. "A party was immediately sent to bring the blacksmith," recalled light infantryman Martin Hunter, "who informed us that we were close to the camp, and that the picquet was only a few hundred yards up the road."[9]

Light rain was falling by the time the British advance guard approached the American picket post on the Lancaster Road just east of the Admiral Warren Tavern. The head of Grey's column was comprised of two dragoons, a company of light infantry, and Ferguson's riflemen, about 120 men. The American picket post commanded by Lt. Edward Fitz Randolph of the 4th Pennsylvania Regiment totaled 19 men. Lieutenant Richard St. George, a British light infantryman who had been shot in the heel at Brandywine and was still hobbling during the attack on Wayne's camp, recalled what happened next: "A piquet fired upon us at a distance of fifteen yards miraculously without effect—This unfortunate Guard was instantly dispatched by the riflemen's Swords"—a reference to the unusually long bayonets affixed to their Ferguson rifles. The unfortunate Lieutenant Randolph lost an eye and was left for dead. One of his men, Pvt. George English, was "very badly wounded in the Head, Shoulder, Arm, and Hand." Grey pushed his column past the decimated picket post and obliterated the next picket in his drive toward Wayne's camp. "We rushd on thro a thick wood and receivd a smart fire from another unfortunate Piquet, as the first, instantly massacred," continued the infantry officer. Captain Andre confirmed the destruction of the American picket posts: "The sentries fired and ran off to the number of four at different intervals.

8 The alignment of regiments from left to right was as follows: 4th Pennsylvania, 8th Pennsylvania, 11th Pennsylvania, 5th Pennsylvania, 10th Pennsylvania, 2nd Pennsylvania, Hartley's Additional Continental Regiment, 7th Pennsylvania, 1st Pennsylvania, and Randall's Independent Artillery Company. McGuire, Paoli, 101-102. Wayne would later blame Col. Richard Humpton for the failure to get the column moving in a timely manner. Undated manuscript detailing Wayne's defense at his Court of Inquiry, Wayne Papers, vol. 4.

9 The British also entered the Admiral Warren Tavern looking for a guide, but innkeeper Peter Mather refused to help. A blacksmith shop still stands across the road from the tavern at the intersection of Warren Avenue and Old Lancaster Pike. Hunter, *Journal*, 31; Brownlow, *Paoli*, 13.

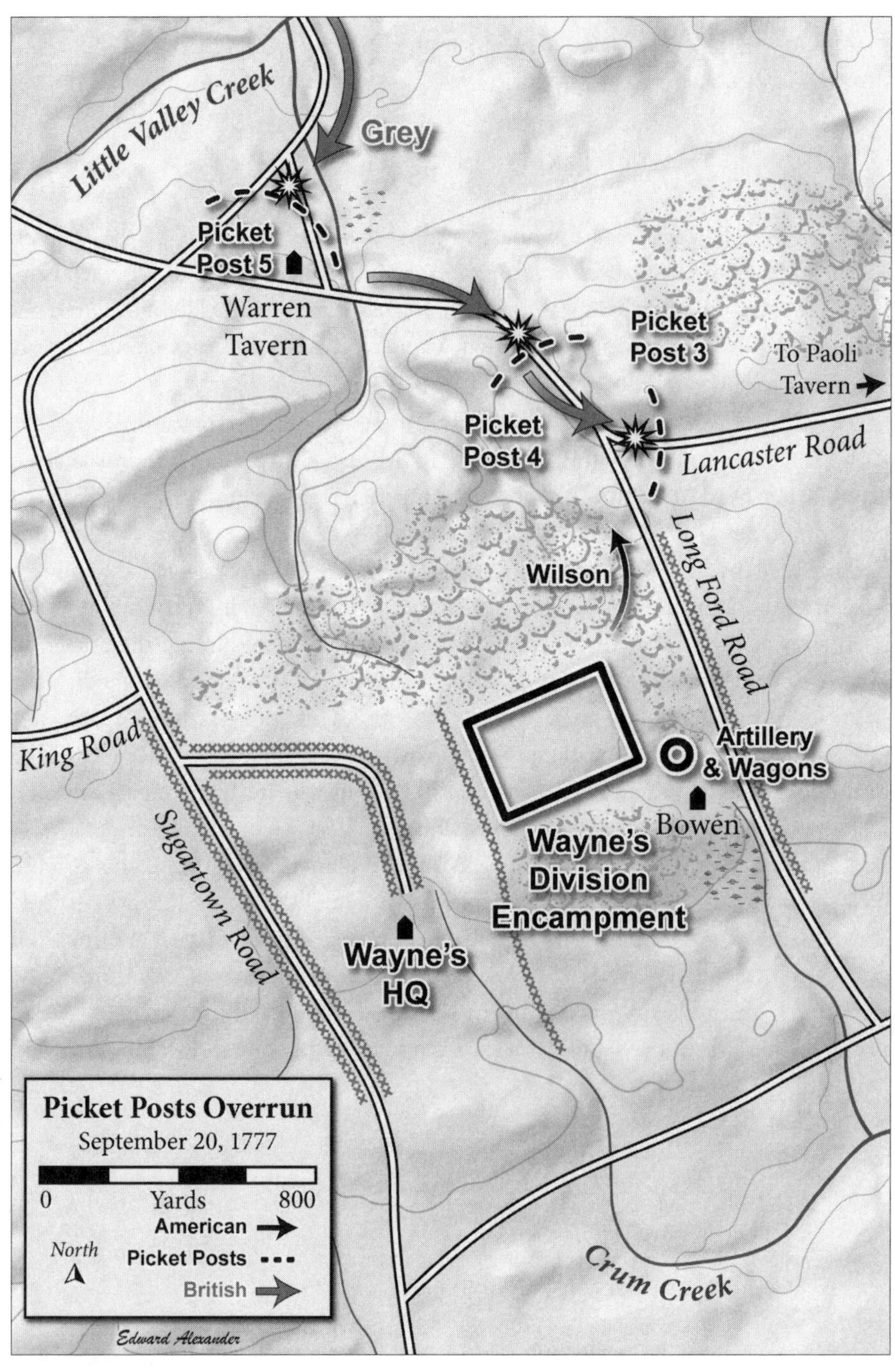
Little Valley Creek
Grey
Picket Post 5
Warren Tavern
Picket Post 3
To Paoli Tavern
Picket Post 4
Lancaster Road
Long Ford Road
Wilson
King Road
Artillery & Wagons
Bowen
Wayne's Division Encampment
Sugartown Road
Wayne's HQ
Picket Posts Overrun
September 20, 1777
0 Yards 800
American
North
Picket Posts
British
Crum Creek
Edward Alexander

The piquet was surprised and most of them killed in endeavouring to retreat." The British were now approaching the American camp up present Warren Avenue. Still unsure of Wayne's exact position, they followed the retreating American pickets hoping they would lead them to the camp.[10]

The fitful small arms fire echoing in the distant night hailed from the direction of Randolph's picket post; the British were coming toward Wayne's right flank. The Pennsylvanian ordered the division to file to the left (west) and head toward Sugartown Road and White Horse Tavern. The artillery would lead the column, followed by about 20 supply wagons. Colonel Richard Humpton's 2nd Brigade would follow the wheeled vehicles, and Col. Thomas Hartley's 1st Brigade would bring up the rear of the main column. Because it was raining, Wayne ordered his men "to take off their Coats and put their Cartridge Boxe's under to save the Cartridges from Damage."[11]

Before the infantry could move, however, Wayne needed to extricate his wagons and artillery, which were simply too valuable to lose. In order to lead the column, Randall's battery had to move from the right side of the division, pass behind the waiting infantry, cross the fields, and reach the road. The same was true of the divisional supply wagons. Once these vehicles were moving down the road, the waiting infantry could leave. To buy time for the guns and wagons, Wayne ordered the 1st Pennsylvania Regiment, about 200 men, to move into the strip of woods along the eastern edge of camp to slow down the British advance. He also sent the 1st Pennsylvania's light company under Capt. James Wilson out to support the pickets about 300 yards down the Long Ford Road.[12]

The British, however, made short work of the light company. "His Orders I Obeyd as Long as Possible," Wilson would later testify, "but the Enimy being too Numerous forsd me to Give Way." Wilson's command fell back to Capt. John Doyle's picket post. Within minutes the British 2nd Light Infantry Battalion advanced and swept away the men holding Doyle's position. Lieutenant Samuel Brady had "laid down with his blanket buckled around him," he recalled. The

10 McGuire, *Campaign*, vol. 1, 311; Richard St. George letter, dated September 11, 1777. The letter, with several additions made after its beginning date of September 11, was captured by Wayne's division at the Battle of Germantown and is today in the Society Collection, Anthony Wayne papers, Historical Society of Pennsylvania, Philadelphia, PA; Andre, *Journal*, 50; McGuire, *Paoli*, 100.

11 Undated manuscript detailing Wayne's defense at his Court of Inquiry, Wayne Papers, vol. 4.

12 Wilson's testimony at Wayne's Court of Inquiry, original documents in the Library of Congress, transcription in McGuire, *Paoli*, 103-104, 211. Wilson's position was roughly at the modern intersection of Longford Avenue and West Broad Street.

advancing British were nearly upon them before a sentinel fired into the darkness. Brady ran, but as he jumped a fence "a soldier struck at him with a musket and pinned his blanket to a rail. He tore the blanket and dashed on." When a dragoon overtook him and yelled for him to halt, "He wheeled and shot the horseman dead, and got into a small swamp, supposing no one in it but himself."[13]

Assaulting the Camp

"General Grey . . . came to the head of the battalion, and cried out—'Dash on, light infantry'! Without saying a word, the whole battalion dashed into a wood," wrote British light infantryman Martin Hunter in his journal, "and, guided by the straggling fire of the piquet, that we followed close up." Having overwhelmed and scattered Wayne's pickets, the British light infantry emerged from the woods and into Wayne's camp, striking his column from the right. When "we entered the camp," continued Hunter, the British "gave such a cheer as made the wood echo." The Americans, he added, "were completely surprised; some with arms, others without, running in all directions in the greatest confusion."[14]

"By this Time the Enemy and we were not more than Ten Yards Distant—a well directed fire mutually took Place, followed by a charge of Bayonet—Numbers fell on each side," Wayne informed Washington. Although it may have appeared to have unfolded that way, the Pennsylvanian was clearly mistaken, for the British had no flints with which to fire their muskets. In fact, the officers of the 1st Pennsylvania had witnessed their own pickets firing in defiance at the oncoming British and ordered their men to take aim; the Pennsylvanians, however, leveled their muskets and accidentally fired into their own men. The volley disclosed the position of the Americans—as Andre would later write, "we knew the foe to be wherever fire appeared"—and the British, bayonets affixed, charged upon the reloading Pennsylvanians of the 1st Regiment. More than half of the regiment was armed with rifles that could not hold bayonets. Reloading a musket was time-consuming, but the process to load a rifle, especially during combat, was

13 Ibid., 211. J. Smith Futhey and Gilbert Cope, *History of Chester County Pennsylvania* (Philadelphia, 1881), 86. The next morning, Brady found fifty-five other men hiding in the swamp.

14 Hunter, *Journal*, 31.

exasperatingly slower. Wayne's rearguard never had a chance against the bayonet-wielding British.[15]

After being driven back from the picket line, Captain Wilson of the 1st Pennsylvania rejoined what was left of his regiment near the eastern end of the division column. With the enemy pouring out of the darkness upon them, he and some comrades fell back to what he called "the middle Fence, Where I Rallied about thirty men, and Gave them the Last Fire." The 1st Pennsylvania was the first unit hit, but the British were unable to close with the bayonet before most of the men fled. As a result, it lost only one man killed, 11 wounded, and three captured out of the 200 men engaged. Regimental quartermaster Lt. Andrew Johnston was wounded in the left leg, George Beiler was stabbed in the shoulder by a bayonet, and drummer John Hutchinson "received a wound in the thigh with a Bayonet."[16]

The rout of the 1st Pennsylvania would not have been nearly as disastrous if Wayne's column had followed the artillery and wagons out of the camp as planned. When the rifle-toting Pennsylvanians ran out of the woods into the field containing the American camp, however, they stumbled upon the stationary division silhouetted against blazing campfires. Just behind them were the charging, disciplined British troops, cheering wildly. The routed men melted away in every direction. The 7th Pennsylvania was at the rear of the stalled column and one of its members, Maj. Samuel Hay, recalled nearly three weeks later what happened next. "They Came up upon our Right and left and by the light of our fires which was both in front and Rear of the line," wrote Hay. "I discovered the Enemy by their Clothes Close after the Infantry. I then Ordered the Plattoons that was faced to fire which they did and Continued to do so for some time which kept the Enemy back until the Other Plattoons was Moving on Smartly but the Enemy got up Round us and wounded An officer and some of the Privates on the Parade before we Stired."[17]

15 Letter, Anthony Wayne to George Washington, September 21, 1777, Wayne Papers, vol. 4; Andre *Journal*, 49-50.

16 John Blair Linn and William H. Egle, eds., *Archives*, Series 2, 17 vols. (Harrisburg, PA, 1880), vol. 10, 323. Other casualties included Surgeon's Mate Christian Reinick, who was killed. Company clerk Sgt. Atchinson Mellen, Sgt. William McMurray, Pvt. William Brown, and Pvt. John Hutchinson were wounded, and Pvt. William McCormick was captured in the melee. Thomas Lynch Montgomery, ed., *Archives*, Series 5, 8 vols. (Harrisburg, PA, 1906), vol. 2, 632-633, 649, 729; Linn and Egle, eds., *Archives*, Series 2, Vol. 10, 369, 594; Montgomery, ed., *Archives*, Series 5, Vol. 4, 534; RWPF, file W4701; McGuire, *Paoli*, 216-217.

17 Hay's evidence at Wayne's court of inquiry, original documents in Library of Congress, transcription in McGuire, *Paoli*, 199.

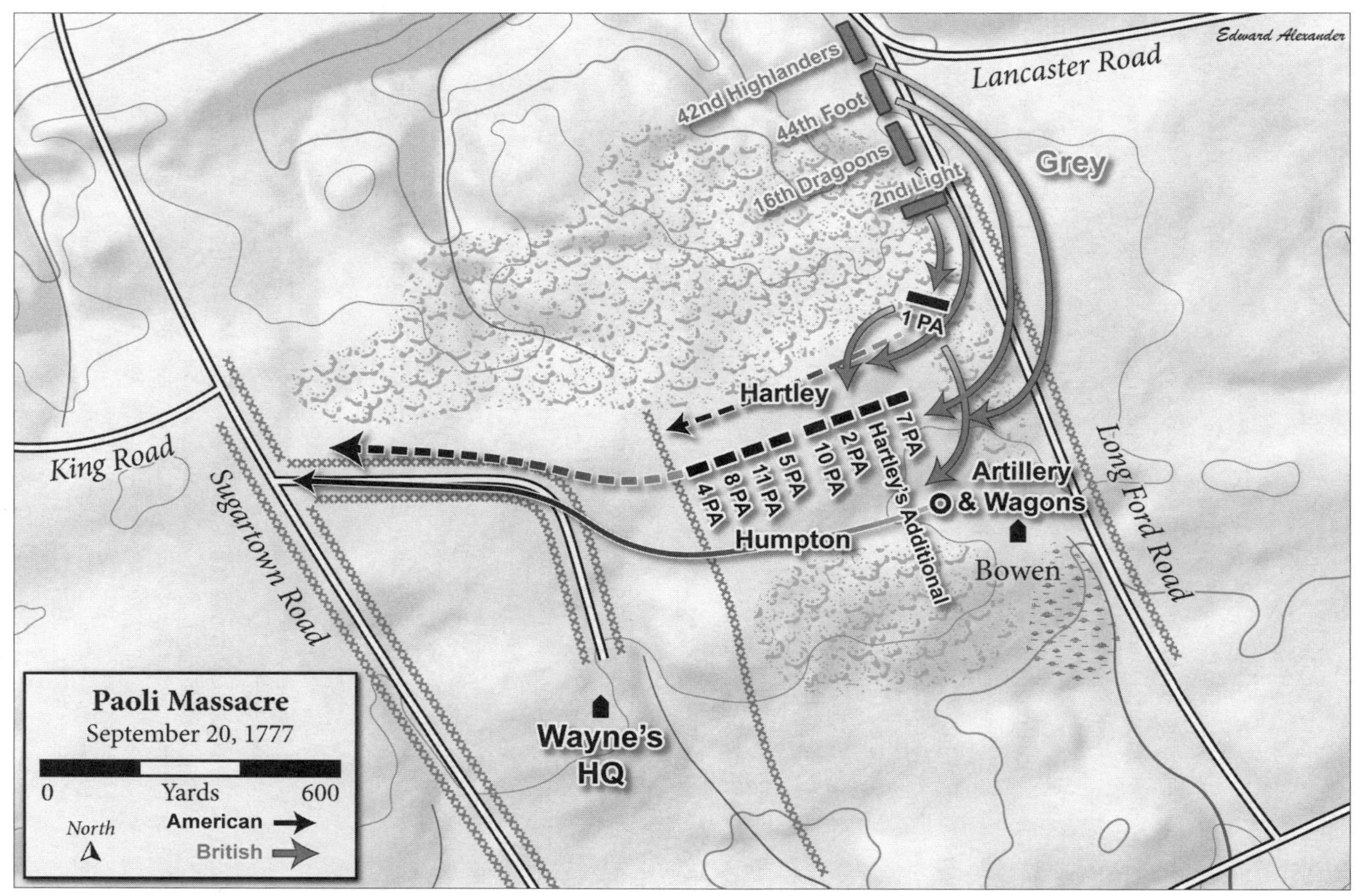
Edward Alexander
Lancaster Road
42nd Highlanders
44th Foot
16th Dragoons
2nd Light
Grey
1 PA
Hartley
7 PA
Hartley's Additional
2 PA
10 PA
5 PA
11 PA
8 PA
4 PA
Artillery & Wagons
Humpton
Bowen
Long Ford Road
King Road
Sugartown Road
Wayne's HQ
Paoli Massacre
September 20, 1777
0
Yards
600
North
American
British

When the Pennsylvanians of the 1st Regiment dispersed into the darkness, the brunt of the British assault fell upon the 7th Pennsylvania. In a letter written on September 29, Hay recalled the horrors of that night, claiming that "[t]he annals of the age cannot produce such a scene of butchery. All was confusion. . . . I need not go on to give particulars, but the Enemy rushed on, with fixed bayonets, and made use of them they intended. So you may figure to yourself what followed." One of the enemy soldiers rammed his bayonet into the side and against the spine of Hay's commander, Lt. Col. David Grier, a thrust that left Hay in command of the regiment. Grier would survive but would never serve in the field again. Other casualties included Capts. Robert Wilson and Andrew Irvine. The former was stabbed in the side and had a musket's cocknail driven into his forehead, while the latter suffered seventeen different stab wounds. Fife Major Richard Stack was stabbed thirteen times before being taken prisoner. Pvt. Samuel Gilman went down with a wound in the left arm. In all, 56 of the 325 men present with the 7th Pennsylvania were killed or captured.[18]

Lieutenant Martin Hunter of the British light infantry was one of the few British casualties suffered at Paoli. "Captain Wolfe was killed, and I received a shot in my right hand soon after we entered the camp," recalled Hunter. "I saw the fellow present at me, and was running up to him when he fired. He was immediately put to death." Captain John Andre, Grey's aide, also recalled the chaotic and bloody scene. "On approaching the right of the Camp we perceived the line of fires, and the Light Infantry being ordered to form to the front, rushed along the line putting to the bayonet all they came up with, and, overtaking the main herd of the fugitives, stabbed great numbers and pressed on their rear till it was thought prudent to order them to desist." Some Pennsylvanians were too afraid to leave their wigwams and fight even as the British set the shelters on fire. "Many of the Enemy would not come out," explained Thomas Sullivan of the 49th Regiment of Foot, "chusing rather to suffer in the Flames than to be killed by the Bayonet."[19]

The British 2nd Light Infantry Battalion swarmed through Wayne's camp and surrounded the rear of the stalled column. Captain Sir James Baird led the light infantry of the 71st Highlanders into the fight. Loyalist James Parker described

18 Linn and Egle, eds., *Archives*, Series 2, Vol. 10, 614. The regiment's colonel, William Irvine, was a prisoner on parole at the time. Linn and Egle, eds., *Archives*, Series 2, Vol. 10, 618; RWPF, Richard Stack file (no file number); McGuire, *Paoli*, 108, 219-221.

19 Hunter, *Journal*, 31; Andre, *Journal*, 50; Thomas Sullivan, *From Redcoat to Rebel: The Thomas Sullivan Journal, Joseph Lee Boyle*, ed. (Bowie, MD, 1997), 138.

Baird's narrow escape and how he turned his anger against the Americans: "He push'd a rebel musket past his breast, which kill'd a Sergent behind him; he paid them, for he put 16 of them to death with his own hands." The next wave of Grey's attack—the 44th Regiment of Foot and the detachment of the 16th Light Dragoons—lined up along Long Ford Road near bodies of Wayne's pickets and prepared to enter the close-quarters combat.[20]

Confusion was spreading through the ranks of Wayne's command. Farther up the stalled column, men scattered to save themselves, climbing over fences and fleeing into the woods. Many were caught by the pursuing British while still on the fences and bayonetted. Hartley's Additional Continental Regiment was the next unit in the column beyond the 7th Pennsylvania and thus the next to receive the British wrath. "The Seventh Regiment having no Front towards the Enemy—as well as my own Regiment—were attacked in their flank and Rear & tho' there were attempts made to form them with another Front," Hartley testified, "yet the enemy were so amongst them it was impracticable—nor could they retreat regularly, as the left Wing had been so long a Moving. Confusion followed—Several Men fell on both Sides—the Troops in the Rear pressed on those in the Front & the Passage on the Left being narrow sacrificed Many of the Troops." Hartley's 265 men suffered 14 killed and wounded in just a few minutes, among them Pvt. George Blakely, who was stabbed three times in the body and captured.[21]

The affair would go down in history as the "Paoli Massacre" because of a series of atrocities committed by Grey's troops. One particularly gruesome account comes from militiaman William Hutchinson, who was stationed at McClellan's Tavern, 25 miles west of the battlefield. "The second morning after the Paoli massacre . . . a stranger, came to our quarters and brought with him a man which he said he had found lying in the woods whose clothes, coat, vest, and trousers were stiff with gore . . . they would have stood alone when taken off him." The poor man, continued Hutchinson,

> had been singled out . . . as a special object for the exercise of the savage cruelty of the British soldiers. He told us that more than a dozen soldiers with fixed bayonets formed a cordon round him, and that every one of them in sport had indulged their brutal ferocity by stabbing him in different parts of his body and limbs, and that by a last desperate effort, he

20 Parker Journal, September 21, 1777 entry, Parker Family Papers.

21 Hartley's testimony at Wayne's Court of Inquiry, original documents at Library of Congress, transcription in McGuire, *Paoli*, 204, 222-223; Montgomery, ed., *Archives*, Series 5, Vol. 3, 752.

> got without their circle and fled. And as he rushed out, one of the soldiers struck at him to knock him down as the finis to the catastrophe, in which only the front of the bayonet reached his head and laid it open with a gash as if it had been cut with a knife. . . . He had neither hat, shoes, nor stockings, and his legs and feet were covered with mud and sand which had been fastened to his skin by mixing with his own blood as it ran down his limbs.[22]

Hutchinson continued his horrific description:

> We then procured the means of washing and cleansing the wounded man, and upon examining him there was found . . . forty-six distinct bayonet wounds in different parts of his body, either of which were deep and sufficiently large to have been fatal if they had been in vital parts. But they were mostly flesh wounds, and every one of them had bled profusely, and many of them commenced bleeding again upon being washed. [23]

"The greatest Cruelty was shewn on the side of the Enemy," recorded Lt. Col. Adam Hubley of the 10th Pennsylvania. "I with my own Eyes, see them, cut & hack some of our Poor men to pieces after they had fallen in their hands and scarcely shew the least Mercy to any." Hubley himself was lucky to escape, and described the ruse he used to do so. "I unfortunately fell in the Hands of some of the British Troops. . . . When they took me, I damn'd them for a parcel of Scoundrels, ask'd them what they meant taking one of their own Officers." One of the British troopers "beg'd my pardon, and I desir'd him to follow on. . . . He came on with me until I got him amongst a Party of our Men." When surrounded by fellow Americans Hubley ordered the man to surrender, "which he refus'd . . . I then ordered him to be shot which was instantly done, and I brought off his Horse, Accoutrements, &c. I was closely Persued but luckily got off safe." Of the 170 men present, the 10th Pennsylvania lost just eight wounded. Private Frederick Wilt was stabbed in the right arm and leg, while Pvt. James Reed "was left for dead with numerous bayonet wounds . . . and continued weak and feeble till after the close of the war—and wholly unable to rejoin the army."[24]

22 John C. Dann, *The Revolution Remembered: Eyewitness Accounts of the War for Independence* (Chicago, 1980), 149-150.

23 Ibid., 150.

24 Letter, Adam Hubley to William Atlee, et al, September 23,1777, Peter Force Papers, Library of Congress, Washington, DC; Letter, Adam Hubley to William Atlee, et al, September 21, 1777, Peter

The British were engulfing the eastern end of Wayne's crumbling column when a roar erupted from the tree line where the 1st Pennsylvania had made its stand: the second wave of British attackers—the 44th Regiment of Foot and a dozen troopers from the 16th Light Dragoons—had stepped off from the Long Ford Road. As the light infantry formed along the edge of the field as a reserve, the cavalrymen fanned out and "came on sword in Hand. The Shreiks Groans Shouting imprecations deprecations, the Clashing of Swords & Bayonets &c &c &c . . . was more expressive of Horror than all the Thunder of the artillery &c on the Day of Action," was how Lt. Richard St. George recalled the attack.[25]

Pockets of Pennsylvanians attempted to stem the crimson tide from behind stout fences, but nothing they could do stopped the surge of British Regulars pouring through the camp. The wounds inflicted by the 16th Light Dragoons were especially gruesome. Daniel St. Clair, a drum major for Hartley's Additional Continental Regiment, took multiple saber slashes to his head and body. When he raised his left arm to protect himself, another blow took off all the fingers on his left hand and carved out an eye. Now formed behind the attacking dragoons, the 44th Regiment of Foot advanced in a solid line to sweep the field of everything before it. Hartley's brigade disintegrated before its commander's eyes:

> After we had gone 200 or 300 Yds. several Attempts were made to rally the Men—but the Enemy pressing so close, upon the left of the Retreat, which was chiefly My Brigade & so Many Interuption of Fences that it was impossible to rally Any Men 'till We had got to some Distance from the Enemy. The Men were extremely intimidated with the Noise of the Enemys Horse[.] at the Fences considerable opposition was made by some of the best Men—but many of them suffered.

Unwilling to wait for Humpton's brigade, which was at the head or western end of the column, Hartley's men ran past the stalled troops, scrambled over a fence, and turned to make a stand from behind the barrier.[26]

Force Papers, Library of Congress, Washington, DC; Montgomery, ed., *Archives*, Series 5, Vol. 3, 583; McGuire, *Paoli*, 221; RWPF, file S16236.

25 St. George letter dated September 11, 1777.

26 RWPF, file W2188; Hartley's evidence at Wayne's Court of Inquiry, original documents in Library of Congress, transcription in McGuire, *Paoli*, 204. At least three fence lines blocked Wayne's route of retreat.

Wayne had his men in column with enough time to extricate them from the approaching danger, but the order of march doomed his command at Paoli. Twenty-nine wheeled vehicles, including wagons and four artillery pieces, had to move from the right side across the entire rear of the column, and then pass through a fence line to reach the Sugartown Road. In the darkness and with the confusion of battle, it is no surprise that the movement took longer than expected. Humpton's Brigade was stalled while waiting for the artillery and wagons to clear out. "The Brigde was for'd in as short a time as possible—at least I saw no delay, they remain'd form'd a few Minutes waiting for orders," recalled Humpton. "The Artillery & wagons was driving very fast along our left flank . . . the Artillery & Waggons greatly incommoded Us either for Action or a retreat." When Humpton rode forward to investigate what was holding up the withdrawal, he discovered to his dismay that the fence rails had not been knocked down prior to the retreat. Once the confusion at the head of the column was dealt with and the fence laid low, the troops began to move.[27]

Soon after entering the road, Wayne informed Washington, "one of the [artillery] Pecies met with Misfortune near the field of Action which Impeded us a Considerable time." The carriage of the field piece, remembered Lt. Col. Adam Hubley, "had lost the hind wheels." The officer "ordered another Horse to be hitched to the piece & drag'd it along which was done, and brought of[f] the piece." Once the disabled gun was hauled out of the way, the column marched into an adjoining field and attempted to make a stand. "The Enemy were upon us, in our rear," recalled Hubley, "and with their charg'd Bayonets, we push'd forward and got into a field adjoining the One in which we were Attacked, we endeavoured to form Our Men, but found it impracticable, the Enemy being then almost mix'd with us, at the same time calling out No quarters &c, which in my humble Opinion," he continued, "caused our Men to make a disparate and indeed obstinate stand, a most severe Bayoneting was the Consequence."[28]

The handling of Wayne's artillery was not the fault of the battery's commander, Capt. Thomas Randall. Captain Randall, "after getting one of his pieces away," recalled fellow artillery officer Samuel Shaw, "was taken [prisoner] while he was

27 Humpton's testimony at Wayne's Court of Inquiry, original documents in Library of Congress, transcription in McGuire, *Paoli*, 212-213.

28 Letter, Anthony Wayne to George Washington, October 22, 1777, Wayne Papers, vol. 4; Hubley's testimony at Wayne's Court of Inquiry, original documents in Library of Congress, transcription in McGuire, *Paoli*, 210-211.

anxiously exerting himself for the security of that, and another [gun], which, under the cover of the night, was also got off. On finding himself in their hands, he endeavoured to escape, but the enemy prevented it by knocking him down and stabbing him in eight places." Randall's wounds were so severe that the British left him at a nearby house rather than take him along as a prisoner.[29]

Grey, already easily winning the battle, had yet to insert the 600 men of the 42nd Royal Highlanders; they now entered the fight. Wayne's command had harassed these men during the *petit guerre* in northern New Jersey back in June; now the Highlanders had their chance to exact revenge. A wall of men swept across the fields, burning what was left of Wayne's camp and killing or wounding everyone in their path. Grey had not given any orders regarding prisoners, and the enlisted men took matters into their own hands, including setting tents and wigwams afire. "At this time the whole army were so inveterate against the Americans that they seldom gave any quarter," admitted Martin Hunter.[30]

Wayne rode to the head of the column and rallied remnants from other regiments around the 4th Pennsylvania to provide covering fire for the retreat. Major Marion Lamar, a member of the 4th Pennsylvania, shouted, "Halt, boys, and give these assassins one fire!" Moments later, recalled Capt. Benjamin Burd, Lamar was "bayonetted on horseback." The major collapsed from his horse mortally wounded, the highest-ranking American killed at Paoli. Of the 135 men engaged, the 4th Pennsylvania suffered two killed and six wounded. Casualties included Pvt. William Farrell, who was wounded in the head and arm. The demoralized Pennsylvanians fell back to a wooded rise near the road leading to White Horse Tavern, where Wayne hoped to make a stand. Brigade Major Michael Ryan recalled that he and Wayne "rally'd a Number of Men, whome was again form'd to Cover the Retreat." As Wayne struggled to regain control of the situation, he ordered Maj. Caleb North of the 10th Pennsylvania to ride west on King Road, find Smallwood's militia command, and bring it forward at once.[31]

29 Randall was the only casualty from his 37-man company. Shaw, Journals, 38; McGuire, *Paoli*, 223.

30 Hunter, *Journal*, 29.

31 Linn and Egle, eds., *Archives*, Series 2, Vol. 10, 548; RWPF, files S40788 & S42192; McGuire, *Paoli*, 118, 218; McGuire, *Campaign*, vol. 1, 316; Ryan's evidence at Wayne's Court of Inquiry, original documents in Library of Congress, transcription in McGuire, *Paoli*, 205.

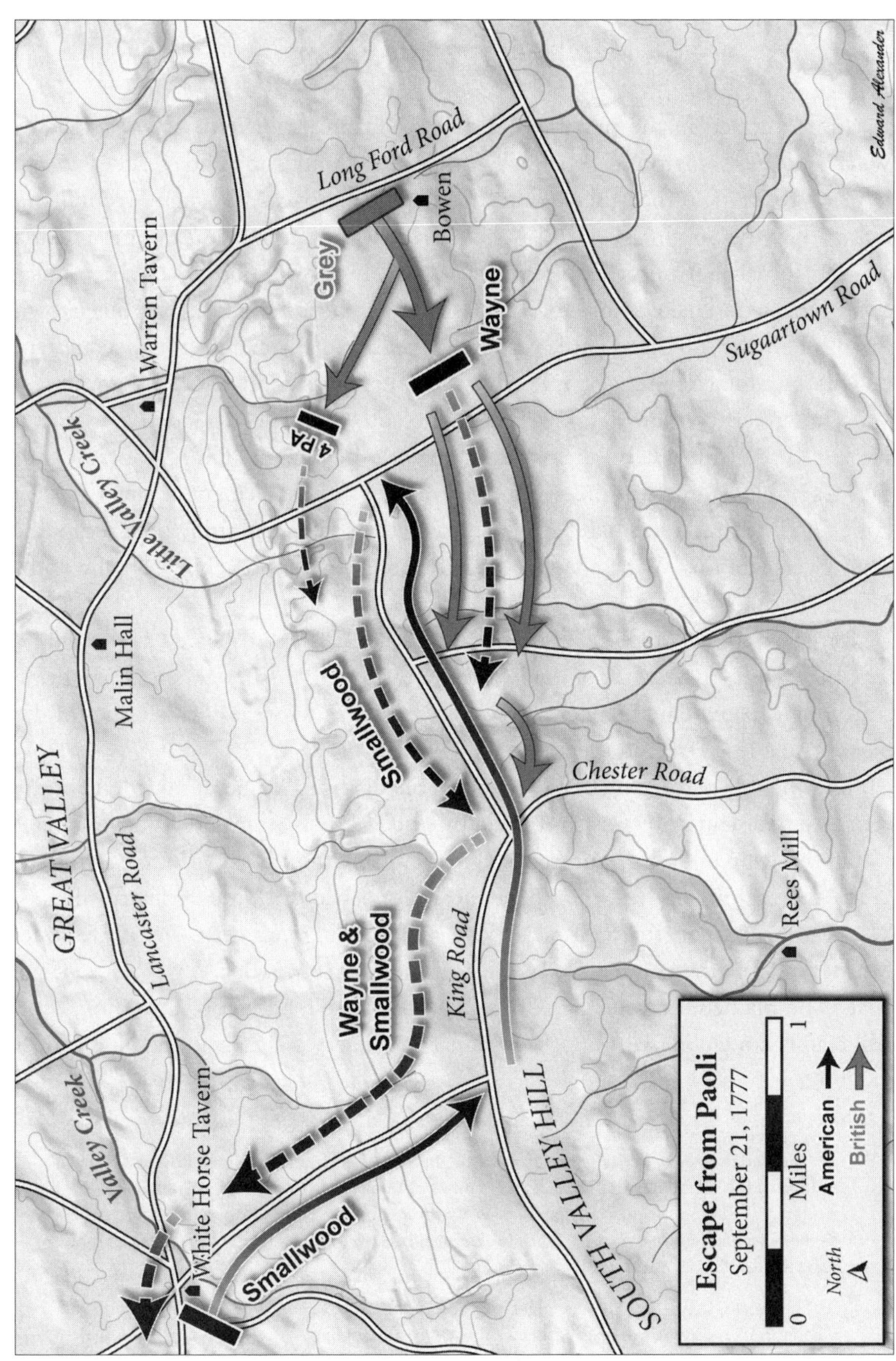
Escape from Paoli
September 21, 1777
North
0
Miles
1
American
British
Long Ford Road
Bowen
Grey
Wayne
Warren Tavern
4 PA
Sugaartown Road
Little Valley Creek
Malin Hall
Smallwood
Chester Road
GREAT VALLEY
Lancaster Road
Wayne & Smallwood
King Road
Rees Mill
Valley Creek
White Horse Tavern
Smallwood
SOUTH VALLEY HILL
Edward Alexander

Marylanders to the Rescue?

As described in the previous chapter, William Smallwood was heading for Wayne, not Washington. When Smallwood's 2,100 Maryland militia reached White Horse Tavern, he turned the column right onto the road to Goshen Meeting and tramped up the South Valley Hill. When it reached the top, the head of the militia column turned left onto King Road toward Wayne's division about three miles away. Smallwood halted close to Wayne's camp at the intersection with Sugartown Road, where the sounds of battle carried on the dark night air and convinced him to pull his untrained militia back onto what he thought was good defensible ground.[32]

The attack continued to be pressed relentlessly. The wounded Lt. Martin Hunter of the British light infantry kept up with the pursuit "until I got faint with the loss of blood, and was obliged to sit down." With the element of surprise long gone, the British soldiers had begun replacing their flints and firing their weapons. They were driving Wayne's men, and were now approaching Smallwood's Maryland militia.[33]

Smallwood reported pulling back, but to the British it appeared as though he was being driven back. "For two Miles We drove Them now and then firing scatteringly from behind fences & trees &c," wrote St. George. "The flashes of the pieces had a fine effect in the Night."[34]

During this part of the battle, reported Smallwood, "[o]ne of our Men abt the centre of the Main Body was shot Dead by some of their Stragglers [Wayne's men], which threw great Part of our Line in great consternation, many flung down their Guns & run off, & have not been heard of since . . . the Artillery Men & Waggoneers cutting their Horses loose and running off with them." Colonel Mordecai Gist, who commanded a brigade under Smallwood, also wrote about the chaos and blamed it on the lack of experience of the men involved, adding, "you will readily conclude that Militia unused to an Attack especially in the Night must

32 The road they took is today's Planebrook Road. In the 18th century, Planebrook Road continued south over the hill. Modern rail lines and the campus of Immaculata University have obliterated the road trace. When Smallwood was approaching Wayne's camp, the militia was near the intersection of the King and Sugartown roads. Smallwood pulled back to form a line near the intersection of King Road with Route 352. McGuire, *Paoli*, 119-120.

33 Hunter, *Journal*, 31-32. Hunter might have been left behind had his friend, Lt. Richard St. George, not realized he was missing and went back to look for him.

34 St.George letter dated September 11, 1777.

be thrown into some Confusion." Gist rallied his brigade, "by which time several stragglers of Wanes Division retreated to us."[35]

Smallwood and Gist were doing their best to stabilize the new line forming as a rearguard when Smallwood was nearly killed for his efforts by his own men. "The Rear taking us for British light Horse fired a Volley on us within 15 or 20 Foot, wounded several, and killed a light Horseman alongside of me in waiting for Orders," reported the militia commander. "In this confusion several more would have been killed by our own People had I not flung myself from my Horse and called aloud that I shu'd have been glad to have seen them as ready to fire on the Enemy as they now seemed on their Friends." Thankfully, continued Smallwood, "they knew my Voice and ceased." Gist described the final "stand" by the militiamen. "A party of the Enemy by this time had got a head of us and lay in ambuscade the firing from them was so close and unexpected that they [the militia] immediately broke & left us no possibility of rallying them." Gist was trying to extricate himself from the fleeing men when his "Horse received two Balls through his Neck but fortunately only fell on his Knees and Hams otherwise I must have received the Bayonet or fallen into their Hands." The confusion that night had nearly killed the two highest ranking Marylanders in Washington's army.[36]

The rabble that was the Maryland militia was disintegrating when Maj. Caleb North of the 10th Pennsylvania found Smallwood and delivered Wayne's orders for help. "There was nothing left but to order the Retreat to be made," explained Smallwood in a letter three days later to Maryland's Governor Thomas Johnson. Many of his men threw away their arms and equipment, and more than 1,000 deserted outright. "If our wrong headed assembly cou'd only be here to see these mens behavior and be a little pestered in restraining and regulating their conduct," lamented a disgusted Smallwood. Gist echoed Smallwood's complaints. "Desertion is since become so frequent that it is impossible to ascertain the

35 Letter, William Smallwood to Governor Johnson, September 23, 1777, Maryland Historical Society, Baltimore, MD; Letter, Mordecai Gist to John Smith, September 23, 1777, Emmet Collection, New York Public Library, New York, NY.

36 The horseman killed beside Smallwood was Pvt. Jones Dean of Bland's Light Dragoons. Letter, Smallwood to Johnson, September 23, 1777; McGuire, *Campaign*, vol. 1, 317; Letter, Gist to Smith, September 23, 1777. This dangerous action involving Smallwood and Gist likely took place south of King Road but above Forest Lane. The east and west boundaries for this action were, respectively, Hickory Lane and Route 352. In fairness to Gist (and everyone who wrote about that night), distances and the identity of commands were nearly impossible to accurately identify. No British troops had gotten ahead (west) of Gist's men, so if this took place as he relates, they may have been some of Wayne's refugees, frightened and firing into the militia.

number missing," he wrote to John Smith on September 23. "I hope the Governor will exercise his authority by Imprisonment or otherwise of these Miscreants while the Brave and Virtuous continue with fortitude to encounter the hardships of War, until an Opportunity may offer to retrieve the reflection and Disgrace thrown upon the State of Maryland by their unmanly Behaviour."[37]

Captain Thomas Buchanan of the 1st Pennsylvania, who was with Smallwood when the militia broke, rode off down the road to Downingtown to stop the flood of refugees. "On coming to these, I found where some of his [Smallwood's] artillery had thrown a field-piece into a limekiln and had broken the carriage. I went on to Downingtown and fixed a guard on the road to stop the runaways; got a wheeler and blacksmith to mend the carriage," he added, "and went down and put the cannon on the carriage."[38]

Taking Account

Despite the close-quarter fighting and darkness, according to Captain von Muenchhausen of Howe's staff, the British assault force lost only three men killed and nine wounded. Grey's men rounded up between 70 and 80 prisoners, many of whom were suffering from multiple stab wounds. Grey's aide, John Andre, recalled bringing away "near 80 prisoners, & of those who escap'd a great number were stab'd with bayonets or cut with broad swords, as great a number at least never stopped till they got to their own homes, in short this harassing corps is almost annihilated by the loss of that night & by the subsequent desertions." The horrific condition of the wounded and the mutilated bodies of the dead infuriated the survivors, who swore to gain revenge in their next fight. Lieutenant Martin Hunter of the 52nd Foot's light company knew that a massacre had taken place. "I don't think that our battalion slept very soundly after that night for a long time," he confessed. Hunter, who would see service around the world and eventually would rise to the rank of general, described Paoli as "the most dreadful scene I ever beheld." Lieutenant William Keugh, adjutant of the 44th Regiment of Foot, agreed. "The Carnage was Amazing & terrible—I confess it is most shocking to think that such Extremities are unavoidable in the prosecution of War, but think w[ha]t Baneful Consequences must have ensued to Us, had it not have been put in

37 Letter, Smallwood to Johnson, September 23, 1777; Letter, Gist to Smith, September 23, 1777.

38 Montgomery, ed., *Archives*, Series 5, vol. 2, 622.

Execution, as They (knowing We were to March th[a]t Morn[in]g) were getting under Arms for the purpose of Assassinating Our Army, at the time Gl. Gray reach'd them, & so unexpectedly frustrated their Cowardly Diabolical Intentions."[39]

Since Howe planned to cross the Schuylkill, Grey called off the pursuit and returned to the British camp by the Lancaster Road, leaving the American dead and many of the wounded in the fields where they fell. Grey's command linked up with Musgrave's column at Paoli Tavern and moved back into Tredyffrin by the same route Musgrave had taken earlier that night.[40]

The area around Wayne's former camp was littered with the dead, the wounded, and the detritus of war. Many of Wayne's men had taken to the woods and swamps to wait out the night. Some of the more severely wounded were "taken to nearby houses" by the British, but many more remained where they had fallen. Howe had no intention of dealing with them, especially since he was about to make a move to cross the Schuylkill, and he sent a message to Washington to send surgeons. "[L]ose no Time in sending whom you shall think proper for this Purpose," suggested the general who had brought about the carnage. "Agreeable to your request," Washington responded, "I have sent Dr. [Lewis] Wilson to take charge of the Wounded Officers & Men of the Army under my command who have fallen into your hands at Howels Tavern & the neighbouring Houses. The Doctor," he continued, "has direction to give a receipt for All that are delivered him, and they will be considered Your prisoners."[41]

39 Von Muenchhausen, *At Howe's Side*, 34. One of the killed was Capt. William Wolfe of the 40th Regiment of Foot's light infantry company. John Andre manuscript letter dated September 28, 1777, with a postscript dated October 8, original in the American Philosophical Society, Philadelphia, PA, transcription in McGuire, *Campaign*, vol. 2, 298; Hunter, *Journal*, 31-32; Letter likely written by Lt. William Keugh dated September 28, 1777, original in the American Philosophical Society, Philadelphia, PA, transcription in McGuire, *Campaign*, vol. 2, 282.

40 Many of the American dead were buried by local inhabitants immediately after the battle in the corner of the field where they fell. Five-year-old Cromwell Pearce grew up on the farm that became half of the battlefield, and he later became colonel of the 16th United States Infantry during the War of 1812. After that war he returned home and helped organize an effort to remember the American dead from the Battle of Paoli. On September 20, 1817 (the 40th anniversary of the battle), the Republican Artillerists, a Philadelphia militia organization, and other Chester County residents erected a monument over the burial mound. A newer monument also stands nearby. The remains of 53 of Wayne's men now rest under a marble obelisk marking the site of the "Paoli Massacre." Chambers, *Memories*, 90.

41 Von Baurmeister, "Letters," 412; Chase and Lengel, eds., Papers, vol. 11, 283-284.

1817 Paoli monument erected on the 50th anniversary of the battle over the graves of Wayne's dead. *Photo by author*

Wayne, meanwhile, spent the morning hours of September 21 reorganizing his division before marching west to join with the remnants of Smallwood's shattered command. Together, they retreated to Red Lion Tavern, nine miles from the former camp, marching west on Swedesford Road and then northwest on Ship Road before turning right onto Pottstown Pike (modern Route 100). The column turned left onto South Village Avenue to reach the tavern.[42]

Despite being taken by surprise, and in spite of the brutality of the fight that followed, Wayne managed to extract most of his division, including all four of his precious artillery pieces. The officers and men, however, lost most of their baggage and personal effects.[43] All told, Wayne suffered about 300 killed, wounded, or captured out of 2,200 men, or about 13.5 percent of his strength. In a way, the darkness, which shielded Grey's men during their advance and added to the terror of the sudden attack, also aided the Continentals, though to a lesser extent. Grey did not know the exact location of Wayne's camp, and maneuvering men during a night attack was a confusing endeavor; Wayne thus managed to extract many of his men.[44] A prideful man,

42 McGuire, Paoli, 252.

43 Letter, John Doyle to Joseph Howell, January 30, 1786, Letters sent to J. Howell, Comm. Accounts, RG 93, National Archives and Records Administration, accessed online at www.wardepartmentpapers.org on April 15, 2014.

44 Brownlow, *Paoli*, 20. Besides the casualties already mentioned, two men in the 8th Pennsylvania suffered their second wounds of the war. Pvt. Robert Hunter had been wounded at Bound Brook in northern New Jersey early in the campaign and suffered the same fate at Paoli. Pvt. John Holton was wounded in the thigh ten days earlier at Brandywine, and suffered a bayonet wound at Paoli. Regimental commander Daniel Broadhead suffered a slight wound as well. The 8th Pennsylvania

1877 Paoli monument erected on the 100th anniversary of the battle. *Photo by author*

Wayne's reputation suffered from the Paoli affair. The Pennsylvanian ached to avenge the manner in which his men had been treated. He would get his chance for revenge when he unleashed his frustration on the enemy in a similar fashion two years later at Stony Point, New York.[45]

The supplemental British force posted near Paoli Tavern, comprised of Lt. Col. Thomas Musgrave's 40th and 55th Regiments of Foot, never got into the fight. Some, however, went looking for Wayne at his family home of Waynesborough about a mile away. "A number of the British troops surrounded your House in serch of you," wrote Wayne's brother-in-law to the general, "but being disappointed in not finding you they took poor Robert & James [two of Wayne's slaves]." The British, he continued, "behaved with the utmost

had a total of nine men wounded out of 225 engaged. The 11th Pennsylvania suffered six casualties out of 200 engaged. The 5th Pennsylvania suffered 24 casualties out of 245 men, including Ensign William Magee (killed) and Pvt. James Reed (wounded). Reed had also been wounded at New Brunswick, New Jersey, earlier in the campaign. Lieutenant Charles McHenry took saber blows to the head and collarbone. The 2nd Pennsylvania had 22 casualties out of 187 engaged, including Lts. John Irwin and Major Walbron. Walbron was killed and Irwin (the regimental adjutant) was badly wounded and left for dead on the field. Irwin had jammed his company orderly book into his waistcoat, and the book likely saved his life when it absorbed multiple bayonet thrusts. Private John Fagain was wounded in the cheek and leg by bayonets, and Pvt. Peter Jacobs was wounded in the side. Montgomery, ed., *Archives*, Series 5, Vol. 3, 10, 87, 312, 627; Linn and Egle, eds., *Archives*, Series 2, Vol. 10, 407; McGuire, *Paoli*, 111, 154, 217-219, 221-222.

45 After the Battle of Germantown Wayne requested a court of inquiry to defend his actions at Paoli. The court, which announced its findings on November 1, 1777, acquitted him of any wrongdoing. McGuire, *Paoli*, 183.

politeness to the Women and said they only Wanted the General. They did not disturb the least Article." Wayne was lucky the enemy did not ransack or burn his home that night. Most British officers would not have been so kind.[46]

Virginia loyalist James Parker summed up the lesson he hoped Wayne had learned. "Genl. Wean, tho' an Old [fox] but a Young General, taught now by experience, it is to be hop'd . . . will keep further from our rear."[47]

46 Letter, Abraham Robinson to Anthony Wayne, September 22, 1777, Wayne Papers, vol. 4.

47 Parker Journal, September 21, 1777 entry, Parker Family Papers.

Chapter 5

Washington Outmaneuvered, Again

September 21-25, 1777

"If the rebels had the least spirit or resolution they might have defended this pass [ford]; not that they would have prevented our getting over, but they might have killed us a number of men."[1]

— Capt. Francis Downman, Royal Artillery, September 23, 1777

Once Grey's column returned from the successful Paoli operation, William Howe put his army in motion. With the threat that Wayne posed to his rear eliminated, Howe moved ahead with his plans to cross the Schuylkill River.

The British army departed its camps, turned up the Baptist Road (modern Route 252), bore left at Gulph Road into the Valley Creek watershed, and marched up Nutt Road (modern Route 23) where Cornwallis's detachment remained on the hills watching the fords. The column moved past the forge ruins on Nutt Road and marched as far as the bridge over French Creek in Charlestown Township before halting. Howe established headquarters in the home of William Grimes along Pickering Creek, roughly halfway back down the column, with his army stretched

1 F. A. Whinyates, ed., *The Services of Lieut.-Colonel Francis Downman, R.A. in France, North America, and the West Indies, Between the Years 1758 and 1784* (Woolwich, 1898), 35.

1907 marker in Phoenixville, PA denoting furthest inland advance of the British army. The British, however, actually advanced beyond the location of this marker.

Photo by author

along a seven-mile front.[2] "[W]e found the houses full of military stores," recalled Engineer John Montresor. "This country abounds with Forage, but the cattle drove off." With the army's left flank at French Creek and its right at Valley Forge, Howe had six river crossings in front of him: Gordon's, Long, Richardson's, and Fatland Fords, and Pawling's and Davis's Ferries. By the time Howe arrived the Continental Army stretched for nine miles and covered the Schuylkill River fords across from the British.[3]

Crossing the Schuylkill River

Howe's arrival put his army almost half way between Reading and Philadelphia. It was painfully obvious to Washington that Anthony Wayne's loss at Paoli had altered the strategic situation. Washington had intended to prevent

2 A monument at the intersection of Route 23 and Route 113 in Phoenixville, on a traffic island opposite the former Fountain Inn, marks the deepest inland penetration of the British army. The monument was erected by the Pennsylvania Society Sons of the Revolution on September 21, 1907. British and Hessian troops, however, actually moved deeper inland to and across French Creek. Ethan Allen Weaver, ed. *Annual Proceedings Pennsylvania Society of Sons of the Revolution 1907-1908* (Philadelphia, 1908), 23. From Phoenixville, the British front stretched all the way back to the heights where Gulph Road and Innerline Drive meet today in Valley Forge National Historical Park. Reed, *Campaign*, 180-181; McGuire, *Campaign*, vol. 1, 318. An 1870s history of Phoenixville claims Cornwallis accompanied the column into that village, but no contemporary source confirms his departure from Valley Forge. Samuel Whitaker Pennypacker, *Annals of Phoenixville and its Vicinity: From the Settlement to the Year 1871, Giving the Origin and Growth of the Borough, with Information Concerning the Adjacent Townships of Chester and Montgomery Counties and the Valley of the Schuylkill* (Philadelphia, 1872), 104.

3 Montresor, "Journals," 456. Gordon's Ford was near the mouth of French Creek. Richardson's Ford was at the location of Bridge Street in Phoenixville. Long Ford was located along Long Ford Road in present-day Oaks. Reed, *Campaign*, 181.

Howe's crossing of the Schuylkill by raiding his rear and seizing his baggage. "Paoli had allowed Howe not only to regain the strategic advantage," summarized historian Thomas McGuire, "but also to successfully turn the tables and seize full control of the military situation."[4]

Washington faced a Hobson's Choice, for the storehouses at Reading needed to be protected, but to do so would uncover Philadelphia, which, politically speaking, could not be surrendered without a fight. His options were bleak: lose Reading and the supply depots of the Pennsylvania backcountry, or lose the colonial capital at Philadelphia. If he shifted troops to guard the city, Howe could seize the iron manufacturing region to the west. To the poorly supplied army, protecting those backcountry regions was more important than the psychological loss of Philadelphia. It was obvious, however, that Howe could move rapidly west, capture the Continental supply centers, and return for Philadelphia, winning both major prizes. No matter what Howe decided to do, Philadelphia was all but lost. The defeat at Paoli had drastically altered the strategic equation.[5]

Howe's moves seemed to signal that he was about to march toward Reading and the iron manufacturing region. In fact, Howe had informed George Germain that he had utilized the water route to the Chesapeake earlier in the campaign to threaten the storehouses in the Pennsylvania backcountry. Any British advance in that direction would force Washington to move accordingly, leaving Howe the option of reversing course and marching for the lower fords of the Schuylkill River and into the capital city. Howe had utilized flanking maneuvers to turn Washington's positions at least six times, most recently at Brandywine just ten days earlier. His current move toward the American right flank appeared to be more of the same.

Washington was unaware of the supply situation within the British army, but there was little chance Howe would move even farther from a rendezvous with the fleet. "Howe's supplies were none too plenty," wrote one modern historian, "and [he] would probably have to fight to get to [Reading]. . . . To fight, Howe would have to do so on ground of Washington's choosing, at the fords of the river or against high, defensible hills."[6] Neither option would have appealed to the British. Washington decided to obstruct the fords leading toward Reading, and ordered

4 McGuire, *Paoli*, 150-151.

5 Ibid.

6 Risch, *Washington's Army*, 34-35.

Gen. John Sullivan to send parties "to break up and throw Obstructions in the landing places of all the Fords from Richardson's at least as high as parkers." With the failure to watch all the fords along the Brandywine fresh in his memory, Washington urged Sullivan to "[a]dvise the Officers who superintend, not to neglect such [fords] as the Country people tell them are difficult, because at such places the Enemy will be most likely to pass, thinking we shall pay least attention to them. A subaltern and twelve Men," he continued, "[will] constantly remain at each of the Fords to give Notice of the approach of the Enemy." Washington was determined to avoid repeating the mistakes of Brandywine. Colonel Stephen Moylan of the light dragoons, an Irish immigrant and wealthy merchant from Philadelphia who began the war on Washington's staff, was ordered to send detachments across the river to watch Howe.[7]

The American commander's mounting problems included the deplorable condition of the survivors of Paoli. Wayne's division had lost about 13 percent there, hundreds of muskets and invaluable camp equipment had been left behind, and at least one-half of Smallwood's Maryland militia had deserted. Both officers, wrote Ephraim Blaine to William Buchanan, the Commissary General of Purchases, were "much distress'd for the Necessary supplies for their People." The amount of equipment and commissary stores lost, he added, hadn't been "properly ascertain'd, but [were] Considerable." Wayne now had about 1,500 Pennsylvanians under arms—some 700 fewer than he had immediately before the battle—but many of them were not "effectives," meaning they were sick, unarmed, or otherwise could not be relied upon to fight. Smallwood's command had been whittled down to 1,100 men, about 1,000 fewer than he had before the evening of September 21. Rumors, few of them favorable to Wayne, circulated through the army, and morale in his division plummeted. Many blamed the general directly for the devastating defeat. Wayne, meanwhile, remained near Red Lion Tavern during the day attending to both his battered division and his wounded ego.[8]

Now convinced Reading was Howe's immediate objective, on the evening of September 21 Washington pulled away from the river fords and shifted his army west to better protect that supply center. The Americans moved west on Ridge Road through Trappe to Limerick, where they veered away from the river onto Faulkner Swamp Road, eventually moving into the Crooked Hills surrounding

7 Chase and Lengel, eds., *Papers*, vol. 11, 277.

8 McGuire, *Paoli*, 151-152; Joseph Lee Boyle, ed., *"My Last Shift Betwixt Us & Death": The Ephraim Blaine Letterbook 1777-1778* (Berwyn Heights, MD, 2001), 10.

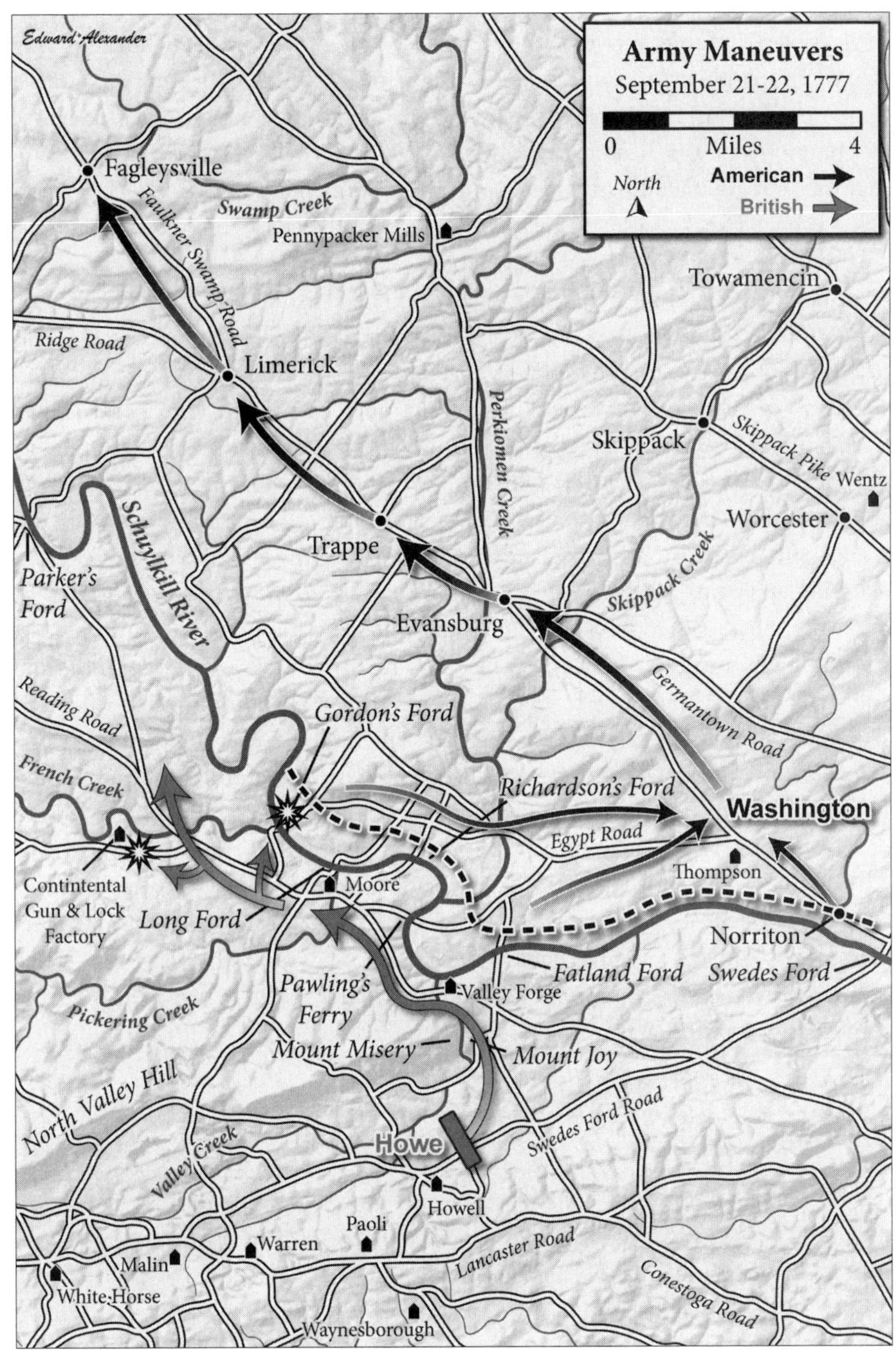
Edward Alexander
Army Maneuvers
September 21-22, 1777
0 Miles 4
North
American
British
Fagleysville
Faulkner Swamp Road
Swamp Creek
Pennypacker Mills
Towamencin
Ridge Road
Limerick
Perkiomen Creek
Skippack
Skippack Pike
Wentz
Worcester
Schuylkill River
Trappe
Skippack Creek
Parker's Ford
Evansburg
Germantown Road
Reading Road
Gordon's Ford
French Creek
Richardson's Ford
Washington
Egypt Road
Thompson
Moore
Contintental Gun & Lock Factory
Long Ford
Norriton
Fatland Ford
Swedes Ford
Valley Forge
Pawling's Ferry
Pickering Creek
Mount Misery
Mount Joy
North Valley Hill
Swedes Ford Road
Howe
Valley Creek
Howell
Paoli
Warren
Malin
Lancaster Road
White Horse
Conestoga Road
Waynesborough

Fagleysville. The risky movement exposed the lower fords of the Schuylkill River to the British; other than some militia detachments, Washington's army was gone.

The next morning Howe sent detachments west to further convince Washington he was heading that way. One body of troops skirmished with Pennsylvania militia and stumbled upon the Continental Gun and Lock Factory along French Creek. Earlier in the year, Congress had established the factory and a small powder mill; the latter had exploded in March, soon after it became operational. The complex was four miles from Phoenixville and eight from Valley Forge. While the militia was supposed to protect it, they were too unreliable to depend upon, so Continental soldiers who were prisoners on parole helped defend the complex. The parolees would not put up much of a fight either, because they were not supposed to be assisting the army while on parole.[9]

Hessian officer Johann Ewald noted in his diary that he and his jaegers approached the complex around 8:00 a.m. and found the American parolees and militiamen "behind the houses and fences and fired several shots, to which no attention was paid," whereupon he ordered his force to move within 150 paces of the Americans. As they drew near, "the enemy fled into the wood so hastily that not a single man was caught." Ewald recalled finding the "blown-up powder magazine and a rifle factory, in which several pieces of fabricated and unfinished rifles and sabers of all kinds were stored." The Hessian "ordered everything smashed to pieces, set fire to the factory, and marched back." An unidentified officer with the British 2nd Light Infantry Battalion heard about the day's events and recalled the news by noting, "[a] Recnghting party found Pouder Mill A Magazien and Some Armers Shops and Store houses Which they Burnt and Distroid all that Came to hand & With Stores of Provisions and Furage." At least one American militia officer would have disagreed with these descriptions of the damage. "They destroyed very little property," wrote Isaac Anderson, "as it had been sent off sometime before to Lancaster, guarded by the militia."[10]

9 McGuire, *Campaign*, vol. 1, 321. The powder mill was also built for the Continental government. The nearby gun factory apparently suffered little or no damage from the explosion and continued to operate. Most sources state the mill never went back into production, but several British and Hessian accounts note that it was operational in September 1777. Dan Graham, "French Creek Continental Powder Works and Gun Manufactory, Chester County, Pennsylvania," *The Local Historian* (Morgantown, PA, Fall 2011), 1-7. The Continental Gun and Lock Factory had been moved to this location in 1776 by Benjamin Rittenhouse. Smith, *Manufacturing*, 15.

10 Ewald, *Diary*, 90-91. The site of this action was along Rapps Dam Road in Kimberton, between the National Guard Armory and the covered bridge over French Creek. British Officer's "Memorandum List of 1777," *George Washington Papers, Series 6, Military Papers, 1755 to 1798, Subseries*

To further convince Washington that he was headed west, Howe ordered forward Hessians under Gen. William Erskine, a column consisting of 200 grenadiers commanded by Capts. von Westerhagen and Schimmelpfennig, as well as 20 mounted and 60 foot Jaegers led by Capts. Richard Lorey and Carl von Wreden, respectively. The Hessians moved to Gordon's Ford (present-day Phoenixville) and, supported by artillery fire, crossed the river and made a noisy demonstration that prompted Washington to pull even more of his militia away from the lower river crossings. Once it was clear Washington was heading west toward Reading, the Hessians withdrew to the south side of the river and Howe issued orders for the entire army to move east for Fatland Ford, away from Reading. Washington, meanwhile, moved his army 15 miles west before realizing he had been duped yet again.[11]

Elsewhere, the remnants of Anthony Wayne's and William Smallwood's forces retreated from Red Lion Tavern to Morgantown. Marching 14 miles, they moved up Little Conestoga Road to Ridge Road (Route 23) and camped near the Little Conestoga Creek, just over the Berks County line, 20 miles west of the British position near David Jones's tavern. Some of the Paoli wounded traveled with the column. "I went to the ground to see the wounded," recalled Maj. Samuel Hay of the 7th Pennsylvania. "The scene was shocking—the poor men groaning under wounds, which were by stabs of Bayonets and cuts of Light-horsemen's swords. . . . Captain Wilson stabbed in the side, but not dangerous, as it did not take the guts or belly. He got also a bad stroke on the head with the cock nail of the locks of a musket. Andrew Irvine was ran through the fleshy part of the thigh with a bayonet. They are all laying near David Jones' tavern. I left Captn McDowell with them to dress and take care of them, and they are in a fair way of recovery."[12]

Farther north, wagons carrying church bells from Philadelphia, including the Liberty Bell, arrived in Bethlehem. "The wagon in which was loaded the State House bell [the Liberty Bell], broke down in the street, and had to be unloaded." Ultimately, the Liberty Bell would end up in the basement of Zion Church in

---

6C, Captured British Orderly Books, 1777-1778: Captured British Officer's Accounts Ledger, 1769 to 1771, and Diary, 1774; 1777, retrieved from the Library of Congress, www.loc.gov/item/mgw6c00015/, accessed August 19, 2017; Anderson, "Historical Sketch," 30.

11 McGuire, *Campaign*, vol. 1, 321-322; McGuire, *Paoli*, 160.

12 McGuire, *Paoli*, 152. The tavern is believed to have stood on the north side of Route 23 just west of Route 401, between Elverson and Morgantown. Linn and Egle, eds., *Archives*, Series 2, Vol. 10, 614-615. Ultimately, many of Wayne's wounded found their way to a hospital in Lancaster. Gillett, *Medical Department*, 210.

Allentown. The Congressional archives also reached Bethlehem, escorted from Trenton by 50 cavalrymen and 50 infantrymen.[13]

"Painful as it is to me to order and as it will be to you to execute the measure," wrote Washington to Alexander Hamilton on September 21, "I am compelled to desire you immediately to proceed to Philadelphia, and there procure from the inhabitants, contributions of blankets and Cloathing and materials to answer the purpose of both, in proportion to the ability of each. . . . As there are also a number of horses in Philadelphia both of public and private property," he continued, "which would be a valuable acquisition to the enemy, should the city by any accident fall in their hands, You are hereby authorised and commanded to remove them thence into Country to some place of greater security and more remote from the operations of the enemy."[14]

The Brigade of Guards under Brig. Gen. Edward Matthew, led by its grenadier and light companies, formed the vanguard of the British column driving across the Schuylkill River that night. Having tricked Washington into moving west away from the Schuylkill River fords, the British army crossed to the north side of the river unopposed. The units crossed at Fatland and Richardson's fords under a bright moonlight that made for a challenging, but not exceedingly difficult, passage. The water, recalled Grenadier John Peebles, came "up to a Gr[enadie]rs breetches pockets." Once on the far side, "the Troops took up ground as they arrived, made fires, & dryed themselves till about 7 or 8 oclock."[15] Luckily for the British, the river passage was not challenged by American fire. The Schuylkill, recalled Gen.

13 Jordan, "Bethlehem," 74. Numerous bells had been ordered removed from Philadelphia. Several of the smaller ones were submerged in the Delaware River while the larger ones were sent north by wagon. Two Lehigh Valley farmers, Frederick Leasor and Jacob Mickley, were forced to haul the bells after they arrived in the city with produce. The State House Bell was originally loaded into Mickley's wagon, but the vehicle broke down on the hill between Monocacy Creek and the Brethren's House in Bethlehem. The bell then was transferred to Leaser's wagon, which safely hauled the heavy bell to the Zion Church, at the corner of Church and Hamilton streets in Allentown. The bell remained in the church's basement until it was returned to Philadelphia in June 1778. Richmond E. Myers, *Northampton County in the American Revolution* (Easton, PA, 1976), 47-50; Kidder, *Crossroads*, 207; Reed, *Campaign*, 183-184; McGuire, *Campaign*, vol. 2, 183-184.

14 Chase and Lengel, eds., *Papers*, vol. 11, 282-283.

15 Fatland Ford road cut sharply downhill from modern Route 23, near the Washington Chapel in Valley Forge National Park, through a roadbed that is still visible, except where modern railroad tracks intervene. Entering the Schuylkill, the road passed over the upper tip of Fatland Island (now joined to the mainland), ran down the middle of the island, and then bore left into the back channel of the river. The road then ascended the bluffs of the bank through another still-visible roadbed before skirting the Fatlands property on the present Chapel View Road, and entering Pawlings Road. Peebles, *Diary*, 137.

James Grant, who commanded two of Howe's infantry brigades, was "a very difficult Creek indeed much more formidable than the Brandy Wine if it had been defended." Captain Francis Downman of the Royal Artillery agreed. "If the rebels had the least spirit or resolution they might have defended this pass [ford]," chided Downman, "not that they would have prevented our getting over, but they might have killed us a number of men. . . . The rebels fly before us; they run whenever we advance." Before crossing the Schuylkill, the British burned the Valley Forge mill complex and any supplies they could not haul away.[16]

Once they realized what had happened, on September 23 the Pennsylvania militia defending Swedes' Ford, in the only earthwork built west of Philadelphia, abandoned their position, along with four cannon. With most of Howe's troops between them and Washington's army (which was 20 miles away in New Hanover and Limerick Townships), the militiamen failed to spike the cannon in their haste to abandon the position.

Once his army had dried their uniforms and equipment, Howe moved up Egypt Road, made a right onto Ridge Road, and marched into Norriton Township before going into a long linear camp along Stony Creek. Howe positioned his left flank at Swedes' Ford on the Schuylkill and his right flank on Germantown Road five miles away. The British were now firmly positioned between Washington and Philadelphia; no more combat was needed for them to seize the colonial capital, but the fighting was far from over.[17]

Royal artilleryman Francis Downman recalled that the area around Norriton Township had essentially been abandoned. "Very few of the inhabitants have remained in their houses, those who have alone saving their effects," he penned in his journal. "It is otherwise with the deserted houses." Several structures met the torch, including Thompson's Tavern, which had been Washington's headquarters. After serving as Howe's headquarters, Col. John Bull's plantation was burned to the ground. Howe's chief engineer, John Montresor, described the region as "very

16 Grant to Harvey October 20, 1777, Grant Papers. The British dried out after the crossing in modern Audubon. Rowland Evans, who ran a mill in the area, later reported the destruction wrought by the passing British troops. "Two of the bolting cloths having been torn by the British Soldiers when the Army went by, and some fences burnt by them; The Times rendering the Mill of very little value." Letter, Evans to Physick, March 2, 1778; Whinyates, *Services*, 35. The Valley Forge complex remained in ruins for many years. After the war, Isaac Potts rebuilt the complex on a larger scale. None of the industrial buildings stand today. Bining, *Iron Manufacture*, 51.

17 Reed, *Campaign*, 184; Martin, *Campaign*, 97.

rebellious. All the manufactures about this country seem to consist of Powder, Ball, Shot and Cannon, firearms, and swords."[18]

Howe's move across the river impacted much more than just the military situation. The plunder of John Bayard's home in Plymouth Township offers an insightful example of what civilian destruction and thievery truly entailed. Bayard was not only a militia colonel but also speaker of the Pennsylvania Assembly. A few wagons were engaged "to carry the furniture to places of safety," explained James Wilson, "but could not, on such short notice, dispose of all the family stores . . . They had to be left for the plunder of the soldiery." Wilson, remembering the event from his childhood, continued:

> [T]he enemy arrived and took possession of the house. . . . They found much that was gratifying, and some things which proved amusing in the way of destruction. The library was a thing which could do them no good; they found many religious books, and concluded they belonged to some Presbyterian parson, and, of course, a rebel. They made a pile of them and amused themselves in shooting at them; in all directions, the fragments and some few volumes remaining scattered over the court yard. . . . The wine was a great prize, and proved the means of saving the house which was doomed to destruction. But the officer, in gratitude for this unlooked for luxury, instead of ordering the house to be burnt, wrote a very polite note [to Bayard], thanking him for his entertainment.[19]

Christopher Marshall, an elderly apothecary who had a shop in Philadelphia, had moved out to the country that spring in a failed attempt to escape from the political tensions pulsing through the capital. There "are many instances of the wanton cruelty they [the British] exercised in his neighbourhood," he wrote in his diary,

> amongst which is the burning of the house where Col. [Joseph] Reed did live, the house where Thompson kept tavern, with every thing in it, all the hay at Col. Bull's, fifteen hundred bushels of wheat, with other grain, his powder mill and iron works; destroyed all the fences for some miles, with the Indian corn and buckwheat, emptied feather beds, destroyed furniture, cut books to pieces at Col. Bayard's; at one place emptied some feather beds, and put a cask of yellow ochre, cask of Spanish Brown [and] cask of linseed oil, and

18 Whinyates, *Services*, 35. Bull was a militia colonel. McGuire, *Campaign*, vol. 1, 323; Montresor, "Journals," 457.

19 James Grant Wilson, "A Memorial of Colonel John Bayard," *Proceedings of the New Jersey Historical Society*, 13 vols. (Newark, NJ, 1879), 2nd series, vol. 5, 150-151.

> mixed them all together. So brutal and cruel are their steps marked, it would be tiresome tracing them with a pen.[20]

Local Loyalists rode into Howe's camp and provided the British with crucial intelligence. John Roberts, a Quaker miller from lower Merion Township, was one of those who showed up; the Americans would hang him as a traitor in November 1778.[21]

Howe was above the river and held all the strategic cards except one: he desperately needed to be resupplied by the British fleet. The general, however, did not have a full understanding of the difficulties facing his naval officer brother. After the victory at Brandywine, Admiral Richard Howe needed to move the frigates and supply ships to the mouth of the Delaware River to better support the army. It would be several weeks before the fleet could return to the Delaware from the Chesapeake. At the outset of the campaign, Admiral Howe had waited at the Elk River for word of his brother's progress, and news of his victory at Brandywine did not reach him until September 13. The admiral acted immediately by detaching the *Isis*, a 50-gun ship-of-the-line, for the Delaware River, along with a dozen supply ships jammed with food and ammunition for his brother's army. Howe then ordered the rest of his fleet to follow. Sailing ships, however, are subject to the vagaries of weather, and unfavorable winds kept the resupply convoy and the balance of the fleet in the Chesapeake for another ten days.[22]

While Howe's men were busy plundering Norriton Township, Washington sought to replace his losses from the campaign. Smallwood and Wayne had yet to rejoin the main army. Washington, however, expected a brigade of Connecticut Continentals under Alexander McDougall from the Hudson River Valley within the week, as well as New Jersey militia under Gen. David Forman, to reinforce his army. He urged McDougall to "use all the diligence and dispatch in your power to join this army." As for the New Jersey militia, Maj. Gen. Philemon Dickinson informed Washington that it was unclear how many militiamen would gather for service in Pennsylvania, and that he feared many would desert once they crossed

20 Christopher Marshall, *Passages from the Diary of Christopher Marshall, Kept in Philadelphia and Lancaster During the American Revolution*, ed. William Duane (Philadelphia, 1839-1849), 152.

21 Nagy, *Spies*, 102.

22 Gruber, *Howe Brothers*, 248-249.

1913 marker in New Hanover Township, PA denoting the site of Washington's Camp Pottsgrove. *Photo by author*

the Delaware. Malcolm's Additional Continental Regiment, operating in the Hudson Highlands, also received orders to reinforce Washington's army.[23]

The Continental Army was now positioned near Pottsgrove, a region encompassing most of modern-day northwestern Montgomery County. The large-scale battle at Brandywine, various skirmishes and engagements (including Paoli), long marches, and stretches without adequate food and supplies had worn down the army. His troops, Washington informed Congress, were short of clothing, blankets, and especially shoes; nearly 1,000 men were in the field barefoot despite efforts to shod them. The Virginia general called a council of war to decide whether the army should wait where it was for reinforcements, or move toward an engagement with the enemy, for which it was not yet ready. In spite of its problems, the army had to be ready to fight, so Washington ordered each regiment to make as many cartridges as possible and hold them in storage for future use.[24]

23 Forman, a native of New Jersey, was born in 1745. He was authorized to raise Forman's Additional Continental Regiment and was made a brigadier general of the New Jersey militia in the spring of 1777. Chase and Lengel, eds., *Papers*, vol. 11, 271, 275-276; Wright, *Army*, 216.

24 Washington established his headquarters at the home Frederick Antes, a militia colonel. The Antes house still stands along Colonial Road in Fagleysville. A stone marker erected in 1913 identifies the camp location near the intersection of Swamp Pike and Faust Road. The American camp occupied by Washington's army in New Hanover Township, Montgomery County, was still marked by physical remains nearly six decades after the event. In a reminiscence of the "camp at Pottsgrove" written at the beginning of the twentieth century, a landowner recalled that in his childhood (circa 1820s), the area occupied by the American camp was characterized by enough "leaden musket balls, and grape and canister balls and broken shells [to fill] a straw bread-basket." Benjamin Bertolet, "The Continental Army at Camp Pottsgrove," *Historical Sketches: A Collection of Papers Prepared for the Historical Society of Montgomery County, Pennsylvania* (Norristown, PA, 1905), vol. 3, 25-26; Chase and Lengel, eds., *Papers*, vol. 11, 293, 302.

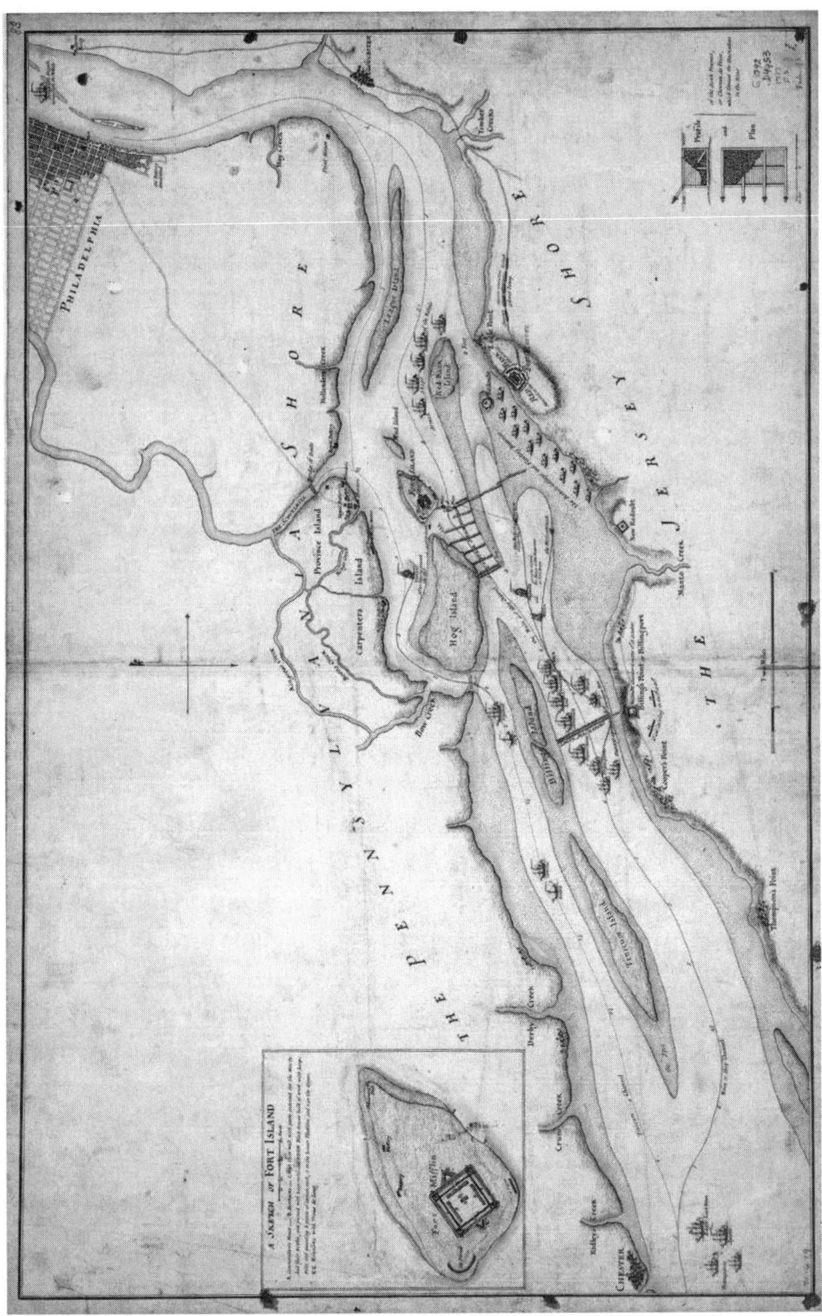

1777 map showing 'The course of Delaware River from Philadelphia to Chester, exhibiting the several works erected by the rebels to defend its passage, with the attacks made upon them by His Majesty's land & sea forces.' *Library of Congress*

Having accepted the fact that Philadelphia was doomed, Washington decided to cause as many problems as possible for the British by controlling the Delaware River. If Washington could bar the Royal Navy access to Philadelphia, he might be able to starve Howe's army into submission. Initially, he thought it best to put Commodore John Hazelwood's Pennsylvania Navy in command of the river defenses at Fort Mifflin, Billingsport, and Fort Mercer. Specifically, Washington wanted Hazelwood to remove 200 to 300 men from his ships to garrison Fort Mifflin on Mud Island, just south of Philadelphia on the Pennsylvania side of the river. At the time, there were no Continentals or militia garrisoning the fort, so sending seamen who could operate the artillery was a reasonable option. Washington apparently was unaware that many of Hazelwood's ships were still at anchor because they did not have enough men to put out to sea. Stripping bodies off stationary ships to garrison a fort was out of the question. Washington requested that all boats be gathered to prevent any attempts against the fort. As Fort Mifflin sat on an island, the approaching British army would be unable to occupy it without ships. "If we can stop the Enemy's fleet from coming up & prevent them from getting Possession of the Mud fort, & they take Possession of the City & our Army moves down upon the back [of the city]," Washington informed the commodore, "it will be the most effectual method of ruining General Howe's Army. . . . If you think it necessary for the Security of the Fort to lay the Island under water, let it be done immediately."[25]

Hours later Washington changed his mind and assigned command of the defenses to the Continental Army. He placed Col. Heinrich D'Arendt in command of Fort Mifflin and ordered Lieut. Col. Samuel Smith of the 4th Maryland Regiment to garrison the fort with a detachment of Continentals. Unfortunately D'Arendt, a man of exceptional engineering ability and thus a logical choice for the assignment, was ill and would not arrive at the fort for some time. "If it [reinforcement] succeeds and they with the Assistance of the Ships and Gallies should keep the obstructions in the River," wrote Washington to John Hancock, "General Howe's Situation in Philada will not be the most agreeable, for if his supplies can be stopped by Water it may be easily done by land. To do both shall be

25 The Pennsylvania Navy consisted of a conglomeration of vessels of varying sizes raised by the Pennsylvania Assembly to defend the Delaware River. It answered to the Assembly, not the Continental Congress. John W. Jackson, *Fort Mifflin: Valiant Defender of the Delaware* (Norristown, PA, 1986), 24; Chase and Lengel, eds., *Papers*, vol. 11, 303. Fort Mifflin was erected on a mud bog called Mud Island. Dikes along its shoreline kept the river water out of the fort. If the dikes were cut, they could flood the island and make its occupation impossible.

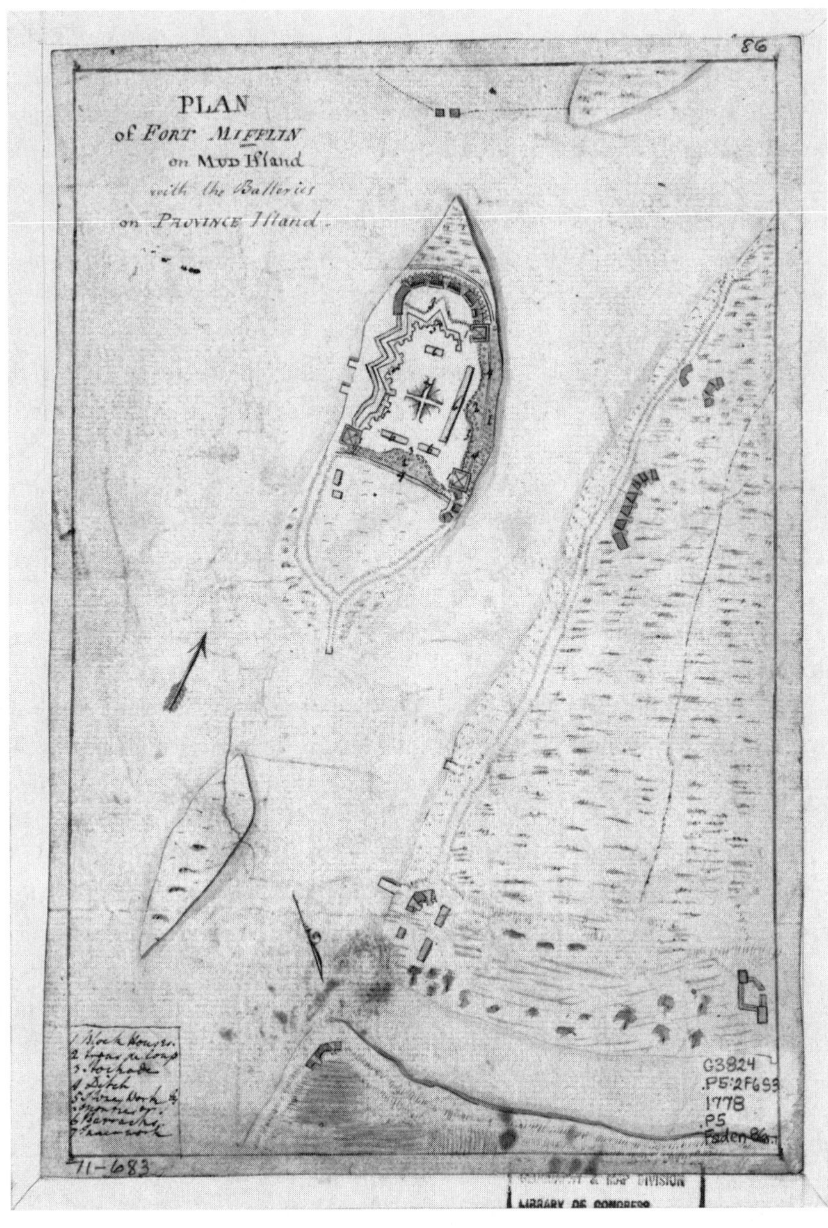

1778 map showing 'Plan of Fort Mifflin on Mud Island, with the batteries on Province Island.' South is at the top of this image.

Library of Congress

my utmost endeavor, and I am not yet without hope that the acquisition of Philada may, instead of his good fortune, prove his Ruin." Keeping the fort in American hands, he added, was "of very great Importance." Knowing that squabbles between the two branches were both common and detrimental to the cause of liberty, Washington appealed to the army and navy commanders to work together to maintain control of the Delaware. "Let us Join our Force & Operations both by land & Water in such a manner as will most effectually work the Ruin of the Common Enemy, without confining ourselves to any particular Department," he urged.[26]

All vessels on the Philadelphia waterfront had to be removed to keep them from falling into the hands of the approaching British. Washington issued the necessary order on September 23. The docked vessels above the Market Street wharf were ordered to make for Burlington, New Jersey, while those downstream of the wharf were sent to Fort Mifflin with orders to report to Commodore Hazelwood. Public and private goods remaining in the city were to be removed by any vessel available for the task. Small craft uninvolved with the evacuation were hidden up New Jersey creeks. Any boats found along the river the next day were to be destroyed.[27]

While the Continentals scrambled to reinforce the Delaware River line, Washington took a few minutes out of his busy day to send a situation report to Israel Putnam, commander of the defenses along the lower Hudson River around West Point, New York. "The situation of our affairs in this Quarter calls for every aid, and for every effort," he explained. "Genl. Howe by various Maneuvrs & marching high up the Schuylkill, as if he meant to turn our right Flank found means by countermarching to pass the river last Night several miles below us, which is fordable almost in every part, and is now fast advancing towards Philadelphia." Washington implored Putnam to send reinforcements. He also sent a situational report to Congress. "The Enemy, by a variety of perplexing Maneuvers thro' a Country from which I could not derive the least intelligence being to a man disaffected," he wrote, "contrived to pass the Schuylkill last Night at the Flat land and other Fords in the Neighbourhood of it. They marched immediately towards

26 Jackson, *Navy*, 129; McGuire, *Campaign*, vol. 2, 137. Colonel Heinrich D'Arendt's late arrival at the fort, created command issues there. Samuel Smith had enlisted in the Maryland Line at the beginning of the war as a sergeant and quickly rose through the ranks. Chase and Lengel, eds., *Papers*, vol. 11, 302-303.

27 Jackson, *British Army*, 15.

Philada and I imagine their advanced parties will be near that City to Night." Howe's maneuver induced Washington "to believe that they [the British] had two objects in view, one to get round the right of the Army, the other perhaps to detach parties to Reading where we had considerable quantities of military Stores. To frustrate those intentions I moved the Army up on this side of the River to this place [Pottsgrove], determined to keep pace with them, but early this morning I recd intelligence that they had crossed at the [lower] Fords [behind us]."[28]

September 24 was a busy day for the Americans. Commodore Hazelwood, who was patrolling Philadelphia's waterfront aboard a Pennsylvania Navy vessel, ordered two fieldpieces onto the Market Street wharf along with a naval detachment, apparently to determine whether the British had entered the city; he removed them when no enemy forces were discovered. Following this reconnaissance, Hazelwood returned downriver with his vessels. To the southwest, near Morgantown, Generals Wayne and Smallwood broke camp and marched to join the main army. Washington's baggage train of 700 wagons, escorted by 200 men under Col. Thomas Polk of the 4th North Carolina Regiment, reached Bethlehem with many of the Brandywine wounded. "They encamped on the south side of the Lehigh, and in one night destroyed all our buckwheat and the fences around the fields," noted an anonymously penned Moravian diary. "With them came a crowd of low women and thieves, so that we had to maintain a watch at the Tavern [the Sun Inn]. No services could be held of late—it is a time of confusion!" Prominent officers wounded at Brandywine were already in town when the wagon train of wounded arrived, including the Marquis de Lafayette, a French major general who at that time held no command, and Brig. Gen. William Woodford, commander of the 3rd Virginia Brigade. "Many complaints are Daily made by the Country people of Robberys and other disorders committed by these Scum of the Army," Woodford reported to Washington. "I have taken every method to detect the delinquents & bring them to Justice, but they have heitherto proved ineffectual." There was no rest for the weary teamsters, for as soon as they offloaded the injured they were dispatched to Trenton to retrieve army supplies stored there.[29]

28 Fifty-nine-year-old Israel Putnam had risen to lieutenant-colonel during the French and Indian War after extensive service and was an energetic leader of the Connecticut Sons of Liberty prior to the American Revolution. Chase and Lengel, eds., *Papers*, vol. 11, 201-302, 305.

29 Jackson, *British Army*, 15-16; McGuire, *Paoli*, 167; Jordan, "Bethlehem," 73-74; Chase and Lengel, eds., *Papers*, vol. 11, 371; Kidder, *Crossroads*, 207.

An army constantly on the move is difficult to keep supplied, and Washington's troops had not remained in one place for longer than a few days since Brandywine. "Should the Army keep at one place the supply would be much easier," confessed Washington's commissary general to William Buchanan. "I am quite discouraged about our proceedings, God knows how it may end; The English seem to get the Advantage upon every movement of our people, where the fault lays, am not able to judge."[30]

Occupation of Germantown

On September 25, Howe marched his army in two columns (one along the Germantown Road and the other on the Ridge Road) 11 miles into Germantown, which was just five miles from Philadelphia. Germantown, explained Loyalist James Parker, was a "[v]illage of one Street & two Miles in Length Inhabited Chiefly by German Stocking Weavers, Waggon Makers &c who are Chiefly of the Rebellious Cast, & look down on this Occasion." "Their whole army seemed in complete order," recalled resident John Ashmead decades later. He was just 12 when the British arrived in Germantown. "The display of officers, the regular march of red coated men, and refugee greens [the Queen's Rangers], the highlanders, grenadiers, their burnished arms, &c. There was, however, *no* display of colours, and *no* music—every thing moved like machinery in silence. . . . Sundry men occasionally came up and said, 'Can you give us a little milk or any cider.'" Howe dispatched troops to cover the approaches to the town from the north and west. The Queen's Rangers took up a position near Kensington on the road to Frankford, while Lt. Col. Ludwig von Wurmb's jaegers moved along Wissahickon Creek near the Schuylkill River. The main camp ran parallel to School House Lane along a two-mile front centered on Germantown's market square. Howe posted Maj. John Maitland's 2nd Light Infantry Battalion two miles north of the square on Mount Pleasant, with pickets spread out 400 yards on Mount Airy. The 1st Light Infantry Battalion under Col. Robert Abercromby was deployed at Luken's Mill with pickets covering the crossroads of Limekiln Pike and Abington Road (present Washington Lane), and Lt. Col. Thomas Musgrave's 40th Regiment of Foot was posted behind Benjamin Chew's country home at Cliveden. Howe established

30 Boyle, ed., *Letterbook*, 10.

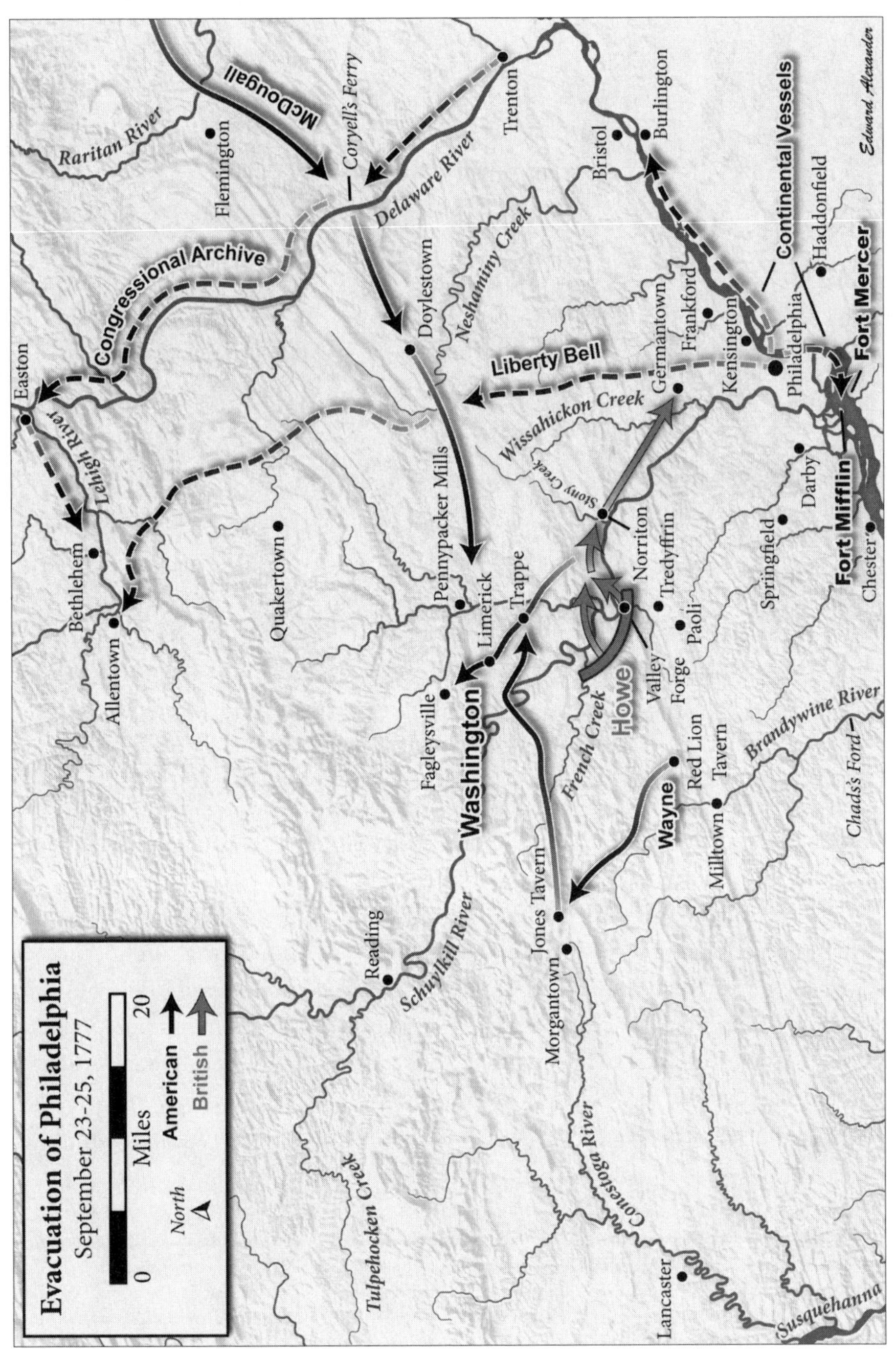
Evacuation of Philadelphia
September 23-25, 1777
0
Miles
20
North
American
British
Reading
Schuylkill River
Tulpehocken Creek
Morgantown
Jones Tavern
Conestoga River
Lancaster
Susquehanna
Washington
Fagleysville
Limerick
Trappe
Pennypacker Mills
Quakertown
Allentown
Bethlehem
Lehigh River
Easton
Congressional Archive
Flemington
Raritan River
McDougall
Coryell's Ferry
Trenton
Delaware River
Doylestown
Neshaminy Creek
Liberty Bell
Wissahickon Creek
Stony Creek
Germantown
Frankford
Kensington
Bristol
Burlington
Continental Vessels
Philadelphia
Haddonfield
Fort Mercer
Fort Mifflin
Chester
Darby
Springfield
Norriton
Tredyffrin
Paoli
Valley Forge
Howe
French Creek
Wayne
Red Lion Tavern
Milltown
Brandywine River
Chads's Ford
Edward Alexander

The Stenton House, used by William Howe as British headquarters during the occupation of Germantown. *Photo by author*

headquarters at Stenton, the same home Washington had used about a month earlier when his army was on its way to Delaware.[31]

"[T]he inhabitants are mostly Germans but were against us, the most ill-natured people in the world, who could hardly contain their anger and hostile sentiments," scribbled a surprised Capt. Johann Ewald in his diary. "One old lady, who was sitting on a bench before her front door, answered me in pure Palatine German when I rode up to her and asked her for a glass of water: 'Water I will give you, but I must also ask you: What harm have we people done to you, that you Germans come over here to suck us dry and drive us out of house and home? We

31 Parker *Journal*, September 25, 1777 entry, Parker Family Papers; John F. Watson, *Annals of Philadelphia and Pennsylvania, in the Olden Time; Being a Collection of Memoirs, Anecdotes, and Incidents of the City and its Inhabitants*, 2 vols. (Philadelphia, PA, 1855), vol. 2, 51; McGuire, *Germantown*, 15-16. Mount Airy was the country seat of William Allen. Stenton was the country seat of the Logan family; the large brick home was built in 1730 but was not occupied in 1777. The original owner had passed away the previous year and his heir was studying medicine in Scotland. McGuire, *Campaign*, vol. 1, 100.

have heard enough here of your murderous burning. Will you do the same here as in New York and in the Jerseys? You shall get your pay yet!'" While Ewald marveled at the treatment they received at the hands of fellow Germans, John Andre studied the make-up of the population. "A good many people came in from Philadelphia," he observed, most of whom "represented that place as in the greatest confusion and expressed fears of its being burnt."[32]

As he took up his position in Germantown, General Howe had no idea of the problems that continued to plague his brother's fleet in its laborious journey to reach the Delaware River. Contrary winds had held up Admiral Howe's armada in the Chesapeake until September 23, and the impatient admiral had pushed ahead with two warships—the *Eagle* and the *Isis*—to try to make contact with his brother's army. On September 25—the same day the army marched into Germantown—a severe storm slammed into the two ships and blew them so far out to sea that it took more than a week before they reached the Delaware River. The longer the navy took to link up with Howe's army, the greater risk of starvation.[33]

Panic in the Capital

As John Andre intimated, Philadelphia was in a state of pandemonium. That morning, the Americans loaded supplies and munitions stored in the city on every movable boat (whether Continental, state, or privately owned) and shipped them north up the Delaware River to Trenton. There wasn't a person in the capital that did not know it was about to change hands. "It has rained all this afternoon, and to present appearances, will all night," teenage Sally Wistar told her journal. "In all probability the English will take pocession of the city to-morrow or next day. What a change will it be! May the Almighty take you under His protection, for without His divine aid all human assistance is vain. . . . The uncertainty of our position engrosses me quite," she confessed. "Perhaps to be in the midst of war, and ruin, and the clang of arms. But we must hope the best."[34]

32 Ewald, *Diary*, 91; Andre, *Journal*, 52.

33 Gruber, *Howe Brothers*, 248-249.

34 Jackson, *Navy*, 122; Sally Wister, *Sally Wister's Journal: A True Narrative Being a Quaker Maiden's Account of her Experiences with Officers of the Continental Army, 1777-1778*, ed. Albert Cook Myers (Philadelphia, PA, 1902), 72-73.

Privateer Capt. Charles Biddle helped townspeople intent on escaping before the British arrived. "I took on board every person that applied to go up until we had as many as we could stow," recalled the compassionate officer. "Many of these unfortunate people who were leaving the city knew not how they were to subsist. Some of them had wives and children without a morsel of provisions to give them." Biddle sailed north to Bristol, where he landed "and found the place full of people flying from Philadelphia, many of whom were my acquaintances."[35]

Quaker and inveterate journalist Elizabeth Drinker kept a careful record of what took place during those tumultuous times. "This has been so far, a day of great Confusion in the City . . . the English were within 4 or 5 miles of us . . . they are expected by some this Evening in the City," she penned in what would eventually be a 2,100-page diary. "Things seem very quiate and still . . . a great number of the lower sort of the People are gone out to them [the British] . . . tis said that tar'd faggots &c are laid in several out Houses in different parts, with [mischievous] intent." Elizabeth would face the approaching British occupation alone, for her husband had been rounded up by the Pennsylvania authorities as an "undesirable." Loyalist and former delegate to the First Continental Congress Joseph Galloway thought the transition would be as smooth as possible, all things considered. "[T]he Inhabitants must take care of the Town this Night, and they would be in, in the Morning," said Galloway, who added that "all things appear peaceable at present, the Watch-Men crying the Hour without Molestation." Diarist Sarah Logan Fisher wasn't as sanguine, and worried the city would be put to the torch: "Many people were apprehensive of the city's being set on fire, & near half the inhabitants, I was told, sat up to watch."[36]

"Most of the warm people [patriots] have gone off . . . the inhabitants of this place were threatened with great inconvenience and distress, thro want of provisions and necessaries, from the country," explained Loyalist Robert Proud to his brother. "The rebel army had left it very bare and destitute, having at their departure, a few days before the British forces arrived not only carried off almost every thing of that nature, except only what was immediately wanted for the present use of the inhabitants, [but had also] taken away every boat and vessel in the

35 Charles Biddle, *Autobiography of Charles Biddle, Vice-President of the Supreme Executive Council of Pennsylvania, 1745-1821* (Philadelphia, PA, 1883), 102.

36 Elizabeth Sandwith Drinker, *The Diary of Elizabeth Drinker*, Elaine Forman Crane, ed., 3 vols. (Boston, MA, 1991), vol. 1, 235; Fisher, "Diary," 450. Drinker's remarkable and invaluable diary first appeared in print in 1889 and covers a host of topics on life in Philadelphia, politics, Quaker culture, and of course, the American Revolution.

harbor, under pretence that if they were left, they might be serviceable to their enemies." The Americans carried away everything they thought "might be of use to the English army, besides what they apprehended might be wanted by themselves," continued Proud,

> which they chiefly took from Quakers, and such at least favoured them; as blankets, carpets, cloathing, etc. They likewise took away all the lead and leaden pipes and all the bells in the city, except one; and they drove off with them about 4000 head of fat or feeding cattle from the island and meadows round the city, with most of the horses they could get, leaving the city and remaining inhabitants in much straight and destitute; they likewise cut the banks of the meadows, island etc. and laid them under water, having seemingly done all the mischief in their power before their departure.

General Howe was desperately short on supplies and was about to achieve his objective: the capture of a destitute city.[37]

Washington's chief staff officer, Timothy Pickering, was disgusted with the lack of support from the local population. "Here [Pennsylvania] we are, in fact, in an enemy's country. I am told upwards of sixty-five thousand men are enrolled in the militia of Pennsylvania; yet we have not two thousand in the field, and these are of little worth and constantly deserting," complained the frustrated aide. "After the action on the 11th [Brandywine], and the enemy took possession of Wilmington," Pickering continued,

> almost all the militia of Delaware State also ran home. Some Maryland militia join us to-morrow, perhaps a thousand men. Many that marched from home have deserted . . . I had heard at home so much contempt and ridicule thrown by the southern gentlemen on the New England militia, that I expected something better here; but no militia can be more contemptible than those of Pennsylvania and Delaware; none can be spoken of more contemptuously than they are by their own countrymen. And how astonishing is it, that not a man is roused to action when the enemy is in the heart of the country, and within twelve miles of their grand capital, of so much importance to them and the Continent! How amazing, that Howe should march from the head of Elk to the Schuylkill, a space of sixty miles, without opposition from the people of the country, except a small band of

37 Letter, Robert Proud to William Proud, December 1, 1777, Robert Proud memoranda and letter copies, 1770-1811, Historical Society of Pennsylvania, Philadelphia.

militia just around Elk! Such events would not have happened in New England. I rejoice that I can call *that* my country. I think myself honored by it.[38]

Washington's stationary position in Pottsgrove allowed General Wayne the time he needed to march into the vicinity on September 25. General Smallwood with his Maryland militia tramped behind Wayne and joined the army soon thereafter. After crossing the Schuylkill at Parker's Ford, Wayne moved his division to Trappe, just six miles from Washington. General John Armstrong and his Pennsylvania militia marched east and also camped near Trappe. Armstrong would remain there until ordered to cooperate in the attack on Germantown nine days later. Other reinforcing troops also headed toward Washington's army; Gen. Alexander McDougall's Connecticut brigade from the Hudson Highlands crossed the Delaware and marched into Pennsylvania. Worried that McDougall was moving too close to the British camp at Germantown, Washington ordered him to march for Pennypacker's Mills and wait there for the army. Washington also ordered Lord Stirling to send light horse and guides to make sure the Connecticut brigade moved in the proper direction.[39]

Although he had been beaten at the Brandywine and maneuvered out of position outside Philadelphia, Washington was eager to strike the British. The army's current position, however, precluded any attempt to do so because the Continentals were not within easy striking distance of the British position at Germantown. Washington wanted to move along the Perkiomen Creek at Pennypacker's Mills, and sent officers to scout the position to see if the area would be a convenient location to assemble the army and launch an assault against the enemy camp.[40]

While Washington contemplated his next move, William Howe prepared to march into Philadelphia unopposed.

38 Pickering, *Pickering*, vol. 1, 163-164.

39 Chase and Lengel, eds., *Papers*, vol. 11, 316-317.

40 Brownlow, *Germantown*, 10; Chase and Lengel, eds., *Papers*, vol. 11, 314. "Pennypacker's Mills" or "Pawlings Mill" was used interchangeably in the 18th century, but were actually multiple properties. The modern Pennypacker Mills Historic Site in Montgomery County was owned by Samuel Pannebecker in 1777, and would be greatly enlarged by Pennsylvania Governor Samuel Pennypacker in the 20th century. The site also featured a grist mill owned by Joseph Pawling. Lastly, the "Old Mill House," located in modern Central Perkiomen Valley Park, was known as Pawlings Mill in 1777, and also was owned by Joseph Pawling.

Chapter 6

Philadelphia Captured

September 26, 1777

"The Streets [were] crowded with Inhabitants who seem to rejoice on the occasion, tho' by all accounts many of them were publickly on the other side before our arrival."[1]

— Lieutenant John Peebles, 42nd Highlanders, September 26, 1777

The Setting

Philadelphia was the largest American port, the seat of the government, and the fourth largest city in the entire British Empire. Although established less than a century earlier, it grew more rapidly than the older cities of Boston and New York. The founding Penn family's offers of lucrative land deals, coupled with the province's Quaker tolerance of all faiths, contributed to the heavy and steady influx of immigrants to both the city and its picturesque surrounding countryside. Within the Empire, only Dublin, Edinburgh, and London had larger populations.[2]

1 Peebles, *Diary*, 138.

2 McGuire, *Campaign*, vol. 1, 124.

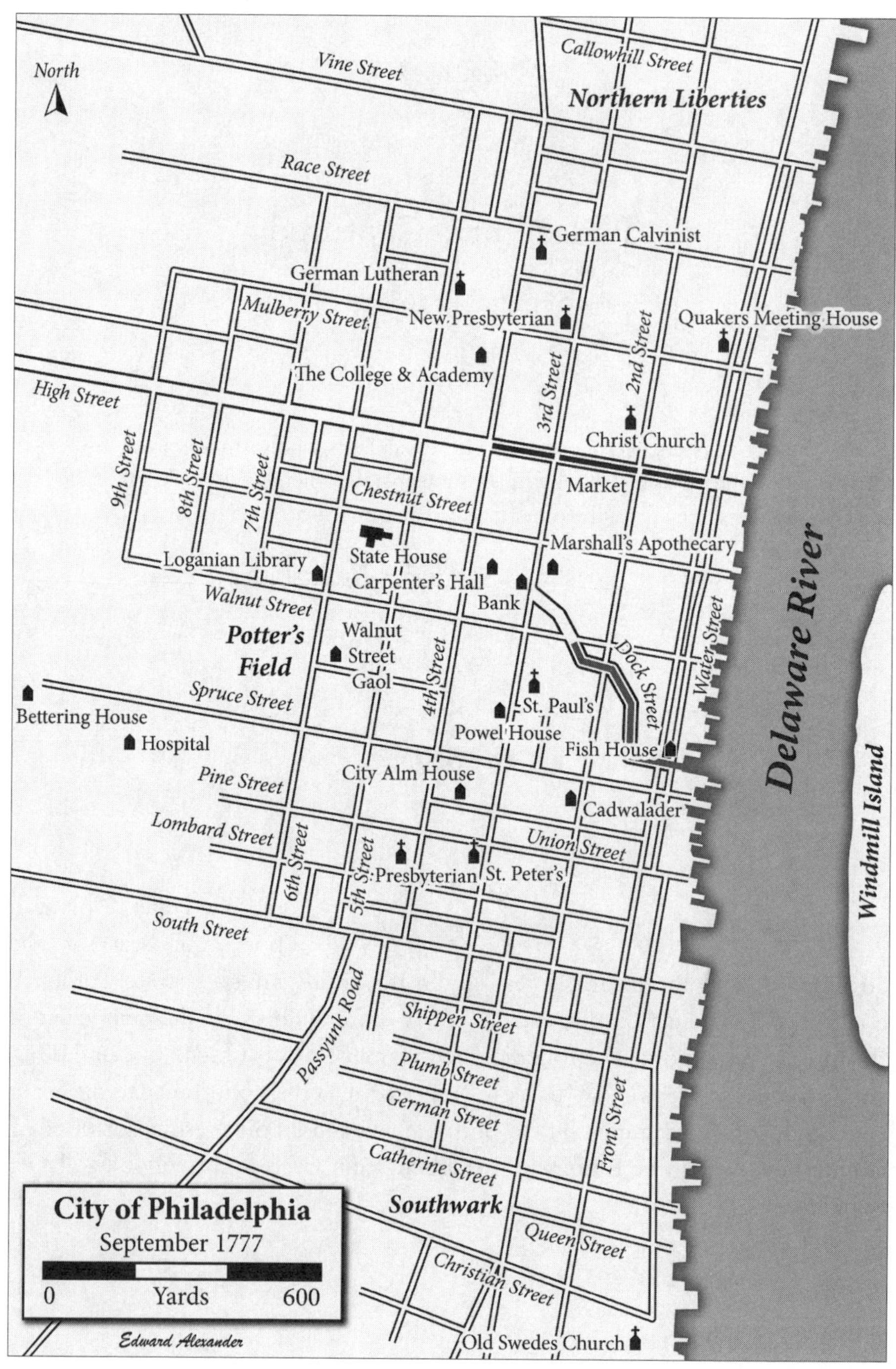
North
Vine Street
Callowhill Street
Northern Liberties
Race Street
German Calvinist
German Lutheran
Mulberry Street
New Presbyterian
Quakers Meeting House
The College & Academy
High Street
3rd Street
2nd Street
Christ Church
9th Street
8th Street
7th Street
Chestnut Street
Market
Logonian Library
State House
Marshall's Apothecary
Carpenter's Hall
Bank
Walnut Street
Potter's Field
Walnut Street Gaol
4th Street
Dock Street
Water Street
Delaware River
Spruce Street
St. Paul's
Bettering House
Powel House
Hospital
Fish House
Pine Street
City Alm House
Cadwalader
Lombard Street
Union Street
6th Street
5th Street
Presbyterian
St. Peter's
Windmill Island
South Street
Passyunk Road
Shippen Street
Plumb Street
German Street
Front Street
Catherine Street
Southwark
Queen Street
Christian Street
Old Swedes Church
City of Philadelphia
September 1777
0 Yards 600
Edward Alexander

Philadelphia was laid out in a grid pattern, with (mostly numbered) north-south streets running parallel to the Delaware River, and east-west streets named after trees and other plants. Streets were 50 feet wide, paved with cobblestone, and lined with sidewalks of brick or flagstone. An exception was High Street, a 100-foot wide thoroughfare with a market shed running down the middle of three blocks starting at the old courthouse at Second Street. Other than a scattering of church steeples and other cupolas, no building was taller than four stories. By 1777, the city of 30,000 to 40,000 citizens boasted more than 5,000 houses and 3,000 other buildings including warehouses, merchant facilities, and small workshops. These mostly red-brick structures were erected within one square mile of each other. The city extended eight blocks west from the Delaware River. If the suburbs of Northern Liberties and Southwark are included, the boundaries were 14 blocks north-to-south from Callowhill to Christian Streets. Beyond the organized streetscape were verdant fields and farmland, stands of trees, and a sprinkling of country houses.[3]

Politics divided the population. The Scotch-Irish Presbyterian Protestants favored American independence. Members of the Church of England, or Anglicans, were divided between loyalty to the Crown and support for their homes and livelihoods. Protestant Germans, who composed about half of Philadelphia, were neutral for religious reasons or supported the war effort. Members of the large Quaker contingent preferred neutrality, but their default position was passive loyalty to the crown. The small number of Jews, Irish, and German Catholics kept a low profile.[4]

Unfortunately for the colonial cause, the spirit and enthusiasm for revolution was waning. "I soon discovered that a material change had taken place during my absence from Pennsylvania," observed Alexander Graydon, a Philadelphia captain captured by the British at Fort Washington and home on parole, "and that the pulses of many that, at the time of my leaving it, had beaten high in the cause of Whiggism and liberty, were considerably lowered." While this was generally true among urbanites, most people in the countryside remained enthusiastic about the war.[5]

3 McGuire, *Campaign*, vol. 1, 125; Sullivan, *Disaffected*, 13.

4 McGuire, *Campaign*, vol. 1, 126.

5 Alexander Graydon, *Memoirs of a Life, Chiefly Passed in Pennsylvania, within the Last Sixty Years* (Edinburgh, 1822), 299.

Philadelphia's disenchantment with the rebellion offered the British an opportunity. Pennsylvanians remained less militant than New Englanders to the northeast or Virginians to the south because of its long-standing lack of a true militia. Much of this was because of the state's diversified economy, which was less affected by Parliament's taxation policies. Many believed they profited from the imperial connection, so why sever it? They enjoyed, wrote historian John Luzader, the "kind of society that other Americans aspired to, and it had become a reality without needing a revolution."[6]

From the outside the city appeared to be solidly behind independence. A closer look revealed that more than half the population was disinterested in war or loyal to the King. The large population of Quakers in Pennsylvania made it unique among the colonies. Belief in nonviolence kept them politically neutral. While many agreed with the patriot cause, the vast majority refused to take up arms or support the war in any way. Likewise, Pennsylvania supported Loyalists within its borders. The combination of Quakers and Tories put the patriots of Pennsylvania in the minority.

Philadelphia Captured

Philadelphia was eerily quiet on Friday morning, September 26, 1777. The entire city was at a standstill. The usual throng of people who entered the city from the countryside to sell their produce and wares at Saturday's market day failed to materialize, and the wharves were still and largely vacant. Entire sections of Philadelphia were empty of inhabitants who had fled ahead of the British. After a night of rain, the weather had cleared and gradually gave way to sunshine.[7]

Charles Cornwallis, afforded the honor of leading a column of troops into Philadelphia to occupy and garrison the colonial capital, selected about 3,000 troops and marched them in from Germantown. Two squadrons of the 16th Light Dragoons under Lt. Col. William Harcourt formed the head of the column. Behind Harcourt was the brigade of British grenadiers and two battalions of Hessian grenadiers (the von Linsing and von Lengerke battalions commanded by Col. Carl von Donop). As a further show of force, six medium 12-pounders and four howitzers brought up the rear.

6 Luzader, *Saratoga*, 5.

7 McGuire, *Campaign*, vol. 2, 6-7.

Several notable Tories trotted their mounts ahead of the column symbolizing the return of Royal government. One was Andrew Allen, the former attorney general of Pennsylvania and delegate to the Second Continental Congress, and the other his brother, William Allen, Jr., a former officer in the 2nd Pennsylvania Battalion. Both had changed allegiances after the signing of the Declaration of Independence. Their brother John was with them as well. Loyalist Joseph Galloway, a member of the First Continental Congress and a former friend of Ben Franklin's, rode with the Allen brothers, returning to the city he had abandoned the previous year. Philadelphia Loyalists Phineas Bond and Enoch Story guided the long column, which comprised a quarter of Howe's effective force. The shifting of troops to Philadelphia significantly weakened the garrison left behind at Germantown.[8]

Cornwallis had formed his column that morning on the heights above Nicetown, just southeast of Germantown. From there, the British could see Philadelphia about four miles away. The men stepped off down the Germantown Road about mid-morning and tramped past the Rising Sun Tavern at the Old York Road. It was an impressive display of pomp and might. The sun gleamed off the distant Delaware, beyond which shimmered the pine forests of New Jersey. Shaping the skyline were the spires of Christ Church and the Pennsylvania State House, known today as Independence Hall. Off to the right meandered the chocolate-colored water of the Schuylkill River, which the army had crossed to organize the celebratory march. Although Philadelphia was the object of William Howe's campaign, he did not ride into the city that morning. Instead, wrote Captain von Muenchhausen, the general "accompanied them half way and then rode back after the grenadiers had passed in review to the accompaniment of martial and other music."[9]

The column approached Second Street and the small suburb of Northern Liberties, which spread out for a mile above the city boundary at Vine Street. Behind it a half mile away stood the village of Kensington along the Delaware River. When the head of Cornwallis's column reached Second Street, it turned right and crossed Cohocksink Creek and marched past the large brick French and Indian

8 McGuire, *Germantown*, 18; McGuire, *Campaign*, vol. 2, 8-12, 14; McGuire, Paoli, 2; Jackson, *British Army*, 288.

9 McGuire, *Campaign*, vol. 2, 10-11. Unfortunately, Germantown and the region between it and Philadelphia are enveloped by urban sprawl. In the eighteenth century, this area was home to several country estates owned by prominent Philadelphians. Thankfully, many of the homes have been preserved as part of Fairmount Park. Muenchhausen, *At Howe's Side*, 36.

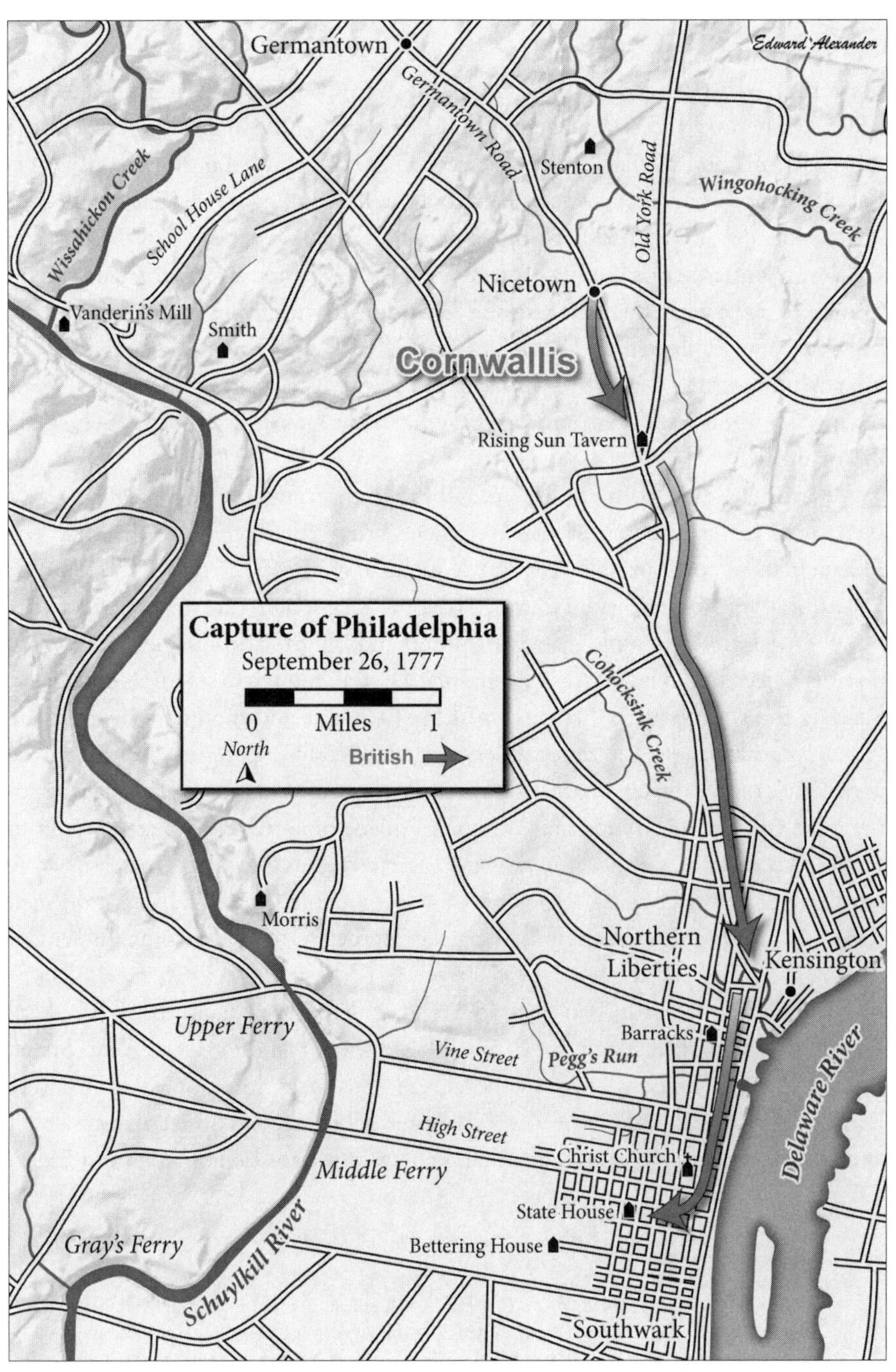

Edward Alexander
Germantown
Germantown Road
Stenton
Old York Road
Wingohocking Creek
Wissahickon Creek
School House Lane
Nicetown
Vanderin's Mill
Smith
Cornwallis
Rising Sun Tavern
Capture of Philadelphia
September 26, 1777
0 Miles 1
North
British
Cohocksink Creek
Morris
Northern Liberties
Kensington
Barracks
Upper Ferry
Vine Street
Pegg's Run
Delaware River
High Street
Christ Church
Middle Ferry
State House
Gray's Ferry
Schuylkill River
Bettering House
Southwark

War-era barracks, which was capable of housing up to 3,000 men. A mixed aroma greeted the marchers, including reeking tanneries, boiling cabbage, and the malty fumes of breweries and distilleries. Crossing over Pegg's Run, the men ascended a low ridge to Callowhill Street and approached the city limits, where the muddy road gave way to cobblestone.[10]

"First came the light horse . . . nearly 200 I imagine in number, clean dress & their bright swords glittering in the sun," wrote Sarah Logan Fisher, wife of a Philadelphia Quaker merchant, in her diary. After that came the foot," she continued,

> headed by Lord Cornwallis. Before him went a band of music, which played a solemn tune, & which I afterward understood was called 'God save great George our King.' Then followed the soldiers, who looked very clean & healthy & a remarkable solidity was on their countenances, no wanton levity, or indecent mirth, but a gravity well becoming the occasion seemed on all their faces. After that came the artillery & then the Hessian grenadiers, attended by a large band of music but not equal to the other. Baggage wagons, Hessian women, & horses, cows, goats & asses brought up the rear.

One of the men riding with the artillery observed by Sarah Fisher was Captain Downman. "[T]he roads and streets were crowded with people who huzzaed and seemed overjoyed to see us," recalled the officer. "Whether they were pleased or not at our entrance, they must have been struck with the appearance of a body of such fine fellows as the British grenadiers. It was a fine sight." Lieutenant Peebles of the 42nd Highlanders agreed: "The Streets [were] crowded with Inhabitants who seem to rejoice on the occasion, tho' by all accounts many of them were publickly on the other side before our arrival."[11]

Continuing down Second Street, the conquerors tramped past Christ Church, one of the city's two Anglican churches. Two very different men, Joseph Galloway and Anthony Wayne, had been married inside. Just up the road from Christ Church the troops crossed the 100-foot wide intersection at High Street (modern-day Market Street), where market sheds stretched down the middle of the road for three blocks. They marched past the old Court House, where independence was proclaimed on July 8, 1776, and one block farther turned right on Chestnut Street, moving beyond Christopher Marshall's apothecary shop. As they crossed Third

10 McGuire, *Campaign*, vol. 2, 12-13.

11 Fisher, "Diary," 450; Whinyates, *Services*, 36; Peebles, *Diary*, 138.

Street, the elegant town houses of men like Benjamin Chew and Samuel Powel came and went, and, beyond that, Carpenter's Hall, where the First Continental Congress had met three years earlier.[12]

Fifteen-year-old Debby Norris watched the procession from a second-floor window. "They looked well, clean, and well clad," she began, and "the contrast between them and our own poor barefooted and ragged troops was very great, and caused a feeling of despair—it was a solemn and impressive day—but I saw no exaltation in the enemy, nor indeed in those reckoned favourable to their success." The head of the lengthy column halted in front of the State House, where Galloway had served as speaker of the Pennsylvania Assembly for more than a decade, and Andrew Allen as attorney general. The British would soon convert the State House into the Captain's Main Guardhouse. A ten-year-old boy watching the historic event recalled little beyond how the Hessian grenadiers terrified him. "Their looks to me were terrific—their brass caps—their mustaches—their countenances, by nature morose, and their music, that sounded better English than they themselves could speak—plunder—plunder—plunder—gave a desponding, heart- breaking effect, as I thought, to all; to me it was dreadful beyond expression." The British troops impressed the young boy as much as the Hessians frightened him: "I went up to the front rank of them when several of them addressed me thus—'How do you do, young one—how are you, my boy'—in a brotherly tone, that seems still to vibrate on my ear; then reached out their hands, and severally caught mine, and shook it, not with an exulting shake of conquerors, as I thought, but with a sympathizing one for the vanquished."[13]

"[T]o the great relief of the inhabitants who have too long suffered under the yoke of arbitrary Power," recalled a 17-year-old supporter of the Crown named Robert Morton, "[they] testified their approbation of the arrival of the troops by the loudest acclamations of joy." Joseph Galloway exaggerated the welcome Cornwallis and his troops received upon entering Philadelphia. "His entry was truly triumphant," declared the prominent Loyalist. "No Roman General ever received from the citizens of Rome greater acclamations than the noble General did on this occasion from the loyal citizens of Philadelphia." What he failed to mention was that most of the patriot citizens had fled the city. Captain John Andre had a more sober view of what was transpiring. Galloway, he wrote in his journal, "valued the

12 McGuire, *Campaign*, vol. 2, 16-18. High Street (Market Street today) was the main business thoroughfare, running east-west.

13 Watson, *Annals*, vol. 2, 283-284; McGuire, *Campaign*, vol. 2, 19.

number of inhabitants who have quitted Philadelphia, at one-sixth; some respectable Quakers said one-third."[14]

After this triumphant show-of-force parade, Cornwallis deployed his men to cover the city's approaches. The 1st Battalion of British Grenadiers moved into Southwark, a suburb below the city's southern boundary at South Street, while the 2nd Battalion of British Grenadiers and the Hessian Grenadier Battalion von Lengerke took up station at the Bettering House west of town. The Hessian Grenadier Battalion von Linsing occupied the barracks in Northern Liberties. The two squadrons of Light Dragoons, meanwhile, rode out to the Schuylkill Stables, a mile outside town, west of the Common at Center Square, and below the Middle Ferry on the road to Gray's Ferry. The light field guns remained with their respective battalions while the heavy artillery was divided along the river front. Two 12-pounders and a pair of howitzers were unlimbered at the upper end of Northern Liberties. Engineers placed four 12-pounders and two more howitzers on high ground south of town near the 1st Battalion of British Grenadiers, and also constructed platforms to mount the heavy artillery. The occupation unfolded without a hitch, which Captain Andre attributed to the fact that "a great many desperados" had left the city. Wherever the British and Hessian units camped, explained civilian Robert Morton, the area began "to show the great destruction of the Fences and other things, the dreadful consequences of an army however friendly."[15]

Cornwallis ordered artillery redoubts erected to protect the vulnerable waterfront south of the city, one near present Reed and Swanson streets and another near Swanson and Christian (close to Old Swedes Church). The British also reactivated the old Association Battery at what is now the foot of Washington Avenue and placed another battery on a wharf near Cohocksink Creek, north of the city in the neighborhood of what is today Noble Street and Christopher Columbus Boulevard.[16]

14 Morton, "Diary," 7-8; Joseph Galloway, *Letters to a Nobleman on the Conduct of the War in the Middle Colonies* (London, 1779), 77; Andre, *Journal*, 54.

15 The Bettering House, or Quaker Alms House, sat on the south side of Spruce Street between the present 10th and 11th Streets. In 1777, the city did not extend beyond 9th Street. The stables built for use by the Pennsylvania and Continental light dragoons had only recently been evacuated. McGuire, *Philadelphia Campaign*, vol. 2, 28-29; Reed, *Campaign*, 409; Samuel Steele Smith, *Fight for the Delaware*, 1777 (Monmouth Beach, NJ, 1970), 7; John Andre's narrative of the Philadelphia Campaign, McGuire, *Campaign*, vol. 2, 298; Morton, "Diary," 8.

16 Jackson, *Navy*, 123.

Boats of any kind in the vicinity were seized immediately. Fifty craft were located, including a Durham boat in Frankford Creek that could hold at least 50 men. Scows, flatboats, and other types of vessels were found hidden in the marshes and on Windmill Island. Washington had ordered Capt. Charles Alexander of the Continental Navy to remove from the area anything that could float, but there simply was not enough time for Alexander to put the plan into effect.[17]

Cornwallis issued orders to survey public and private buildings capable of being converted into barracks—and for good reason. Philadelphia would eventually house some 18,000 soldiers and noncombatants traveling with Howe's army. When news of the capital's fall spread, thousands of Loyalist refugees flocked to the city.[18]

So began what would be a nine-month occupation, one month and one day after Howe had landed his army at Turkey Point. The campaign that had started back in June had taken nearly three months to complete. Howe had planned to move quickly, capture Philadelphia, and return with sufficient forces to New York to assist John Burgoyne. That may have been possible two months earlier if he had ascended the Delaware River in July; instead, he had managed to meander both on land and at sea. He fought several engagements along the way, including the major battle along the Brandywine on September 11. The 80-day endeavor isolated and doomed Burgoyne, who would surrender his army at Saratoga in another month. "Here it may be observed that if so much Time was expended in obtaining the possession of an Inland City at the Expence of Thousands of pounds (in money) & the loss of a great number of Men," explained Capt. Samuel Massey of the Pennsylvania militia, "how could the possibility of Conquest be supported, the Space between New York [and Philadelphia] being 90 Miles; the Distance of (the) Conquest [of the colonies] being comprized in ab(ou)t 1800 Miles from New Hampshire to Georgia by the Roads, exclusive of the Number of Villages, Towns &c. that composed the United States, that there could be the least probability of Conquest(?)"[19]

17 Smith, *Fight for the Delaware,* 6-7.

18 John W. Jackson, *The Delaware Bay and River Defenses of Philadelphia, 1775-1777* (Philadelphia, 1977), 13.

19 Samuel Massey, "Journal of Captain Samuel Massey, 1776-1778," *Bulletin of the Historical Society of Montgomery County Pennsylvania,* John F. Reed, ed. (Norristown, PA, 1976), vol. 20, no. 3, 226. Howe's campaign consumed 80 days from the time he embarked in New York Harbor to the day he entered Philadelphia.

It was important that Howe's actions be seen as the reestablishment of civil government, but he established one in name only. Samuel Shoemaker was installed as mayor and Joseph Galloway as police commissioner. Neither wielded any power without the weight of the British military. As time passed, the British pushed Shoemaker and Galloway aside in deference to military control.[20]

With the city now in hand, Howe needed to keep the Continental Army at bay while his own command, with the assistance of the British fleet, strived to open the Delaware River in order to provide provisions and supplies to his army. The Pennsylvania galleys patrolled the river, and could rake the streets of Philadelphia. Fort Mifflin, with a newly arrived garrison of Continentals, was in position to prevent British naval access to the city. The Pennsylvania Navy under Commodore John Hazelwood assembled several watercraft near Fort Mifflin to prevent the approach of the Royal Navy. This flotilla contained the Continental frigate *Delaware*, the 32-gun frigate *Montgomery*, the 8-gun sloop *Fly*, a floating battery, several gondolas, and fire ships. Congressman Charles Carroll believed "[i]f the garrison at the fort will hold out a few days perhaps Mr. Howe may repent his going into Ph[iladelphi]a. General Washington is assembling & collecting troops from all sides. His army is much broken down with their late marches but a few days rest I hope will revive their strength & spirits." William Howe's looming tasks were formidable.[21]

Not only was the river approach closed, but Washington had the foresight to train and plant spies in the colonial capital. Back in April, Washington had instructed his quartermaster general and Pennsylvania native, Thomas Mifflin, to create a spy system in Philadelphia. If Howe occupied the city, the spies were "to remain among them under the mask of Friendship," instructed Washington. "I would have some of those in Bucks County, some in Philadelphia, and others below Philadelphia about Chester. . . . I would therefore have you set about this work immediately, and give the persons you pitch upon [choose], proper lessons. Some in the Quaker line, who have never taken an active part, would be least liable to suspicion from either party." Now was the time for those spies to pay dividends.[22]

20 Reed, *Campaign*, 190.

21 Jackson, *Navy*, 123; McGuire, *Campaign*, vol. 2, 29; Smith, et al., eds., *Letters*, vol. 8, 18.

22 Fitzpatrick, *Writings*, vol. 7, 385.

The situation was rather simple. If the British could gain control of the Delaware River, Philadelphia would remain in the hands of the Crown. If they could not navigate the *Delaware* at will, they would not have sufficient supplies to remain in place and would almost certainly have to evacuate the capital. Howe "can neither support his Army in Philada if he is cut off from comm[u]nication with his ships," concluded Washington, "neither can he make good a Retreat should any accident befall him."[23]

Continental Movements

When Cornwallis entered Philadelphia, the last vestiges of colonial resistance slipped out. A New Jersey militia detachment, which had been sent across the Delaware by Gen. Silas Newcomb, escaped into New Jersey. The Jerseymen had served under James Potter of the Pennsylvania militia, who pulled his men south across the Schuylkill River when Cornwallis entered the city from the north.[24]

After several days on the run and a roundabout route to get there, members of Congress showed up in Lancaster, 60 miles west of Philadelphia. While Congress ultimately ended up governing in York during the British occupation of Philadelphia, for a time they operated out of Lancaster. New supply depots had to be created for the army, and Congress scrambled to make it so. The previous summer the Congress had ordered a gunpowder factory constructed at Carlisle, and had designated the old French and Indian War works as a Quartermaster Depot and Commissary Magazine; this work was still underway when Howe marched into Philadelphia.[25]

On September 26, Washington and his army crossed Perkiomen Creek from Camp Pottsgrove and arrived at Pennypacker's Mills, ten miles closer to Philadelphia but still more than 20 miles outside the captured capital. The Continentals established their new camps thoroughly exhausted, having marched some 140 miles in the past eleven days. Washington took up residence at the home of Samuel Pennypacker, where he established his headquarters.

23 Smith, *Fight for the Delaware*, 6; Chase and Lengel, eds., *Papers*, vol. 11, 347.

24 Smith, *Fight for the Delaware*, 6.

25 Frantz & Pencak, eds., *Beyond Philadelphia*, 130. Carlisle was rapidly developing into a major supply center for the Continental Army. Before the end of the year 11 buildings would be constructed there. Carlisle remains a U.S. military post and houses the U.S. Army War College. Smith, *Manufacturing*, 98-99.

1897 marker denoting the location of Washington's campsite before and after the Battle of Germantown at Pennypacker Mills.

Photo by author

To Washington's relief, Alexander McDougall's Connecticut brigade, some 1,000 strong, arrived to reinforce the army. McDougall's command was the first significant Continental reinforcements the army had received since the campaign began back in June, and others were on the way. Brig. Gen. David Forman and 600 New Jersey militia were across the Delaware and approaching the new camp. Like McDougall before him, Forman was marching too close for comfort to the British camp, and Washington had to warn him to take a wider route in order to safely link with the army.[26]

The arrival of the Continental army along Perkiomen Creek introduced plundering to the neighborhood. "Before dark on the first day of the camp every fence on Samuel Pennypacker's place had disappeared," recalled Pennypacker's descendent and owner of the property, Gov. Samuel Whitaker Pennypacker, in 1902. "Four stacks of wheat were pulled down and used for straw. Every chicken, duck, and goose perished save one old hen who was wasting her existence in the effort to raise a late brood. In anticipation, the woolen blankets, which represented nights of industry upon the part of the women, had been hidden beneath the floors, and the horses upon whose labor the men depended for the produce of the farm had been driven to the distant woods." Washington understood the needs of an

26 As was his practice, it was likely that Washington's marquee was pitched in the yard of the Pennypacker home for the general to sleep, and he never physically occupied the house. No primary evidence exists to suggest that Washington inconvenienced the family by occupying the home. A marker erected by the Historical Society of Montgomery County in 1897 marking Washington's encampment sits near the modern entrance of Pennypacker Mills, a Montgomery County Historic Site. Reed, *Campaign*, 199. Though considerably altered, the Pennypacker home still stands. Later, the property became home to Governor Samuel Pennypacker from 1900-1916. Brownlow, *Germantown*, 12.

army in the field, but reminded his men in a general order on September 26 that they were not to steal from civilians. The thievery, which he labeled a "base and wicked practice," was ongoing "notwithstanding all former orders," he fumed, and "in some cases, in the most atrocious manner."[27]

Washington was working to keep the Delaware River in American hands while simultaneously attempting to hide and disperse any supplies that could help the British army in the short term. Also on September 26, he ordered his commissary general, Clement Biddle, to "impress all the Blankets, Shoes, Stockings and other Articles of Clothing for the use of the Army, that can be spared by the Inhabitants in the Counties of Bucks Philada and Northampton, paying for the same at reasonable Rates, or give Certificates." While the British stripped the countryside, Washington needed the support of the locals—even as his roving foragers took from them what his army needed to subsist. Washington always maintained that his men left enough for their survival, but being caught between the two armies left the civilian population in a perilous situation. While the Virginia commander dealt with these issues, news arrived of Burgoyne's defeat in upstate New York. The defeat of a British army energized the Continentals.[28]

Also on September 26, Lt. Col. Samuel Smith's detachment of Continentals from Washington's main army arrived at Fort Mifflin. Smith's command of 200 officers and men joined the roughly 60 invalids already stationed there. Just reaching the post required a roundabout route since the British army blocked the main roads, and what Smith discovered upon his arrival shocked him. "[E]very-thing in the utmost Confusion, not as many Cartouches [gun cartridges] as will last one day," wrote Smith to Washington, "& the very necessary Cartouches for the Block houses not sufficient for an hour: 60 untrained Militia, are all the artillery men in the Fort, the provisions almost out." Smith's reference to "60 untrained Militia" referred to men under Col. Lewis Nicola, who commanded the Corps of Invalids, an official Continental Army unit established the previous summer to garrison posts with troops unfit for field duty, thus freeing up combat units. Smith was also shocked to find not a single engineer, artillery officer, or artillery crew in the fort. He arrived with three officers—Majors Robert Ballard and

27 Samuel Whitaker Pennypacker, *Pennypacker's Mills in Story and Song: With the Incident of the Settlement, The French and Indian War, and the Encampment of Washington's Army September 26th to October 8th, 1777, Before and After the Battle of Germantown* (Norristown, PA, 1902), 20; Chase and Lengel, eds., *Papers*, vol. 11, 323.

28 Chase and Lengel, eds., *Papers*, vol. 11, 324.

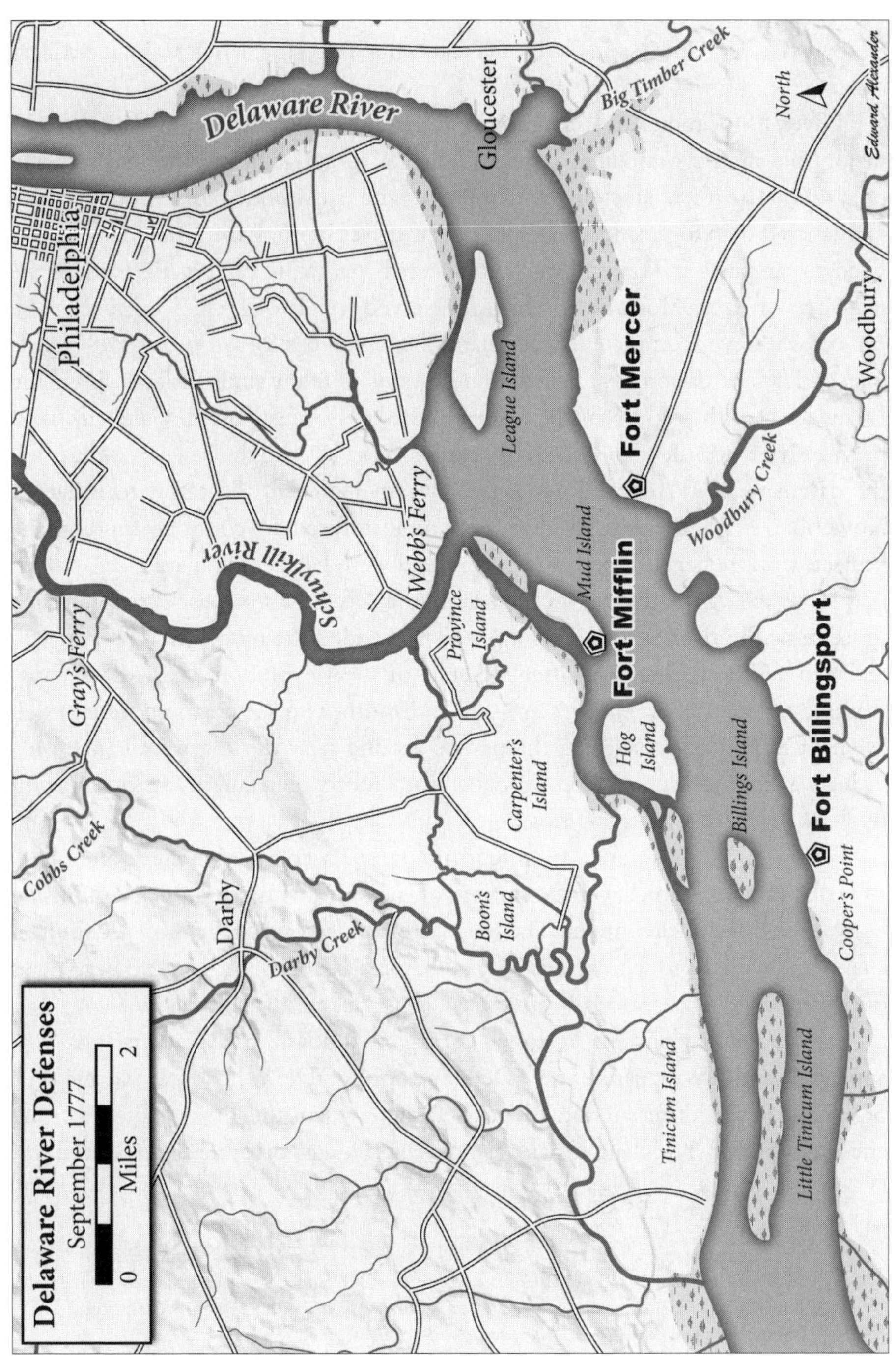
Delaware River Defenses
September 1777
0
Miles
2
Delaware River
Philadelphia
Gloucester
Big Timber Creek
North
Edward Alexander
League Island
Fort Mercer
Woodbury
Woodbury Creek
Webb's Ferry
Schuylkill River
Mud Island
Fort Mifflin
Province Island
Gray's Ferry
Fort Billingsport
Hog Island
Carpenter's Island
Billings Island
Cobbs Creek
Darby
Boon's Island
Darby Creek
Cooper's Point
Tinicum Island
Little Tinicum Island

Simeon Thayer, and Capt. Robert Treat—but only the latter was an artillery officer.[29]

Given its location and strategic importance, Fort Mifflin was destined to play a major role in the campaign. It was neither a thing of beauty nor engineering precision. The fort, erected on a mudflat and surrounded by a swamp, was constructed with logs, ship spars, and pine rafts set in mud, the same material that filled its ramparts and dikes. British engineers began work on it in 1771 under the guidance of John Montresor, who now served as Howe's chief engineer. The project was never completed. Mud Island, on which the fort stood, was 400 yards long and 200 yards across at its widest point, one of many similar islands lining the Delaware near the mouth of the Schuylkill River. Loyalist Joseph Galloway, who previously owned the island, sold it to the colony in 1771 so the English could build the defensive work there. When winter weather ground the effort to a halt in November 1773, the Pennsylvania Assembly refused to continue funding the project; work never resumed, and left behind were barracks and a zig-zag wall of gray stone facing the river. Two years later, the Assembly established a committee to examine the river defenses. The Americans added the mud and earth parapets and two additional barracks after the start of the Revolution. Fort Mifflin now featured barracks along the western wall and another on the northern wall, as well as an officer's barracks across the parade ground near the south wall. The only viable way to reinforce or supply the fort was to ferry men and provisions in from the New Jersey side of the Delaware.[30]

The fort was positioned to defend the western end of the chevaux-de-frise river obstructions, which were comprised of large bins with iron-tipped logs jutting outward and facing downriver. The bins were connected with heavy wrought iron chains and were filled with stones so that they sank beneath the water. These types of obstructions were especially effective against deep-draft vessels.

Notorious for shifting channels, shoals, sandbars, and mud islands that appeared and disappeared, the Delaware presented a host of navigational problems. Two different situations became evident in the building of the chevaux-de-frise. The channel passage between Billingsport and Billings Island was

29 McGuire, *Campaign*, vol. 2, 137, 184. Smith's troops and everyone who arrived thereafter had to march to Bristol, and from there cross the river to Burlington, New Jersey, march south through Haddonfield to either Gloucester or Red Bank, and then be ferried over to Fort Mifflin. Chase and Lengel, eds., *Papers*, vol. 11, 334; Wright, *Army*, 136.

30 McGuire, *Campaign*, vol. 2, 182.

narrow, but somewhat deeper than the channel at the second line of defense between Mud Island and the New Jersey shore. The latter was wider but contained two sand bars that created a main channel between Hog and Mud Islands on the west and the large shoal to the east. East of the shoal was a secondary channel with another sandbar near the New Jersey shore. The main river channel was deep enough to permit the passage of any eighteenth-century ship, but was slightly shallower than the passage at Billingsport. Of the blocking chevaux-de-frise, 24 were placed in two irregular lines at Billingsport, and another 43 were positioned near Mud Island in four groupings. The redoubt at Darby Creek on Tinicum Island had limited effectiveness against small ships and cruisers, but a major thrust by the British fleet would leave the post isolated. With the fall of Philadelphia, the earthwork near Darby Creek was abandoned and the fire rafts there were towed above Fort Mifflin.[31]

To solidify the waterborne command on the Delaware, Washington placed Commodore John Hazelwood of the Pennsylvania State Navy in charge of the combined State and Continental fleets. Hazelwood's familiarity with the changing shoals of the Delaware River, coupled with the fact that most of the effective elements of the fleet (galleys, floating batteries, and fire ships) were State Navy vessels, made him a wise choice to lead the combined fleet. The commodore was a long-time resident of Philadelphia and had spent much of his life piloting merchant ships along the Delaware. The Continental Board of Admiralty told Capt. Charles Alexander, the Continental naval officer Hazelwood superseded, that "the Fort and the passage of the River if bravely and properly defended, the possession of Philada will probably turn out to be the ruin of the British Army." Washington hoped Hazelwood would unify and energize the fragmented elements defending the river, but Continental officers distrusted and looked down upon State officers, so the appointment had the opposite effect. How this would play out remained to be seen.[32]

Foreshadowing what was to come, pockets of American militia hovered around the British camps and a minor skirmish broke out near Germantown. A "large party of the Enemy unperceived attacked the Queen's Rangers, shot the sentry and another, but were repulsed with great alertness, one of their Lieutenants

31 Jackson, *Navy*, 353-361.

32 Smith, *Fight for the Delaware*, 6; Charles Oscar Paullin, ed., *Out-Letters of the Continental Marine Committee and Board of Admiralty: August, 1776-September, 1780*, 2 vols. (New York, 1914), vol. 1, 159; Jackson, *Navy*, 121-122.

we found dead on the field," reported John Montresor. Royal Engineer Montresor had his own close call scouting positions for batteries along the Delaware when he "and [a]servant [were] near being taken at Gloucester Point by the enemy's galley stationed there."[33]

Reactions to Washington's Decisions and the Fall of Philadelphia

James Allen, a former member of the Pennsylvania Assembly, left the city and went into self-imposed exile in Allentown to escape the war. While most of his family remained loyal to the Crown, he "retreated to his country home where he and his acquantances endeavored to 'banish Politics' from their lives and conversations." Allen recorded his thoughts on the capture of Philadelphia in his diary. "This is a great event & tho' our people affect to consider the loss of this metropolis as nothing yet it strikes deep. . . . Every day some of the inhabitants of Phila are coming up to settle here. The road from Easton to Reading, by my house, is now the most travelled in America," complained the man who was doing his best to avoid the war's impact. "The minds of people are much changed by the loss of Phila & the prospect of a total stop to the necessaries of life, becomes alarming. This will be a terrible winter," concluded the dejected former assemblyman.[34]

Lieutenant Colonel Adam Hubley of the 10th Pennsylvania Regiment, part of Anthony Wayne's command, scratched out a letter to friends on September 26, unaware the city was being occupied as he wrote. "You, before this, heard of the Enemies crossing Schuylkill, and also the easy and cheap passage they had," he explained. "I dare say his Excellency is censur'd, by many, for his conduct in this matter. But wise Men will suspend their Judgments—Time—indeed, little time, will convince the World, he did it for the best." Hubley added that he hoped the "people are not dispirited, about these movements—depend on it, Howes ruin is

33 Montresor, "Journals," 458-459.

34 John K. Heyl, "Trout Hall and Its Owner James Allen: Excerpts from Diary of James Allen," *Proceedings of the Lehigh County Historical Society*, 40 vols. (Allentown, PA, 1862), vol. 24, 81-82. Allen served in the militia earlier in the war. "Disheartened and disillusioned, he abandoned the militia and retreated to his country estate, hoping in vain to avoid participation in the conflict happening on his doorstep, and wondering what had become of his country and the glorious cause of liberty in which he had once believed," noted historian Aaron Sullivan. Allen's home, "Trout Hall," is the only remaining pre-Revolution structure standing in Allentown. Sullivan, *Disaffected*, 8. 20.

working fast." Thomas Hartley, one of Wayne's brigadiers, wrote about the potential loss of the city three days before Hubley recorded his thoughts on the matter. "These are the fortunes of war; the little checks we meet with tend to make the survivors soldiers and statesmen, and God knows we want both Statesmen and Generals sometimes," Hartley wrote on September 23 to William Atlee, his friend in Lancaster. "Our Worthy Commander in Chief feels for his Country. He is sorry to loose an inch of ground, but the loss of Cities may sometimes be the salvation of States."[35]

Major Samuel Shaw of the Continental Artillery was livid about how others outside the army were treating the loss of Philadelphia. "Here, again, some blustering hero," he began,

> in fighting his battles over a glass of madeira, may take upon him to arraign the conduct of our general, and stigmatize the army as cowards. Leaving such to enjoy their own sagacity, it must appear obvious to men of sense and reflection, duly impressed with the importance of the great contest in which we are engaged, that a general action ought, on no pretence, to be risked under disadvantageous circumstances; nor should the safety of a single city be brought into competition with the welfare of posterity. Giving these considerations due weight, the absurdity of risking too much is evident: for, should we miscarry, posterity would execrate, and the world call us fools.[36]

Washington's adjutant general, Timothy Pickering, thought the people in and around the city deserved what had befallen them. "I feel in some degree reconciled to Howe's entering Pennsylvania and Philadelphia, that the unworthy inhabitants (of which 'tis apparent a majority of the State is composed) may experience the calamities of war, which nothing but their own supineness and unfriendliness to the American cause would have brought them," he penned in his journal. "Possibly Heaven permits it in vengeance for their defection, that their country should be the seat of war."[37]

"I rest satisfied at all times, that the loss of a battle, or of a town, will detract nothing finally from the Americans," concluded an anonymous observer, "and the

35 Letter, Adam Hubley to William Atlee, et al, September 26, 1777, Peter Force Papers, Library of Congress, Washington, DC; Letter, Thomas Hartley to William Atlee, et al, September 23, 1777, Peter Force Papers, Library of Congress, Washington, DC.

36 Shaw, *Journals*, 39.

37 Pickering, *Pickering*, vol. 1, 165.

acquisition of victories and of territory, will serve only to weaken General Howe's army, and to accelerate the period when America shall establish her freedom and independence, upon the permanent foundation of public virtue, and military knowledge."[38]

The Marquis de Lafayette was resting in Bethlehem recovering from a wounded leg suffered at Brandywine when the city fell. The Frenchman arely hesitated to express his opinion, and he took the opportunity to do so with vigor on this occasion in a letter to his wife on October 1:

> I must give you your lesson, as the wife of an American general officer. [Your friends] will say to you, 'They have been beaten:' you must answer—'That is true; but when two armies of equal number meet in the field, old soldiers have naturally the advantage over new ones; they have besides, had the pleasure of killing very many more of the enemy, many more than they have lost.' They will afterwards add: 'All that is very well; but Philadelphia is taken, the capital of America, the rampart of liberty!' You must politely answer, 'You are all great fools! Philadelphia is a poor forlorn town, exposed on every side, whose harbor was already closed; though the residence of congress lent it, I know not why, some degree of celebrity. This is the famous city which, be it added, we will, sooner or later, make them yield back to us.'[39]

Benjamin Franklin heard the news while in France negotiating a treaty of alliance, and offered the same basic opinion held by the Marquis de Lafayette, though in his usual clever manner. "Instead of saying Sir William Howe had taken Philadelphia," he quipped, "it would be more proper to say, Philadelphia has taken Sir William Howe."[40]

The Loyalist New York paper *Royal Gazette* was proud to announce the taking of the colonial capital. "A large detachment, under the command of the Right Hon. Earl Cornwallis," began the editorial,

> entered this city [Philadelphia], marched through Second-street, and after placing the proper guards, encamped to the southward of the town. The fine appearance of the

38 New Jersey *Gazette*, January 7, 1778, microfilm copy at David Library of the American Revolution, Washington Crossing, PA. Film 241, Reel 1.

39 Marquis de Lafayette, *Memoirs, Correspondence and Manuscripts of General Lafayette: Published by his Family*, 3 vols. (New York, 1837), vol. 1, 103-104. The Marquis de Lafayette returned later that fall to command a division in Washington's army.

40 John C. Miller, *Triumph of Freedom, 1775-1783* (Boston, 1948), 220.

soldierly, the strictness of their discipline, the politeness of the officers, and the orderly behavior of the whole body immediately dispelled every apprehension of the inhabitants, kindled joy in the countenances of the well-affected, and gave the most convincing refutation of the scandalous falsehoods which evil and designing men have been long spreading to terrify the peaceable and innocent. A perfect tranquility has since prevailed in the city. Numbers who have been obliged to hide themselves from the former tyranny, and to avoid being forced into measures against their conscience, have appeared to share the general satisfaction, and to welcome the dawn of returning Liberty.[41]

41 *New York Royal American Gazette*, November 6, 1777, Library of Congress, Washington, D.C.

Chapter 7

Preparing for Battle

September 27-October 2, 1777

"We are always on the advanced Post of the army—our Present one is unpleasant. . . There has been firing this Night all round the Centrys—which seems as they endeavor to feel our situation."[1]

— Lieutenant Richard St. George, 52nd Regiment of Foot, October 2, 1777

The Naval War Begins

The citizens of Philadelphia were greeted with the sound of cannon fire rolling across the waters of the Delaware on the morning of September 27. None of them knew what to make of it.

Unaware that General Cornwallis had actually entered the colonial capital, Commodore Hazelwood had issued orders to Capt. Charles Alexander of the Continental frigate *Delaware* to "[d]o Every Thing in your Power, with the Force with you, to annoy the Enemy should they attempt to Come in to our City, & should you see them preparing any works for Cannon or Hauling Cannon near the river," he added, "you are in that case to send a Flag on shore & warn them if they do not desist in making any preperations of Fortifying any where, that you will in

1 St. George letter dated September 11, 1777.

that case fire on the City." Hazelwood left "the Conduct & management of the whole" to Alexander's "prudent & effectual management."[2]

The combined Continental and State fleet that morning consisted of the 24-gun *Delaware* and her 150-man crew in the lead, together with the 24-gun State guard ship *Montgomery*, the Continental 8-gun sloop *Fly*, and five row galleys, each carrying a single gun. When the *Delaware* rounded Gloucester Point, British drummers alerted the garrison, and Royal artillerymen and grenadiers of the 1st British Battalion formed up to prepare for whatever was coming their way.[3]

Captain-Lieutenant Francis Downman was in command of the artillery at the southern edge of the city—a six-gun battery consisting of four 12-pounders and two Royal howitzers. His defensive preparations, however, remained incomplete. The earthwork being built to hold his half-dozen guns remained unfinished, and only two of the 12-pounders were in place that morning. His remaining four pieces, deployed along the riverbank, were completely exposed. The army's chief of artillery, Gen. Samuel Cleaveland, arrived on the scene after the alert was given and ordered Downman "not to fire at the ships until they fired at me," recorded the captain-lieutenant in his journal, a directive that made him "extremely uneasy." Two light 6-pounders attached to the 1st Battalion of British Grenadiers raced to the river to bolster the waterfront defenses. Downman found a good spot for one cannon and instructed Lt. George Wilson, the commander of the other light fieldpiece, to move his gun about 150 yards to a wharf that offered a good firing position. Wilson, who had performed well at Brandywine, raced south downriver to the lower end of the shipyards, manhandled the piece onto the end of a wharf jutting 50 yards into the river, and trained the gun in the direction of the approaching warships.[4]

Downman, meanwhile, under orders to hold his fire, watched with nervous trepidation as the enemy flotilla edged closer to his position. "The situation was disagreeable," recalled the officer, "for the largest ship was within 400 yards, and in another tack or two would have been alongside our guns." Lieutenant Wilson, however, was unaware of Cleaveland's order because Downman had failed to inform him. When the *Delaware* moved within range Wilson ordered his crew to

2 Hazard, et al., eds., *Archives*, Series 1, vol. 5, 637. Jackson, *Navy*, 124. The September 27 order is headlined "Off Fort Mifflin." The course of the river and surrounding terrain blocked Hazelwood's view of the occupation, which explains why he sent Alexander to investigate the current situation.

3 McGuire, *Campaign*, vol. 2, 30; Reed, *Campaign*, 202; Jackson, *Navy*, 123.

4 Whinyates, *Services*, 36; McGuire, *Campaign*, vol. 2, 31.

fire. He managed to get off two shots before Downman ordered him to cease fire, but by that time it was too late. Captain Alexander reasonably concluded it would be "prudent & effectual" to defend himself, and ordered the *Delaware's* 12-pounders to reply. Within seconds the guns discharged blasts of screaming grapeshot toward the wharf, forcing Wilson and his gunners to dodge the deadly iron rounds. Wilson's pair of shots and Alexander's reply were an open invitation for everyone to join the contest. Downman's guns along the waterfront thundered and recoiled, their iron balls arcing their way 400 yards in the air or plunging harmlessly into the muddy water near the hulls of the enemy ships, which hurled in reply a mixture of 12-, 18-, 24-, and 32-pound shot. When Wilson realized the dozen rounds he had brought with him were gone, he ran back up the wharf in search of more, leaving his gun without an officer. Exposed on the wharf to a fire that could kill or maim the entire gun crew with a single blast, Wilson's gunners abandoned the piece until Capt. James Moncrieff ordered them to return and extricate the gun. By the time Wilson returned, his men and his gun had disappeared.[5]

The noisy gunfire drew curious citizens out of their homes and into the streets, where they streamed down to the waterfront to witness the combat. Elizabeth Drinker watched the fighting from her home on Front Street at the upper end of town. "The people in General, especially downwards, exceedingly Allarm'd," she scribbled in her diary, "part of this scean we were spectators of, from the little Window in our loft." Elizabeth, who did her best to remain neutral, wrote that her primary focus was "the security and well-being of her family, her home, and her neighbors."[6]

Those aboard the *Delaware* felt anything but secure as British rounds began striking the frigate. "We opened upon them and the artillery [was] extremely well directed [against] their best Frigate the Delaware," wrote Howe's chief engineer John Montresor in his journal. To the dismay of Captain Alexander and his crew,

5 Whinyates, *Services*, 37; McGuire, *Campaign*, vol. 2, 31-32. Six months later, Lt. George Wilson was court-martialed for "misbehaving himself before the Enemy by improperly quitting his Post on the 27th Sept. 1777." Despite several heroic actions before and after September 27, Wilson was found "Guilty of unofficer-like conduct in leaving his gun twice, which was not from fear or cowardice, based on the supporting testimony of his character, but was nevertheless improper." His sentence was a reprimand before the Brigade of Royal Artillery. British War Office, Judge Advocate General Office, Court Martial Proceedings and Board of General Officers' Minutes: WO71/86, March 31-April 1, 1778, Film 675, Reel 9, 66-84, David Library of the American Revolution, Washington Crossing, PA; Montresor, "Journals," 459.

6 Drinker, *Diary*, vol. 1, 236; Sullivan, *Disaffected*, 6.

the American warship, to use Montresor's words, "got somewhat grounded. She was 2 or 3 times on fire owing to one of our shot having drove through her caboose [cook house]," observed Montresor, "it not being easily extinguished." Flaming embers flew in every direction and spread small deck fires that threatened to engulf the ship. Confusion mounted on the *Delaware* as Alexander attempted to turn his ship about. Amid the chaos, his sailors mismanaged the sails as a British howitzer round crashed through the foredeck near the bow, setting the hull ablaze. Confusion abounded and the men, recalled Downman, neglected "the management of the sails, and she ran aground" on the lower end of Windmill Island, within 250 yards of the barking British guns. Alexander's crew tried to return fire as best they could but were overwhelmed by the weight of British metal. With his ship stuck fast and portions of it in flames, Captain Alexander had little choice but to strike her colors. By the time he did so, one crewman was dead and six wounded out of his 152-man crew.[7]

The British immediately dispatched a boat with 10 grenadiers, together with engineer Capt. James Moncrieffe and several carpenters, to take possession of the *Delaware* and extinguish the fires. Once aboard, the carpenters swung axes, cut away the burning parts of the ship, and tossed them into the river. The Continental sailors, meanwhile, were loaded into the boat, taken ashore near Old Swedes Church, and marched to jail near the State House. Captain Alexander, the *Delaware's* commander and the fleet's senior Continental officer, was among the prisoners.[8]

While the *Delaware* was being neutralized, the British artillery turned its collective attention to the other ships that were now rapidly withdrawing. The *Fly* took repeated hits, had her foremast shot away, and suffered four killed and six wounded. She ran aground on the New Jersey shore. The *Montgomery* did not venture "near enough to receive much damage," reported John Andre, and "returned to her station near Mud Island." The American schooner *Mosquito* later tried to run the gauntlet from upriver past the city but was fired on by the British

7 Whinyates, *Services*, 37; McGuire, *Campaign*, vol. 2, 33. Windmill Island was a long, narrow mud flat that was home to a single windmill and wharf in the middle of the river. Smith, *Fight for the Delaware*, 7.

8 McGuire, *Campaign*, vol. 2, 34. Once British engineers completed the river battery near Kensington located near the modern intersection of Richmond Street and Girard Avenue, they towed the captured *Delaware* there for repairs. Smith, *Fight for the Delaware*, 7.

battery deployed at the upper end of town, struck at least once, and forced aground along the New Jersey shoreline. Her precise fate thereafter remains a mystery.[9]

What was not in doubt was the outcome of the naval battle. "Thus ended the insolent attempt of their boasting Commodore, with two frigates and five galleys, each carrying a 32 or 24 pounder, opposed by only four 12 pounders and two howitzers, three of those being drawn up on the bank without the least covering," bragged Francis Downman. The British would later float the *Delaware* off the sandbar and repair her for their own use. "The same afternoon a number of rebel sailors entered voluntarily on board of her to fight on our side," bragged Francis Downman. Howe sent grenadiers to Chester to escort part of the crew of the HMS *Roebuck* (53 men) back to the city to crew the *Delaware*.[10]

This hour-long engagement around the shipyards of Philadelphia marked the beginning of the fighting for control of the Delaware River that would consume the next two months. Despite the capture of the *Delaware* and the ease with which the American fleet had been turned back, the British worried that the river forts and obstructions were likely to cause grave long-term injury to the army. "She is an acquisition & a great security to the Town," admitted Gen. James Grant, referring to the captured frigate, but "those Rebell ships & Gallies, the Fort upon Mud Island & the Chevaux de Frize which they have sunk in the River prevent the Fleet getting up, retard our operations—obstruct our supplys & are likely to give much trouble." Grant was right. The British now controlled a warship stronger than any other vessel the Continentals could muster, but the American obstructions blocked the fleet and the delivery of supplies. With the *Delaware*, however, Howe could now

9 Reed, Campaign, 202-203. Despite his poor performance Alexander never faced a court of inquiry, though he also never received another assignment. Many of the captured crewmen from the *Delaware* chose to serve the British rather than rot in jail or die inside the hulk of a prison ship. Jackson, *British Army*, 289; Jackson, *Navy*, 127; McGuire, *Campaign*, vol. 2, 34. According to Cpl. Thomas Sullivan of the 49th Regiment of Foot, the grenadiers who boarded the ship were from a Royal Marine Company. The two Royal Marine companies, however, were attached to the 2nd British Grenadier Battalion and so were unlikely to have been at the scene because they were stationed on the west side of the city. The 1st British Grenadier Battalion was much closer as it was stationed on the south side of the city. Sullivan's account is problematic and secondhand because his regiment was in Germantown, not Philadelphia, at the time of the action. Sullivan, *Journal*, 140; Andre, *Journal*, 53. The *Fly* was refloated that night and returned downstream to the fleet. Jackson, *Navy*, 124.

10 McGuire, *Campaign*, vol. 2, 34; Whinyates, *Services*, 36-37. With the British fleet stuck below Fort Mifflin, the *Delaware* provided amphibious access to New Jersey from Philadelphia. Reed, *Campaign*, 203. Following the British landing at Turkey Point back in August, Capt. Andrew Hamond and the *Roebuck* had been ordered back to the Delaware along with the frigates *Pearl*, *Camilla*, and *Liverpool*. Jackson, *British Army*, 20; Jackson, *Navy*, 125, 131.

safely ferry troops to New Jersey to conduct foraging or military operations. With access to New Jersey (i.e., north of Fort Mifflin) assured, Howe set his eyes on breaking through the river defenses by assaulting the unfinished American defensive point at Fort Billingsport, New Jersey, about two miles below Fort Mifflin on the opposite bank of the river.[11]

The news of the *Delaware's* loss angered several members of Congress. "The preservation of the water Defences of the River Delaware greatly depend upon retaking this ship out of the hands of the Enemy," argued New York delegate James Duane. Connecticut delegate William Williams expressed similar angst at the ship's loss, though his facts were woefully wrong. "The enemy have taken the Delaware Frigate in the River, not by their Ships which had not been able to get up, but that the Master who commanded her . . . came up to the Wharf, & tis supposed gave or sold her. With her help," he continued, "I expect they will demolish the other Ships & Fire Craft &c &c which were confident of defending the river."[12]

Congressman Duane was about to suffer additional disappointment. Cornwallis's quick move into Philadelphia prevented the Americans from removing or hiding all the river craft there. As a result, the British accumulated about 50 boats of various types. One, a large, wooden, flat-bottomed and double-ended Durham boat, was found in Frankford Creek, while others were discovered in the marshes south of the city and on Windmill Island. Without vessels, Howe's men would have been forced to remain on the Pennsylvania side of the Delaware River. The capture of the frigate and 50 additional vessels, however, offered Howe a host of possibilities.[13]

On the day the *Delaware* surrendered, elements of Admiral Howe's British fleet re-entered Delaware Bay. With the fleet finally approaching, General Howe knew he needed to reduce or destroy the American defenses blocking the Delaware River. Before he could withdraw the Germantown garrison blocking Washington's access to Philadelphia, however, a line of earthworks had to be constructed to protect the land side of the city. Until that was accomplished, Howe simply did not have enough troops to confront Washington's army and move along the river to help procure access for the fleet. "This afternoon began to reconnoitre the heights near this city, for forming the defense of it, by Field Works, running from the

11 Grant to Harvey, October 20, 1777, Grant Papers; Jackson, *Navy*, 125.

12 Smith, et al., eds., *Letters*, vol. 8, 44, 94.

13 Jackson, *Navy*, 125.

Schuylkill to the Delaware rivers," wrote British engineer John Montresor. "This I was given to understand was our present grand object."[14]

Continental Concerns

As one drama was playing out on the Delaware River, another was continuing for Anthony Wayne at the Continental camp at Pennypacker's Mills. There, rumors continued to fly regarding the general and his conduct at the Battle of Paoli. His biggest critic was Col. Richard Humpton, one of Wayne's brigade commanders and the second ranking officer in his division. "[T]he officers of the Division have protested against Genl Wayne's conduct & lodged a complaint, & requested a court of Inquiry, which his Excellency [Washington] has promised they shall have," wrote Maj. Samuel Hay of the 7th Pennsylvania on September 29. "This has brought down his [Wayne's] pride a little already." Wayne, of course, wanted to clear his name and wrote to Washington requesting a court of inquiry to examine his conduct. "I feel myself much Injured until such time as you will be kind Enough to Indulge me with an Enquiry into my Conduct Concerning the Action of the night of the 20th Instant," he implored his superior officer. "Conscious of having done my duty I dare my Accusor's to a fair and Candid hearing—dark Insinuations and Insidius friends I dread—but from an Open and avowed enemy I have nothing to fear."[15]

While Wayne tried to clear his name, Washington focused on how to concentrate all available forces for another strike at Howe. The army had grown with the recent arrival of Alexander McDougall's four Connecticut regiments, and 600 New Jersey militiamen under David Forman were but a short march away. Anthony Wayne and the balance of his division, together with William Smallwood's Maryland militia, all told some 2,500 troops, finally arrived in camp on September 29. In truth, Wayne's and Smallwood's men were not ready for combat. Wayne's division had suffered reasonably heavy losses at Paoli, and nearly 1,000 men from Smallwood's demoralized command had deserted in the aftermath of that defeat. Those Marylanders who remained were poorly armed and mostly untrained. A column of Virginia militia also was moving toward the army, as

14 Martin, *Campaign*, 123; Reed, *Campaign*, 204; Montresor, "Journals," 459.

15 Letter, Samuel Hay to William Irvine, September 29, 1777, Irvine Papers within the Draper Manuscripts, the David Library of the American Revolution, Washington Crossing, PA, series AA, vol. 1, film 60, reel 70; Chase and Lengel, eds., *Papers*, vol. 11, 336.

Washington recorded on September 28: "a Body of Militia was coming from Virginia, & that part had arrived at Lancaster. That he understood from Report, that the number of 'em amounted to near 2,000 men [commanded by Col. William Rumney], but that from good authority, he was advised they were badly armed & many of them without any at all."[16]

The concentration helped swell Washington's numbers but caused other problems in the region by accelerating the destruction of civilian property. Reverend Muhlenberg, for example, complained about how militiamen had abused his church. "The church was crowded with officers and privates with their guns. The organ loft was filled, and one man was playing the organ while others sang to his accompaniment," wrote the distraught man of the cloth. "Down below lay straw and manure, and several had placed the objects of their gluttony, etc. on the altar. In short," he concluded, drawing upon a biblical analogy, "I saw, in miniature, the abomination of desolation in the temple."[17]

Most of the men in the Pennsylvania militia were set to complete their terms of service, which meant a fresh batch (with even less experience) would be replacing them. Pennsylvanian John Armstrong was doing his best to keep the men in line. The 59-year-old brigadier, one of Washington's acquaintances from their service together in the French and Indian War, also was trying to get his men to remain in the army beyond the terms of their enlistments. Private James Patten of Dunlap's Partisan Regiment was back with the impending disbanding of the Light Infantry. Dunlap's unit was an ad hoc formation of riflemen mobilized earlier in the campaign because of the absence of Daniel Morgan's riflemen. Maxwell's light infantry brigade (which had fought at Brandywine and at the Battle of the Clouds) was disbanded prior to Germantown. Dunlap's men returned to their original commands—many of which were militia units. Armstrong, recalled Patten, made "a speech to the troops requesting the militia to volunteer a little longer as they now had some experience and as more confidence could be placed in them than in raw troops; but where they were going or what particular service he desired them to perform he did not at that time disclose."[18]

16 Chase and Lengel, eds., *Papers*, vol. 11, 338-339.

17 Muhlenberg, *Journals*, vol. 3, 80. Muhlenberg is describing the destruction of Augustus Lutheran Church in Trappe, PA.

18 *RWPF*, file S30629. Armstrong's militia force soon moved to Norriton Township.

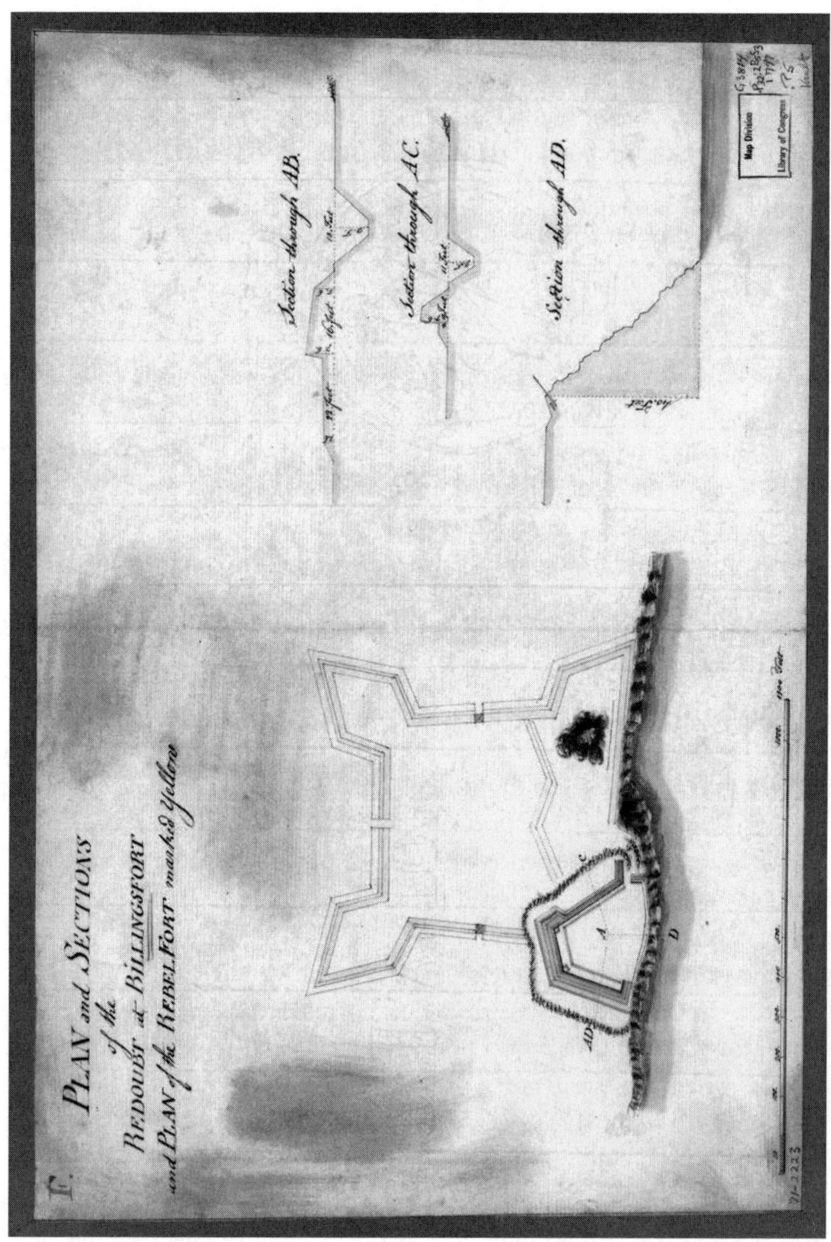

1777 Plan and sections of the redoubt at Billingsfort and plan of the rebel fort.

Library of Congress

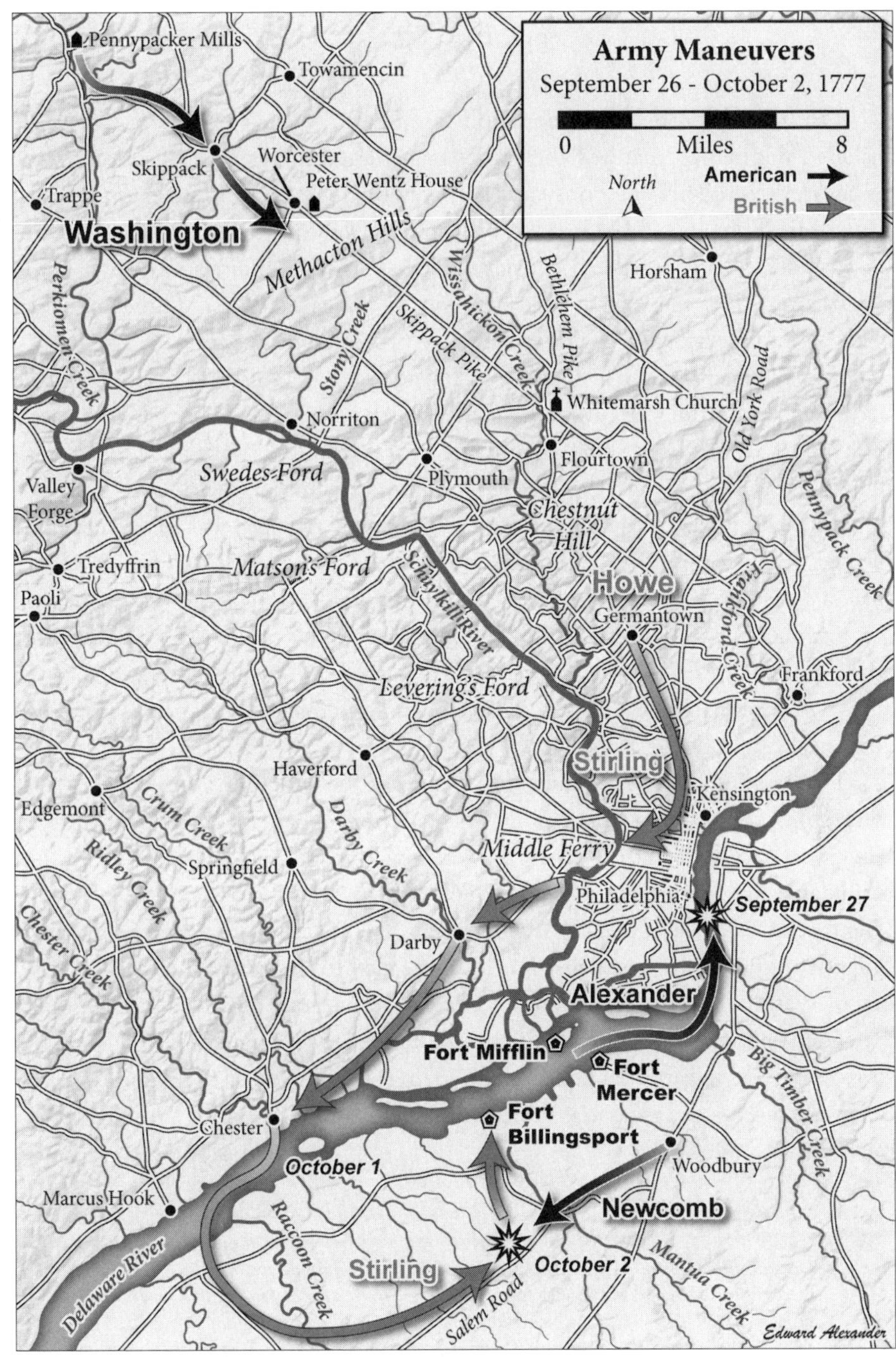

Army Maneuvers
September 26 - October 2, 1777
0
Miles
8
North
American
British
Pennypacker Mills
Towamencin
Skippack
Worcester
Peter Wentz House
Trappe
Washington
Methacton Hills
Horsham
Perkiomen Creek
Stony Creek
Skippack Pike
Wissahickon Creek
Bethlehem Pike
Old York Road
Whitemarsh Church
Norriton
Plymouth
Flourtown
Valley Forge
Swedes Ford
Chestnut Hill
Pennypack Creek
Tredyffrin
Matson's Ford
Paoli
Schuylkill River
Howe
Germantown
Frankford Creek
Frankford
Levering's Ford
Haverford
Stirling
Kensington
Edgemont
Crum Creek
Darby Creek
Ridley Creek
Springfield
Middle Ferry
Philadelphia
September 27
Chester Creek
Darby
Alexander
Fort Mifflin
Fort Mercer
Big Timber Creek
Fort Billingsport
Chester
Woodbury
October 1
Marcus Hook
Newcomb
Raccoon Creek
Delaware River
Stirling
October 2
Mantua Creek
Salem Road
Edward Alexander

The River Forts

The host of problems Washington faced and the decisions he had to make included the management of the vitally important American defenses along the Delaware River. This line consisted primarily of three forts: Mercer (on the east bank of the river at Red Bank in New Jersey); Mifflin (directly across from Mercer on a mud island on the Pennsylvania shore); and Billingsport, two miles downstream on the same side of the river as Mercer. Three lines of chevaux-de-frise blocked the river and were protected by the forts.

Fort Billingsport, the farthest from Philadelphia, was also the least defensible because it was unfinished, undermanned, and poorly designed. The 96-acre parcel on which it sat had been purchased by the Pennsylvania Committee of Safety with money authorized by the Continental Congress on July 5, 1776—the first land purchase ever made by the United States. Its original purpose was to protect a line of river obstructions placed there the previous year. The fort's Achilles' Heel was that it was indefensible from the land side. Plans for the work proved overambitious. The original design was significantly larger than what the British went up against in early October: an undermanned, unfinished square fort on 15 acres with a bastion on each corner, some abatis, and five cannon (four 9-pounders and one 12-pounder).

Two floating batteries holding 18-pounders (one with nine guns and the other with ten) were anchored near Billings Island. American engineers hoped the "land being very low and narrow, these batteries will be able to produce above it, a formidable fire against the frigates, which may present themselves, to attack the Line of cheveaux de frize, opposite to Billing's port," explained French engineer Philippe du Coudray on August 6. The fort failed to impress Nathanael Greene, one of Washington's finest generals. "There have been prodigious sums of money expended on that place," he informed his commander on August 7, 1777, "[yet the] fortress renders the approaches easy, the enemy can make good their landing a little below the work—the ground is very favorable but a small distance from the fort to open Batteries."[19]

19 Jackson, *British Army*, 26; Jackson, *Navy*, 133; Smith, *Fight for the Delaware*, 8; Worthington Chauncey Ford, "Defences of Philadelphia in 1777," *The Pennsylvania Magazine of History and Biography* (Philadelphia, 1894), vol. 18, 13; Nathanael Greene to George Washington, August 7, 1777, Washington Papers online, Library of Congress, series 4, General Correspondence, accessed February 5, 2017.

Two miles upriver on the same side was the 14-gun Fort Mercer, the best constructed of the trio of forts. Mercer's earthen walls mounted a log palisade fronted by a deep ditch about 320 yards long and 50 yards wide, with protruding bulwarks on the landward corners. A separate redoubt north of the fort had been erected but was unmanned. Although designed for a garrison of 1,500 men, the Continentals would never have anywhere near that many men available to defend it.

Fort Mercer overlooked and helped protect Fort Mifflin on the southern tip of a mud flat on the far side of the river. Surrounded by swamp, the mud island was separated from Hog Island. When Lt. Col. Samuel Smith took command, Mifflin barely deserved to be called a fort. While it looked imposing, it was in fact an engineering monstrosity impossible to defend. A line of palisades made of pine logs 15 inches thick extending along the northern and western perimeter joined the stone wall on the east and south. A poorly conceived battery built in front of the south wall left it open on the east to enfilade and ricochet fire from enemy men-of-war. Engineers had dug a ditch on three sides but left the south exposed, thinking the battery erected there made it unnecessary. Wooden blockhouses in the northeast, northwest, and southwest corners of the fort left the southeast side exposed to enemy rounds. A floating chain extended along the western side of the works to prevent landing parties from launching an assault from the Pennsylvania side, and a line of chevaux-de-frise blocked the river between Mud Island and Fort Mercer. At high tide much of the island was underwater, and the entire island, including the fort, could be flooded by cutting the dikes on the western side of the river.[20]

Smith and Commodore Hazelwood were particularly concerned with defending Mifflin, and together examined the 600-yard back channel between the fort and Province and Carpenter's islands and the potential problem posed by the vexing geography. The two islands, along with much of the land at the mouth of the Schuylkill River, had been diked to keep the water out and create a large meadow. Separated by nothing more than small tidal streams, at ground level the pair of islands appeared to be part of the mainland. Smith, aghast at the danger posed to Fort Mifflin if the British seized either island, related his concern to Commodore Hazelwood. The confident naval officer waved away Smith's apprehension by replying that "a musquito could not live there under the fire of my guns." Smith disagreed. The difference of opinion between the Army and Navy regarding how

20 Jackson, *Navy*, 156-157.

best to defend Mifflin, as well as the other forts, was just the beginning of the problems facing the Continentals.[21]

On September 29, Washington ordered the Pennsylvania militia garrisoning Billingsport to take "any Stores there, [and] remove them to Ft. Mifflin." Despite the general air of confidence exuded by Hazelwood, the river defenses were ripe for the taking. Earlier, Washington had ordered the destruction of the works at Billingsport, but a lack of manpower and the fear exhibited by the Pennsylvania Navy at the suggestion delayed the fulfillment of the order.[22]

Washington remained upbeat about his chances of holding the river and beating Howe. The seat of the American government had fallen, but Congress reestablished itself in the Pennsylvania backcountry. Where it operated was not nearly as important as the fact that it was still in existence. The major supply depot in Reading remained intact, and was still supplying the growing army. If the war had demonstrated anything thus far, it was that occupying a city meant little in a sprawling multi-colony revolution like this one. The British had once occupied Boston but had been forced to leave. New York had been lost, but the war continued apace. It was slowly becoming clear that who held which major city meant much less in this war than it did on the European continent.

"Washington," wrote an uneasy Capt. John Andre in a letter to his mother on September 28, "is taking breath about 26 miles from us. When we lay still," he continued, alluding to the main British garrison encamped at Germantown just north of Philadelphia, "their treacherous engines go to work[;] they get intelligence[,] they harass us & retrieve their losses." Major Benjamin Tallmadge of the 2nd Continental Light Dragoons, might have agreed with Andre. "Although defeated at the Brandywine, and foiled in several smaller encounters," concluded Tallmadge, "our American Fabius retained his full determination to give these hostile invaders no repose." Henry "Light Horse Harry" Lee continued in the same

21 McGuire, *Campaign*, vol. 2, 184; Smith, *Fight for the Delaware*, 13. The back channel is now filled and Mud Island as a distinct entity is no longer visible. Much of this area is now the Philadelphia International Airport. Samuel Smith, "The Papers of General Samuel Smith," *The Historical Magazine and Notes and Queries, Concerning the Antiquities, History and Biography of America* (2nd series, no. 2), February 1870, vol. 7, 86.

22 Hazard, et al., eds., *Archives*, Series 1, vol. 5, 644; Chase and Lengel, eds., *Papers*, vol. 11, 347. The precise order for the destruction of the post does not appear in Washington's papers, but a reference to such an order can be found in Lt. Col. Smith's letter to Washington on September 27. Chase and Lengel, eds., *Papers*, vol. 11, 338-334.

vein, noting later that, "Cautious as Washington undoubtedly was, his caution was exceeded by his spirit of enterprise."[23]

Washington used the news of Burgoyne's defeat at Saratoga to raise the morale of his army by ordering artillery salutes and extra rations of rum. "[H]ere [Pennypacker Mills] were fired 13 Pieces of Cannon for our successes to the Northward," was how Marylander William Beatty, a lieutenant in the 7th Maryland Regiment, recorded the event. The news made the naturally aggressive Washington more anxious to match the exploits of the northern army and strike his own decisive blow. Captain Andre was right: Washington was resting, observing, gathering intelligence, and reinforcing his army. The only questions were when and where he would attack.

On September 28, the commander-in-chief held a second war council and posed the same question he had asked five days earlier: Should the American army attack Howe? The first council had generated a unanimous vote against launching an assault. This time, of the 15 commanders present, five voted in favor of an attack while 10 voted against it. The recommendation was that "the Army should move to some Grounds proper for an Encampment within about 12 Miles of the Enemy, and there wait for further Reinforcement, or be in readiness to take advantage of any favourable Opportunity that may offer for making an Attack."[24]

With the main Continental Army protecting the approaches to the major supply depot at Reading, making sure the supplies evacuated from Philadelphia to Trenton remained safe became a top priority for Washington. He had his doubts. As the Commissary General of Issues, Charles Stewart, reported,

> an amazing quantity of Stores in the different departments on the wharfs[,] unguarded in shallops and wagons . . . there are a number of people but no person seems to have command. I have ordered all waggons & Boats to this side of the River But it is not in my

23 Smith, *Fight for the Delaware*, 7. Archibald Robertson, *Archibald Robertson, Lieutenant General Royal Engineers: His Diaries and Sketches in America, 1762-1780, ed. Harry Miller Lydenberg* (New York, 1930), 151; John Andre manuscript letter, September 28, 1777. The original letter is in the collection of the American Philosophical Society, but has been transcribed and reproduced in McGuire, *Campaign*, vol. 2, 298; Benjamin Tallmadge, *Memoir of Col. Benjamin Tallmadge* (New York, 1858), 22; Lee, *Memoirs*, vol. 1, 26.

24 Beatty, "Journal," 110; Chase and Lengel, eds., *Papers*, vol. 11, 339. The officers who voted to move closer to the enemy, but were against an attack, included Alexander McDougall, Henry Knox, Francis Nash, Peter Muhlenberg, Thomas Conway, John Sullivan, Nathanael Greene, Lord Stirling, Adam Stephen, and John Armstrong. Those who voted in favor of an immediate attack included William Smallwood, Anthony Wayne, James Potter, James Irvine, and Charles Scott.

power to procure even for now a Guard, and as I expect many days will elapse before wagons are procured to carry off the most Valuable.[25]

Stewart asked Governor William Livingston to order 150 militiamen to assemble at the Trenton wharves, hoping the move might save the colonies millions of dollars and prevent the loss of "vast quantitys of powder[,] cloathing[,] spirits & provisions."' Col. Jonathan Mifflin was requested to remove all stores to Bethlehem and Easton.[26]

Within a few days, the British began making progress along the Delaware River, and, with reports of the poor security at Trenton, Washington wanted the stores removed from the town immediately. "The situation of our public Stores, particularly those of the Ordnance kind at Trenton gives me great uneasiness—I have directed every exertion to be employed for their Removal—I must entreat that any assistance you [Gov. William Livingston] can give in Waggons &c. may be afforded—Also that a body of Militia, under a Spirited Officer, if it is possible, may be ordered there as a Guard till they can be removed."[27]

British Philadelphia

Moving forward with plans to defend the city, on September 28 engineer John Montresor and Gen. Cornwallis surveyed the terrain in the Northern Liberties Montresor had selected for a line of fortifications. It was the same ground Israel Putnam had chosen in December 1776 when the British were threatening Philadelphia. Montresor explained to Cornwallis that the defensive line required 10 redoubts along with two demilunes and a ravelin, along with a front covered by a ditch and abatis, and the escarpment of the earthworks fraised (pointed stakes driven into the ramparts in a horizontal or inclined position). Cornwallis agreed with the engineer and work began. When the line was finished around October 18, it stretched from below Kensington to a hill called Fairmount overlooking the Upper Ferry of the Schuykill River, a distance of about 5 ½ miles. The works could

25 Chase and Lengel, eds., *Papers*, vol. 11, 359.

26 Letter, Charles Stewart to William Livingston, 28 September 1777, William Livingston Papers, David Library of the American Revolution, Washington Crossing, PA, Film 293, Reel 5. Reed, *Campaign*, 212.

27 Chase and Lengel, eds., *Papers*, vol. 11, 359.

Present day view looking down the Delaware River from the site of Fort Billingsport.

Photo by author

be manned by rotating detachments of the main army, and Howe would then have the bulk of his army freed up for operations against the Delaware River forts.[28]

The Continental Camp

On September 29, the day after Montresor and Cornwallis rode along the Northern Liberties front, Col. Christopher Greene with two Rhode Island regiments left the Hudson Highlands and marched south to reinforce Washington. David Forman and his 600 New Jersey militia arrived and increased the size of the Continental Army, which Washington moved closer to the British. The wind was from the northeast and the day, recorded a British journal, "very cold" as the troops marched down Skippack Pike five miles to the Mennonite Church in the village of

28 Jackson, *British Army*, 22. One redoubt was constructed on each road leading into the city. Eventually, two additional advanced redoubts were added to the plan 250 yards north of the main defensive line, one on Wissahickon Road (Ridge Pike) and the other on Fourth Street just below Germantown Road. A demilune is an outwork resembling a bastion with a crescent-shaped gorge; a ravelin is a v-shaped structure outside the main ditch, covering the works between two bastions. McGuire, *Philadelphia Campaign*, vol. 2, 143; Jeffery M. Dorwart, *Fort Mifflin of Philadelphia: An Illustrated History* (Philadelphia, 1998), 36.

Present day view looking up the Delaware River from the site of Fort Billingsport. The modern Philadelphia skyline is visible in the distance. *Photo by author*

Skippack, where the army went into camp once more for what turned out to be three days of rest. Washington intended to "reconnoitre and fix upon a proper Situation, at such distance from the Enemy, as will enable us to make an attack should he see a proper opening," he wrote to John Hancock on September 29, "or stand upon the defensive till we obtain further reinforcements." The army, Washington assured Jonathan Trumbull on October 1, got "the rest and refreshment it stood in need of—and our men are in very good spirits."[29]

Fire on the River

No American accounts verify the story of the fire rafts, a fascinating event on the cold evening of September 29 whose genesis and execution remain wrapped in mystery. The Continentals' standing concern was that Howe's Royal fleet would ascend the Delaware, and a rather creative action was undertaken to impede that possibility. "This night," wrote the usually reliable John Montresor, "the rebels sent down 3 large Fire rafts to burn some of our Ships of war who kept a smart cannonade upon them." Some of Admiral Howe's fleet had arrived in the Delaware

29 Montresor, "Journals," 461. Christopher Greene was the third cousin of Gen. Nathaniel Greene. Washington established headquarters in the home of Joseph Smith, along the west bank of Skippack Creek and north of Skippack Pike not far from Forty-Foot Road. Reed, *Campaign*, 211; Chase and Lengel, eds., *Papers*, vol. 11, 346, 365.

River following their trip from Chesapeake Bay. According to Montresor, the hour was late, the tide reversed, and the burning craft "returned with the Flood to their Own Shipping."[30]

With American quartermasters stripping resources from the region surrounding Philadelphia and army patrols blanketing the area, it would only get progressively harder to obtain quantities of forage and provisions from the countryside sufficient to supply the British army. Winter was coming. The men would need cold-weather clothing, and the Delaware River would begin to freeze in early December. If he was going to maintain his grip on Philadelphia, Howe would have to open the river to his supply ships soon. To do so, he needed to move against the American forts blocking access to the Delaware.

On September 29, engineer Capt. Archibald Robertson, together with Lord Cornwallis, rode to the mouth of the Schuylkill River to study Fort Mifflin from its land side. They arrived opposite Province Island "but did not cross [to] it, the land so low [flooded] we could not see it." To the young engineer and combat general, reaching Mifflin from the western land approaches was not going to be easy. Assaulting the fort or constructing siege batteries would have to be done with wet feet.[31]

While Cornwallis and Robertson conducted their reconnaissance on the northern end of the American river line, General Howe decided to move first against the southernmost enemy position on the river at Billingsport, New Jersey. On September 28, he assigned this task to the 10th and 42nd Regiments of Foot (nearly 1,000 troops) under Lt. Col. Thomas Stirling, together with a pair of six-pounders from the 3rd British Brigade. Stirling's column left Germantown and arrived that evening at the Middle Ferry on the Schuylkill. The next morning (September 29), they tramped into Chester and met up with two battalions of the 71st Highlanders, which had come up from Wilmington, Delaware, after protecting the depot being established there. The plan called for Stirling's column to cross the Delaware in long boats, march inland, turn north, and seize the

30 Montresor, "Journals," 461. Martin (*Campaign*, 126) provides a different version of the fire raft story; he claims the 10th and 42nd Regiments of Foot arrived in Chester a day early and were in the process of being ferried across the Delaware River in long boats when the fire rafts appeared. The long boats towed the other ships out of harm's way, allowing the rafts to drift harmlessly past. Unfortunately, Martin offered no documentation to support his version of events. Montresor ("Journals," 461) confirms the tide was the more likely reason the fleet escaped harm that night. Jackson, *British Army*, 26.

31 Robertson, *His Diaries*, 151.

unfinished fort, which would effectively remove the first line of obstructions blocking the river.[32]

Germantown Camp

While Cornwallis reconnoitered and Howe planned to move against Fort Billingsport, tensions rose north and west of Philadelphia. September 30th found Washington sending out scouting parties to observe the British at Germantown. Dragoon commander Casimir Pulaski was to "immediately form a detachment of at least fifty Horse of which part are to be Colo. Moylans in their Red Uniforms, which will serve to deceive both the Enemy and Country people." Elements of Continental Light Dragoons wore captured British uniform coats, which Washington hoped would trick the British. Washington's former adjutant general, Joseph Reed, and John Cadwalader of the Pennsylvania Militia also wore red coats while scouting along Wissahickon Creek and would have been captured if not for being mistaken for British troops.[33] One jaeger officer described his picket post "at the bridge across the Wissahickon at Van Dering's Mill, where this river [creek] flows into the Schuylkill. Everything bound for the left flank of the army therefore had to come in through the pass. As a precautionary measure," he added, "I had this bridge barricaded with old wagons, tables and lumber during the night, to be safe from an ambush."[34]

32 Jackson, *Fort Mifflin*, 29; Jackson, *British Army*, 26; Letter, Wilhelm von Knyphausen to the Landgrave, October 17, 1777, translated copy located in Hessian Documents of the American Revolution, Morristown National Historical Park, New Jersey, copy in the David Library of the American Revolution, Washington Crossing, PA, microfiche 10, letter AA, 83; McGuire, *Campaign*, vol. 2, 46; Reed, *Campaign*, 206-207.

33 Chase and Lengel, eds., *Papers*, vol. 11, 354; McGuire, *Campaign*, vol. 2, 46-47. Accurate intelligence was critical. Three brothers living on Green Lane (the modern neighborhood of Manayunk) named Andrew, Jacob, and John Levering operated as spies for Washington between there and Philadelphia. Jacob, disguised as a farmer, canoed down the Schuylkill to sell produce and bring back military intelligence he acquired going door-to-door. Once home, he dispatched a brother to deliver the intelligence to American officers. On September 30, British light dragoons looking for John arrested Jacob during one of his canoeing trips, thinking he was his brother. Jacob had a pass from Washington that he managed to chew and swallow before being searched. The dragoons took him to an oak tree on a hill leading to the middle ferry in Manayunk and were preparing to hang him when neighbors arrived to testify that he was, in fact, Jacob. The British released him. Colonel Stephen Moylan reported the news to Washington. Nagy, *Spies*, 61.

34 von Feilitzsch, *Journal*, 95.

In August, when his army landed in Maryland, Howe had issued a proclamation offering amnesty to anyone who wished to publicly support the Crown. Because few Pennsylvanians accepted the offer, he now canceled the amnesty option. "A Proclamation dated yesterday [September 28] was issued this day by the Commander-in-Chief, signifying no further indulgences to Rebels, all other former proclamations being void." Suspicious persons were arrested for the slightest of reasons, which increased disaffection inside the city and across the countryside. Military and civilian prisoners were crammed into the Walnut Street Gaol across from the State House, where commandant Capt. William Cunningham and his guards watched over them. Hundreds died under his care, and were dragged off to Potter's Field. Securing Philadelphia was one thing, but now Howe needed to plan for a long-term occupation. Quarters were needed for the army, its followers, and for Loyalist refugees. Howe asked Joseph Galloway to "tally all houses and stores and determine if they were occupied, apprehend any residents suspected of being dangerous to the security of the city, and confiscate any weapons in their possession." Hundreds of vacant houses and stores were requisitioned for army use. The British considered taking over everything, including Carpenters' Hall, the Academy (the modern University of Pennsylvania), large schools, the Fish House, and the stores of Robert Morris and Samuel Shoemaker. "Officers are going about this day [September 29] Numbering the Houses, with chalk on the Doors" to identify houses available for officers' quarters and possibly barracks for soldiers, recalled Elizabeth Drinker. Churches were used as hospitals, and riding academies were created for officers.[35]

Continental Concerns as September Closed

In addition to supply and reinforcement issues, Washington had to deal with command matters that threatened the potency of his army. General William Maxwell, the former commander of the New Jersey Brigade who had organized and led a provisional Corps of Light Infantry at Cooch's Bridge and Brandywine, was removed from the command and his brigade disbanded. Maxwell's problems stemmed from his partisan accuser, William Heth. A Virginian, Heth had earned a

35 Montresor, "Journals," 460; Reed, *Campaign*, 204. Potter's Field is today's Washington Square, where a monument stands to the unknown dead. Jackson, *British Army*, 20-22; Drinker, *Diary*, vol. 1, 237. Within a few weeks, hospital space would be required for the sick and wounded of the battles of Brandywine, Germantown, and the assault on Fort Mercer.

reputation as a fighter under Daniel Morgan during the failed 1775 Canadian campaign, where he lost an eye in the assault on Quebec. Heth was one of the 1000 men Maxwell assembled from the army's 10 brigades to form Washington's Light Infantry Brigade, and he had served admirably under Maxwell at Cooch's Bridge and Brandywine before turning against him in the weeks leading up to Germantown. Rumors were circulating through the army that Maxwell had been intoxicated at Brandywine and the Battle of the Clouds. Maxwell had served well in a partisan capacity in northern New Jersey earlier in the campaign and had followed his orders at Cooch's Bridge and Brandywine. The American retreat after the Battle of the Clouds days later was falsely attributed to him by Heth. Many of the light infantrymen on detached service returned to their own units, vowing never to serve under Maxwell again. The undeserved backstabbing resulted in Maxwell's demotion and he returned to command his New Jersey Brigade. With Daniel Morgan detached from the army, Washington would fight his next battle without the benefit of a light infantry force.[36]

The respective forces closed September 1777 with Howe in Philadelphia and moving to open the Delaware River, the British fleet poised to sail up and supply him, and Washington's Continentals about 20 miles northwest of the city seeking an opportunity to strike. It had been a tough month for the Americans. Despite fighting well at Brandywine on the 11th, poor intelligence and a mishandling of the army had resulted in its defeat and the loss of hundreds of men. The aborted Battle of the Clouds five days later risked the army and could well have led to its destruction had the rain not interceded to save it. Wayne's Pennsylvania division had been roughly handled at Paoli, another defeat attributable to the mishandling of intelligence. Philadelphia had fallen, Congress was on the run to York, and the strongest American warship on the river, the *Delaware*, had been lost and would soon be in the service of the British. One of Washington's division commanders (Wayne) was seeking a Court of Inquiry for his actions at Paoli, another (Sullivan) was being investigated by Congress for misconduct at Brandywine, and the army's senior brigadier general (Maxwell) had been removed from his independent command.

Despite these and other problems, Washington knew the Continental Army could not afford to sit outside Philadelphia and wait for winter, or remain idle and

36 McGuire, *Campaign*, vol. 2, 38.

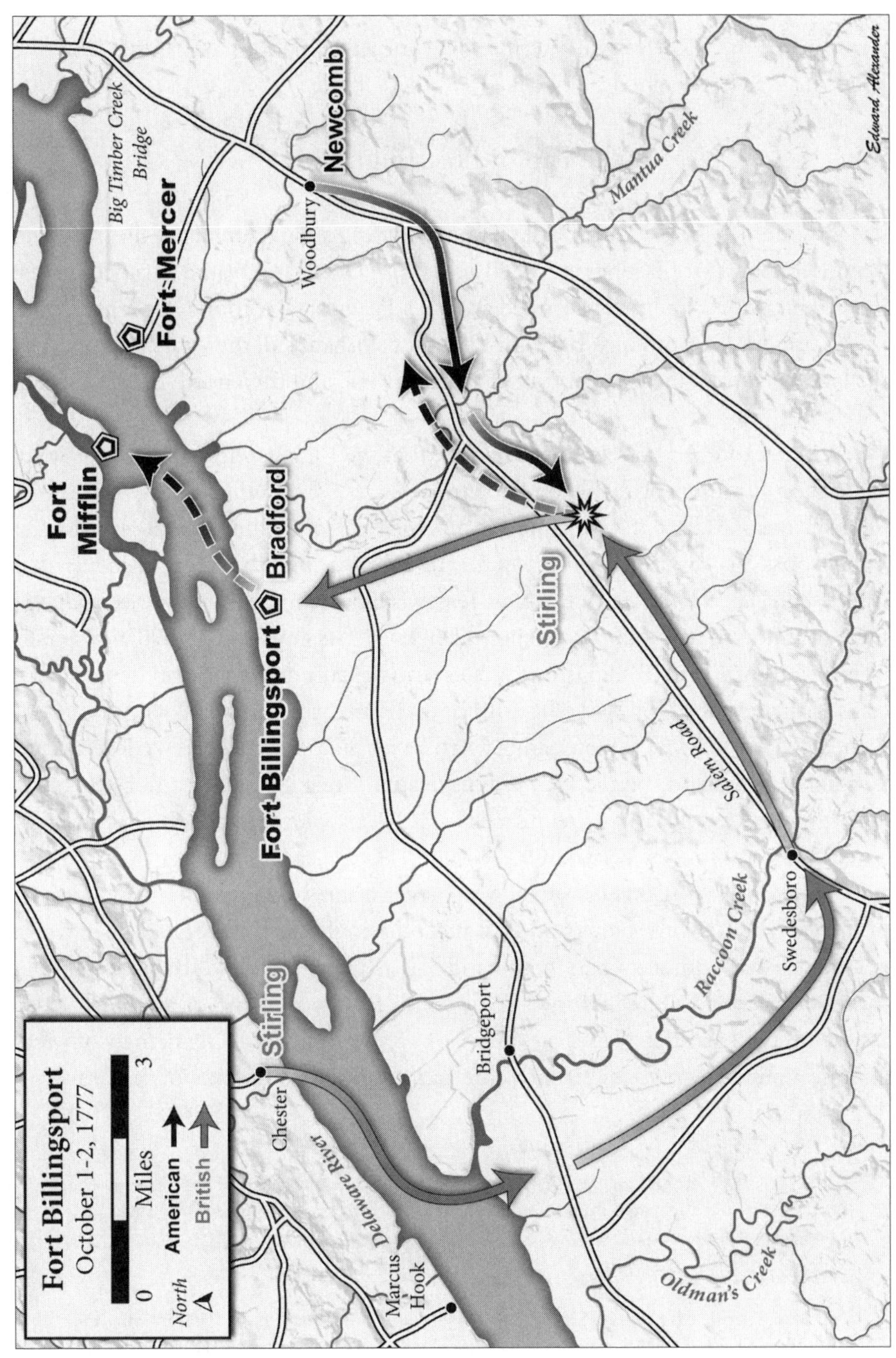
Fort Billingsport
October 1-2, 1777
0 Miles 3
North
American
British
Fort Mercer
Big Timber Creek Bridge
Newcomb
Woodbury
Mantua Creek
Fort Mifflin
Bradford
Fort Billingsport
Stirling
Salem Road
Swedesboro
Raccoon Creek
Bridgeport
Stirling
Chester
Delaware River
Marcus Hook
Oldman's Creek
Edward Alexander

receive an attack on Howe's terms. The initiative had to be seized, and the Virginian was determined to take it.[37]

The Fall of Fort Billingsport

October opened with Lt. Col. Thomas Stirling's detachment of the 10th and 42nd Regiments of Foot being ferried across the Delaware for the advance against Fort Billingsport. The troops landed at Paul's Point on Raccoon Creek, just south of the present Commodore Barry Bridge. Once organized, they pushed east from the landing site on the present Center Square Road, and then north on the present Kings Highway.[38]

Washington had known for some time that the Billingsport position was weak and issued an order (probably on September 27) for Col. William Bradford of the Pennsylvania Militia to assume command of the militiamen garrisoning Billingsport. To Bradford's surprise, he arrived on September 29 to discover that Brig. Gen. Silas Newcomb of the New Jersey Militia, who he thought was in charge there, was not in the fort at all, and had taken one of its guns and his 300 New Jersey troops with him. Fort Billingsport was essentially an unmanned and demoralized post. "I there found Col. Will of the 4th Battn [Pennsylvania militia] with about 100 men, & Captn Massey['s] Company of Artillery which was reduced by desertion to 12 men," Bradford penned to Pennsylvania President (Governor) Thomas Wharton. "After I got in was reinforced by 100 Jersey Militia and the next day with about 50 more [sent by Newcomb.]"[39]

Newcomb, wrote one historian, was "never where he should be, and indecisive in the extreme. A very pious and well-meaning individual, he should never have been entrusted with a military command." Washington discovered precisely that earlier in the war and had removed Newcomb from command of the New Jersey Line. "Notwithstanding I believe that Colo. Newcomb is a Gentleman of great goodness and integrity, and cannot entertain the Slightest doubts of his Bravery,"

37 York was chosen by Congress since it was close to the edge of Pennsylvania civilization. The town was a four day march from Philadelphia, thus providing plenty of time to flee should the British army move inland.

38 Reed, *Campaign*, 207.

39 Hazard, et al., eds., *Archives*, Series 1, vol. 5, 644. Letter, Silas Newcomb to William Livingston, October 4, 1777, William Livingston Family Collection, Reel 1, Massachusetts Historical Society, Boston, MA.

explained Washington, "yet I am too well persuaded that he is not equal to such a Command.—Many qualities, independent of personal Courage, are requisite to form the good Officer."[40]

On October 4, General Newcomb wrote what was the equivalent of a battle report to Gov. William Livingston of New Jersey. On September 29, he explained, he had made his headquarters at Woodbury (7 miles northeast of Billingsport) rather than at the fort itself. He then posted a "guard of about 50 men at Big Timber creek bridge; with a sergts. guard at each of the ferries [Coopers and Gloucester] to serve as piquet, & to prevent any boats going over to the enemy." The militia officer also placed "a guard of about 40 men at Thompson's point, 4 miles below Billingsport . . . about 150 men I sent to Billingsport [to assist Col. Bradford in the defense of the fort] . . . reserving only a small guard at Woodbury."[41]

On the evening of October 1, continued Newcomb, "I was informed that a party of the enemy was landg on this shore, opposite Marcus Hook. Their number said to be about 400." Newcomb decided it was better to advance and engage the British as far from the fort as possible, and did precisely that. "Immediately called in my out guards & marched to a Height, on the Salem Road, about 15 miles below Philada and about 3 ½ miles from Billingsport [near modern Mount Royal]," explained Newcomb to the governor.[42]

Lieutenant Colonel Stirling, meanwhile, was advancing inland with his column when he spotted the militia deploying to oppose him. "About 9 in the morning . . . the Enemy advanced within a few hundred yards of where we were drawn up, with 2 or 3 field pieces," wrote Newcomb, "when a pretty brisk fire, from both sides, issued-we now discover their numbers to be greatly superior to what they had been represented." To Newcomb's dismay, he was not facing 400 men but "not less than 1500." The Americans watched as Stirling shook out "strong flanking parties" to turn Newcomb's line. The tactic may have driven back the heavily outnumbered New Jersey militia, or, as Newcomb later claimed, "[w]e might soon have been

40 Jackson, *Navy*, 133. Fitzpatrick, *Writings*, vol. 7, 134.

41 Letter, Silas Newcomb to William Livingston, October 4, 1777.

42 Ibid. Newcomb added a fascinating, if somewhat cryptic, comment before describing the fighting that followed: "Genl Washington had written to the Commanding Officer at Billingsport, that, if he thought it undefensible, he ought to evacuate it, and destroy the works, which accordingly was done, it being the unanimous opinion of the officers there that the place could not be defended against any considerable force." If accurate, the Americans were already destroying the unfinished fort at Billingsport before the British arrived.

surrounded, I thought it prudent to retreat, which we did in tolerable good order, keeping up a constant fire in our rear."[43]

Stirling drove Newcomb past the intersection of Salem Road and the road leading west to Fort Billingsport, about 3 ½ miles distant, and up to Mantua Creek, which Newcomb crossed before turning to make a stand. The British crossed after him and a short engagement followed. With the pesky militia out of the way, Stirling decided to ignore the New Jersey defenders and turned his attention westward toward the fort. Newcomb extricated his men from this tight spot and withdrew to Woodbury, New Jersey, just a short march from Fort Mercer. The militia general had had the foresight to move valuable stores from Billingsport to Woodbury, saving them from the hands of the enemy. "I believe we had none killed, nor many badly wounded," he informed the governor, though "several are missing, but I believe they are mostly, if not all, gone home. The enemy had 3 or 4 killed at Mantua creek bridge. I have at present," he concluded, "not quite 300 men under my command; & as it is impossible to get any more, under the old Militia law."[44]

Bradford heard the fighting from inside the unfinished fort and knew he could not resist a serious effort to take Billingsport. The Pennsylvania officer "ordered the People into Boats and sent most of them to Fort Island [Mifflin], spiked up all the Cannon we could not carry off, and set the Barracks & Bake House on Fire, but the Dwelling House some how escaped." After sending away the small garrison, Bradford remained behind with Capt. Isaiah Robinson of the brig *Andrea Doria* to determine the size of the British force. "About 12 o'clock the Enemy came on so close thro' a corn field that they were not more than 30 yards from us, and began to fire on us before our Boat put off the shore," reported Bradford, and "we returned the fire with 6 muskets we had on board, and a Guard Boat we had with us also fired on them, and all got off, one man only being wounded."[45]

Lieutenant Colonel Stirling's men moved in to occupy the vacant fort while American row galleys shelled the position. Four British warships supporting the operation from downriver arrived and opened on the American vessels, driving them back upriver. The embarrassing affair was enough to convince several

43 Ibid.

44 Smith, *Fight for the Delaware*, 10. Salem Road is the modern Kings Highway. Letter, Newcomb to Livingston, October 4, 1777. The action between Stirling and Newcomb was in present-day Clarksboro, New Jersey.

45 Hazard, et al., eds., *Archives*, Series 1, vol. 5, 644.

American seamen to desert to the British, prompting Capt. Andrew Hamond of the *Roebuck* to offer pardons to the entire American fleet. Commodore Hazelwood vowed that evening in response to the offer that "he should defend the Fleet to the last, and not give them up, and was not afraid of all the Ships they could bring, and desired they would send no more such flags."[46]

The loss of Billingsport meant the loss of the first line of chevaux-de-frise river obstructions. The British Navy began removing them immediately, but the tedious process would require three weeks to complete. Howe, meanwhile, ordered the gun carriages, artillery platforms, and barracks destroyed and the unfinished earthworks leveled. With the line of river obstructions breached, however, there was no reason for the Americans to attempt the fort's recapture.

Like a line of dominoes, the fall of Billingsport exposed Fort Mercer, just to the north, to any aggressive British commander willing to make the effort. Loyalist Joseph Galloway later insisted that Stirling's request for permission to advance on Fort Mercer had been denied. "Colonel Stirling saw the necessity of forming a post at Red Bank, not yet occupied by the Rebels . . . Colonel Stirling desired permission to take possession of Red Bank—but it was not granted him." What Howe seems not to have known was that Fort Mercer and Bush Island were ungarrisoned, the cannon and works without a caretaker except for a few laborers at the former location. If Stirling had advanced and occupied Fort Mercer, the Americans would have had no choice but to evacuate Fort Mifflin immediately.[47]

The unhappy news that Billingsport had fallen to a British strike soon reached Washington. The Virginian had ordered that the fort be abandoned, but "[o]ur Reason for not dismantling Billingsport," explained Lt. Col. Samuel Smith the day after it fell, "was the great discontent in the State fleet who already are much scar'd & from whom the greatest desertions of Captains, Lieuts. & men has been. So general a discontent and panic run through that part of the fleet that neither Officer nor men can be confided in," he continued, and "they conceive the River is lost if the enemy gets possession of Billingsport nothing can convince them of the contrary & I am persuaded as soon as that fort is taken that almost all the fleet will desert." Bradford's sudden appearance at Fort Mifflin with the remnants of the Billingsport garrison triggered a panic in Smith's command. Responding to Smith's concerns at Mifflin but needing to reassure him of the fort's importance,

46 Smith, *Fight for the Delaware*, 10-11.

47 Reed, *Campaign*, 207-208; Dorwart, *Fort Mifflin*, 33; Jackson, *British Army*, 27; Galloway, *Letters to a Nobleman*, 79-80.

Washington responded to Smith's dispatches, writing that he was "sorry to hear that you found Matters so much out of order at Fort Mifflin. Much must depend upon your activity and that of other Officers in Garrison."[48]

Honing in on a Plan

Construction on the defensive line sketched out north of Philadelphia by Montresor and approved by Cornwallis began in earnest on the first of October. The line of works eventually would begin at Lemon Hill on the Schuylkill River, pass above the city limits on the present Spring Garden Street, and end on the Delaware River opposite the Schuylkill. It was a strong line with ten separate redoubts interlinked by lighter entrenchments and abatis. Howe intended to quarter the army in a continuous line behind the works, ready to man them at a moment's notice if necessary. Until they were completed, however, he left the bulk of his command in Germantown. Montresor, who intended to use civilians to assist in the construction, found it difficult to rouse the interest of the local populace. Only a "few of the Inhabitants" wanted to help make "a kind of beginning at the Redoubt[s]," he complained. The engineer had barely begun work on the redoubts when Howe ordered him to oversee the building of gun emplacements on Carpenter's and Province islands to hold the cannons that would bombard Fort Mifflin. With Mifflin still controlling river access to Philadelphia, Howe was forced to conduct intermittent communication with the fleet over a long and unsecure land route that required heavy guards of troops. Until the British reduced the American defenses, the victualling of the army would be impossible. Howe wanted Fort Mifflin eliminated. The exhausted Montresor had too much to do and too little time to do it.[49]

Dissatisfaction among the city's residents only increased when Howe issued a proclamation requiring everyone to take an oath of allegiance. Enoch Story, a Philadelphia Loyalist, was "appointed to administer the oath of allegiance to those who come in and put themselves under his Majesty's protection."[50]

48 Chase and Lengel, eds., *Papers*, vol. 11, 364, 368-369.

49 Reed, *Campaign*, 205; Montresor, "Journals," 461. Montresor engaged citizens to supervise the construction, including mason John Palmer and carpenters Samuel Griscomb and Elias Smith. Jackson, *British Army*, 22-23.

50 Reed, *Campaign*, 208-209; Morton, "Diary," 12.

Washington Prepares to Strike

Washington had the Continental Army moving again on October 2. The march took the men four miles beyond the crossroads in Worcester Township onto Methacton Hill, where Washington established his headquarters at the home of Peter Wentz, Jr. The high ground provided an excellent viewing platform toward Philadelphia, and a strong defensive position should one be needed. Washington was now fewer than 20 miles from the city limits and about half that from Germantown. Even as he edged closer to Howe, the Virginia commander threw out his net far and wide for more troops, and continued seeking reinforcements from the northern theatre of operations. Lee's Additional Continental Regiment was the latest to be ordered down from Boston. Once the army arrived at Methacton Hill, Cornet Baylor Hill with 15 dragoons rode with Col. Joseph Reed to scout the British positions between Chestnut Hill and the Delaware to make sure the position was secure and to locate the closest British outposts.[51]

Despite the best efforts of the Americans to keep supplies away from the British, the army's deputy commissary general received word that a local agent had sold 100 head of cattle to Howe's commissary. The animals were pastured on the islands along the Delaware River. This same agent promised to provide Howe's army with more food. The news infuriated Washington, whose own army was desperately short of food.[52]

Rumors trickled into British headquarters of the Americans' advance and offensive plans. Howe was isolated from his Tory spies in the countryside and could not verify such reports. Washington's dragoons and militia patrols had cut off access to the city by anyone outside the British lines. The British manning the picket posts at Germantown were becoming increasingly concerned. Lieutenant Richard St. George, picketing with the 52nd Regiment of Foot, knew the Americans "threaten retaliation, vow that they will give no quarter to any of our

51 Reed, *Campaign*, 213. Greene's and Stephen's divisions, as well as the militia of Smallwood and Forman, were positioned on Bethel Hill, a half mile south of the crest of Methacton Hill. Greene established his headquarters on the Cassel farm on Bethel Road. Sullivan, Wayne, and Stirling, along with Armstrong's militia, were on Methacton Hill. Washington's headquarters at the Wentz house was just north of Methacton Hill. Jackson, *British Army*, 30-31; Wright, *Army*, 216; McGuire, *Campaign*, vol. 2, 59.

52 Risch, *Washington's Army*, 208. According to John Chaloner, "Ludwick Karchar has engaged to procure Cattle for General Howe, and he is now using all his diligence to provide for our Enemys." Boyle, ed., *Letterbook*, 12.

Battalion, we are always on the advanced Post of the army—our Present one is unpleasant." American pickets advanced and exchanged rounds with the British sentries. "There has been firing this Night all round the Centrys—which seems as if they endeavor to feel our situation," confirmed St. George. "I am fatigued & must sleep—Couldst Thou sleep thus?" he continued. "My Ear is susceptible of the least Noise." Washington, he added ominously, "intends to move nearer us to try the Event of another Battle."[53]

53 St. George letter dated September 11, 1777.

Chapter 8

The Continental Army

October 3, 1777

"General Washington never knew within 3,000 men what his real numbers were."[1]

— Dr. Benjamin Rush, October 1, 1777

By October 3, 1777, George Washington's Continental Army had been actively campaigning for more than four months, had marched hundreds of miles, had fought a major battle along the Brandywine, and had been involved in several smaller engagements. Now, the exhausted American army was positioned in the western reaches of Philadelphia County, poised to strike a formidable British garrison in Germantown.

The army included Continentals and militia, and not just Americans, but Canadians and Europeans as well. Like every army in history, even women and children marched with it. Historian Thomas McGuire provided an outstanding summary of the Continental command: "Pulled together from a wide spectrum of backgrounds and beliefs, they were often proud, self-reliant, fractious, and provincial. To secure ultimate victory, Americans had to learn to cooperate with

1 L.H. Butterfield, ed., *Letters of Benjamin Rush*, 2 vols. (Princeton, NJ, 1951), Vol. 1, 156.

each other despite their differences. Though many were familiar with hunting or outdoor living, they were impatient with military life and discipline."[2]

The army Washington gathered around him on Methacton Hill on October 2 was a mixed bag of veterans and raw recruits. While many of the men and officers had invaded Canada, had fought in the battles around New York City, and had taken part in the fighting at Trenton and Princeton, just as many others had seen no action at all. Most of the first set of enlistments had expired the previous year, and it took Washington the entire spring and much of the summer to rebuild his command. Many officers were new to their roles, and many of the regiments did not exist in their current form the previous year. All this was true a month earlier, and except for some recent additions, most of the army had learned the lessons of war the hard way at places like Cooch's Bridge, Brandywine, along the South Valley Hills, and in the terrifying darkness at the end of a bayonet at Paoli. The training and professional transformation through which all of these men would pass during the winter months at Valley Forge lay ahead. Still, in recent weeks they had displayed an amazing amount of grit in the face of the professional legions fielded by the British. There was something to work with, and perhaps win with, in that army.

Desertion and the refusal to serve more than a single term of enlistment were constant problems for Washington, and had been since the day he assumed command in 1775. The bulk of the men, enlisted or otherwise, left the ranks for what they believed were legitimate reasons. They had farms to run, businesses to keep out of debt, and wives and children who had been left alone for months on end. More mundane concerns also drove them away. They were cold, hungry, lacking proper clothing, unpaid, and angry about missing promised bonuses. Others left because they refused to report to French officers. And as it was in any army, some men simply hated taking orders, and despised officers. Many feared contracting smallpox and other diseases common to the army. "One of the hallmarks of army culture was the filth in which enlisted men lived," explained one historian. "It also reflected common American resistance to European regular army-style discipline, as their British enemies maintained relatively more hygienic

2 Today, this region is part of Montgomery County, which split away from Philadelphia County in 1784. McGuire, *Paoli*, 45.

camps." It was not uncommon for troops to desert after just a few weeks of service.[3]

Washington had informed Congress in September 1776 that he realized the soldiers had "such an unconquerable desire of returning to their respective homes, that it not only produces shameful, and scandalous Desertions among themselves, but infuses a like spirit in others. Men accustomed to unbounded freedom, and no control," he continued, "cannot brook the Restraint which is indispensably necessary to the good order and Government of an Army; without which, licentiousness, and every kind of disorder triumphantly reign."[4]

The 1776 campaign confirmed that the enthusiasm of the early months of the conflict would not sustain a long war effort. The grueling campaign pushed the men to the limits of what a "highly motivated but short-term, half-trained, insufficiently organized, partly disciplined, and poorly equipped force could accomplish against seasoned regulars," concluded a pair of scholars. A well-trained and experienced army was needed if independence was going to be achieved. John Adams, a congressman from Massachusetts, had lobbied for a standing army in an August 1776 letter to artilleryman Henry Knox. "I am a constant Advocate for a regular Army, and the most masterly Discipline, because, I know, that without these We cannot reasonably hope to be a powerfull, a prosperous, or a free People, and therefore," he concluded, "I have been constantly laboring to obtain a handsome Encouragement for inlisting a permanent Body of Troops."[5]

During the 1776 campaign that resulted in the Battle of Trenton, Congress authorized the recruitment of 88 regiments. The legislators authorized Washington to raise an additional 16 infantry regiments, three artillery regiments, 3,000 dragoons, and a corps of engineers. At full strength, each regiment contained 35 officers, 32 sergeants, and 640 privates and corporals. By the middle of May 1777, 43 regiments had been assembled averaging 200 men each. The Continentals modeled their regiments after British formations, but they were not exact copies. For example, American regiments did not have grenadier and light infantry

3 Bruce Chadwick, *The First American Army: The Untold Story of George Washington and the Men Behind America's First Fight for Freedom* (Naperville, IL, 2005), 171; Gregory T. Knouff, *The Soldiers' Revolution: Pennsylvanians in Arms and the Forging of Early American Identity* (University Park, PA, 2004), 87; Pancake, *1777*, 74-5.

4 Fitzpatrick, Writings, vol. 6, 110-111.

5 Martin and Lender, "*Respectable Army*," 63. Edmund C. Burnett, ed., *Letters of Members of the Continental Congress*, 7 vols. (Washington, D.C., 1923), vol. 2, 61.

companies. British colonels never commanded their regiments in the field, but American colonels did exactly that until January 1778. The number of companies and the strength of regiments varied from colony to colony throughout the long war. Each regiment's high ratio of officers to enlisted men, explained historian Robert Wright, recognized the greater need for control under conditions specific to America. The use of the two-rank battle formation emphasized American faith in musketry rather than shock.[6]

Despite Congressional authorization, organizing the new regiments was a slow process. Only 1,000 of the 1776 Continental veterans reenlisted. The situation was so bleak that Washington was incapable of confronting Howe as late as May 1777. Continental strength did not reach its peak until October 1777, with 39,443 men in the ranks throughout the country, including militia. That figure was 8,000 fewer than the peak strength of the previous year. New financial incentives did little to increase enlistments. Most recruits after 1776 were from the lowest rungs of society, including drifters, unemployed servants, and slaves. Few were independent farmers, merchants, or tradesmen. The latter class of people, if they served at all, usually chose the militia over Continental service so they spent less time away from home. Most recruits were in their late teens and early twenties, but some were under the age of fourteen. Few owned property. Many were unemployed laborers, recent immigrants to the colonies, and, on occasion, criminals who were allowed to avoid punishment by enlisting for service. Every northern colony, plus Maryland and Virginia, allowed the enlistments of white indentured servants, free blacks, and slaves. Although forbidden by regulations, some British and Hessian deserters also found their way into American ranks. With many regiments below strength, Washington was forced to issue rank and file muskets to sergeants and junior officers to augment the power of his firing lines. Despite these variables and circumstances, new recruits continued to arrive throughout the campaign, and by the time he had his army on Methacton Hill outside Germantown, Washington fielded a respectable force of 14,000 men, though not all battle ready.[7]

6 Wright, *Army*, 47, 65; Luzader, *Saratoga*, 226-227. A grenadier was once a specialized soldier who threw a primitive form of hand grenade. By the 18th century grenade-throwing had been phased out, but grenadiers were still chosen for their physicality to lead assaults in battle. In January 1778, Congress created the rank of lieutenant colonel, commandant to make the exchange of captured regimental commanders easier.

7 Martin and Lender, *"Respectable Army,"* 90-91; Mark Edward Lender and Garry Wheeler Stone, *Fatal Sunday: George Washington, the Monmouth Campaign, and the Politics of Battle* (Norman, OK, 2016), 62-63; Wright, *Army*, 125.

The new recruits with the army outside Germantown were different from their predecessors. Much of the patriotic ardor of the war's early months had long ago worn off. The setbacks of 1776 had a direct impact on the social status of many recruits and on the willingness of others to join. Military discipline, high mortality rates, and the rigors of camp life discouraged reenlistment. Paying cash bounties to induce young men of low economic status with few other options to join the army became common.[8]

Many factors attracted recruits throughout the war, including boredom, friendship, the excitement of war, bounties, a desire to see the world or get away from parental supervision, and support for the political cause. As time passed, it became more difficult for recruiters to locate suitable replacements. After Congress introduced troop quotas for each colony in 1777, wrote one historian, "recruiters began to turn a blind eye to race in an effort to get men in the service." British deserters, Africans, and drifters were not accepted in 1775, but all that changed two years later. "By 1777 a more realistic attitude dictated the acceptance of such undesirables, slaves and convicts. This was often the result of state laws which permitted men called to duty to furnish substitutes, and if the price was right recruiters accepted almost anyone."[9]

When Congress turned the responsibility for recruitment over to the colonies, bounties and promises of land helped them meet their quotas. Such incentives made it clear that, for many troops, a sense of duty was not enough to get them—or keep them—in the ranks. Nearly all the troops had stronger ties to their local townships and colonies than to any national cause. That, too, became obvious by the end of 1777, when Washington observed, "we may fairly infer that the country has been pretty well drained of that class of Men, whose tempers, attachments and circumstances disposed them to enter permanently, or for a length of time, into the army; and that the residue of such men, who from different motives," he added, "have kept out of the army, if collected, would not augment our general strength in any proportion to what we require."[10]

By the beginning of 1776 Washington had authorized the enlistment of free blacks. The next year Rhode Island, New York, and Maryland approved enlisting slaves, who were promised their freedom in exchange for honorable service. By the

8 Caroline Cox, *A Proper Sense of Honor: Service and Sacrifice in George Washington's Army* (Chapel Hill, NC, 2004), 3.

9 Ibid., 12,17.

10 Fitzpatrick, *Writings*, vol. 10, 366.

fall of 1777, Africans were mixed in among the regiments poised to strike Germantown. Though a black soldier was subjected to the same racial prejudices found elsewhere in eighteenth-century society, the army provided him with food, clothing, and shelter. His service consisted of undesirable duties, such as orderly, cook, teamster, and other forms of laborious work. Given their situation, there was little incentive for these men to desert, so they usually served out their full terms of enlistment.[11]

The officers in Washington's army almost all came from the upper social strata. "In the deferential society of eighteenth-century America," explained scholar Robert Wright, "members of the leading families naturally assumed leadership in the regular forces just as they did in the militia, in politics and law, in the church, and in business." While it was possible for enlisted men to rise to the ranks of the officer corps, "Washington's desire to maintain a distance between officers and men as a disciplinary tool kept most of the latter from rising far."[12]

While Washington overcame long odds to rebuild the army during the winter of 1776-1777, his troops were still new to army life. Even after several months of campaigning, discipline was lacking within most units. "The men were by nature individually independent, and no officer at hand had the required time, experience and popularity to administer drill with needed severity," was how one historian described the situation. "It was only the dream of liberty, and love for the Commander-in-Chief that kept the army in any measure cohesive." Most of these men believed in Washington and would have followed him anywhere, willing to endure anything he required of them.[13]

Just as Washington's troops often lacked discipline, his officers often lacked maturity, which constituted a major discipline problem in its own way. Unfortunately for the commander-in-chief, he had to spend inordinate amounts of time settling petty problems between his officers. Disputes over rank were a typical and thorny issue. Aggrieved officers often submitted requests for permission to resign, which obligated Washington to smooth hurt feelings to keep his men

11 Pancake, *1777*, 75-76.

12 Wright, *Army*, 184.

13 Reed, *Campaign*, 54. Most companies included both a drummer and a fifer. These individuals often massed behind their regiments during battle to help signal orders rather than inspire morale. The sound of beating drums could carry for miles under good conditions, and when grouped could be heard above the chaos of battle. Musicians also administered corporal punishment, maintained regimental guard rooms, and assisted in the evacuation of casualties. As early as 1777, many also carried firearms.

together. Many officers refused to lead by example, which added to the lack of discipline. Officers committed the same offenses as the enlisted men, including desertion, gambling, drunkenness, and pillaging. "It behooves every Man to exert himself," Washington asserted to Congress in September 1776. "It will not do for the Commanding Officer of a Regiment to content himself, with barely giving Orders, he should see (at least know) that they are executed. He should call his men out frequently and endeavor to impress them with a Just and true sense of their duty, and how much depends on subordination and discipline." Washington knew that the officers needed to set themselves apart from their men, or their subordinates would treat them as equals and regard them "as no more than a broomstick, being mixed together as one common herd; no order, nor no discipline can prevail; nor will the Officer[s] ever meet with that respect which is essential to due subordination." Problems with officers went all the way to the top. Three of his most senior commanders were under a cloud even as the army was set to take the offensive outside Germantown. General John Sullivan was under Congressional investigation for his actions at Staten Island and Brandywine, Anthony Wayne had sought a court of inquiry into his actions at Paoli, and Washington had demoted William Maxwell pursuant to charges of incompetence at Cooch's Bridge, Brandywine, and the Battle of the Clouds.[14]

Despite internal squabbling, Washington made strides in turning his officers into a professional cadre. He issued orders for them to use their spare time reading military texts—a sign of growing professionalism within the Continental Army, aided by a number of foreign observers who contributed their time and advice to the Americans struggling to understand military science. Though some units had combat experience, many regiments remained green, and dealing with harsh discipline, the boredom of camp life, long absences from home, and combat losses and disease simply proved too much. Desertion was rampant, with some regiments losing as much as 20 percent of their strength in just the past few months. In some cases officers were no more dependable than the men in the ranks, and Washington feared their loss would "shake the very existence of the Army."[15]

By regulation, the members of the army were entitled to a substantial daily ration of one pound of beef, ¾ pound of pork, or a pound of salted fish, together with a pound of bread or flour. They were also to get three pints of peas or beans

14 Fitzpatrick, *Writings*, vol. 6, 110.

15 Wright, *Army*, 140; Lender and Stone, *Fatal Sunday*, 63-64; Fitzpatrick, *Writings*, vol. 11, 285.

per week to supplement their meat and bread rations. A pint of milk each day was added, along with a half-pint of rice or a pint of Indian meal each week. A quart of spruce beer or cider to fight scurvy also was supposed to be issued daily. While the regulations read well on paper, reality was something else entirely. The men were rarely supplied in this manner, especially during active campaigning. Through most of his enlistment, the standard Continental soldier subsisted on bread and meat alone, with the Commissary Department judged upon its ability to supply those two important staples. "Vegetables," observed historian Erna Risch, "were usually lacking, and vinegar, later included in the ration for antiscorbutic purposes, was often omitted by commissaries. Beer and cider . . . were never plentiful." Sutlers followed the army selling provisions, and Washington allowed farmers to sell products at markets set up in the camps when time allowed. "Soldiers, however, had little money to buy supplementary foods," observed Risch, a scholar of Washington's army, "but in the Revolution, as in later wars, they were good at 'liberating' provisions."[16]

A popular misperception has American soldiers uniformly clothed in a blue and off-white uniform, something that was the exception rather than the rule. Washington sported a blue and ivory (or "buff") uniform early on, the same worn by the Fairfax County troop of horse, of which he had served as colonel before being elevated to command the Continental Army. The predominant uniform colors throughout much of the war, however, were green and brown. In fact, blue was not adopted as the official color of the Continental Army's uniforms until early October 1779. It was a rare sight to see even a single regiment, let alone the entire army, uniformly clothed. This was not for lack of trying. The army's Clothier General, James Mease, attempted in 1777 to uniformly clothe each regiment and left the choice of color to the respective regimental commanders. This approach, however, did not factor in the military implications of their individual choices. Stephen Moylan, for example, chose to outfit his dragoons in scarlet coats, which closely resembled British dragoon uniforms. Washington wisely ordered that all red clothing be dyed to avoid any confusion in combat, and preferred brown coats with white or buff facings to the scarlet worn by the enemy. By the fall of 1777, obtaining sufficient amounts of quality cloth was a huge problem. As one scholar noted, even men sick or injured in hospitals often were unable to return to the army when healthy because they were so poorly clothed. The fact that Washington was

16 Risch, *Washington's Army*, 190-191.

able to keep an army of any size in the field while facing shortages of nearly everything is remarkable.[17]

The state of the army and the quality of its opposition would have discouraged anyone other than George Washington. Luckily for him, and the American cause, General Howe's delays and fitful approach to the 1777 campaign allowed what one observer described as the "haphazard organization of the Continental Line [to] become more stabilized. Both the regiments and Washington's generals had acquired experience in troop movement and administration. Combat experience had also been gained over the previous month. The army was now organized into divisions, and several major generals were beginning to emerge as competent commanders."[18]

Another common misconception is that the Continental Army that defeated the British was composed of Indian fighters and men had who spent their lives wielding their deadly muskets or rifles. While it is certainly true that some such men were sprinkled throughout the army, the majority of Washington's soldiers—perhaps as many as nine out of 10—were recruited from the cities and villages east of the Appalachian Mountains and were at least one generation removed from the frontier of today's imagination. Many in his army that fall had never seen an Indian or fired a shot in anger until the Battle of Brandywine. Most, however, had some familiarity with firearms, had hunted game, or had defended their livestock from predators, but that was a far cry from combat experience.[19]

The Americans were armed with two basic types of muskets: the .75 caliber British Long Land pattern smoothbore flintlock musket (more commonly called the "Brown Bess"), and the French Charleville .69 caliber smoothbore flintlock musket. American manufacturers produced muskets patterned on both types. The model 1763 French Charleville was the standard American weapon by 1777. The smoothbore fired a one-ounce lead ball, could be fitted with a 14-inch bayonet, and was more reliable and accurate than the British musket. Since the Continental Army placed more emphasis on musketry than shock tactics, the Charleville was an ideal weapon. Professional armies of this age no longer loaded loose ball and powder into muskets. Instead, the men were issued cartridges made of a paper or cloth filled with a single musket ball and gunpowder for one shot. The cartridges

17 Risch, *Washington's Army*, 283, 285-286, 289.

18 Pancake, *1777*, 165.

19 Ibid., 66.

were held together with string and stored in cartridge boxes slung around a shoulder. A soldier tore open one end of a cartridge with his teeth, dumped the gunpowder down the barrel, and then used a ramrod to seat the round lead ball.[20]

Most of Washington's men carried smoothbores rather than rifled weapons. Smoothbores were accurate up to 50 yards and took about 30 seconds to reload. Even when fired at a pointblank range of 25 or 30 yards, hitting an enemy soldier was problematic. Effective firepower was generated by organizing men into disciplined ranks so volleys could be "concentrated and controlled" against similarly arranged enemy lines. Although Washington insisted the Continental Army be trained according to the principles of European military science, the army that fought along the Brandywine and that would attack the British at Germantown had little or no such training, and would not possess it until after the long winter at Valley Forge.[21]

Questionable recruiting practices, rawness of the recruits, and diminishing patriotism did not mean these men were poor soldiers. Many proved themselves and became the backbone of the army that ultimately achieved victory at Yorktown. Some senior officers had fought in the French and Indian War, which made them familiar with British tactics and practices. Much of the organization and logistics that Washington attempted to instill were based upon British precedents. Many of the junior officers who had been too young to serve in the earlier war had read British publications and English translations of various French and German studies of military science and tactics. Although the end of enlistments had damaged the army, it was not completely starting over from scratch, for many regular and noncommissioned officers had gained significant experience during the prior two years of service.[22]

Camp followers attached themselves to every army in history, and the Continental Army was no exception. Hundreds of hangers-on gathered in the fields outside Philadelphia, including sutlers, women, wives, and children. Washington discouraged the practice and issued orders against their presence, but he realized these people helped hold his army together. "He came to accept the followers who helped root the men within the army," explains one historian. "Followers, in turn, further promoted that acceptance through their labor" as

20 Smith, *Manufacturing*, xviii; Wright, *Army*, 113.

21 Pancake, *1777*, 66.

22 Luzader, *Saratoga*, 207.

laundresses and nurses. They mostly traveled with the baggage train, received rations, and were expected to follow camp regulations just like the troops.[23]

Exactly how many men Washington had in the field in October 1777 remains a subject of debate. Analyzing the size of the Revolutionary armies is difficult. According to the British Annual Register for 1776, "all calculations of this nature, though founded upon the best official information, will far exceed, even at a much nearer distance than America, the real effective number that can ever be brought into action." Unfortunately, few troop returns exist for Washington's army. Two strength reports survive that are of particular interest to this study. One, dated May 20, 1777, details army strength several months before the September bloodlettings at Brandywine and elsewhere. Another, dated November 3, 1777, records the army's strength after the fighting at Germantown. The numbers used in this work are based on those returns and a few additional sources.

Most accounts on the Battle of Germantown agree that Washington took about 11,000 men into the battle. According to my research, the Continental Army outside Germantown was comprised of some 14,000 men (3,000 fewer than were at Brandywine) divided into six divisions, plus four unattached brigades. It is unlikely that many men could have physically accompanied the army into Germantown. "I heard of 2,000 who sneaked off with the baggage of the army to Bethlehem," complained Dr. Benjamin Rush to John Adams. "General Washington never knew within 3,000 men what his real numbers were."[24]

A few months after the Philadelphia Campaign concluded, Capt. Johann Heinrichs of the Hessian jaeger Corps penned his summation of the effectiveness of the American troops in his letter-book. Washington's army, he admitted, was not "to be despised; as there are many Englishmen, Irishmen, Scotchmen, Frenchmen and others in their service, and are per se a brave nation, which bravery

23 Holly A. Mayer, "Wives, Concubines, and Community," in John Resch and Walter Sargent, eds., *War & Society in the American Revolution: Mobilization and Home Fronts* (DeKalb, IL, 2007), 238. The women attached to the army included the wives of soldiers, laundresses, and servants, and others, not all of good reputation, who performed "a multitude of feminine tasks, good and bad, to ease the lives of soldiers." Men, like teamsters and drivers, and children also were among them. Camp followers added approximately 50 percent more people traveling with the armed personnel of the Continental Army. Reed, *Campaign,* 79-80.

24 The Annual Register, or a View of the History, Politics, and Literature for the Year 1776 (London, 1788), 166; Jackson, *British Army*, 34; Butterfield, ed., *Letters*, vol. 1, 155-56. Rush was born outside of Philadelphia in 1745, and attended West Nottingham Academy, the College of Philadelphia, and Edinburgh University. In 1777, he was appointed surgeon general of the middle department of the Continental Army.

is surprisingly enhanced by the enthusiasm engendered by falsehood and vagaries, which are drilled into them. . . . It but requires time and good leadership to make them formidable," he concluded with prescience, "but the great thing wanting with them is subordination; for their very spirit of independence is detrimental to them." The full quality and advantages inherent in that American spirit were something the Hessian captain would never truly understand.[25]

Army Administration

Any analysis of the inner workings of the Continental Army at Germantown must begin with Washington's personal staff—the men responsible for managing the army's operations. Chief among them were Col. Timothy Pickering, his adjutant general; Brig. Gen. Henry Knox, his chief of artillery; and Maj. Gen. Thomas Mifflin, his quartermaster general. After becoming commander-in-chief of the Continental Army in 1775, Washington was authorized by Congress to appoint a personal staff of one military secretary and three aides-de-camp. Throughout the war he supplemented his staff with voluntary aides. Congress authorized generals who served under Washington and commanded divisions or other detachments just two official aides-de-camp each.[26]

25 Johann Heinrichs, "Extracts From the Letter-Book of Captain Johann Heinrichs of the Hessian Jäger Corps, 1778-1780," *PMHB*, Julius F. Sachse, trans. (Philadelphia, 1898), vol. 22, 139.

26 Washington's staff officers included: Col. Timothy Pickering (adjutant general), Brig. Gen. Henry Knox (chief of artillery), Maj. Gen. Thomas Mifflin (quartermaster general), Col. Henry Emanuel Lutterloh (deputy quartermaster general), Lt. Col. Joseph Thornbury (wagonmaster general), Lt. Col. Benjamin Flower (commissary general of military stores), Clement Biddle (commissary general of forage), William Buchanan (commissary general), Ephraim Blaine (deputy commissary general), Col. Elias Boudinot (commissary general of prisoners), James Mease (clothier general), Dr. William Shippen (director general of the medical department), Dr. Benjamin Rush (surgeon general of the army), Dr. John Cochrane (chief physician of the army), Casimir Pulaski (chief of the dragoons), Lt. Col. Robert Hanson Harrison (general military secretary), Lt. Col. Alexander Hamilton (aide-de-camp), Lt. Col. Tench Tilghman (aide-de-camp), Maj. John Fitzgerald (aide-de-camp), John Laurens (volunteer aide), Peter Thornton (volunteer aide), Lt. Col. Richard Kidder Meade (volunteer aide), and Capt. Caleb Gibbs (captain of the guard). Marylander Benjamin Flower moved to Philadelphia in the 1770s to work as a hatter. He joined the army in 1776. Smith, *Manufacturing*, 28. Elias Boudinot was born in 1740 and was a prominent New Jersey attorney and member of that colony's Assembly when the war began. Appointed to his position in April 1777 by Washington, Boudinot's role was supervising prisoner of war compounds and ensuring that American prisoners of war were receiving proper treatment. Philadelphia merchant James Mease was responsible for preparing estimates, purchasing and storing clothing, and issuing items through regimental quartermasters. He also oversaw turning the hides produced by the army's consumption of beef into needed leather goods. Wright, *Continental Army*, 114-115. Elias Boudinot, *"Their Distress*

An aide-de-camp, explained the *Universal Military Dictionary* in 1779, was

> an officer appointed to attend a general officer, in the field, in winter-quarters, and in garrison; he receives and carries their orders, as occasion requires. He is seldom under the degree of a captain, and all aids-de-camp have 10s. a day allowed for their duty. This employment is of greater importance than is generally believed: it is, however, often entrusted to young officers of little experience, and of as little capacity; but in most foreign services they give great attention to this article.[27]

"The military secretary's job was to compose letters and orders," explained historian Arthur Lefkowitz. "He was selected for his writing skills and discretion since he frequently had access to confidential information. He might be asked, for example, to attend councils of war and keep minutes." While the secretary was to maintain the general's paperwork, the aides with Washington served as "administrative assistant[s] and personal representative[s]" of the general. "Aides were generally entrusted to deliver important dispatches and other privileged information in camp, on the march, and in battle. During a battle, if there was no time to write a note or dispatch, a general would use one of his aides to deliver verbal orders."[28]

The fact that Washington was responsible for molding the army about to face Howe's professionals outside Philadelphia, as well as all the other Continental units spread across the colonies, is often overlooked. He did all he could to maintain contact with the units he had left in the Hudson Highlands, the army under Horatio Gates that had dealt the fatal blow to Burgoyne's invading command in the Hudson River valley, and other detached garrisons. Washington also was responsible for staying in contact with Congress. As a result, he had no choice but to rely "on a small cadre of trusted subordinates—primarily his aides—to help him manage the affairs of the army," continued Lefkowitz, "and these men quickly found themselves enmeshed in a multitude of critical issues." Washington had no choice but to pick the best men he could, trust them, and rely upon their discretion. They had access to sensitive documents "concerning strategy, troop location and

---

is almost intolerable": The Elias Boudinot Letterbook, 1777-1778, Joseph Lee Boyle, ed. (Westminster, MD, 2008), v. William Buchanan was a Baltimore merchant prior to taking his post on August 5, 1777. Risch, *Washington's Army*, 173.

27 George Smith, *A Universal Military Dictionary* (London, 1779), 3.

28 Arthur S. Lefkowitz, *George Washington's Indispensable Men: The 32 Aides-de-Camp Who Helped Win American Independence* (Mechanicsburg, PA, 2003), 5-6.

movements, the supply situation, unrest in the army, and spy operations," and they often attended councils of war.[29]

The Continental Army's logistics were based on the British model, with a Commissary Department looking after food and other supplies. When stocks ran low in the Middle Colonies, flour was transported from the grain plantations along the James, Rappahannock, and Potomac rivers in Virginia. Salted meat was hauled by wagon from New England over a long and inhospitable route.[30]

While quartermaster departments are the mainstay of any army, the Continental Congress failed to adopt regulations for that department until May 14, 1777—just as the summer campaign was getting underway. The highlights of the regulations included a separation of the Forage & Wagon Department and the Quartermaster Department. Thomas Mifflin, the quartermaster general, could finally appoint a deputy quartermaster for each military department, and each division and brigade of the army was now authorized to retain a staff officer to manage such duties. On July 1, Washington named Col. Emanuel Lutterloh as his deputy quartermaster general for the main Continental Army. Lutterloh's staff included a clerk, paymaster, and assistant deputy quartermaster general; a second staffer, with two assistants, supervised and issued stores. An assistant deputy quartermaster general, with four hostlers, was placed in charge of the Continental horse yards. Pennsylvania housed many supply manufactories, so Mifflin's assistants were scattered among them; these included Robert Lettis Hooper in Easton, Mark Bird in Reading, John Davis in Carlisle, and George Ross in Lancaster. Christopher Ludwick, a man perhaps both loved and loathed, was a German baker from Philadelphia who was paid 75 dollars a month and two rations a day to serve as the director of baking for the entire army.[31]

Having enough wagons on hand for the army's needs was a constant problem. Hiring civilian wagons was the most desired method of procurement, but impressment became more common as the army continued to operate in Pennsylvania. The demand for wagons pushed up the cost of hiring them beyond the 30 shillings a day for a wagon, four horses, and driver that Congress had authorized. Few civilians would work for such a low rate, and those who did often failed to receive payment for their services, which compounded the army's supply

29 Ibid., xvi-xvii, 203.

30 Fischer, *Crossing*, 268.

31 Risch, *Washington's Army*, 36-38, 195.

problem. Impressing wagons, however, angered civilians, who began concealing their wheeled vehicles to keep them away from Washington's army.[32]

With his army as large and as well-organized and supplied as it was likely to be that fall, Washington determined that the time had arrived to assault the British position at Germantown.

John Sullivan's Column

John Sullivan headed into Germantown at the head of two divisions and an additional attached brigade. Washington rode with him. The army commander retained confidence in the New Hampshire major general despite the scrutiny that had surrounded him since Brandywine. Perhaps he accompanied the column to keep a closer eye on Sullivan, but in all likelihood it was because Lord Stirling's reserve column was slated to follow Sullivan's troops. The column of 3,700 men consisted of Sullivan's own division, Brig. Gen. Anthony Wayne's Pennsylvania division, and Brig. Gen. Thomas Conway's Pennsylvania brigade.

Sullivan's 1,500-man, two-brigade division was composed of soldiers from Maryland, Delaware, and Canada. William Smallwood was nominally in command of one of his brigades. With Smallwood still detached and leading the Maryland militia, Col. John Stone remained in command of the brigade he had led at Brandywine. Stone had been with the army since the beginning, rising from a major in the Maryland Line to colonel and in command of a brigade consisting of the 1st, 3rd, 5th, and 7th Maryland regiments and the Delaware Regiment. Preudhomme de Borre, who had led Sullivan's other brigade at Brandywine, had resigned after that debacle, leaving a vacancy that had to be filled immediately. Colonel Moses Hazen should have been installed in de Borre's place, but was exercising tactical command of the division, with Sullivan commanding the column. Colonel Thomas Price, by virtue of seniority, commanded Hazen's brigade. Like Stone, Price had risen from captain in the Maryland Line. His brigade consisted of the 2nd, 4th, and 6th Maryland regiments, the German Regiment, and Hazen's French Canadians. The German Regiment, recruited from German communities in Pennsylvania and Maryland, was created to counterbalance British efforts to use German soldiers from Europe against the colonies. Sullivan's division was 300 men smaller than it had been before Brandywine, where it was mauled thanks to de Borre's poor

32 Ibid., 83.

leadership. The division was going into battle at Germantown with colonels commanding at all levels.[33]

With Benjamin Lincoln absent leading militia in Horatio Gates's army in New York, Brig. Gen. Anthony Wayne remained in command of his division. After putting 1,800 men into the fight at Brandywine, his the losses there (about 240), compounded with the pummeling they received at Paoli, whittled the division down to 1,300 men. Both of Wayne's brigades were led by colonels. Thomas Hartley commanded the 1st, 2nd, 7th, and 10th Pennsylvania regiments and Hartley's Additional Continental Regiment, while Richard Humpton commanded the 4th, 5th, 8th, and 11th Pennsylvania regiments. The division lacked the leadership of general officers, and many of its remaining officers distrusted Wayne and were seeking charges against him for the massacre at Paoli. This underlying tension aside, the men were looking forward to battle so they could seek revenge for their fallen comrades.[34]

Washington attached Brig. Gen. Thomas Conway's brigade to Sullivan's column. Irishman Conway had been appointed brigadier general that May but was disliked for relentlessly drilling his brigade. His command of 900 men included the 3rd, 6th, 9th, and 12th Pennsylvania regiments and Spencer's Additional Continental Regiment. The brigade had fought well at Brandywine before being overpowered by British grenadiers.[35]

33 Stone, who entered the war in January 1776 as the major of Smallwood's Maryland regiment, rose to lieutenant-colonel in December 1776 and colonel of the 1st Maryland Regiment in February 1777. Price began the war as a captain of a Maryland Rifle Company in June 1775 and rose to major of Smallwood's Maryland Regiment in January 1776. He was promoted to colonel of the 2nd Maryland Regiment in December 1776. The November 3, 1777, strength return had the two brigades with 1,472 men. Washington's brigades lost approximately 120 men each at Brandywine. If we reduce Sullivan's division by 240 men after Brandywine, 1,640 men were left. An estimate of 1,500 soldiers going into action at Germantown is not unreasonable. Harris, *Brandywine*, 170; Charles H. Lesser, ed., *The Sinews of Independence: Monthly Strength Reports of the Continental Army* (Chicago, IL, 1976), 50. Under the Congressional plan for 88 regiments, Maryland was required to furnish seven of them. Patrick K. O'Donnell, *Washington's Immortals: The Untold Story of an Elite Regiment Who Changed the Course of the Revolution* (New York, 2016), 132.

34 Wayne could not be made a major general because Pennsylvania's quota for that rank was already taken up by Thomas Mifflin and Arthur St. Clair. The November 3, 1777, strength return credited Hartley's and Humpton's brigades with 1,342 men. If the division had 1,800 men at Brandywine and lost 240 there, plus another 160 at Paoli, some 1,400 remained. Therefore, 1,300 soldiers in the ranks for Germantown is a reasonable estimate. Harris, *Brandywine*, 169; Lesser, ed., *Sinews*, 50.

35 Several regiments received recruits throughout the campaign. Conway's brigade went into Brandywine with about 750 men, but the November 3, 1777, return, a month *after* Germantown, put

Except for Conway's brigade (which had fought under Lord Stirling at Brandywine), all of the units in Sullivan's column had something to prove. The British Brigade of Guards had decimated Sullivan's troops at Brandywine, and the division remained under questionable leadership going into Germantown. Wayne's men, on the other hand, had performed well at Brandywine, but were going into Germantown with the stain of the Paoli operation hanging over them like a pall.

Nathanael Greene's Column

Like Sullivan, Maj. Gen. Nathanael Greene rode into Germantown at the head of two divisions and an additional attached brigade. Greene was Washington's most capable general and led his column without Washington's direct guidance. His 4,800 men consisted of Greene's own division under Brig. Gen. Peter Muhlenberg, Maj. Gen. Adam Stephen's Virginia division, and Brig. Gen. Alexander McDougall's Connecticut brigade, which Washington attached to Greene's command.

Greene's division had fought well at Brandywine as the army's rear guard and counted about 1,900 men as it marched toward Germantown. With Greene commanding the column, Brig. Gen. Muhlenberg was in tactical command of the division. Colonel William Russell moved up to take command of Muhlenberg's brigade, which consisted of the 1st, 5th, 9th, and 13th Virginia regiments. The second brigade under Brig. Gen. George Weedon contained the 2nd, 6th, 10th, and 14th Virginia regiments and the Pennsylvania State Regiment. The division was blessed with great leadership, as Greene himself was considered the army's best tactician and strategist. His division was also the best organized and disciplined in the army. Washington never hesitated to assign Greene to command on the hottest part of the field.[36]

Greene's second division under Maj. Gen. Adam Stephen consisted of 1,900 Virginians allocated between two brigades led by Brig. Gen. Charles Scott and Col. Alexander McClanachan. Scott commanded the 4th, 8th, and 12th Virginia

---

its strength at 897. Thus, an estimate of 900 men for Germantown is reasonable. Conway's brigade would lead the attack at Germantown and see heavy combat throughout the battle. Harris, *Brandywine*, 172; Lesser, ed., *Sinews*, 50.

36 Russell became colonel of the 13th Virginia Regiment in December 1776. The November 3, 1777 strength return had the two brigades with 1,946 men. If we reduce Greene's division by 240 men after Brandywine, 2,260 men were left. An estimate of 1,900 men going into battle at Germantown is not unreasonable. Harris, *Brandywine*, 168; Lesser, ed., *Sinews*, 50.

regiments and Grayson's and Patton's Additional Continental Regiments. McClanachan (who was in command of the other brigade because Brig. Gen. William Woodford was still recovering from his Brandywine wound) led the 3rd, 7th, 11th, and 15th Virginia regiments. This division also had fought well at Brandywine, though Stephen was often rumored to be under the influence of alcohol in battle.[37]

Brigadier General Alexander McDougall's 1,000-man Connecticut brigade consisted of the 2nd, 4th, 5th, and 7th Connecticut regiments. McDougall's men, who were not on hand for the hard fight along the Brandywine, had yet to see combat. The brigade had only recently arrived from the Hudson Highlands after being called down to reinforce the Continentals in Pennsylvania. Washington had no idea how the command would act under fire, and neither did its own commander.[38]

Except for McDougall's brigade, Greene's column consisted of battle-tested regulars who had performed well at Brandywine. Other than the questionable temperance of Adam Stephen, the column boasted some of the best leadership in the army. Washington expected much from them.

Corps de Reserve

Washington had created a tactical reserve under Maj. Gen. William Alexander (Lord Stirling) when he reorganized the army after Brandywine. Stirling's reserve consisted of two roughly equal-in-size brigades led by Brig. Gens. William Maxwell and Francis Nash. Maxwell's brigade contained about 800 men of the 1st, 2nd, 3rd, and 4th New Jersey regiments (also called the "New Jersey Line"). These troops had fought well at Brandywine under Col. Elias Dayton before British grenadiers pushed them off Birmingham Hill. Maxwell had been demoted for accusations of drunkenness at Brandywine and the Battle of the Clouds. "Were I to describe the

37 Charles Scott began the war as lieutenant colonel of the 2nd Virginia before gaining command of the 5th Virginia in May 1776. He rose to brigade command in April 1777. Fischer, *Crossing*, 153. McClanachan entered the war as lieutenant colonel of the 7th Virginia Regiment in February 1776 before rising to colonel in March 1777. The November 3, 1777 strength return credited the two brigades with 2,006 men. If we reduce Stephen's division by 240 men after Brandywine, 1,860 men were left. An estimate of 1,900 men available to fight at Germantown is not unreasonable. Harris, *Brandywine*, 171; Lesser, ed., *Sinews*, 50.

38 The November 3, 1777 strength return had the brigade with 1,087 men. An estimate of 1,000 men going into battle at Germantown is not unreasonable. Lesser, ed., *Sinews*, 50.

hardships and the difficulties we underwent from this time until the 4th of October," recalled Ensign George Ewing after the fight at Germantown, "no person but those who were with us would credit my relation; therefore I choose to pass it over in silence rather than those who should see this work should think me guilty of an hyperbole." Stirling's second brigade under Francis Nash, a North Carolina outfit of 800 men, was composed of the 1st through 9th North Carolina regiments. The North Carolinians had seen little combat heading into Germantown.[39]

The Dragoons and the Artillery

The remaining Continental units in Washington's army consisted of the Light Dragoons Brigade, commanded by Brig. Gen. Casimir Pulaski, and the Artillery Brigade. Congress did not authorize dragoon regiments until March 1, 1777, just eight months before Germantown. The legislation dictated that each of the four authorized regiments were to have six troops (companies), each comprised of a captain, lieutenant, cornet, and 41 enlisted men. Including regimental staff, each prescribed regiment numbered 280 men. Due to supply shortages, expense, desertion, and occasional outright mutiny, these regiments rarely numbered more than 150 men. The 4th Continental Light Dragoons, for example, was down to a mere 80 men by the middle of July 1777, and it was not an exception. It is reasonable to conclude that Washington had a dragoon brigade consisting of four regiments, numbering about 500 mounted personnel, led by regimental commanders Col. Theodorick Bland, Col. Elisha Sheldon, Lt. Col. Francis Byrd, and Lt. Col. Anthony White. After Washington's mounted arm turned in a miserable performance at Brandywine, he assigned Brig. Gen. Casimir Pulaski, an experienced European officer, to command his cavalry. Washington believed the primary purpose of dragoons was reconnaissance, not combat. According to historian Robert Wright, Washington's troopers were to use "inconspicuous dark horses and ordered the officers to recruit native-born Americans rather than

39 George Ewing, "Journal of George Ewing, a Revolutionary Soldier, of Greenwich, New Jersey," *American Monthly Magazine*, 42 vols. (1911), vol. 38, 7. The November 3, 1777 strength return had the brigades with 1,582 men. These two brigades went into Brandywine with about 1,800 men. An estimate of 1,600 men available for the battle at Germantown is not unreasonable. Harris, *Brandywine*, 172; Lesser, ed., *Sinews*, 50. When the North Carolina Brigade arrived in Philadelphia in July, it numbered only 1,100 men, with just two of the regiments being able to muster over 200 effectives. Wright, *Army*, 108.

immigrants whose loyalty was less certain." Filling the ranks was complicated by the need to procure enough horses, weapons, and special equipment. Both men and horses needed specialized training. How Washington would use his troopers, and how they would perform under fire with Pulaski at their head, remained to be seen.[40]

Primary records provide little information on the composition and number of guns at Germantown. The Artillery Brigade, commanded by Brig. Gen. Henry Knox, consisted of about 600 men in three regiments. Each regiment consisted of between eight and a dozen companies. Knox attached portions of the brigade to each infantry division. It is unclear which specific units were so assigned, and which remained with the general artillery reserve. By 1777, it was common practice to assign an artillery company to each brigade of the army, while other companies served as part of a general reserve. The ideal armament for each brigade was two 6-pounders, although this caliber gun required the largest crew—12 to 15 men—of any field piece with the army. Concentrating fire against enemy infantry was the goal, so rate of fire and maneuverability were more important than range. The performance of Washington's long arm, which had sustained heavy losses in personnel and equipment at Brandywine, would bear watching in the upcoming fight.[41]

The American Militia Problem

Washington had long believed the fledgling country needed a professional army to win a war against Great Britain, and that relying too much on militia was a losing proposition. Congress believed otherwise, and many of its members argued that the maintenance of a standing army was one of the chief American complaints against England. Besides, a militia was cheaper and easier to maintain.[42]

Washington's experience with militia dated back to the French and Indian War. When that war broke out in North America, British officials hoped militia could augment British Regulars. As was quickly discovered, the mechanism for incorporating civilians into military service no longer functioned properly. Eligible men, explained historian Edward Lengel, "ignored the call to enlist, and county

40 Stephen E. Haller, *William Washington: Cavalryman of the Revolution* (Bowie, MD, 2001), 32.

41 Wright, *Army*, 104-107. Unfortunately, strength returns do not indicate the number and types of guns possessed by the Continentals

42 Lefkowitz, *Indispensable Men*, xvi-xvii, 76-77.

officials, who for years had neglected elementary record-keeping, did not know who lived under their jurisdictions." It was within this context that Washington was tasked with raising a force to defend the Virginia frontier. "Washington," continued Lengel, who was a Provincial officer during the French and Indian War, "sulked for two weeks . . . waiting futilely for men to answer his call, before giving up and returning . . . in humiliation."[43]

Washington's experience as commander of the Virginia provincial regiment contributed to his belief in the necessity of an established, well-trained military force. He believed soldiers fought best within the European system, which was characterized by professional management, supply stockpiles, plentiful transportation, and high standards for training and discipline. Washington was wise enough to know that there were ways to use militia effectively, but professional soldiers ruled the battlefield.[44]

In June 1775, after being named commander-in-chief by Congress, Washington rode to the outskirts of Boston and found himself face-to-face with the militia issue once more. The Virginian "quickly discovered that commonly no one gave or obeyed any orders," observed historian James Flexner. "The militiamen, having elected their officers, expected due subservience to the sovereign voters." Washington's experience with the militia during and after the New York Campaign of 1776 did nothing to alter his low opinion of them. Their conduct disgusted Washington, whose desire for an army of professionals increased. Depending upon one-year enlistments and militia, he believed, was a recipe for failure.[45]

On September 25, 1776, Washington wrote a scathing letter to John Hancock. "To place any dependence upon militia is assuredly, resting upon a broken staff," Washington informed the president of the Continental Congress, before moving on to justify his reasoning:

> Men just dragged from the tender Scenes of domestick life, unaccustomed to the din of Arms; totally unacquainted with every kind of Military skill, which being followed by a want of confidence in themselves, when opposed to Troops regularly trained, disciplined, and appointed, superior in knowledge, and superior in Arms, make them timid, and ready to fly

43 Lengel, *Washington*, 30-31.

44 Ibid., 61-62.

45 Flexner, *Indispensable*, 68; Arthur S. Lefkowitz, *The Long Retreat: The Calamitous American Defense of New Jersey, 1776* (New Brunswick, NJ, 1999), 11-12.

> from their own Shadows. The Jealousies of a standing Army, and the Evils to be apprehended from one, are remote, and in my judgment, situated and circumstanced as we are, not at all to be dreaded.

Ultimately, concluded Washington, "If I was called upon to declare upon Oath, whether the Militia have been most serviceable or hurtful upon the whole, I should subscribe to the latter."[46]

One major issue with militia was the system of rotation practiced by most colonies. A portion of eligible men left for the front at a given time, but rotated home after a few weeks or months and were replaced by others. What little discipline and training had been instilled within these men was lost when they rotated back home. Additionally, most of them had never seen combat before joining the army, whatever experience they gained during a campaign or battle was lost when they left the front. It was a vexing cycle that taxed the patience of the commander-in-chief. "Men who have been free and subject to no controul, cannot be reduced to order in an Instant," complained Washington, "and the Priviledges and exemptions they claim and will have, Influence the Conduct of others, and the aid derived from them is nearly counterbalanced by the disorder, irregularity and confusion they Occasion."[47]

When Washington withdrew from New York and entered New Jersey in 1776, hope rose that the New Jersey militia would rise to support the army. Such was not the case, explained historian Arthur Lefkowitz, for New Jersey's militia was poorly organized and weak. Few were willing to leave their homes and families unprotected, and fewer still turned out to support Washington. Most New Jersey men at that time would not even turn out to defend their own colony.[48]

The American militia, wrote Edward Lowell, were "in some respects, more like the clans of Scotch Highlanders in the civil wars of the seventeenth and eighteenth centuries than like modern soldiers. They came or went, as patriotism or selfishness, enthusiasm or discouragement, succeeded each other in their breasts." Even though they were "often intrepid in battle, they were subject to panics, like all undisciplined troops," he continued, "and were such uncomfortable customers to

46 Philander D. Chase and Frank E. Grizzard, Jr., eds., *The Papers of George Washington*, Revolutionary War Series, 25 vols. (Charlottesville and London, 1994), vol. 6, 396-397.

47 Fitzpatrick, *Writings*, vol. 6, 5-6.

48 Lefkowitz, *Retreat*, 55-6.

deal with that it was equally unsafe for their generals to trust them or for their enemies to despise them."[49]

After the Battle of Princeton Washington openly decried the militia's sense of independence and lack of discipline—attributes that infuriated him. "They come and go when they please," he complained to Jonathan Trumbull on March 6. Washington again stressed the importance of building a strong professional army that would be large enough to make militia obsolete for the coming year. His complaints fell on mostly deaf ears.[50]

Once Washington rebuilt his army during the spring of 1777 and set out to face Howe in the campaign to take Philadelphia, it became clear that militia once more would play a major role in the undertaking. Congress passed a resolution recommending that Maryland call out 2,000 men and Delaware another 1,000, and resolved that Pennsylvania collect 4,000 of its militia to help repel the threatened attack against the colonial capital. Virginia, too, was expected to send militia to help the cause.[51]

Their poor reputation preceded the arrival of Pennsylvania's militiamen. Due to the longstanding influence of Quakerism on the Pennsylvania Assembly, the colony had no official militia system prior to or during the early months of the Revolution. Militia was notoriously ill-trained and poorly disciplined, but these problems were compounded in Pennsylvania. The New Jersey militia may have been considered next to worthless, but the Pennsylvania militia was even worse. The Pennsylvania Militia Act, passed on March 17, 1777, called for obligatory military service for the first time since the French and Indian War. The legislation required service from all white males between the ages of 18 and 53 able to bear arms. The act exempted Congressional delegates, members of the Executive Council, judges of the Supreme Court, masters and faculty of colleges, ministers of the gospel, and servants. Militiamen organized into companies within their respective counties. Eight companies formed a battalion. Under the Act, militia units were to train regularly, and when absenteeism became a problem, members would be fined for missing training. The Act included a provision that allowed the Executive Council to activate portions of the militia in the event of invasion. The

49 Edward J. Lowell, *The Hessians and the Other German Auxiliaries of Great Britain in the Revolutionary War* (Gansevoort, NY, 1997), 290-291.

50 Frank E. Grizzard, ed., *The Papers of George Washington*, Revolutionary War Series, 25 vols. (Charlottesville, VA and London, 1998), vol. 8, 531-32.

51 Hazard, et al., eds., *Archives*, Series 1, vol. 5, 539.

period of active duty was limited to a mere 60 days. "Instead of the Country rising for their defence & surrounding & harassing the Enemy in every Movement," complained Congressman Eliphalet Dyer of Connecticut to Commissary General Joseph Trumbull on September 28, "the Militia which were Collected have principally run off & left the General [Washington] with his Continental forces to shurk for himself."[52]

By the time Washington arrived on Methacton Hill outside Germantown, a powerful undercurrent of distrust existed within the army toward anything having to do with the militia. Three states forwarded a total of 3,100 militia to Washington before the move toward Germantown. The largest contingent, about one-half, was comprised of Maj. Gen. John Armstrong's Pennsylvanians. Armstrong's 1,500 men contributed little besides their mere physical presence at Brandywine, where most fled without firing a shot. Now, in early October, Armstrong was going into battle at Germantown with about half the force he had commanded at Brandywine, but one-third of it was still operating south of the Schuylkill River. Brigadier General William Smallwood herded 1,000 Marylanders into the army camps. Smallwood had left Maryland with double that number, but at least half of his force had deserted in the aftermath of Paoli. The final contingent consisted of Brig. Gen. David Forman and his 600 New Jersey militia, together with his own understrength Additional Continental Regiment.[53]

Thus was the mixed American force that mustered itself west of Germantown to meet Howe's professional army. The motley collection of manpower included many talented and experienced officers and men within its ranks, but the militia, with their questionable organization, leadership, and training, remained shaky at best. Most were dedicated to Washington as commander-in-chief, but their attachment to the national cause, in competition with colonial, local, and family

52 Samuel J. Newland, *The Pennsylvania Militia: The Early Years, 1669-1792* (Annville, PA, 1997), 146-7; Smith, et al., eds., *Letters*, vol. 8, 24.

53 These men often came and went on their own, and how many would be in the ranks on a given day was unpredictable. The Maryland militia battalions were provisional organizations of varying sizes. Maryland's policy called out several classes from each battalion of a county and assembled them into provisional battalions. No undue burden was therefore placed on any particular county. New Jersey and Pennsylvania had similar polices. Forman's Regiment was formed in early 1777 and was largely recruited in New Jersey, with particular ties to Forman's home county of Monmouth. The regiment was constantly understrength and probably only had about 40 men in its ranks at Germantown. The unit likely received captured British uniforms of red coats faced with buff intended for the 31st Regiment of Foot. Waistcoats and breeches appear to have come from the same source and would have been buff.

concerns, was at best thin. Supply deficiencies and distractions in camp and back home vexed the soldiers. No one, least of all Washington, had any real idea how this iteration of the Continental Army would perform when facing professionals in scarlet uniforms and perfect ranks tramping toward them with bayonets fixed. But Washington was sure about one thing: He was about to ask these men to undertake their first offensive against the main British army in North America.

Chapter 9

The British Army

October 3, 1777

"Officers and soldiers became known to each other; they had been engaged in a more serious manner, and with greater disadvantages than they were likely again to meet with in the common chance of war."[1]

— Capt. John Simcoe, Queen's Rangers, October 20, 1777

While there were similarities between William Howe's professional European army deployed around Philadelphia and Washington's American command, the differences were striking.

Great Britain had all the material advantages. The population of the 13 colonies hovered around 2.5 million in 1775, including 500,000 mostly enslaved African Americans. In contrast, the British home isles were home to eleven million souls, 48,000 of whom served in the standing army. The Royal Navy boasted 139 war vessels in various states of disrepair; nearly all were shorthanded. The outbreak of war brought with it a massive recruiting campaign. The British military establishment was one of the first global bureaucracies. Separate departments

1 John Simcoe, *Simcoe's Military Journal: A History of the Operations of a Partisan Corps, Called the Queen's Rangers, Commanded by Lieut. Col. J.G. Simcoe, During the War of the American Revolution* (New York, 1844), 17-18.

existed for barracks, boatmen, commissaries, engineers, hospitals, ordnance, and quartermasters. Officers worked long hours filling out endless detailed reports.[2]

Like their American counterparts, most British soldiers wanted to be in the army because of its promise of adventure and the supposed attractions that came with a military life. This was not an army of outcasts and criminals. Many were farmers, weavers, and laborers with clean records. Prior to 1775, soldiers enlisted for life, and most were veterans of long service in faraway places—every one of them fiercely proud of their regiments. Recruiting during wartime was often difficult, so the British offered three-year enlistments to fill the ranks. When the line regiments arrived in North America in 1776, recruiting parties left behind forwarded replacements throughout the war.[3]

The regiment was the basic unit of the British Army. "Regiment," however, was an administrative rather than a tactical term. The administrative commander of a regiment was its colonel, with whom the King contracted to raise and equip the organization. Except for the Royal regiments, the colonels owned their commands and intended, as one noted historian explained, to "profit financially and socially from that species of property by selling commissions, receiving a bounty for each recruit, negotiating lucrative contracts for uniforms, and retaining for each colonel the captaincy of one company." The financial logistics of running a regiment guaranteed some level of corruption. The government provided the colonel with an annual sum intended to pay the soldiers, buy clothing for the regiment, and enlist replacements. Any remaining money found its way into the colonel's pocket. In the field, colonels also often held the rank of general. Generals did not have a pay scale, so the salary of each general officer depended on his being the colonel of a regiment, which did not have to be part of his command.[4]

While "regiment" was the administrative term for British army units, in tactical terms the unit was called a "battalion." The terms are synonymous for purposes of discussing eighteenth-century operations since virtually every British regiment consisted of a single battalion. Because colonels often functioned as generals in

2 Fischer, *Crossing*, 34.

3 Ibid., 39.

4 Luzader, *Saratoga*, 226. Examples of Royal regiments included the 1st (Royal) Regiment of Foot and 4th (King's Own) Regiment of Foot, as opposed to the non-Royal 10th Regiment and others. Royal regiments bore the names of the monarch or other members of the Royal family.

field armies, they did not physically command their regiments on campaign. Normally this privilege was borne by the regiment's lieutenant colonel.[5]

Prior to the Revolution, the British army was composed of 70 regiments of foot (infantry). With the onset of war, the army was expanded by creating new regiments and adding battalions to existing regiments. In October 1775, the British government directed that every regiment in America or slated for service there be enlarged to provide stronger units for field service and to "enhance the recruiting and training infrastructure to accommodate wartime attrition." By the end of the war, 105 regiments were on the rolls.[6]

Every British regiment was composed of eight battalion companies and two flank companies. One flank company was composed of grenadiers, and the other of light infantry. On paper each full-strength regiment consisted of a colonel, a lieutenant colonel, a major, nine captains, 14 lieutenants, 10 ensigns, one chaplain, an adjutant, a quartermaster, a surgeon and his mate, 36 sergeants, 36 corporals, 24 drummers, two fifers, and 672 privates, all for a grand total of 811 men. Every regiment was understrength because of attrition, illness, and other factors. Enlisted soldiers wore black shoes with brass buckles, with heavy linen half or full gaiters over the top. Their breeches and waistcoats were of white linen or wool.

Howe's decisions were shaped by the need to preserve his army's fighting capacity. It was difficult to replace troops lost in battle, especially so far from the home country. The mechanism for replacements in Great Britain was archaic, and the 3,000-mile Atlantic voyage consumed both time and lives. The revulsion Howe experienced as a witness to the bloody frontal assaults against Breed's Hill explains his repeated use of flanking movements thereafter. The difficulty inherent in replacing veteran troops in the eighteenth century caused considerable concern amongst general officers, who strove to avoid unnecessarily losing troops through sickness and desertion, or by exposing them to short rations or inclement weather. This conservative mindset, in turn, limited field mobility, tying armies to magazines, bread ovens, and baggage trains.[7]

5 Luzader, *Saratoga*, 226.

6 Don N. Hagist, comp., *British Soldiers, American War: Voices of the American Revolution* (Yardley, PA, 2012), 11.

7 Spring, *With Zeal*, 9.

Battalion Companies

Privates in the battalion companies were armed with the 10-pound flintlock known as the Brown Bess. Most American and British soldiers carried this smoothbore musket, which fired a large .75 caliber lead ball and sported a 17-inch bayonet that made it a fearsome close-quarters weapon, but diminished its already limited accuracy. A dozen separate motions were required to fire the weapon. The soldier ripped away one end of a paper cartridge with his teeth, sprinkled a small amount of black powder into the priming pan, and used his ramrod to seat the cartridge and ball down the muzzle. A well-trained soldier could get off at least two and as many as three shots a minute under combat conditions. A mounted bayonet made the loading process even more difficult, and many soldiers could only depend upon a single effective shot per minute. The inaccuracy of the musket made volleys a preferred method of fire delivery, and the difficulty in loading was one of the reasons the British made the bayonet charge their primary assault tactic.[8]

There is a common misconception that the British army fought in rigid lines of battle, arrayed shoulder-to-shoulder. Each line of battle consisted of two ranks (with a small interval between each) with the men formed in open order about arm's-length apart. Even in open order, however, the men were not spread out to the extent they operated independently. They presented a solid mass (and thus a ready target) and delivered volleys at a similarly compact enemy formation, often at point-blank range. The first two ranks were responsible for delivering the battalion's firepower. Six paces behind them stood a rank of file closers ready to step up and fill gaps created by the wounded and the dead.

Since it was desirable to withhold firing until within 50 yards of an enemy line, maintaining fire discipline was essential. The prevailing professional opinion espoused that it was better to receive rather than deliver the initial round of fire, and thus sustain some level of casualties so that when the fire was returned, one's own men were near enough for every shot to find its mark. This required strict combat discipline, and this type of fire training was the British army's greatest attribute.[9]

British soldiers rarely picked individual targets and fired at their own pace. Instead, the men loaded and fired on command at an enemy line. Smoothbore

8 Luzader, *Saratoga*, 224.

9 Ibid..

muskets were inaccurate beyond 50 yards and there was little interest in target practice, since the cost of lead and powder was not worth the expense and time. When a battalion delivered a volley, the "objective was to lay down a curtain of fire ahead of one's troops at the desired rate of one shot every fifteen or twenty seconds, assuring at least two volleys before closing with the enemy," explained one historian. "The men then resorted to clubbing with their muskets or stabbing with the bayonet, with which the British were famously effective."[10]

Specific accuracy may have been superfluous, but organized and controlled speed in both firing and movement was essential. The faster the defenders could load and fire, the more damage they could inflict upon the approaching enemy. The faster the attackers could close with the enemy while simultaneously maintaining unit cohesion, the fewer casualties they would sustain and the stronger they would be when they reached their objective. Since cartridge boxes could only hold 30 or fewer rounds, uncontrolled fire would quickly exhaust the limited ammunition supply. Once firing began, the thick black powder smoke that enveloped the battlefield made it even harder for officers to maintain effective control of their men. The beating drums and tooting fifes, coupled with flags waving above the center of the battalion, could be heard and seen above the chaos, and helped maintain control.[11]

The strict discipline and harsh living conditions that made life difficult for the average British soldier also molded him into a well-trained and formidable opponent. The monotonous and repetitive drill created a soldier who reacted to orders with predictable speed and precision. British generals lost several battles during the American Revolution, but not because of a lack of discipline in their ranks.

The officers who led these men achieved their positions through either social rank or money. Officers purchased commissions, rising through the ranks from subaltern to colonel, requiring either the death of an officer, an officer's retirement, or the sponsorship of a higher-ranking officer or government patron. Many officers owed their position to someone else. This system created officers devoutly loyal to certain colonels or generals, but who sometimes undermined others within the army. Military competence played little role in the promotion of officers. Officer corps service was a respectable career that offered both status and the

10 Luzader, *Saratoga*, 224-225.

11 Ibid., 225.

potential for advancement. Some historians have noted that the purchase system was "institutionalized corruption, but its purpose was to ensure that British officers had a stake in their society and were not dangerous to its institutions." This system, argued David Hackett Fischer, "kept the army firmly in the hands of Britain's governing elite, mainly its small aristocracy, who controlled much of the wealth and power in the nation."[12]

Officers rarely criticized their colleagues in public, choosing instead to have political patrons do the dirty work for them, thereby mixing partisan politics with military affairs. Senior commanders often ignored the chain of command and communicated directly with political and government officials.[13]

British officers had no official schooling. Although well-read in military literature, they obtained the vital knowledge of their profession through experience. Senior sergeants supported young subalterns in their companies who were learning the ropes during their teenage years, proving the old adage that sergeants are the backbone of any army. Most officers entered the army as young amateurs and learned to handle their commands in combat. They took their obligations seriously and compiled impressive service records. "Combine purchase rank with political influence, and it should come as no surprise that the system pinned epaulets on its share of fops and blockheads, though it also provided the army with generally competent leadership," argued the historians of the Monmouth campaign.[14]

Flank Companies and Additional Units

The elite soldiers of the eighteenth-century were assigned to the flank companies of their regiments. Throughout most of the Revolution, flank companies rarely served with their parent regiments and instead "brigaded" together to form battalions of light infantry or grenadiers, depriving the regiments of their best men. To offset this practice, the battalion companies supplied reinforcements to the flank companies.[15]

12 Martin and Lender, "*Army*," 13; Fischer, *Crossing*, 34.

13 Lender and Stone, *Fatal Sunday*, 55.

14 Pancake, *1777*, 71-72; Lender and Stone, *Fatal Sunday*, 55-56.

15 Wright, *Army*, 48.

The tallest and strongest men in the regiment made up grenadier companies. Originally, their function was to throw primitive grenades into fortifications, but grenades were no longer in use by the Revolution. The grenadier's uniform included a short sword and a tall bearskin cap instead of the cocked hats worn by the battalion men. The light infantry company consisted of fit men who functioned as rangers or scouts. They cut their coats short (for fast movement and to avoid entanglement in rough terrain), wore leather caps and red waistcoats, and carried small cartridge boxes and hatchets.

Like their comrades, grenadiers and light infantrymen were armed with muskets, although at least some British light infantry were armed with short rifles. Only a small number of these weapons were sent to North America, and there is evidence that each light company received some, though not enough to arm the entire company. While only a few British light troops were so armed, all of the Hessian jaegers (the German equivalent of light infantry) were armed with short jaeger rifles.

A corps of guides and pioneers under Maj. Samuel Holland moved at the front of the marching army to clear obstructions. Holland's corps of 172 men was equipped with axes, saws, and shovels in addition to muskets; they wore heavy leather aprons, gloves, and leather caps, and were permitted to grow beards. A significant number were of African descent.[16]

Artillery

The British organized their field artillery into four battalions of eight companies each. Each company consisted of six officers, eight noncommissioned officers, nine bombardiers, 18 gunners, and 73 matrosses (or privates). The British artillery system was somewhat unique in that the gunners and matrosses were enlisted men, but the drivers were hired civilians. The 4th Battalion of the Royal Artillery Regiment was deployed to the colonies in 1775. Hard service over the next two years reduced the strength of the battalion, and 300 Loyalists from New York were recruited when it became difficult to find suitable replacements. Howe took all eight companies to Pennsylvania.[17]

16 McGuire, *Campaign*, vol. 1, 140.

17 Lender and Stone, *Fatal Sunday*, 53-54.

The men of the Royal Artillery were clothed in dark blue rather than the traditional red, and artillery officers were promoted through merit rather than through the purchase of commissions. Given the scientific aspects of artillery, its officers were among the most highly trained in the service. The Woolwich Military Academy taught mathematics, engineering, and chemistry to prospective artillery officers. Artillerymen were armed with carbines, which were shorter and lighter versions of an infantryman's musket. Fusilier regiments, such as the 23rd of Foot (Royal Welch Fusiliers), were originally formed to escort artillery, but served as infantry in North America.[18]

Field guns ranged in size from large 24-pounders to small 3-pounders. The latter light brass cannons became popular for their mobility in the rough terrain of North America. Developed by William Congreve and James Pattison, these light guns could be moved by pack horses or by eight men. Since 12-pounders required many horses to haul them, and maintaining horses in North America was difficult, the British preferred 6-pounders and 9-pounders. It was customary to allot two guns (known as "battalion guns") to each infantry regiment. Some officers criticized this practice because it spread the guns out and prevented concentration of fire on a single point, position, or objective.[19]

The maximum range of the most powerful piece in the British artillery was about 2,000 yards, but no field gun was considered effective beyond 1,200 yards (and many of the smaller caliber much less than that). The guns were capable of firing solid shot, grape, or canister.[20]

Most field pieces delivered their fire on a fairly flat trajectory. Howitzers, however, fired projectiles along a high arc, which made them effective for lobbing shells over entrenchments or walls. The howitzer's shorter barrel reduced its effective range of fire.[21]

18 Pancake, *1777*, 68; Edward E. Curtis, *The British Army in the American Revolution* (Gansevoort, NY, 1998), 6-7; O'Donnell, *Immortals*, 43; Fischer, *Crossing*, 37. When matchlocks were common in the British infantry, fusilier regiments were armed with flintlocks, or *fusils* in French.

19 O'Donnell, *Immortals*, 43-44; Fischer, *Crossing*, 37.

20 Artillerymen used solid shot against fortifications or opposing artillery. Grapeshot consisted of clusters of iron balls about two inches in diameter, which either devastated infantry or knocked down fence lines or hedges. Canister, a container filled with musket balls, was an effective anti-personnel weapon.

21 Pancake, *1777*, 68-69.

Cavalry

The British had heavy cavalry within its service, but North American terrain precluded its use. As a result, light cavalry in the form of the 16th and 17th Light Dragoons were dispatched to America. Only the 16th was with Howe during most of the Philadelphia Campaign. Each regiment consisted of six troops (the equivalent of an infantry company), each of which contained three officers, four noncommissioned officers, and 38 privates. Few of these units were at full strength.[22]

Support

Regulations called for the British army operating in North America to be provisioned from England. The most important provisions included beef, pork, bread, flour, oatmeal, rice, peas, butter, and salt. Less important provisions, such as cheese, bacon, suet, fish, raisins, and molasses, also found their way to the colonies. Many types of vegetables, including potatoes, parsnips, carrots, turnips, cabbages, and onions, also were dispatched by sea, although they were not always fresh or edible when they reached the men at the front. Most of these vegetables were intended for soldiers recovering in hospitals. Onions, sauerkraut, porter, claret, spruce beer, malt, vinegar, celery seed, and brown mustard seed were used as anti-scorbutics to help ward off scurvy.

Commissary generals complained of moldy bread, biscuits teeming with insects, rancid butter, rotten flour, worm-eaten peas, and maggot-ridden beef. Not surprisingly, men frequently attempted to supplement their diet by foraging (or outright looting) in the countryside, which led to depredations against civilians.[23]

By 1777, the British high command hoped the army would no longer need to be reliant on supplies from Great Britain, but the army's commissary general often noted that North America could not be depended upon for supplies. The alternative was the provision train. "No eighteenth-century commander raised in the European tradition would think of taking the field without such a train," explained R. Arthur Bowler, historian of British logistics during the Revolution. "Armies of the period tended to be small and expensive to the point that even

22 Wright, *Army*, 105.

23 Curtis, *Army*, 88 93.

victories attended by considerable losses were unacceptable. Aware of the problems of health and morale that accompanied poor and short rations, few commanders willingly trusted the feeding of their armies to the chance that sufficient food could be obtained along the line of march." Simply put, long provision trains were a necessity.[24]

Daniel Wier, Howe's commissary general, knew from experience that depending on North American supplies rather than on shipments from England was less than ideal. He had served as a commissary official in Germany during the Seven Years' War and in the East and West Indies, where he learned armies could live well off the land in Europe, but the Americas were an altogether different proposition. Many of the provisions he brought from New York for Howe's army were spoiled. Of the 2,000 bags of bread landed with the army, "300 were condemned as unfit for Men to eat and of the 254 Bags carried on the March 50 or 60 were left on the way on the same Account." Rats and other vermin damaged or destroyed much of the food, while careless storage damaged other provisions. Obtaining fresh supplies from the countryside was critical to the health and well-being of Howe's men.[25]

Provision trains required healthy horses in large numbers, which in turn required tons of fodder—a precious commodity the British sought to obtain from the countryside, which in turn required even more horses to haul it. Howe estimated he would need at least 3,662 horses, and all their requisite supplies, for his Philadelphia campaign. Exactly how many horses he left with from New York is unknown, but we do know many died and many more became ill during the difficult voyage to the Chesapeake. The mobile workshops of blacksmiths, carpenters, harness-makers, and other tradesmen also required draft horses.[26]

Howe's army was forced to sit idle several times during the campaign while foragers roamed the countryside seeking food and horses. Even though Washington issued orders to clear supplies out of Howe's path, there was not enough time to strip the countryside bare. As a result, since landing at the Head of

24 R. Arthur Bowler, *Logistics and the Failure of the British Army in America, 1775-1783* (Princeton, NJ, 1975), 49, 55-56.

25 Daniel Wier to John Robinson, October 25, 1777, "Copies of Letters from Danl. Wier, Esq., Commissary to the Army in America, to J. Robinson, Esq., Secretary to the Lords Commissioners of the Treasury; and from John Robinson, Esq., in Answer thereto in the Year 1777," Dreer Collection, Historical Society of Pennsylvania, Philadelphia, PA, case 36.

26 Bowler, *Logistics*, 58.

Elk, the army had been issued fresh provisions from the well-developed farms of Pennsylvania every other day.[27]

By the time of the American Revolution, England had long had a standing army, and had long recognized the need for a different kind of support system for it. Each company had an authorized quota of women. The return for the British army in New York for May 1777 showed one woman present for every eight men in the ranks. The presence of women reduced desertions, and they performed work like mending, cooking, nursing, and laundering. The women who accompanied the army to North America were supposed to be the wives of enlisted soldiers (wives of officers rarely accompanied them on campaign). The marital statuses of these women were questionable, for proof of a legal marriage was not always required. The women traveled with the baggage wagons on the march and did not accompany the men directly.[28]

German Auxiliaries

In an attempt to bolster the British war effort, King George III hired German forces to serve with his army. Great Britain was a global empire, with military commitments across the world in places like Gibraltar, India, Canada, the Caribbean, the American colonies, and of course, the home islands. British military manpower was stretched to its limits when the American Revolution began in 1775.

The German soldiers sent to North America were not mercenaries in the traditional sense, but rather armies from another country hired for use in the colonies. The soldiers were not paid by Great Britain directly and received nothing more than their regular army pay and rations. Instead, England paid the various German princes for the use of their troops. German officers commanded the German soldiers, and they were not subject to British military discipline.[29]

Six German rulers hired out their soldiers to Great Britain: Frederick II, Landgrave of Hesse-Cassel; William, his son, the independent Count of Hesse-Hanau; Charles I, Duke of Brunswick; Frederick, Prince of Waldeck; Charles Alexander, Margrave of Anspach-Bayreuth; and Frederick Augustus,

27 Bowler, *Logistics*, 58-59, 70.

28 Curtis, *British* Army, 10-11; Hagist, *British Soldiers American War*, 148-149.

29 Fischer, *Crossing*, 63-65.

Prince of Anhalt-Zerbst. Because the German troops sent to North America hailed from separate principalities, they were not all "Hessians," though traditionally they have been referred to by that name. All but one company of jaegers who fought at Germantown were true Hessians.[30]

One reason George III was able to acquire these troops was because he was from the royal house of Hanover. Frederick II (not to be confused with his more famous namesake), of Hesse-Cassel, was married to George's sister. William, the oldest son of Frederick II, not only was the grandson of George II, but was also the ruler of Hesse-Hanau. Duke Charles I of Brunswick had his son, Prince Charles William Ferdinand, marry another of George's sisters. Beyond family obligations, Charles Alexander of Anspach-Bayreuth was so deeply in debt that he felt compelled to supply troops to England. The princes of Waldeck were known to raise soldiers for use by other countries, so providing men to England was merely an extension of an existing program. Frederick Augustus of Anhalt-Zerbst sent only a small number of men, most of whom had to be recruited from other provinces.[31]

The British Parliament was not overly enthusiastic about hiring auxiliary troops, and protests erupted in the House of Lords. The arguments expressed the supposed danger and disgrace of the foreign treaties involved, which acknowledged to all Europe that Great Britain was unable, either from want of men or their disinclination toward the intended service, to furnish enough natural-born subjects for the campaign. Others felt it better to send more foreign troops rather than drawing off the national troops and leaving Britain exposed to potential assaults and invasions by powerful foreign nations, particularly France and Spain. There was another side to the argument. "We have, moreover, just reason to apprehend that when the colonies come to understand that Great Britain is forming alliances, and hiring foreign troops for their destruction," came one Parliamentary protest, "they may think they are well justified by the example, in endeavoring to avail themselves of the like assistance; and that France, Spain, Prussia, or other powers of Europe may conceive that they have as good a right as Hesse, Brunswick, and Hanau to interfere in our domestic quarrels."[32]

30 Lowell, *Hessians*, 5-21.

31 Ibid.

32 Ibid., 30-31.

Unlike their British counterparts, Hessian officers were well trained. They attended Collegium Carolinum to study languages, engineering, and mathematics, becoming experts in military cartography, tactics, and logistics. Promotion was achieved through merit and often in the field for outstanding service. Many of the officers boasted years of field experience.[33]

Enlisted Hessians were recruited in a process designed to serve the needs of their rulers. Those whose civil occupations were deemed indispensable, including skilled artisans, farmers owning more than fifty acres, and anyone making a major contribution to the economy, were exempted from service. Everyone else was encouraged to enlist, especially the sons of poor peasant families. Jaegers tended to be sons of gamekeepers and foresters, while most artillerymen grew up in the cities as sons of industrial workers. Soldiers were paid more than servants and unskilled farm workers, thus encouraging enlistment. Military families were exempted from onerous taxes. Others, like school dropouts, bankrupt tradesmen, and the unemployed, were all but forced into the army.[34]

Unlike British soldiers, Hessians were eligible for prize money from seizures made while on campaign, which encouraged plundering of the countryside. Contributing to this practice was the need for rations. If a Hessian ate British-issued rations, money was deducted from his pay. If that same Hessian sought forage in the countryside, his pay was not docked.[35]

Both British and Hessian regiments were short of officers, which affected their command and control in battle. British regiments did not have enough officers in part because of the American habit of targeting officers in battle, but illness and exhaustion associated with campaigning also took a toll. Hessian regiments were organized with a higher soldier-to-officer ratio, which put them at an immediate disadvantage. Sickness and battle casualties also took their toll on the regiments. Replacing both officers and men was difficult at best with more than 3,000 miles separating them from home.[36]

33 Fischer, *Crossing*, 55.

34 Ibid., 59-60.

35 Ibid., 64.

36 Ibid., 152.

Howe's Staff

Much like the staff Washington assembled, a select group of officers served William Howe. Chief among them were Brig. Gen. James Paterson (adjutant general), Brig. Gen. Samuel Cleaveland (chief of artillery), and Brig. Gen. William Erskine (quartermaster general).[37]

By early October 1777, managing the army was a difficult proposition. Howe needed to maintain contact with the New York City garrison and other detachments in North America while simultaneously spreading his own army out in the Delaware River valley. The garrison at Germantown, for example, consisted of two nominal divisions and several detached units serving on outpost duty. Charles Cornwallis commanded the garrison at Philadelphia (which did not include Germantown), and two smaller garrison forces were posted at Wilmington, Delaware, and Chester, Pennsylvania. Unlike Washington, Howe had thus far had suffered relatively light casualties during the campaign and could still field a respectable force of about 15,000 men. Because of the detachments necessary to manage long supply lines, however, about 6,000 of that number were not in Germantown on the morning Washington decided to attack.[38]

37 Howe's staff also included Lt. Col. Stephen Kemble (deputy adjutant general); Captain Henry Bruen (deputy quartermaster general); Daniel Wier (commissary general); Capt. John Montresor (chief engineer); Capt. Archibald Robertson (engineer); and Capt. Robert McKenzie (military secretary). Six aides served Howe at Germantown: Majs. Cornelius Cuyler, Nesbitt Balfour, and William Gardiner, and Capts. Henry Fox, Henry Knight, and Friedrich von Muenchausen. Stephen Kemble had been promoted to major in 1772 and later became deputy adjutant general of British forces in North America. General Erskine was responsible for the army's non-nutritional needs, from tents, camp kettles, and rope, to candles, shovels, and pickaxes. However, his most important duty was procuring wagons to transport the army's needs. Bowler, *Logistics*, 25. Before becoming the adjutant general in April 1776, Brig. Gen. Paterson had been the lieutenant colonel of the 63rd Regiment of Foot. Robert McKenzie was a captain in the 43rd Regiment of Foot; Cornelius Cuyler was the major of the 55th Regiment of Foot; Henry Bruen was a captain in the 63rd Regiment of Foot; Nesbitt Balfour was the major of the 4th Regiment of Foot; Henry Fox was a captain in the 38th Regiment of Foot; William Gardiner was the major of the 45th Regiment of Foot; and Henry Knight was a captain in the 43rd Regiment of Foot.

38 Strengths are based on commissary reports following the landing at Head of Elk a little over two weeks prior to the Brandywine fight. See "Copies of Letters from Danl. Wier." From these reports, losses for the campaign through early October 1777 are factored to create the strength estimates in this study. One unit with the army was 75 New Jersey Volunteers. Earlier in the campaign, they marched with the baggage train. It is unclear if the baggage train remained at Germantown or had moved into Philadelphia with Cornwallis. Therefore, it is not certain where the New Jersey Loyalists were located during the Battle of Germantown.

British Outposts

Approximately 1,600 men were detached from the main Germantown garrison and positioned along the roads leading out from town. These "buffer" units were the closest to Washington's lurking army. The outposts were manned by both battalions of the British Light Infantry Brigade, Lt. Col. Thomas Musgrave's 40th Regiment of Foot, and Maj. James Wemys's Queen's Rangers.

The light infantry brigade was composed of the 1st and 2nd British Light Infantry Battalions. These battalions were formed by brigading together the various light infantry companies from regiments stationed in North America. The 1st Light Infantry Battalion, commanded by Lt. Col. Sir Robert Abercrombie of the 37th Regiment of Foot, was composed of the light companies of the following Regiments of Foot: 4th, 5th, 7th, 10th, 15th, 17th, 22nd, 23rd, 27th, 28th, 33rd, 35th, and 38th. The 2nd Light Infantry Battalion, under Maj. John Maitland of the Royal Marines, was composed of the light companies of the 37th, 40th, 42nd, 43rd, 44th, 45th, 46th, 49th, 52nd, 54th, 55th, 57th, 63rd, and 64th Foot, and two companies from the 71st. One unit no longer with Howe's army was the detachment of riflemen that had fought under Patrick Ferguson at Brandywine. After Ferguson was severely wounded there, Howe dispersed the command into the light infantry battalions. These men took their Ferguson rifles with them and could fire up to six shots a minute.

Flank battalions in general and light infantry battalions in particular were filled with battle-hardened veterans who had seen severe and successful service in the army. British officers were proud to serve in the light companies. William Dansey of the 33rd Regiment of Foot wrote his mother that he considered the light infantry "the most dangerous and difficult Service of this War, therefore you will rejoice with me in my good Fortune in being able to do my Duty as a Soldier in a line that must be of infinite Service to me here after, for the Preference in all Promotions is given to Light Infantry Officers." The light infantry battalions saw hard service at Brandywine, and the 2nd Light Infantry Battalion had stormed Wayne's camp at Paoli, though it suffered only minor casualties in doing so. They were down about 100 men by the time Germantown became a name to remember.[39]

While the 40th Regiment of Foot saw relatively little action in Pennsylvania, the Queen's Rangers—also detached from the main Germantown garrison—had

39 Spring, *With Zeal*, 62; William Dansey to Mrs. Dansey, letter dated March 15, 1777, original in the William Dansey Letters, the Delaware Historical Society, Wilmington, Delaware.

lost a quarter of its strength at Brandywine. Little is known about James Wemys other than that he was a captain in the 40th Regiment of Foot and commanded the Queen's Rangers at Germantown. The Rangers were Americans recruited in 1776 from the Loyalist population to serve the British. The government clad British regiments in the scarlet red coats for which they are famous, but the Queen's Rangers wore distinctive green jackets with white breeches.[40]

John Simcoe assumed command of the Queen's Rangers eleven days after Germantown. The Rangers, he explained, had "suffered materially in the action at Brandywine, and [were] too much reduced in numbers to be of any efficient service [at Germantown]. [B]ut if the loss of a great number of gallant officers and soldiers had been severely felt," he continued,

> the impression which that action had left upon their minds was of the highest advantage to the regiment; officers and soldiers became known to each other; they had been engaged in a more serious manner, and with greater disadvantages than they were likely again to meet with in the common chance of war; and having extricated themselves most gallantly from such a situation, they felt themselves invincible.[41]

James Grant's Wing

Major General James Grant commanded 3,000 men divided between the British Brigade of Guards and the 1st and 2nd British Brigades in the Germantown garrison. Howe attached a squadron of the 16th Light Dragoons to Grant's command. Except for the British Guards, Grant's men saw relatively little combat in the campaign. The Brigade of Guards smashed John Sullivan's division at Brandywine and suffered little damage in return.[42]

The records are unclear as to who led the two British infantry brigades at Germantown. The First Brigade contained the 4th, 23rd, 28th, and 49th Regiments of Foot. The 23rd Regiment of Foot (The Royal Welch Fusiliers), however, was serving with the Philadelphia garrison, leaving the brigade shorthanded. The

40 Additional units were dressed in shades other than red. Hessian regiments were clothed in blue coats with various styles of trim. The Jaeger Corps wore green jackets faced with red.

41 Simcoe, *Journal*, 17-18. Simcoe was wounded at Brandywine and was not present at Germantown.

42 This information is based upon my own analysis of the British army following Brandywine and Archibald Robertson's map of the British camp and battlefield. Archibald Robertson manuscript map of the Battle of Germantown, Windsor Castle Collection, 734029.d.

Second Brigade contained the 5th, 10th, 27th, 40th, and 55th Regiments of Foot. Like its sister brigade, the Second brigade also was understrength because the 40th Regiment of Foot was serving with the British outposts, and the 10th Regiment of Foot was on its way back to Chester from its excursion to Billingsport.[43]

Brigadier General Edward Mathew, who commanded the British Brigade of Guards, was born in 1729 and became an ensign in the Coldstream Guards in 1746. By 1775 he was a colonel and aide-de-camp to King George III. He was made commander of the Brigade of Guards when the Revolution erupted, and fought throughout the 1776 campaign in New York. The Brigade of Guards was a special composite force made up of 1,000 men chosen by lottery from the three regiments of Foot Guards. Fifteen men from each of the Guard's 64 companies were selected to serve in America. The army had three regiments of Foot Guards during the eighteenth century: the First Guards (also known as the Grenadier Guards); the Second (the Coldstream Guards); and the Third Guards (the Scots Guards). All three were stationed in London or Westminster as bodyguards for the King. The Brigade of Guards was divided into two battalions of 500 men each and, unlike other British regiments, retained its flank companies while on campaign. The Guards functioned like a light infantry unit in America and used common-sense, flexible tactics when faced with heavy gunfire. All the Guards wore uniforms modified for campaign service, including shortened jackets without ornamentation and round hats, under which they wore cropped hair.[44]

Other than Mathew's Guards, Grant commanded a numerically weakened "division" at Germantown. If surprised and hit hard, would he have enough firepower to stop a determined assault?

Wilhelm von Knyphausen's Wing

The senior Hessian officer in North America was Lt. Gen. Wilhelm von Knyphausen, who oversaw 4,500 men at Germantown. His command was composed of the 3rd and 4th British Brigades, Lt. Col. Ludwig von Wurmb's Hessian jaegers, and a brigade of Hessian infantry. Knypahusen's command had a mixed record in the campaign. The 4th British Brigade was stopped and bloodied by Nathanael Greene's rearguard action at Brandywine, while the jaegers fought

43 Ibid.

44 Curtis, *Army*, 3.

well at both Brandywine and the Battle of the Clouds. The 44th Regiment of Foot from the 3rd British Brigade fought at Paoli, but the rest of the brigade had yet to see significant action. The Hessian infantry had been only lightly engaged.[45]

Charles Grey, commander of the 3rd Brigade, was born in 1729 in Northumberland, England. In 1744, Grey purchased a commission as ensign in the 6th Regiment of Foot and took part in suppressing the Jacobite rising the following year. Grey spent time in Gibraltar, rose to captain, and took command of a company in the 20th Regiment of Foot. During the Seven Years' War he served as an adjutant on the staff of Duke Ferdinand of Brunswick and was wounded at the Battle of Minden. In 1772, Grey was promoted to colonel and served as aide-de-camp to George III. His brigade included the 15th, 17th, and 44th Regiments of Foot and the 42nd Highlanders, the latter being detached under Lt. Col. Thomas Stirling to conduct the Fort Billingsport operation. After sitting in reserve with his brigade at Brandywine, Grey led the bloody attack at Paoli with two of his regiments. There, he became one of the more infamous British generals of the Revolution, gaining the moniker "No Flint Grey" for ordering his men to remove their musket flints and kill Americans with cold steel.[46]

Brigadier General James Agnew, at the head of the 4th British Brigade, was born in 1719 in England. He arrived in Boston in 1775 as a lieutenant colonel, fought on Long Island, and rose to brigade command. Early in 1777 he took part in the raid into Connecticut to seize supplies, and in September two of his regiments suffered heavy losses at Brandywine. He would command the 33rd, 37th, 46th, and 64th Regiments of Foot at Germantown.[47]

Major General Johann von Stirn, in command of the Hessian Brigade, was born in Borken in October 1712 and entered the Hessian service in 1728. He rose through the ranks of the Regiment Prinz Friedrich and was a major by 1757. By the time the Revolution began he was colonel of the Leib Regiment Infanterie and commanded a brigade in the Hessian army. Through the New York Campaign von Stirn commanded a Hessian brigade under Howe. His brigade consisted of the Leib Regiment, the von Mirbach Regiment, the Combined Regiment von Loos, and the von Donop Regiment. Two of von Stirn's units, the von Mirbach Regiment

45 This information is based upon my own analysis of the British army following Brandywine and Archibald Robertson's map of the British camp and battlefield. Archibald Robertson manuscript map of the Battle of Germantown, Windsor Castle Collection, 734029.d.

46 Ibid.

47 Ibid.

and the Combined Regiment von Loos, were on garrison duty in Wilmington. The Combined Hessian Battalion contained the men from the von Lossberg, von Knyphausen, and Rall regiments who had survived the various actions around Trenton the previous December. Since most of the Hessian grenadiers were part of the Philadelphia garrison, the Hessian Grenadier Battalion von Minnegerode also fell under von Stirn's command at Germantown.[48]

While Knyphausen's "division" was not as depleted as Grant's, there was a disproportionate number of Hessians in the wing. Often criticized for being slow and methodical in battle, could the division respond quickly in a crisis?

The Philadelphia Garrison

Lt. Gen. Charles Cornwallis commanded the 4,000 men of the Philadelphia garrison. His troops included the British Grenadier Brigade, the battalions of Hessian grenadiers under Col. Carl von Donop, the 23rd Regiment of Foot, two squadrons of 16th Light Dragoons, and the army's heavy siege artillery. While Howe's heavy guns were with Cornwallis, the light battalion pieces remained spread out with the regiments. The 23rd Regiment had been only lightly engaged at Brandywine and had thus far suffered few casualties in the campaign.

The British Grenadier Brigade was comprised of the 1st and 2nd British Grenadier Battalions. Much like the light infantry companies, Howe had consolidated the grenadier companies of the regiments stationed in North America into these battalions. The 1st British Grenadier Battalion was composed of the grenadier companies from the following Regiments of Foot: 4th, 5th, 7th, 10th, 15th, 17th, 22nd, 23rd, 27th, 28th, 33rd, 35th, and 38th. Maj. Edward Mitchell led the battalion at Germantown while Lt. Col. William Medows recovered from his Brandywine wound. The 2nd Grenadier Battalion, commanded by Col. Henry Monckton of the 45th Regiment of Foot, consisted of the following grenadier companies: two Royal Marine companies, and those from the following Regiments of Foot: 37th, 40th, 42nd, 43rd, 44th, 45th, 46th, 49th, 52nd, 54th, 55th, 57th, 63rd, 64th, and 71st. The grenadiers, heavily engaged at Brandywine, were short 150 men by the time of Germantown.

48 This information is based upon my own analysis of the British army following Brandywine and Archibald Robertson's map of the British camp and battlefield. Archibald Robertson manuscript map of the Battle of Germantown.

Carl von Donop's brigade of Hessian grenadiers contained the von Linsingen, von Minnigerode, and Lengerke grenadier battalions. The von Minnigerode battalion, however, had been detached on temporary service and remained in Germantown under Maj. Gen. von Stirn. Though Hessian units were often considered elite soldiers, they had many detractors among the British officer corps. One officer, describing a commonly-held belief, wrote that the Hessians "were led to believe before they left Hesse-Cassel, that they were to come to America to establish their private fortunes," and "hitherto they have certainly acted with that principle." Before Germantown, the Hessian grenadiers had done little fighting in the campaign.[49]

The Chester Garrison

Another 800 men detached from Germantown included the 10th and 42nd Regiments of Foot under Lt. Col. Thomas Stirling of the 42nd. The troops had captured Fort Billingsport in New Jersey and were now part of the garrison in Chester, Pennsylvania. The 42nd Royal Highlanders had fought at Paoli but only suffered light casualties. The 71st Highlanders also were present at Chester, having moved north from Wilmington.[50]

The Wilmington Garrison

The British army had been relatively fresh and concentrated when Howe attacked at Brandywine. On September 12, Howe dispatched Lt. Col. Archibald Campbell and his 71st Highlanders, together with the Hessian von Mirbach Regiment and the Combined Hessian Battalion (all under Campbell's command), to Wilmington in order to garrison the Delaware River town and await the arrival of the British fleet. The selection of these 1,200 troops weakened the army unnecessarily, since none of them had seen heavy action at Brandywine. Prior to the Billingsport raid, the 71st Highlanders moved north to Chester.[51]

On the eve of battle, Howe's army was spread far and wide, with just over one-half of his available force deployed in Germantown.

49 Lowell, *Hessians*, 86.

50 This information is based upon my own analysis of the British army following Brandywine.

51 Ibid.

British Tactics

The British army trained its troops to fight with line-of-battle discipline and skills. In Europe, whatever guerilla activities occurred were a nuisance with little or no effect upon the outcome of a battle, let alone a war. While some partisan combat took place in the 1740s and early 1750s, the British military refused to adopt any formal changes to its basic battlefield tactics, instead remaining convinced that experience and training in European warfare would always prove superior when fighting others following any other tactical doctrine. All of that changed when the Seven Years' War (the French and Indian War) reached North America.[52]

This new method of fighting forced the British to create new organizations and to develop frontier-style, hit-and-run tactics. The objective was to damage the enemy with the smallest force possible and retreat as necessary. Lord Loudon (John Campbell, the 4th Earl of Loudon), overall commander of British armies during the French and Indian War, emphasized the importance of these units and observed that conventionally trained British Regulars were unsuited for such a task. Initially the British relied on American frontiersmen distributed between Regulars in the hope that the former would acquire some discipline, and the latter some woodsmen skills. These and other changes would impact the coming Revolution.[53]

Lord Loudon also introduced light infantry units to Regular regiments. By the summer of 1758, every regiment had been trained to deal with ambushes, and had issued rifles to their best marksmen. The new Regular light infantry units were capable of scouting, fast strikes, and service in traditional lines of battle, where they were trained to impart their mobility to the line infantry around them. "The art of War," observed one British officer at the time, "is much changed and improved here. . . . The Highlanders have put on breeches. . . . Swords and sashes are degraded, and many have taken up the Hatchet and wear Tomahawks."[54]

52 Peter E. Russell, "Redcoats in the Wilderness: British Officers and Irregular Warfare in Europe and America, 1740-1760," *LW524: Student Reading Package, APUS Faculty, Fall 2009* (Charles Town, WV, 2009), 152-153; Ian K. Steele, *Warpaths: Invasions of North America* (New York, 1994), 196.

53 Russell, "Redcoats," 141-142; John Ferling, *Struggle for a Continent: The Wars of Early America* (Arlington Heights, IL, 1993), 163.

54 Steele, *Warpaths*, 209; John K. Mahon, "Anglo-American Methods of Indian Warfare, 1676-1794," *LW524: Student Reading Package, APUS Faculty, Fall 2009* (Charles Town, WV, 2009), 131; Daniel J. Beattie, "The Adaptation of the British Army to Wilderness Warfare, 1755-1763," *Adapting to Conditions: War and Society in the Eighteenth Century, ed. Maarten Ultee* (Birmingham, AL, 1986), 73.

The officer most responsible for revolutionizing the British light infantry was George Howe, the older brother of William and Richard Howe. The elder Howe ordered Regulars assigned to light infantry units to cut the tails off their coats and to remove the queues (ponytails) from their heads. Heavy packs were to be left behind and leggings were added for better protection against brush and other impedimenta. He even had them brown their musket barrels to reduce the glint of the sun.[55]

British army officer Henry Bouquet took Howe's innovations one step further. Bouquet implemented physical conditioning like running long distances, leaping logs and ditches, and carrying heavy loads. During the French and Indian War, Bouquet trained his light infantry to perform on the run and he made sure they could shoot from kneeling or prone positions. He also taught them how to disperse and rally in response to non-verbal signals.[56]

By the end of the French and Indian War, British infantry tactics had been transformed significantly. British troops no longer needed to fight in rigid European lines of battle and were better able to adapt to changing tactical conditions. The most important lessons instilled within the officer corps and the men in the ranks were the abilities to launch fast strikes and to skirmish in heavy woods or difficult terrain. These tactics became the exclusive domain of specially equipped and trained Regular light infantry. For the last three years of the war, redcoats aimed their muskets at specific targets, rather than firing volleys in the general direction of the enemy. "The army employed specialized units on a scale that would have been extraordinary in Europe," was how one historian described the transformation. In North America that meant fewer grenadiers and more light infantrymen—so many more that the army created entire battalions of light infantry. These spry men could move fast through various types of terrain to secure the flanks of heavy columns marching on the roads. The innovative creation and use of light infantry would help to modernize the British Army.[57]

The British continued to improve upon their light infantry system during the years between the French and Indian War and the American Revolution. In 1772, Lt. Gen. George Townshend issued instructions to his light infantrymen in Ireland

55 Mahon, "Methods," 131.

56 Ibid,

57 Spring, *With Zeal*, 245; Fred Anderson, *Crucible of War: The Seven Years' War and the Fate of Empire in British North America, 1754-1766* (New York, 2000), 411; Howard H. Peckham, *The Colonial Wars: 1689-1762* (Chicago, 1964), 153.

to enable the light companies to skirmish in woods independently, either with their parent regiments or as part of a light battalion. Townshend took a step away from the British army manual of 1764 by adopting the two-deep firing line at open intervals. He also taught his men to maneuver and form by files, and he enabled his officers to maintain control over loosely deployed light infantrymen. Firing was to occur in pairs rather than in volleys, which required each file to work together so at least one man always had a loaded firearm.[58]

In 1774, William Howe issued a light infantry drill focusing on light battalions as opposed to Townshend's emphasis on individual companies. As in Townshend's manual, most of the maneuvers allowed the battalion to change its formations and facings with men moving by files rather than by wheeling entire ranks. Howe not only expected individual companies to detach themselves from the battalion to act semi-independently during combat, but that the battalion itself would maneuver more quickly than its opponent so it could outflank an enemy line. The army trained the soldiers themselves to break ranks when under fire and seek cover instead of standing pat and remaining vulnerable to enemy lead.[59]

Even though these changes suggest that the British had learned their lesson in the previous war, they could never bring themselves to apply those lessons, regardless of which doctrine was preached. Though it is unclear whether Regular line infantry was trained in these tactics, the opening actions of the Revolution indicated they were not. When hostilities erupted in 1775, the British failed to put their new theories into practice and for the most part never adapted to conditions in the colonies. (In contrast, American colonists effectively used a type of guerilla warfare to harass them from the very beginning.) British light infantry battalions continued to fight in line of battle using the same linear formations and bayonet-oriented tactics as the rest of the infantry. British leaders entered the Revolution confident that European soldiers led by competent officers possessed the cohesion needed to dominate and destroy untrained American militiamen.[60]

Many British officers in North America believed bayonet shock tactics were as effective in heavy woods as in open fields. Events proved otherwise during the spring 1775 fighting around Lexington and Concord, in which the Americans used the varied terrain and cover to harass and slaughter their opponents all the way

58 Spring, *With Zeal*, 246-247.

59 Ibid., 247-248, 253.

60 Ibid., 260.

back to Boston. The deadly withdrawal, argued one historian, proved that "[u]nder certain favorable conditions a small force of well-armed and woods-wise colonists could rout a much larger, more ponderous formation of professional European soldiers."[61]

Beginning in 1776, General Howe ordered all units—including grenadiers and Regular infantry battalions—to fight in loose order, with their men arrayed in two ranks and at arm's length from each other, rather than shoulder-to-shoulder. Hessian officer Carl von Donop confirmed that Howe's orders were still in effect along the Brandywine when he wrote just nine days before the battle, "I hope . . . that we . . . may be a bit more closely drawn together for the attack. For unless we are, I cannot yet reassure myself that infantry with its files four feet apart can capture intrenchments by escalade." The doubting Von Donop went on to observe the Americans had been "drilled by French officers; and I am none too sure how our general is going to get himself out of this affair."[62]

While the British failed to practice what they sometimes preached, the Americans continued to show their frontier skills during the war by developing light infantry units armed exclusively with rifles. The task of these specialized troops was to scout ahead to help advance infantry lines. Most American units were incapable of maneuvering and fighting against the professional British in open-field combat. Fighting in wooded areas, however, neutralized the principal American weakness. "In short," concluded one historian, "all but the rebels' best troops were probably most effective when they operated in loosely directed swarms in broken terrain."[63]

* * *

British military development in North America during the eighteenth century is a study in contradictions. When confronted with Indian-style warfare during the French and Indian War, British leadership realized the need for new tactics, relied initially on American frontiersmen to conduct guerilla operations, and eventually created Regular units of light infantrymen to employ new fighting methods. After the 1763 peace treaty, the army continued to improve upon the light infantry

61 Spring, *With Zeal*, 252; Douglas Edward Leach, *Roots of Conflict: British Armed Forces and Colonial Americans, 1677-1763* (Chapel Hill, NC, 1986), 165.

62 McGuire, *Campaign*, vol. 1, 207; Von Donop, "Letters," 499.

63 Spring, *With Zeal*, 259.

system and produced drill manuals to effect substantive change. When the Revolution erupted, however, the British remained convinced the colonists were incapable of successfully fighting their professional soldiers. While the Americans used tested guerilla tactics that had been employed in the colonies in a variety of ways for decades, the British steered away from their light infantry doctrines, determined to fight a conventional war against an unconventional enemy.

The teachings of William Howe notwithstanding, the British were incapable of overcoming their own prejudices against the American fighting man. They would excel at light infantry tactics in the nineteenth century, but during the Revolution they largely forgot the valuable lessons learned during the French and Indian War.

Chapter 10

The Eve of Battle

October 3, 1777

"Early this morning orders were issued for the troops to be furnished with two days cooked provisions, and each man served with forty rounds of ammunition. At noon the sick were sent to Bethlehem, which indicates that a sudden attack is intended."[1]

— Lt. James McMichael, Pennsylvania State Regiment, October 3, 1777

The Theater of Operations

When the Revolution began, a large German immigrant population lived in an area north and east of the Schuylkill River. Many had emigrated from the Palatinate region along the Rhine River, where they had witnessed religious wars and bloodshed for hundreds of years. Boasting a mix of religions, the German-speaking population included pacifists such as Mennonites, German Baptists or "Dunkers," and Seventh-Day Adventists. Most feared armies thanks to their experiences with German princes. So many Germans settled near Philadelphia that the village of Germantown was founded on the edge of the city in 1683, after negotiations with William Penn for 6,000 acres on which to do so. Two years later, Francis Daniel Pastorius, a German agent for the Frankfurt Company, moved to Germantown and became one of its

1 McMichael, "Diary," 152.

leading citizens. As one historian put it, "Considering that a large portion of the King's army in Pennsylvania was comprised of Hessian soldiers [in 1777], it is no surprise that the inhabitants greeted Howe's army with a combination of uncertainty fear and anger." Though not entirely a German community, the village had a "decidedly more Germanic flavor than colonial Philadelphia." By 1753, "a German-language newspaper claimed a readership of four thousand."[2]

By 1748, Germantown boasted one two-mile thoroughfare called Germantown Road. Four main roads approached Germantown from the north. Germantown Road formed the village's main street. The Germantown Road left Germantown, through Bebberstown, the northern "suburb" of Germantown spread out along a mile of good road running to Mount Airy, a mile from the town's limits. From there, the road extended another mile to Chestnut Hill, where it split, with one branch leading to Reading and the other to Bethlehem. Several fenced lanes ran off the main road. To the west of and parallel to the main thoroughfare was Ridge Road, which followed the bank of the Schuylkill. To the east of Germantown Road was Limekiln Road, which intersected the main route at Germantown's market square. Farther to the east ran Old York Road, which formed a junction with Germantown Road south of the market square.[3]

Germantown's inhabitants "enjoy such privileges, as they are not possessed of any where else," thought visitor Peter Kalm in 1770. Most residents were tradesmen who produced various goods in "quantity and perfection." While most houses were constructed of stone, several were made of brick. "They were commonly two stories high, and sometimes higher. The roofs consisted of shingles of the white cedar wood," continued Kalm. Many of the upper stories had balconies, windows sported shutters, and each house included "a fine garden," the whole usually surrounded by thriving orchards. "Many of the houses were fronted with stoops—wide steps with seats or benches, often shaded by a door hood, pent roof, or overhang—and some had 'piazza' or roofed porches." Each property was long and narrow, and situated perpendicular to Germantown Road. "Behind the houses were acres of orchards and vegetable gardens, often protected by paling or picket fences, and a sprinkling of outbuildings reached into the long, rolling fields, which typically ended in clumps of woods and thickets down the many ravines and

2 McGuire, *Germantown*, 9; McGuire, *Campaign*, vol. 2, 326; Russell F. Weigley, ed., *Philadelphia: A 300-Year History* (New York, 1982), 25. Peter Kalm, *Travels into North America*, 2 vols. (Warrington, 1770), vol. 2, 89-90.

3 Brownlow, *Germantown*, 6-7.

rock clefts in the area."[4] The land along the Germantown Road was mostly cleared, but it also presented obstacles to armies on the move. Successive rows of heavy fencing promised to hinder any troop advance.

Four churches existed at the time of the battle—one for Lutherans, another for Protestants, a Baptist meetinghouse, and a Quaker meetinghouse. The houses of worship "were small and plain, one or two stories high, and for the most part built of local gray stone, with rail or picket fences between them." While the first churches were built by Dutch- and German-speaking Quakers, by 1726 the community boasted a German Reformed Church and a German Lutheran Church.[5]

Six miles from the center of Philadelphia, Germantown established its own industrial economy that became known throughout the colonies for the "excellence of the goods it produced." By 1777 its citizens were providing grain to Washington's army, and Christopher Mong's vinegar house doubled as a storehouse for hospital supplies. Two men, John Bringhurst and William Ashmead, made wagons for the Continental Army. The initial inhabitants were mostly linen weavers and were not skilled at farming. Nestled in the Wissahickon Creek valley west of Germantown was the Rittenhouse mill complex, where Jacob and Abraham Rittenhouse operated their paper mill. Across the creek from the mill was their brother Nicholas Rittenhouse's grist mill, and between that and the paper mill was another grist mill owned by Abraham.[6]

Several homes were located on the periphery of the village. Wealthy members of Philadelphia society, "intent on escaping the heat and smell of the city in summer," built these seasonal homes 200 feet above the street level of Philadelphia. On the east side of Germantown Road, just north of the village, was Benjamin Chew's country estate Cliveden, built in 1767 and named after the country house of Frederick, the Prince of Wales. One writer described the structure as "the most elegant country estate Germantown had yet seen and indeed one of the most elegant in all the colonies." Chew, who served as attorney general of

4 Jackson, *British Army*, 291; McGuire, *Campaign*, vol. 2, 66. Several sources refer to the area around Mount Airy as "Beggarstown," but the area actually was named after Matthias Bebber and called Bebberstown by the locals.

5 Kalm, *Travels*, vol. 2, 89-90; Weigley, ed., *Philadelphia*, 25; Brownlow, *Germantown*, 7.

6 The Nicholas Rittenhouse grist mill stood near modern Hermit Lane. Abraham Rittenhouse's grist mill was located near the Blue Stone Bridge on Forbidden Drive, within the Wissahickon Valley Park. John L. Cotter, Daniel G. Roberts, and Michael Parrington, *The Buried Past: An Archaeological History of Philadelphia* (Philadelphia,1993), 322-323.

Present day view of Cliveden. The 40th Regiment of Foot camped in the rear of the house and would soon turn it into a stronghold. *Photo by author*

Pennsylvania from 1755 to 1769 and chief justice of the province in 1774, was being held prisoner by the Americans because of his open loyalty to the British.[7]

Farther north between Cliveden and Chestnut Hill stood the Allen family's country house, Mount Airy. The house was 495 feet above sea level on a small hill along Germantown Road. William Allen, former chief justice of the Pennsylvania Supreme Court, built the country estate on 47 acres in 1750 and named it after the area's fresh breezes. Daniel Fisher, an Englishman who had moved to Williamsburg, visited Mount Airy in 1755. "The House was small, built of stone, as most of the Houses thereabouts are," he wrote in his journal, and "stands close to a large much frequented Road, which often occasions the Dust to be very troublesome. The spot, doubtless from its elevated situation, must be as healthy as

7 Cotter, Roberts, and Parrington, *Buried* Past, 324, 347-349. Today, Germantown offers urban blight and industrial decay, efforts to redevelop the area in recent years notwithstanding. It also boasts a collection of lovely restored historic houses. Brownlow, *Germantown*, 27. Cliveden is one of the finest examples of Georgian architecture in America.

any thereabouts, but to me it appeared very naked, much exposed to the sun and to bleak winds. A small Portico, facing the South East," he continued, "is a good contrivance and to my thinking the very best about the house." The portico extended over the sidewalk, providing passersby with a refuge from the weather.[8]

South of the village and east of Germantown Road stood James Logan's country estate, Stenton, the earliest example of Georgian architecture in the area. Logan, who had immigrated to the colonies to serve as William Penn's secretary, built the large home in 1728 and named it after his father's birthplace in Scotland. At the time of the battle the home sat on 500 acres, but today the site is a condensed urban park surrounded by bustling streets and city life. In 1777 Stenton was being maintained by a caretaker following the death of Logan and his son. When the British occupied Germantown, Howe established headquarters in the home.[9]

British Dispositions

The camps of Gens. James Grant's and Wilhelm von Knyphausen's wings of the British army stretched perpendicularly across the Germantown Road. The entire line faced generally northwest, with Grant's command on the right side and Knyphausen's on the left closest to the Schuylkill River with the Germantown Road cutting through the line where the two commands met.[10]

Knyphausen's men were camped between modern Coulter Street and School House Lane, extending from the market square to the Schuylkill. Brigadier General

8 Daniel Fisher, "Extracts from the Diary of Daniel Fisher, 1755," *PMHB* (Philadelphia, 1893), vol. 17, 269. The Allen home no longer exists. It was near the intersection of Allens Lane and Germantown Avenue. Today, the site is occupied by the Lutheran Theological Seminary. The 1840s Italianate administration building was built on the approximate footprint of the original house. Prior to being razed, Mount Airy housed the Mount Airy College, and after 1826 was home to the American Classical and Military Lyceum.

9 Cotter, Roberts, and Parrington, *Buried Past*, 325-343. Three other prominent structures are "Wyck," "Grumblethorpe," and the Deshler house. Owned by the descendants of Hans Milan, Wyck stands on the west side of Germantown Road north of the market square. At the time of the battle, the home was occupied by a tenant farmer, and it served as a field hospital after the fighting. In 1744, John Wister built Grumblethorpe on 200 acres on the edge of Germantown. The diary of his granddaughter, Sally Wister, is often used when researching the Philadelphia Campaign. After the arrival of the British army, General James Agnew and his entourage set up headquarters at the house. Just up the road stands David Deshler's home. The Deshler House would later gain fame as the temporary "white house" for George Washington during yellow fever outbreaks in Philadelphia in 1793 and 1794.

10 Archibald Robertson manuscript map of the Battle of Germantown, Windsor Castle Collection, 734029.d.

Present day view of the home of David Deshler. Later the home would be used as George Washington's "White House" during the 1793 yellow fever epidemic. *Photo by author*

James Agnew's 4th Brigade was closest to the market square with the 37th, 64th, 46th, and 33rd Regiments of Foot arrayed west to east. To Agnew's left sat Maj. Gen. Charles Grey's 3rd Brigade, with the 17th, 44th, and 15th Regiments of Foot (west to east). Across Township Line Road (modern Wissahickon Avenue) rested Stirn's Hessian Leib and von Donop regiments. About halfway between Stirn's camp and the Schuylkill was the Hessian grenadier battalion von Minnigerode. Knyphausen's long main line covered a front two and one-half miles long.[11]

11 Ibid.

Grant's brigades ran parallel to modern Coulter Street and Church Lane, continuing the British line from near the market square east to Wingohocking Creek (where Wingohocking Terrace is today). Grant's 2nd Brigade was camped closest to the market square, with the 55th and 5th Regiments of Foot (west to east). The 1st Brigade (the 49th and 4th Regiments of Foot) extended the line to the northeast. These four regiments covered a front one-half mile in length.[12]

Several detachments were fanned out in front of the camps to watch the approaches. The 1st Light Infantry Battalion was on high ground above the heavily wooded eastern bank of Wingohocking Creek, 300 yards off the right flank of James Grant's camp. Three picket posts were established farther out on the roads and another three-quarters of a mile east of the main battalion camp at Luken's Mill on Limekiln Road. Another post was set up off to the north, three-quarters of a mile away at the intersection of Bristol Road (modern Haines Street) and Township Line Road (modern Stenton Avenue). A third 1st Light Battalion picket was farther out at the intersection of the Abington Road (modern Washington Lane) and the Limekiln Road.[13]

The Queen's Rangers held the far right of the long British front positioned, to monitor Old York Road just below the modern intersection of Old York Road and

Present day view of Wyck. The home would be used as a field hospital following the battle. *Photo by author*

12 Ibid.

13 Archibald Robertson manuscript map of the Battle of Germantown, Windsor Castle Collection, 734029.d.

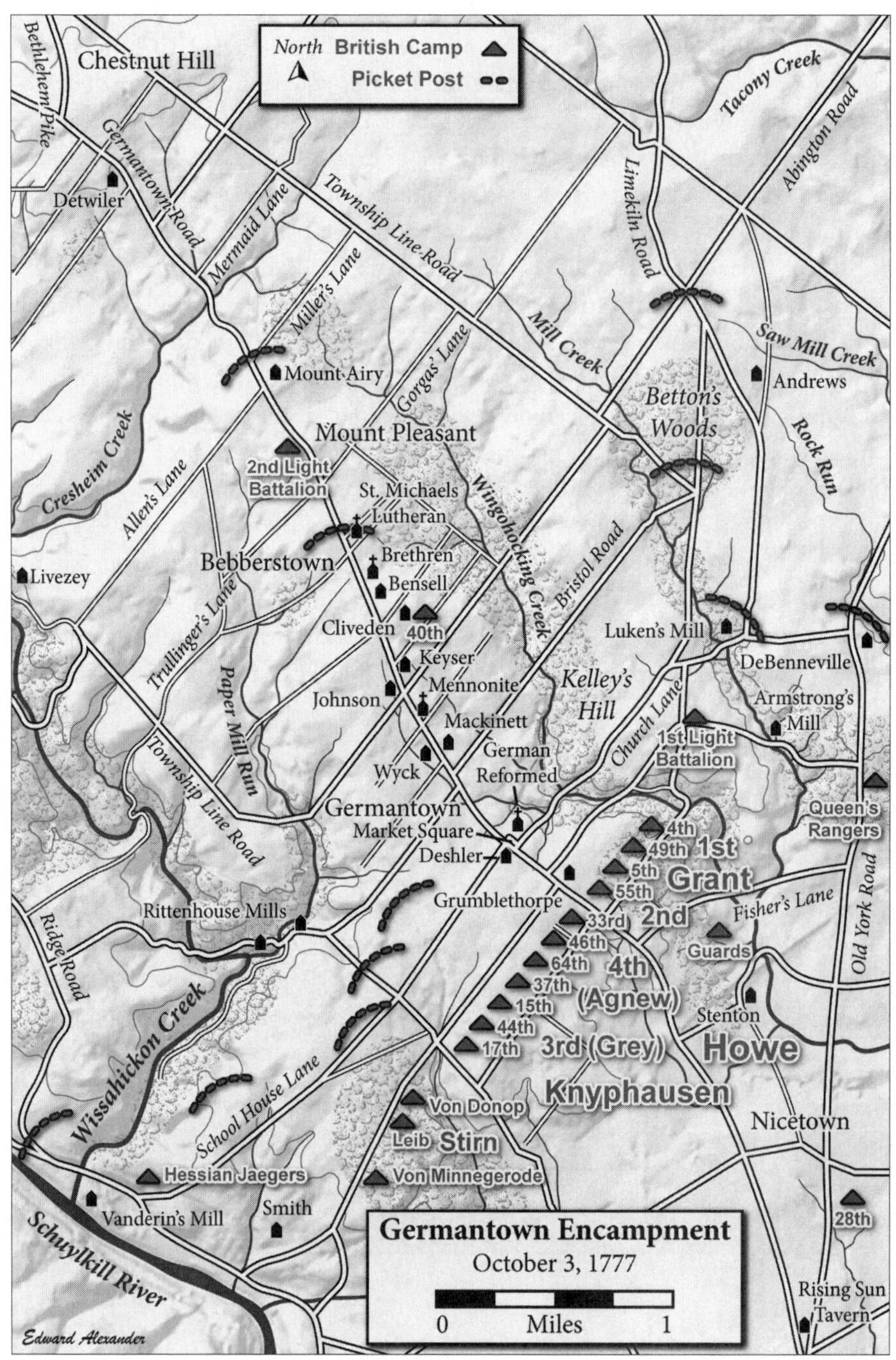
North
British Camp
Picket Post
Germantown Encampment
October 3, 1777
0 Miles 1
Chestnut Hill
Bethlehem Pike
Germantown Road
Detwiler
Mermaid Lane
Township Line Road
Miller's Lane
Mount Airy
Mount Pleasant
2nd Light Battalion
St. Michaels Lutheran
Bebberstown
Brethren
Bensell
Cliveden
40th
Keyser
Mennonite
Johnson
Mackinett
German Reformed
Wyck
Germantown
Market Square
Deshler
Grumblethorpe
Gorgas' Lane
Wingohocking Creek
Bristol Road
Mill Creek
Limekiln Road
Tacony Creek
Abington Road
Saw Mill Creek
Andrews
Betton's Woods
Rock Run
Luken's Mill
DeBenneville
Armstrong's Mill
Kelley's Hill
Church Lane
1st Light Battalion
Queen's Rangers
Old York Road
4th
49th
1st
Grant
5th
55th
2nd
33rd
46th
4th
64th
37th
(Agnew)
15th
44th
17th
3rd (Grey)
Fisher's Lane
Guards
Stenton
Howe
Knyphausen
Von Donop
Leib
Stirn
Von Minnegerode
Hessian Jaegers
Nicetown
28th
Rising Sun Tavern
Cresheim Creek
Allen's Lane
Livezey
Trullinger's Lane
Paper Mill Run
Township Line Road
Rittenhouse Mills
Ridge Road
Wissahickon Creek
School House Lane
Vanderin's Mill
Smith
Schuylkill River
Edward Alexander

Green Lane. In support farther south along Old York Road were the light and grenadier companies of the Brigade of Guards.[14]

Above the east bank of Wissahickon Creek at the intersection of the Manatawny Road (modern Ridge Avenue) and School House Lane was the camp of the Hessian Jaegers. The jaegers had a picket post on the west side of the creek at the intersection of Manatawny Road and a secondary road following the Schuylkill River toward Levering's Ford (modern Main Street in Manayunk). The pickets were a mile down the Manatawny Road from the jaeger camp near the Octagon, the country villa of William Smith, Anglican minister and provost of the College of Philadelphia. Vanderin's Mill was on the south side of Wissahickon Creek where it empties into the Schuylkill near a stone bridge, with the creek itself passing through a deep and nearly impassable gorge that could double as a natural defensive barrier.[15]

The British 2nd Light Infantry Battalion was positioned on Mount Pleasant, two miles northwest of the main camp, with a picket 400 yards farther north at Mount Airy. It was "the close of the campaign," observed Lt. Martin Hunter of the 52nd Regiment of Foot's light company in his journal on October 4, "[so] our battalion was very weak. They did not consist of more than three hundred and fifty men and there was no support nearer than Germantown, a mile in our rear." Hunter's battalion of more than 600 men had landed at Head of Elk, Maryland, at the beginning of the campaign that summer, and had seen hard service since then, especially during the past month and a half. The battalion camp was spread out on both sides of the main road behind some isolated buildings, with picket posts deployed on the northern slope of Mount Airy. A pair of 6-pounders supported the battalion. The 300 men of the 40th Regiment of Foot supported the light infantry from its camp behind the Chew House, halfway between the 2nd Light Infantry Battalion and Grant's and von Knyphausen's camps.[16]

The British Brigade of Guards, supporting Grant's division, was camped on the grounds of Stenton on both sides of Wingohocking Creek just south of Fisher's

14 Several sources claim that small redoubts were built at each end of this line of encampment. However, Archibald Robertson's map of the battlefield and the camp provides no evidence of any such earthworks. Luken's Mill no longer stands and modern streets have completely changed this area. McGuire, *Campaign*, vol. 2, 66-7.

15 Archibald Robertson manuscript map of the Battle of Germantown, Windsor Castle Collection, 734029.d.

16 Hunter, *Journal*, 34.

Lane (modern Logan Street). With the 27th and 28th Regiments of Foot detached and camped near the intersection of the road leading to the village of Frankford, Grant's division was woefully understrength. One squadron of the 16th Light Dragoons set up camp immediately behind Grant's main line.[17]

Little effort was made by Howe's army to prepare defenses for its long front-line encampment. If Washington could break through Grant and Knyphausen, Howe would be hard pressed to stop the Continentals short of Philadelphia. "We imagined that the defeat of Brandywine had dispirited the enemy to such a degree that it would be utterly impossible for Washington to give us any further trouble, for some time at least," confessed Capt. Richard Fitzpatrick of the British Guards, "in consequence of which I Believe we had not much considered the strength of the Position we took at Germantown." Captain William Scott, the commander of the 17th Regiment of Foot's light company, was unimpressed with the position, thinking it had been "taken up during rain, and not on ground originally intended; the army by mistake not having been halted soon enough" when it occupied Germantown. With a beaten, rag-tag enemy army roaming about the countryside, no one was going to go to the trouble of altering the front.[18]

Howe did not prepare earthworks or other defenses for the camp, but his Germantown front was not "open" ground inviting attack. The rough country in front of the British camp, dominated by Wissahickon and Wingohocking creeks, was generally well suited for defensive operations.[19]

The Eve of Battle

While Washington contemplated an assault on Germantown, operations continued apace elsewhere. Captain John Montresor of the Royal Engineers, along with an officer and 20 grenadiers, crossed to Province Island in two skiffs to survey

17 McGuire, *Campaign*, vol. 2, 56, and 58; Reed, *Campaign*, 218; Archibald Robertson manuscript map of the Battle of Germantown, Windsor Castle Collection, 734029.d.

18 Letter, Fitzpatrick to his Brother, October 28, 1777; William Scott, "Memorandum on the Battle of Germantown," original located in the American Philosophical Society, Philadelphia, PA, transcription in McGuire, *Campaign*, vol. 2, 291.

19 The redoubts surveyed and under construction were laid out between Germantown and Philadelphia. Even if they had been finished by this point, they were not positioned to protect Germantown. Howe's plan was to complete them so he could pull out of his blocking position at Germantown and move more troops into Philadelphia, freeing up men for operations against the Delaware River forts.

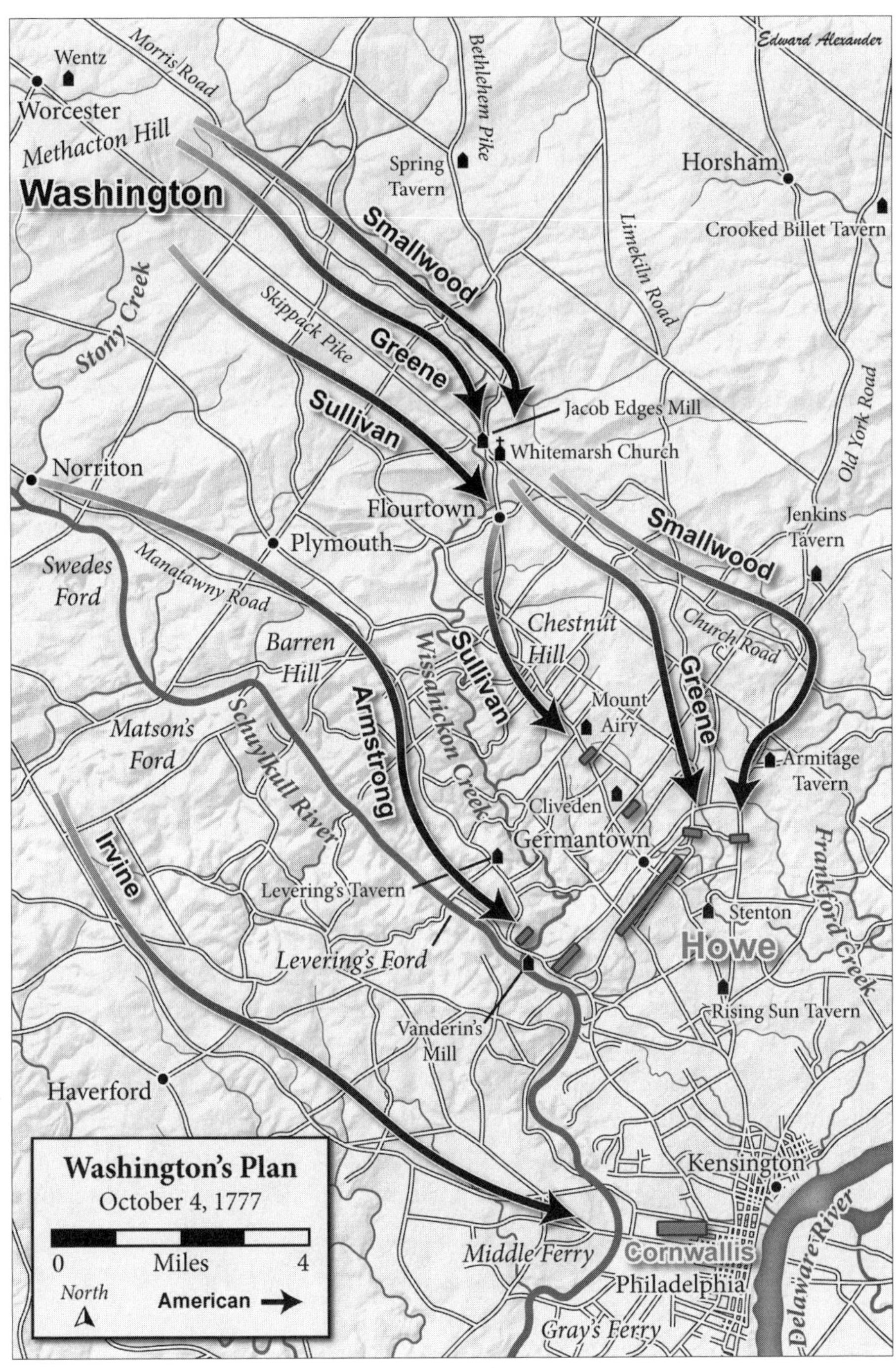
Edward Alexander
Wentz
Worcester
Methacton Hill
Morris Road
Bethlehem Pike
Spring Tavern
Horsham
Washington
Smallwood
Crooked Billet Tavern
Limekiln Road
Stony Creek
Skippack Pike
Greene
Sullivan
Jacob Edges Mill
Whitemarsh Church
Old York Road
Norriton
Flourtown
Jenkins Tavern
Smallwood
Plymouth
Swedes Ford
Manatawny Road
Church Road
Chestnut Hill
Barren Hill
Sullivan
Wissahickon Creek
Armstrong
Greene
Mount Airy
Matson's Ford
Schuylkill River
Armitage Tavern
Cliveden
Germantown
Frankford Creek
Irvine
Levering's Tavern
Stenton
Howe
Levering's Ford
Rising Sun Tavern
Vanderin's Mill
Haverford
Kensington
Delaware River
Middle Ferry
Cornwallis
Philadelphia
Gray's Ferry
Washington's Plan
October 4, 1777
0 Miles 4
North
American

the high ground and flooded marshes near Fort Mifflin. The scouting operation was no secret, and the reconnaissance prompted the Americans to abandon the island, including the Pest House, the hospital for contagious diseases they had established on its northern end. The evacuation of Province Island cleared the way for a British assault on Mud Island's Fort Mifflin. While commencing operations against Fort Mifflin was important, maintaining a safe supply route between the fleet anchored off Chester and Howe's army was at least as critical to the survival of the British troops in Philadelphia. Howe dispatched Lt. Col. Benjamin Bernard's 23rd Royal Welch Fusiliers from the 1st British Brigade of James Grant's wing of the army, about 300 men, from Germantown to Philadelphia to form a guard at the Middle Ferry and to help keep the supply route to Chester open.[20]

Washington's Plan of Attack

"Having received intelligence through Two intercepted letters, that Genl Howe had detached a part of his force for the purpose of reducing Billingsport and the Forts on Delaware," Washington wrote John Hancock on October 5, "I communicated the Accounts to my Genl Officers, who were unanimously of Opinion, that a favorouable Opportunity offered to make an Attack upon the Troops, which were at & near German Town. It was accordingly agreed, that it should take place." The reading of Howe's private correspondence had detailed to Washington the decision to weaken the Germantown garrison. Washington estimated that Howe's army had lost between 1,000 and 2,000 men during the entire campaign. With the 23rd Royal Welch Fusiliers now serving elsewhere, some 3,000 grenadiers ensconced in Philadelphia, and 2,000 Scots and Hessians at Wilmington and Chester, Washington and his staff calculated the remaining British forces in Germantown to number perhaps 8,000 men. Just as important was the fact that the overall quality of the troops in Germantown was subpar. The British Light Infantry, Hessian Jaegers, and the Brigade of Guards were quality veteran units, but most of the grenadiers, the elite Royal Welch Fusiliers, and two large Highland Regiments were absent. Most of the troops remaining in the Germantown camp were regular line infantry, not the "shock" troops Howe preferred to use in battle.[21]

20 Jackson, *Navy*, 138.

21 Chase and Lengel, eds., *Papers*, vol. 11, 393.

Ten-year-old Hance Suppllee later claimed he witnessed the American council of war in a field along the Skippack Pike, in which Washington called on Nathanael Greene and the pair of generals held a long talk by themselves. The next day, wrote Suppllee, "Washington called again with other officers on foot and mounted, and they went into the meadow. Forming a semi-circle they faced General Washington holding their swords in front of their faces. They stayed in this position for quite a long time, after which each officer went to his command."[22]

It had taken less than two days for Washington to plan his assault on Germantown and gain the full consent of his generals for the undertaking. Surprise was a key element of the plan, which would require a great deal of discipline, coordination, and good luck. Once approved, Washington intended to divide his army into four columns designed to meet on the northern and western edges of Germantown simultaneously at 5:00 a.m. the next day. The columns would move silently through the darkness for 14 to as many as 20 miles over a series of poorly marked roads. The Continental Army had camped around Germantown twice during the campaign, so the senior officers had some familiarity with the road network. These movements would show whether the army was capable of a nighttime march and a coordinated surprise attack. The Americans had tried to execute a similar plan at Trenton nearly nine months earlier, but two of the four columns had failed to reach their objectives. Washington had learned through hard experience that stand-up fights against the British were a losing proposition; thus, his preferred tactic was to strike isolated enemy detachments, which is precisely what he was attempting to do against the depleted British garrison holding Germantown.[23]

"Although defeated at the Brandywine, and foiled in several smaller reencounters," noted dragoon Benjamin Tallmadge, "our American Fabius retained his full determination to give these hostile invaders no repose." James Monroe, a young aide to Lord Stirling and a future president of the United States, recorded his thoughts on the matter later in life. "General Washington was attentive to the conduct of the enemy. He perceived that the British force extended over a large surface and that the body which was at Germantown was not well

22 Samuel Kriebel Brecht, ed., *The Genealogical Record of the Schwenkfelder Families*, 2 vols. (Pennsburg, PA, 1923), vol. 2, 1441.

23 McGuire, *Campaign*, vol. 2, 52; *Pancake*, 1777, 193.

supported by that at the city and below it," he explained. "He resolved to attack it, and with that view made secretly the necessary preparations."[24]

In truth—as Washington well knew—the plan was bold, complicated, and risky for an army like his to attempt. Similar in scope to but much larger in scale than his designs for the attack on Trenton the previous December, Washington hoped to drive into a major village along four different roads, using timing his men would have to pull off in the dark. Coordinating the movements of each column so that they would arrive in Germantown simultaneously was more than ambitious. On paper Washington counted nearly 14,000 men, but the army that marched and fought on October 4 six miles outside Philadelphia was much smaller; it had been bleeding stragglers and deserters throughout the campaign, and some men had to be left behind to protect the encampment and wagons. Most sources put the number who marched to Germantown at about 11,000. "Our whole army, exclusive of the necessary guards left for the security of the camp, began its march, in four columns, on the evening of the 3d instant," recorded Lt. Samuel Shaw of Proctor's Artillery. Thomas Paine, the infamous pamphleteer and author of *Common Sense*, agreed: the rest of the army remained "as guards for the security of the camp." Regardless of the actual number, Washington was moving a numerically superior force into the fight. It was the first time during the war that Washington launched his own army in a major attack against the main British force.[25]

Militia comprised two of Washington's four columns. John Armstrong's 1,500 Pennsylvania militiamen formed the army's far right closest to the Schuylkill River. Brigadier General James Potter, with an escort of Philadelphia Light Horse and four artillery pieces, marched up Ridge (or Manatawney) Road with about 1,000 of those men to strike the Hessian jaeger camp at Vanderin's Mill along the Wissahickon, which served as the British left flank. Armstrong's objective was to "pass by Leverings tavern & take guides to cross Wessahiecon creek up the head of John Vandeering's mill-dam so as to fall above Joseph Warners new house."

24 Tallmadge, *Memoir*, 22; James Monroe, *The Autobiography of James Monroe*, Stuart Gerry Brown, ed. (Syracuse, NY, 1959), 28-29. Fabius is a reference to Quintus Fabius Maximus Verrucosus (280-203 B.C.), who earned a lasting reputation fighting Hannibal's forces in the Second Punic War by targeting supply lines and waging smaller combats on ground of his choosing rather than gambling his entire army in one pitched battle.

25 "Operations," 288; Shaw, *Journals*, 40; Henry Knox, Washington's chief of artillery, would later claim, however, "We were more numerous after the battle of Brandywine than before." Francis S. Drake, *Life and Correspondence of Henry Knox, Major-General in the American Revolutionary Army* (Boston, 1873), 52.

Washington hoped that by successfully carrying out these movements, the Pennsylvanians could turn Howe's left flank. Johann Stirn's Hessian Brigade and the Hessian Grenadier Battalion von Minnigerode were camped behind the British line on heights south of the creek, above the Falls of the Schuylkill River, in support of the jaegers. If Armstrong's men performed as intended, the militia would freeze these veteran troops in place and keep them from responding to the American threat against the center of the line. Armstrong's remaining 500 Pennsylvania militia, under Brig. Gen. James Irvine, would operate on the south side of the Schuylkill in order to distract the British garrison in Philadelphia.[26]

William Smallwood's Marylanders and David Forman's New Jerseymen, on the army's extreme left, constituted the second militia force. With Smallwood in overall command of the 1,600-man column, Mordecai Gist was probably in charge of the Marylanders. The plan called for these troops to hit Howe's right flank (held by the Queen's Rangers) so the column on Smallwood's right under Nathanael Greene would have an easier time reaching the right side of the main British camp, which was commanded by Gen. James Grant.

Smallwood's men faced a long and rather complex march of about 20 miles. The militia would head down the road "by a mill formerly danl Morris' and Jacob Edges mill into the White marsh road at the Sandy run: thence to white marsh Church [modern St. Thomas Episcopal Church], where take the left-hand road, which leads to Jenkin's tavern on the old york road, below Armitages, beyond the seven mile stone half a mile from which [a road] turns off short to the right hand, fenced on both sides, which leads through the enemy's encampment to German town market house." They needed to go two miles beyond the Limekiln Road intersection to reach the turn onto the Old York Road. Following these directions at night would be difficult, even for veteran troops. If they arrived at the correct point down the Old York Road, they would come out behind Howe's right flank near Stenton, thus threatening his rear.[27]

26 Chase and Lengel, eds., *Papers*, vol. 11, 375. John Vanderen's mill was located on Wissahickon Creek near its confluence with the Schuylkill River, next to the bridge where Ridge Road crossed the creek. Levering's Tavern was near Levering's Ford, a short distance northwest of the mill. Letter, John Armstrong to Horatio Gates, 9 October 1777, Horatio Gates Papers, Microfilm 23, Reel 5, 977-978, David Library of the American Revolution, Washington Crossing, PA; McGuire, *Campaign*, vol. 2, 49-50.

27 Chase and Lengel, eds., *Papers*, vol. 11, 375. These convoluted orders required Smallwood to march down Morris Road from Methacton Hill to Bethlehem Road and turn south to its junction with Skippack Road in Whitemarsh. Daniel Morris's and Jacob Edge's mills were on Wissahickon Creek near its confluence with Sandy Run, just north of Whitemarsh. From Whitemarsh, the

The main attack envisioned by Washington would be delivered by his two center columns. The right-center column under Maj. Gen. John Sullivan included his own division of Maryland, Delaware, and French Canadian troops (1,500 men), together with Brig. Gen. Thomas Conway's Pennsylvania Brigade and Brig. Gen. Anthony Wayne's Pennsylvania Division (another 2,000 men). Sullivan's men would march down the Skippack Pike, to the Bethlehem Pike, then to the Germantown Road in Chestnut Hill to attack the left-center of the British line, a distance of about 10 miles. Conway's brigade would spearhead this column. Washington had disbanded his light infantry brigade in the aftermath of the Battle of the Clouds and consequently had no mobile force to screen the army's advance. With a cloud hanging over Sullivan's head after Brandywine and the investigation into his conduct there still underway, Washington personally followed this column with the Corps de Reserve. The 1,500-man reserve, commanded by Maj. Gen. Lord Stirling, consisted of the New Jersey Brigade under Brig. Gen. William Maxwell and Brig. Gen. Francis Nash's North Carolina Brigade.

The left-center column of the main attack—the largest of the four—was under the command of Maj. Gen. Nathanael Greene. It consisted of Greene's Virginia Division under Brig. Gen. Peter Muhlenberg (1,700 men) and Maj. Gen. Adam Stephen's Virginia Division (another 1,700 men). Marching with this column was the recently arrived Connecticut Brigade of 1,000 troops under Alexander McDougall. Like Conway with Sullivan's column, McDougall was charged with spearheading this advance. These troops followed Smallwood down Morris Road and into Whitemarsh before turning onto Whitemarsh Church Road (modern Route 73) and entering Germantown via Limekiln Road to assault the right of the main British camp. The Limekiln Road intersection was four miles from the Bethlehem Pike. Washington hoped Greene would crumple the British right flank and drive it southwest into Sullivan's oncoming attack.

The size of the columns was weighted toward the American left. "The Reason of our Sending So many Troops to attack their right was because it was supposed That if This wing of the Enemy could be forced," explained John Sullivan to the governor of New Hampshire, "their army must have been pushed into the Sculkill or have been compelled to Surrender. Therefore Two Thirds of the Army at Least were Detached to oppose the Enemys Right." "It was a grand enterprise, an

---

column turned left onto Church Road (modern Route 73) to the Old York Road intersection where William Jenkins's tavern stood. The column would then turn right onto Old York Road past Benjamin Armitage's tavern and march to the Church Lane intersection in Germantown.

inimitable plan," concluded Lt. Col. William Heth of the 3rd Virginia, "which nothing but its God-like author could equal."[28]

To achieve maximum effect and complete surprise, it was imperative that each of the four columns reach its assigned location at the same time—a rather tall order given that each column had to march a different distance in the dark. Coordinating the timing of departure was crucial; any such errors could throw the entire attack plan off and result in piecemeal assault, leaving the British to concentrate troops as each attack developed. A final key to the battle plan was destroying Howe's Germantown garrison before any reinforcements could arrive from Philadelphia, six miles away.[29]

Washington's orders were straightforward enough, but the devil was in the details:

> [The] Pickets on the left of Vanderin's mill to be taken off by Armstrong: one at Allen's house on Mount-Airey by Sullivan—One at Lucans Mill by Greene. Each Column to make their disposition so as to attack the pickets in their respective routs, precisely at five OClock, with charged bayonets and without firing, and the columns to move to the attack as soon as possible. The Columns to endeavor to get within two miles of the enemy's pickets on their respective routs by two OClock and there halt 'till four and make the disposition for attacking the pickets at the time above mentioned. The Columns of Cont[inental]: troops & militia to communicate with each other from time to time by light horse. Proper flanking parties to be kept out from each Column.[30]

"It was a complicated plan, one that would have taxed the energy and skill of officers and men far more experienced than Washington's Continentals," concluded campaign historian John Pancake. If all went according to plan, the Americans would have a six-mile semicircle formation with each column separated by broken country and deep ravines. Maintaining effective communication under combat conditions "by light horse" would be next to impossible.[31]

28 Otis G. Hammond, ed., *Letters and Papers of Major-General John Sullivan: Continental Army,* 3 vols. (Concord, NH, 1930), vol. 1, 543; Henry Steele Commager and Richard B. Morris, eds., *The Spirit of Seventy-six: The Story of the American Revolution as Told by its Participants* (Edison, NJ, 2002), 629.

29 Reed, *Campaign*, 217.

30 Chase and Lengel, eds., *Papers*, vol. 11, 376.

31 Any attempt to achieve complete surprise would require the capture of all British picket posts before they could spread any warnings. Several sources claim Washington ordered the men to put pieces of white paper in their hats to distinguish themselves during the night march. However, this

"This army—the main American Army—will certainly not suffer itself to be out done by their northern Brethren—they will never endure such disgrace," wrote Washington in his General Orders of October 3, referencing Horatio Gates' victory at Saratoga. "[W]ith an ambition becoming freemen, contending in the most righteous cause, rival the heroic spirit which swelled their bosoms, and which so nobly exerted, has procured them deathless renown." Prior to their departure on the evening of October 3, Washington exhorted his men in general orders read to them by their commanders. "Covet! my Countrymen, and fellow soldiers! Covet! a share of the glory due heroic deeds!" he began. "Let it never be said," Washington continued,

> that in a day of action, you turned your backs on the foe—let the enemy no longer triumph—They brand you with ignominious epithets—Will you patiently endure that reproach? Will you suffer the wounds given to your Country to go unrevenged? Will you resign your parents—wives—children and friends to be the wretched vassals of a proud, insulting foe? And your own necks to the halter? General [Howe] has promised protection to such as submitted to his power; and a few dastard souls accepted the disgraceful boon—But his promises were deceitful—the submitting and resisting had their property alike plundered and destroyed: But even these empty promises have come to an end; the term of Mercy is expired—General Howe has, within a few days proclaimed, all who had not then submitted, to be beyond the reach of it; and has left us no choice but Conquest or Death."

"Nothing then remains, but nobly to contend for all that is dear to us," he added. "Every motive that can touch the human breast calls us to the most vigorous exertions—Our dearest rights—our dearest friends—our own lives—honor—glory, and even shame, urge us to the fight—And my fellow soldiers! when an opportunity presents, be firm, be brave, shew yourselves men, and victory is yours."[32]

After inspiring his army, Washington issued more mundane battle orders. The men were to leave their "Packs & blankets" and carry "their provisions in their Haversacks, or any other manner least inconvenient. All the pioneers of each

---

author could not find any such statement in Washington's general orders immediately before or after the battle. Pancake, *1777*, 193.

32 Chase and Lengel, eds., *Papers*, vol. 11, 373-375.

division who are fit to march are to move in front of their respective divisions, with all the axes they can muster."[33]

"Early this morning orders were issued for the troops to be furnished with two days cooked provisions, and each man served with forty rounds of ammunition," wrote Scotsman James McMichael of the Pennsylvania State Regiment in his diary. "At noon the sick were sent to Bethlehem, which indicates that a sudden attack is intended." Sixteen-year-old Joseph Plumb Martin, a veteran of the fighting around New York in 1776, noted later in life, "Their provisions (what they had) were all cooked, and their arms and ammunition strictly inspected and all deficiencies supplied."[34]

On the eve of the operation, as the men packed their gear, wrote their letters, and prepared for the combat ahead, Anthony Wayne found the time to dash off a quick note to his wife. "I have often wrote to you on the eve of some expected and uncertain event—but never on any equal to the present—before this reaches you the Heads of many and worthy fellow will be laid low," wrote the division leader. "Dawn is big with the fate of thousands . . . have the most happy presage of entering Philadelphia at the head of troops covered with laurels before the close of day."[35]

* * *

Continental dragoon and scout Baylor Hill set out early in the morning of October 3 "to Jinkin's Town then down on the Enemys lines to Frankford Town 5 miles from Phila from thence to Jno. Hollowells on Skippack Road at night." Hill was but one of many scouts employed by Washington to ride ahead of the advancing army. Deploying scouts was a calculated risk that may well have prevented an ambush, but it also offered the threat that one would fall into enemy hands and be forced to reveal the army's plans.[36]

33 Ibid., 375.

34 McMichael, "Diary," 152; Joseph Plumb Martin, *Private Yankee Doodle*, George F. Scheer, ed. (Fort Washington, PA, 2000), 72.

35 Letter, Anthony Wayne to Polly Wayne, 3 October 1777, Anthony Wayne Papers, Historical Society of Pennsylvania, Philadelphia, PA, vol. 4.

36 John T. Hayes, ed., *A Gentleman of Fortune: The Diary of Baylor Hill, First Continental Light Dragoons, 1777-1781*, 3 vols. (Ft. Lauderdale, FL, 1995), vol. 1, 78.

"It is reported that the advance troops of the American army are on the march tonight," German Lutheran pastor Henry Muhlenberg wrote in his diary on October 3 from Trappe, about seven miles west of Washington's camp, "and that they intend to attack the outposts of the British army in Germantown . . . at daybreak."[37] Somehow Muhlenberg had caught wind of the movement. Fortunately for the Continentals, he was not in a position to tell the British before the marching columns reached Germantown.

37 McGuire, *Campaign*, vol. 2, 47-48; Muhlenberg, *Journals*, vol. 3, 82.

Chapter 11

Marching to the Attack

October 3-4, 1777

"We had not above two hours notice of their advancing,
& then gave no credit to it."[1]

— Capt. Richard Fitzpatrick, 1st British Foot Guards, October 28, 1777

George Washington concocted an ambitious plan for assaulting the British force at Germantown. His young Continental Army had a long night of marching ahead of it.

No lights, noise, or talking were permitted along the way. Clouds blocked the moonlight and the temperatures dropped into the fifties. "The night was dark and it looked like rain, but it remained dry," recorded Rev. Henry Muhlenberg in his journal. Stark darkness greeted the men as they tramped southeast in silence. To shorten the march and arrive in the proper order "to attack the different parts of the Enemy's lines," wrote an anonymous American officer to George Clinton, the governor of New York, the day after the battle, "Conway, Sullivan & Wayne followed by the Reserve marched down one Road, Green Stevens & McDougall another, Armstrong a third, & Smallwood & Foreman a fourth Road."[2]

1 Letter, Fitzpatrick to his Brother, 28 October 1777.

2 Muhlenberg, *Journals*, vol. 3, 82; McGuire, *Campaign*, vol. 2, 53; *Public Papers of George Clinton, First Governor of New York, 1777-1795 — 1801-1804*, 10 vols. (New York, 1900), vol. 2, 367-368.

Smallwood's Column

As it had the longest march of anyone that night, William Smallwood's Maryland and New Jersey militia column was the first to leave the American camp. The militia descended Methacton Hill using the Morris Road (a mile to the left of Skippack Road), turned right onto Bethlehem Pike, and headed for the Whitemarsh Church intersection, where they turned left down Church Road heading farther east to the Old York Road intersection. After crossing Tacony Creek, the militiamen turned right onto Old York Road a quarter mile south of Jenkin's Tavern. With a little luck Smallwood's men would then approach Germantown and come out on the right rear of the British camp. Old York Road was fifteen miles from camp, and they would need to march another three or four miles before encountering the enemy. According to Smallwood, he left "about 6 o'clock in the evening of the 3rd." James Vance of New Jersey's Hunterdon County militia remembered "they fixed pieces of white paper on their hats by which to know one another" in the darkness. Another New Jerseyman, Aaron Hageman of the Somerset County militia, recalled how they "Marched all night, halted in the road about break of day so as not to be there too soon." It was Smallwood's task to drive the Queen's Rangers away at daybreak.[3]

Three miles after turning onto Church Road the head of Smallwood's column approached Limekiln Road, down which some of the flankers marched in error. Each step down the wrong road moved them closer to the camp of the British 1st Light Infantry Battalion. Later, the capture of one of these flankers provided an early warning to the British that the enemy was near.[4]

Greene's Column

Nathanael Greene, who commanded the largest column in the Continental Army, had to wait for Smallwood to clear out before getting his own men on the road. Sources claim Greene was moving by 6:00 p.m., but with Smallwood using the same narrow road and claiming to have left about the same time, it is more likely

3 Morris Road took Smallwood's men to the Bethlehem Pike, where they would turn right. Just down the road was the Skippack Road intersection at Whitemarsh Church. Church Road is modern Route 73. Letter, William Smallwood to unknown recipient, October 9, 1777, reproduced in *PMHB* (Philadelphia, 1877), vol.1, 401; RWPF, files S4697 and S819.

4 McGuire, *Campaign*, vol. 2, 62.

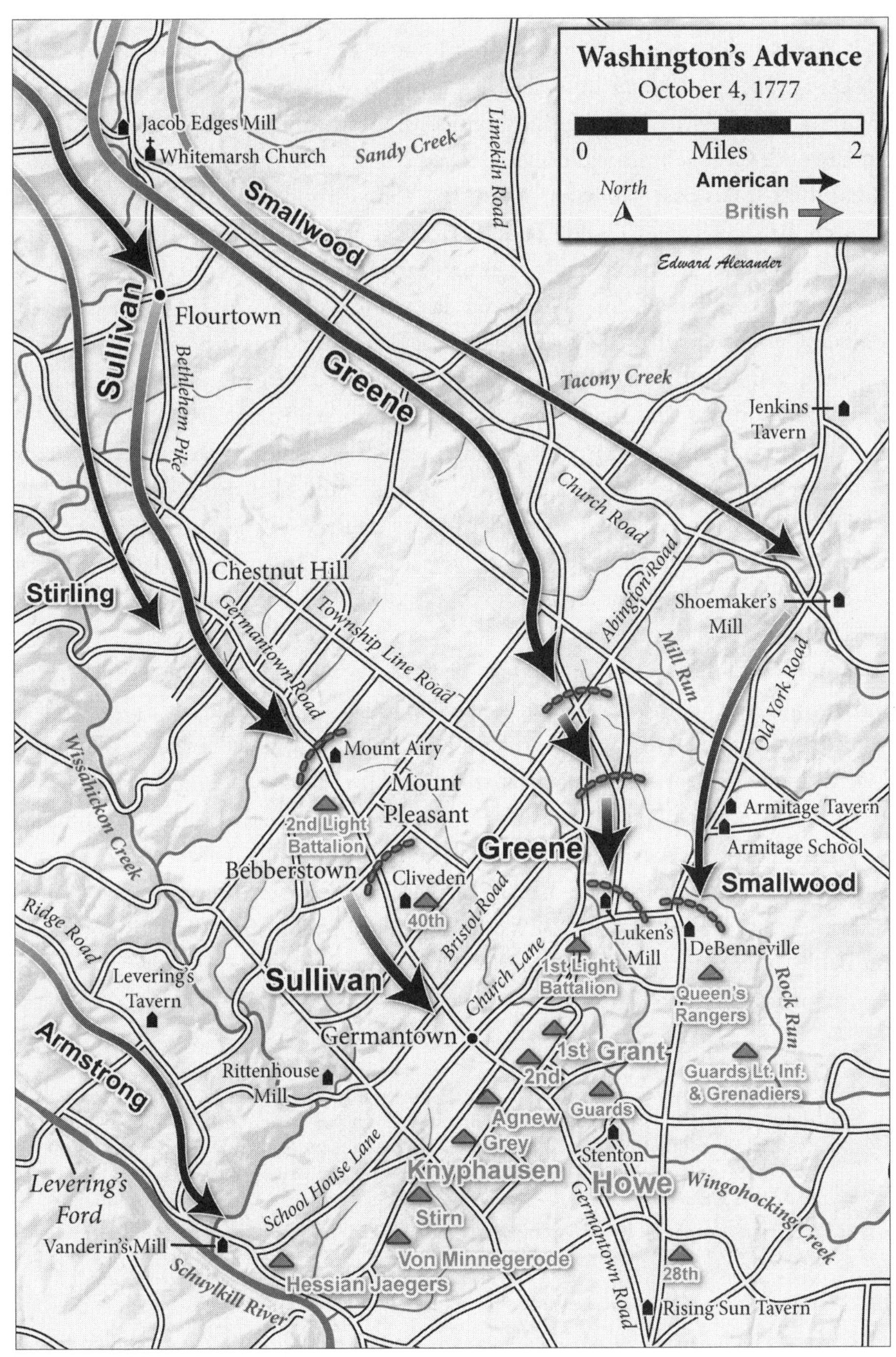
Washington's Advance
October 4, 1777
0 Miles 2
North
American
British
Edward Alexander
Jacob Edges Mill
Whitemarsh Church
Sandy Creek
Limekiln Road
Smallwood
Flourtown
Sullivan
Bethlehem Pike
Greene
Tacony Creek
Jenkins Tavern
Church Road
Abington Road
Chestnut Hill
Stirling
Germantown Road
Township Line Road
Shoemaker's Mill
Mill Run
Old York Road
Mount Airy
Mount Pleasant
Wissahickon Creek
2nd Light Battalion
Armitage Tavern
Armitage School
Bebberstown
Cliveden
Greene
Smallwood
40th
Bristol Road
Ridge Road
Luken's Mill
DeBenneville
Levering's Tavern
Sullivan
Church Lane
1st Light Battalion
Queen's Rangers
Rock Run
Armstrong
Germantown
1st Grant
2nd
Guards Lt. Inf. & Grenadiers
Rittenhouse Mill
Agnew
Guards
Grey
Stenton
Levering's Ford
School House Lane
Knyphausen
Howe
Wingohocking Creek
Stirn
Vanderin's Mill
Von Minnegerode
Germantown Road
28th
Schuylkill River
Hessian Jaegers
Rising Sun Tavern

that Greene did not get started until at least 6:30 p.m. or thereafter. Alexander McDougall's Connecticut brigade led the movement followed by Greene's own division, with Adam Stephen's Virginia division bringing up the rear. Like Smallwood, Greene tramped down Church Road but turned right onto Limekiln Road three miles past Whitemarsh Church. (Smallwood had marched farther out Church Road to get to Old York Road.) The movement to Limekiln Road separated Greene from Sullivan's column to the northeast by more than two miles. If all went as planned, Greene would slam into the British 1st Light Infantry Battalion just after sunrise beyond Luken's Mill. The roads were poorly marked and the night dark, so the march was slower than desired. Greene arrived in position about half an hour later than Sullivan's men off his right flank.[5]

"I left my baggage and my Bible which my father bought for me when I was six years old, in my trunk," recalled Lt. James Morris of the 5th Connecticut Regiment, McDougall's brigade. "I marched with only my military suit, and my implements of war, without any change of dress or even a blanket." Morris also took note of "Samuel Stannard my waiter," a servant he described as "a strong athletic man [who] carried my blanket and provisions with a canteen of Whiskey." Ensign Jonathan Todd of the 7th Connecticut Regiment of the same brigade remembered moving all night "without so Much as speaking A Loud word. Just at day we arriv'd within a Mile from Town Where we formed." The 4th Connecticut's Joseph Plumb Martin made it clear that specific instructions for the attack had been withheld from the men when he observed that he "naturally concluded something serious was in the wind. We marched slowly all night. In the morning there was a low vapor lying on the land which made it very difficult to distinguish objects at any great distance." Similarly, Col. Charles Webb, the commander of the 2nd Connecticut, recalled "marching the whole night" and arriving "at the day dawn . . . at Germantown."[6]

5 McGuire, *Campaign*, vol. 2, 55; Reed, *Campaign*, 220-221; Edgar, *Campaign*, 57. It is important to note that commanders' watches were not synchronized. Greene has been criticized for being misled by his guide down the Morris Road. Had Greene taken the Skippack Road with Sullivan's column, however, more than three-quarters of Washington's army would have been using the same road to approach the Whitemarsh Church intersection. Despite later criticism by such campaign historians as Thomas McGuire and John Reed, it was wise for Greene to utilize Morris Road to spread the army out over multiple routes. Some writers claim this change of roads forced his troops to countermarch to return to his intended route, but no contemporary accounts from Greene's column mention any such needless marching.

6 Letter, Jonathan Todd to his Father, October 6, 1777, Jonathan Todd Letters, Revolutionary War Pension Files, reel 2396, National Archives, Washington, DC; Martin, *Yankee Doodle*, 72;Ryan, ed.,

Lieutenant James McMichael of the Pennsylvania State Regiment, part of George Weedon's Virginia brigade marching behind the Connecticut men, recorded a curious order he received as the column passed Whitemarsh Church. "Major J[ohn] Murray, Capt. [John] Nice and I were ordered at the head of 80 men to feel their advance pickets, and if we conveniently could to attack. Owing to the picket being within a mile of their main body, we were unsuccessful, and rejoined our regiment at daybreak." These Pennsylvania troops represented the only locals in Greene's entire column, and using them to probe ahead of the column on the dark night made sense.[7]

Few accounts agree on the distance marched that night, which is not surprising since the men were moving in column along strange roads in the dark, uncertain of their destination. Brigade commander Weedon believed his men marched about "22 miles to the Ground, did not arrive so soon as we Expected so that it was near six in the Morning" by the time they reached their jump-off point. Morris of the 5th Connecticut echoed Weedon's estimate when he recorded the march covered "a distance of about twenty miles." Sergeant Charles Talbot of the 6th Virginia, Weedon's brigade, however, thought the march much shorter, covering just "12 or fourteen miles," as did Col. Walter Stewart of the Pennsylvania State Regiment, who wrote that he and his men marched "about 12 miles; on account of the darkness of the night and badness of some Roads we did not arrive at our appointed place until past 6 O'Clock." The shorter estimates were in fact the most accurate gauges of the distance from the American camps to the point designated for the opening of the attack.[8]

Adam Stephen's division moved out behind Weedon's brigade at the end of Greene's column. Like the rest of the recorded departure times, when it did so is

---

Salute to Courage, 103; "Contemporary Account of the Battle of Germantown," *PMHB* (Philadelphia, 1887), vol. 11, 330. Greene's march was conducted well and without serious incident. The record shows that one officer, Lt. Joseph Fish of the 4th Connecticut, was charged with "Leaving the regiment and platoon, he belonged to, while on the march towards the enemy . . . and also with being much disguised with liquor." After the battle he was tried and acquitted of the first charge but found guilty of being inebriated "and sentenced therefore, to be reprimanded, by the Brigadier General, in the presence of the officers of the brigade." Chase and Lengel, eds., *Papers*, vol. 11, 605.

7 McMichael, "Diary," 152.

8 Letter, George Weedon to John Page, 4 October 1777, original in Weedon Letters, Chicago Historical Society, Chicago, IL; Charles Talbot, "Letters of Charles Moile Talbot to Charles Talbot," Mrs. J. B. Friend and Elizabeth V. Gaines, eds., *The William and Mary Quarterly* (Williamsburg, VA, 1931), vol. 11, 318; Letter, Walter Stewart to General Gates, October 12, 1777, reproduced in *PMHB* (Philadelphia, 1877), vol. 1, 400.

uncertain. Captain John Marshall, who had turned 22 a week earlier and later would serve as the country's fourth chief justice of the Supreme Court, recalled that "the army moved from its ground about seven o'clock in the afternoon." Stephen's adjutant, Joseph Clark, observed that they left "about sunset" but only took with them "about half the pieces out of the [artillery] park, leaving the rest with a guard, of such as were less fit to go on with the army, who had orders to put all the baggage and tents in the wagons, and to wait further orders." Lieutenant Colonel William Heth of the 3rd Virginia, part of Charles Scott's brigade, described the column being "disposed of in such a manner as to march by several ranks, so as to arrive at the enemys picquets by 2 o'c[lock] . . . but from shrt marches and frequent halts it was near 6 before the first volley of small arms were heard."[9]

Armstrong's Column

John Armstrong's Pennsylvania militiamen, marching on the right flank of Washington's army that night, had the shortest distance to cover and were the first to arrive at the point of attack. Armstrong left Norriton Township down Manatawny Road (modern Ridge Avenue), west of and generally parallel to the rest of the army. The militiamen had 15 miles to cover before arriving at Vanderin's Mill to confront the Hessian jaegers, who were manning the posts closest to the Schuylkill River. John Donaldson of the Philadelphia Light Horse recalled moving down the "Ridge Road towards Vandeerens mills . . . having orders to turn the left flank of the enemy & attack him in the rear. The cavalry were silently to scour the roads & to keep up the communication with the head of the columns."[10]

Sullivan's Column

In order to provide time for Smallwood and Greene to get underway, the last of the army's four strike columns, commanded by John Sullivan, did not move until

9 John Marshall, *The Life of George Washington, Commander in Chief of the American Forces, During the War Which Established the Independence of His Country, and First President of the United States*, 5 vols. (Philadelphia, 1804), vol. 3, 178. Marshall later became chief justice of the U.S. Supreme Court. Joseph Clark, "Diary of Joseph Clark," *Proceedings of the New Jersey Historical Society* (Newark, 1855), 100; Commager and Morris, eds., *Spirit of Seventy-six*, 629.

10 Capt. J. H. C. Smith, "History of the 1st City Troop," based largely on the recollections of Trooper John Donaldson, First City Troop Archives, Philadelphia, PA. The Philadelphia Light Horse is still an active military unit (Philadelphia 1st City Troop, Pennsylvania National Guard).

about 8:00 p.m. Sullivan's men took the direct route down Skippack Road (modern Route 73). "[T]he whole Army march from their encampments leaving only a sufficient number to guard the Camp," wrote Pvt. Ephraim Kirby of the light dragoons to his father five weeks after the battle. "[T]he march of the Army was very silent." Light dragoon Baylor Hill, who was exhausted by nightfall because he had been out all day scouting the British lines, was resting along Skippack Road in Whitemarsh Township when Sullivan's men tramped past. "This night our army at 8 oClock began to march by this place towards the Enemy lines," he wrote.[11]

Sullivan halted his column just short of Whitemarsh Church about six miles after leaving camp. According to Washington's adjutant general, Timothy Pickering, the "halt being occasioned by information from a prisoner, that half a battalion of the enemy's light infantry had the preceding evening advanced on the same road a considerable way beyond their picket. It was necessary, therefore," continued Pickering, "to make a disposition to secure that party of light infantry, that their opposition might not frustrate the principal design. Such a disposition was in fact made; but the enemy had retired about midnight to their camp."[12]

Rather than continue, Sullivan turned right and moved straight down Bethlehem Road to Germantown Road through Flourtown, and eventually into Chestnut Hill, which was about three miles beyond Whitemarsh Church. The march, Sullivan reported, took "all night." Benjamin Tallmadge, another member of the light dragoons, recalled that the head of the column got into position earlier than did Sullivan: "by 3 o'clock the next morning we found ourselves close in upon the scene of action."[13]

The Corps de Reserve under Lord Stirling trudged along behind Sullivan's column. Ensign George Ewing thought it was "[a]bout eleven at night they marched off." Elias Dayton, colonel of the 3rd New Jersey, recalled the difficulties in making a timely march: "Unfortainately for us the Night proved very dark which

11 Letter, Ephraim Kirby to his father Abraham Kirby, November 12, 1777, Ephraim Kirby Papers, Duke University Library, Durham, NC; Baylor Hill, *A Gentleman of Fortune: The Diary of Baylor Hill, First Continental Light Dragoons, 1777-1781*, John T. Hayes, ed., 3 vols. (Ft. Lauderdale, FL, 1995), vol. 1, 78.

12 Pickering, *Pickering*, vol. 1, 167-168. The prisoner was referencing a detachment of the 2nd Light Infantry Battalion that had been ordered out on patrol by General Howe based upon a report that Washington's army was fast approaching. Smallwood and Greene had just moved through this same area without incident. This halt could have been to avoid British patrols as Pickering later stated, but it also may have come about because the road was clogged with Greene's men.

13 Hammond, ed., *Papers*, vol. 1, 544; Tallmadge, *Memoir*, 22.

so retarded our march that we did not reach the Enemys Advanced post until sunrise, whereas our design was to Attack them at first dawn of day." According to artillery chief Henry Knox, the combined troops of Sullivan and Stirling moved "from 15 to 20 miles" and "arrived a little after break of day [opposite] the respective posts of the enemy."[14]

Four decades after the battle, Charles Cotesworth Pinckney, an unattached South Carolina officer tagging along with Washington's staff, leveled an accusation against the army's cavalry commander that evening. "[Casimir] Pulaski who commanded the Cavalry drew it off," Pinckney claimed in an 1820 letter, "& when the head of Sullivan's Division arrived near the point of attack, we found he had lain down, & gone to sleep; for which he was very severely reprimanded by the General [Washington]." Timothy Pickering recalled no such incident. "I did not know at the time, nor do I recollect ever to have heard, that Pulaski was found asleep," scoffed the adjutant general to a confidante. "Nor do I remember to have heard him censured for any neglect of duty, in the case referred to, the battle of Germantown. [T]he distance the army had to march, from its encampment on the Skippack road to Germantown, is estimated to be about sixteen miles," he continued, "and, therefore (although I do not recollect it) a very temporary halt might have taken place; but certainly not long enough for an officer, or private, to have retired to indulge in sleep in a farmhouse."[15]

Washington wanted his columns to arrive and attack the British at Germantown simultaneously, a complex move that would have been hard to pull off under the best of circumstances. Pickering, who was in the thick of the planning at Washington's elbow, later explained this initial failure of coordination. "The right column under General Sullivan, which Washington accompanied, marched on the direct road to Germantown," he wrote in a letter to early American historian Jared Sparks on August 23, 1826. "Greene, with his column, was obliged to make a circuit to the left, to gain the road which led to his point of attack. The columns being entirely separated, and at a distance from each other, no calculations of their

14 Ewing, "Journal," 7; Ryan, ed., *Salute to Courage*, 100; Letter, Henry Knox to Lucy Knox, 6 October 1777, Gilder Lehrman Collection, New York Historical Society, New York, NY; Drake, *Correspondence*, 52.

15 Letter, Charles Cotesworth Pinckney to Henry Johnson, November 14, 1820, in *The Historical Magazine: Notes and Queries, Concerning the Antiquities, History and Biography of America* (Morrisania, NY, 1866), vol. 10, 203; Letter, Timothy Pickering to Jared Sparks, August 23, 1826, reproduced in *The North American Review* (Boston, 1826), vol. 23, 425-426.

commanders could have insured their arriving at the same time at their respective points of attack."[16]

The "disposition [of the troops] appears to have been well made; but to execute such a plan requires great exactness in the officers conducting the columns, as well as punctuality in commencing the march, to bring the whole to the point of action at once," observed Pickering. "For this end it is absolutely necessary that the length and quality of the roads be perfectly ascertained, the time it will take to march them accurately calculated, and guides chosen who [are] perfectly acquainted with the roads. It is also necessary to assign proper halting-places, if either column would arrive before the appointed hour. All these points," he concluded, "I believe were attended to in the present case." As far as Washington and his adjutant general were concerned, they had planned for every possible contingency. The friction of war, however, had a mind of its own.[17]

The British Forewarned?

Hessian jaeger Johann Ewald's diary contains a revealing entry for the night of October 3 that goes a long way toward explaining what happened at Germantown. "Toward evening Professor Smith from Philadelphia came to me, who owned a country seat close to the jager post, for which I had provided protection. He asked me to take a little walk with him, which I was quite willing to do since we had enjoyed several days' rest." Smith led Ewald "behind the camp, and when he thought no one would discover us, he addressed me with the following words: 'My friends, I confess to you that I am a friend of the States and no friend of the English government, but you have rendered me a friendly turn. You have shown me that humanity which each soldier should not lose sight of. You have protected my property. I will show you that I am grateful. You stand in a corps which is hourly threatened by the danger of the first attack when the enemy approaches.'" Smith continued his discussion with Ewald. "Friend, God bless your person! The success of your arms I cannot wish.—Friend! General Washington has marched up to

16 Pickering to Sparks, August 23, 1826, 429.

17 Pickering, *Pickering*, vol. 1, 167. Pickering went on to state, "I understood that the guide of the left wing [Greene's] mistook the way." My research has not discovered any primary sources that confirm Greene's column took a wrong turn.

Norriton today!—Adieu! Adieu!' This grateful man," ended Ewald, "took the road to Philadelphia without saying one word more."[18]

The information stunned Ewald, who "stood for quite a while as if turned to stone. I thought over this man's entire conversation, hurried into camp, and reported to Colonel [Ludwig von] Wurmb, who immediately mounted his horse to report this information to General Knyphausen and to headquarters. General Knyphausen took his precautionary measures at once." When Howe heard the news, recorded the German, he purportedly uttered, "That cannot be!" Since the entire countryside was devoted to him, no person except this honest man would let us know it," continued Ewald. "We could not learn much from our patrols because they were constantly betrayed by the country people and attacked, and did not dare to venture farther than they could get support."[19]

Howe's scoffing notwithstanding, jaeger commander Ludwig von Wurmb instructed Ewald to order "the pickets which were posted from the Schuylkill along the Wissahickon Creek doubled at midnight. The creek covered the army's front on the left. The colonel ordered me to patrol steadily both roads near the Schuylkill and the highway to Norriton. I did this unceasingly, and assigned each part of the picket its place, which should be taken at the first shot." The road forked west of the stone bridge across Wissahickon Creek; the lower fork hugged the Schuylkill while the upper route carried Ridge Road up the hill past the jaeger picket post. The *Jaeger Corps Journal* does not mention Ewald's report specifically, but it does note that the army was forewarned, and that von Wurmb prepared accordingly: "About two o'clock in the morning, we received reports of his [Washington's] approach. Lieutenant Colonel von Wurmb immediately moved out with the Jaeger Corps . . . and occupied the bridge over the Wissahickon, near the Vanderen's house."[20]

Wilhelm von Knypausen, commanding the army's left wing, made no mention of Ewald's warning that night after the battle in his report to Frederick II, Landgrave of Hesse-Cassel. "We only received information at daybreak about all these movements," was how Knypausen described the events. Despite von Knyphausen's opinion, Lieutenant Colonel von Wurmb, commander of the

18 Ewald, *Diary*, 92.

19 Ibid., 92-93.

20 Ibid., 93. The lower road is now Main Street in Manayunk. Marie E. Burgoyne and Bruce E. Burgoyne, eds., *Journal of the Hesse-Cassel Jaeger Corps and Hans Konze's List of Jaeger Officers* (Westminster, MD, 2008), 21. The *Jaeger Corps Journal* was a record of events kept in the field from June 23, 1777 to April 20, 1784.

jaegers, appears to have heeded Ewald's warning and alerted his command to the approach of the Continentals. If some of the army was unprepared for a surprise attack, the jaegers were ready. Unbeknownst to John Armstrong's Pennsylvania militiamen, they would not have the element of surprise on their side.[21]

Captain John Andre, who served as an aide to brigade commander Charles Grey, wrote that the enemy's approach along Knyphausen's left wing was not totally unexpected. "Some intimation had been received the 3rd of the designs of the Rebels to attack us, which were very little credited." Captured Americans, Andre continued, claimed "Washington's whole Army had marched the preceeding evening from the 19th mile-stone; that he was within a very small distance." Lieutenant William Keough, adjutant of the 44th Regiment of Foot, which was camped in the left center of Knyphausen's division line, believed the intelligence from the captured Americans "[e]nabled Our Army to get speedily under Arms for their reception."[22]

On the British army's far right, meanwhile, where the Queen's Rangers were camped supported by the light infantry and grenadier companies of the British Brigade of Guards, orders arrived on the evening of October 3 from the commander himself. "Sir William Howe came to the quarters I was in, with his Aids-de-camp, a little before sunset," testified Sir George Osborne of the Guards before Parliament, "and gave me orders to move in front, with the grenadiers, and light-infantry of the guards, to Major Simcoe's [the Queen's Rangers picket] post, about a half a mile in front of the line of infantry." According to Osborne, Howe made it clear "I might expect the enemy at day-break next morning. I can therefore add, that the firing of the enemy, on the morning of the attack of German-Town, began exactly, or near the time, that Sir William Howe acquainted me the night before it would do." It was because of Howe's personal warning, continued Osborne, "I was not in any danger of being surprised." If Osborne is to be believed and Howe alerted the light infantry and grenadier companies of the Brigade of Guards to support the picket post of the Queen's Rangers, no such warning reached the main Guards camp. Captain Richard Fitzpatrick of the 1st Foot Guards (Brig. Gen. Edward Matthew's Brigade of Guards) remembered being surprised "indeed in every sense of the word, for we had not above two hours

21 Letter, Wilhelm von Knyphausen to the Landgrave, October 17, 1777, 83.

22 Andre, *Journal*, 54-55; Narrative letter, September 28, 1777, probably by Lt. William Keough, adjutant of the 44th Regiment of Foot, American Philosophical Society, quoted in full in McGuire, *Campaign*, Vol. 2, 284.

notice of their advancing, & then gave no credit to it." When Smallwood's Maryland and New Jersey militia approached the right end of the British line, they ran into an alert picket outpost of the Queen's Rangers supported by the grenadier and light infantry companies of the Brigade of Guards. The main Guards camp, however, was completely unprepared for battle.[23]

To the north or front of the Brigade of Guards sat the camp of the 1st Light Infantry Battalion. Captain William Scott of the 17th Regiment of Foot's light company heard "Rumours of general attack." Scott remembered seeing officers "in front of advanced posts as if to reconnoiter; partial attack thought likely; army in the fullest confidence." According to Scott, their sister command, the 2nd Light Infantry Battalion camped about 1 ½ miles in front of the army near Mount Pleasant, was ordered to "advance some miles on the main [Germantown] road in the night." About 8:00 p.m., seven companies of Maj. John Maitland's battalion began to patrol down the Germantown Road from the 2nd Light Infantry Battalion's camp, but "returned without making any discovery." (Sullivan's American column, it will be recalled, had taken a prisoner or deserter who warned that a British scouting party was out looking for the approaching enemy, and halted its advance for an undetermined length of time.) Scott's comment about patrols from the 2nd Light Infantry Battalion moving out on Germantown Road is intriguing. Once beyond Chestnut Hill, a mile and a half distant from their camp, they would not have encountered any Americans since Sullivan did not enter the Germantown Road until the head of his column arrived in that area via the Bethlehem Road.[24]

While the patrol from the 2nd Light Infantry Battalion did not find signs of enemy activity during its short march beyond Chestnut Hill, pickets watching the front of the 1st Light Infantry Battalion uncovered the enemy approach. "Capt.

23 *Narrative*, 108-109. Simcoe did not command the Queen's Rangers at Germantown. He was recovering from his Brandywine wound and was assigned the command after Germantown. Letter, Fitzpatrick to his Brother, 28 October 1777.

24 Scott "Memorandum," 292. According to Scott, the "Advanced post" of his battalion, "About ½ mile to the right and rear of 2nd Light Infy. Consisted of 17th, 28th, 38th companies commanded by Capt. [St. Lawrence] Boyd 38th." The order for the patrol read: "After orders 8 at Night 3rd Octor. 1777. The 55th, 57th, 63rd, 64th, 71st, 37th, and 40th Companys to parade with arms and accoutrements at Major Maitland's Quarters immediately." George Washington Papers, Series 6, Military Papers, 1755-1798, Subseries 6B, Captured British Orderly Books, 1777-1778: Captured British Army 64th Light Infantry Orderly Book, September 14 - October 3, 1777, Library of Congress, Washington, D.C. This was the last entry made in the orderly book, whichwas captured the next day in the company's camp.

Boyd waked me [at Luken's Mill]" to say they had captured a prisoner, wrote Captain Scott. When Boyd questioned him, the captive admitted he "belongs to two brigades that marched forward as candles were lighting, to attack us; he had lost his way." The infantry companies, added Scott, were "ordered to stand to their arms an hour before day." The prisoner was one of Smallwood's flankers who had moved down the wrong road in the dark and was later sent to battalion commander Col. Robert Abercromby.[25] The captive informed Abercromby that Washington's entire army was on the march that night. Abercromby immediately mounted a horse and rode to inform Brig Gen. Sir William Erskine; the two officers decided the news was credible enough to alert Maj. Gen. James Grant. The intelligence alarmed the veteran general, who immediately dressed and "ordered the line to accouter." Grant and Abercromby rode out to Scott's picket outpost with orders "to remain till [the] enemy advanced in force; then to fall back on the battalion."[26]

According to Lt. Frederick Augustus Wetherall of Scott's light infantry company, the prisoner from Smallwood's militia column was never "[e]xamin'd by any of the Generals [Howe's] Family." Wing commander Grant in fact rode to the front and issued orders to the 1st Light Infantry Battalion to prepare for a surprise attack. The 2nd Light Infantry Battalion and the 40th of Foot camped "a mile in Front of the Line were by mistake omitted in the Order to Accoutre & the 2nd L.I. having made a patrole in the Night discover'd nothing but some Fires at Whitemarsh, of course had little Reason to expect a general Attack." Like other areas of the line that night, not everyone received the word to be prepared for a surprise attack. Captain Charles Cochrane of the 4th Regiment of Foot's light company later recorded that Washington "was close upon us by the morning

25 Scott, "Memorandum," 292. Scott also delineated activity on his picket post: "A captain and 2 Subs. Walking about, or sitting down occasionally in the house which served the officers as a barrack: men in a sort of wigwam camp ready to stand to their arms in an instant; strong picket at night: duty eased in the day. Officers and men off duty slept in the night half dressed." Scott also detailed how the prisoner was caught: "On the lime kiln road one sentry was posted. . . . This being a cross road, and near other sentries, one had been judged sufficient. Sentry heard a man approaching; bent on one knee, thought him armed and a deserter, but resolved to secure him; night dark man approached close. Sentry challenged gently; answer it is I, it is Fynn, don't you know me; throw down your arms or I will put you to death." Lt. Frederick Augustus Wetherall of Scott's company also recalled the prisoner. "A Centinel of the 20th L[ight]. I[nfantry]. [company] belonging to an Out Post. . . . discovering a Man coming toward him conceal'd himself till this Man was so near he made him Prisoner." Frederick Augustus Wetherall, *Journal of Officer B*, Sol Feinstone Collection of the David Library of the American Revolution, Washington Crossing, PA, Item No. 409.

26 Scott, "Memorandum," 292-293.

without our having any good Intelligence of his motions," despite the fact that Cochrane was assigned to the supposedly alert 1st Light Infantry Battalion.[27]

Grant recalled the advance warning in a letter two weeks after the battle to Gen. Edward Harvey, adjutant general of the British Army. "None of the Inhabitants gave information of Washingtons march but We had an Hours notice by the lucky accident of one of his Flankers missing his Road & falling into the Hands of a Light Infantry Patrole," he explained. After being informed of the incident by Colonel Abercromby, added Grant, he "got a Horseback, put the 1st & 2nd Brigades under Arms, sent to Head Quarters & to Genl. Grey who was upon the Left of the Line of British & rode on to the advanced post of the 1st Lt. Infantry." There, Brig. Gen. William Erskine, the army's quartermaster general, approached the general and, with a laugh, called him "the most Alert Man in the Army." Grant told Erskine that he "knew & thought they [the Americans] were equal to such an Attempt, but that for once Hussar-like I had taken the Alarm, had faith in a Battle that morning and had acted accordingly." Like Armstrong's militiamen off to the southwest, Nathanael Greene's column, aiming for the other end of the British line, would arrive near the camp of the 1st Light Infantry Battalion only to find the enemy waiting for them to step within killing range.[28]

Because of its advanced position between the jaegers and the 1st Light Infantry Battalion, the 2nd Light Infantry Battalion was destined to be assaulted first that morning. Martin Hunter, a lieutenant in the 52nd Regiment of Foot's light company, in the camp of the 2nd Light Infantry Battalion on Mount Pleasant, remembered it was about one in the morning when "we had information from a deserter, as he said he was, but I rather think he had lost his way. He was brought in by one of our patrols, and positively said that he had left General Washington and his whole army on their march to Chestnut Hill." The prisoner, continued an irritated Hunter, was sent to "Captain [Nesbitt] Balfour, one of General Howe's aide-de-camps, who was too lazy to get up to examine him." According to Hunter, "the first that General Howe heard of General Washington's marching against us was the attack upon us at daybreak."[29]

Lieutenant Richard St. George, an exhausted officer in Hunter's light company of the 52nd Regiment who was trying to get some rest, heard the fitful firing of

27 Wetherall, *Journal of Officer B*; Letter, Charles Cochrane to Andrew Steuart, 19 October 1777, Stuart Steven papers, MS5375, 35-42 ff., National Library of Scotland, Edinburgh.

28 Grant to Harvey, October 20, 1777, Grant Papers.

29 Hunter, *Journal*, 33.

distant opposing pickets late that evening while writing a letter. "There has been firing this night all round the Centrys, which seems as they endeavour to feel our situation. I am fatigued & must sleep. Coud'st Thou sleep thus?" Despite a patrol pushing out beyond the picket post, the 2nd Light Infantry Battalion was unprepared for the approaching column of John Sullivan.[30]

Despite claims to the contrary by several historians, many British and Hessian units did receive, in fact, intelligence of the American approach and reported as much to Howe's headquarters. According to contemporary sources, only the 2nd Light Infantry Battalion was not expecting an attack that morning. As Howe later reported, "at three o'clock in the morning of the 4th the patroles discovered the enemy's approach, and upon the communication of this intelligence the army was immediately ordered under arms." Engineer officer Archibald Robertson, of Howe's staff, recalled that "at 4 in the morning. . . . Got on horseback with Sir William immediately. The lines all turn'd out between 5 and 6."[31]

Orders spread through the lines at Germantown to prepare for action. The command farthest from Howe's headquarters—Major Maitland's 2nd Light Infantry Battalion—was not under arms when sunrise arrived one minute before 6:00 a.m. that Saturday morning. The light infantrymen lounging around Mount Airy were in for the shock of their lives.

30 St. George letter dated September 11, 1777.

31 Stockdale, *Register*, vol. 10, 431; Robertson, *His Diaries*, 151. American brigade commander George Weedon wrote in a letter to the lieutenant governor of Virginia on the night of the battle, "all their [British] Troops from Phila was call'd up, the Enemy before which makes me think they got wind of our situations notwithstanding the precautions used to prevent it." It may have seemed that way to Weedon, but such was not the case. Letter, George Weedon to John Page, October 4, 1777.

Chapter 12

Sullivan & Armstrong Strike

October 4, 1777
5:00 a.m. to 6:30 a.m.

"When our Men first made the attack we had the most pleasing prospect before us."[1]

— Maj. Gen. John Sullivan, Continental division commander, October 1777

It was still dark when John Sullivan's large column marched down Bethlehem Road to Chestnut Hill and turned onto the Germantown Road. The Americans were just one mile from the British 2nd Light Infantry Battalion's picket outpost at Mount Airy and three miles from the main British camp in Germantown. No one knew whether any of the other three columns had reached their jump-off points and were in position to strike. Sullivan, anxious to get into position and attack before the rising sun revealed his presence, began shaking his troops into lines of battle.[2]

The first objective was to overrun the British picket post at Mount Airy. Sullivan detached and sent ahead two regiments—Lt. Col. Josiah Harmar's 6th Pennsylvania from Conway's brigade and Col. Josiah Hall's 4th Maryland from Price's brigade—and ordered the balance of Conway's brigade to follow them.

1 Hammond, ed., *Papers*, vol. 1, 567.

2 In 1777, Chestnut Hill was nearly uninhabited, unlike the busy shopping district it contains today.

Present day view of Widow Mackinett's Tavern. *Photo by author*

Sullivan's own division under Moses Hazen's command came next, with Anthony Wayne's Pennsylvania division trailing. The 6th Pennsylvania and 4th Maryland regiments moved down the south side of Chestnut Hill and crossed Cresheim Creek around 5:30 a.m. Major John Eager Howard of the 4th Maryland later recalled that as the men "descended into the Valley near Mount Airy, the sun rose, but was soon obscured." A heavy, thick fog began to develop just at daybreak, and the air was still. Soon, gunpowder smoke and small brush fires would combine with the fog to obscure the terrain and add to the confusion of battle.[3]

Captain Jacob Bower's company of the 6th Pennsylvania led the way toward the British outpost. Recruited largely from the Philadelphia area, the regiment was fighting on its home turf. Both Lieutenant James Glentworth and Ensign John Markland had been born in the colonial capital. Ensign Charles Mackinett had been

3 Hammond, ed., *Papers*, vol. 1, 544; McGuire, *Campaign*, vol. 2, 67; "Col. John Eager Howard's Account of the Battle of Germantown writing to Timothy Pickering in 1827," *Maryland Historical Magazine* (Baltimore, 1909), vol. 4, 314.

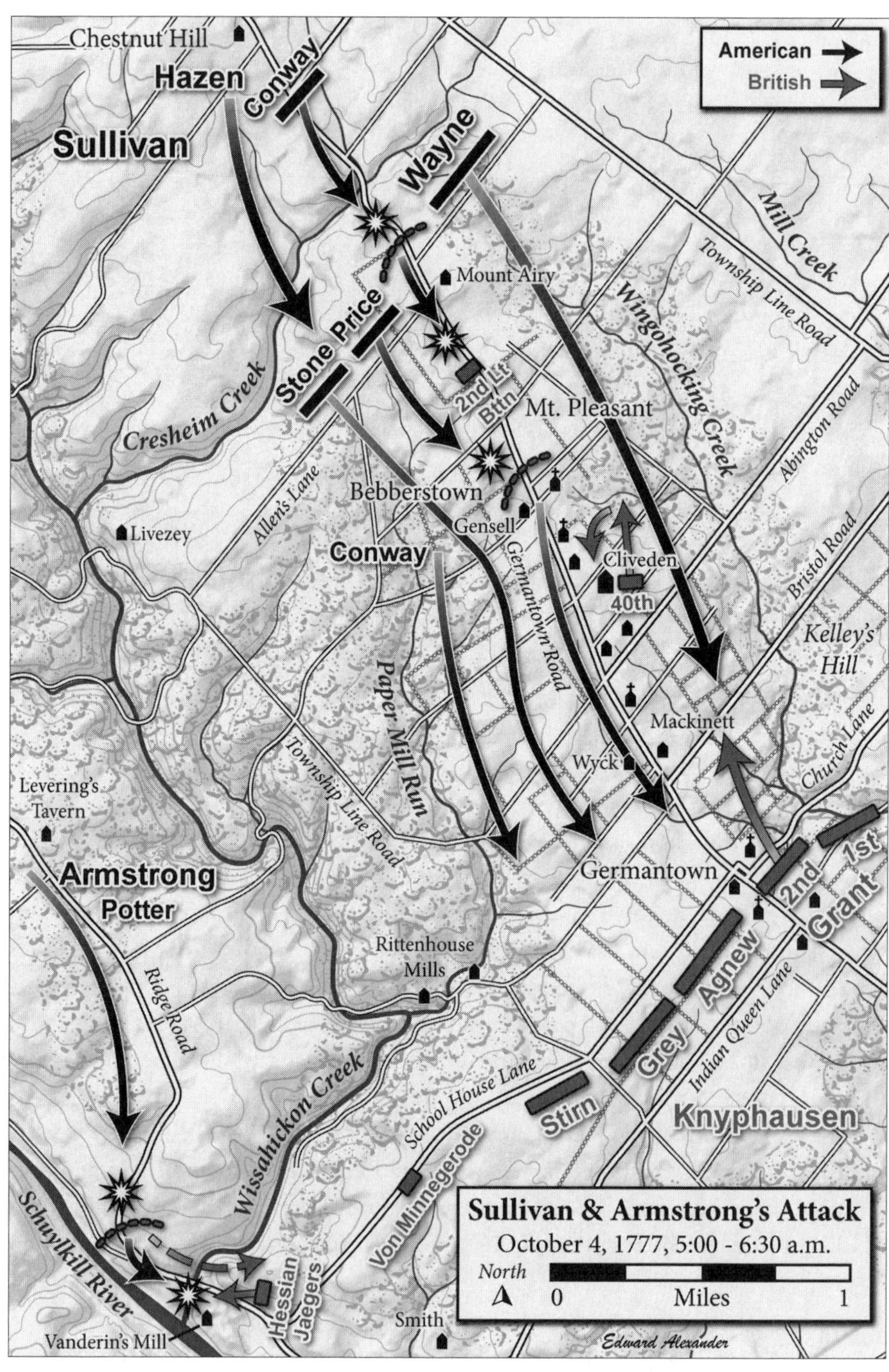

Sullivan & Armstrong's Attack
October 4, 1777, 5:00 - 6:30 a.m.
North
0 Miles 1

raised in Germantown and his mother ran "Widow Mackinett's Tavern," just a half mile down the road from Cliveden. After crossing Cresheim Creek, Bower's company advanced in a steady line up Mount Airy with bayonets fixed. The morning mist grew thicker with each passing minute. A detachment of 4th Continental Light Dragoons under Capt. Allen McLane of Delaware trotted along in support. The men were not sure exactly what awaited them, but they soon discovered it was three companies of British light infantry: Capt. William Wood's company of the 45th of Foot, Lt. Mark Saurin's of the 46th of Foot, and Lt. Alexander Forbes's of the 40th of Foot.[4]

The British pickets caught their first glimpses of the enemy as the Pennsylvanians tramped through the mist during their ascent of Mount Airy. Two 6-pounders fired a round at the figures stepping out of the gloom. The deep-throated booms alerted both armies that something was afoot. The staccato of small-arms fire a few moments later confirmed that a battle was underway.

Conway deployed the rest of his brigade in order to overwhelm the British picket post as quickly as possible. "The troops were put in motion," recalled Benjamin Tallmadge of the light dragoons in his memoir, "and in a few moments the firing commenced." Taken almost completely by surprise, "the out-posts and advanced guards of the enemy were driven in with great precipitation." One anonymous American, in a letter to New York's governor penned the next day, thought it "about ten minutes before Six o'Clock in the morning [when] a firing began between the head of Conway's Column & the Enemy's pickett." Tench Tilghman, one of Washington's most trusted staff officers, remembered in a letter two days later how "[t]he first Guard was at Mount Airey," and was "carried without much resistance." With the British picket quickly overwhelmed, Sullivan needed to keep moving if he had any hope of taking out the rest of Maj. John Maitland's 2nd Light Infantry Battalion 3/4 of a mile ahead on Mount Pleasant.[5]

The initial fighting at the picket posts alerted the balance of the 2nd Light Infantry Battalion to get organized and under arms. "On the first shots being fired at our piquet the battalion was out and under arms in a minute," claimed Lt. Martin Hunter of the 52nd of Foot. "So much had they in their recollection Wayne's affair

4 McGuire, *Campaign*, vol. 2, 65 and 67. The tavern building still stands at 6023 Germantown Avenue in Philadelphia. After the war, Mackinett returned to Germantown to run his mother's tavern. McGuire, *Germantown*, 93.

5 Tallmadge, *Memoir*, 22-23; *Papers of Clinton*, vol. 2, 368; Tench Tilghman, *Memoir of Lieut. Col. Tench Tilghman, Secretary and Aid to Washington, Together with an Appendix, Containing Revolutionary Journals and Letters, Hitherto Unpublished* (Albany, NY, 1876), 160.

[Paoli] that many of them rushed out the back part of the huts." The day "had broke about five minutes, but it was a very thick, foggy morning, and so dark that we could not see a hundred yards before us," he continued. "Just as the battalion formed the piquet ran in and said the enemy were advancing in force." During the retreat Lt. Alexander Forbes of the 40th Foot fell wounded.[6]

Hunter thought their initial defeat could have been much worse. "It was a very fortunate circumstance for us that we had arranged our quarters two days before from the houses in Beggarstown to wigwams outside the town," he explained, "for I am certain, had we been quartered in the town the morning we were attacked, we should all have been bayonetted." Indeed, thoughts of "Wayne's Affair" hung over the light infantry like an ill-fitting shroud.[7]

Sullivan Deploys his Division

Once the picket post broke and fled, reported John Sullivan, the British "were Suddenly reinforced by all their Light Infantry." Sullivan can be forgiven for his exaggeration. The heat of battle, pall of fog, and low light made it difficult to see fully what was transpiring. In fact, what he faced was the balance of the now fully alert 2nd Light Infantry Battalion. Their appearance, continued Sullivan, "[c]ompelled General Conway to form his Brigade to Sustain the attacking Regiment & to Repulse the Light Infantry—they maintained their ground with great Resolution till my Division [under Hazen] was formed to support them." Lieutenant John Markland of the 6th Pennsylvania, part of Conway's brigade, recalled the moment of contact as the command "was marching in close column to the attack of Germantown, in front, when they were fired on by the enemy." While Conway deployed, Hazen formed his two brigades in lines of battle west of Germantown Road. "Sullivan's division in the Valley [of Cresheim Creek] left the road and moved to the right through fields and formed in a lane running from Allen's house towards the Schuylkill," was how Maj. John Howard of the 4th

6 Hunter, *Journal*, 33.

7 Ibid. Another picket was stationed at the modern intersection of Westview and Germantown avenues a little south of Mount Airy. In 1777, the property was owned by Jacob Gensell, an immigrant from Wurttemburg. In November 1985, the skeletal remains of a soldier were discovered during renovations of a post office building at the intersection. Later research identified the remains as those of light infantryman Pvt. John Waites of Capt. George Hamilton's 52nd Regiment of Foot. The remains subsequently were interred in the British plot in Northwood Cemetery at 15th and Haines streets in Philadelphia. Cotter, Roberts, and Parrington, *Buried Past*, 351-353.

Maryland described the maneuver in a letter to Timothy Pickering in 1827. Sullivan's left was about 200 yards from the Allen House, with Col. Thomas Price's 2nd Maryland Brigade on the far left of the line and Col. John Stone's 1st Maryland Brigade extending the line toward the Schuylkill.[8]

As the Maryland division formed and Anthony Wayne extended the line to the left along Miller's Lane, Conway drove the British light infantrymen from their positions. "The action," recalled Lieutenant Markland in an 1826 paper, "continued very heavy for some time, the enemy retreating until our troops had expended all their ammunition. A fresh supply arriving in a few minutes, the American line again advanced, and after pressing the British very severely for some time, the brigade halted in order that the line might be more completely formed, when information was brought that the British had driven our troops on the left." Conway sent Markland and others to respond to this threat "and after some hard fighting the British were again forced to retire."[9]

Conway's push carried his men toward the main camp of the 2nd Light Infantry Battalion, about 400 yards away on Mount Pleasant. The pickets "had not well joined the battalion when we heard a loud cry of 'Have at the Bloodhounds! Revenge Wayne's affair!' and immediately fired a volley," remembered the 52nd of Foot's Lieutenant Hunter. This initial volley by Conway's Pennsylvanians into Maitland's battalion toppled Lt. Richard St. George of the 52nd of Foot's light company, rendering him unconscious with "a shocking wound in the head," recalled Hunter. The glancing round ball fractured St. George's skull. "He was carried off the field by [Cpl. George] Peacock," who served as St. George's waiter, and "behaved like himself, otherwise St. George must certainly have been taken prisoner."[10]

The British lights responded to the attack with their own volley. "We gave them another in return, a cheer, and charged," wrote Hunter. "On our charging they gave way on all sides but again and again renewed the attack with fresh troops and greater force. We charged them twice, till the battalion was so reduced by killed and wounded that the bugle sounded to retreat," he continued. "Indeed, had we

8 Hammond, ed., *Papers*, vol. 1, 544; "Howard's Account," 314. "Revolutionary Services of Captain John Markland," *PMHB* (Philadelphia, 1885), vol. 9, 107. The lane is modern Allens Lane.

9 "Revolutionary Services of Captain John Markland," vol. 9, 107.

10 Hunter, *Journal*, 22, 33-34; McGuire, *Campaign*, vol. 2, 69.

not retreated at the time we did, we should have been all taken or killed, as the columns of the enemy had nearly got round our flanks."[11]

The initial drive cost Conway's brigade numerous injured and killed. "In this part of the action among the many who were killed or wounded was a very gallant soldier, Abraham Best, who had his leg shot off just below the knee. Markland, who was alongside, had his pantaloons covered with the poor fellow's blood and had him immediately removed to the wagons in the rear, appropriated for the wounded. Notwithstanding the severity of the wound, Best recovered and repaid the service with his thanks." Moments later a lead ball struck Markland's arm, and he "fell into the arms" of Ensign Charles Mackinett.[12]

General Sullivan shifted his units around to meet the fully deployed 2nd Light Infantry Battalion. "The Enemy Endeavoring to flank us on the Left I [Sullivan] ordered Colo. Fords [6th Maryland] Regiment to the other side [of] the Road to Repulse them till General Wains Division arrived." There was no sign or word of Nathanael Greene's column joining the attack to Sullivan's left. Sullivan "was oblidged to form General Wains Division on the East of the Road to attack the Enemys Right." With Wayne forming on the left of the rapidly developing line, Sullivan "then Directed General Conway to Draw off Such part of his Brigade as were formed in the Road & in front of our Right & fall into my Rear & file off to the Right to flank my Division." When this formation was completed, 3,700 men were poised to overwhelm and destroy the British 2nd Light Infantry, with Wayne's Pennsylvanians on the left, Sullivan's two brigades under Hazen in the center, and Conway's Pennsylvanians on the right. Lieutenant Samuel Shaw of the Continental artillery enthusiastically noted in his journal that "our lads, encouraged by so prosperous a beginning, pushed on with the utmost resolution."[13]

Once deployed on the right side of the road, Sullivan's division pushed forward and drove back all resistance. Plagued by their disgraceful performance at Brandywine, these men were eager to redeem themselves. "We had orders to move

11 Hunter, *Journal*, 34.

12 "Services of Markland," 107. This source about Markland's war service was written in 1826, but the author's identity is unclear. It could have been Markland, writing on occasion in the third person. At the end of the paper, three officers who served with him attest to his war service, but there is no mention whether they had a hand in producing the document. Abraham Best was sent to a hospital in Reading and was awarded a pension of $5.00 a month in 1785. RWPF, file S322381. Markland also was sent to a hospital in Reading. While he did not lose his arm, it caused him problems for years. McGuire, *Germantown*, 92-93.

13 Hammond, ed., *Papers*, vol. 1, 544; Shaw, *Journals*, 40.

on," explained the 4th Maryland's Major Howard, "and advanced through a field, three or four hundred yards to the encampment of the British light infantry in an orchard, where we found them ready to receive us."[14]

"We pushed down all fences in our front and marched to the battle. It was a very foggy morning," remembered Captain Enoch Anderson of the Delaware Regiment. "Bullets began to fly on both sides," he continued, "some were killed—some wounded, but the order was to advance. We advanced in line of the division—the firing on both sides increased—and what with the thickness of the air and the firing of guns, we could see but a little way before us." Anderson soon found himself opposite a line of British infantry positioned behind a small breastwork. There, he wrote, "began the hardest battle I was ever in—at thirty feet distance." Both sides kept up a steady fire, shrouded in powder smoke and fog—or as Anderson described it, "all in darkness." The enemy rounds took a toll, continued the captain, and his "men were falling very fast. I now took off my hat and shouted as loud as I could—"Charge bayonets and advance!"' According to Anderson, every man in the line advanced as ordered under a tremendous "roar of cannon and small arms." He later claimed that "the British heard me and [ran] for it," but their retreat was the result of a destructive American fire pressed by a bayonet attack, not a shouted order that would have been impossible to hear above the din of combat. "I lost four men killed on this spot, and about twenty wounded."[15]

While Enoch Anderson's Delaware men battled to the west along Sullivan's line, Marylander John Eager Howard recalled that "a close and sharp action" against Maitland's infantry, lasting about 15 or 20 minutes, erupted closer to the Germantown Road. The line had "inclined to the left, until we reached the [Germantown] road," he continued, "and in the action one Company, commanded by Capt. Daniel Dorsey, crossed the road." From what little Howard could see, "no other part of the army was up at that time." In fact, the battle smoke and heavy fog obscured his view of Wayne's division advancing off Howard's left and driving back the light infantrymen. "My Division were ordered to advance which they Did with Such Resolution," boasted General Sullivan, "that the Enemys Light Infantry were soon compelled to Leave the Field & with it their Encampment."[16]

14 "Howard's Account," 314.

15 Anderson, *Recollections*, 45.

16 "Howard's Account," 314-315; Hammond, ed., *Papers*, vol. 1, 544.

Colonel Josias Hall, the commander of the 4th Maryland, was advancing on foot and instructed the mounted Major Howard to carry a message to Captain Dorsey to return with his company from beyond the Germantown Road. Howard spurred his horse after the errant command but found the men "engaged from behind houses, with some of the enemy, who, I supposed, had belonged to the picket." Utilizing discretion he may not have been given, Howard "judged it not proper to call them off, as it would expose our flank." When he returned with this information, an angry Hall appropriated Howard's horse and set out to bring back Dorsey's company. "Riding one way and looking another," recalled Howard, "the horse run him under a cider-press, and he was so hurt that he was taken from the field."[17]

Since the unit's lieutenant colonel was on detached duty, Hall's injury left Howard in command of the regiment. With the British line broken and in retreat, the major "pushed on through their encampment, their tents standing, and in the road, we came opposite to Chew's house, took two six pounders, which I supposed were those that had been with the picket, but as the drag ropes had been cut and taken away, we could do nothing with them." Major Henry Miller of the 1st Pennsylvania, part of Wayne's division fighting on Sullivan's left, had a similar recollection. "The artillery, &c., which had first fallen into our hands," he wrote in his memoir, could not be moved, the gunners "having stabbed their horses." Howard, who also recalled orders to keep the regiment on the right side of the Germantown Road, pressed his men past Cliveden (the Chew house), where they were "fired at from the upper windows but received no injury." Enemy stragglers "were discovered among the houses on the right of the road, probably wounded," added the major, "and we fired at them as they were making their escape." The Marylanders, together with most or all of the balance of Sullivan's division, pressed on "to the rear of several stone houses, four or five hundred yards to an orchard" before Colonel Hazen arrived and ordered the 4th Maryland to halt and reorganize.[18]

Cliveden was a mile from Mount Pleasant and about the same distance from the main British camp in Germantown. Sullivan's division was advancing more quickly and meeting heavier resistance than Washington had expected. The commanding general had not yet reached the vicinity, but was already worried that

17 "Howard's Account," 314-315.

18 Lieutenant Colonel Samuel Smith was in command of the Fort Mifflin garrison at the time. "Memoir of Miller," 427; "Howard's Account," 315-317.

Sullivan's Marylanders were expending too much ammunition. He dispatched Timothy Pickering "forward with an order to Sullivan to preserve it [his ammunition]. This was before we came in sight of Chew's house," recalled the aide in an 1827 letter, "and when Sullivan's whole right wing must have passed it."[19]

Sullivan's description of his early success makes it clear that the terrain, coupled with the fog and smoke, had already affected command control. "When our Men first made the attack we had the most pleasing prospect before us," he recalled. "The plan was evidently good, & the compleat surprise given the Enemy promised a glorious victory. They were routed, pursued, and charged with fury." Unfortunately, he continued, "I had the misfortune to drive the enemy upwards of a mile with my own division before I received assistance . . . and though the enemy made a stand at every wall and hedge and fence, we drove their left wing near three miles [a] great part of the time, shouldered arms and charged bayonets." Sullivan exaggerated the distance, but there was no doubt that he had indeed driven the enemy in almost abject rout. Despite their proximity, Sullivan was somehow unaware that Wayne's Pennsylvanians also had advanced in line with the rest of his column on the east side of the Germantown Road. Likewise, Conway was keeping abreast of Sullivan's right flank, as Sullivan had ordered. The thick fog and black powder smoke made it almost impossible for the Continental commanders to maintain command and control. The fog and smoke, remembered adjutant general Timothy Pickering, "from the stillness of the air, remained a long time, hanging low and undissipated."[20]

Control between major units was fraying, as was the relationship between one of the army's generals and his brigade. Nine days after the battle, Benjamin Rush, Washington's surgeon general, informed John Adams that Gen. Thomas Conway had "wept for joy when he saw the ardor with which our troops pushed the enemy from hill to hill, and pronounced our country free from that auspicious sight." Another account penned decades later by Pennsylvania officer Alexander Graydon, however, was devoid of laurels of any kind. Graydon contended that, during the fighting, Conway "was found in a farm-house" by two Pennsylvania militia officers. "Upon their inquiring the cause, he replied, in great agitation, that his horse was wounded in the neck. Being urged to get another horse, and, at any

19 Letter, Timothy Pickering to the *National Intelligencer*, January 5, 1827, Pickering Papers, Massachusetts Historical Society, Boston, microfilm copy at the David Library of the American Revolution, Washington Crossing, PA, Film 220, Reel 51.

20 Hammond, ed., *Papers*, vol. 1, 567 and 576; Pickering, *Pickering*, vol. 1, 169-170.

rate, to join his brigade, which was engaged, he declined it, repeating, that his horse was wounded in the neck."[21] Whether Conway actually exhibited cowardice during the battle is unknown; what is certain is that his brigade, fighting alongside the Marylanders, performed admirably and suffered accordingly.[22]

Sullivan's drive into the outskirts of Germantown came at a price. While the reported casualties for Washington's army are not broken down by division or regiment, some Marylanders detailed individual losses within the division. Maryland Congressman Samuel Chase documented in detail for the state's governor the casualties suffered by Sullivan's Marylanders. Brigade commander Col. John Stone was "wounded in the Ankle," while Maj. Uriah Forrest of the 3rd Maryland "had his Thigh broke by a Musquet Ball," reported Chase. Captain Benjamin Brookes, also of the 3rd Maryland, "received a Ball through his Mouth which split his Tongue & went out the back of his Jawbone," while Capt. William Bowie of the 4th Maryland "was wounded slightly in the shoulder." Captain Levin Lawrence of the 6th Maryland was but "slightly wounded"; additional subordinates were "killed and several other wounded."[23]

21 Butterfield, ed., *Letters*, Vol. 1, 158. After the "Conway Cabal" (a treasonous plot by a group of senior officers in late 1777 and early 1778 to replace Washington as commander-in-chief), General John Cadwalader (who supported Washington) accused Conway of cowardice at Germantown and the men fought a duel. "The duel which afterwards took place between Generals Conway and Cadwalader, though immediately proceeding from an unfavourable opinion expressed by the latter of the conduct of the former at Germantown. . . . Not that General Cadwalader was induced from the intrigue to speak unfavourably of General Conway's behavior at Germantown. That of itself was a sufficient ground of censure. . . . Upon Conway's applying to Congress, some time after, to be made a Major-general, and earnestly urging his suit, Cadwalader made known this conduct of his at Germantown; and it was for so doing that Conway gave the challenge, the issue of which was, his [Conway's] being dangerously wounded in the face from the pistol of General Cadwalader. He recovered, however, and sometime after, went to France." Graydon, *Memoirs*, 318.

22 Several officers and men of Conway's brigade became casualties. Lieutenant William Campbell of the 6th Pennsylvania was wounded and captured, Lt. James Glentworth was shot in the right arm, and Ensign Joseph Cox fell into enemy hands. In that same regiment, Sgt. John Kerner lost two fingers and Pvt. Abraham Best lost a leg. Lieutenant William Whitman of the 9th Pennsylvania was shot through the body and captured. Whitman later was paroled. Casualties in the 12th Pennsylvania included Lt. John Carothers (killed), Pvt. John Gallant (lost right arm), and Pvt. Robert Polston (wounded). Private Christian Pemberton of the 3rd Pennsylvania was wounded. "A Partial List of Pennsylvania Troops Killed, Wounded, and Captured at the Battle of Germantown," *PMHB* (Philadelphia, 1916), vol. 40, 241-242; Montgomery, ed., *Archives*, Series 5, vol. 3, 688; Linn and Egle, eds., *Archives*, Series 2, vol. 10, 483; McGuire, *Germantown*, 93.

23 William Hand Browne, ed., *Archives of Maryland: Journal and Correspondence of the State Council March 20, 1777-March 28, 1778*, 865 vols. (Baltimore, 1897), vol. 16, 396. Major Forrest later had his leg amputated.

According to Lt. William Beatty, his 7th Maryland Regiment lost "four Men Killed and 28 Wounded and four Officers Wounded." Beatty, who was "in the action the Whole time and in the hottest fire . . . Received a Dead Ball On my thigh the Very first fire the Enemy made, But did me no harm Only made the place a little Red, I Know no Body fell Except Unkle Michael and he fell Dead on the Spot, Capt Naff Received a flesh Wound in the thigh but is like to do Well." Corporal James Keland, also of the 7th Maryland, later claimed in his pension application that he was shot "through the body, the ball extracted from the side of the back bone."[24]

In addition to the Marylanders, Sullivan had with him the Delaware Regiment, the only Delaware troops in the entire army. Its colonel and future governor, 25-year old David Hall, fell wounded and Lt. Richard Wilds and Capt. Thomas Holland were disabled.[25] Captain Thomas Randall of the artillery was wounded and taken prisoner. The entire division had fought well, concluded Tench Tilghman of Washington's staff. "The Maryland Regulars bore the brunt of the day," he wrote, and "they behaved amazingly well and suffered more in proportion than the others."[26]

Wayne Enters the Fight

Thus far Sullivan had done all that could have been asked of him and more, but he needed support to continue his advance. "I then Detached my Aid De Camp

24 Letter, William Beatty to his father, October 6, 1777, Papers of Captain William Beatty of the Maryland Line, Maryland Historical Society, Baltimore. The identify of "Capt. Naff" remains uncertain as he does not appear in the Army Officer register. Francis B. Heitman, *Historical Register of Officers of the Continental Army During the War of the Revolution, April, 1775, to December, 1783* (Washington, D.C., 1914). RWPF, file S38110. Private Richard Atkinson of the 5th Maryland claimed several decades after the battle that he had a "bayonet run in his breast, which wound to this day, he can feel when eating or drinking." RWPF, file S37691.

25 Wilds's widow sought back pay for her husband in 1787. He had resigned from the army on August 1, 1778, for "being unable to perform the Duties of his Office, Owing to a wound he received in the Battle of Germantown." Letter, Charles Pettit to John Pierce, 29 May 1787, National Archives and Records Administration, Letters sent to J. Howell, Comm. Accounts, RG 93.

26 Tilghman, *Memoir*, 161. Colonel Henry Arendt's German Regiment of Col. Thomas Price's brigade lost Sgt. Philip Gleim with a wound in his left shoulder, Pvt. Henry Waggoner with a wound to his leg, Pvt. John Rybaker with wounds to his head and shoulders, and Pvt. John Snyder with a wound to his leg. Another regiment in Price's brigade—Congress's Own Regiment, under Col. Moses Hazen—also suffered casualties, including Sgt. Edward Bradley, who dropped with a wounded arm. Overall, Hazen's regiment lost three officers and 19 men killed and wounded. "A Partial List," 241-242; Montgomery, ed., *Archives*, Series 5, vol. 3, 79-832; Linn and Egle, eds., *Archives*, Series 2, vol. 11, 78; Hawkins Journal.

Major [Lewis] Morris to Inform his Excellencey [Washington] who was in the main [Germantown] Road that the Enemys Left wing had given way & to Desire him to order General Waine to advance against their Right." It was a curious request. General Anthony Wayne's Pennsylvanians, who had been put under Sullivan's command the previous night for the march and attack against Germantown, were already engaged and were pushing back some of the British infantry. It is possible that Wayne's status had not been clearly communicated to Sullivan. Confusion swirled within the American high command that morning, and it had little or nothing to do with the heavy ground fog.[27]

Despite what many in the Maryland division believed, Wayne's command participated in overrunning the British light infantry camp. About the same time Sullivan's Marylanders formed opposite the Allen house, Wayne's division formed east of the Germantown Road in the fields several hundred yards behind and to the left of Sullivan's two-brigade line. By this point, Conway's brigade had shifted to the right of Sullivan's division to take up a position on the right flank of the attack formation. Wayne advanced both brigades in a long single line, with Col. Thomas Hartley's 1st Pennsylvania Brigade next to the Germantown Road and Col. Richard Humpton's 2nd Pennsylvania Brigade extending the front farther left (east) into the undulating fields beyond.

East of the 2nd Light Infantry Battalion's camp on Mount Pleasant were two other British picket posts, on Abington and Bristol roads, manned by the light company of Capt. Matthew Johnson's 46th of Foot. "I was on Picket and happily had Captain [Mathew] Johnson & Lt [Alexander] Cameron with me two steddy Soldiers," recalled Lt. Loftus Cliffe of Capt. Johnson's company in a letter to his brother three weeks later. "[W]e who were a good distance on the right of the Light Infantry moved towards them and see them quite broke, flying like Devils," he continued. "[W]e heard the word, stop Lt Infantry stop, which made us wait expecting they wd rally, when a devil of a fire upon our front & flank came ding dong about us." According to Cliffe, "we had but 60 men could not cope, were obliged to fly. For the first time I ever saw the 46 turn, but alas it was not the last that Day."[28]

27 Hammond, ed., *Papers*, vol. 1, 545.

28 Letter, Loftus Cliffe to brother, Jack Cliffe, October 24, 1777, William Clements Library, Loftus Cliffe Papers.

The "devil of a fire upon our front & flank" was coming from the barrels of muskets wielded by the 2nd Pennsylvania Brigade of Wayne's division. The British picket post, wrote Lieutenant Cliffe,

> had 2 killed and 8 or 9 Wounded. The Regt had no opertunity of engaging with many others; I was far from regretting the excessive fatigue I had on this Picket. The greatest I ever suffered as it pleased God our little Body came off so well owing entirely to the prudence & Conduct of Johnson & Lt. Cameron not much his inferior & made me (as yet a young Soldier) quite happy this Days Business has made them quite inactive with us since.[29]

Major Maitland's 2nd Light Infantry Battalion was not strong enough to stop the momentum of the unfolding American assault. "[T]he Unparalleled bravery of the troops surmounted every Difficulty, and the enemy retreated in the utmost Confusion," Wayne wrote in a letter to his wife, Mary. "When we advanced on the Enemy with Charged Bayonets—they broke at first without waiting to Receive us," he boasted, "but soon formed again—when a heavy and well directed fire took place on each side—The Enemy again gave way." The Pennsylvanians, remembering the bloodbath at Paoli, "took Ample Vengeance for that Nights Work—Our Officers Exerted themselves to save many of the poor wretches who were Crying for Mercy—but to little purpose; the Rage and fury of the Soldiers were not to be Restrained for some time—at least not until great numbers of the Enemy fell by our Bayonets." As the division surged past the Chew House, a ball fired from one of the windows struck Pvt. William Butler of the 2nd Pennsylvania in the left arm and right leg.[30]

Sullivan and his Marylanders may not have seen Wayne's advance off their left flank, but the British had no doubt who was attacking them. "General Wayne commanded the advance of the army, and fully expected to be revenged on the 'Bloodhounds,'" wrote Lt. Martin Hunter of the 52nd Regiment of Foot. Ironically, Wayne was driving his men into the camp of the same British light infantrymen who had assaulted his encampment at Paoli just two weeks earlier.

29 Abington Road is modern Washington Lane, and Bristol Road is modern Haines Street. Letter, Loftus Cliffe to brother, Jack Cliffe, October 24, 1777. The young Cliffe had seen enough of fighting and wrote his brother 20 days later to express satisfaction that he had not experienced more combat after Germantown. McGuire, *Campaign*, vol. 2, 77. It is also possible some of the firing into the light infantry's flank was coming from Adam Stephen's late arriving division. See Chapter 13.

30 Stille, *Anthony Wayne*, 96. The source for the Butler account is *Waldie's Select Circulating Library, Furnishing the Best Popular Literature, Novels, Tales, Travels, Memoirs, Biography, &c.*, a copy of which, dated 1838, is located in the Pennypacker Mills Archives, Schwenksville, PA.

Despite the bravery of these British regulars, the long and exhausting campaign had taken a toll on them. Those who survived later told Virginia Loyalist James Parker that the Americans charged into battle shouting, "Now is the time to take Vengeance of the bloody Infantry!"[31]

Wayne had a close call with death during the advance and described the incident for his wife shortly after the battle. "My Roan Horse was killed under me within a few yards of the Enemy's front—and my left foot a little bruised by one of their Cannon shot," he wrote to Mary Wayne, "but not so much as to prevent me from walking—my poor horse Received one Musket Ball in the breast—and one in the flank at the same Instant that I had a slight touch on my left hand—which," he assured her, "is scarcely worth mentioning."[32]

"On our side (the left) our Men behav'd with the greatest bravery, and repuls'd the Enemy, and with the charge of the Bayonet took their Encampments, &c., and pushed them before us Hard," wrote the 10th Pennsylvania's Lt. Col. Adam Hubley, one of Wayne's regimental commanders, in a letter to several friends on October 9. The same light infantrymen who had attacked Wayne at Paoli were now being overrun in their camps at Germantown by Wayne's survivors. "Almost every Man expended 40 rounds, excepting our Division . . . who came to the charge of Bayonets immediately. This little Division, which is now become small thro' their bravery, behav'd, indeed, like Veterans, and if I was to pass them, both Officers & Men in silence, I should do them the greatest injustice & Act against my Conscience. Altho it may be, & indeed is call'd cruel by the Enemy," he continued, "the Treatment they receiv'd from our Division but, Justice call'd for retaliation." If the readers of Hubley's letter had any doubt of his meaning, he made it clear when he admitted that his Pennsylvanians "paid in the same Coin that we received on the bloody Night, on which our Division was surpriz'd. I must confess, our people shew'd them No quarter and without distingishon put their Bayonets thro's all ye came across, at the same time reminding them of their Inhumanity on that Night. It was a very remarkable Circumstance that the same troops, who engag'd us on that Night, also engag'd us in this Battle," he marveled, "so that our behavior to them is

31 Hunter, *Journal*, 33; Parker Journal, October 4, 1777 entry, Parker Family Papers. Hunter is referencing the ruthless fashion in which the British light infantrymen had treated Wayne's division at Paoli.

32 Stille, *Anthony Wayne*, 96.

still more justifiable, in short, as in our Division we neither gave nor took quarters."[33]

Lieutenant Hunter of the 52nd of Foot had a hard time believing what he was witnessing. "This was the first time we had ever retreated from the Americans," he confessed, "and it was with great difficulty that we could prevail on the men to obey our orders." It was about this time that General Howe "had come up" somewhere between Mount Pleasant and Cliveden, continued Hunter, "and seeing the battalion all broke, he got into a great passion, for We were always his favourites." Like the lieutenant, Howe was shocked that his men were being driven from the field. "For shame, Light Infantry! I never saw you retreat before. Form! Form! It is only a scouting party!" shouted Howe to no avail.[34]

Yet the commanding general, continued Lieutenant Hunter,

> was very soon convinced that it was more than a scouting party, as the heads of three columns of the enemy appeared—one [Sullivan's] coming through Beggarstown with three pieces of cannon in their front, which they immediately fired with grape at the crowd that was standing with General Howe under a large chestnut-tree. I think I never saw people enjoy a discharge of grape before, but really all the officers of the 2nd Battalion appeared pleased to see the enemy make such an appearance, and to hear the grape rattle about the Commander-in-Chief's ears, after he had accused us of having run away from a scouting party.[35]

Convinced by the hissing iron grapeshot or the pressing need to organize his defense, or both, Howe spurred his mount and galloped toward the rear. The overwhelming American force drove the bloodied 2nd Battalion of Light Infantry after him into the outskirts of Germantown. "It was not possible for them to make a stand against General Washington's whole army," argued Hunter.[36]

33 Letter, Adam Hubley to William Attlee et. al., October 9, 1777, Peter Force Papers, Box IX: 21, Reel 104, Library of Congress, Washington, D.C.

34 Hunter, *Journal*, 34.

35 Ibid., 34-35.

36 Ibid. Despite Howe's exhortations, this was not the first time the light infantry had retreated in North America. With Howe personally leading them, they had fled down the beach of the Mystic River during the Battle of Bunker Hill following the failure of their first assault. Likewise, they had been forced to retreat after advancing too far and too fast during the attack on Harlem Heights. McGuire, *Campaign*, vol. 2, 76.

Colonel Thomas Musgrave's 40th Regiment of Foot was camped near the Chew House to support the 2nd Light Infantry Battalion. Musgrave temporarily stabilized the line with "well-timed and heavy discharges," remembered an anonymous British officer on October 10. Howe's aide Friedrich von Muenchhausen agreed. The 40th Regiment of Foot, he told his diary, "held off the vehemently attacking enemy for a time, but then had to retreat, after heavy losses. I arrived just at that time, and was astounded to see something I had never seen before, namely the English in full flight."[37]

Captain Muenchausen had taken a roundabout route to reach the front. Earlier that morning, Howe had sent him into Philadelphia to deliver a message to Cornwallis. "I was close to Philadelphia about half past five in the morning when I heard cannon shots behind me," he recorded. "I immediately rushed to Lord Cornwallis's quarters and asked one of his aides to report the firing to his lordship, who was still asleep." When it became clear that the army was under attack, the Hessian captain left in search of General Howe. The five-mile uphill ride back to Germantown carried him to Howe's headquarters at Stenton, but the general was nowhere to be found. "Since I knew that the General [Howe] would always be where firing was heaviest, I rode, without asking where I could find him, in the direction of the heaviest fire, and there I found him," with the 2nd British Light Infantry Battalion. Von Muenchhausen arrived about the time Howe was swept up in the retreat of Maitland's infantry.[38]

Although the 2nd Light Infantry Battalion was taking a beating, so too were Wayne's Pennsylvanians, who suffered a heavy toll in officers. The fact that so many were taken prisoner suggests the proximity of the firing lines. In the 1st Pennsylvania, Lt. Peter Weiser, son of famed Indian agent Conrad Weiser, was wounded and captured, and Lt. Abraham Skinner also was captured. The 4th Pennsylvania lost several key officers, including Capt. John McGowan and Lts. Thomas Campbell and Erskurius Beatty to wounds, and Lt. George Blewer as a prisoner. The 7th Pennsylvania's Lt. Samuel Bryson collapsed from a severe wound in his right leg, while Lt. Samuel Smith of the 8th Pennsylvania was killed. Adjutant Thomas Lucas of the 11th Pennsylvania was killed outright. Major William Williams, commanding the 2nd Pennsylvania, got lost at some point in the swirling

37 "Extract of a Letter from an English Officer serving with the Hessians in America, dated Philadelphia, Oct. 10, 1777," *London Chronicle*, January 3-6, 1778, reproduced in *PMHB* (Philadelphia, 1887), vol. 11, 112; Von Muenchhausen, *At Howe's Side*, 38.

38 Von Muenchhausen, *At Howe's Side*, 38.

smoke and fog. He never emerged, taken by a British soldier who marched him into captivity. The British also captured Capt. Robert Sample of the 10th Pennsylvania. These men were only the beginning of the losses sustained by Wayne's men at Germantown.[39]

While Wayne and Sullivan drove back and broke apart Maitland's battalion and pushed aside the 40th of Foot, Maj. Gen. James Grant, a veteran of the French and Indian War and former governor of Florida, used his 5th and 55th Regiments of Foot to obstruct Wayne's advance as the Pennsylvanians reached and passed the Chew house.[40] The two regiments marched rapidly to the Cliveden area in order to bolster the crumbling light infantry, and took a pounding trying to hold the line with the 40th Regiment and remnants of Maitland's light infantry. The 5th, which had passed through Brandywine relatively unscathed, lost 10 killed and 46 wounded of the 350 men who marched into battle at Germantown. Its officer corps was especially hard hit. Lieutenant Colonel William Walcott went down with a dangerous wound, as did three other regimental officers.[41]

39 Eleven-year-old drummer John Geyer of the 1st Pennsylvania was wounded in the heel, and his father, Pvt. Peter Geyer, was wounded by a bayonet in the groin and by a ball in the leg. Peter Geyer's wife (John's mother) accompanied the regiment as washer-woman. The 1st Pennsylvania also lost Pvt. James Smith, who was shot through the head and wounded in the knee with a bayonet, and Pvt. Patrick Sullivan with a wound to his leg. Pvt. Daniel McCay of the 2nd Pennsylvania sustained a head wound. The 4th Pennsylvania lost Sgt. Isaac Brown with a wound in his left side, and Pvt. Casper Stone. Private Henry Hoover of the 5th Pennsylvania was wounded in the leg. In the 7th Pennsylvania, losses included Sgt. Timothy O'Neill; Cpl. James McCann, wounded in the wrist and shoulder; and Pvt. John Walsh, who was hit with a ball through the body near the Chew house. The 8th Pennsylvania lost Pvt. John Churchfield, wounded in the leg, and Pvt. Neal Murray, who was captured. Private Michael Lynch of the 10th Pennsylvania collapsed with wounds in both legs. The 11th Pennsylvania saw Pvt. Christian Derr wounded with three ribs broken and three balls in his body, and Pvt. Bingley Mark Worrell, who lost his right leg. Jacob Hout of Hartley's Additional Continental Regiment was wounded in the knee, causing him to be lame the rest of his life. "A Partial List," 241-242; Montgomery, ed., *Archives*, Series 5, Vol. 2, 630-1090; Linn and Egle, eds., *Archives*, Series 2, Vol. 10, 235 and 651; Montgomery, ed., *Archives*, Series 5, Vol. 3, 79-832; Montgomery, ed., *Archives*, Series 5, Vol. 4, 588; Linn and Egle, eds., *Archives*, Series 2, Vol. 11, 78.

40 McGuire, *Campaign*, vol. 2, 68; Stille, *Anthony Wayne*, 95. The 55th lost Lt. Garret Fisher to a wound. For their troubles, the regiment lost 18 killed and wounded. Narrative letter, probably by Lt. William Keough, 285.

41 The other officers that were wounded were Lt. William Charlton (who later died from his wounds), Ens. William Thomas, and Ens. James Stewart. Walcott died of his wounds on November 16, 1777. *Remembrancer; or, Impartial Repository of Public Events for the Year 1777* (London, 1778), 418; George Inman, ed., "List of Officers Killed Since the Commencement of the War 19th April 1775, Regiments Etc. and Officers of Marines Serving on Shore," *PMHB* (Philadelphia, 1903), vol. 27, 176-205; Steven M. Baule and Stephen Gilbert, *British Army Officers Who Served in the American Revolution, 1775-1783* (Westminster, MD, 2008).

British officer Loftus Cliffe of the 46th of Foot's light company was one of the men of the 2nd Light Infantry Battalion who rallied around the temporary line formed by the 5th, 40th, and 55th regiments. "The engagement became general [and] our Battalions [a reference to the three regiments they rallied around] moved up and on all sides of us was the hottest fire I ever heard," Cliffe recalled. "Our little body looking for an equal Enemy, fell in with a body that we could not cope with were a second time put to flight." British resistance to Sullivan's column collapsed. The 5th and 55th regiments, along with Maitland's survivors still at the front, streamed in full flight into Germantown. Musgrave, together with three of his 40th of Foot companies, took refuge in Cliveden while the remainder of the 40th streamed to the rear with the others.[42]

Maitland's battalion was on the field less than an hour before it was broken and began retreating with the other troops who had done their best to hold the line against the American tide pouring off Mount Pleasant. Of the 500 men who entered the fight with the 2nd Light Infantry Battalion that morning, nine were killed outright, 59 more were wounded, and another five captured. In less than a month the elite battalion had lost about 130 men out of 550, or nearly 22% of its effective strength. Even if the battalion managed to regroup later in the day, its combat effectiveness would be limited. Baggage belonging to officers, including orderly books and private papers, fell into American hands when the camp was overrun.[43]

* * *

"After a Sharp conflict, the Enemy gave ground, and in a Short time retreated with precipitation," was how an anonymous Continental officer described the stunning tactical victory to Gov. George Clinton of New York the next day. "Our Troops pursued them with ardour, and with as much haste as the nature of the Ground would admit, which was exceedingly incuntered with fences, the pulling down of which not a little retarded us. During the Enemy's flight," he continued, "our men kept up brisk firing upon them, & pursued them above two miles, took

42 Letter, Loftus Cliffe to brother Jack, October 24, 1777.

43 The battalion lost several officers that morning. Captain Sir James Baird and Ens. John Campbell of the 71st of Foot and Capt. John Weir of the 43rd of Foot were wounded. Also, Capt. Edward Speake of the 37th of Foot was captured. *Remembrancer*, 418; Inman, ed., "List of Officers," 176-205. Several of these captured items now reside in Washington's Papers at the Library of Congress.

possession of their upper Camp which they left with all their furniture, orderly Books & victuals remaining in it, and chased them as far as Chew's large House in German Town. Much to the Honour of our men none Staid to plunder their Camp."[44]

The ubiquitous fencing outside Germantown wreaked havoc on the American lines. The British "made a Stand at Every Fence wall & Ditch they passed which were numerous—we were Compelled to Remove Every Fence as we past which delayed us much," complained John Sullivan.[45] General Wayne's Pennsylvanians drew abreast of the Marylanders and "past Chews House while mine [Hazen's command] was advancing on the other side of the main Road," Sullivan continued. "Though the Enemy were Routed yet they took advantage of every yard House & Hedge in their retreat which kept up an Incessant fire Through the whole pursuit."[46]

While Sullivan's reporting on the early fighting was cautiously optimistic, Wayne's was ecstatic, leaving little doubt he expected a complete victory. "Fortune smiled on our arms for full three hours—the Enemy were broke, dispersed, & flying in all Quarters—we were in Possession of their whole Encampment, together with their Artillery park, etc., etc," gushed Wayne to Horatio Gates on November 21. Major Henry Miller of the 1st Pennsylvania, part of Colonel Hartley's brigade, believed the British were completely routed "and nothing but the following unfortunate circumstance [the assault on Cliveden] prevented a complete victory."[47]

After routing Maitland's infantry and the three British regiments that had come to their aid, Sullivan's command advanced several hundred yards beyond the Chew house. Exhaustion was setting in, and Hazen's Marylanders and Conway's Pennsylvanians were running low on ammunition. Washington ordered Lord Stirling's two-brigade command to march for the front in order to allow Sullivan the time he needed to reorganize his men and replenish his powder and shot. Brigadier General William Maxwell's New Jersey brigade moved up behind Hazen's Marylanders to the northwest of the Chew house, while Brig. Gen. Francis

44 *Papers of Clinton*, vol. 2, 368-369.

45 Hammond, ed., *Papers*, vol. 1, 544-545.

46 Ibid., 545.

47 Letter, Anthony Wayne to Horatio Gates, 21 November 1777, Horatio Gates Papers, Microfilm copies at The David Library of the American Revolution, Washington Crossing, PA, Film 23, Reel 6; "Memoir of Miller," 427.

Nash's North Carolinians backed up Wayne's Pennsylvania troops. "His Excellency immediately Detached part of the Reserve on my Right & part on the Left of the Road," was how Sullivan recalled the much-needed support. [48]

Initial Success and Analysis

While Sullivan, Wayne, and Conway collapsed the British line, Washington pressed ahead along the Germantown Road in the thick of it all "and was very much exposed during the greatest part of the action," recalled a Continental officer the next day. "He did every thing to gain us Success & to insure it." The conduct of his men and their officers impressed the commanding general. "[T]hings appeared in a very favorable way once, as the column under the command of Genl Sullivan (who behaved extremely well) continued to gain ground upon the enemy . . . thro the encampment of the light Infantry, which was abandoned with their baggage &c.," explained Washington in a letter to Congressman Benjamin Harrison the following day. The morning's weather, however, made it harder than it otherwise may have been. "Among other misfortunes that attended us," continued Washington, "was a hazy atmosphere without a breath of air, so that the Smoke of our artillery & small arms often prevented us from seeing thirty yards; and this not for an instant but of long continuance for want of wind to take it off."[49]

By 7:00 a.m. the Americans were in the heart of Germantown. The enemy fire, terrain, fencing obstacles, and deep advance, however, had unwound the Continental Army's organization. The meteorological conditions worked with the other factors to conspire against a decisive American victory. "For more than an hour we had a bright prospect of success, and began to anticipate a glorious triumph," confessed Joseph Ward, Washington's commissary of musters, in a letter to Massachusetts politician James Bowdoin five weeks later. "But a thick fog together with the smoke rendered it so dark our General could not so well improve the decisive advantages they had gained, by reinforcing where we were too weak and pushing the enemy with more vigour where necessary." Anthony Wayne agreed. "The fog, together with the smoke Occasioned by our Cannon, and

48 Hammond, ed., *Papers*, vol. 1, 545.

49 *Papers of Clinton*, vol. 2, 370; Chase and Lengel, eds., *Papers*, vol. 11, 401.

Musketry—made it almost as dark as night," wrote the general to his wife two days later.[50]

"A very heavy fog prevented our *corps* from discovering one another, so as to distinguish, in some cases, friend from foe," recalled light dragoon Benjamin Tallmadge in his memoir. "Hitherto the progress of our troops had been entirely successful, and it seemed as if the victory must be ours. Some of the regiments on the flanks had reached the centre of the village, and had then more prisoners than troops of their own." Artillerist Henry Knox also mentioned the ubiquitous fog in a letter his wife Lucy two days after the fighting. "All things were in a most happy way the enemy [retreating] from every part—when a fog which was but moderate at first became so thick from the continued firing of Cannon and musquetry that it absoulutely became impossible to see an object at twenty yards distance."[51]

The army "drove the enemy before them a mile or two to the very centre of Germantown," recalled adjutant general Timothy Pickering. "All this time we could not hear of the left wing's [Greene] being engaged, for the smoke and fog prevented our seeing them, and our own fire drowned theirs."[52]

Baylor Hill, of the 1st Light Dragoons, guided his horse across the battlefield to see "where many on both sides were killed." Private Ephraim Kirby, also of the Continental dragoons, did the same and admitted in a letter to his father five weeks later that "the enemy in their Camp . . . made a good defence but being Over powered fled before us near 3 miles leaving all their tents standing and baggage in them, which fell into our hands as recompence for our valor & courage." The cavalryman "rode through the field over the dead bodies where they lay as thick as the stones in a stony felowfield, shocking to behold the horrors of the Day. I am not able to describe but must leave you to judge. While the Action lasted," continued, Kirby who enjoyed the added advantage of serving as a mounted courier, "I was sent three or four times from right to left of the whole with orders where I had a fine prospect of the whole field, & I am certain that there was four of the enemy lay dead to one of ours."[53]

50 Letter, Joseph Ward to James Bowdoin, November 12, 1777, "The Bowdoin and Trumbull Papers," *Collections of the Massachusetts Historical Society*, 6th series (Boston, 1897), vol. 9, 410; Stille, *Anthony Wayne*, 96.

51 Tallmadge, *Memoir*, 23; Letter, Henry Knox to Lucy Knox, 6 October 1777.

52 Pickering, *Pickering*, vol. 1, 170-171.

53 Hayes, ed., *Diary*, vol. 1, 79; Letter, Ephraim Kirby to his father Abraham Kirby, November 12, 1777.

Lieutenant Colonel John Lacey, a Pennsylvania militia officer without an official command, "rode forward to where the Main Army was engaged and had an opertunity of seeing the manner in which the affare was conducted—We had full possession of the Enemies Camp which was on fire in many places Dead and Wounded Men laying strewed about on all Quarters."[54] Captain Enoch Anderson, whose Delaware Regiment had waged an old-fashioned stand-up fight against Maitland's infantry at just 30 paces until he ordered a bayonet attack that helped break the line, remembered driving "into the heart of Germantown," where he and his men "soon were in possession of a part of their artillery—about thirty pieces—and among their tents."[55]

The Pennsylvania Militia Column

While John Sullivan's column was advancing and driving back the right-center of the British line, John Armstrong's Pennsylvania militia was hugging the bank of the Schuylkill River two miles farther west on Ridge Road in an effort to strike the left flank of the enemy beyond Wissahickon Creek simultaneously. Ridge Road roughly paralleled the Germantown Road, but Wissahickon Creek carved up the landscape, separating Sullivan's and Armstrong's troops. The twisting ravine was overgrown with brush and difficult to cross under ideal circumstances. The thick foliage along the creek, coupled with the morning fog, made communication between the two columns impossible. Sullivan complained to the governor of New Hampshire on October 25 that "no Evidence being given of General Armstrongs arrival I was oblidged to Send a Regiment from Wains & another from my own Division to keep the Enemy from Turning our Right. I also Detached Colo Moylands Regiment of Light Horse to watch their motions in that Quarter." Sullivan may have felt abandoned by Armstrong's militia, but Armstrong was in position and engaged with the left flank of the British line at the time.[56]

54 "Memoirs of Brigadier-General John Lacey, of Pennsylvania," *PMHB* (Philadelphia, 1902), vol. 26, 106. Lacey had served as a captain under Wayne on the Canadian frontier in 1776, but the officers butted heads and Lacey resigned his commission in disgust and rode home. He returned to the army in 1777. He was an outstanding officer and was promoted to brigadier general in the Pennsylvania militia in January 1778.

55 Anderson, *Recollections*, 45.

56 Hammond, ed., *Papers*, vol. 1, 544.

Armstrong's militia had not performed well at Brandywine and had done nothing to redeem themselves thereafter. Regaining the confidence of the Continental Regulars two miles off their left seemed an unreachable goal, for Armstrong's orders were to march, locate, and engage the British near the mouth of Wissahickon Creek at the same time Sullivan struck the line farther east, and to drive the enemy back toward Philadelphia. Washington expected Armstrong to link his left with Sullivan's right eventually, but the Wissahickon Creek ravine precluded such a union. Armstrong would be on his own throughout the day.

The day did not begin well for the militia. About the same time Conway's brigade was overwhelming the British pickets at Mount Airy, "[t]heir Light Horse [mounted jaegers] discovered our approach a little before sunrise," Armstrong informed the president of Pennsylvania, Thomas Wharton, by letter the following day. The horsemen had ridden out beyond the jaeger's picket post just north of Wissahickon Creek, which at that point cut across Armstrong's axis of advance before spilling into the Schuylkill River. General Wilhelm von Knyphausen's men had no idea a strong enemy column was so close, and were completely unaware that anything was amiss. "Long before daybreak, canonfire could be heard from the direction of Germantown," scribbled Lt. Heinrich von Feilitzsch of the Ansbach jaegers in his diary. The firing prompted Lt. Col. Ludwig von Wurmb, commander of the Hessian jaegers, to ride "up and down the camp [shouting] Jagers be alert!" The Hessian officer also dispatched a foot patrol, but when it "did not return [another], from the cavalry, was dispatched."[57]

"Although everything was still quiet where our outposts were, the Colonel soon had us take up our arms," continued von Feilitzsch, "and shortly thereafter we heard besides the canons, also small arms fire, which was constantly coming closer." The sound of small arms was getting nearer because Armstrong was pushing his own advance hard. "We could not take off (as was designed) but beat in the enemies pickquets, so that the surprise was not total but partial," he explained. Joseph Armstrong, an enlisted man in the American ranks that morning, remembered years later that the initial confrontation erupted "before daylight," and soon thereafter orders circulated "to attack the pickett guard of the British Army, who returned a Fire and retreated and we pursued them." Knyphausen's aide, Maj. Carl von Baurmeister, confirmed the details of the encounter: "Shortly

57 Hazard, et al, eds., *Archives*, Series 1, vol. 5, 646; Von Feilitzsch, *Journal*, 97. The Hessian picket post was located at the modern intersection of Ridge Avenue and Main Street on the edge of the Manayunk neighborhood.

before sunrise a Hessian jager patrol from our left wing encountered 300 enemy troops one English mile from our most advanced outpost, and by daybreak we were convinced of the actual approach of the enemy army."[58]

When the mounted German patrol "moved up the hill on the opposite bank of the Wissahiccon," continued Lt. von Feilitzsch, "they noticed the enemy marching briskly. They withdrew quietly and sent the fastest horse back to camp with the report." The mounted rider, continued the lieutenant, broke protocol by "calling from afar, 'the rebels are coming like sand in the sea!' for which he got 30 lashes after the battle." This collision, coupled with the shouted warning, provided all the proof the German troops needed, and within minutes Knyphausen's Hessians were under arms along Wissahickon Creek, waiting for the Americans to arrive.[59]

Pushing ahead, Armstrong deployed his 1,000 militiamen and engaged the jaegers near the mouth of the Wissahickon, with the attack focused on taking the bridge over the waterway. "We cannonaded from the heights on each side of the Wissahickon, whilst the Riflemen on opposite sides acted on the lower ground," reported the militia commander. Armstrong's ill-trained troops had little hope of driving back 550 elite Hessian jaegers posted on the opposite bank, and the low light and increasing fog worked against them. "The enemy sent a small detachment across the Wissahiccon against our picket," recorded an Anspach jaeger, "but his artillery and infantry remained on the other side of the rise, wherefrom they shot at us, without knowing where we stood, because it was very foggy."[60] "[T]he enemy's cannonade forced us to retreat from the bridge and occupy the height," reported von Wurmb. Maj. Carl von Baurmeister of von Knypahusen's staff did not mention the fog, but he did confirm the American push across the creek. "General [James] Potter and his column . . . rushed upon the jager picket at the bridge so furiously that it was compelled to fall back a little," he explained, "but after a company of jagers had advanced to its support, our men regained their post this side of the bridge." Once there, the Hessians deployed along the steep slope of the Wissahickon ravine and held that position "until the end of the engagement."[61]

58 von Feilitzsch, *Journal*, 97; RWPF, file S22090; von Baurmeister, "Letters," 415.

59 von Feilitzsch (*Journal*, 97) confirms that Conway's assault at Mount Airy was underway before Armstrong launched his own attack.

60 Hazard, et al., eds., *Archives*, Series 1, vol. 5, 646; von Feilitzsch, *Journal*, 97.

61 Letter, Lt. Col. Ludwig von Wurmb to Gen. Friedrich von Jungkenn, Court Chamberlain of Hesse-Kassel, 14 October 1777, Henry Retzer and Donald Londahl-Smidt, eds., "The Philadelphia Campaign, 1777-1778: Letters and Reports from the von Jungkenn Papers. Part 1—1777," *Journal of*

According to the *Jaeger Corps Journal*, Armstrong supported his thrust with four 6-pounder field pieces: "Our Corps had to give up the bridge, but took position on a height opposite and defended it with rifle fire against the enemy's repeated attempts to force a crossing. The four enemy cannon fired continuously upon the jaegers, while our 3-pounders could not reach the enemy." Jaeger Capt. Johann Ewald wrote that the picket post withdrew "under constant fire to the defile that I had to defend. I immediately ordered the rocky heights occupied from the left bank of the Schuylkill along the ravine and bridge, which were at Vanderen's Mill, and awaited the enemy."[62]

Once under arms, the Anspach jaegers moved from the main jaeger camp behind Vanderin's Mill toward the Wissahickon with the unmistakable sounds of Sullivan's assault on Mount Pleasant echoing in their ears. "Our attack was lively and fast," recorded jaeger officer Lt. Heinrich von Feilitzsch in his journal. "[T]hose 200 men [of the Pennsylvania militia] that had come over to this side of the river to engage our picket in the valley," he continued,

> were thrown into the water right away, either shot, killed with the hunting knife or taken prisoner; we on the rise on the other hand were shelled with heavy artillery and small arms fire for ¾ of an hour; because the enemy had posted besides his riflemen a corps of 4000 men against us in the woods. The river and the steep hill prevented us to attack them en fronte from up closer, they also had much advantage on account of their long rifles.

As von Feilitzsch indicated, the jaegers were waging one aspect of the fight at a disadvantage. Jaeger rifles had a maximum killing range of about 200 yards, but most of Armstrong's militia were armed with Pennsylvania long rifles, which could kill at 300 yards and beyond. Additionally, the creek bank was 100 to 150 feet higher on the Pennsylvanians' side, which allowed the militia to shoot down into the jaegers.[63]

John Donaldson of the Philadelphia City Troop, Armstrong's small mounted command, remembered the prolonged exchange along the creek later in life. The "morning was so dark from the heavy fog from the river & from Vandeerens

---

the Johannes Schwalm Historical Association (Pennsauken, NJ, 1998), vol. 6, no. 2, 11; von Baurmeister, "Letters," 416-417. The site of this engagement is west of modern School House Lane, which leads into Germantown. Of the two brigades of Pennsylvania militia with Washington's army, only James Potter's brigade was with Armstrong on Ridge Road.

62 McGuire, *Campaign*, vol. 2, 79; Burgoyne and Burgoyne, eds., *Journal*, 22; Ewald, *Diary*, 93.

63 von Feilitzsch, *Journal*, 98; McGuire, *Campaign*, vol. 2, 80.

[Vanderin's] dam that General Armstrong . . . could not make an attack on the Hessians with any certainty," recalled the cavalryman. "Only about ten of the Troop were with him at this time, some skirmishing took place & some of the troop reconnoitering made prisoner of a Hessian Lieutenant & brought him off."[64]

Unbeknownst to both armies, the climax of the fight at Wissahickon Creek had already come and gone. Armstrong would not cross to the far side of the creek a second time or drive away von Wurmb's jaegers. The heated engagement along the stream would peter out and Armstrong would remain in place, satisfied with a prolonged, fitful exchange of small arms fire that would stretch into the final stage of the battle later that morning.

Besides being something of a nuisance on the British left flank, Armstrong had done little to aid the American cause that morning. Washington expected him "to attack their left wing in flank & rear." The weak effort to cross the creek failed to divert British troops from Sullivan's front in the American center as Washington intended, and he certainly did not get into the rear of Howe's army. Armstrong's diversion kept von Wurmb's Hessians from marching east and striking Sullivan's exposed right flank, but Washington intended and expected more than simply holding the jaegers in place.[65]

Unattached militia officer Lt. Col. John Lacey placed some of the blame for the day's misfortunes at the doorstep of the militia. "Had they equally acted their part with that of the Senter, commanded in person by Genl Washington and pushed the Enemies flanks with spirit and alairity, as they ought to have done," he later argued, "they must have been prevented of forming a second line, as they did without opposition." If Armstrong had crossed the Wissahickon and driven away the jaegers, he could have thrust deep into the enemy rear and created real havoc. Jaeger commander Ludwig von Wurmb later confirmed that, while fighting at the

64 Capt. J. H. C. Smith, "History of the 1st City Troop." It was not uncommon for applicants to exaggerate their roles during the war when applying for pensions decades later to increase their chances of receiving the government pension. William Hutchinson, for example, fought with Armstrong's militia that morning but claimed he "had the honor of firing many rounds at the enemy entrenched in Chew's house, at which time declarant was wounded in the right arm by a musket ball from the enemy while his arm was elevated in ramming down a charge in his own gun, the mark of which yet distinctly remains to be seen." Hutchinson may have been wounded at Germantown, but he did not fight within two miles of Cliveden. In all likelihood he was wounded in the manner he describes, but somewhere along Wissahickon Creek instead. Dann, *Revolution Remembered*, 150.

65 Chase and Lengel, eds., *Papers*, vol. 11, 375.

creek, his command was unsupported, "as the Minnegerode Grenadier Battalion was located almost two miles from us."[66]

Armstrong placed his losses that day at "not quite 20 men on the whole, & hope we killed at least that number, besides diverting the Hessian Strength from the General [Washington] in the morning." According to Capt. Johann Ewald, "The jagers, of which only the picket had been engaged, counted three killed and eleven wounded, most of whom died from their severe wounds after several days."[67]

* * *

The right-most American command, operating as a diversionary force on the far side of the Schuylkill River, was another Pennsylvania militia brigade, 500 men led by Brig. Gen. James Irvine. The Pennsylvanians, who likely had spent much of the night marching, approached Philadelphia on the Lancaster Road opposite the Middle Ferry, far from the scene of the main assault. Irvine's precise orders remain unknown.[68]

Loyalist Robert Morton was out early that morning to inspect his family's country house near Gray's Ferry. The 16th Light Dragoons were camped nearby, and he was worried that the cavalrymen might be plundering the home. "I went this morning . . . to the middle ferry, where I saw a number of the citizens with about 30

66 "Memoirs of Lacey," 106; Letter, Lt. Col. Ludwig von Wurmb to Gen. Friedrich von Jungkenn, Court Chamberlain of Hesse-Kassel, 14 October 1777, 11.

67 Hazard, et al., eds., *Archives*, Series 1, vol. 5, 646. Among Armstrong's losses were two artillerymen. James Dunn was wounded and Joseph Smith was wounded and captured. Private George Deiker was killed and Pvt. William Gundy was wounded in the neck. Private Nicholas Toy was captured. Other wounded included Sgt. Thomas Scotland and Pvts. James Barr, Thomas Clark, Samuel Lewis, William Russell, and Daniel Dougherty. "Partial List," 243; Montgomery, ed., *Archives*, Series 5, Vol. 4, 575; Ewald, *Diary*, 93.

68 Irvine's participation in this phase of the battle is a bit of a mystery. His specific orders for that morning have not been located, and his role set forth herein has been pieced together from circumstantial evidence. A militia force was operating in Chester County prior to Germantown. Potter's brigade accompanied Armstrong, so that force was almost certainly Irvine's command. He and his men may have camped with Armstrong's militia in Norriton Township prior to the battle, and could have crossed the Schuylkill River at Swedes Ford in order to approach Philadelphia. If Irvine was already in Chester County, he would have marched his men down the Lancaster Road to threaten the city at the Middle Ferry. If he split off from Armstrong, Irvine would have approached via modern Route 23. Though unlikely, it is possible that Armstrong directed this diversion without Washington's approval, but no such order has been found and such a thing runs counter to what we know about John Armstrong.

of the [British] Light Dragoons on Foot watching the motions of the enemy on the other side," he recorded in his diary. Morton continued:

> I waited there about an hour during which time there were several shots from both sides without much execution, when 3 columns of the Americans with 2 field pieces appeared in sight marching tow'ds the River. The Dragoons were order'd under arms and an express sent off for a reinforcement immediately, after which the Americans fired a field piece attended with a volley of small arms. . . . The Americans afterwards came down to the River side with 2 Field Pieces, which they fired with some small arms and run and left them; soon after they returned and brought them back without any considerable loss, 1 man being wounded on their side and none on the other.

Morton had seen enough and "thought it advisable to leave the Ground, and rode off as fast as possible."[69]

If Washington hoped the diversion would be delivered with enough vigor to convince the British that a serious, direct attack was being made against Philadelphia, thus pinning the garrison there in place, Irvine's role was but another in a string of disappointments that day. "To alarm our garrison at Philadelphia, Washington, immediately after he started to attack us, had some . . . of the militia show themselves on the other side of the Schuylkill and on the other side of the Delaware, on the Jersey shore," was how Capt. von Muenchhausen described the tepid affair in his diary. The effort was a complete failure, for "Lord Cornwallis, who soon realized that these were feints, came flying to Germantown." The Irvine diversion tied up some British dragoons, but the more important relief column—the British grenadiers under Charles Cornwallis—were unaffected by the American militia and were gearing up for a march to Germantown.[70]

69 McGuire, *Campaign*, vol. 2, 75; Morton, "Diary," 13. The action described by Morton occurred near the modern Market Street Bridge.

70 von Muenchhausen, *At Howe's Side*, 39. British engineer John Montresor, who was in Philadelphia preparing for the bombardment of Fort Mifflin, noted in his journal that the mood inside the city changed when the citizenry realized the Americans were attempting to recapture it: "During the action of this day, the countenances and actions of many of the Inhabitants of Philadelphia were rather rebellious and seem to indicate their wish for the rebels to regain the city." Montresor, "Journals," 462.

Chapter 13

Greene and Smallwood Join the Fight

October 4, 1777
5:30 a.m. to 7:00 a.m.

"I suppose a hotter fire was Never known both of small Arms & Field Pieces."[1]

— Ensign Jonathan Todd, 7th Connecticut Regiment, October 6, 1777

The complicated four-column approach adopted by Washington required Nathanael Greene to march his men farther than John Sullivan's troops, but to attack the enemy simultaneously. Scouts had led both Washington and Greene to believe that the first contact with the enemy would come in the vicinity of Luken's Mill. They were wrong.

Greene's column, with McDougall's brigade in front, followed by Greene's division under Peter Muhlenberg and Stephen's division bringing up the rear, left Bethlehem Pike and entered Church Road, moved a few miles and turned right onto Limekiln Road, and continued on toward Germantown. The head of the attack force stumbled upon a picket post of the British 1st Light Infantry Battalion about one and a half miles earlier than anticipated, near the intersection of the Abington and Limekiln roads. Despite having a longer march, Greene entered the

1 Letter, Jonathan Todd to his Father, October 6, 1777.

fight a short time after Brig. Gen. Thomas Conway launched his brigade (which was part of Sullivan's column) against the picket post at Mount Airy.[2]

Multiple accounts agree that the head of Greene's command engaged the enemy at roughly the same time Sullivan's men went in about two miles or so off their right. James McMichael, who belonged to Col. Walter Stewart's Pennsylvania State Regiment (Brig. Gen. George Weedon's brigade), believed Greene's men went in just "after 5 o'clock." One week after the battle Colonel Stewart, McMichael's commanding officer, wrote to Horatio Gates that both Sullivan and Wayne were engaged after 6:00 a.m., and his men "join'd in about 15 minutes." Virginian James Wallace recalled in an October 12 letter that he and his comrades "attacked the enemy early in the morning before it was quite light." While Greene did not strike simultaneously with Sullivan, his contact with the enemy came soon after the opening shots of the battle. Sullivan and others in his command would later claim that Greene's column was late in arriving that morning, but the terrain, ground fog, and black powder smoke obscured visibility and made it impossible to determine what was transpiring a couple miles off their left flank.[3]

The British light infantry manned an advanced picket post northeast of Cliveden and north of Betton's Woods—well short of Luken's Mill. Much like Sullivan had caught the British unprepared at Mount Airy, Greene surprised the three British companies (one each from the 17th, 28th, and 38th Regiments of Foot from Col. Robert Abercromby's 1st Light Infantry Battalion) at the picket post. Captain William Scott of the 17th Regiment of Foot's light company later recalled that he and his comrades started the day listening to the fighting on Sullivan's front around Mount Airy while impatiently waiting for orders. "At last the advanced

2 Jackson, British Army, 32. Much of the original route of the Limekiln Road has been altered by the Route 309 expressway. However, sections of the original road remain, especially the final stretch where it meets Abington Road (modern Washington Lane). The approximate location of the intersection of Church Road and the Limekiln Road is on the modern campus of Arcadia University. Greene began forming his lines of battle roughly where Cheltenham Avenue and Limekiln Pike intersect today.

3 McMichael, "Diary," 152; Letter, James Wallace to Michael Wallace, 12 October 1777, Horace Edwin Hayden, Virginia Genealogies: A Genealogy of the Glassell Family of Scotland and Virginia, Also of the Families of Ball, Brown, Bryan, Conway, Daniel, Ewell, Holladay, Lewis, Littlepage, Moncure, Peyton, Robinson, Scott, Taylor, Wallace, and Others, of Virginia and Maryland (Wilkes-Barre, PA, 1891), 707; Letter, Walter Stewart to General Gates, October 12, 1777, 400; Commager and Morris, eds., *Spirit of Seventy-six*, 629. As McDougall's Connecticut brigade led Greene's column during the night march, it is unclear why they did not lead the attack down Limekiln Road. Perhaps Greene pulled them aside to allow his own division to lead the assault, thus causing some of his delay in launching the attack.

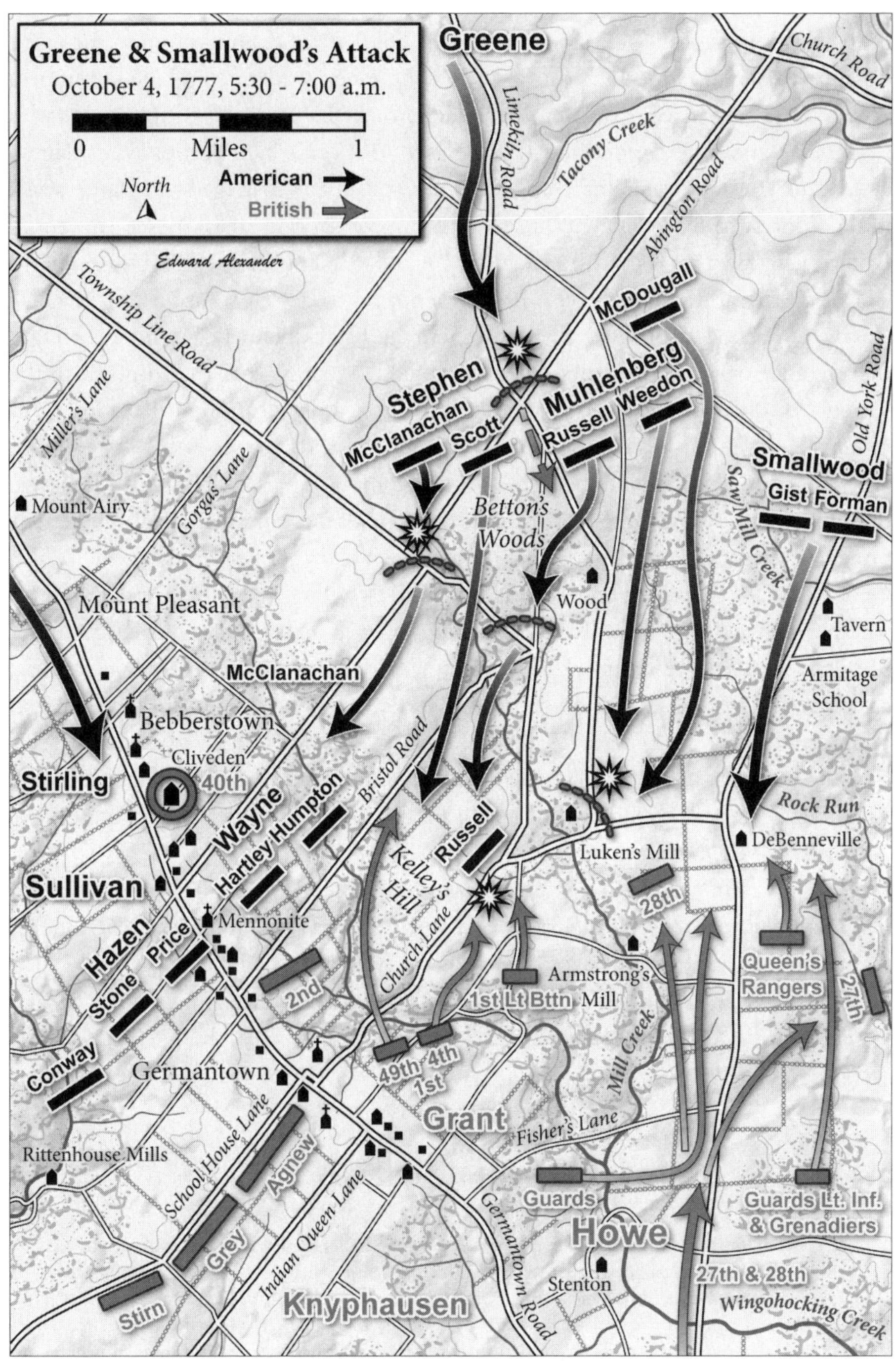
Greene & Smallwood's Attack
October 4, 1777, 5:30 - 7:00 a.m.
0 Miles 1
North
American
British
Edward Alexander
Greene
Limekiln Road
Tacony Creek
Church Road
Abington Road
Township Line Road
McDougall
Stephen
Muhlenberg
Weedon
McClanachan
Scott
Russell
Old York Road
Smallwood
Gist Forman
Saw Mill Creek
Miller's Lane
Gorgas' Lane
Mount Airy
Betton's Woods
Wood
Tavern
Mount Pleasant
McClanachan
Armitage School
Bebberstown
Cliveden
40th
Stirling
Wayne
Hartley Humpton
Bristol Road
Russell
Rock Run
DeBenneville
Kelley's Hill
Luken's Mill
Sullivan
28th
Hazen
Price
Mennonite
Church Lane
Stone
2nd
Armstrong's Mill
1st Lt Bttn
Queen's Rangers
27th
Mill Creek
Conway
Germantown
49th 4th
1st
Grant
Fisher's Lane
Rittenhouse Mills
School House Lane
Agnew
Indian Queen Lane
Guards
Guards Lt. Inf. & Grenadiers
Howe
Grey
Germantown Road
Stenton
27th & 28th
Wingohocking Creek
Knyphausen
Stirn

sentry fired; and soon after distinguished the head of the enemys column throwing down the rails of a wood in front of our right. Enemy advancing," he continued, "the companies fired and fell back according to orders." Captain Charles Cochrane, who commanded the 4th Regiment of Foot's light company, explained in a letter two weeks later that Washington's army managed the large-scale, multi-front surprise attack because of the universal bane that beset the entire British army that morning: the weather. "A most uncommon thick Fog favour'd Their scheme and enabled them [the Americans] to get close upon our advance Posts ere we had any other intelligence, there the Attack being began. They brought their whole Army against ours," he continued, "which was at that time from the variety of objects necessary to attend to extreamly scattered. [Emphasis in original.][4]

While the primary sources remain murky about what actually unfolded once the attack on the main British army units began in earnest, the initial deployment of Greene's divisions prior to overrunning the picket post is fairly clear. Major General Adam Stephen's men tramped to the right (west) of the Limekiln Road, where Stephen formed his 1,900-man, two-brigade division with Col. Alexander McClanachan on the right and Brig. Gen. Charles Scott's command on the left, closest to the road. Greene's own division under Brig. Gen. Peter Muhlenberg, also numbering about 1,900 men, deployed east of the road with Col. William Russell's brigade on the right closest to Scott and Brig. Gen. George Weedon's on the left. Brigadier General Alexander McDougall shook out his Connecticut brigade, about 1,000 strong, on Greene's left-rear.[5]

Little about this arrangement pleased Lt. Col. William Heth, whose 3rd Virginia Regiment marched with McClanachan's brigade in Stephen's division. "It was near 6 before the first volley of small arms were heard [Sullivan's attack], when Genls. Green and Stephen's divisions, who were to oppose the enemy's right," explained the deputy regimental commander, "were then, from some

4 Lambdin, "Battle of Germantown," 383; Scott, "Memorandum," 293; Letter, Charles Cochrane to Andrew Steuart, October 19, 1777.

5 The information in this paragraph is largely based on circumstantial evidence and Archibald Robertson's manuscript map. Robertson Map, Windsor Castle Collection, 734029.d. According to the Robertson map, a second picket post was located at the Abington Road and Township Line Road intersection off Stephen's right flank. The identity of the picket is uncertain, but it was probably the light company from the 46th Regiment of Foot, which was part of the 2nd Light Infantry Battalion.

mismanagement, only forming at more than a mile's distance."[6] Why Greene formed so far from the British picket post baffled Heth. When the order came to step off, it quickly became obvious that the American troops were in for a difficult time. "[Ou]r wing, by another piece of bad conduct, attempted to march in line of battle, till that order was found impracticable," continued an irate Heth, "which from the great number of post and rail fences, thickets and in short [ev]ery thing that could obstruct our march, threw us frequently into the greatest disorder, and as the heavy fire before us urged us on to a dog trot, we were nearly exhausted before we came to the first field of action." Ensign George Inman of Captain Scott's light company, who was on the receiving end of the first attack by Greene's leading troops, would have been surprised by Heth's description of the action. Inman was on picket early that morning and later wrote that the American advance was so quick and deadly that "several of my men [were] killed and wounded before I was ordered in."[7]

"The two Divisions formd the Line of Battle at a great distance from the Enemy," admitted General Stephen, "and Marching far through Marshes, Woods &c strong fences; before we came up with the Enemy. The first party of them that we discovered was to our left," one-half mile from their starting point. To overwhelm it, Stephen "detachd Col. [George] Mathews [with his 9th Virginia Regiment], who was nearest to me & advancing wt. Spirit." Colonel Mathews, however, was part of Russell's brigade, advancing in line and holding Russell's right flank. Stephen, who would be accused of being under the influence of alcohol during the battle, had ridden left behind his division and had given orders to an officer over whom he had no control. Stephen also dispatched a staff officer to determine if there was a chance to move around the exposed left flank and "[a]ttack the Enemy in the Rear if possible." Stephen ordered Maj. William Darke with a portion of the 8th Virginia, advancing on the left side of Scott's brigade, to support Mathews and flank the enemy line. In all likelihood, Stephen joined this movement and left his division to fend for itself. According to a later court of inquiry, Stephen was not always with his men; his after-action report to Washington made this clear

6 Commager & Morris, eds., *Spirit of Seventy-six*, 629

7 Commager and Morris, eds., *Spirit of Seventy-six*, 629; "George Inman's Narrative of the American Revolution," PMHB (Philadelphia, 1883), vol. 7, 242. Heth's confusion likely stems from his regiment's position in the formation. While McClanchan's brigade encountered no resistance until approaching Township Line Road (about a mile away), those units closest to Limekiln Road (Scott's brigade) had to contend with the British picket post at the intersection of the Abington and Limekiln roads.

when he assured the army commander that he had "been informd by My Aid de Camp that our troops behavd gallantly & drove the Enemy after a hot encounter."[8]

The eruption of gunfire just before dawn surprised the region's civilians as well as the British. Saturday was market day in Philadelphia, which normally meant the inhabitants of Germantown rose before dawn and traveled into the city to sell their produce and wares. The growing conflagration ended that possibility and convinced the wisest among them to gather in their cellars and wait out the metal maelstrom. Some, however, threw caution to the wind and climbed onto their roofs to watch the unfolding action. The surging Americans pushed back the advance British pickets along the Limekiln Road onto property owned by Isaac Wood. According to an 1843 history of the fighting, Wood was "peeping out at the battle" from his cellar door when he was killed by an errant musket round.[9]

Greene's initial thrust may have been tactically messy, but it was completely effective. While Sullivan was driving the British back at Mount Airy off his right, Greene pushed his lines ahead, collapsed the advanced light infantry picket post of the British, and continued south in pursuit of the fleeing enemy. The routed 17th, 28th, and 38th companies of light infantry fell back all the way to Luken's Mill, where they regrouped in order to offer some semblance of opposition. Several minutes later, while peering through the thick fog, they caught glimpses of a massive wall of men bearing down on them. At that moment, any doubt whether this was merely a probe vanished. The unnerving sight tightened a handful of trigger fingers and convinced the officers to order a second retreat. The scarlet-clad

8 McGuire, Campaign, vol. 2, 78; Chase and Lengel, eds., Papers, vol. 11, 468. Why Stephen believed he could give an order to Mathews, who commanded the 9th Virginia Regiment in Colonel Russell's brigade (Greene's division), may reflect his mental state, for he was later accused of being intoxicated. Mathews was wounded and captured later that morning, as was Major Darke, and neither appears to have left a detailed account of the battle. Stephen later faced a Court of Inquiry for his erratic conduct at Germantown.

9 Watson, Annals, vol. 2, 53. Wood was killed near the current location of the Philadelphia National Cemetery. An unsubstantiated account was written in the early 1880s by Jacob Miller, who claimed that he and several others "went across the road to an old house . . . they secured themselves in the cellar, from the door of which they saw cannon balls streaking through the air." Townsend Ward, "The Germantown Road and Its Associations," part 3, PMHB (Philadelphia, 1881), vol. 5, 248. The retreating British picket post was halted to regroup at the modern intersection of Washington Lane and Stenton Avenue.

infantry fell back southwest toward their battalion camp, where they spread the alarm.[10]

Earlier that morning, when warnings filtered into British lines that Washington's army was approaching Germantown from the north, Maj. Gen. James Grant put his two infantry brigades under arms. When the fighting to the northwest intensified, he dispatched his 5th and 55th Regiments of Foot to obstruct General Wayne's advance after Sullivan's column had crushed Maj. John Maitland's 2nd Light Infantry Battalion on Mount Pleasant. Greene's noisy advance to the north, along with the presence of British light infantry pickets around Betton's Woods and elsewhere, convinced Grant to push Lt. Col. Henry Calder's 49th Regiment of Foot north across Wingohocking Creek. As the fighting drew closer, Lt. Col. James Ogilvie's 4th Regiment of Foot moved a short distance northeast to support the 1st Light Infantry Battalion.[11]

Ogilivie's veteran 4th Regiment had opened the war at Lexington and Concord, charged up Bunker Hill, and battled the Continentals off Long Island and at Brandywine. The confident regulars moved briskly from the main camp to the location indicated by Grant and formed into line just short of Church Lane, a fenced road running southwest from the general vicinity of Luken's Mill into Germantown. Ogilvie's left was close to the road, but his line ran east and angled away from Church Lane, meaning the right side of his line was much farther from the road than was his left. The 4th Regiment was in the act of deploying when Colonel Abercromby arrived with eleven companies—the balance of his 1st Light Infantry Battalion—and deployed them on Ogilvie's right.[12]

It was at this time that Captain Scott and the three light picket companies arrived after retreating across Mill Creek at Luken's Mill. The exhausted pickets found the balance of the light infantry battalion "drawn up in a buck wheat field a little in front of its camp, with a woody height and road [Church Lane] running in front of the left company into the town." The three newly arrived companies formed on the left side of Abercromby's battalion. Knowing what was about to hit them, Scott surveyed the landscape and was shocked by what he described as "the

10 Scott, "Memorandum," 293. Archibald Robertson's invaluable manuscript map of the Battle of Germantown, which he drew himself, is the best overall primary source for the basic locations of the opposing forces. Robertson Map, Windsor Castle Collection, 734029.d.

11 Robertson manuscript map of the Battle of Germantown; Grant to Harvey, October 20, 1777, Grant Papers.

12 Scott, "Memorandum," 293; Robertson manuscript map of the Battle of Germantown.

naked front the battalion presented." He knew the advancing Americans would overwhelm Abercromby and outflank him on the right. Scott sought out Capt. St. Lawrence Boyd of the 38th Regiment's light company and "pressed him to go with me to the Col. [Abercromby] to state the danger." Unsure what to do, Boyd froze—but only for a moment, for at that instant lead balls fired from Virginia muskets zipped through the air around them, killing "a very fine soldier of 17th." That was enough to convince Boyd to act. Once the pair of captains found Colonel Abercromby near the right side of the battalion, they assured him that they had "not fallen back till we saw the enemy advancing in force, that if he staid on his ground five minutes, half the battalion would be knock'd down." The experienced Abercromby, also a veteran of Long Island and Brandywine, quickly grasped the danger. "I agree with you as to the ground," he replied. "I would not have drawn the battalion up here, but Genl. Grant ordered me to form line on the right of [the] 4th Regt." The right side of Abercromby's battalion was but a short distance from a large stand of woods, leaving his command blind as to what was coming. The colonel made it clear that orders were orders when he ended his explanation with, "What can I do?"[13]

While Ogilvie formed his 4th Regiment of Foot and a pair of British captains and their commanding officer debated the merits of their position, mortal danger in the form of Col. William Russell's brigade of Greene's division got closer with each passing second. In the foggy confusion—and behind the woods that blinded Abercromby—Russell's 900 men pushed across the wooded banks of Mill Creek in column, reached Church Lane, and marched west down the road toward Germantown. Part of Church Lane was sunken, which, coupled with the heavy ground fog and the deployment of the British, further served to hide the advancing Americans from Ogilvie's 4th Regiment of Foot (whose line angled away from the road) and Abercromby's light infantrymen (whose front was even farther away and mostly behind woods). Someone in Russell's brigade, however, realized that an enemy line of battle was within killing distance on their immediate left. In short order Russell had his column stop, turn left, advance to the heavy fence lining Church Lane, stick their Virginia muskets between the rails, and open fire.[14]

Captains Scott and Boyd were still talking with Abercromby when the "enemys column following the road leading to German town which run along the whole front of 4th Regt. and probably not having seen the 1st Battn.," recalled Scott,

13 Lambdin, "Battle of Germantown," 383; Scott, "Memorandum," 293.

14 Robertson manuscript map of the Battle of Germantown.

"faced to the fence, and leaning their pieces on the bottom rail for it was a hollow road in that part, fired on the 4th Regt." The point-blank volley, continued the captain, "knock'd them down 50 men." Lieutenant Frederick Wetherall of the 17th Regiment of Foot's light company witnessed the same surprise encounter. "The Rebels moving on lined a Bank & Rail under cover of the Fog & threw in a most severe fire upon the 4th Regt., which had been order'd to the left of the 1st L. I. & which knoc'd down almost the whole of their Right Wing," wrote Wetherall in his journal. A surprised Abercromby responded to the heavy volley by "instantly" attempting to wheel his battalion to face the threat and "dash at the Enemy," continued Wetherall. The companies on the right of the battalion, however, either did not hear the command or did not respond with alacrity, and before they could perform the wheel "the left hand Companys had pressed forwards."[15]

Captain Scott also recalled the effort to maneuver in the face of the killing volley and the temporary loss of tactical control. Colonel Abercromby, wrote Scott, "called to the battalion to advance, and pressing forward rapidly to the spot [where] the fire came from, wheeled towards the left in line." Scott, whose 17th Regiment of Foot's light company held the far left flank of the battalion line, ran back to his command with Boyd and other officers, "but they neither hearing, or seeing the movement at first from the fog, the companies on the right got a start." Scott tried to march his troops in a giant wheel in order to link them with Ogilive's men lining Church Lane, "yet the right passed them got into the wood and followed the enemy. The left," continued Scott, "was then completely separated." Abercromby did not yet realize it, but his battalion had broken into two unequal parts. The smaller portion, with the 4th, 17th, 28th, and 38th companies, would have to fight on its own hook.[16]

Unable to keep up with the battalion, which may not have been in sight any longer, Scott, Boyd, and the other two captains of the separated companies tried to pivot their line "towards the right from whence they expected to fall in [make contact] with the enemy." The fog cleared sufficiently for a few moments for Scott to spot "a number [of them] breaking down the fence from an orchard." Russell's Americans were climbing the fence lining Church Lane while Ogilvie's 4th Regiment was likely breaking for the rear. At this time Scott heard "loud shouting in the town which the soldiers thought their own people." After a quick discussion,

15 Scott, "Memorandum," 293; Wetherall, Journal.

16 Scott, "Memorandum," 293-294.

the captains "judged otherwise and as the shouting gained upon us, [we] were apprehensive of being surrounded." For the third time in the space of an hour, Scott gave the order to retreat and the four companies "fell back towards the left of our camp, hoping to regain our battalion, or some part of the army."[17]

Exactly what transpired next remains uncertain, as does what befell Colonel Ogilvie's 4th Regiment after it received the devastating fire from Russell's brigade. The four light companies with Captain Scott had attempted to support the embattled 4th Regiment, to no avail, and both bodies fell back. The balance of Colonel Abercromby's battalion had drifted northeast into Mill Creek's wooded trough, where they ran into the onrushing brigade of George Weedon (and perhaps Alexander McDougall's as well). Such a collision in the smoky and foggy woods would have erupted at close quarters and ended quickly, with the approximately 2,000 Virginia, Pennsylvania, and Connecticut troops routing Abercromby's poorly-formed force of roughly 500 men. "The morning was so foggy that their Coloms cou'd hardly be distinguished at Twenty paces distance," complained British officer Henry Stirke of the 10th Regiment of Foot's light company, one of the units still under Abercromby's control.[18]

Weedon's four Virginia regiments and lone Pennsylvania command used the fog and battle smoke to slip out of the woods in pursuit of the retreating light infantry, which at times tried to make a stand only to be pressed back steadily. Weedon's men continued across the buckwheat field where Abercromby had formed his battalion just minutes earlier. It is possible that, while shoving Abercromby's crumbling command farther south, the Americans were able to work their way behind Scott's four light infantry companies. "[W]e drove them immediately & so continued to drive them," boasted Sgt. Charles Talbot of the 6th Virginia Regiment, Weedon's brigade. "We ran over their dead in Grate Numbers." The Pennsylvania State Regiment's Lt. James McMichael remembered driving the British "with the utmost precipitation" through buckwheat fields. "The Action became very general, at the distance sometimes of twenty and sometimes forty

17 Ibid.

18 Stirke, "Journal," 172. Stirke's account suggests they ran into an unexpected line of the enemy (i.e., Weedon and McDougall). The light infantry already knew precisely where Russell's men were located.

yards," recalled Col. Walter Stewart of the Pennsylvania State Regiment. "We however began to gain Ground on them."[19]

The Americans did indeed "gain Ground on them," but their success came at a cost for Greene. His brigade and regimental leaders were losing control of their commands, unable to see where they were going or who was on their flanks. Some stopped their units and held their ground while others continued through the fog, uncertainty growing with each passing step. American regiments undoubtedly passed within a stone's throw of enemy formations, and visa versa, without either side realizing it. Ironically, the confusion left isolated pockets of British troops behind the advancing Americans, and Americans operating between Germantown and British units. It was a confused mess that was about to get even more chaotic.

Colonel Stewart's Pennsylvania State Regiment, advancing on the left side of Weedon's line out of the woods and into the buckwheat field, stumbled upon a pair of light infantry companies that had been driven back from the fighting farther north and had rallied around the battalion's guns. We "engag'd the 5th and 38th," declared Stewart, the former company having just been driven out of the woods with Abercromby's section of the 1st Light Battalion, and the latter unit belonging to Captain Boyd. Both, he continued, "ran lustily and I took a little flush redoubt with three pieces of Cannon from them I had cursed hot Work for it before they left them." The field pieces, he added, were "behind a V-shaped earthwork on the angled crossroads between Luken's Mill and the front of their camp. Our success," he added, "was great."[20]

While Weedon was overrunning the two light field pieces, the survivors of Ogilvie's 4th Regiment of Foot (and most of the 1st Light Infantry Battalion companies) were streaming around, and perhaps through, his command south and west of the captured earthwork and beyond the gorge of Winghocking Creek, near the right end of the camp of Maj. Gen. James Grant's division. Weedon's brigade, with McDougall's Connecticut troops somewhere off its left, continued in the same general direction, approaching the north bank of the creek. Riding

19 Talbot, "Letters," 318; McMichael, "Diary," 153; Letter, Walter Stewart to General Gates, October 12, 1777, 400. Stewart's casualties in the battle included Pvt. William Watson with a wound in his right knee joint and Lt. William Moore, who also was wounded. Montgomery, ed., Archives, Series 5, Vol. 3, 717; Linn and Egle, eds., Archives, Series 2, Vol. 10, 788; McGuire, Campaign, vol. 2, 103.

20 Letter, Walter Stewart to General Gates, October 12, 1777, 400; Robertson manuscript map of the Battle of Germantown. While Stewart claims he captured three guns, the Robertson map depicts two guns.

somewhere behind his front line that morning, Nathanael Greene was elated by how well the battle was unfolding. It was a rare sight to see British troops retreating on any field, and it was something he had never witnessed. Decisive success, he believed, was within the army's grasp. "Notwithstanding the Fog depriv'd us of the Opportunity of seeing how to Conduct our near approaches at the Enemy's confusion and giving them a Compleat route which beyond a Doubt we should have done if the Weather had been Clear," believed Greene; "nevertheless," he had "the satisfaction to assure the Troops, the Enemy suffer'd very severely."[21]

George Weedon was nearly as elated as his division commander: "The Enemies whole force was Collected, we drove them two miles with Considerable loss." Weedon, who had served with Washington in the French and Indian War and had taken part in some of the Revolution's bloodiest battles, felt compelled to record the "Great numbers of the Enemy Slain as we drove them." "Seeing, is believing," he added in case the recipient of his letter did not fully believe him, "and I can with truth say they lay very thick in the Ground in which I pursued them over." The Virginia native was proud of his brigade. "Our men behaved with the greatest intrepidity," he wrote soon after the battle, "Driving them from their Camps, Field pieces, Stone walls, House &c, Trofies lay at our feet, but so Certain were we of making a General defeat of it, that we pass them by in the pursuit, and by that means lost the Chief part of them again." Weedon was confident that "Victory was Declairing in our Favor."[22]

In a letter penned a couple weeks after the battle to the army's adjutant general in London, the bombastic Gen. James Grant, commander of the British right wing, minimized the severity of the situation while refusing to credit the Americans with an exceptionally well-planned attack. "I need not tell you that the General," he wrote, referencing himself in the third person, "was soon prepared & active in bringing Troops to support, but there was such a Fog that one could not see Ten Yards, it was difficult to ascertain where they were, but from the noise. . . . The

21 Showman, McCarthy, and Cobb, eds., Papers, vol. 2, 171.

22 Letter, George Weedon to John Page, October 4, 1777; Letter, George Weedon to John Page, October 8, 1777. James Wallace, a surgeon in Weedon's brigade, listed casualties of the 2nd Virginia Regiment of Weedon's brigade: "We lost one officer out of our Regiment, which was Mr. [Jonathan] Die of Capt. Willises company. Our Lieutenant Col. [Richard] Parker was wounded in the leg." Letter, James Wallace to Michael Wallace, 12 October 1777. Captain John Willis did not command his company at Germantown, as he had been captured at Brandywine. Colonel Alexander Spottswood of the 2nd Virginia Regiment resigned after Germantown and went home.

attempt was bold," he finally admitted in passing, "but when it came to the push they failed Totally in the execution. I was uneasy for Ten Minutes."[23]

Grant may have exuded confidence in the weeks following the battle, but it was unlikely he felt that way on the field that day. He knew there were no troops from his command left to stop the advancing Americans. Weedon's brigade, most of Russell's command, and likely McDougall's brigade as well were approaching Wingohocking Creek and were within just half a mile of the Germantown Road. Cutting off British access to Philadelphia and trapping a large number of troops was now within their grasp. Off to the northwest, General Wayne's Pennsylvanians had driven back the 5th and 55th Regiments of Foot, and Grant's 49th Regiment of Foot had run into Scott's brigade of Adam Stephen's advancing Virginia division. Grant's 4th Regiment of Foot under Colonel Ogilvie had been ambushed with heavy losses along Church Lane by Russell's deadly musket volley and was now in full retreat, while Weedon's troops had pushed through and dispersed pieces of various British commands during the foggy pursuit to and through the buckwheat fields. Who was left to stop them?

Adam Stephen Joins Greene's Advance

Once the initial 1st Light Battalion picket post at the intersection of Abington Road and Limekiln Road was overrun about dawn, Stephen's two brigades continued advancing, with Col. Alexander McClanachan's brigade on the right and Brig. Gen. Charles Scott's brigade on the left. Without a firm guiding hand, Stephen's command angled southwest, away from Greene's division under Muhlenberg. A long and deep stretch of woods covered their front. Off Stephen's right, another British picket post, composed of the light company from the 46th Regiment of Foot, was straddling the Abington Road.[24]

The division was starting to fall apart and no one was in control. Earlier, Stephen had dispatched Major Darke with part of the 8th Virginia (Scott's brigade) to help Russell's men flank the first light infantry picket post off his left near Betton's Woods. Darke's detachment, which did not rejoin the division for the rest of the day, appears to have advanced with Stephen himself on the right of Russell's command (Muhlenberg's division) all the way south to Church Lane. In his

23 Grant to Harvey, October 20, 1777, Grant Papers.

24 Robertson manuscript map of the Battle of Germantown. The makeup of the picket post is based upon a reasonable supposition given the circumstantial evidence available.

confused and disjointed report to General Washington, Stephen explained that "a Body of the Enemy Appeard in front of the Right of Genl Greens Division, & left of Mine," and that he led his men "on to the Attack—They advanced with great Chearfullness, and the Enemy were drove Back with their Artillery." Stephen's description could only have referred to Ogilvie's 4th Regiment of Foot beyond Church Lane.[25]

While Stephen was fighting with most of Darke's 8th Virginia and Russell's brigade against Ogilvie's 4th Regiment of Foot and perhaps some of Abercromby's 1st Light Infantry Battalion companies, the rest of his division off to the northwest continued to advance. McClanachan overran the 46th Regiment's light company on the Abington Road and headed due west through heavy terrain. McClanachan's advance separated his left flank from the right flank of Scott's weakened brigade, which by this time consisted of just the 4th and 12th Virginia regiments, Patton's and Grayson's Additional Continental Regiments, and part of the 8th Virginia. Scott continued generally southwest, on a collision course with a fresh British regiment marching north to stop them.

The last unengaged element of James Grant's command began moving forward when Stephen's two brigades were advancing against the 1st Light Infantry Battalion's pickets. Henry Calder marched his 49th Regiment of Foot out of its camp south of Church Lane between the Germantown Road and Wingohocking Creek, crossed the stream, and headed nearly due north above Bristol Road and into the woods beyond, where it ran into General Scott's Virginians. Stephen, who apparently had realized that he was not a regimental commander but the leader of a division, rode back north and met up with Scott's Virginians. He later reported the sudden appearance of Calder's 49th Regiment, and that he "sent Mr. Black who acted as Aid de Camp, to order up a Body of troops unemployed on my Right; to Attack the Reinforcement; They moved towards the Enemy." According to Stephen, these "unemployed" troops "consisted of I understand . . . Col. Spencer [with] his Rgt that Movd & Patton's [Additional Continental Regiment]." Colonel Walter Patton's regiment was part of Scott's brigade, but there was no officer named Spencer under Stephen's command. The drunken division commander had taken it upon himself once again to give orders to a unit that did not belong to his division.[26]

25 Chase and Lengel, eds., Papers, vol. 11, 468-469.

26 Chase and Lengel, eds., Papers, vol. 11, 468. Based on his later court martial, Stephen had to be informed about the conduct of his own division by his aide-de-camp, and may or may not have been

The two regiments under Patton and Spencer, in conjunction with Scott's Virginians, struck Calder's 49th Regiment somewhere in the woods east of Wingohocking Creek. The British infantrymen were likely exhausted by their quick move north and may not have been fully deployed when the Americans struck them. Whatever the circumstances, the assault "pushd the Enemy so Closely, that I calld to them 'give them the Bayonet'" claimed Stephen, who further alleged that, "Upon hearing this, The Enemy Officers on horse back rode to their Rear out of Sight; Many of their Men running After them." Some of the British approached the Americans begging to be spared. Appearing out of the fog at what Stephen described as "this flattering Juncture" was "a large Corps dressed in blue." The Americans, at least a regiment from Col. Richard Humpton's brigade of General Wayne's division, were marching southeast into the left-rear of Calder's 49th Regiment. The Pennsylvanians, "mistaking the Enemy who had Surrendered, for a party coming up to Charge them as I suppose," attacked the surprised British. Stephen attempted to stop the bloodshed by shouting that they were already defeated and "hastend to them . . . but to No purpose."[27]

Having helped defeat Ogilvie's 4th Regiment below Church Lane and driven back Calder's 49th Regiment, Stephen's separated brigades continued moving fitfully west; they crossed Winghocking Creek, reformed, and moved south by southwest toward the Germantown Road and the heart of Germantown itself. General Washington's plan had called for an uninterrupted front between the columns of Greene and Sullivan, but the fog, terrain, the presence of advanced British picket posts, and Stephen's chaotic tactical leadership prevented what had seemed achievable on paper. Instead of a long, firm front, Stephen's division was in two widely separated pieces, intertwined with two columns. McClanachan's brigade had inserted itself into Sullivan's column between Wayne's southward marching division on its left and elements of the army's advancing reserve under Maj. Gen. Lord Stirling on its right. Ahead, perhaps a quarter of a mile distant,

back with his division during this part of the advance. The only known "Spencer" commanding a regiment at Germantown was Col. Oliver Spencer of Spencer's Additional Continental Regiment, which belonged to Brig. Gen. Thomas Conway's brigade (Sullivan's column), operating about half a mile to the west. The only logical explanation for Stephen's statement is that Spencer was left behind or forgotten in the fog when Conway's brigade shifted to the far right of Sullivan's developing assault. This would have placed Spencer in this general vicinity at the time. The casualties in Patton's Additional Continental Regiment included Lt. William Patton, who was killed, and Pvt. Thomas Cox, who was wounded in the thigh. Montgomery, ed., *Archives*, Series 5, vol. 2, 631; "Partial List," 242; McGuire, *Campaign*, vol. 2, 98.

27 Chase and Lengel, eds., *Papers*, vol. 11, 468.

stood Benjamin Chew's country home at Cliveden. Scott's brigade, meanwhile, had continued southwest and was somewhere in advance of Wayne's men (perhaps astride the Bristol Road), with Muhlenberg's brigades (Greene's division) fighting off to the southeast.[28]

"Some of the regiments pursuing with vivacity while others endeavoured to proceed more circumspectly, they were entirely separated from each other, so that their weight was broken, and their effect very much weakened," wrote Capt. John Marshall of the 15th Virginia (McClanachan's brigade) while explaining the loss of tactical control. "The same cause which facilitated the separation of the regiments, prevented their discerning the real situation of the enemy. They consequently did not improve their first impression, nor direct their efforts to the most advantage."[29]

Stephen's drive toward the middle of Germantown seems to have been the least organized and most poorly led of the American efforts. His supposed drunken state, combined with the fog, caused his division to drift right and into the rear of Wayne's command. Stephen's men fired a volley into the backs of the Pennsylvanians, halting Wayne's forward surge. "The country through which the enemy was pursued, abounded with strong and small enclosures which every where broke the line of the advancing army," wrote Captain Marshall in an effort to explain how such a thing could have happened. "The darkness of the morning rendered it difficult to distinguish objects, even at an inconsiderable distance."[30]

When the fighting began, Stephen's Virginians faced the least British resistance of any of Washington's divisions; they should have been able to keep pace with Muhlenberg's command on their left and easily reach the heart of Germantown. Instead, poor leadership, heavy terrain, and fog interfered with their movements, funneled them into friendly units, and threw the division into confusion.

Connecticut Troops Enter the Battle

The final element of Greene's column to enter the fighting was Brig. Gen. Alexander McDougall's Connecticut brigade, which had only recently joined the army from the Hudson Highlands. As the divisions under Muhlenberg and Stephen entered the fight, "the curs [muskets] began to bark first and then the

28 Robertson manuscript map of the Battle of Germantown.

29 Marshall, Life, vol. 3, 180.

30 Ibid.

bulldogs [artillery]," remembered Pvt. Joseph Plumb Martin of the 4th Connecticut Regiment. McDougall moved ahead in the left rear of Muhlenberg's division. "We saw a body of the enemy drawn up behind a rail fence on our right flank," he recalled. "We immediately formed in line and advanced upon them. Our orders were not to fire till we could see the buttons upon their clothes, but they were so coy that they would not give us an opportunity to be so curious, for they hid their clothes in fog and smoke before we had either time or leisure to examine their buttons. They soon fell back," added Martin, "and we advanced, when the action became general." Ensign Jonathan Todd of the 7th Connecticut, also of McDougall's command, found it difficult to identify any troops in the swirling fog and smoke. "The Morning was very foggy which was a great disadvantage to us," he wrote his father two days later, and "we could scarce know our men from the Enemy." Todd's regiment continued advancing into a field, "where the smoke was so thick that I could't see a man 3 rods—I dres'd 17 or 18 Men Wounded in different Parts—I extracted 4 balls by cutting in the opposite side from where they went in."[31]

Coming up onto the left flank of Muhlenberg's division, the Connecticut men helped flank the three 1st Light Infantry Battalion companies; the British fell back closer to Luken's Mill, where they again were easily driven back by the sheer weight of heavy American numbers. With nothing in his front, McDougall drove his brigade across Mill Creek below Luken's Mill and continued west, with Brig. Gen. George Weedon's brigade advancing on his right. The assault carried the Connecticut men out of the woods and into the buckwheat field, with Abercromby's light infantry falling back in front of them. Private Martin and his comrades drove the British "quite through their camp. They left their kettles, in which they were cooking their breakfasts, on the fires, and some of their garments were lying on the ground, which the owners had not time to put on. Affairs went on well for some time. The enemy were retreating before us." The swirling sounds of close combat were deafening. "The crackling of thorns under a pot, and incessant peals of thunder only can convey the idea of their cannon and musketry," recalled the 2nd Connecticut's Col. Charles Webb in a letter written two days after the battle. "The enemy . . . soon gave us the ground from all parts; repeated huzzas were heard from our people who took possessions of their encampments, tents,

31 Martin, Yankee Doodle, 72-73; Letter, Jonathan Todd to his Father, October 6, 1777.

&c." In Ensign Todd's opinion, "a hotter fire was Never known both of small Arms & Field Pieces."[32]

The Connecticut men, along with Weedon's Virginians to the north and elements of Russell's brigade, continued to advance; they soon arrived on the banks of Wingohocking Creek, with the edge of Germantown looming before them. Taking the town, however, would not be as easy as it appeared. British infantry elements from General Grant's division rallied and positioned themselves behind the fences, houses, and outbuildings lining the Germantown Road. Colonel Webb, with the 2nd Connecticut,

> thought the day our own but every house in the town soon became a garrison for British troops, who put their high field pieces into the chambers; (the houses built with stone were proof against small arms), the town lying low, it being a foggy morning, the smoke of the fire of cannon and musketry, the smoke of several fields of stubble, hay and other combustibles, which the enemy fired combined, made such a midnight darkness that [a] great part of the time there was no discovering friend from foe but by the direction of the shot, and no other object but the flash of the gun.

The bloody, smoky confusion, Webb continued, was "to the enemy's advantage, who knew perfectly well the ground, to which our general and troops were total strangers with other misfortunes."[33]

The result was a stand-up exchange of lead, with one side well-protected and the other mostly out in the open. "Our Regt. far'd as well as any, & shew'd as much Obedience to Orders," recalled the 7th Connecticut's Ensign Todd. "We lost 4 or 5 [killed] & had 4 Wounded." One of the injured was company commander Capt. Theodore Woodbridge, who was struck in the shoulder and arm by two musket rounds. According to Todd, "the other Regts. In [the] division far'd much wors than we did. Colo [Philip] Bradley [5th Connecticut Regiment] has 67 Men Missing." Casualties were mounting and obstacles remained, but the Americans

32 Martin, Yankee Doodle, 73; "Contemporary Account," 330; Letter, Jonathan Todd to his Father, October 6, 1777. Large quantities of bullets supposedly found on Armstrong's Hill near Luken's Mill after the war suggest that heavy action took place there. If such fighting occurred, it was done by the Connecticut men before they advanced toward Germantown. Unfortunately, this whole area has been obliterated by development and modern roads. Lambdin, "Battle of Germantown," 385.

33 "Contemporary Account," 330-331. The British who took up positions in the houses and along fences likely included the 5th and 55th Regiments of Foot.

were on the verge of success, "and victory in the out-Setting seemed to march on our standards."[34]

Thus far the combined assault by Greene's division (under Muhlenberg), Stephen's division, and McDougall's Connecticut brigade had mauled Abercromby's 1st Battalion of Light Infantry and Ogilvie's 4th Regiment of Foot, and had driven back Calder's 49th Regiment of Foot. Supporting the light infantrymen proved a deadly task for Ogilvie's 4th Regiment of Foot, which was crippled with nine killed, 56 wounded, and three missing in a matter of minutes. If the 33 men it had lost in the attack across Chads's Ford at Brandywine are also counted, the 4th had suffered 28% casualties thus far in the campaign.[35]

Future jurist John Marshall of the 15th Virginia (Stephen's division) was amazed by the army's success. "Every thing as yet had succeeded to the utmost expectation of general Washington, and the prospect of victory was extremely flattering," he wrote. "The attack had been made with great spirit; several brigades had penetrated into the town; there was much reason to believe that a separation of the two wings of the British army would be effected, and that they would be entirely routed."[36]

The Maryland and New Jersey Militia Arrive

The last of Washington's four-column battle plan included the Maryland and New Jersey militia under Brig. Gen. William Smallwood, about 1,600 men. With Smallwood in overall command of the column, Col. Mordecai Gist likely commanded the Maryland militia contingent, which consisted of eight battalions, or some 1,000 soldiers. The native Marylander and regular army officer had been fighting since the war's early weeks. Later, he would serve as a brigadier general in

34 Letter, Jonathan Todd to his Father, October 6, 1777. Todd elaborated on the losses in his regiment: Capt. [Albert] Chapmans Company 1 [man] shot thro the thigh—Capt [Titus] Watsons company 1 [wounded] in the Arm. Capt. [Stephen] Halls one [man] slightly wounded in the Neck. Capt Halls & [Aaron] Stevens Companies fard well." It wasn't just high-ranking officers who faced scrutiny after the battle. Lieutenant Nathaniel Ferris of the 7th Connecticut was later charged with "[being drunk and incapable of doing his duty" during the fighting. Ferris was found guilty and was cashiered on October 25, 1777. Chase and Lengel, eds., *Papers*, vol. 11, 605.

35 Ten officers were wounded in the 4th regiment: Capts. Thomas Thomlinson and Francis Thorne; Lieuts. John Rowland, John Arbuthnot, and Peter Kemble; and Ensigns William Dickson, Henry Schoen, Robert Hadden (who died of his wounds in December), and Joseph Blenman. Adjutant James Hunt also was wounded. Inman, ed. "List of Officers," 176-205.

36 Marshall, Life of Washington, vol. 3, 179.

the Southern colonies at Camden, and would happily witness Cornwallis's surrender at Yorktown. In October of 1777, however, Gist was less than enthused with his undisciplined command. The Maryland militiamen had failed him and Smallwood at Paoli. Their performance in the Germantown operation would do little to alter Gist's low opinion of them.

The New Jersey militia contingent of seven battalions and a severely understrength Continental regiment of about 600 men was led by Brig. Gen. David Forman. Born in New Jersey in 1745, Forman commanded the New Jersey State Regiment in 1776. He was authorized to raise Forman's Additional Continental Regiment and was promoted to brigadier general of the New Jersey militia in the spring of 1777. He would go on to serve at Monmouth in 1778 and acted as a liaison to the French fleet later in the war. Forman's militia had seen but little action by this point in the Revolution, and their reliability was suspect. Many histories of the battle claim that Smallwood's militia wing never entered the fighting at Germantown, but eyewitness accounts say otherwise.

The militia column had the longest march that morning and entered the fight to the left of Greene's command, directly east of Luken's Mill. After turning off Church Road onto the Old York Road, Smallwood deployed his command north of Saw Mill Creek, with the Maryland men on the right and the New Jersey militia on the left. Once deployed, the troops pushed south past the school of Joseph Armitage into the low ground formed by Rock Run (which no longer exists), just above the DeBenneville family property. It was there that they ran up against a picket post manned by Maj. James Weyms's Queen's Rangers, who were positioned on the east side of the Old York Road a few hundred yards south of an unnamed road (modern Church Lane) leading to Luken's Mill.[37]

According to a letter Gist wrote to Maryland's governor on October 31, the combat opened with a sudden bout of cowardice. The enemy pickets, he explained, "began a Scattering fire upon the front of our Column, when the Colonel [Henry Hooper] was Immediately attack'd with some qualms of Sickness which obligd him to Retreat with precipitation to Maryland. As Mankind cannot be Answerable at all

37 Rock Run, which no longer exists, is today's Godfrey Avenue. All that is left of the DeBenneville property is the family burial ground, where several British officers killed or mortally wounded during the battle were eventually laid to rest. Once Smallwood entered the battle, the American line, from left to right (east to west), was as follows: Smallwood (New Jersey and Maryland militia), McDougall's Connecticut Brigade, Greene's division (Muhlenberg), Stephen's division, Wayne's division, Sullivan's division (Hazen), Conway's brigade, and the Pennsylvania militia near the Schuylkill River.

times for the weakness & frailty of the Human Heart," opined Gist. The "feelings" of the frightened officer, who had ridden into the battle next to Gist without a formal command, "demanded more pitty than resentment which led me to conceal his Error." This "weakness & frailty" seems to have had no effect on the balance of the Marylanders, who "drove them from several redoubts." These "redoubts" were likely fleches erected at the outposts manned by the Queen's Rangers and the light and grenadier companies of the British Guards. Like so many this day, Gist lamented the heavy ground fog and its effect on the militia's attack. "A thick foggy air prevaild throughout the whole of this Action, as if designd by Providence to favor the Brittish Army which with the smoak of Gunpowder prevented our discovering the situation of their line."[38]

The militia and the British pickets exchanged fire, the fog notwithstanding. The first Jerseymen to be killed fell here. "Lieut. [John] Brokaw . . . was killed by [my] side on the ground near the British picket," testified Pvt. Joseph Stull many years later. Ephraim Carle, a New Jersey militia private, marched into the battle on the left side of Forman's line. "We came across a picket guard, the British were from that across [a] Corn field, to a larger house and there they commenced firing upon us," he recalled in a postwar pension application. "[T]hey killed one of our men, we crossed a mill pond about knee deep in mud . . . went through a buckwheat field and a rifle ball cut the buckwheat down close to my legs," continued Carle. "[W]e got into the woods and there we were stationed but not in firing distance of the Enemy."[39]

The militia proved too strong to stop; they pushed aside the loyalist pickets and drove ahead, striking the main line. On the right, the Maryland troops came up against the Queen's Rangers, about 300 men all told, while the New Jersey militia met the light and grenadier companies of the British Brigade of Guards, which

38 Letter, Mordecai Gist to Gov. Thomas Johnson, 31 October 1777, Mordecai Gist Papers, Letterbook MS 2348, Maryland Historical Society, Baltimore. Gist wrote that Henry Hooper was a colonel, but Heitman had him as a brigadier general of Maryland militia. Heitman, *Historical Register*, 299. Gist went on to complain that Hooper spread falsehoods about the battle after returning home. "I am since Informd that he reported . . . in his Neighbourhood at Home that the Maryland Militia was placd in front at the Engagement, and were entirely cut off," explained Gist. "This with many other Absurdities propogated by him to the prejudice of the Army, has had its tendency to prevent the Second Class of Militia from turning out so generally as they otherwise would have done." Letter, Mordecai Gist to Jno. McClure, October 10, 1777, Gist Papers. McGuire, Campaign, vol. 2, 105. The pickets of the British Guards consisted of their grenadier company and Light Infantry company.

39 RWPF, file S23953; RWPF, file S3121.

totaled perhaps 100 men. Once the initial firing began, the two Guards companies moved up to the right of the Queen's Rangers from their own picket post farther south. Captain Richard Fitzpatrick of the British Guards remembered being "suprized by their Army coming down upon us & making a most desperate attack, surprising indeed in every sense of the word." Fitzpatrick wrote that the British "had not above two hours notice of their advancing, & then gave no credit to it."[40]

"During said Battle," testified one eyewitness, "General Forman cursed and swore most vehemently during the time of the action." The militiaman who wrote this account claimed that he "distinctly recollects that the Genl. observed to his men that the Damned Little Bullets of the British would hurt no man. That the horse rode by the general during the action was slightly wounded." Forman's Additional Continental Regiment wore red coats, which naturally enough caused confusion—especially under foggy conditions. Koert Schenk of Forman's regiment recalled fighting "by the side of a company (commanded by Captain John Burrows) who all wore red coats, and were fired upon by some of our troops through mistake." According to American Maj. Asher Holmes of the 1st Battalion of Monmouth County militia, "[t]he Jersey Militia and Red Coats [Forman's Additional Continental Regiment] . . . and the Maryland Militia . . . drove the enemy, when we first made the attack. . . . The fire was very severe, and the enemy ran."[41]

The retreat did not last long, for the Americans soon ran up against a solid British line (the Queen's Rangers on the left and the light and grenadier companies of the Guards on the right), most of whom were using a fence for protection. "They brought a fieldpiece to fire on us with grapeshot," continued Holmes. Private Elijah Hummel never forgot the deadly result of one of the blasts from that lone gun. "Col. [William] Chamberlin's son was killed that day. He was at the other end of the regiment from where I was," testified Hummel. The colonel's oldest son, 18-year-old Lewis Chamberlin, was visiting his father when he learned that a battle was in the offing. Although a civilian, he remained and, apparently with the permission of his father, went into the action. The large grapeshot tore apart Lewis's knee and severed an artery, and "for the want of prompt medical

40 Letter, Richard Fitzpatrick to his Brother, October 28, 1777. Richard Fitzpatrick Papers, Library of Congress.

41 RWPF, file S16273; Asher Holmes, "Letter Concerning the Battle at Germantown, 1777," *Proceedings of the New Jersey Historical Society: A Magazine of History, Biography and Notes on Families* (Newark, January 1922), vol. 7, no. 1, 34-35; RWPF, file S748.

attention," he bled to death on the field. Thomas Peterson later remembered that his commander, "Captain [Rynear] Staats was wounded in the same battle." Additionally, Lieutenant Colonel Peter Vroom was wounded and Lieut. John Brocaw was killed.[42]

Despite Forman's tenacity, the Queen's Rangers and the light and grenadier companies of the Guards proved more than enough for the militia, so much so that the main line of the Brigade of Guards never pulled a trigger. Although their march, deployment, and initial advance started well, the militia did not have enough discipline and experience to drive home their attack against veteran troops. "The Guards [the two battalions of the Brigade of Guards, some 800-900 men] were not Engaged, though we had a column of the enemy in our front who I suppose waited only for the success of their main attack to begin theirs," surmised a British captain in a letter to his brother. The attack was so timidly made that the Brigade of Guards "lost but three privates." Fortune continued to smile on the Guards, who had now passed through two major battles in the campaign with just 10 total casualties.[43]

Once the Queen's Rangers and the light and grenadier companies of the Guards realized they were facing militia, they "Immediately took the advantage of our Feelings and drove us from the Ground," reported Mordecai Gist on October 10. Some of the men, continued Gist, sounded the false alarm that "a Party of Hessians was making round on our left in order to Surround us." The universal fear of Hessians was not uncommon in the ranks of the American army, but there were no Hessian units anywhere near Smallwood's column. The confusion may have been the result of Marylanders mistaking the green uniforms of the Queen's Rangers for those worn by Hessian jaegers; this had happened at Brandywine as well. Major Asher Holmes made the same claim in a letter two days after the battle when he wrote, "by the thickness of the fog the enemy got into our rear," and "our

42 Holmes, "Letter Concerning the Battle at Germantown, 1777," 34-35. RWPF, files S2277, S4520, and S5899. For information on Chamberlin and his son, see www.findagrave.com/memorial/15121363/william-chamberlin. Just one member of the Queen's Rangers was wounded in the battle. After their bloodletting at Brandywine, the Loyalists could ill afford another battle with heavy casualties. Remembrancer, 418.

43 The George Osborne papers are in a private family collection in England and were not accessible to this author. The quote provided herein is from McGuire, Campaign, vol. 2, 49. The only other known account for the Brigade of Guards at Germantown comes from Lord Cantelupe, though it provides few details of the battle. "At six in the morng The Rebel Army came down in 3 or 4 Columns & attack'd the Left of Our Army in German Town but was totally routed by 12 oclock at noon a thick fog continued till ten oclock." Entry for October 4, Lord Cantelupe Diary, the Grey Papers, Durham University, England.

Monmouth men stood firm until their ammunition was nearly exhausted and the enemy advancing round our right flank." Gist responded to the fearful shouts of a British flanking party by deploying "part of my Brigade in a Wood in order to receive" the advance of the enemy and moving off "with a small party to the left, where I placed them in order to cover and Guard our Flank and give Intelligence of their Approach, but on my return to the place found that the whole had retreated."[44]

Smallwood's militia was not as successful as other elements of Washington's army, but they advanced far enough, and, contrary to most sources, fought long enough to sustain casualties. Maryland militiaman George Welsh took quill in hand to pen a note to the young widow of a comrade. "Your loving husband, and America's best friend," he began,

> nobly defending his country's cause, having repulsed the enemy, driving them from their breastworks, received a ball through his body, by which he expired in about three-quarters of an hour afterwards. He was carried off the field to a house, his most valuable things secured, and as our people lost the ground, we were obliged to leave him there; the people of the house promised to have him interred.[45]

General Smallwood wrote to the governor of Maryland to detail the colony's casualty figures: "Capt. [James] Cox, of Baltimore, a brave and valuable officer, with Lieut. Crost, of [Baker] Johnson's regiment, and several other brave officers and men, were killed within twenty paces of the enemy's lodgment before they were dispossessed of it." Colonel Luke Marbury, a 32-year-old colonel of the Lower Battalion of Militia from Prince George's County, was listed as missing.[46]

44 Holmes, "Letter Concerning the Battle at Germantown, 1777"; Letter, Mordecai Gist to Jno. McClure, 10 October 1777, Gist Papers.

45 J. Thomas Scharf, The Chronicles of Baltimore; Being a Complete History of "Baltimore Town" and Baltimore City from the Earliest Period to the Present Time (Baltimore, 1874), 165-166. Unfortunately, the only known account from the Queen's Rangers that covers this period of the war proves unhelpful in reconstructing the battle. Stephen Jarvis recorded that "when the battle took place I was under the operation of medicine the Surgeon had given me that morning, and therefore had not the Honour of engaging with my brave comrades in the action." John T. Hayes, ed., *Stephen Jarvis: The King's Loyal Horseman, His Narrative 1775-1783* (Fort Lauderdale, 1996), 16-17.

46 Browne, ed., Archives, vol. 16, 396. Cox's corpse was taken to the home of the Wilson family on the Old York Road above Nicetown, where he was buried. McGuire, Campaign, vol. 2, 107. Marbury was held prisoner until his exchange on March 21, 1781, Heitman, *Historical Register*, 379.

Major Asher Holmes thought they were lucky to suffer so few losses, as the heavy fog certainly helped impede British marksmanship. "Providence seems to have protected our Monmouth Militia in a particular manner, as we have lost very few, if any, killed, and not many wounded, although the Enemy was within 120 yards of us in the hottest of the fire, and their fieldpiece firing on us with grapeshot [a] great part of the time. I have escaped without being hurt, although I was much exposed to enemy's fire."[47]

* * *

Except for Lord Stirling's reserve division, once Smallwood went into action the American line was fully formed and mostly driving the British units. "The different attacks being made at the same time distracted the enemy's attention so much, that after about an hour's engagement they began to give way on every part," explained artilleryman Henry Knox in a letter to Maj. Gen. Artemas Ward on October 7. "[M]ost unfortunately for us," he continued, "a fog which had arisen about daybreak became so excessively thick from the continued firing that it was impossible to discover an object at twenty yards' distance."[48]

Of more concern than the fog and the smoke was the musket and artillery fire emanating from the grounds at Cliveden. Although no one knew it yet, the heavy clattering of small arms, occasionally punctuated by the deeper bark of field artillery, signaled the climax of the Battle of Germantown, when the well-planned American surprise attack slipped from victory into defeat. If the American attack had taken place after the training Washington's army would receive at Valley Forge that winter, the next couple of hours may well have been very different.

47 Holmes, "Letter," 35.

48 Drake, Correspondence, 52.

Chapter 14

Decision at Cliveden

October 4, 1777
7:00 a.m. to 8:00 a.m.

"It was proposed (for our advanced brigades had driven the enemy some way beyond it) to send a flag to summon the enemy posted there to surrender, it being urged as dangerous to leave them in our rear."[1]

— Colonel Timothy Pickering, George Washington's adjutant general, October 4, 1777

By 7:00 a.m. on October 4, ten brigades of Continentals, supported by three brigades of militia, had overrun the British picket posts and camps, crushed the enemy right flank, and were poised to sever the Germantown Road, potentially cutting off a large segment of the reeling British army. "[T]here was," scribbled artilleryman Elisha Stevens in his journal, "a very fair prospect of our gaining the Day." What Stevens and others did not know was that actions were being set in motion that would alter the entire course of the morning.[2]

1 Pickering, *Pickering*, vol. 1, 169.

2 Elisha Stevens, *Fragments of Memoranda Written by him in the War of the Revolution* (Meriden, CT, 1893), pages not numbered. The artillery structure in the Continental army is unclear. Stevens was likely attached to one of the independent batteries.

Musgrave Fortifies the Chew House

About dawn, when the head of General Sullivan's American column struck the British outposts at Mount Airy, Lt. Col. Thomas Musgrave's 40th Regiment of Foot was camped well to the rear in a supporting position for Maitland's embattled 2nd Light Infantry Battalion. The American spearhead quickly broke Maitland's lines and drove his men rearward while Musgrave pushed his regiment ahead to reinforce the collapsing front. According to an anonymous British account, Musgrave "had been sparing of his ammunition, [and] told the light infantry that he would cover their retreat, which he did in a most masterly manner." Within a half hour of the beginning of the fighting, however, Musgrave's men were battling for their lives, surrounded on three sides with no prospect of holding a line that had mostly disintegrated.[3]

Musgrave was 40 years old at Germantown, the sixth son and only surviving heir of Sir Richard Musgrave, 4th Baronet of Hayton Castle. He had been in the British army for 23 years and in the American colonies since the early days of the war and had led his regiment in battle at Brandywine. Now, nearly surrounded and with retreat the clear and most viable option, he opted to do something else entirely. "At this critical moment," recalled Maj. Benjamin Tallmadge of the American light dragoons, "Col. [Thomas] Musgrave . . . threw his regiment into a large stone house . . . from which he poured a heavy and galling fire upon our troops." In an instant, Benjamin Chew's large country home—Cliveden—had become a castle-like fortification in the middle of the new American front.[4]

By the time Musgrave made that fateful decision, Sullivan's men were pressing almost within musket-swinging reach. Musgrave had his men fire into the closing enemy ring while others stuffed themselves into the Chew house as fast as they could squeeze through the door. Musgrave, wrote General Howe's Hessian aide Capt. Friedrich von Muenchhausen, "saw the light infantry and the 5th regiment falling back toward him, whereupon he detached half his regiment forward to support the retreating troops. Musgrave, with the other half of the 40th," he continued, "threw himself into a massive building that was situated close between the two roads on which the two enemy columns were advancing." Although many

3 "Extract of a Letter from an English Officer," 112-113.

4 Tallmadge, *Memoir*, 23.

accounts claim Musgrave packed half a dozen companies into Cliveden, in reality he moved into the house with half that number, about 100-120 men.[5]

According to an unknown British officer writing a week later, Musgrave "ordered all the window-shutters of the ground floor to be shut, as the enemy's fire would otherwise have been too heavy upon them there: he placed, however, a certain number of men at each window, and at the hall doors, with orders to bayonet every one who should attempt to come in; he disposed of the rest in the two upper stories," continued the anonymous officer, "and instructed them how to cover themselves, and direct their fire out of the windows." He also dispatched soldiers to the roof and others into the basement to man the windows. Musgrave, continued the officer, detailed to his troops why he was ordering them into the mansion:

> That their only safety was in the defence of that house; that if they let the enemy get into it, they would undoubtedly every man be put to death; that it would be an absurdity for any one to think of giving himself up, with hopes of quarter; that their situation was nevertheless by no means a bad one, as there had been instances of only a few men defending a house against numbers; that he had no doubt of their being supported and delivered by our army; but that at all events they must sell themselves as dear as possible to the enemy.[6]

"This house of Chew's was a strong stone building, and exceedingly commodious," explained adjutant general Timothy Pickering, "having windows on every side, so that you could not approach it without being exposed to a severe fire; which, in fact, was well directed, and killed and wounded a great many of our officers and men." Benjamin Chew's country home, which had been empty when Washington's army passed it earlier that morning, was two and a half stories tall on a raised basement, with a finished attic and an observation deck on the back roof.

5 McGuire, *Campaign*, vol. 2, 84, 318; Muenchhausen, *At Howe's Side*, 38. The three companies were commanded by Lt. Col. Thomas Musgrave, Capt. William Harris, and Capt. Samuel Bradstreet. Technically speaking, pay for battalion officers in British regiments was predicated on their being the titular head of a company in the regiment.

6 "Extract of a Letter," 113. Historian Thomas McGuire (*Campaign*, vol. 2, 58-59, 83-84) repeatedly claims the 40th of Foot acted as light infantry throughout the campaign, but he does not provide any documentation for his assertion. While Musgrave was a veteran light infantry officer who had been shot in the face during the New York campaign, this author has yet to find any documentation to support McGuire's conclusion. Howe had instilled light infantry concepts into all the regiments of his command, including the wearing of overalls and fighting in open order. That does not mean, however, that they were equipped as light infantry.

The home was adorned with classical motifs and the grounds included statuary. Like many Germantown structures, it was built of Wissahickon schist, a medium-grade metamorphic rock formed from mudstone or shale. The large ashlar blocks of the front façade were two feet thick, and the equally thick side and rear walls were rubble stone covered with stucco. The elegant interior featured high ceilings, wide hallways, fine woodwork, and a grand staircase. The property boasted four outbuildings: a kitchen, laundry, stone barn, and carriage house. The kitchen was off the northeast corner of the house, with the symmetrically placed laundry building erected off the southeast corner. (A 1776 colonnade connected the kitchen to the main house.) A low stone wall ran along Germantown Road at the edge of the front lawn, while the driveway leading to the house was lined with cherry trees. A small kitchen garden surrounded by a paling fence sat behind the house.[7]

The fighting around Cliveden would last for some two hours. The infantrymen who packed the house only had with them the limited ammunition inside their cartridge boxes, so it is more than likely that ammunition had been stored in the house before the battle began. Cliveden's first floor windows sported thick, paneled wooden shutters that locked from the inside. The iron-barred basement windows were small. The structure sported three entrances: the ornamental double French doors that opened into the elegant main hallway; a solid, heavy back door that entered the rear of the hallway; and a paneled servant's entrance on the north side near the kitchen. Musgrave's men locked the shutters and doors and blocked the three entrances with tables and chairs. Jaeger Capt. Johann Ewald, who rode across the battlefield the next day, explained that the "house was built of baked stones, two stories high, and the three entrances to the building could be barricaded only with tables and chairs, due to the rapid advance of the enemy."[8]

While Musgrave jammed three companies of infantry inside Cliveden, Sullivan pushed his brigades past the structure, isolating them inside. According to Timothy

7 Pickering, *Pickering*, vol. 1, 168-169. There is no evidence that anyone was living at the home while the British were in Germantown. Circumstantial evidence suggests the presence of an observation deck that no longer exists. The attic contained a finished winder staircase that stopped at the roof. Most contemporary images of Cliveden depict some type of flat roof, which (if accurate) would have provided a magnificent view of the area, including the distant Delaware River. It is highly probable that the roof was heavily damaged during the battle, which resulted in the current roof configuration when the house was repaired in 1779. McGuire, *Campaign*, vol. 2, 81-83, 317. The house was significantly altered after the war; a pantry was added in the 1780s, and a large addition was built onto the rear of the house in 1868.

8 McGuire, *Campaign*, vol. 2, 83; Ewald, *Diary*, 96.

Pickering, Musgrave's command did not cause a problem for the Americans until after they had pushed past the structure deeper into Germantown. "I saw not one dead man until I had passed it [Cliveden], and then but one, lying in the road near where I fell in with General Sullivan," claimed the staff officer in a letter decades later. "I presume that, following close on the heels of the British battalion of light infantry and half the 40th regiment, which were retiring before him, Sullivan, with his column, had passed Chew's house, without annoyance from it." Pickering concluded that it "must have taken some time for Colonel Musgrave . . . to barricade and secure the doors, and the windows of the lower story, before he would be ready to fire from the chamber windows; and it was from them that the firing I saw proceeded." Pickering was riding next to General Washington down the Germantown Road in the wake of Sullivan's advance when they heard "a very heavy fire of musketry. General Sullivan's divisions, it was evident, were warmly engaged with the enemy; but neither was in sight."[9]

Washington took a moment to survey the situation and turned to Pickering. "I am afraid General Sullivan is throwing away his ammunition; ride forward and tell him to preserve it." Washington had ordered the Americans to husband their ammunition and fire carefully at well-defined targets, but "the exhilaration of the victorious advance caused the men to be careless and they poured shots at many indefinable targets that proved to be illusory." Pickering recalled that Washington was "apprehensive that Sullivan, after meeting the enemy in his front, kept up his brisk and incessant fire, when the haziness of the air, and its increased obscurity, from the burning of so much powder, prevented his troops having such a distinct view of the enemy, as would render their fire efficient." With his orders in hand, Pickering later claimed he spurred his horse along the road "three or four hundred yards beyond Chew's house, met Sullivan, and delivered to him the General's orders."[10]

Once his task was completed, Pickering spun his mount around and galloped back toward Washington. It was at this point in the battle that he first took notice of Cliveden. "At this time I had never heard of Chew's house; and had no idea that an enemy was in my rear," he explained. "The first notice I received of it was from the whizzing of musket balls, across the road, before, behind, and above me, as I was returning, after delivering the orders to Sullivan." Pickering turned to the right

9 Letter, Timothy Pickering to Jared Sparks, August 23, 1826, 427.

10 Ibid., 427-428.

Present day view of the Bensell House, where the argument over assaulting Cliveden took place. *Photo by author*

and "saw the blaze of the muskets, whose shot were still aimed at me, from the windows of a large stone house, standing back about a hundred yards from the road." Fortunately for Pickering, he and his mount were barely within musket range of Cliveden.[11]

While British infantrymen were drawing beads on Pickering, American artillerymen were firing on the stone structure. "Passing on, I came to some of our artillery, who were firing very *obliquely* on the front of the house," he recalled. Four guns were lobbing rounds at Cliveden—two belonging to the Pennsylvania battery under Thomas Proctor and two 6-pounders captured from the British light infantry that morning. All four were unlimbered across the road from Cliveden in the yard of the present Upsala house. From the back of his horse, Pickering shouted to the gunners that "in that position their fire would be unavailing, and that the only

11 Ibid., 427-428. Pickering found Sullivan in the fields west of the Mennonite meetinghouse.

chance of their shot making any impression on the house, would be by moving down and firing *directly* on its front." The artillerymen took Pickering's suggestion to heart and shifted their fire, moving the guns by hand to face the front of the building, about 120 yards distant, and bombarded the strongest side of the house, which was protecting Musgrave's men with its two-foot thick walls.[12]

Indecision at the Highest Levels

Large numbers of Continentals, including the fresh New Jersey and North Carolina brigades from Lord Stirling's division, surrounded the bristling Cliveden house. The three companies of the 40th Regiment of Foot, explained Washington in a letter to John Hancock the next day, were "in a situation not to be easily forced, and had it in their power from the Windows to give us no small annoyance, and in a great measure to obstruct our advance." What was to be done with them? The question prompted a heated and prolonged debate amongst Washington's staff officers that continued through the morning, as well as across the next several decades.[13]

Leaving the booming artillery pieces, Pickering rode on and rejoined Washington, "who, with General Knox and other officers, was in front of a stone house (nearly all the houses in Germantown were of stone) next northward of the open field in which Chew's house stood." The officers were discussing "in Washington's presence, this question; Whether the whole of our troops then behind should immediately advance, regardless of the enemy in Chew's house, or first summon them to surrender?" Pickering and chief of artillery Henry Knox began debating the best course of action. Knox wanted to call back the infantry to attack Cliveden because "it would be unmilitary to leave a castle in our rear."[14]

Knox's position stunned Pickering, who adamantly opposed assaulting the edifice. "Doubtless that is a correct general maxim; but it does not apply in this case," Pickering shouted above the cacophony of battle. "We know the extent of the castle (Chew's house); and to guard against the danger from the enemy's sallying, and falling on the rear of our troops, a small regiment may be posted here to watch them; and if they sally, such a regiment *will take care of them*. . . . [T]o

12 Letter, Timothy Pickering to Jared Sparks, August 23, 1826, 428; McGuire, *Campaign*, vol. 2, 86-87. There were no structures on the Upsula property at the time of the battle.

13 Chase and Lengel, eds., *Papers*, vol. 11, 394.

14 Pickering, *Pickering*, vol. 1, 168.

summon them to surrender will be useless," he protested. "We are now in the midst of the battle; and its issue is unknown. In this state of uncertainty, and so well secured as the enemy find themselves, they will not regard a summons; they will fire at your flag." As he later explained, the annoying fire coming from Cliveden "absolutely stopped our pursuit—not necessarily." The frustrated Pickering believed the army should keep pushing into Germantown with Stirling's division, and that stopping to deal with a handful of enemy men in the house was not only unnecessary but bordered on madness. The better policy, he advocated, was "to have pushed our advantage, leaving a party to watch the enemy in that house."[15]

Charles Cotesworth Pinckney, a South Carolina officer voluntarily attached to Washington's entourage, witnessed the exchange and wrote about it in an 1820 letter. Musgrave's men, he recalled, had

> commenced a brilliant & incessant firing from the windows, without being able to see very clearly what [they] fired at, for the Fog was very thick, & kept the Smoke down so low, that the battle was fought without the adverse parties scarcely seeing each other, & the only way we knew of the Enemy's being drawn up in opposition to us, was by their fire & the whistling of their Balls, and it was some time after they retreated before we knew of it, & that only by our not hearing the whistling of their Balls, & seeing no flashes in our front.[16]

A French engineer with the army told Pinckney that he remembered a similar event occurring in Italy, "but the Army passed on & gained the Victory, & the Cassino full of soldiers fell into their hands," and "requested that I [Pinckney] would state it to the General." General Knox, meanwhile, continued to argue "against the impolicy of leaving an inimical armed force in our rear."[17]

Captain Henry "Light Horse Harry" Lee provided a detailed account of the debate in his memoir. "The halt at Chew's house," began the cavalryman, "was taken after some deliberation (as the writer well recollects; being for that day in the

15 Letter, Timothy Pickering to Jared Sparks, August 23, 1826, 428. This argument took place a couple of hundred yards north of Cliveden near the Bensell house. Today known as the Bensell-Billmeyer House, the structure had been built about 1730 by John George Bensell. Michael Billmeyer, a printer, purchased the home in 1789, and it was significantly enlarged in 1793. Today, the house stands at 6505 Germantown Avenue in Germantown. At the time of the battle, the house was the nearest stone structure adjacent to the northern fields of the Cliveden property. One account has Washington standing on a carriage-stone to get a better view of the action. Brownlow, *Germantown*, 30; McGuire, *Campaign*, vol. 2, 318; Reed, *Campaign*, 227.

16 Letter, Charles Cotesworth Pinckney to Henry Johnson, November 14, 1820, 203-204.

17 Ibid.

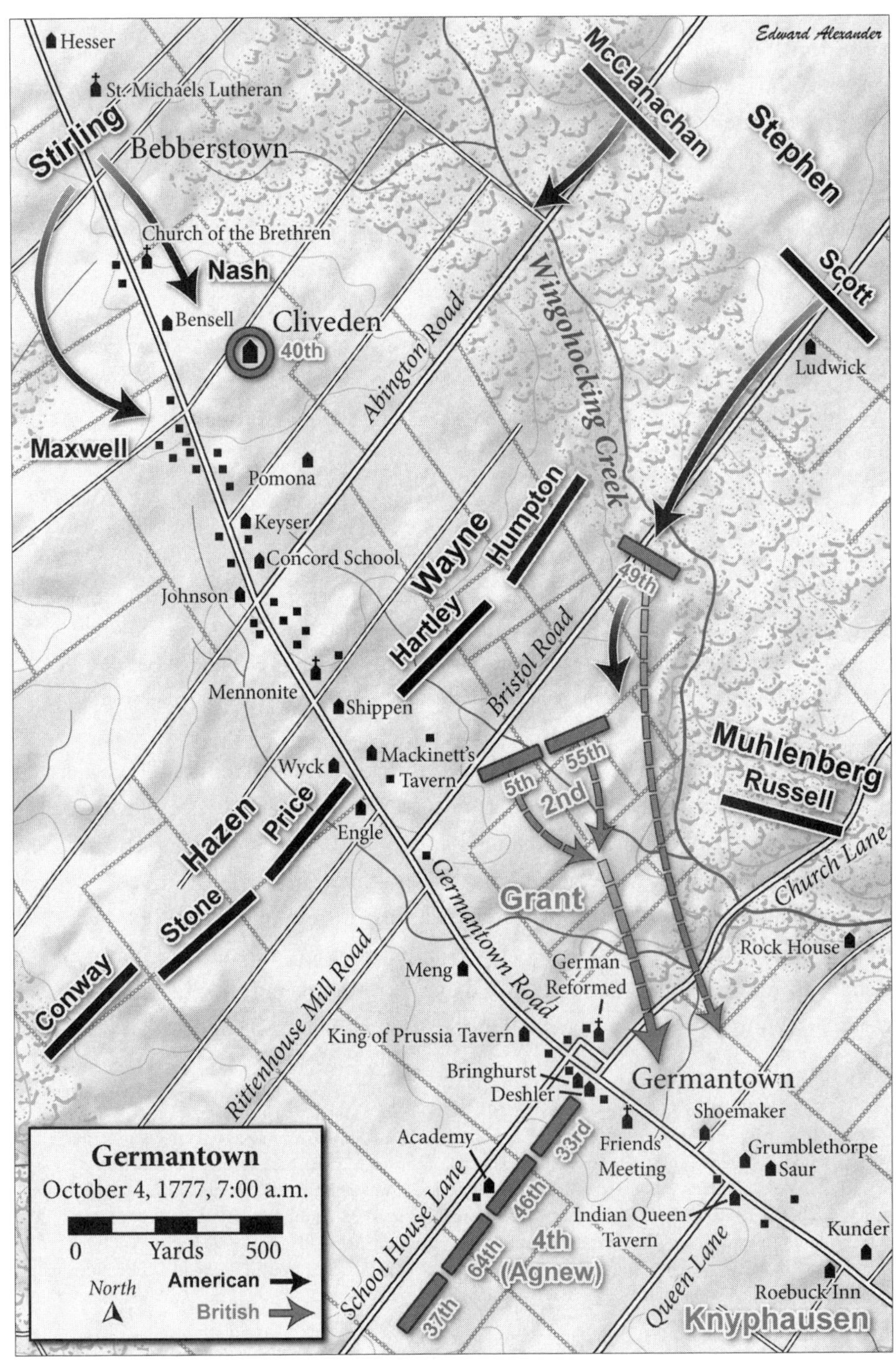
Edward Alexander
Hesser
St. Michaels Lutheran
Stirling
Bebberstown
McClanachan
Stephen
Church of the Brethren
Nash
Bensell
Cliveden
40th
Abington Road
Wingohocking Creek
Scott
Ludwick
Maxwell
Pomona
Keyser
Concord School
Johnson
Wayne
Humpton
Hartley
49th
Bristol Road
Mennonite
Shippen
Mackinett's Tavern
Wyck
Muhlenberg
Russell
5th
55th
2nd
Hazen
Price
Engle
Germantown Road
Grant
Church Lane
Stone
Rock House
Conway
Rittenhouse Mill Road
Meng
German Reformed
King of Prussia Tavern
Bringhurst
Deshler
Germantown
Shoemaker
Academy
33rd
Friends' Meeting
Grumblethorpe
Saur
46th
Indian Queen Tavern
Kunder
School House Lane
64th
4th (Agnew)
Queen Lane
37th
Roebuck Inn
Knyphausen
Germantown
October 4, 1777, 7:00 a.m.
0 Yards 500
North
American
British

Present day view looking across the front lawn toward Cliveden from west of the Germantown road. It was on these grounds that the New Jersey Continentals fought.

Photo by author

suite of the commander in chief, with a troop of dragoons charged with duty near his person.)." According to Lee, several junior officers, "at the head of whom were colonel Pickering and lieutenant colonel [Alexander] Hamilton, urged with zeal the propriety of passing the house." Knox, however, "opposed the measure with earnestness, denouncing the idea of leaving an armed force in the rear; and, being always high in the general's confidence, his opinion prevailed."[18]

Despite the admonitions of Pickering, Hamilton, and perhaps others, "[i]t was proposed (for our advanced brigades had driven the enemy some way beyond it) to send a flag to summon the enemy posted there to surrender." Washington, Knox, and others believed Musgrave's position was dire and that capitulation was the natural course any officer would choose given his predicament. Lieutenant Colonel William Smith, the army's deputy adjutant general, offered to carry a flag of truce and approach the house to make the offer. Because many Americans had refused to take prisoners that morning (likely without Washington's knowledge), this tactic was unlikely to succeed. Sullivan's advance toward Cliveden and beyond was marked by Wayne's Pennsylvanians exacting revenge for Paoli—not the seizure of prisoners. Musgrave likely witnessed this himself and was less than prone to accommodate Washington. While Smith was preparing to walk to Cliveden,

18 Lee, *Memoirs*, vol. 1, 29.

A surviving example of the Cliveden statuary showing battle damage. *Photo by author*

"appropriate bodies of troops were prepared to compel his submission." Pickering fully expected the British to shoot the flag bearer dead. "I imagined they would pay no respect to the flag, they being well posted, and the battle far enough from being decided," he declared. "The event justified my apprehensions: in a few minutes Mr. Smith was brought back with his leg broken and shattered by a musket-ball fired from the house." The lieutenant colonel had reached the gate at the road in front of the house when an unnamed soldier fired from one of the windows. Smith lingered in agony for nearly three weeks before succumbing to his gruesome wound. "Thirsting after military fame, and devoted to his country," wrote Light Horse Harry Lee, Smith "obeyed with joy the perilous order; advanced through the deadly fire pouring from the house, presuming that the sanctity of his flag would at length be respected: vain expectation! He fell before his admiring comrades, a victim to this generous presumption." No extant British accounts mention any such attempts to get the Cliveden garrison to surrender.[19]

19 Pickering, *Pickering*, vol. 1, 169. Major Caleb Gibbs, the commander of Washington's Life Guards (a special unit charged with the protection of the commander-in-chief), later told Pickering, "While you were absent I offered to carry the flag; I thank my stars that the offer was not accepted." Letter, Timothy Pickering to William Johnson, January 25, 1825, Pickering Papers, Massachusetts Historical Society, Boston, microfilm copy at the David Library of the American Revolution, Washington Crossing, PA, Film 220, Reel 16. Another officer almost certainly volunteered before the ill-fated Smith. "General Washington thought that if the commander of this post were summoned, he would readily surrender: M. de Mauduit was therefore requested to take a drum with him, and make this proposal; but on his observing that he spoke bad English, and might not, perhaps, be understood, an American officer was sent, who being preceded by a drum, and displaying a white handkerchief, it was imagined, might not incure the smallest risk; but the English replied to this officer only with musket fire, and killed him on the spot." Marquis de Chastellux,

The grievous wounding of the staff officer angered Washington's entourage. Henry Knox advanced the next proposal to remove the threat posed by the fortified Chew house. According to Benjamin Tallmadge, "[a]ll attempts to dislodge them were ineffectual, and although they would have been harmless in a few minutes if we had passed them by, yet through the importunity of Gen. Knox (which I distinctly heard), Gen. Washington permitted him to bring his field artillery to bear upon it, but without effect."[20]

Benjamin Rush, a signer of the Declaration of Independence and a surgeon with the army, also witnessed the high-level debate. Rush left the impression that the staff quarreled as Washington passively listened to their arguments. Rush saw an officer "low in command give counterorders to the Commander in Chief," he wrote to John Adams on October 13, "and the Commander in Chief passive under that circumstance, his distress and resentment exceeded all bounds." Knox's view prevailed with Washington; Musgrave had no interest in surrendering, and the only option left was to drive him out of the Chew house.[21]

Assault on the Chew House

While the debate raged regarding what to do about the enemy holed up inside the Chew house, General Sullivan's front stabilized in a strong advanced position about 1,000 yards farther south. Colonel Moses Hazen's division was in line west of

Travels in North America in the Years 1780, 1781 and 1782, 2 vols. (Chapel Hill, NC, 1963), vol. 1, 139-140; Pickering, "Account," 220; McGuire, *Campaign*, vol. 2, 88; Lee, *Memoirs*, vol. 1, 29-30.

20 Tallmadge, *Memoir*, 23.

21 Butterfield, ed., *Letters*, Vol. 1, 158. Several decades later Pickering engaged in a prolific exchange of correspondence about what happened that morning within the high command. It seems to have begun with the publication in 1822 of William Johnson's *Sketches of the Life and Correspondence of Nathanael Greene*. Pickering had numerous issues with Johnson's history of events including what happened at Cliveden, and he wrote extensively about it. Pickering was adamant that Washington listened to the discussion, and that "[Light Horse Harry] Lee, commanding a troop of horse, on that day on duty near the General's person, accounts for his [Lee's] determination to send the summons. . . . Further I must remark, that the general officers . . . were then in their proper places, with their divisions and brigades. Knox alone, of the general officers, was present. Commanding in the artillery department, and the field pieces being distributed among the brigades of the army, he was always at liberty, in time of action, to attend the commander in chief. . . . The truth is," continued Pickering, "that General Washington, not sanguine in his own opinions, and his diffidence being probably increased by a feeling sense of his high responsibility, as Commander in Chief, was ever disposed, when occasions occurred, to consult those officers who were near him, in whose discernment and fidelity he placed a confidence; and certainly his decisions were often influenced by their opinions. This is within my own knowledge." Letter, Timothy Pickering to Jared Sparks, August 23, 1826, 430.

the Germantown Road, with the left flank of Col. Thomas Price's brigade near the Engle house and Col. John Stone's brigade on Price's right. Brigadier General Thomas Conway's Pennsylvania brigade angled southwest in its advance to take up a position on Stone's right. Opposing the brigades west of the road, perhaps 600 yards distant, was the 3rd and 4th British Brigades of Wilhelm von Knyphausen's wing of Howe's army just south of School House Lane. Brig. Gen. James Agnew's 4th Brigade had its right flank just west of the Germantown Road and positioned off the left flank of Agnew was Maj. Gen. Charles Grey's 3rd Brigade.[22]

Wayne's division was in line on the east side of the Germantown Road opposite Hazen's division, with the right side of Col. Thomas Hartley's brigade near Mackinett's Tavern and Col. Richard Humpton's brigade extending the line east into the rougher wooded ground near Wingohocking Creek. The small Virginia brigade under Brig. Gen. Charles Scott, part of Adam Stephen's scattered division of General Greene's column, was in the rough creek terrain facing generally west, roughly perpendicular to Wayne's front. Stephen's other brigade under, Col. Alexander McClanachan, had crossed Wingohocking Creek several hundred yards to the north behind Wayne's command and was advancing toward Cliveden from the east. Facing them to the southeast of the Bristol Road were the rallied 5th and 55th Regiments of Foot and perhaps the 49th Regiment of Foot that had been pushed back earlier by the advance of Wayne and Stephen. A lull occurred in the fighting about this time, which may have come about because many of the American units were running low on ammunition. In addition, Wayne's advance had been stalled for a time when McClanachan's Virginians stumbled into his rear and opened fire. Several British units, meanwhile, were regrouping in their front.[23]

Washington ordered Lord Stirling's reserve division to provide any support needed because he expected that a bombardment of Cliveden would drive out the enemy infantry. Thomas Proctor's Pennsylvania battery, meanwhile, continued shelling the house. The British had overrun the same battery at Chads's Ford at Brandywine, and the gunners were more than happy to take out their vengeance against the stone house. The first shot, wrote an anonymous British officer, "burst open both the hall-doors, and wounded some men with the pieces of stone that flew from the wall." To better coordinate his defense of the house, Colonel

22 Robertson Map, Windsor Castle Collection, 734029.d.

23 Ibid.

Present day view looking into front yard of Cliveden from a 2nd floor window. This shows the view the British soldiers had of the area where many of the New Jersey Continentals were shot down. *Photo by author*

Musgrave placed Capt. William Harris one of his company commanders in command of the ground floor. When the artillery round smashed through the doors, Harris reported this to Musgrave, "and that he had thrown chairs, tables, and any little impediments he could before the door, and that he would endeavor to keep the enemy out as long as he had a single man left." His efforts, continued the British account, were "very soon put to the test, for the rebels directed their cannon (sometimes loaded with round, sometimes with grape shot) entirely against the upper stories."[24]

American troops farther south quickly discovered that the artillery fire was generally ineffective. "This was found very Difficult as the House being Stone was almost impenetrable by Cannon & Sufficient proof against musketry," explained General Sullivan. "The Enemy Defended themselves with great Bravery & annoyed our Troops much by their fire." An anonymous American officer agreed with Sullivan in a letter to the governor of New York: "Four pieces of artillery were

24 "Extract of a Letter," 113. Cliveden's original front doors survived the battle and were kept as relics. Periodically, they were put on display in the hall of the house. Unfortunately, a carriage house fire in 1970 destroyed them. McGuire, *Germantown*, 70.

ordered to play upon it but as our metal was not heavy & the Walls were very thick our Execution was then but trifling."[25]

The artillery shells, recalled Tench Tilghman, one of Washington's aides, made little impression on the building even though "a vast number was fired thro' it." The cascade of iron caused hellish conditions inside the Chew home. The solid iron rounds knocked large chunks of stone out of the walls and slammed through the wooden shutters on the ground floor, spraying "the occupants in the dark hallway with broken glass, splinters, and stone fragments," wrote one historian of the battle. Grapeshot struck the building like giant iron hail from an angry sky, chipping the front steps, grooving fine stonework, splintering cornices, and shattering the glass windows. The balls thudded into plaster walls, sending clouds of dust and debris in every direction. Cedar paneling was transformed into kindling, and the handsome stone urns were destroyed. The flying balls severed limbs and heads from the life-size marble statues decorating the grounds, and knocked some off their pedestals.[26]

Proctor's small guns were fully capable of inflicting heavy damage, but they were of insufficient caliber to significantly degrade the structural integrity of the house's thick walls. "With its [Cliveden's] massy [massive] walls Musgrave had probably become well acquainted while encamped in its neighborhood, and, as an able and experienced officer, knew it was proof against the light field artillery with which alone he would reasonably conclude the American army, on such an expedition would be furnished. In other words," concluded Timothy Pickering decades later in a letter that evidenced his ongoing frustration with the course taken, "Musgrave threw his troops into that house, because he knew it was tenable." The British officer, continued Pickering, "must also have considered, that if the Americans were in the end victorious, the condition of his party could be no worse than by a present surrender, that is, they would be, prisoners of war." Pickering wanted nothing to do with "attacking, what to our artillery was an impregnable castle. *"Then, and not till then,"* he added, *"came the posting of [Mathias] Ogden's [1st] New Jersey regiment* [emphasis added]." The adjutant general was referring to 22-year-old Col. Mathias Ogden, the commander of one of William

25 Hammond, ed., *Papers*, vol. 1, 545-546; *Papers of Clinton*, vol. 2, 369.

26 Tilghman, *Memoir*, 160-161; McGuire, *Campaign*, vol. 2, 89. The damage to the home was so severe that it took three carpenters the entire winter of 1777-1778 to restore its woodwork. Reed, *Campaign*, 228.

Maxwell's New Jersey regiments; Ogden's unit would form the tip of a spear that was never intended to be hurled against the embattled Chew house.[27]

After at least thirty minutes (and perhaps as much as an hour) of shelling, Washington had seen enough and called upon Lord Stirling's infantry. Maxwell's New Jersey brigade was positioned in the fields 200 yards west of the Germantown Road, while Francis Nash's North Carolina brigade was about the same distance away, north of Cliveden and east of the road. Nash's men and Maxwell's 2nd and 4th New Jersey regiments were laying down a heavy fire against the house when Ogden's 1st New Jersey left Maxwell's line and charged toward it with the 3rd New Jersey following suit.[28]

This spirited assault notwithstanding, it was never Washington's intent to launch infantry against the stone fortress. According to a letter written by Charles Cotesworth Pinckney in 1820, Ogden was ordered "to remain with his Regiment to watch the house, & to fall on the soldiers in it, if they attempted to quit it." Indeed, Washington urged caution. "[T]here never was a battle in which a Commander took more care to insure success, than General Washington did at the battle of Germantown," explained Pinckney. Perhaps it was the adrenaline of battle coursing through Ogden's young veins, or perhaps he simply misunderstood his orders. Whatever the reason, Ogden attacked with his regiment down the Chew lane and closed on the house, "but the doors were too strong and too firmly barricaded to be forced by any means in possession of the assailants."[29]

Ogden was the first to storm the enemy stronghold, but his movement soon was followed up by Col. Elias Dayton's 3rd New Jersey. Ensign John Kinney of Dayton's regiment recalled being "ordered to storm a stone house." An hour had passed, he continued, "without demolishing, or making a break on the house." The two New Jersey regiments charged in column about 100 yards up the estate's driveway toward the front of the house and attempted to break through the main entrance. While the head of the column attempted to gain entry, the following

27 Letter, Timothy Pickering to *The National Intelligencer*, January 5, 1827.

28 McGuire, *Campaign*, vol. 2, 89; Letter, Timothy Pickering to *The National Intelligencer*, January 5, 1827. In his letter, Pickering added that "Governor Howell of that state [New Jersey] mentioned to me, that he was with the troops who made the bold attempt to force their way into the house." Richard Howell (1754-1803), a major in the 2nd New Jersey who later served as governor of the state (1793-1801), was with the 2nd regiment at Germantown, but that unit did not participate in the assault. If Howell took part in the attack, he left the ranks in order to do so.

29 Letter, Charles Cotesworth Pinckney to Henry Johnson, November 14, 1820, 204.

companies and the 3rd New Jersey likely fanned out pouring musketry toward the window openings.[30]

Timothy Pickering later wrote that the firing from Cliveden was "well-directed, and killed and wounded a great many of our officers and men." Proctor rolled his guns "within musket-shot of it, and fired round balls at it, but in vain," continued Pickering. "The enemy, I imagine, were very little hurt; they still kept possession" of the building. The same could not be said for the attackers, for a British ball struck and blinded Cpl. Nicholas Copple, one of Proctor's artillerists.[31]

An anonymous British officer who confirmed Pickering's account of a stout defense provided some additional details. The Americans, he wrote six days after the battle, "sent some of the most daring fellows under cover of their artillery; to do them justice, they attacked with great intrepidity, but were received with no less firmness." The men on the second floor, under Musgrave, put down a "well-directed [fire]" into which "the rebels nevertheless advanced." Ogden's men made it all the way to the doors and windows. "Several were killed with bayonets getting in at the windows and upon the steps, attempting to force their way in at the door."[32]

Only a handful of accounts from members of the 40th Regiment of Foot who fought in the house that day survive. Two members of Musgrave's command discussed the attack and defense of the Chew house at the court martial of Martin Hurley, an ensign. Hurley previously deserted from the 44th Regiment of Foot and fought as an ensign with the 1st New Jersey Regiment at Cliveden. Private Matthew

30 RWPF file S33357.

31 Pickering, *Pickering*, vol. 1, 169; Linn and Egle, eds., *Archives*, Series 2, Vol. 11, 212. Archaeological work done in the 1970s uncovered few battle related artifacts in the rear of Cliveden. Only a single gun flint was found. It was speculated that this was a result of most of the fighting having occurred on the front side of the house. The area behind the Chew House has been significantly altered and developed with modern housing precluding a true archaeological study of the area. Cotter, Roberts, and Parrington, *Buried Past*, 350.

32 "Extract of a Letter," 113-114. The New Jersey troops in the yard took a beating from Musgrave's defenders. Col. Elias Dayton detailed the New Jersey losses in his campaign narrative written soon after the battle. "We suffered considerable in Advancing by a party of the Enemy had thrown into a large stone House.... at this place fell Capt. [Andrew] McMyer & Ensign [Martin] Hurley of Col. Ogdens Regiment, Capt. [John] Conwey, Capt. [Isaac] Morrison, & Capt. [Daniel] Baldwin [losing a leg] & Lt. [Robert] Robinson wounded of the same Regiment, together with about 20 men; of my Regmt. Lt. [William] Clark & Ensign [Jarvis] Bloomfield wounded & 18 men killed & wounded, my horse was shot under me at same place within about 3 yds, of the Corner of the House." Ryan, ed., *Salute to Courage*, 101; Harry M. Ward, *General William Maxwell and the New Jersey Continentals* (Westport, CT, 1997), 79. Hurley was not actually killed. He was wounded and captured and then court martialed for being a British deserter. McGuire, *Campaign*, vol. 2, 131-132.

Fitzgerald testified seeing "the prisoner [Hurley] with a drawn Sword, in his hand, come up with a number of rebels to the Attack; that he there saw him wounded and fall." When the 40th left the house, "he saw the prisoner laying on the ground, at the place where he had seen him drop." Corporal William Yates "saw the prisoner standing in the road wounded & bleeding, and he was then dressed in a blue coat faced with red; that having known him before, he taxed him with being a Deserter from the 44th Regiment, but this he denied." After taking Hurley into custody, Yates "prevented some Soldiers from putting him to Death."[33]

When the unordered direct assault failed, Col. John Laurens of Washington's staff, together with Thomas-Antoine de Mauduit du Plessis (a young French officer serving as aide to Washington), and Majs. John White and Edward Sherburne of Sullivan's staff decided it was necessary to burn the British out. The Marquis de Chastellux, a brigadier general in the French army, visited Germantown in 1780 with several American veterans who had fought there including Maj. John Howard of the 4th Maryland, part of Col. Price's brigade. Someone, recalled one of the veterans, suggested to "get from a nearby barn some straw and hay which they would pile up against the front door and set afire." Colonel Laurens and his three cohorts, straw apparently in hand, approached close enough to light a fire, but the British infantry drove them back.[34]

Major Howard, who would marry into the Chew family after the war, explained to the Marquis that the officers "also attempted to burn it by putting fire to the window shutters which were very strong and well fastened." John White, who acted as a volunteer aide to General Sullivan during the battle, was one of the brave men who advanced through the hail of bullets to reach the stone house. "He was so close that they could not fire at him from the upper windows," continued Howard, "and he with several others were killed from the cellar windows." Major Edward Sherburne, Sullivan's aide-de-camp, was mortally wounded in the attempt and succumbed the next day. "During the whole of the action," Sullivan wrote to

33 Judge Advocate General Office: Court Martial Proceedings and Board of General Officers' Minutes, Great Britain, War Office, October 6, 1777, Court Martial Testimony, WO71/84/342-345, microfilm copy at the David Library of the American Revolution, Washington Crossing, PA, film 675. Despite his protestations, Hurley was found guilty of desertion at a court martial on October 6 and was hanged two days later at the Royal Artillery Park near the center of Germantown. Von Muenchhausen, *At Howe's Side*, 39.

34 Chastellux, *Travels*, 139.

Sherburne's family, "he behaved with such coolness and bravery, that his memory will be ever dear to AMERICA."[35]

One of those wounded in the yard of the Chew house was Washington's staff officer John Laurens, whose father Henry was a member of Congress. "Our Friend Laurens behaved in a very Spirited manner during the Engagement and has established his Reputation for intrepidity," explained an anonymous American officer in a letter to Governor Clinton of New York. Early in the attack on the house, a musket ball passed through "the fleshy part" of Laurens' right shoulder but missed the bone. The painful wound "did not in the least abate his ardour," continued the letter writer. Sword still in hand, Laurens managed to charge all the way up to the door of the house. Unable to make it inside, he "received afterwards a blow on his side from a Spent ball as he was coming from Chew's House." Luckily, the injury "only occasioned a Swelling in the part Struck."[36]

While the effort to reduce Cliveden continued, troops from Sullivan's and Wayne's divisions (which had advanced well south of the Chew property) took notice of the escalating gunfire to their rear. There are several things no soldier ever wants to encounter on a battlefield, and one of the most frightening of these is the eruption of fighting directly behind him. As far as Wayne was concerned, the firing could only mean one thing: The British had flanked and defeated Sullivan's troops and were now in his rear. It was impossible for Wayne to see Sullivan's right flank well to the west of the Germantown Road, and he had no way of knowing with certainty whether most of Sullivan's men were still in place. If he did not act quickly, the enemy could completely cut off and trap his entire division. He decided to act.

Wayne issued orders to his subordinates to face about and advance north to confront the unexpected threat. In truth, exactly how the movement was organized will never be known. Some of his men may have already been falling back. At least one of Stephen's regiments had fired into the backs of Wayne's troops a short time earlier. Given the fog and confusion, few of them realized the flying lead came from friendlies. The eruption of fresh firing reinforced the mistaken belief that the British were behind them.

35 "Howard's Account," 317-318. White, who died from his injuries on October 10, supposedly received his mortal wound near the basement window at the northwest corner of the house, to the right of the servants' entrance. *The Continental Journal and Weekly Advertiser*, November 21, 1777. "I saw some years afterwards the marks of the fire on the shutters."

36 *Papers of Clinton*, vol. 2, 372-373.

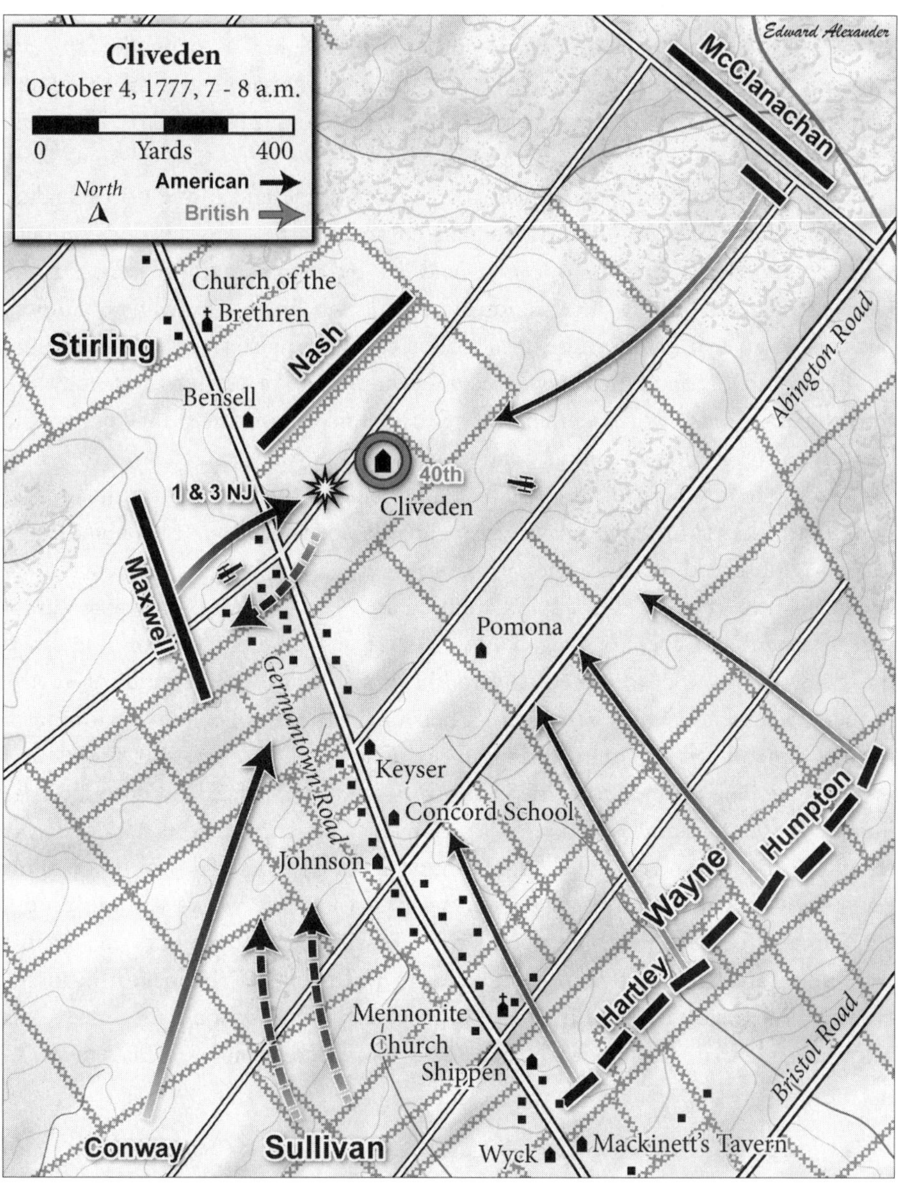

Wayne's about-face "Totally uncovered the Left Flank of my Division," explained General Sullivan in a letter to the governor of New Hampshire three weeks later. Just before Wayne pulled out, Sullivan's own troops "were Still advancing against the Enemies Left. The firing of General Greens Division was very Heavy for more than Quarter of an hour but then Decreased & Seemed to Draw further from us." Wayne described what was taking place in his rear as a "wind Mill attack . . . made on a House into which six light Companies had thrown themselves to avoid our Bayonets." He later admitted that he and his men were "deceived by this attack, taking it for something formidable [and] fell back to assist in what [we] deemed a Serious matter."[37]

Wayne was not the only officer to reverse course and move north against Cliveden. Thomas Conway, who advanced into battle with his independent brigade, ended up on the opposite end of Sullivan's division west of the Germantown Road. How much control he had over his men remains unknown, but what *is* known is that most or all of his command also marched toward the swirling combat around the Chew house. Within perhaps a quarter-hour Conway's troops were moving north to the west of the Johnson house and then across the Germantown Road at an oblique angle, into the cauldron of fire.[38]

Almost before he knew it, Capt. John Markland of the 6th Pennsylvania found himself attacking Musgrave's nearly impregnable position. One of his men, Philip Ludwig, "observed a handsome British musket leaning against the fence." He cheerfully turned to the captain and announced, "I will make an exchange; this is much better than mine." Ludwig, who was described as "a brave fellow," grabbed the Brown Bess and advanced toward the house immediately in front of the captain. He had taken only a few steps when a British ball drilled into his forehead, killing him instantly. "The firing from Chew's house was tremendously severe—the balls seemed to come in showers," was how Markland described the intense firefight. During the height of Conway's attack, Captain Markland was struck by a ball that shattered his right arm near the shoulder. The only linen in his possession was the shirt he had been wearing for three weeks. By the time a surgeon was found to dress his wound, the right shirtsleeve was saturated and stiff with blood, and he had no choice but to cut it off. In need of a bandage, the doctor cut off the left sleeve to use for that purpose, leaving Markland with a sleeveless shirt he wore another three weeks before he could find a suitable replacement.[39]

37 Hammond, ed., *Papers*, vol. 1, 546; Letter, Anthony Wayne to Horatio Gates, November 21, 1777.

38 As detailed in Chapter 12, Conway was accused of abandoning his brigade after his horse was shot despite being urged by others to exercise his brigade command. He would later fight a duel defending his honor against the accusers.

39 "Services of Markland," 108-109. As noted earlier, the author(s) of this account is unknown. It may have been Markland writing in the third person. Markland's arm "continued to be extremely painful, and pieces of broken bone, one to two inches in length, were frequently extracted. On one

Some of Sullivan's units also reversed course and moved toward the combat at Cliveden, though likely without that general's explicit order to do so. One was Col. David Hall's Delaware Regiment, which belonged to Stone's brigade of Hazen's division. Delaware Capt. Enoch Anderson had a corporal in his company named Manuel Trayson, a flamboyant German soldier-of-fortune who was about 36 years old. According to Anderson, Trayson spoke "in his broken English, more like a Frenchman than a German. Some old soldiers in Europe—(perhaps in this country too)," he continued, "have got a conception that by some cant words or prayer, they can ward off all bullets in battle." A few days before Germantown, Trayson had stepped into the captain's tent to speak with him.

"Vell Ca-pe-a-teen, I does vant to spake vid you," he announced.

"Sit down, Manuel," replied the officer, who made it clear he was alone.

"If you vil gif me de von quart visky, I dell you a barticular brayer," continued the German, "shall touch you not von bullet in all battles."

"A canteen of whiskey stands by the tent-pole," Anderson replied, encouraging him to take a drink. The corporal willingly did so. "But suppose I [lack] confidence and faith in this prayer?"

"Den I pe sorree—vairy sorree, sar—for mitout de fait[h], it too you no cood." With that, the corporal exited the tent.[40]

During the assault a bullet pierced "the face of his [Trayson's] cocked hat—of which he was not a little proud." A few days later Captain Anderson spoke with him again. "Well, Manuel," he asked, alluding to the bullet hole in his hat. "What do you think of that particular prayer you wanted to learn me before the battle?"

Trayson stamped his right foot three or four times on the ground. "I vil tell you, Ca-pe-a-teen, vat I tink ov dem dings—de brayer pees vairy coot and strong vor de small pullets—but for tem tam crape-shot; I don't know vat do dink!"[41]

Elements of Greene's column, fighting off to the east, also headed toward Cliveden. As noted earlier, Stephen's two-brigade division battled the fog, combat confusion, rough terrain disrupted by fences and Wingohocking Creek, and the lack of a firm command hand. As a result, Col. Alexander McClanachan's brigade

---

occasion the pain was so great that, no physician being at hand, he availed himself of the assistance of an intelligent farmer, who, with a penknife, laid open the arm and extracted a large piece of bone."

40 Anderson, *Recollections*, 51-52.

41 Ibid., 52. Manuel was convinced that a piece of grapeshot fired from the one of the windows, was responsible for ripping through his hat. There is no evidence to support his conclusion, and it is much more likely that friendly artillery fire was the source.

marched west away from Brig. Gen. Charles Scott's brigade, whose Virginia regiments moved southwest in front of Wayne's line. Stephen's location remains a mystery. The westward trek of McClanachan's Virginians carried them out of the creek bottomland, through more woods, and into the cleared fields east of the Chew House. Stepping out of the fog as they did triggered a temporary panic, recalled Maj. Henry Miller of the 1st Pennsylvania (Hartley's brigade). "A column of our men coming up in the rear of those at the house, were mistaken in the fog of the morning and the smoke of the action for the enemy, and threw our left into confusion." The identity of the new arrivals was sorted out, and when some of the Virginians stepped within musket range, a heavy fire from inside the house brought the chaotic advance to a ragged halt. McClanachan, who had two pieces of artillery with him, unlimbered the pieces and had them open fire against the back of the structure.[42]

The rear of the Chew mansion was not as well constructed as the front of the house, and McClanachan's iron rounds caved in portions of the walls and blew open the rear door. If General Washington had concentrated his available artillery against the back of the home (which he did not realize was more vulnerable) earlier in the fighting, the course of the battle may have been very different. With American artillery now pounding two sides of the house (Proctor's against the front, and McClanahan's against the rear), it was inevitable that some of the rounds that overshot the structure would continue on and hit their own men. With McClanachan's men closing in from the east, Maxwell's New Jersey troops approaching from the west, Nash's North Carolinians coming from the north, and Wayne's Pennsylvanians flowing up from the south, any hope Musgrave maintained of slipping away vanished. His companies were surrounded and their defensive bastion was beginning to crumble.[43]

The Americans were running out of ammunition. It was about 8:00 a.m. Some five brigades totaling approximately 4,000 men had either been held back from continuing the successful attack or had been used to surround and attack three small British companies trapped in a house. Hundreds of other British troops, meanwhile, fired their muskets from inside and around individual homes dotting

42 "Memoir of Miller," 427. The information in this paragraph is largely based on circumstantial evidence and Archibald Robertson's manuscript map. Robertson Map, Windsor Castle Collection, 734029.d.

43 Lambdin, "Battle of Germantown," 384; McGuire, *Campaign*, vol. 2, 95-96. Some American accounts claim the British fired artillery from the house. Overshot friendly fire is the more likely explanation.

the landscape off to the south. According to Commissary General of Prisoners Elias Boudinot, the enemy "through necessity . . . took to the Stone Houses of the lower End of Germantown, from whence they galled us much." Despite their best efforts, he continued in a letter to his wife, "It [was] impossible to drive them from these Houses with small Arms, and our Ammunition being almost expended." Continental troops, he lamented, began drifting to the rear. "We had brought no more ammunition than the men could carry in their Cartouches," wrote staff officer Tench Tilghman, "and that being nearly expended and the Men fatigued with marching all Night."[44]

Washington's army had shot its bolt.

44 Letter, Elias Boudinot to his wife Elisha, 5 October 1777, Emmet Collection, New York Public Library, New York, NY; Tilghman, *Memoir*, 161.

Chapter 15

British Counterattack

October 4, 1777
8:00 a.m. to 10:00 a.m.

"7 battalions stemm'd the torrent[;] two of these drove them from the village rushing up the Street & scrambling thro' the gardens & orchards under a pretty heavy fire & not without some loss."[1]

— Captain John Andre, aide to British Maj. Gen. Charles Grey, October 8, 1777

General Washington had a clear choice on the morning of October 4: He could push Lord Stirling's reserve division southward to join Sullivan's and Wayne's victorious troops at the front and defeat the British troops waiting there to stop them, or he could halt Stirling's advance and assault the Chew house, inside which three companies of enemy infantry had taken refuge. In spite of his adjutant general's protestations, Washington decided to follow the latter course. It was a fateful decision, and one that would have a direct impact on the outcome of the battle.

The British put the delay to good use. Although the record is mostly silent, the credit for coalescing the British front and the large-scale assault that followed belongs to two veteran officers: Maj. Gen. James Grant east of the Germantown Road, and Lt. Gen. Wilhelm von Knyphausen west of it.

1 Letter, John Andre to his mother, September 28, 1777, with a postscript dated October 8.

General Grant called upon three strong commands—Brig. Gen. Edward Matthew's Brigade of Guards, Lt. Col. John Maxwell's 27th Regiment of Foot, and Lt. Col. Robert Prescott's 28th Regiment of Foot—to move immediately to support his beleaguered right flank. Matthew marched his Guards due north from their camp on a hill straddling Wingohocking Creek just north of Howe's headquarters at Stenton to a supporting position behind the Queen's Rangers, who were battling William Smallwood's Maryland and New Jersey militia. Maxwell's 27th Regiment moved from its camp south of Stenton at the Frankford Road intersection and marched north up Old York Road into a supporting position behind the light infantry and grenadier companies of the British Guards, some of which were also engaged with Smallwood's militiamen. The 300 men of the 27th—technically part of the 2nd British Brigade of Grant's command—had been bivouacked behind the main British encampment in order to watch the road to Frankford. Like the 27th, Prescott's 28th Regiment was camped at the Frankford Road intersection, but was detached from Grant's 1st Brigade. Prescott's men (also about 300 strong) moved up the Old York Road but veered left behind the Brigade of Guards to help fill the void created by the collapse of Abercromby's 1st Battalion Light Infantry and Ogilvie's 4th Regiment of Foot.[2]

With the right flank stabilized, the left side of the British position needed to be organized for a counterattack. Once the firing a couple of miles to the north made it clear that a major battle was underway, General Knyphausen assembled his troops near their encampments. His Hessians formed with their left near the Schuylkill River, their line stretching east to the 3rd and 4th British brigades. The Hessian jaegers under Lt. Col. Ludwig von Wurmb were anchored on the Schuylkill, with Lt. Col. Ludwig von Minnigerode's battalion of Hessian grenadiers in support. Major General Johann Daniel Stirn's Hessian brigade extended the line east, with Lt. Col. Philip Heymell's von Donop Regiment holding Stirn's left and Col. Friedrich von Wurmb's Leib Regiment on the right. Von Wurmb's jaegers had been busy since dawn thwarting the efforts of Armstrong's American militia to cross Wissahickon Creek. All told, the Hessians numbered about 2,000 men.[3]

2 Robertson manuscript map of the Battle of Germantown.

3 See Chapter 12 for details of von Wurmb's fight against Armstrong's militia. The von Minnigerode Battalion had been detached from its parent brigade, Col. Carl von Donop's Hessian Grenadier Brigade, which was in Philadelphia. It almost certainly was under General Stirn during the battle (it is listed this way in the order of battle in Appendix A), but it could have reported directly to General Knyphausen. Von Wurmb's jaegers were independent and reported directly to

Knyphausen's two remaining brigades formed on Stirn's right in the fields just south of School House Lane. The first of these, Maj. Gen. Charles "No Flint" Grey's 3rd Brigade, continued the long line toward the Germantown Road, with the 17th Regiment holding the left and the 44th and 15th regiments next in line. The last of Knyphausen's brigades, Maj. Gen. James Agnew's 4th, comprised the 37th, 64th, 46th, and 33rd regiments (west to east), with the 33rd's right flank anchored just west of the Germantown Road. Together these two brigades numbered about 2,000 fresh men. The front was composed of veteran, rested troops, but when the time came to attack, they would not advance together.[4]

While the 3rd and 4th brigades and Stirn's Hessians waited and listened, the Americans from Sullivan's and Greene's columns collapsed the British lines east of the Germantown Road. The 1st and 2nd Light Battalions, together with the 4th, 5th, 49th, and 55th Regiments of Foot, were driven back (and especially in the case of the 4th Regiment, roughly handled), and were either trying to get out harm's way or were regrouping well south of Church Lane. General Grant's command needed assistance. The Americans on Knyphausen's front were not advancing, and a short lull fell upon the field west of the Germantown Road. The respite allowed Knyphausen to dispatch two regiments— Lt. Col. John Bird's 15th from Grey's brigade and Maj. James Cousseau's 37th from Agnew's brigade—to march east in order to bolster Grant's reorganizing front. It was this ad hoc force that would regroup and counterattack east of the Germantown Road.[5]

The 3rd and 4th brigades went over to the attack about a quarter of an hour after Knyphausen's regiments had left the line to move east to help Grant. Stirn's Hessians soon moved out in a supporting role. Perhaps Knyphausen ordered his men ahead on his own, or perhaps he coordinated with Grant; maybe an order arrived from General Howe to press ahead. Regardless, the tide of battle was about to turn.

Knyphausen. This information is based on my general analysis of the campaign and how the battle was conducted.

4 Robertson manuscript map of the Battle of Germantown.

5 Robertson manuscript map of the Battle of Germantown; Letter, John Andre to his mother, September 28, 1777, with a postscript dated October 8.

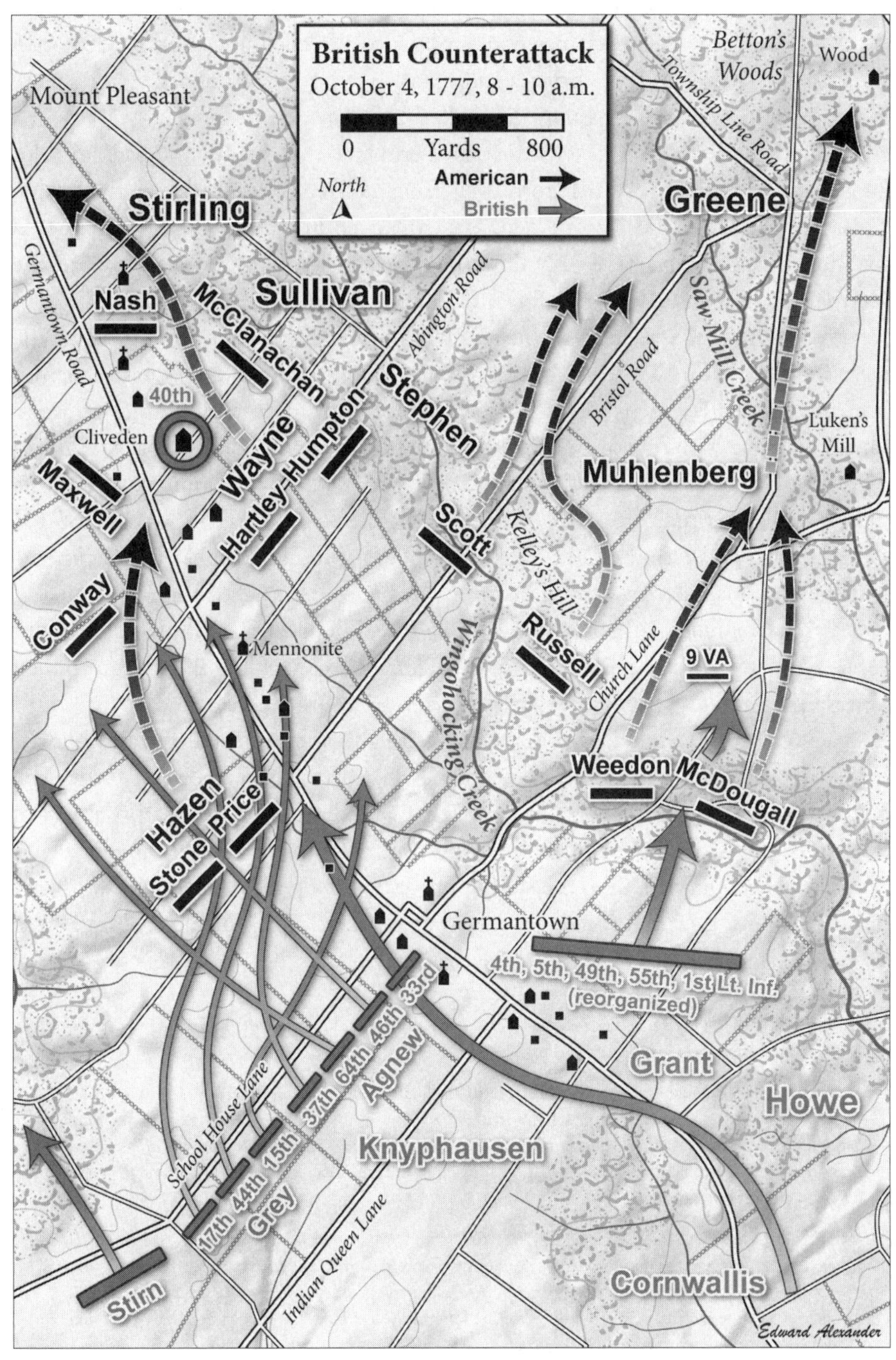
British Counterattack
October 4, 1777, 8 - 10 a.m.
0 Yards 800
North
American
British
Mount Pleasant
Betton's Woods
Wood
Township Line Road
Stirling
Greene
Germantown Road
Nash
McClanachan
Sullivan
Abington Road
Saw Mill Creek
Bristol Road
40th
Cliveden
Wayne
Hartley-Humpton
Stephen
Luken's Mill
Maxwell
Muhlenberg
Scott
Kelley's Hill
Conway
Mennonite
Wingohocking Creek
Russell
Church Lane
9 VA
Weedon
McDougall
Hazen
Price
Stone
Germantown
4th, 5th, 49th, 55th, 1st Lt. Inf.
(reorganized)
33rd
46th
64th
37th
15th
44th
17th
Agnew
Grant
Howe
School House Lane
Knyphausen
Grey
Indian Queen Lane
Stirn
Cornwallis
Edward Alexander

"The line now began to move in support of the advanced Corps," recorded Capt. John Andre, Grey's brigade adjutant. Two fresh British brigades were marching to confront John Sullivan's stalled column.[6]

"On the left and on the West side of German Town the 4th and 3rd Brigades and Hessians moved forward from their Encampment," recalled Captain Andre. This organized, relentless movement was advanced in a methodical, professional manner. When it began, the only fighting in progress was taking place east of the Germantown Road, where the 15th and 37th Regiments, along with the rallied 5th Regiment, engaged Greene's troops. Agnew's 4th Brigade stepped off first. The 64th Regiment, Lt. Col. Enoch Markham's 46th Regiment, and Lt. Col. James Webster's 33rd Regiment moved straight ahead, keeping the Germantown Road on their right flank. Slowly and steadily they pushed back Moses Hazen's command.[7] Grey's 3rd Brigade (stripped down to just two regiments) began its march a short time later, but veered east to sweep down and east of the Germantown Road on the right flank of Agnew's command. These five regiments had the responsibility of driving Anthony Wayne's command. East of the road, meanwhile, the rallied 4th, 5th, 49th, and 55th regiments and 1st Battalion of Light Infantry, along with the 15th and 37th regiments, comprised the counterpunch James Grant intended to deliver against Nathanael Greene's command.[8]

According to Captain Andre, Agnew's 4th Brigade marched several hundred yards before running into stiff resistance. "The 4th Brigade received Orders by inclining to their right to enter German Town and drive the Enemy from it. From some misunderstanding, or from receiving some fire, they did not immediately go into the village, but halted on the skirts of it, and kept up a very heavy fire against a distant Column they had some intimation of in front." The "distant column" was

6 Andre's use of "advanced corps" was a reference to the light infantry battalions which had been overrun earlier in the day.

7 Robertson manuscript map of the Battle of Germantown; Letter, John Andre to his mother, September 28, 1777, with a postscript dated October 8. Bird's men (15th Regiment) were confronting Scott's small Virginia command (Stephen's division). The 64th Regiment's Maj. Robert McLeroth had been severely wounded at Brandywine, and it is unclear who was in command of the regiment at Germantown.

8 Andre, *Journal*, 55-56. General Grey was fortunate he did not fall into American hands. Many wanted him to pay fcr his actions at Paoli. Grey, wrote Adam Hubley, was "the same Catiff that commanded in the Night of our Surprize. . . . He had given positive orders that no Quarters should be given to the Rebels. . . . Would to God he had fell in our Hands—proper notice by our Men would certainly have taken him." Hazard, et al., eds., *Archives*, Series 1, vol. 5, 666; McGuire, *Campaign*, vol. 2, 96-97, 115.

comprised of Sullivan's Maryland brigades (Price and Stone), and perhaps elements of Conway's Pennsylvania brigade west of the Germantown Road near Widow Mackinett's Tavern.[9]

With Agnew's brigade slowed to a crawl, General Grey led his two remaining regiments, Lt. Col. Charles Mawhood's 17th and Lt. Col. Robert Donkin's 44th (some 650 men), northeast behind Agnew's men and into the heart of Germantown, near the intersection of the Germantown and Bristol roads. Grey positioned himself with the 44th Regiment and may have led it from the front. Because isolated pockets of Americans were firing from within the village, "the 17th and 44th Regiments were therefore ordered to wheel to the right and drive out the Rebels." This done, the 44th crossed the village and moved up the skirts on the east side of the road, with the 17th advancing on both sides of the thoroughfare. The two regiments drove the Americans "from the village rushing up the Street & scrambling thro' the gardens & orchards under a pretty heavy fire & not without some loss."[10]

Civilian John Watson never forgot that eventful day. "The roar and rattling of discharges of musketry and cannon, was incessant, and the whistling of balls, were occasionally heard," he recalled several decades later. "Combatants could be seen, from the house top, occasionally in conflict, then obscured by smoke, and then again exposed to view. The battle was but little witnessed *in the town*, after the first onset," he continued, "and but few of the military were seen along the main street. It was chiefly on the north-eastern side, on the tillage ground; and the fences were mostly down." In one 10-acre field across which some of Greene's command had advanced, a "great number of leaden bullets" were found "for years afterwards." Jacob Keyser was a young lad during the battle and watched the unfolding action from his family home. "Its high position above the street" he explained, allowed the Keysers, "by placing an apple under the cellar door, to peep abroad and see the battle in the opposite field, distinctly." Some eight decades later, Keyser remembered that he could "see . . . those who fell under successive peals of musketry."[11]

9 Andre, *Journal*, 56. Conway's men may have already fallen back toward Cliveden by the time Agnew advanced. The sources are unclear on this point.

10 Andre, *Journal*, 56; Letter, John Andre to his mother, September 28, 1777, with a postscript dated October 8.

11 Watson, *Annals*, vol. 2, 48, 52. This house was located at the modern intersection of Duval Street and Germantown Avenue. It is no longer standing.

At some point either before or just after the British advance began, Anthony Wayne's Pennsylvanians heard the fighting around Cliveden, and discovered the movement of men toward their left-rear. This was enough for them to reverse course. Whether the about-face was conducted without undue panic or disorganization remains an open question. The commander of the 10th Pennsylvania, Lt. Col. Adam Hubley, had no doubt that the division broke and ran. Colonel Richard Humpton's brigade, he observed, began "to break & retreat towards us which threw our Men in Confusion also, and the whole began their Retreat no body knowing the cause of it, until we arriv'd about three Mile, beyond Germantown, where we halted." Not everyone fell back, however; a substantial number of Wayne's men remained behind in the houses and yards exchanging fire with Grey's advancing regiments.[12]

It was during their return north toward Cliveden that the unfortunate Pennsylvanians were mistaken a second time for enemy soldiers, and once again were fired upon by their own men. An hour earlier, in the foggy confusion, part of McClanachan's brigade of Stephen's division (Greene's column) had driven west across Wingohocking Creek toward Cliveden and fired into the backs of Wayne's men. This time, troops from Stephen's other brigade, under Charles Scott, may have made the fatal mistake of emptying their muskets into the Pennsylvanians—and vice versa—as they moved back north. "A large body of troops were Discovered Advancing on our left flank—which being taken for the Enemy we retreated," explained Wayne to his wife. The various bodies of troops often mistook one another for the enemy, he continued, and "frequently Exchanged several shots before they discovered their Error." After a long retreat of some two miles, continued the frustrated general, "we found it was our own people—who were Originally Designed to Attack the Right Wing of the Enemy's Army. . . . The fog and this mistake prevented us from following a victory that in all Human probability would have put an end to the American War."[13] In a letter to Gen. Horatio Gates on November 21, Wayne expressed little doubt that the Americans "ran away from the Arms of Victory ready [and] Open to receive us." Another anonymous American agreed. "Our men went up to the attack with the

12 Letter, Adam Hubley to William Attlee, et. al., October 9, 1777.

13 Stille, *Anthony Wayne*, 96.

greatest ardour & alacrity imaginable & in general, 'till the retreat, behaved as well as any men could do."[14]

While Grey drove the stubborn remnants of Wayne's command out of Germantown and Agnew engaged whatever was left of Sullivan's division west of the village, Hessian units from Johann Stirn's brigade moved forward to support the advance. Knyphausen's aide, Maj. Carl von Baurmeister, ordered Col. Friedrich von Wurmb's Leib Regiment to advance. Captain von Muenchhausen, Howe's Hessian aide, "rode up to the Leib Regiment and the v. Donop Regiment who were already under arms, and gave them orders to march off at once to Germantown to that part where the heaviest firing was going on. It is true," continued the *Leib Regiment Journal*, that "General Howe had not ordered him [von Muenchhausen] to do so, he had done it of his own accord, because immediate help was absolutely necessary, otherwise the whole army would probably have been defeated and scattered, which would certainly have had the most disastrous consequences for us, seeing that we were so far distant, from our ships and were cut off from all supplies."[15]

According to Knyphausen's October 17 report, the "von Donop Regiment advanced from their camp to reinforce the pickets of the 3rd and 4th Brigades, as well as those of the Landgrave's [Leib Regiment] and von Donop's Regiments." With orders in hand, "the Regiments [von Donop and Leib] set off at once, marched to Germantown with drums beating."[16] Lieutenant Colonel Ludwig von Minnegerode's Grenadier Battalion, however, "remained at its post on the left to support the jagers."[17] The Regiment von Donop and the von Minnigerode Battalion of Hessian grenadiers, "who were initially to advance with the line, had to cover the left flank of the Hessian Leib regiment, though a little farther back, forming a hook on the height," was how Howe's aide von Muenchhausen described these movements.[18]

14 Letter, Anthony Wayne to Horatio Gates, November 21, 1777; Papers of Clinton, vol. 2, 371.

15 "Journal of the Remarkable Events Which Occurred to the Hon. Leib Infantry Regiment," Hessian Documents of the American Revolution, Lidgerwood Collection, letter V, 21-22, microfiche 312, Morristown National Historical Park, Morristown, NJ, a copy of which is located at the David Library of the American Revolution, Washington Crossing, PA.

16 Letter, Wilhelm von Knyphausen to the Landgrave, October 17, 1777, 85.

17 Von Baurmeister, "Letters," 416.

18 Von Muenchhausen, *At Howe's Side*, 39.

Present day view of Grumblethorpe, where Brig. Gen. James Agnew died of his wounds.

Photo by author

Now reinforced, Agnew pressed his attack into the maelstrom. Hazen's brigades extracted a high price for each yard of ground as they slowly gave way. The brunt of the British thrust was borne by the 46th and 64th Regiments of Foot, both of which had suffered heavily at Brandywine three weeks earlier. Captain Andre believed the two units suffered a disproportionate number of casualties compared to the Americans they went up against, and he believed he knew why. "They wound many more of ours in proportion as they make use of Buck Shot," explained Andre. "My horse receiv'd 4 or 5 that hurt him so little that I wish I receiv'd them myself to make people stare with the story of 5 wounds in one day[.]"[19]

American lead also took a high toll on Howe's officer corps. Hessian brigade commander Johann Stirn "was wounded in the left arm and had to leave the field in

19 Letter, John Andre to his mother, September 28, 1777, with a postscript dated October 8.

The graves of Brig. Gen. James Agnew and Lieut. Col. John Bird in the DeBenneville Family Burial Ground in Philadelphia, PA. *Photo by author*

order to be bandaged." General Agnew was pushing the British attack up the west side of the Germantown Road with his advance troops just ahead of him. Agnew rode into the village with only his personal servant, Pvt. Alexander Andrew, at his side, and turned left (north) down the Germantown Road. "He had not rode above 20 or 30 yards, which was the top of a little rising ground, when a party of the enemy, about 100, rushed out from behind a house," recalled Andrew.[20]

"The General," he continued,

> being then in the street, and even in front of the piquet, and all alone, only me, he wheeled around, and, putting spurs to his horse, and calling to me, he received a whole volley from the enemy. The fatal ball entered the small of his back, near the back seam of his coat, right side, and came out a little below his left breast. Another ball went through and through his right hand. I, at the same moment, received a slight wound in the side, but just got off in time enough to prevent his falling, who, with the assistance of two men, took him down, carried him into a house, and laid him on a bed, sent for the doctor, who was near.[21]

20 Ibid.; Johann Stirn, "Diary Installment from Major General Johann Daniel Stirn," Henry Retzer and Donald Londahl-Smidt, eds., "The Philadelphia Campaign, 1777-1778: Letters and Reports from the von Jungkenn Papers. Part 1—1777," *Journal of the Johannes Schwalm Historical Association*, vol. 6, no. 2 (Pennsauken, NJ, 1998), 7; "Journal of the Regiment von Donop"; Hagist, *British Soldiers*, 230. The "little rising ground" was the hill in front of the Mennonite meetinghouse, a few hundred yards south of Cliveden. Andrew estimated the distance from the enemy as 500 yards, but given Agnew's immediate concern for his safety and the fatal gunfire that followed, the enemy troops were considerably closer. It is possible that he wrote 50 yards rather than 500, and the extra zero was a transcription error. McGuire, *Campaign*, vol. 2, 111.

21 Hagist, *British Soldiers*, 230.

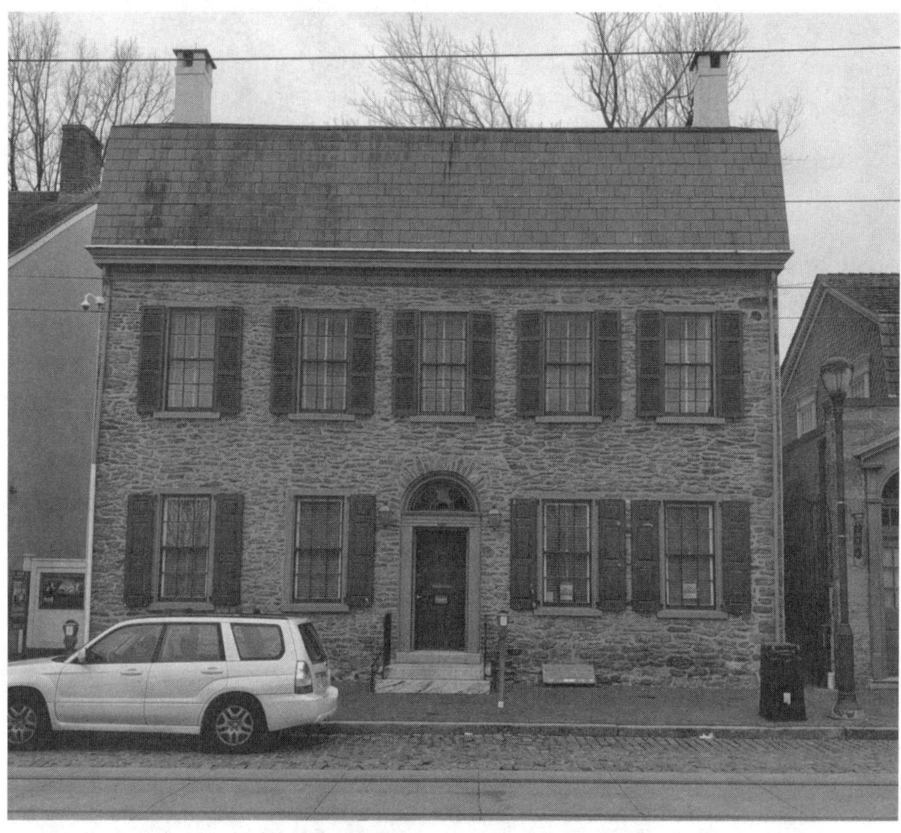

Present day view of Bringhurst, where Lieut. Col. John Bird died of his wounds.

Photo by author

Agnew was hit near the Mennonite meetinghouse on the Germantown Road by a ball that severed his spine, paralyzing him. He was taken back to his quarters in the John Wister House (known as "Grumblethorpe"). "When he [the doctor] came he could only turn his eyes, and looked steadfastly on me with seeming affection," wrote Andrew. "The doctor and [acting Brigade] Major [John] Leslie just came in time enough to see him depart this life, which he did without the least struggle or agony, but with great composure, and calmness, and seeming satisfaction, which was about 10 or 15 minutes after he received the ball, and I believe between 10 and 11 o'clock." Agnew died in the northwest room on the ground floor.[22]

22 Ibid. Alfred Lambdin's 1877 history of the battle claims Agnew was shot by a civilian named Hans Philip Boyer, but no primary source is provided to support that claim. Lambdin, "Battle of

Another casualty in the British officer corps was Lt. Col. John Bird, commander of the 15th Regiment of Foot. John Andre was an aide to Bird's brigade commander, Charles Grey, and as such was "particularly acquainted with [Bird], a veteran of the greatest merit, & most estimable Character."[23] Ensign Nathaniel Phillips of the 17th Regiment of Foot also was killed, and the 37th of Foot's Lt. Charles Buckeridge and Ensign David Stark of the 44th of Foot were wounded.[24]

While Grey's and Agnew's regiments swept generally north into Germantown and then on toward Cliveden, General Grant's hastily assembled command punched back east of the Germantown Road. Adam Stephen's staggered westward advance into and behind Wayne's left flank, followed by the confused, fitful withdrawal of the Pennsylvanians, left empty a large section of front between the Germantown Road and the Limekiln Pike. The fog, smoke, and rolling terrain made it doubtful that Grant could see the broad, unmanned front, but the wily veteran certainly sensed as much from the slackening fire and the lack of advancing enemy troops. The American commands that had torn apart his right were still off to the northwest and no longer were in vigorous pursuit of his men, which gave Grant the time he needed to reorganize. It was now time to exploit these advantages.

Germantown," 388. Andrew carefully detailed how he attended Agnew's corpse. "I then had his body brought to his former quarters, took his gold watch, his purse, in which there was four guineas and half a Johannes, which I delivered to Major Leslie as soon as he came home. I then had him genteelly laid out, and decently dressed with some of his clean and best things; had a coffin made the best the place could produce. His corpse was decently interred the next day in the churchyard, attended by a minister and the officers of the 44th regiment." A large stain, supposedly from Agnew's blood, is still visible on the floor, but it is more likely that it was caused from bleach used to clean the blood stain sometime after the war. The general was initially buried in the Lower Burial Ground of Germantown. Prior to the British evacuation of Philadelphia in 1778, Agnew's body, together with those of other British officers who had been killed in action, was moved to the DeBenneville Family Burial Ground.

23 Bird died in the house known as "Bringhurst," and later was buried next to Agnew. Bringhurst is the stone house immediately northwest of the Deshler-Morris House. Reed, *Campaign*, 233; Letter, John Andre to his mother, September 28, 1777, with a postscript dated October 8. The 15th Regiment of Foot lost several other officers, including Ensign Anthony Frederick, who was killed. Among the wounded were Capts. John Goldfrapp and Harry Ditmas, Lieut. George Thomas, and Ensign Robert Walker. The 15th of Foot suffered a total of 55 casualties. Lieutenant Henry Harding of the 46th of Foot was wounded. Overall, the 46th lost 8 men at Germantown. Narrative letter, probably by Lt. William Keough, 285; *Remembrancer*, 418.

24 Narrative letter, probably by Lt. William Keough, 285; Baule and Gilbert, *Army Officers*, 24. The 17th of Foot suffered 30 casualties, the 37th of Foot lost 24 men, and the 44th of Foot lost 40 men. *Remembrancer*, 418.

Nathanael Greene's men were exhausted. George Weedon's brigade of Virginians and Pennsylvanians (part of Greene's division under Peter Muhlenberg), together with Alexander McDougall's Connecticut troops and parts of Col. William Russell's Virginia brigade, had marched all night, broken through the British right, and driven back Abercromby's 1st Light Infantry Battalion and Ogilvie's 4th Regiment of Foot. Fragments of all these American commands had forged ahead west and southwest to Wingohocking Creek, where the advance seems to have stalled. By this time, the attackers were becoming disorganized, and were running short of ammunition.

Though their precise alignment is unknown, Grant's reorganized troops included Abercromby's light infantry battalion, Ogilvie's 4th Regiment of Foot, the 49th Regiment of Foot, and perhaps the rallied remnants of the 5th and 55th regiments from his own 2nd Brigade. The British attack pushed north and east across Wingohocking Creek and struck the disorganized Americans. "By some means or other the Right wing [Sullivan's command] gave way, which encouraged the Enemy to Rally and press forward," was how Weedon later described the Continentals' collapse. "The left [Greene's command including Weedon's brigade] shortly after was also Broke, and a General repulse took place instead of a victory the most important (had we attained it)." Once the men started falling back, continued Weedon, the "utmost exertions to rally them again was in vain, And a few minutes viewed the absolute majority of drawing them off in the best manner we could."[25]

The Pennsylvania State Regiment, part of Weedon's brigade, was on the left side of the brigade front and was one of the last units to fall back. The regiment was under fire "from front, left and part to the rear," explained Lt. James McMichael, "when Gen. Stephen ordered Col. Stewart to evacuate the ground from the right of subdivisions by files." Thus far, Adam Stephen had accompanied part of the 8th Virginia of Scott's brigade all the way south to Church Lane, had fought against Ogilvie's 4th Regiment, and had moved on to Wingohocking Creek, leaving the balance of his division far to the northwest to fend for itself. Stephen's order to Stewart's men was the third recorded time he had issued commands to a regiment belonging to someone else during the battle. "Every thing appeared in our favour when the Unfortunate retreat took place, which cannot yet be accounted for,"

25 Letter, George Weedon to John Page, 4 October 1777; Letter, George Weedon to John Page, 8 October 1777.

confirmed Col. Walter Stewart, the commander of the Pennsylvania State Regiment. It was "Genl. Stevens who certainly gave the order to the left wing."[26]

The Virginia regiments were hit particularly hard. Lieutenant Colonel Richard Parker of the 2nd Virginia (Weedon's brigade), reported an anonymous source, "a brave officer, got wounded in the leg, and it is said the bone is broke." Colonel James Hendricks, commander of the 1st Virginia from Russell's brigade, took a bullet below the left eye, but "was likely to recover; he behaved with such heroism, that he was the admiration of the field." Captain John Eustace, also of the 1st Virginia, "was killed dead on the spot," while Capt. Edmund Dickinson was slightly wounded in the knee.[27]

Like their Virginia counterparts, McDougall's Connecticut soldiers also collapsed. In his pension application, Pvt. Ephraim Andrews of the 8th Connecticut remembered that the British received reinforcements and that he and his comrades were "driven off the field with much loss our Regt lost several men there out of our Company." Private Joseph Plumb Martin of the 4th Connecticut blamed the lack of ammunition for their inability to stave off the enemy. "Some of the men unadvisedly calling out that their ammunition was spent, the enemy were so near that they overheard them," explained Martin; the British "first made a stand and then returned upon our people, who, for want of ammunition and reinforcements, were obliged in their turn to retreat."[28]

The presence of Adam Stephen with Greene's frontline troops raises the question of what Nathanael Greene actually did after his troops engaged the British pickets about dawn. The sources are silent on the matter. Many members of Greene's stunned command, however, did not remain silent. Surgeon James Wallace of the 2nd Virginia was dumbfounded by the manner in which the battle unfolded. "The whole of the affair appears a mystery to me," admitted the doctor to his brother a week later. "Many of the officers have told me that when they were ordered to retreat they were then persuing the enemy, who were flying before them;

26 McMichael, "Diary," 153; Letter, Walter Stewart to General Gates, October 12, 1777, 400.

27 An anonymous account detailed several casualties suffered by the Virginia Continentals: Lt. John Cornet Baylor of the 3rd Light Dragoons "had one half of his foot shot away." Major John Jameson of the 2nd Light Dragoons had his horse killed under him, but he himself was unhurt. Captain Thomas Edmonds of the 15th Virginia (McClanachan) was so badly wounded that he died in a few hours. Captain John Holcombe of the 4th Virginia (Scott) also was among the wounded. Anonymous letter written from York, PA, October 8, 1777, *North Carolina Gazette*, October 31, 1777.

28 RWPF, file W1795; Martin, *Yankee Doodle*, 73.

they were astonished to the last degree when they retreated from the highest expectations of success."[29]

Caught out of position, Greene tried to pull his command back a short distance from Wingohocking Creek in order to stabilize and reposition his line and present a solid front against Grant's approaching infantry. Instead, he lost control when the Virginians, Pennsylvanians, and Connecticut men thought the partial retreat order was actually a call to withdraw from the battlefield entirely. The frustrated general admonished his division on that very point three days later. Though Greene assured his troops that he had "the highest Confidence" in them and appreciated "the Spirit and good Conduct of the Officers," the "best information" available gave him "the mortification to assure the Troops they fled from Victory." Greene went on to explain that he "wishes most ardently, that the Troops may be convinced of the necessity of retreating and rallying briskly, and that a Partial Retreat to change a position is often necessary," but a "particular retreat," as he called it, "is not to be Considered general without the order is such."[30]

With Adam Stephen seemingly everywhere on the battlefield except where he should have been, his own disorganized division, comprised of Scott's and McClanachan's brigades, also fell apart and fell back. The latter brigade was already far to the north, intermingled with Wayne's retreating men, while Scott's troops were somewhere east of the Mennonite church with both flanks exposed. Grant's advance had driven Greene's men north and east across Church Lane toward Saw Mill Creek, which left Grant well beyond the left and rear of Scott's advanced position. The assault by General Grey's infantry east of Germantown put additional pressure on Scott. In trying to assess what happened that morning, Capt. John Marshall of the 15th Virginia, McClanachan's brigade, demonstrated the same ability as a wordsmith that he would later put to use as the chief justice of the Supreme Court. "The face of the country, and the extreme darkness of the morning, co-operating with the want of discipline in the army," Marshall wrote in his 1803 biography of George Washington, "blasted all the flattering appearances of the moment and defeated an enterprise which promised in its commencement the most happy and brilliant result." The British regrouped, he continued, and "attacked the regiments which had penetrated furthest into Germantown, where a part of Muhlenberg's [Russell's] and Scott's brigades were surrounded and made prisoners. The different broken parts mistook each other for the enemy," added

29 Letter, James Wallace to Michael Wallace, October 12, 1777, 707.

30 Showman, McCarthy, and Cobb, eds., *Papers*, vol. 2, 171.

Marshall. Senior officers did their best to maintain the initiative. "Great efforts were made to rally the American troops, when this retrograde movement first commenced, but they were ineffectual. A general confusion prevailed, and the confidence felt in the commencement of the action was entirely lost."[31]

Joseph Clark, Stephen's adjutant, recorded in his diary that they were "obliged to draw off to prevent being surrounded, as our flanks were not able to oppose the columns that came against them. This threw the whole into disorder, and occasioned a retreat in some confusion." There was "a considerable slaughter on both sides," scribbled Clark, "though I think it may be said with truth that the enemy in this action also suffered both in killed and wounded a great deal more than our army." The 3rd Virginia's Lt. Col. William Heth, also of McClanachan's brigade, was far less sanguine than Clark in his assessment of why the precipitous retreat took place. "The heavy smoke, added to a thick fog, was of vast injury to us," he asserted. "It undoubtedly increased the fear of some to fancy themselves flanked and surrounded, wh[ich] like an electrical shock seized some thousands, who fled in confusion, without the appearance of an enemy."[32]

Several accounts accuse Adam Stephen of giving the retreat order, and he would be court martialed for being drunk during the battle. Stephen tried his best to explain what happened that morning in an October 9 letter to General Washington. After detailing the initial portion of the battle, Stephen curiously noted that Col. Charles Lewis of the 14th Virginia (part of Weedon's brigade, not Stephen's division), together with Col. James Wood of the 12th Virginia (Scott's brigade), "kept the field with their Regiments until they were Orderd to Retire; when the Enemy were advanced agt them on All Quarters." If Stephen is accurate, Lewis and Wood managed to keep their regiments together during the collapse of Greene's column and served as a kind of rear guard. Artilleryman Elisha Stevens, who may have been serving with a battery attached to Stephen's division, put the blame for the retreat—and by extension, the defeat—squarely at Stephen's feet: "General Stevens gave orders to Retreat." That command, Stevens continued, put

31 Marshall, *Life*, vol. 3, 179-181. Grant's men captured most of Col. George Matthew's 9th Virginia of Col. William Russell's brigade. See page 361 for more details.

32 Clark, "Diary," 101; Commager and Morris, eds., *Spirit of Seventy-six*, 629-630. Lt. Joseph Blackwell of the 3rd Virginia Regiment described some of the casualties. "Capt. John Eustace got kild. . . . Three men of Capt. Tho Blackwell Compa. got Slitely wounded. Got my Breeches cut Just by the knees with a bullet." Ryan, ed., *Salute to Courage*, 102.

Washington's army "in confusion So that they was a Bliged to Retreat and Loos the Day."[33]

The tidal wave of retreating Continental troops washed into William Smallwood's Maryland and New Jersey militia, which was positioned east of Greene's troops. "Part of the centres retreating [Greene and Sullivan] composed of Continental Troops, set the example to others to retreat," wrote a disgusted Smallwood a few days later,

> and the sentiment that it was necessary, from the impression of so bad an example in the first instance, lead many more . . . which to our reproach was shameful to abandon in the midst of Victory. The enemy was generally repulsed, and drove . . . when our Ammunition on the right [Greene and Sullivan] and in some other parts grew scarce . . . which together with our Troops in the Centre [Greene and Sullivan] being flushed with success, and their officers not attending to preserve order, they got into Confusion by the pursuit, and contributed to loose one of the most glorious victories perhaps that America for some time may have an opportunity of gaining.[34]

Two days after the battle, Maj. Asher Holmes of the Monmouth County (New Jersey) militia blamed the Continentals on his right for the defeat. Brigadier General David Forman "ordered us to retreat, which we did in pretty good order," claimed Holmes, "until our Continental troops broke and ran a second time, and their running through our men broke them entirely."[35]

In the confusion following the collapse of Nathanael Greene's entire wing and Smallwood's command, James Grant pushed forward his reorganized units into the buckwheat fields near the camp of the 1st Light Infantry Battalion, east of Wingohocking Creek and northwest of Armstrong's mill. There, perhaps while trying to make a stand, Col. George Matthew's 9th Virginia (Russell's brigade) found itself alone and was surrounded and captured almost to a man. According to James Wallace, a surgeon with the 2nd Virginia (Weedon's brigade), the "9th Virg'a Reg. was all taken to a man; the manner in which they were taken does them much honour . . . on the army's retreating they were left without any support, and were surrounded and all taken." Sergeant Charles Talbot of the 6th Virginia of the same

33 Chase and Lengel, eds., *Papers*, vol. 11, 468-469; Stevens, *Fragments of Memoranda*, pages not numbered.

34 Letter, William Smallwood to unknown recipient, October 9, 1777, 402.

35 Holmes, "Letter," 35.

brigade noted in an October 10 letter that "the Enemy Retook the Ground & drove our army under some loss & retook a Number of prisoners & many Waggons & other things which we had taken." Major Oliver Towles, one of Sergeant Talbot's officers, was captured during this advance. "All of a sudden we retreated in a very confused state," Talbot explained, and in doing so "left many of our wounded on the field." In a postwar letter to adjutant general Pickering, Maj. John Howard of the 4th Maryland wrote that Colonel Matthews of the 9th Virginia "defended himself with great bravery, and did not surrender until the most of his Officers and men were killed or wounded. He himself received several bayonet wounds."[36]

Earlier that morning, the 9th Virginia, along with the rest of Russell's brigade, had ambushed Ogilvie's 4th Regiment of Foot just below Church Lane, had helped embarrass and drive back Abercromby's 1st Battalion of Light Infantry, and had overrun the light infantry camp. The regrouped and infuriated light infantry retook their camp and exacted revenge on Matthew's Virginians. The company commander of the 4th Regiment of Foot's light company, Capt. Charles Cochrane, left a detailed account of one of the battle's most dramatic events. "My Compy and the 42nd Light Compy having in the pursuit of some of them to the right separated in the Fog from the rest of the Battalion were seeking for It," Cochrane began,

> when we observed a considerable Body which turned out to be the 9th Virginia Regt in our Rear, and between us and our own Hutts. At first they were supposed to be our own people But on further examination proved to be Rebels who had contrived to get around us. It occurred to me that their intention was to come in from the appearance of some of them coming forwards [to surrender]. I therefore called to them to throw down their arms but was soon undeceived by their beginning to fire. We made the best haste we could to them, drove there into and through our own Hutts . . . with our bayonets: It afterwards appeared that they had been [to the huts] before we fell in with them, in my Companys Wigwams & the 42d had taken out our Bread and divided it among themselves so certain they then were of carrying the Day.[37]

36 Letter, James Wallace to Michael Wallace, October 12, 1777, 707; Talbot, "Letters," 318. After the battle, Towles and several other officers were confined in Philadelphia. Letter, William Dangerfield to Mary Towles, November 20, 1777, Thomas Addis Emmet Collection, New York Public Library Digital Collection, accessed February 6, 2019; "Howard's Account," 319.

37 Letter, Charles Cochrane to Andrew Steuart, October 19, 1777. Captain Cochrane lost an officer and five men.

Captain Cochrane apparently failed to realize that other light infantry companies had closed in and attacked the Virginians at the same time. "Having approached the camp to our astonishment, saw a line of the enemy drawn up opposite the camp, their backs to us, a thin broken hedge only separating, some of our men started back with surprise," reported Capt. William Scott of the 1st Battalion of Light Infantry. "Officers hallowed out loudly charge, charge, enemy turned [ab]out, fired and run forward through the camp. One of my Lts. was mortally wounded, and a very few others; pursued the enemy who were forming and threw down their arms."[38] Lieutenant Frederick Wetherall of the 17th Regiment of Foot's light company also witnessed the collapse of the 9th Virginia:

> Some Rebels were perceived in the Wigwams in moving towards them the 9th Virginia Regt. that under cover of the Fog had penetrated was drawn up with their Backs to the Light Infantry, upon which the Officers with the most determined Bravery encouraging the Men, they charg'd them tho' very inferior to their numbers & effectively routed them those that Escap'd the Bayonet run into the Camp . . . threw down their Arms & beg'd for Mercy.[39]

Lieutenant Colonel Henry Calder's 49th Regiment of Foot had also regrouped below Wingohocking Creek and had moved up during General Grant's attack in order to support the advancing 1st Battalion of Light Infantry. "We fell in with a party of the Enemy, that had surrounded three Companies of the 1st Light Infantry and made them Prisoners," recalled Cpl. Thomas Sullivan of the 49th Regiment. "After we fired the first Volley, they ran towards the Center, leaving the Prisoners loose, which latter formed immediately & took to their Arms, firing upon the enemy with the greatest ardour. The left hand Company of our Regiment," continued Sullivan, "took 63 of that party who upon their approach, threw down their Arms; the Battallion still pushing on."[40]

General Grant later claimed that many of the captured Americans were drunk. "They got Rum three times," he asserted. "Before they set out— halfway—and at

38 Scott, "Memorandum," 294.

39 Wetherall, *Journal*, np.

40 Sullivan, *Journal*, 145. The 49th Regiment of Foot lost 12 men to wounds. *Remembrancer*, 418.

Chesnut Hill, when they drew near if I may judge from the situation I found a Colonel & two Majors in, they were certainly all drunk."[41]

The 1st Light Infantry Battalion whose effectiveness had been reduced by a casualty rate of 20% since the beginning of the campaign (including Brandywine and other actions), suffered six killed, 39 wounded, and two missing at Germantown.[42]

American resistance east of the Germantown Road, east of Wingohocking Creek, and south of the Bristol Road had collapsed. Along both sides of the Germantown Road, General Knypahusen's men had driven back Sullivan's and Wayne's troops and were approaching the grounds of Cliveden. "The enemy, who already penetrated far into Germantown and were firing from gardens and behind houses, which here are set far apart," reported the *Hessian Corps Journal*, "were now attacked so fiercely that they gave up the attack on the house defended by Colonel Musgrave."[43] With Germantown and the fields east and west of it cleared, Agnew's and Grey's commands had an unobstructed approach to the Chew house. The Americans "broke, & were Effectually Drove on both hands, leaving the Ground thickly Strew'd with their Dead & Wounded," wrote Lt. William Keough of the 44th Regiment of Foot. "By this time, the Greater part of Our Army Engaged them, the Canonade & firing was on every Quarter."[44] Lieutenant Colonel Robert Donkin's 44th Regiment of Foot moved north up the road, reached the embattled house, and liberated the survivors of Musgrave's three 40th Regiment of Foot companies. Captain John Andre wrote an account of the action to his mother soon after the battle:

> As we went up the street we releas'd Col. Musgrave with part of the 40th Regiment . . . who with great presence of mind & equal gallantry had maintaind themselves in a house, strewing the yard, garden, avenue &c. with a prodigious number of rebel Dead who pass'd by in their flight or were hardy enough to attempt assaulting . . . the house, pierced with hundreds of shot both Cannon & Musketry, with the dead within & without, told its own

41 Grant to Harvey, October 20, 1777, Grant Papers.

42 Among the losses were two wounded lieutenants: Marcus Anthony Morgan of the 17th's light company (who later died from his wounds) and Forbes Champagne of the 4th's light company. *Remembrancer*, 418.

43 Journal of the Hessian Corps in America, Letter FZ, 124.

44 Narrative letter, probably by Lt. William Keough, 285. According to historian John Reed, "Most of the American dead, and probably the British, who fell in this unfortunate attack still sleep in unmarked graves within the wall that circumvallates the mansion's park." Reed, *Campaign*, 229.

> story without necessity of comment, upon our troops appearing, the 40th reg. sallied out, and joined the pursuit.[45]

Once Sullivan's and Wayne's men retired past Cliveden, recalled Maj. John Howard of the 4th Maryland, "the enemy sallied out [of the house], one hundred or more, and fired on our rear." His troops, continued Howard, "faced about, and gave them a fire, which killed the Officer in front, and checked them. We then retreated at leisure."[46]

Cliveden's grounds resembled a charnel house. The day after the battle, jaeger Capt. Johann Ewald surveyed the carnage and "counted seventy-five dead Americans, some of whom lay stretched in the doorways, under the tables and chairs, and under the windows, among whom were seven officers. The rooms of the house were riddled by cannonballs and looked like a slaughter house because of the blood splattered around."[47] Musgrave, through his bold decision and magnificent performance, had altered the course of the battle single-handedly. His 40th Regiment of Foot suffered four killed, 29 wounded, and three missing at Germantown. Among the wounded were Lts. John Doyle and John Forbes and Ensign John Campbell. The regiment had passed through Brandywine relatively unscathed, but lost eight percent of its strength at Germantown. How many fell in the house itself will never be known.[48]

Knyphausen's regiments had brought with them their own artillery; they unlimbered their guns just south of Cliveden and fired at William Maxwell's and Francis Nash's Continentals. The New Jerseymen and North Carolinians had taken up a position north and west of the house, which proved untenable when the most prominent man amongst the Carolinians became one of the casualties. A round shot from a British artillery piece ricocheted down the road, tore through the right side of General Nash's horse, ripped through his left leg, and smashed into the side of the head of Maj. James Witherspoon, aide to William Maxwell, creating a hideous cloud of blood, flesh, brains, and bone. The bloodied horse collapsed and

45 Letter, John Andre to his mother, September 28, 1777, with a postscript dated October 8. Chew family tradition holds that only one British soldier died in the house—in the upper northwest room. McGuire, *Campaign*, vol. 2, 117.

46 "Howard's Account," 315.

47 Ewald, *Diary*, 96.

48 *Remembrancer*, 418; Inman, ed., "List of Officers," 176-205; McGuire, Germantown, 82.

pinned Nash and his nearly severed leg beneath it.[49] "We have lost Poor Genl Nash in the Battle," was how Capt. Cosimo de Medici of the North Carolina light horse lamented Nash's death in a letter to the state's governor. "There we lost our General, Frank Nash," wrote Pvt. Hugh McDonald of the 6th North Carolina. According to McDonald, the cannon ball "struck his horse behind the right thigh and, passing through, cut off [Nash's left] thigh, except [a] small bit of skin on the fore part, which was cut before he was raised, and put in the carriage with him." The grievously wounded Nash was extricated from the bloody heap, his leg tightly bound to slow the bleeding, and carried nearly twenty miles back to camp. The unfortunate officer lingered for five long days before succumbing.[50]

Most histories of the battle attribute little or no role to the North Carolina brigade, but primary accounts prove otherwise. The command, congressman Cornelius Harnett informed the governor of North Carolina, "lost several other brave officers and many wounded, the latter were all brought off the field." Another member of the congress, John Penn, wrote that "most of the North Carolina Troops were engaged, and behaved well. . . . Col. [Thomas] Polk's [4th North Carolina] son wounded, not bad." And there were others. "Lt. McKenzie of Daniel Williamson's company, from Duplin county, the only son of two old Irish people in that county, said to be the handsomest man in our regiment, also fell there," confirmed Pvt. Hugh McDonald. "Lt. [Joshua] Hadley, of [Thomas]

49 The ball killed Witherspoon, the son of John Witherspoon, the president of Princeton College and a signer of the Declaration of Independence, instantly. Witherspoon and six others were buried in the front of the house, near the modern intersection of Westview and Germantown Avenues. Today, a mass transit bus lot is located where the house once stood. Later, Witherspoon's remains were removed to St. Michael's Lutheran churchyard in Germantown. McGuire, *Campaign*, vol. 2, 84-85.

50 Letter, Cosimo de Medici to Richard Caswell, October 21, 1777, Walter Clark, ed., *State Records of North Carolina*, 30 vols. (Raleigh, NC, 1895), vol. 11, 661. Nash was buried in the Mennonite churchyard in Kulpsville, Pennsylvania. Lieutenant Colonel William Smith and Maj. John White, who were mortally wounded in the attack on Cliveden, are buried in the same cemetery; McDonald, *Teen-ager*, 12-13. When Nash fell, Alexander Martin, as the senior colonel, assumed command of the brigade. His tenure proved to be short-lived. Several sources claim he was court martialed for his actions at Germantown, but in fact he was brought up on charges of cowardice for his conduct three weeks earlier at Brandywine, while serving with the light infantry. Martin was acquitted but left the army on November 22. Captain Edward Vail of the 2nd North Carolina also found himself before a court martial "charged with . . . Cowardice at the battle of Germantown." Vail was "found guilty of the first charge and sentenced to be dismissed from the service; and that his crime, name, place of abode, and punishment, be published in the news-papers in and about the camp, and that particular state from which he came; and that it shall be deemed scandalous for any officer to associate with him." Fitzpatrick, *Writings*, vol. 10, 191. Eventually, Brig. Gen. Lachlan McIntosh, a Georgian, took command of the North Carolina brigade.

White's company [6th North Carolina], had a split ball hit him on the shin and lodge in the bone. Capt. Armstrong, of the 7th N.C. regiment, who had joined us a few days before, received a similar wound; and we afterwards called him 'Hickory Shins' making out, from his hard visage and lean appearance, that the shin had cut the ball." Colonel Alexander Martin of the 2nd North Carolina also provided details of the North Carolina casualties. "We lost Cap. [Jacob] Turner of the 3d Regiment who fell by a Musquet Shot. This brave Officer greatly distinguished himself under my command in the light Infantry at Chads Ford [Brandywine]."[51]

According to John Andre, "7 battalions stemm'd the torrent"—meaning Grey's and Agnew's brigades, along with one of Grant's units comprised of the 5th, 15th, 17th, 37th, 44th, 46th, and 64th Regiments of Foot.[52] As General Grey's staff officer, Andre can be forgiven for his myopia west of the Germantown Road, but he failed to acknowledge that the 49th and 55th Regiments of Foot, together with the 1st Battalion Light Infantry and possibly the 4th Regiment, had cleared the entire field east of the road. While these latter regiments pushed back the enemy in their fronts, the supporting Hessian command also played a small role, though the details have gone mostly unrecorded. "In this affair one Corporal and three men of the [Leib] Regiment were slightly wounded," confirmed the *Leib Regiment Journal*, while the von Donop Regiment "did not suffer" any casualties.[53] According to Royal artilleryman Francis Downman, "[t]he light 12 pounders and fieldpieces had a share in the day's action, and had several men wounded."[54]

* * *

51 Letter, Cornelius Harnett to Richard Caswell, October 10, 1777, Clark, ed., *State Records of North Carolina*, vol. 11, 647; Letter, John Penn to Richard Caswell, October 16, 1777, in Walter Clark, ed., *State Records of North Carolina*, 30 vols. (Winston, NC, 1895), vol. 11, 654; McDonald, *Teen-ager*, 13; Letter, Alexander Martin to Richard Caswell, November 4, 1777, Governor's Papers, North Carolina Department of Archives and History, Raleigh, NC. Other casualties included Lts. John McCann and Matthew White of the 6th North Carolina, both of whom were killed. The 5th North Carolina lost both its colonel and its lieutenant colonel. Colonel Edward Buncombe was wounded and taken prisoner, and died from his wounds that November while in captivity. Lieutenant Colonel Henry Irwin also was killed.

52 Letter, John Andre to his mother, September 28, 1777, with a postscript dated October 8.

53 "Journal of Leib Infantry Regiment," 21; "Journal of the Regiment von Donop," 19.

54 Whinyates, *Downman*, 39. According to Downman, "[Capt. Peter] Traille, [Capt. John] Stewart and [Capt.-Lieut. William] Huddlestone were with the light 12 pounders." Lieutenant James Frost of the artillery was wounded.

"In less than thirty minutes, our troops began to retire, and from the ardor of the pursuit, were in full retreat. This not being general through the line, of necessity left the flanks of some divisions and brigades uncovered and exposed to the assaults of an exasperated foe," recalled a disappointed Benjamin Tallmadge. "From this moment the prospects of victory were changed, and notwithstanding all our attempts to rally the retiring troops, it seemed impossible to effect it, even by the presence of the Commander-in-Chief."[55]

Washington, who had spent the battle along the Germantown Road, tried to stem the retreat while under a heavy fire. Tallmadge—on Washington's orders—threw his "squadron of horse across the road . . . repeatedly, to prevent the retreat of the infantry; but it was ineffectual." Sullivan, busy trying to get his brigades in some semblance of order, now had Washington to worry about. "I cannot help observing That with great Concern I saw our brave Commander Exposing himself to the hottest fire of the Enemy in such a manner that regard to my Country oblidged me to ride to him & beg him to retire—he to gratify me & Some others withdrew a Small Distance but his anxiety for the fate of the Day Soon brought him up again where he remained till our Troops had retreated."[56]

Washington repeatedly exposed himself to enemy fire, but he never ventured south of the Chew house. "The General did not pass it [Cliveden] at all," remembered Timothy Pickering, who "remained near him until our troops were retreating." With Sullivan's men tumbling rearward, Pickering spurred his mount "to endeavor to stop and rally those I met retiring, in companies and squads; but it was impracticable; their ammunition, I suppose, had generally been expended."[57]

Lieutenant William Beatty of the 7th Maryland part of Colonel Stone's brigade (Sullivan's division), believed the British, aided by "some bad management on our side obliged us to retreat. This was about 9 o'Clock." About that same time, General Sullivan finally succumbed to the inevitable: "Unsupported by any other troops, with scarcely a cartridge left, having in a severe fire of three hours, expended the whole, we were at length obliged to quit the field."[58]

55 Tallmadge, *Memoir*, 23.

56 Ibid.; Hammond, ed., *Papers*, vol. 1, 547.

57 Letter, Timothy Pickering to Jared Sparks, August 23, 1826, 429. Washington's highest ranking officers also had subjected themselves to enemy fire without regard for their personal safety. According to an anonymous American officer, "Generals Wayne & Conway & L'd Sterling had their Horses Shot under them." *Papers of Clinton*, vol. 2, 373.

58 Beatty, "Journal," 110; Hammond, ed., *Papers*, vol. 1, 576.

The American officers, devastated by how close they had come to victory, were frustrated by the series of events that had turned their success into chaotic defeat—none more so than John Sullivan. In hindsight, the collapse of his command was not as sudden as it was inevitable. Washington had been right when he had worried about the expenditure of ammunition; by the time the British advanced, Sullivan's ammunition had run out. The reinforcements he expected at any moment never arrived, for Lord Stirling's reserve division, designed to support Sullivan's anticipated deep advance, had been held back by Washington at Cliveden. The alarm among the troops triggered by the sounds of battle behind them was compounded thereafter when "a light horseman" rode behind the front yelling "that the Enemy had got round us" and turned the right flank. By this time Knyphausen's legions were advancing and General Conway's Pennsylvanians on Sullivan's right "retired with as much precipitation as they had before advanced against Every effort of their officers to Rally them." Sullivan's men "had been Engaged near three Hours which with the march of the Preceeding night rendered them almost unfit for fighting or retreating." All these factors contributed to the sudden retreat of Sullivan's division.[59]

* * *

While Sullivan's and Wayne's exhausted commands fled to the rear and Washington did his best to halt the collapse, Lt. Col. Ludwig von Wurmb's Hessian jaegers, on the far left of Howe's line near the Schuylkill River, took decisive action to end the threat posed by Armstrong's Pennsylvania militia. Once the Americans had been driven back across Wissahickon Creek soon after sunrise, the opposing sides had spent the better part of three long hours exchanging fire, without much effect. According to von Wurmb, "Around 9 AM Lieutenant [Joachim Hieronymus] von Bassewitz, Gen. v. Knyphausen's adjutant, arrived and told me that everything was going well on the right wing and the enemy were driven back. I then attacked, retook the bridge, and followed them," he reported in his clipped German style.[60]

The veteran Hessians simply overpowered the inexperienced Pennsylvanians. "The Jager corps turned left face, went across and moved immediately up in

59 Hammond, ed., *Papers*, vol. 1, 546-547, 576.

60 Letter, Lt. Col. Ludwig von Wurmb to Gen. Friedrich von Jungkenn, Court Chamberlain of Hesse-Kassel, October 14, 1777, 11.

formation, attacked the enemy close by, and drove the enemy from his secure position on the hill," wrote Lieutenant von Feilitzsch. "[T]he enemy retreated in disorder, but managed to keep his canons, repeated attacks upon them by our mounted and unmounted Jagers were without results, they could not be taken. But because the enemy column was moving along in a wide path, and our men were spread about the whole field," he added, "only their canons and the last of their rear guard were able to shoot, they on the other hand, were exposed to our total fire, under which they suffered immensely . . . because our bullets could hardly miss."[61]

Armstrong's men "retreated as soon as they realized Washington was retreating, with the main corps," wrote Hessian quartermaster Johann von Cochenhausen. The terrain made it difficult to launch an effective pursuit, which allowed the Americans to withdraw without losing any prisoners. According to the *Jaeger Corps Journal*, "[a]s the attack had to be continued through a long defile, the enemy had time to retire. Therefore we found only twenty dead and, as the jaegers were much fatigued, without support, and were only three hundred men, there was no further pursuit."[62] The militia "withdrew with great speed," observed one source. The jaegers followed for two miles, all for naught. "Because of the bad terrain, nobody was captured," reported a frustrated Ludwig von Wurmb. "In the Corps was 10 wounded, of which one died, the others have good prognoses." Not surprisingly, Armstrong put a positive face on his effort in his October 5 report to Pennsylvania authorities: "We engaged about three quarters of an hour, but their grape shot & ball soon intimidated & obliged us to retreat or rather file off."[63]

General Howe had no opportunity to use his favorite tactic of flanking the enemy, as he had at Brandywine, but the fighting ended the same way, with the Americans streaming off a hard-fought field of battle. Would Howe vigorously pursue the beaten Continentals and deliver a death blow to Washington's army?

61 Von Feilitzsch, *Journal*, 98-99.

62 Letter, Johann Ludwig von Cochenhausen to Friedrich von Jungkenn, October 9, 1777; Retzer and Londahl-Smidt, eds., "The Philadelphia Campaign," *Journal of the Johannes Schwalm Historical Association*, Vol. 6, no. 2, 3; Burgoyne and Burgoyne, eds., *Journal*, 22.

63 Letter, Lt. Col. Ludwig von Wurmb to Gen. Friedrich von Jungkenn, Court Chamberlain of Hesse-Kassel, October 14, 1777, 11; Letter, Wilhelm von Knyphausen to the Landgrave, October 17, 1777, 85; Journal of the Hessian Corps in America under General von Heister, 1776-June 1777, Hessian Documents of the American Revolution, Morristown National Historical Park (Morristown, NJ), Letter FZ, 124, a copy of which is located at the David Library of the American Revolution, Washington Crossing, PA; Hazard, et al., eds., *Archives*, Series 1, vol. 5, 646.

Chapter 16

The Aftermath of Battle

October 4, 1777
10:00 a.m. to Evening

"I had marched in twenty-four hours 45 miles, and in that time fought four hours, during which we advanced so furiously thro' buckwheat fields, that it was almost an unspeakable fatigue."[1]

— Lt. James McMichael, Pennsylvania State Regiment, October 4, 1777

Peale and Paine

On October 3, 36-year-old Charles Willson Peale bedded down for the night in Bucks County, several miles north of Germantown. He awoke the next morning to the sounds of battle and headed toward the firing. While at Crooked Billet Tavern in Hatboro to get oats for his horse, the painter, who had a keen enthusiasm for the Continental cause, spotted "some of our men coming up the Road from whom I learnt that our men was Retreating." A short distance ahead he met "several of my acquaintance who confirmed the News." Peale rode west to Spring Tavern at the intersection of the Bethlehem and Sumneytown Pikes where he "found very little better news," then cantered south to Skippack Pike (modern Route 73) before eventually reaching "the Encampment

1 McMichael, "Diary," 153.

our men had left the Eveng. before." Peale's winding journey to find his brother and friends who fought in Washington's army consumed the day and evening hours until, too exhausted to ride on, he "went to Coll. Pattens and stayed the night."[2]

Like Charles Peale, Thomas Paine rode toward Germantown in the wake of the Continental Army on the morning of the battle; he wrote about his experiences in a letter to Benjamin Franklin in May 1778. "I met no person for several miles riding, which I concluded to be a good sign," remembered the infamous pamphleteer of *Common Sense.* "After this I met a man on horseback, who told me he was going to hasten on to supply the ammunition, that the enemy were broken and retreating fast, which was true." Soon enough Paine spotted evidence of horrific combat. "I saw several country people with arms in their hands running cross a field towards Germantown, within about five or six miles of which I met several of the wounded in wagons, horseback, and on foot," he wrote Franklin. "I passed Gen. Nash on a litter made of poles, but did not know him." A wave of uneasiness coursed through the writer. "I felt unwilling to ask questions, lest the information should not be agreeable, and kept on." Paine continued about two miles and "passed a promiscuous crowd of wounded and otherwise, who were halted at a house." Colonel Clement Biddle, the army's commissary general of forage, was among them and called out to Paine "that if I went further on that road I would be taken, for the firing which I heard a head was the enemy's."[3]

The more Paine spoke with survivors, the more perplexed he became about the course of the battle. "I never could, and cannot now, learn, and I believe no man can inform truly the cause of that day's miscarriage," he wrote before continuing:

> The retreat was as extraordinary. Nobody hurried themselves. Everyone marched his own pace. The enemy kept a civil distance behind, sending every now and then a shot after us, and receiving the same from us. That part of the army which I was with collected and

2 Lillian B. Miller, Sidney Hart, and Toby A. Appel, eds., *The Selected Papers of Charles Willson Peale and His Family, Charles Willson Peale: Artist in Revolutionary America, 1735-1791*, 5 vols. (New Haven, CT, 1983), vol. 1, 246-248. Crooked Billet Tavern, located near 55 South York Road in Hatboro, was demolished in 1955. Some of the retreating Americans found themselves in Hatboro, far from the roads they had used to reach Germantown, which indicates the scattered nature of the army and its hasty exit from the battlefield.

3 "Military Operations," 288.

formed on the hill on the side of the road near White Marsh Church. The enemy came within three-fourths of a mile and halted.[4]

The sight stunned the always-curious Paine. If the army had been so soundly defeated, why had the enemy stopped?

The American Retreat

When his army began to collapse, Washington ordered his division commanders to retreat. With their ammunition largely expended and the British and Hessians having reclaimed the lost ground, the four columns of disorganized American regiments withdrew down the roads they had confidently advanced along just a few hours earlier. On the far left of the army, William Smallwood's Maryland and New Jersey militiamen headed north up Old York Road back to Church Road before turning left to head back to Skippack Pike. The Virginia, Pennsylvania, and Connecticut troops under Nathanael Greene trodded north along the Limekiln Pike before also turning left on Church Road to reach the Skippack Pike. John Sullivan's Pennsylvania, Maryland, Delaware, and Canadian men returned west to Chestnut Hill, turned right up the Bethlehem Pike, and also marched to the Skippack Pike. John Armstrong's Pennsylvania militia, on the far right flank, retreated west down Ridge Road back toward Norriton Township.

Smallwood's militiamen had marched the farthest the previous day to reach the battlefield, and now his amateur soldiers had no choice but to make the longest retreat. Not surprisingly, Smallwood's command hemorrhaged stragglers. "A Rebel came out of the Wood & Surrendered," recalled Loyalist James Parker, who rode to Germantown from Philadelphia later that morning. "He was of a small party sent to attack a picket on our right but said the main Attack [was] at G.Town, where I met the Corps of Genl. Agnew. . . . I got up with the van of our army on Chesnut hill where Genl. Howe was, they halted & the Rebels fled." The surrendered rebel almost certainly was a member of the Maryland or New Jersey militia.[5]

Greene's column had made the deepest penetration of Howe's front, reaching the fields around Germantown; the column commander now faced the difficult task of extricating Alexander McDougall's Connecticut brigade, his own division

4 Ibid., 288-289. White Marsh Church is modern St. Thomas Church.

5 Parker Journal, October 4, 1777 entry, Parker Family Papers.

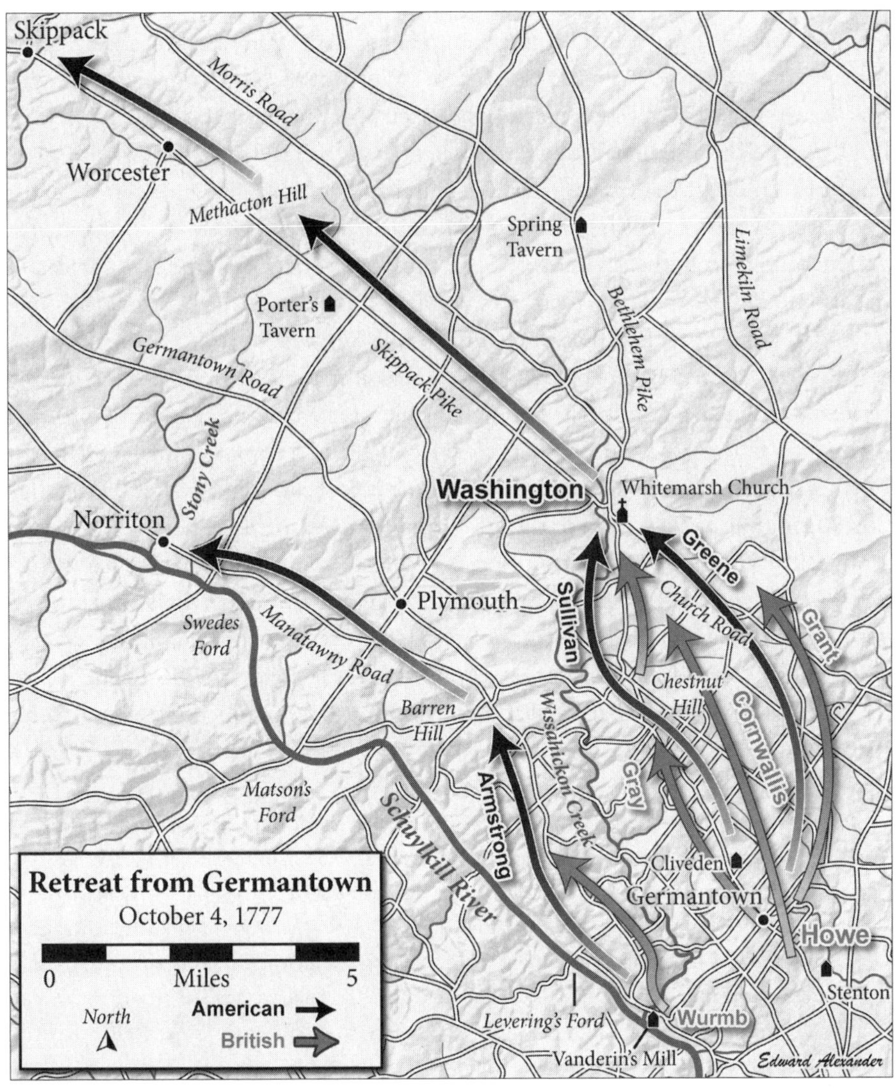

under Peter Muhlenberg, and Adam Stephen's dispersed Virginia division out of harm's way. The Connecticut men had advanced on Greene's left flank to the banks of Wingohocking Creek, but melted away when panic gripped the front during General Grant's well-timed British counter-attack. In a letter to Greene, McDougall said his "endeavors were not wanting to bring off the Troops in order; but [I] could not effect it, as the panic had seized them, and your [Greene's] conduct was far from showing any signs of fear."[6]

6 Showman, McCarthy, and Cobb, eds., *Papers*, vol. 2, 283.

McDougall's men echoed the sentiments their commander shared with Greene. In an October 6, letter, Col. Charles Webb of the 2nd Connecticut prayed that "God Almighty will soon enable us to exchange [the retreat] for that of victory; but I fear the chastisement is not yet sufficient to answer the great design of heaven; but I firmly believe our cause is just and will finally prevail. The retreat in general," continued Webb, "was safe and good, though attended with some confusion, as you may judge from the situation." Webb's regiment had suffered 22 casualties out of about 250 men, "but men are coming in who faned [fainted] through fatigue—hope many missing will return."[7]

Private Edward Yeomans of the 4th Connecticut experienced a harrowing retreat. During the early part of the chaos, a "soldier by the name of Lord, the company's Barber was shot in the back close by him." Yeomans "was in the midst of smoke, drank too much water, became sick & lost his gun Bayonet & cartridge box." Ensign Jonathan Todd of the 7th Connecticut escaped the field thanks to the kindness of another. "I should inivitably have fallen into the Enemies hands had not the Paymaster Lent me his horse to Ride down to the attack. I was as Fatigued with marching all night & day without Eating that I could scarcely walk, my clothes all Blood have none clean to Put on as our baggage is gone up to Bethlehem."[8]

Pvt. Joseph Plumb Martin of the 4th Connecticut described the ordeal in his memoir:

> I had now to travel the rest of the day, after marching all the day and night before and fighting all the morning. I had not eaten nothing since the noon of the preceding day, nor did I eat a morsel till the forenoon of the next day, and I need rest as much as victuals. I could have procured that if I had time to seek it, but victuals was not to be found. I was tormented with thirst all the morning, fighting being warm work; but after the retreat commenced I found ample means to satisfy my thirst. "I could drink at the brook," but I could not "bite at the bank."

The manner in which the retreat was conducted bothered Martin. "There was one thing in such cases as I have just mentioned (I mean, in retreating from an enemy) that always galled my feelings," he began,

7 "Contemporary Account," 331.

8 RWPF, file W11902; Letter, Jonathan Todd to his Father, October 6, 1777.

> and that was, whenever I was forced to a quick retreat to be obliged to run till I was [worn] down. The Yankees are generally very nimble of foot and in those cases are very apt to practice what they have the ability of performing. Some of our men at this time seemed to think that they could never run fast or far enough. I never wanted to run, if I was forced to run, further than to be beyond the reach of the enemy's shot, after which I had no more fear of their overtaking me than I should have of an army of lobsters doing it, unless it were their horsemen, and they *dared* not do it.[9]

Not everyone escaped. Many men were swept up in the confused retreat. Lieutenant James Morris of the 5th Connecticut, one of many grabbed by pursuing British battalions, described the experience in his memoir. "I being in the first company, at the head of one column that began the attack upon the Enemy, consequently I was in the rear in the retreat," explained Morris. "Our men then undisciplined were scattered. I had marched with a few men nearly ten miles before I was captured, continually harassed by the British Dragoons, and the light Infantry. I finally surrender'd to Save life with the few men, then under my command, & marched back to Germantown under a guard."[10]

Like McDougall's brigade, Greene's own division needed to extricate itself from the eastern bank of Wingohocking Creek once Grant's heavy counterassault fractured the American front. "The retreat was one scene of confusion in which many were made prisoners," admitted George Weedon, Greene's brigade commander. Lieutenant James McMichael of the Pennsylvania State Regiment, one of Weedon's units, found it "disagreeable to have to leave the field, when we had almost made a conquest." Nevertheless, McMichael continued, "agreeably to orders, we retreated regularly a short distance, but the enemy taking a different route, we were obliged to march the road from whence we came, in order to head them, but did not fall in with any part of them afterwards."[11]

No accounts by members of Stephen's division detailing their evacuation of the battlefield have been located. Given Stephen's drunken state that morning and his inability to direct his own division in a competent fashion, the conduct of the retreat leaves little to the imagination. Charles Scott's brigade needed to pull away from the eastern fringes of Germantown and did so, likely by following the Bristol Road east to Limekiln Pike. Stephen's second brigade, under Alexander

9 Martin, *Yankee Doodle*, 73-74.

10 Ryan, ed., *Salute to Courage*, 104.

11 Letter, George Weedon to John Page, 4 October 1777; McMichael, "Diary," 153.

McClanachan, moved away from the eastern grounds of Cliveden, probably using the Abington Road to return east to the Limekiln Pike before heading north.

Unfortunately, there are also no known accounts from veterans of Wayne's division about the withdrawal. The Pennsylvanians would have continued their retrograde movement north and west beyond Cliveden to reach the Germantown Road, return to Chestnut Hill, and head up Bethlehem Pike.

Heading up the same roads just ahead of Wayne's troops were John Sullivan's division under Moses Hazen and Thomas Conway's Pennsylvania brigade. Hazen's men, exhausted and out of ammunition, had to disengage from their fight against James Agnew's British infantry northwest of Germantown, and they experienced the same difficult and enervating slog away from the bloody field. "We got to the Perkiomen [Creek, 25 miles to the northwest] again at night. Here, we old soldiers had marched forty miles—fought a battle to three o'clock, P.M.—and marched back to camp again," recalled Capt. Enoch Anderson of the Delaware Regiment. "We eat nothing and drank nothing but water, on the tour!"[12]

On the far right of the line, the last of Washington's columns, under John Armstrong, was ordered to retire and link back up with the main army. "About nine I was called to joine the General [Washington]. . . We proceeded to the left, and above Jermantown some three miles, directed by a slow crossfire of Canon, until we fell into the Front of a superior body of the Enemy, with whom we engaged about three quarters of an hour, but their grape shot & ball soon intimidated & obliged us to retreat or rather file off," was how Armstrong explained part of his retreat the next day. Until that time the Pennsylvania officer "thought we had a Victory." In a letter to Horatio Gates written five days later, Armstrong claimed he "lost but thirty-nine wounded." Whatever the losses, fewer of his Pennsylvania militia retreated up Ridge Road than had taken that route to reach the field that morning.[13]

According to Lt. Col. John Lacey, a 22-year-old officer without a command who was accompanying the Pennsylvania militia, "when the Order for Retreat came the American Troops were in much disorder those in front who had been driven back by the Enemy falling on those in the Rear increased the Confusion," he explained. "It was impossible to form Troops in such order as to oppose the

12 Anderson, *Recollections*, 45-46. It is interesting to note that nearly all other sources agree the battle ended about five hours earlier than Anderson's recorded time.

13 Hazard, et al., eds., *Archives*, Series 1, vol. 5, 646; Letter, John Armstrong to Horatio Gates, 9 October 1777.

advancing Enemy." Lacey, who would be promoted to brigadier general three months later, concluded that "a general retreat was inevitably necessary to save the American Army from a general rout." The Pennsylvania militia returned to their camps of the previous day.[14]

Lord Stirling's reserve division may well have been the last unit to leave the field, holding open the Germantown Road long enough for Wayne and Sullivan to extract their commands safely. This would have been done under the watchful eye of Washington himself. It was during this last segment of the fighting that Brig. Gen. Francis Nash suffered his mortal wound. "At last we were oblig'd to give way in our turn and retreat," wrote the dejected Henry Knox to his wife two days later. The enemy, continued artillery chief Knox, "followed with caution, and we came off without the loss of a single piece of cannon or any thing else, except one empty ammunition wagon." Although much of the initial retreat was chaotic, panic-ridden, and could fairly be described as a rout, the American officers did a magnificent job of herding their men away from the advancing enemy, eventually calming their nerves while reorganizing them for what lay ahead. The retreating Americans that Peale, Paine, and others encountered were not part of any panic-stricken mob.[15]

The British Pursuit

While the Americans fled back up the roads on which they had arrived, the British organized for the pursuit. Captain Friedrich von Muenchhausen, one of General Howe's aides, was on his way to Philadelphia when the battle began and alerted Lord Charles Cornwallis of the fighting in Germantown. Cornwallis "no sooner heard of the rebels' attack upon us, than he hastened with 2 English and our Linsing Grenadier Battalions to our assistance." Within a short time Cornwallis would be leading the three grenadier battalions to Howe's relief. Civilian Jacob Mordecai remembered hearing the firing in Philadelphia by 8:00 a.m., though the fighting had been going on for more than two hours by that time. "Colonel [Henry] Monckton at the head of the British Grenadiers marched at a half trot," and Mordecai "followed them until they reached the Barracks, whence the Hessian Grenadiers had been just marched out, smoking their pipes & marching at a steady

14 "Memoirs of Lacey," 106.

15 Letter, Henry Knox to Lucy Knox, October 6, 1777; Drake, *Correspondence*, 53.

pace on their way to Germantown. They were soon passed by the British Grenadiers," continued Mordecai, "who took the Fourth Street road & were out of sight long before the Hessians were out of view. These troops, though slow, were invincible in battle & hard to beat."[16]

General Cornwallis rushed reinforcements from Philadelphia to Germantown and beyond, dispatching a relief column composed of the two battalions of British grenadiers and one battalion of Hessian grenadiers. Grenadier Lt. John Peebles of the 42nd Highlanders (2nd Grenadier Battalion) was at battalion quarters in the west end of Philadelphia when Washington's attack got underway. "We were relieved off guard at six that the Battn. Might go down towds. Chester but about that time we hear'd a firing at German Town," he penned in his diary, "which grows very heavy and soon after we got an order to march thither in all haste." Peebles and his comrades arrived at Germantown and initiated a pursuit, though "without getting a shot at them but with our 6 pounders." Lieutenant William Hale of the 45th Regiment of Foot (also with the 2nd Grenadier Battalion) confirmed Peebles's account by recalling that he and his men "were only able to get near enough to exchange a few cannon shot with them." Not everyone from the Philadelphia garrison arrived in time to participate in the fighting, or even to watch the artillery lob rounds at the retreating Americans. "[The] part of the Regiment with which I happened to be cantoned near Philadelphia, did not get up till the action was nearly over," noted the frustrated Lt. Col. William Harcourt of the 16th Light Dragoons.[17]

According to General Howe, "the grenadiers from Philadelphia, who, full of ardour, had run most of the way to German-town, could not arrive in time to join in the action. The country in general was so strongly inclosed and covered with wood, that the dragoons had not any opening to charge, excepting a small party on the right, which behaved most gallantly."[18] Captain William Scott of the 17th Regiment of Foot "saw the british Grenadiers on the road hastening from Philadelphia, fell in their rear; saw a few enemys light dragoons brandishing their swords on the road,

16 Von Muenchhausen, *At Howe's Side*, 38; Journal of the Hessian Grenadier Battalion von Minnigerode, Hessian Documents of the American Revolution, Letter K, 83, Morristown National Historical Park, Morristown, NJ, copies of which are located at the David Library of the American Revolution, Washington Crossing, PA; Mordecai, "Addenda," 163.

17 Journal of the Hessian Grenadier Battalion von Minnigerode, 83; Peebles, *Diary*, 140; Walter Harold Wilkin, *Some British Soldiers in America* (London, 1914), 232; Edward William Harcourt, ed., *The Harcourt Papers*, 13 vols. (Oxford, n.d.), vol. 11, 221.

18 Stockdale, *Register*, vol. 10, 433.

to cover their retreat, saw 16th dragoons advance upon them: expected to see a charge: Light infantry ordered on the right flank to protect the dragoons met no enemy, saw them at a distance going off."[19] Although too late to take part in the fighting, Cornwallis's column relieved Howe's beleaguered veterans and helped conduct the pursuit.

Those units at the center of the British line, which also had rescued Musgrave's 40th Regiment at Cliveden, now pursued Sullivan, Wayne, and Stirling down the Germantown Road before turning right up the Bethlehem Pike. "The Leib Regiment and two English regiments from the 4th brigade pursued them along" the Germantown Road, recorded Wilhelm von Knyphausen's aide, Maj. Carl von Baurmeister.[20] The pursuit was delayed briefly at Chestnut Hill, where Wayne's Pennsylvanians formed a temporary rear guard. When General Howe realized the Americans had paused on Chestnut Hill in order to slow the British, he was determined to smash through and capture the beaten army, something he had failed to do after Brandywine. According to an anonymous British account, Howe "ordered Major-General Grey to advance upon it with the seventeenth, thirty-third, forty-fourth, forty-sixth, and sixty-fourth regiments, directing the other corps to follow as fast as possible to sustain; but the rebels did not think [it] proper to maintain that ground, retiring precipitately upon the approach of this small corps."[21]

On the British left, Lt. Col. Ludwig von Wurmb, commander of the jaegers, pursued Armstrong's Pennsylvania militia down Ridge Road for "three English miles." Other units were dispatched to bolster von Wurmb's jaegers. "The Leib Regiment and the 40th English Regiment were sent ahead to take post along the Reading pike [Ridge Road]. Von Donop's Regiment now set out from Germantown along the above-mentioned road and posted small bodies of troops along it to maintain communications," remembered Major von Baurmeister. "About four English miles from Germantown they encountered an enemy corps, [some Pennsylvania militia] which fired from a woods while retreating and wounded slightly several men of the Leib Regiment." Von Baurmeister concluded

19 Scott, "Memorandum," 294.

20 Von Baurmeister, "Letters," 417.

21 Frank Moore, ed., *Diary of the American Revolution: From Newspapers and Original Documents*, 2 vols. (New York, 1860), vol. 1, 505.

that the "army maintained this disposition for several hours, but after the enemy had completely withdrawn, it moved back into its old encampment."[22]

If Howe had indeed been present to order an attack against Wayne's rear guard, he almost immediately set out east toward the British right, where, together with James Grant, he conducted the pursuit of Greene's column up the Limekiln Pike. The sudden turn of events, coming after his men had been routed from the field so quickly at the beginning of the battle, elated Grant. "The Moment the Rebeles were charged they gave Way, got into confusion & fled as usual," he wrote in an October 20 letter. "They were pressed & pursued as least eight Miles & never were so much cut up since the War commenced." Captain Charles Cochrane of the 4th Regiment of Foot agreed in a letter penned one day earlier. "We soon drove Them at full Gallop nine miles back the Road they came and they did not stop till they regained the place they had come from." Gilbert Purdy of the British Corps of Pioneers echoed Grant when he observed that the "Rebels Retreted As usal."[23]

According to Lt. Frederick Wetherall of the 17th Regiment of Foot, part of Abercrombie's 1st Light Infantry Battalion, General Grant "put himself at the head of the Right of the Army, consisting of the Queens Rangers, Guards, 27th & 28th & advancing up the Franckfort [Limekiln] Road pursued the Enemy." As Wetherall soon discovered, catching the Americans was nearly impossible. "The greatest part of their Rear hid themselves in houses, others throwing away their Arms took [off] across the Country." As Capt. John Andre noted in his journal, Grant, "finding it not possible to come up with them, left Abingdon to his right and marched his Column to White-marsh Church, where he joined Lord Cornwallis's rear."[24] "The Fog which did not clear up 'till after the Enemy had begun to move off, covering their Design, they got the Start which they improv'd so nimbly that it was impossible to get up with any numbers," explained Wetherall. Grant described his pursuit of the Americans in an October 20 letter to the army's adjutant general. "In the pursuit from German Town We took sixty Officers & from four to five Hundred Men," he exaggerated, "but they took such care of their Cannon, & are so well supplied with Horses that We could not catch them & yet I pursued their Left for several Miles as fast as the Men could Trot, frequently left our own Guns

22 Von Baurmeister, "Letters," 417.

23 Letter, Grant to Harvey, October 20, 1777, Grant Papers; Letter, Charles Cochrane to Andrew Steuart, 19 October 1777; Gilbert Purdy diary, original located in the Library & Archives Canada (Ottawa), Item MG23-B14, vol. 1.

24 Wetherall, *Journal*; Andre, *Journal*, 56.

behind in Hopes of getting theirs, but it was impossible. The cursed Yankees," Grant continued, "threw away their Blankets & got off the ground in an amazing manner." Although the Americans occasionally stopped and fired at the pursuing British, "at length they dispersed in the woods," wrote Cpl. Thomas Sullivan of the 49th Regiment of Foot.[25]

The limited number of mounted troops under Howe's command had great difficulty closing with the Americans. The 4th Regiment of Foot's Captain Cochrane praised Washington's men: "For Marching and expedition I give them all possible merit and Their Deportments of Waggons and horses for Guns are so vastly well supply'd that it is hardly possible to catch them."[26]

The Rear Guard Action at Whitemarsh Church

The critical road junction for the Continental retreat was where the Bethlehem Pike, Church Road, and the Skippack Pike came together. Whitemarsh Church presided over the critical intersection, which was some five miles from Cliveden. Except for Armstrong's Pennsylvania militia, every other regiment of Washington's retreating army had to pass through this intersection in order to move west down Skippack Pike. According to Wayne, Adam Stephen ordered him to form the rear guard for the army and hold the invaluable junction. "After we left the field of Battle the Troops, who took the Upper Rout[e] were formed at White Ma[r]sh Church under Genl Stephens," Wayne detailed in a report to Washington later that night. "It was thought Advisable to remain there for some time in Order to Collect the Straglers from the Army. The Enemy made their appearance with a party of Light Horse and from 1500 to 2000 Infantry with two fieldpieces—the Troop[s] upon this were Orderd off." Wayne "took the Liberty to call on Col. [Theodorick] Bland to Cover the Rear with the Horse aided by some of the Infantry,"

> but finding the Enemy Determind to push us hard—I Obtained a field piece from Genl. Stephens—and taking the Advantage of a hill that over looked the Road we marched on—they met with Such a Reception as Induced them to Retire back over the Bridge which they had passed. The time we gained by this Stand favoured the Retreat of [a] Considerable

25 Wetherall, *Journal*; Grant to Harvey, October 20, 1777, Grant Papers; Sullivan, *Journal*, 146.

26 Letter, Charles Cochrane to Andrew Steuart, 19 October 1777.

> Number of our men three or four Hundred of which are now Encamped here and I hope will facilitate the Retreat of Almost all those that were Scattered.[27]

Two days later Wayne provided additional details in a letter to his wife. "Gen'l Howe for a long time could not persuade himself that we had run from Victory—but the fog clearing up he ventured to follow us with his Infantry, Grenadiers and Light Horse with some field pieces," he explained. "I, at this time was in the Rear and finding Mr. Howe Determined to push us hard, drew up in Order of Battle—and waited his Approach—When he Advanced near we gave him a few Cannon shot with some Musketry—which caused him to break and Run with the utmost Confusion—this ended the Action of the day." Lieutenant Colonel Adam Hubley of the 10th Pennsylvania praised Wayne in an October 9 letter to friends. "The Enemy finding our people left them, ralied again & . . . March'd after us, thinking to pick up grat numbers of our men," Hubley wrote, "but Genl. Wayne drew up his brave handful of men & wth our field piece, playing on them made the whole to retreat again into Germantown."[28]

True to form, Adam Stephen continued to display a conspicuous lack of leadership during the retreat. According to the report of the Court of Inquiry into Stephen's conduct at Germantown, he was the senior officer present at Whitemarsh Church, where "a stand might have been made on the retreat . . . and that it was necessary to cover straglers which were coming in." Stephen was ordered to form his men and post artillery to check any enemy advance. Instead, the general "went off under pretence to reconoitre ordering off the Artillery at the same Time and left his Division behind; for want of this necessary Disposition tis supposed many Stragglers fell into the Enemys Hands." Wayne, however, remained with his men, performed as instructed, and oversaw the rear guard.[29]

The Continental Army was far more exhausted than its British and German counterparts, but overtaking and forcing a beaten enemy into another battle has always been one of the hardest of military tasks. The aftermath of Germantown was no exception. Any attempt by Howe to conduct a vigorous pursuit was abandoned after the minor action at Whitemarsh Church. Howe's advance

27 Chase and Lengel, eds., *Papers*, vol. 11, 389-390. The hill Wayne describes is near the intersection of the Bethlehem and Skippack Roads in the vicinity of Whitemarsh Church, seven miles from the battlefield.

28 Stille, *Anthony Wayne*, 96; Letter, Adam Hubley to William Attlee et. al., 9 October 1777.

29 Showman, McCarthy, and Cobb, eds., *Papers*, vol. 2, 189.

elements were unable "to catch up with them, even less possible to take their cannon, which they had taken away before their corps retreated," explained Capt. von Muenchhausen. "Furthermore, the roads were very good and they did not suffer from lack of good horses."[30]

Von Muenchhausen's observations were honest, but true to form, Howe's follow-up was faint-hearted at best. "They pursued us very cautiously," confirmed cavalryman Benjamin Tallmadge. "After our army had passed Chestnut Hill, the enemy halted." Another American remembered in a letter to New York's governor that "our Right Wing retreated in tolerable order & was covered by part of our Cavalry. The Enemy did not pursue for Some time, & when they did they never came near our rear, nor did they advance further than White Marsh Meeting House, but I presume they must have picked up, as is always the Case on a retreat many Stragglers." One of Washington's staffers, Elias Boudinot, noted in a letter to his wife the next day that "the Enemy formed again & followed in our rear . . . now & then throwing in a few Cannon Ball at long Shot."[31]

No writings by Cornwallis regarding Germantown have come to light, though we know he accompanied the pursuit column up the Bethlehem Pike to Whitemarsh Church. When an order to stop the pursuit coursed its way through the ranks, the British returned to Germantown and established pickets. Whether it was Howe or Cornwallis who gave this order is unknown, for no records survive detailing its issuance. The Hessian jaegers returned to the mouth of Wissahickon Creek near Van Deering's Mill. "One of the Jagers discovered that the miller was hiding in the cellar with his family," scribbled Lt. von Feilitzsch in his journal. The officer "went down right away and had much trouble to convince them to come up; their house was riddled with large and small bullets." The British grenadiers, wrote Lieutenant Peebles, "return'd in the Evening to Philada. after a march of 4 or 5 & 30 miles."[32]

30 Von Muenchhausen, *At Howe's Side*, 39.

31 Tallmadge, *Memoir*, 23; *Papers of Clinton*, vol. 2, 370; Letter, Elias Boudinot to his wife Elisha, 5 October 1777.

32 Von Feilitzsch, *Journal*, 99; Peebles, *Diary*, 140.

The American Retreat Comes to End

Wayne's rear guard action, coupled with the lackluster British pursuit, allowed the bulk of Washington's defeated army to retreat safely up the Skippack Pike. Atop Bethel Hill, civilians stood along the pike to catch a glimpse of what was transpiring, since the "sounds of guns could be heard." All they saw were dejected Continentals trudging back to their camps in solemn retreat. "In the afternoon the soldiers were seen coming up the Skippack road in full retreat and were in a demoralized condition," recalled Hance Supplee years later. Supplee, who was nine years old at the time of the battle, said that "[a]t times they would travel very slowly, seeming ready to give out; then a report would come that they were being pursued by the British, and they would again go on a full run. A trooper was riding along up the road with a foot soldier riding behind, both on one horse . . . the hindmost soldier dropped off, but the cavalryman rode on as if he did not notice the loss of his companion. The foot soldier was found to be dead, having been shot through the body." The various roads traversed by the army led to Pennypacker Mills. It was a long and tiresome journey. "I retd wth the rest of our army to w[hi]t[e] march Church where we maid a Sm Halt," remarked light horseman Baylor Hill, and "from there up the Skip pack Road to wences [Wentz's] Tavern then to where Genl. Nash was at Porters Tavern, where I stayed with Majr. Jameson till 12 oClock at night then to a farmers House at the 22 mile stone."[33]

The army eventually reached Pennypacker Mills, where they had camped earlier in the campaign, "much fatigued having march'd all night and all day without haulting or refreshing," wrote General Weedon later that night. James McMichael of the Pennsylvania State Regiment thought he and his comrades arrived "to rest at 9 P.M." As the army trudged into the vicinity of the mill along Perkiomen Creek, Thomas Paine thought the soldiers seemed "only sensible of disappointment, not a defeat; and to be more displeased at their retreating from Germantown, than anxious to get to their rendezvous." The exhausted men dropped to the ground where they had halted in a manner much more haphazard and scattered than during their previous stay at Pennypacker Mills.[34]

33 Brecht, ed., *Record*, 1441; Hill, *Diary*, vol. 1, 79. Porter's Tavern stood on the west side of the Skippack Road (modern Route 73) north of Route 202, but south of St. John's Lutheran Church between the "18 and 19 milestones." McGuire, *Campaign*, vol. 2, 324.

34 Letter, George Weedon to John Page, 4 October 1777; McMichael, "Diary," 153; "Military Operations," 289; Pennypacker, *Mills*, 26.

"The whole army retired the same day about 20 miles to Perkiomen & encamped at Skippack," recalled John Donaldson of the Philadelphia Light Horse. Once there, remembered Joseph Armstrong of the Pennsylvania militia, they "encamped, and remained." If these accounts are accurate, the militiamen stopped for the night about four miles short of the rest of the army.[35]

Adjutant general Timothy Pickering was surprised by the extent of the withdrawal. "After the army were all retreating, I expected they would have returned to their last encampment, about twelve or thirteen miles from the enemy at Germantown," he explained, "but the retreat was continued upwards of twenty miles; so that all those men, who retired so far, this day marched upwards of thirty miles without rest, besides being up all the preceding night without sleep." As incredible as it sounds, some units marched as far as 40 miles, and none fewer than 35, during those 24 hours. Pickering was adamant the retreat should have stopped much earlier than it did. "This step appeared to me not of such pressing necessity. It also gave the enemy an idea that we were greatly galled in the action, and thought it necessary to keep well out of their way," he concluded. "On the other hand, I own, had the enemy come out in full force the next day, and we had stayed at our former encampment, it might have put us to much trouble, and perhaps loss, unless we had of ourselves retired early in the morning; which we might have done, and by that means have collected our men with more ease, and saved them much of the preceding day's fatigue."[36]

Given his prominent staff position, Pickering knew the army was in bad shape, especially when it came to supplies. "Certain it is, that we were by no means in a situation to meet the enemy till after we had made up a new stock of cartridges," he wrote. "But, in actions well disputed, the victors are commonly too sore to push their advantages. The refreshing their men, serving them with ammunition, taking care of and removing the wounded, and burying the dead, will usually find them employ[ed] at least for one day." In scenarios in which the victors can pursue immediately, continued Pickering, it is "their duty and interest to do it; for, if the body of the vanquished escape, great numbers of straggling, fatigued, and wounded

35 RWPF, file S22090; "History of the 1st City Troop."

36 Pickering, *Pickering*, vol. 1, 171. An anecdotal story has Washington stopping for tea during the retreat, but no contemporary accounts verify the story. Samuel Hazard, ed., *The Register of Pennsylvania, Devoted to the Preservation of Facts and Documents, and Every Other Kind of Useful Information—Respecting the State of Pennsylvania, vol. 1, January to July 1828* (Philadelphia, 1828), 291. Once in the area of Pennypacker Mills, Washington established headquarters at the Henry Keely house. Reed, *Campaign*, 242.

men may be taken prisoners, with perhaps a part of the baggage." The Americans had marched an average of 14 miles in the dark on October 3-4, attacked veteran commands around dawn, engaged in combat or maneuvers under fire for upwards of five hours, and then retreated another 20 miles in just over 24 hours. All told, it was a remarkable feat.[37]

Feelings in the Countryside

Civilians in and around Philadelphia tried to make sense of what had just happened. The sounds from the battle were heard far and wide. Thirty miles south, near Brandywine Creek, young Phebe Mendenhall Thomas and her family "heard the guns the day of the battle of Germantown. . . . Father was sure there must be a battle somewhere and he thought maybe after night he could see the light, so he went up to the garret window, our house was very high, but he couldn't see anything," recalled Phebe. "Mother went with him, and then I didn't want to be left behind, so I followed . . . Oh! I was afraid. I was only 7 years old then." About 50 miles north in Bethlehem, according to an anonymous diary entry in the Moravian archives, "[l]oud cannonading was heard in the distance to-day." In his memoir, Elkanah Watson remembered riding into Ephrata, 60 miles to the west, "within sound of the thunder of Washington's artillery at Germantown."[38]

John Ashmead, who was just 12 at the time of the battle, witnessed the aftermath of battle and spent the rest of his life trying to forget it. The lad recalled

> several lots of dead, in parcels of sixes and sevens; none of the wounded remaining. They visited Chew's house—there they saw before the house about thirty dead, whom citizens were already beginning to bury, north-west of the house. They went into the house and all over it—saw blood in every room—noticed where a six pounder, which had come in at the front window, had gone through four partitions, and then out at the back of the house. . . . The same persons saw some six or seven bodies of soldiers, partially interred, back of the

37 Pickering, *Pickering*, vol. 1, 171-172.

38 Quoted in McGuire, *Campaign*, vol. 2, 103-104. The website McGuire cites as the source for this information is no longer accessible. Jordan, "Bethlehem," 74; Elkanah Watson, *Men and Times of the Revolution; or, Memoirs of Elkanah Watson, Including Journals of Travels in Europe and America, from 1777 to 1842*, Winslow C. Watson, ed. (New York, 1856), 31.

Methodist meeting-lane; ground was heaped on them just where and as they fell. Their feet were partly uncovered.[39]

The day after the battle, Pastor Henry Muhlenberg dealt with Washington's stragglers moving past his home in Trappe. "From early in the morning until noon the soldiers who marched off from here on October 2 came back again in troops and singly with their wagons to occupy their former places here. They were tired, hungry, and thirsty," observed the pastor. "They will consume all that is left. It was reported that they were only to reassemble here. In fact, they moved off in a side direction during the afternoon." Late that night, the Muhlenbergs were "awakened by loud knocking at the door. Before I could kindle light our womenfolk called out from upstairs and asked what was wanted. Answer: There are four of us on horseback, one of us sick, and we want lodging. Widow Z[immerman] settled the matter with them amicably and they rode on. In these times and circumstances it is dangerous to let a stranger in at night—if he does not force his way in."[40]

The Aftermath of Battle

That night, with the Americans long gone and his own army going into camp, William Howe sat down with his staff for a late evening meal. Delighted with how the day turned out, but cognizant of the reality of war, Howe offered his aide, Capt. Friedrich von Muenchhausen, an English commission. "[D]ue to the losses this day," Howe suggested, "there would be a very good opportunity for advancement." The Hessian declined the offer, wanting instead "to wait to find out whether General von Jungkenn, in Cassel, who has taken good care of me up to now, will find a company for me. This I would rather have then a major's patent in English service." Within a few days Howe moved his headquarters from Stenton to the home of Philadelphia-based merchant David Deshler in Germantown.[41]

The village of Germantown had hosted the battle without a say in the matter and paid the price for that dubious honor. Destruction was visible as far as the eye

39 Watson, *Annals*, vol. 2, 49-50. At the turn of the twentieth century, a mass grave was found south of the Chew House when Johnson Street was being graded. The owner of the house at that time, Mary Johnson Brown Chew, had the remains reburied at the corner of Johnson and Morton Streets. McGuire, *Germantown*, 87.

40 Muhlenberg, *Journals*, vol. 3, 82-83.

41 Von Muenchhausen, *At Howe's Side*, 39.

could see, in all directions, and the smell of death and ashes filled nostrils. The once-stout fences that had interfered with organized lines of battle had been ripped apart or knocked to the ground. Manicured fields and orchards, churned by thousands of feet and gouged by musket balls and cannon fire, lay in ruins. The amber buckwheat, where the British light infantry had been surprised and slaughtered below Church Lane, had been trampled and ruined. Blood stains were visible on trees, fence posts, rocks, and the sides of houses. Cliveden's grounds were strewn with dead Continentals, and American artillery fire had permanently damaged the house's stone walls.[42]

Many citizens ventured out from Philadelphia to visit the war-torn village in order to "satisfie their Curiosity," explained John Miller in his journal. Robert Morton noted that the Chew house "was exceedingly damaged by the Balls on the outside." Elizabeth Drinker heard a report that 18 Americans were lying dead "in the lane from the Road to Chews House." Other homes sustained damage. A Ms. Miller was upstairs in her home "when a Cannon Ball passed thro' a Window very near her."[43]

British headquarters, meanwhile, seethed with anger at the locals. According to civilian Robert Morton, Maj. Nesbitt Balfour, one of Howe's aides,

> is very much enraged with the people around Germantown for not giving them intelligence of the advancing of Washington's Army, and that he should not be surprised if Gen'l Howe was to order the country for 12 miles round Germantown to be destroyed, as the People would not run any risqué to give them intelligence when they were fighting to preserve the liberties and properties of the peaceable inhabitants.[44]

Wilhelm von Knyphausen confirmed this anger by reporting the arrest of several locals "who, during the attack had shown signs of their secret rebel tendencies . . . and all inhabitants were ordered to hand over all arms in their possession within a specified time. Everyone found with arms contrarily retained

42 McGuire, *Campaign*, vol. 2, 126.

43 John Miller Journal, Joseph Reed Papers, New York Historical Society, microfilm copy located at the David Library of the American Revolution, Washington Crossing, PA, Film 266, Reel 2; Morton, "Diary," 15; Drinker, *Diary*, vol. 1, 239.

44 Morton, "Diary," 15.

after the expiration of this time limit," he continued, "was to be treated as a rebel. It was also asserted that…they had shot at the Royal troops from several houses."[45]

* * *

A couple of days after the battle, Thomas Paine had the good fortune to sit down for breakfast with George Washington and listen to the general's comments on the engagement. Fortunately, Paine recalled the discussion in a letter to Benjamin Franklin in May 1778.Washington, he began, "was at the same loss, with every other, to account for the accidents of the day. I remember his expressing his surprise that at the time he supposed everything secure, and was about giving orders for the army to proceed down to Philadelphia, that he saw most unexpectedly a part (I think) of the artillery hastily retreating," remembered the pamphleteer. "This partial retreat was I believe misunderstood, and soon followed by others. The fog was frequently very thick, the troops young, and unused to breaking and rallying, and our men rendered suspicious to each other, many of them being in red. A new army, once disordered," he continued, "is difficult to manage, and the attempt dangerous. To this may be added a prudence in not putting matters to too hazardous a trial."[46]

It took days for the survivors to regain their strength after the trials of Germantown; it would take them a lifetime to unravel the battle's meaning. Lieutenant James McMichael of the Pennsylvania State Regiment "had previously undergone many fatigues, but never any that so much overdone me as this," he confessed. "Had it not been for the fear of being taken prisoner, I should have remained on the road all night. I had marched in twenty-four hours 45 miles, and in that time fought four hours, during which we advanced so furiously thro' buckwheat fields, that it was almost an unspeakable fatigue." Ensign Jonathan Todd of the 7th Connecticut also found it difficult to explain the hardships he had faced. "You, none of you, know the hardships of a Soldiers life—with more the shock it Give[s] to Humane Nature to hear such an Incessant fire & see such Large Columns of smoke & fire & see Garments Rolld in Blood." The exhausted soldiers took out their frustrations on the locals. Farmers near Pennypacker Mills "were not Very well Pleased Becaus they Burnt Every Rail and Took Every Bit of Hay Straw

45 Letter, Wilhelm von Knyphausen to the Landgrave, October 17, 1777, 86.

46 "Military Operations," 289.

grain Chickens And Every thing they Lay hand on," wrote James Pennepacker in 1874.[47]

Casualties

George Washington reported 152 men killed, 521 wounded, and "upwards" of 400 captured, including 54 officers.[48] Unfortunately, no official casualty reports for individual regiments, brigades, or divisions have been found. On average, each Continental brigade lost just under 100 men; the militia suffered negligible casualties as they were not as heavily engaged.

No reports, letters, or diaries have been found detailing the casualties suffered by William Smallwood's Maryland and New Jersey militia. While many histories of the battle imply his militia played little or no role in the battle, a sufficient number of credible primary sources (including pension records) firmly establish that the command was engaged with the enemy, performed at least moderately well, and suffered an undetermined, if modest, number of casualties. The two large Continental columns that fought on Smallwood's right, however, were not so lucky.

Nathanael Greene's column of Virginia, Connecticut, and Pennsylvania troops, which had made the deepest advance into the enemy position around Germantown, suffered about 370 casualties. The largest single regimental loss in the entire army was incurred by Col. George Matthew's 9th Virginia of William Russell's brigade, which was captured nearly to a man during the closing stage of the battle.

John Sullivan's column of Maryland, Pennsylvania, Delaware, and Canadian troops also lost some 370 men. One of the casualties was Maryland brigade commander John Stone, who suffered a painful ankle wound in the fields west of the Germantown Road. Maryland congressman Samuel Chase recalled that Stone "was attended by "Dr Craigg, Cochran & Wallace, his Brother is with him, and several Gentlemen from Philada have offered him their Houses, but he is in too much pain to bear Removal at this Time." Stone underwent a grueling ordeal but

47 McMichael, "Diary," 153; Letter, Jonathan Todd to his Father, October 6, 1777; Letter, James Pennepacker to unknown recipient, 1 November 1874, located in the Pennypacker Mills archives, Schwenksville, PA.

48 A later accounting listed 152 killed, 500 wounded, and 438 captured for the Americans. Howard H. Peckham, ed., *The Toll of Independence: Engagements & Battle Casualties of the American Revolution* (Chicago, 1974), 42.

survived to return to command. Other high ranking casualties included Maj. Uriah Forrest of the 3rd Maryland, who was struck in the thigh by a ball that shattered his femur. Surgeons amputated his leg. Captain Benjamin Brookes of the same regiment "received a Ball through his Mouth which split his Tongue & went out at the back of his Jaw-Bone," an exceedingly painful wound that bothered him for the rest of his life.[49]

The two aides Sullivan lost, Col. John White and Maj. Edward Sherburne, were buried near the army's camp at Pennypacker Mills. According to the *New York Packet* on October 23, White was interred "with the military honours justly due to the sentiment he entertained of liberty, and attended by the friends of freedom in mourning, his remains were committed to the dusty mansions of earth. . . . The bloody plain of Birmingham, by Brandywine, witnessed his coolness and intrepidity; and on the long contended for hills of Germantown, where the division he fought in acquired unfading laurels, his bravery exposed him to that wound which calls upon every passing lover of liberty to shed a tear on his grave."[50]

The same paper observed that Major Sherburne

> was in the severest of the fire for near two hours before he received the fatal wound which forced him from the field; and during the whole time behaved with such uncommon firmness, as the love of freedom only can inspire.... He endured with great constancy the pains occasioned by his wound, and departed this life with a heroic firmness, which well witnessed the satisfaction he felt in suffering for his much injured country. His remains were interred on the 7th inst. with all those military honours which his bravery merited. His funeral was attended by a great number of officers, who all seemed to mourn their own and their country's loss in the truly brave and heroic youth, whose acts of kindness had acquired the love, and his bravery the esteem of all who knew him."

According to an oral history recorded in 1907, Sherburne in his uniform, complete with epaulettes, was buried alongside the main road on the Pennypacker property.[51]

Many of the American wounded suffered mightily on the long journey back to their camps. Captain Thomas Holland of the Delaware regiment (Sullivan's

49 Browne, ed., *Archives*, vol. 16, 396.

50 *New York Packet*, October 23, 1777.

51 Ibid.; Oral history recorded from Abraham Pennypacker on October 14, 1907, a copy of which is located in the Pennypacker Mills archives.

The grave of Brig. Gen. Francis Nash in Towamencin Township, PA.

Photo by author

division) was severely wounded during the attack on Maitland's British 2nd Light Infantry Battalion and the subsequent advance into the fields west of the Germantown Road. At some point during the retreat, Holland was left in a house along the Skippack Pike. Later his comrade, Capt. Enoch Anderson, discussed Holland's plight with Lt. Col. Charles Pope along the banks of Perkiomen Creek. "It was agreed between us that I [Anderson] should go the next day on Colonel Pope's horse, to give our friend Holland what aid and comfort we could," wrote Anderson. Around noon the next day, Anderson borrowed Pope's horse and cantered back along the pike to where Holland was laid up. "In the evening, I saw Holland—he was lying in ruins," lamented Anderson. Desiring to provide what little succor he could for his friend, the captain rode farther east "into Whitemarsh to obtain wine, tea, and sugar." He returned after dark to Holland, provided him with the goods, and "took a long and affectionate farewell of my old friend. I never saw him more." Holland died of his wounds eight days later.[52]

Lord Stirling's reserve division of New Jersey and North Carolina regiments lost about 100 men to all causes. The majority of these casualties were suffered by the 1st and 3rd New Jersey regiments during their assault against the Chew House. The division holds the sad distinction of losing the highest ranking officer to fall in the entire American army: Brig. Gen. Francis Nash. Doctors had "little hopes of

52 Anderson, *Recollections*, 46-47.

saving Genl Nashes life, whose Thigh is Dislocated by a Cannon Ball, Several of our best Colonels are wounded & other good officers of inferior rank, and proportion slain," lamented George Weedon in a letter four days later.[53]

Armstrong's Pennsylvania militia, on the far right of the American line, made what can charitably be called a half-hearted effort to break through the enemy position, or at least to pin the British down and force them to divert their reserves from elsewhere. Armstrong admitted to losing no more than 20 men in the effort, though these numbers may be too low.[54]

The Americans carried away as many wounded as possible, "which was evident from the great amount of blood we could see along the entire road on which we pursued them," observed Capt. von Muechhausen. Churches, houses, and taverns spread out over 25 square miles housed the injured. The dead, who lay in and around Germantown and scattered across the countryside, had to be buried. Churchyards throughout the region served as cemeteries for many of the unfortunate soldiers who fell.[55]

Caring for the wounded, as it was after every major engagement, was a monumental task. In the aftermath of the fighting, Washington's casualties were treated at Evansburg, Trappe, Pennypacker Mills, Faulkner's Swamp, Limerick, Skippack, and other locations before being moved farther north and west when they were able to stand the journey. Men were deposited in homes and churches all along the line of retreat. Pennsylvania militiaman William Hutchinson happened upon a hospital, where "the wounded were dressing and where the necessary surgical operations were performing and there beheld a most horrid sight," he noted in his pension application several decades later. "The floor was covered with human blood; amputated arms and legs lay in different places in appalling array, the mournful memorials of an unfortunate and fatal battle, which indeed it truly was."

53 Letter, George Weedon to John Page, 8 October 1777. Francis Nash succumbed to his gruesome wound on October 8. The general had been carried on a litter to Porter's Tavern on Skippack Pike, then to the DeHaven house in Skippack Township, and finally was brought to the Adam Gotwals home on Forty Foot Road near the army's new camp in Towamencin Township. Washington had sent his personal physician, Dr. James Craik, in an attempt to save the general, to no avail. The Gotwals home was a little over a mile southwest of the Sumneytown Pike intersection. While the campaign continued, Francis Nash was buried at 10:00 a.m. on October 9 at Towamencin Mennonite Meeting House with full military honors. "All Officers whose Circumstances will admit of it, will attend and pay respect to a brave Man who died in defence of his Country," ordered Washington. Chase and Lengel, eds., *Papers*, vol. 11, 452.

54 Hazard, ed., *Pennsylvania Archives*, Series 1, vol. 5, 646.

55 Von Muenchhausen, *At Howe's Side*, 39.

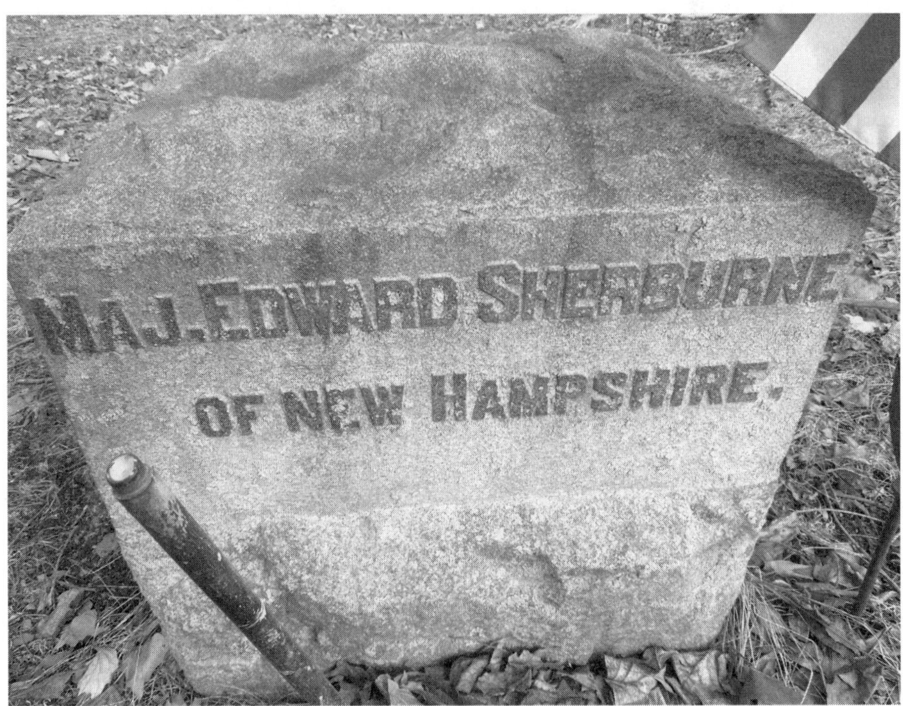

The grave of Maj. Edward Sherburne on the grounds of Pennypacker Mills Historic Site.

Photo by author

Civilian James Hutchinson helped tend to the suffering soldiers. "I am so engaged in Dressing wounded men," he wrote the day after the battle, "that I have scarce time to look around me."[56]

Prominent clergyman Henry Melchior Muhlenberg was concerned over the fate of the Lutheran churches in the region. "The church in Reading has been turned into a hospital and is filled with wounded," he noted, and "the church in the village of Lebanon serves as a prison for captured Hessian soldiers."[57]

56 Gillett, *Medical Department*, 81. As they had after Brandywine, New Hanover Lutheran Church and Falkner's Swamp Reformed Church housed the wounded. Others were moved farther west to Reading. Today, graves of those who succumbed to their wounds may be found at Saint James Church in Evansburg as well as at numerous other churches in the region. Dann, *Revolution Remembered*, 151; Letter, James Hutchinson to James Pemberton, October 5, 1777, James Hutchinson Papers, American Philosophical Society, Philadelphia.

57 Muhlenberg, *Journals*, vol. 3, 82-83.

Many injured Americans reached Bethlehem, the same place most of the casualties had been sent after Brandywine, three days after the battle. Within another three weeks, more than 400 injured men were crammed into the large Single Brethren's House, more than the presiding physicians felt they could care for. While many of the wounded were forwarded to Easton, the seriously injured found care in tents around Bethlehem. Reading, which was already a major supply depot for the American army and a prison camp for many captured Hessians, had to find space for the new wounded. In addition to private homes, the Lutheran Church, the German Reformed Church, and the Quaker Meetinghouse also were used as hospitals, and a large proportion of the casualties eventually made it to the religious community of Ephrata. One interesting story to come out of the treatment of the Germantown wounded centered on Anna Maria Lane, whose husband had enlisted in the army in 1776. Anna apparently dressed as a man, served in the army alongside her husband, and was wounded at Germantown. Historian Holly Mayer summarized Anna Maria's remarkable story: "Her sex may have been revealed when she received treatment for her injury, but, if so, it did not result in banishment from the army. . . . The exact nature of her status remains vague: if she officially enlisted in the army, then her story is that of a soldier; if she did not, then her exploits illustrate the diversity of a female follower's experiences."[58]

By all accounts, the casualties suffered by the Continental Army could have been much worse. The numbers were lower than most expected given the length and severity of the battle. "[R]eturns have since come on and [I] am Doubly happy to find they are very far short of the most favourable number I could suppose from my own Observation, they not exceeding 800 in the whole," wrote the relieved brigadier George Weedon. "And tho' the interprize miscarried, it was well worth the undertaking," he continued, before happily noting, "as from their own [British] Accounts, by Prisoners, & Deserters, their light infantry (the flower of their Army) was cut to pieces."[59]

* * *

58 Jordan, "Bethlehem," 75; Gillett, *Medical Department*, 82; Frantz and Pencak, eds., *Beyond Philadelphia*, 77-78; Holly A. Mayer, *Belonging to the Army: Camp Followers and Community During the American Revolution* (Columbia, SC, 1996), 144-145.

59 Letter, George Weedon to John Page, 8 October 1777.

William Howe's army suffered 80 killed, 426 wounded, and 14 missing among the British troops, and another 24 wounded in the Hessian ranks. Unlike the casualties suffered at Brandywine three weeks earlier, the Germantown losses were incurred within a concentrated area in just four hours of fighting. Howe's casualties at Brandywine had been spread across ten square miles and were incurred over the course of one very long day.[60]

The hardest hit units in the British army were those that had been assaulted first—the two battalions of light infantry under Maitland and Abercromby. Combined, the battalions lost 120 men, which, when added to the casualties they had suffered at Brandywine and other smaller engagements, severely impacted the combat effectiveness of the two elite units. Lieutenant Martin Hunter of the British light infantry lamented the wounding of his friend, Lt. Richard St. George. "It is very extraordinary that I don't get a clink [shot], for I am certain I go as much in the way of it as anybody," the young lieutenant had shared with Hunter earlier in the campaign. By the time the war ended, St. George no longer wondered about his extraordinary luck. He was shot through the heel at Brandywine and took a "shocking wound in the head" at Germantown. If a fellow soldier had not carried him off the field, believed Hunter, "St George must certainly have been taken prisoner." The wound was so severe that it required an extraordinarily gruesome medical procedure. "When he was trepanned, I [Hunter] was the only person he knew, and he desired me to remain with him while the operation was performed. This was the first person I ever saw trepanned, and I am certain it will be the last," promised Hunter. "He bore the whole operation without saying one word. . . . He recovered of the wound to the astonishment of everybody, but had always very bad health afterwards, and was obliged to go the south of France every winter. He wore a little silver plate over the place where he was trepanned."[61]

In its effort to stabilize the collapsing front and defeat the American attackers, James Grant's wing of the army also suffered heavy losses. The 4th, 5th, 49th, and 55th regiments lost 154 killed and wounded, with the 4th and 5th Regiments suffering the highest casualties. As was to be expected, the units fighting against American militia emerged almost completely unscathed. The Queen's Rangers and the Brigade of Guards suffered a mere four wounded against Smallwood's

60 *Remembrancer*, 418.

61 Hunter, *Journal*, 22. Trepanning required boring into the skull and removing part of the bone.

Maryland and New Jersey militia, while von Wurmb's Hessian jaegers lost but 10 men against Armstrong's Pennsylvania militia.[62]

In their drive to push the Americans out of Germantown, Charles Grey's and James Agnew's brigades lost a combined 180 men, including Agnew himself. The mortally wounded brigadier was carried to the John Wister house and laid on the floor in the west parlor. Legend has it that a stain still visible on the floor is from his blood.[63] Stirn's Hessians, who advanced in support of Grey and Agnew, lost just 14 killed and wounded. During the pursuit of the retreating Americans, the 16th Light Dragoons suffered a single man killed. In its support of Maitland's collapsing 2nd Light Infantry Battalion and subsequent defense of the Chew house, Lieutenant Colonel Musgrave's 40th Regiment lost 26 men to all causes.[64]

The British utilized a host of structures as hospitals. At the Wyck House, dark blotches on the floorboards may well be blood stains from operations performed after the battle. It is said that the British soldiers who died there were buried in an area west of the carriage house, where a garden is presently located. The Upper and Lower Burial Grounds in Germantown also served as cemeteries for the battle's dead.[65]

Within days, the British evacuated many of their wounded to Philadelphia. "They brought the wounded back in the number of about sixty, in wagons and put them in the still unfinished Presbyterian Meeting Building in Spruce Street, below 3d and 4th Streets, the City Hospital proper and the Pennsylvania Institution," remembered Royal Navy surgeon Henry Carter. Civilian Jacob Mordecai confirmed Carter's account. "Wagon loads of the wounded of both armies were brought in & lodged in different meeting houses & churches, which were converted into hospitals, more especially in the southern part of the city. Pits were dug in front of some of those meeting houses, where the dead were promiscuously thrown," he continued, and "legs & arms were seen protruding after heavy showers

62 *Remembrancer*, 418.

63 Cotter, Roberts, and Parrington, *Buried Past*, 326, 339.

64 *Remembrancer*, 418.

65 Many of the wounded initially were housed at the Reuben Haines house or at a field hospital located on a hill at the foot of town, today the location of the Loudon Mansion. Lambdin, "Battle of Germantown," 395. The Upper Burial Ground is located near the intersection of Germantown Avenue and Washington Lane, and the Lower Burial Ground is at the intersection of Germantown Avenue and Logan Street.

of rain."[66] Jaeger Capt. Johann Ewald, who rode into Philadelphia to visit the wounded, "found these unfortunate battle victims still lying on the straw, almost without any care. There was still a lack of necessary medicines and bandages, which were requisitioned at first from the city and now awaited from the fleet."[67]

Civilian Robert Morton went "to see the wounded soldiers now in this City, some at the Seceeder meeting house, some at the Presbyterian meeting house in Pine Street, some at the Play House, and some, and those the most, at the Penns'a Hospital, where I see an Englishman's leg and an American's arm cut off." Morton wrote that the "American troops are mostly at 2 new houses in Fourth Street near to the Presbyterian meeting house, amt'g to about 30 and not so much attended to as might be. The British have about 300 wounded in this city." Two days after the battle, a British officer arrived at Elizabeth Drinker's home to "ask if we could take in a Sick or Wounded Captain; I put him off by saying that as my Husband was from me, I should be pleas'd if he could provide some other convenient place, he hop'd no offence, and departed . . . two of the Presbytearan Meeting Houses, are made Hospitals of, for the Wounded Soliders, of which there are a great Number." Some of Mrs. Drinker's acquaintances went in the rain "to the Play House &c. with a Jugg of Wine-Whey and a Tea-Kittle of Coffee, for the Wounded Men."[68]

Prisoners

Caring for the wounded consumed a tremendous amount of resources and manpower, but the British had the additional burden of dealing with American prisoners; they gathered hundreds of Washington's men from the surrounding countryside and marched them into captivity. Lieutenant James Morris of the 5th Connecticut, McDougall's brigade, recalled his rather incredible ordeal in a postwar memoir. Few Revolution-era sources so rich in detail on this subject survive, which makes it especially worthwhile to quote from at length. "Samuel Stannard my waiter [servant] a strong athletic man, carried my blanket and provisions, with a canteen of Whiskey," began Morris. "He had made his escape, and was not taken. Of course I was left without refreshment from break of day in the morning thro'

66 Unpublished diary quote from Dr. Henry Yates Carter of the Royal Navy, reproduced in Robert J. Hunter, "The Origin of the Philadelphia General Hospital," *PMHB* (Philadelphia, 1933), vol. 57, 49; Mordecai, "Addenda," 163.

67 Ewald, *Diary*, 96.

68 Morton, "Diary," 15-16; Drinker, *Diary*, vol. 1, 240-241.

the whole day. Thus I was driven back to Germantown after performing a march of about forty miles from the Evening before at 6 O clock. I reached Germantown a prisoner of War about Sunset fatigued and much exhausted. I was the last officer taken with about twenty men."[69]

After a short rest, Morris and his 20 men were gathered together with other prisoners for the night. "The Evening of the 4th of October was very Cool," he continued,

> [and] I was put under a quarter Guard with the few men with me, in an open field around a Small fire. No provision was made for the Prisoners, the men with me had a little food in their knapsacks, but I had none. A little after Sundown, I was Shivering with the cold and I asked the Sergeant of the Guard if I might see the Commander of the Regiment. He informed me that he quartered in such a house, about 20 rods distant. The Sergeant who was manly and sympathetic waited on me to the house and informed the Commander that there was an American Officer a prisoner at the door who wanted to See him. The Colo. Said he would See him after he had done supper. Accordingly I sat down in the Stoop before the door and after sitting about fifteen minutes the Colo. came out and sat down in the Stoop with me.
>
> He asked me many questions respecting my motives for going into the War and rising up in rebellion against my lawful Sovereign and answered him pleasantly and as evasively as I could consistently with decency. He asked me what I wanted. I told him I was in a suffering condition, I had no blanket or any covering to Shield me from the cold. I wished for Liberty to sleep in the house, and that I Stood in need of some refreshment. The Col. ordered his Servants to get me some victuals and Said I might go into the room where they were. I went into the room, the Servants very politely Spread a table, Set on some good old Spirits and a broiled Chicken, well cooked, with excellent bread and other food of the best kind. The servants Sat off in the room and waited on me in the best manner. This was really the Sweetest meal of Victuals that I ever ate![70]
>
> When I had done supper I asked the Sergeant who had conducted me there, what the Colo. Said respecting my lodging in the house. The Sergeant replyd. that the Colo. told him that I was not on parole, and that he was not authorized to grant a parole of honour, and that I must go out and be with the guard. I then asked the Sergeant if I could be furnished with a blanket for that night. The Soldiers who were waiters to Colo., immediately brought me a

69 Ryan, ed., *Salute to Courage*, 104.

70 Ibid.

> large and clean rose Blanket and said it should be for my use that night. I accordingly went out into the field and lay down among the Soldiers who were prisoners, wrapped myself in the blanket, kept my hat on my head and Slept Sweetly thro the night. Before I lay down the Sergeant informed me that he observed I had a Watch in my pocket and that I had silver knee-buckles if I would give them to his care he would return them to me in the morning, as the soldiers of the Guard would probably rob me of them when I was asleep. I accordingly committed them to his Safe keeping, who very honourably returnd them to me, the next morning.[71]

Most of the men in Colonel Matthew's 9th Virginia, surrounded and captured *en masse*, were "lodged in the church at the market house. The faces of the prisoners and their guards were well blackened about their mouths with gunpowder, in biting off their cartridges," editorialized John Watson in his 1830 *Annals of Philadelphia.* The Americans, observed civilian Jacob Mordecai, were "principally lodged in the New Jail under the direction of Captain [William] Cunningham, the British Provost Marshal, of notorious & execrable memory."[72]

* * *

Both army commanders doled out congratulations to their men. Washington offered "his thanks, to the General and other officers and men concerned in yesterday's attack." The Continental Congress passed a resolution thanking "Washington, for his wise and well concerted attack upon the enemy's army near Germantown . . . and to the officers and soldiers of the army, for their brave exertions on that occasion; Congress being well satisfied that the best designs and boldest efforts may sometimes fail by unforeseen incidents, trusting that, on future occasions, the valour and virtue of the army will, by the blessing of Heaven, be crowned with complete and deserved success."[73]

General Howe's proclamation mimicked Washington's: "Thanks may be given to the General Officers, Commanding Officers of Corps, and to all the Officers

71 Ibid., 104-105.

72 Watson, *Annals*, vol. 2, 48; Mordecai, "Addenda," 163. Among the prisoners was Maj. William Williams, who later took "every possible pains to clear myself of that infamous report, respecting my conduct at Germantown." Letter, William Williams to Anthony Wayne, 18 August 1778, Sol Feinstone Collection, David Library of the American Revolution, Washington Crossing, PA, Item No. 1679.

73 Chase and Lengel, eds., *Papers*, vol. 11, 391; Ford, ed., *Journals*, vol. 9, 785.

and Soldiers that were Yesterday engaged, for their alertness in getting under Arms, and good Services in beating back and effectually routing the Enemy." It also singled out one officer and unit in particular: "[The commanding general] desires his particular Thanks to Lieut.-Col. Musgrave for his well-judged and gallant Defence of the House he took possession of with the 40th Regiment." William Howe had little doubt that Musgrave's decision may well have saved the day at Germantown.[74]

* * *

Something else was saved from the wreckage at Germantown, though what it was and how it happened could never have been predicted. As the Chevalier de Pontgibaud, a Frenchman with Washington's army, recalled, "We were at table at head-quarters—that is to say in the mill, which was comfortable enough—when a fine sporting dog, which was evidently lost, came to ask for some dinner. On its collar were the words, *General Howe*. It was the British commander's dog. It was sent back under a flag of truce, and General Howe replied by a warm letter of thanks to this act of courtesy on the part of his enemy, our General." According to Washington's papers, two days after the battle the Virginian returned Howe's dog with the following dispatch: "General Washington's compliments to General Howe. He does himself the pleasure to return him a dog, which accidentally fell into his hands, and by the inscription on the Collar appears to belong to General Howe."[75]

The battle was over, the dead had been buried, and the wounded were being attended to. The major pieces on the chessboard of war in and around Philadelphia were back in place. With the Americans no longer a direct threat, William Howe turned his eyes to the Delaware River, which was still closed to the ships he needed to support his army during the coming winter.

74 Stephen Kemble, *Journals of Lieut.-Col. Stephen Kemble, 1773-1789* (New York, 1883), 510.

75 Chevalier de Pontgibaud, *A French Volunteer of the War of Independence*, Robert G. Douglas, ed. (New York, 1898), 65-66; Fitzpatrick, *Writings*, vol. 9, 315. The French account implies the dog wandered into camp while the army was wintering at Valley Forge, but Washington's papers make it clear that Washington wrote to Howe on October 6 about returning the dog.

Chapter 17

The Philadelphia Campaign Continues

October-December, 1777

"I found it adviseable to remove to Philadelphia, to expedite the reduction of Mud Island, which proved to be more difficult than was at first supposed."[1]

— Lt. Gen. William Howe, British army commander—April 29, 1779

The day after the Battle of Germantown dawned warm and dry. Elements of the Continental Army trickled into camps spread across the countryside "in troops and singly with their wagons." The men were "tired, hungry and thirsty. They will consume all that is left," complained Rev. Henry Muhlenberg, the leader of Lutheranism in America,who lived in Trappe. Every man in Washington's army needed rest, but for many that luxury remained out of reach. "Small parties of Horse are . . . to be sent up the different Roads above the Present encampment of the Army as much as 10 Miles in order to stop all Soldiers and turn them back to the Army," stated general orders prepared on October 5. Officers read the circular to their men. "The Commander in Chief returns his thanks, to the Generals and other officers and men concerned in yesterday's attack . . . for the spirit and bravery they manifested in driving the enemy

1 *Narrative*, 28.

from field to field. The enemy are not proof against a vigorous attack, and may be put to flight when boldly pushed. This they will remember."[2]

Much needed reinforcements were about to join the beleaguered army. The 1,200-man Rhode Island Brigade under Brig. Gen. James Varnum, which had been detached from the northern army in the Hudson Highlands near Peekskill, New York, on September 29, had reached Coryell's Ferry on the Delaware River en route to reinforce Washington. The approach of Varnum's Continentals heartened the Virginian, but news that Daniel Morgan's rifle corps would not be returning anytime soon—if at all—dampened his mood. Washington's light infantry brigade had been disbanded in late September, and his militia was incapable of effective scouting. Morgan's men were desperately needed in Pennsylvania. Northern army commander Horatio Gates, however, proved reluctant to return them and so informed Washington by letter dated October 5. After describing the proximity of the armies and the likelihood of a significant battle, Gates added, "In this Situation, Your Excellency would not wish me to part with the Corps the Army of General Burgoyne are most Afraid of. From the best Intelligence he has not more than Three weeks provision in Store. . ." As disappointing as it was, Washington knew Gates was right.[3]

While Washington saw to the needs of his army, those of his soldiers unfortunate enough to fall into British hands at Germantown found themselves in crowded conditions in Philadelphia; they had been jammed into the Walnut Street Jail and the State House (Independence Hall) across the street. The latter served as a guardhouse, officer's prison, and hospital. In order to keep Washington apprised of British activities, Thomas Mifflin, the army's quartermaster general, had established a spy ring managed by Maj. John Clark of Nathanael Greene's staff. Both Howe and Washington often allowed citizens to pass into the countryside to obtain flour. While this was certainly a humane gesture, it also provided Washington with valuable information about conditions in Philadelphia.[4]

* * *

2 Muhlenberg, *Journals*, vol. 3, 83; Chase and Lengel, eds., *Papers*, vol. 11, 391-392.

3 Chase and Lengel, eds., *Papers*, vol. 11, 391-392.

4 McGuire, *Campaign*, vol. 2, 134; Nagy, *Spies*, 63; Reed, *Campaign*, 210. Assisting Clark were Col. Elias Boudinot, Capt. Charles Craig, Capt. Allen McLane, Pvt. William Dunwoody, and Cadwalader Jones.

Whatever the conditions there, Philadelphia was now firmly in the grasp of the British. Washington no longer was in a position to recapture it or drive the British away from the colonial capital. His strategy turned instead to starving Howe out of the city. Nearly everything Howe's army needed—including military and medical supplies and food—was stored in the holds of British ships stuck downriver from Philadelphia near Chester, Pennsylvania. The Royal navy still was unable to navigate the Delaware. Several rows of *chevaux-de-frise* prevented the ships from ascending the river, as did the American forts Mercer (on the New Jersey side) and Mifflin (on the Pennsylvania shore on Mud Island). A third fortification at Billingsport had been captured prior to Germantown but was abandoned almost immediately by the British. Given his precarious position, Howe turned his attention back to the war along the river.[5]

The British spent the two weeks after the battle preparing to attack the Delaware River forts, while Washington passed the days inching closer to Philadelphia. With the threat of Billingsport's guns eliminated, the Royal Navy began the tedious process of removing the line of *chevaux-de-frise* blocking the shipping lane in the river west of the former American stronghold. It would not be long until the British fleet could threaten Fort Mifflin, which was precisely what Howe had in mind. Forts Mifflin and Mercer were crucial components of Washington's strategy to tighten the logistical noose around Philadelphia. If the Americans could maintain and protect the *chevaux-de-frise* in the river, the British supply ships would never make it to the city. Doing so required the close cooperation of American land and naval forces, which was akin to asking for the impossible. Washington also spent the next two months harassing the British supply lines in Chester County, usually with militia forces.

The Continental Army, meanwhile, had no choice but to remain north of Philadelphia. Its position there prevented Howe from launching excursions against American supply depots in the Pennsylvania backcountry. The only way this was possible was if the naval forces and river forts kept Howe's British fleet below the *chevaux-de-frise.*

5 No primary source has come to light to explain why the British abandoned Billingsport. Samuel Smith (*Fight for the Delaware*, 11) claims the British force was ordered back to Pennsylvania when a foraging party was harassed by New Jersey militia that some thought might overwhelm the isolated garrison. Another secondary source implies the two British regiments had orders to return to the main army once they destroyed the American works at Billingsport. The entire operation is something of a mystery, considering the British reoccupied the position in late October. Reed, *Campaign*, 41-42.

Work in the flooded, muddy terrain around Fort Mifflin was exceedingly laborious for the British. Building gun positions to assist the navy in opening the Delaware was vitally important for Howe, but completing the line of defensive redoubts north of Philadelphia was also one of his key objectives. Until this was done, he wasn't comfortable removing the garrison from Germantown. With the Schuylkill and Delaware rivers on the east, south, and west sides of the city, a finished line of redoubts to the north would make Philadelphia a veritable island.

At the same time, a different type of conflict was unfolding in the American encampment, where several senior officers faced rebuke for their actions in the field. On October 15, a Court of Inquiry, which had been convened to examine General Wayne's conduct at Paoli, exonerated him for any malfeasance. The Pennsylvanian was still angry about the testimony provided by some of his subordinates and demanded a full court martial proceeding. John Sullivan, William Maxwell, and Adam Stephen would face similar proceedings.[6]

William Maxwell was drunk and woefully incompetent at both Brandywine and the Battle of the Clouds while in command of the Light Infantry Brigade—at least that was the accusation leveled against him by Lt. Col. William Heth of the 3rd Virginia. (Heth, who served under Maxwell in those two engagements, also had the misfortune to be under Adam Stephen's command at Germantown). Maxwell denied Heth's charges and appeared at Nathanael Greene's headquarters on October 15 for the Court of Inquiry, which soon turned into a full court martial. That same day, Washington received news of Horatio Gates's stunning October 7 victory at Bemis Heights in the Second Battle of Saratoga. On October 16, the Court of Inquiry into John Sullivan's actions on Staten Island and Brandywine announced its findings, and cleared him on all charges.[7]

October 18 was memorable for Washington's army, for on that day it received a circular announcing the shocking victory over Burgoyne at Saratoga in upstate New York:

> The General has his happiness completed relative to the successes of our northern Army. On the 14th instant, General Burgoyne, and his whole Army, surrendered themselves

6 Wayne had requested the court martial two days earlier, and it too would clear him of any wrongdoing. Chase and Lengel, eds., *Papers*, vol. 11, 482. For a full account of the Wayne court martial, see McGuire, *Paoli*. For more on Stephen's court martial and his reaction to it, see Appendix B herein.

7 Ward, *Maxwell*, 80-82. Maxwell was acquitted on November 4; Chase and Lengel, eds., *Papers*, vol. 11, 528. See Harris, *Brandywine*, 415-427, for more on Sullivan's court martial.

> prisoners of war—Let every face brighten, and every heart expand with grateful Joy and praise to the supreme disposer of all events, who has granted us this signal success—The Chaplains of the army are to prepare short discourses, suited to the joyful occasion to deliver to their several corps and brigades at 5 O'clock this afternoon—immediately after which, *Thirteen* pieces of cannon are to be discharged at the park of artillery, to be followed by a *feu-de-joy* with blank cartridges, or powder, by every brigade and corps of the army, beginning on the right of the front line, and running to the left of it, and then instantly beginning on the left of the 2nd line, and running on to the right of it where it is to end. The Major General of the day [Adam Stephen] will superintend and regulate the *feu-de-joy*.[8]

"We had . . . a feu de joy through our whole army on the Occasion," exclaimed David Griffith, chaplain of Heth's 3rd Virginia. "Burgoyne was reduced to the most deplorable Situation—His Troops were deserting fast, and they were almost Starved for want of Provisions. They had hardly any thing to Subsist on but Boiled Corn for Several Days before they surrendered." With Burgoyne no longer a threat, Washington recalled most of the northern army to Pennsylvania. "When my last to you was dated I know not," wrote an exhausted Washington to his brother, "for truely I can say, that my whole time is so much engross'd that I have scarce a moment (but sleeping ones) for relaxation, or to endulge myself in writing to a friend."[9]

While the Americans celebrated, William Howe fumed. The attenuated British supply line from Chester to Philadelphia limited his operations and added further stress on the frustrated army commander, who lost his patience with the slow progress along the Delaware. Philadelphia had to be secured and the river opened if his army was going to maintain itself there for the winter.

A change in strategy signaled the end of the occupation of Germantown. In order to free up troops, on October 19 Howe withdrew his units from the battle-scarred village and concentrated his army in Philadelphia. He waited to do

8 Chase and Lengel, eds., *Papers*, vol. 11, 541. A *feu-de-joy* is celebratory gunfire described as a "running fire of guns." Soldiers fire into the air sequentially in rapid succession, creating a cascading sound from the blank cartridges.

9 Letter, David Griffith to Hannah Griffith, October 19, 1777, David Griffith Letters, Virginia Historical Society, Richmond. That same day was one to forget as far as Capt. Peter Priest was concerned. According to Col. Martin Pickett of the Virginia militia, Priest "got Slightly wounded by Accident from one our own guns which went of[f] Struck the Lower part of his testikles I think but skin deep & went through one side of his Peanus which I hope he will soon get well of without any damage to his reputation." Letter, Martin Pickett to William Edmonds, October 18, 1777, Martin Pickett Letters, Virginia Historical Society, Richmond; Chase and Lengel, eds., *Papers*, vol. 11, 551.

this until the line of redoubts north and west of the city were nearly completed so that fewer troops would be needed to block Washington's access to Philadelphia. Howe needed some of the troops to assault the river forts, but occupying Germantown was now pointless. He intended to winter in Philadelphia, and he wanted his men safely settled in before the arrival of cold weather. He also intended to supervise operations along the river in person. His subordinates there had failed him, and time was of the essence. "I found it adviseable to remove to Philadelphia, to expedite the reduction of Mud-Island [Fort Mifflin], which proved to be more difficult than was at first supposed," he later testified to Parliament. "To this end the possession of Red-Bank [Fort Mercer] on the East side of the Delaware engaged my attention. . . . It has been asserted, that an early possession of Red-Bank must have immediately followed by the reduction of Mud-Island, to which I in some measure agree."[10]

Howe's preoccupation with the river operations consumed the next four weeks, which gave Washington the time he needed to rebuild and resupply his army. Colonel Carl von Donop, the commander of the Hessian grenadiers and a distinguished veteran of the Seven Years' War, offered to capture Fort Mercer. Howe, who was more than anxious to see the matter done, gave his blessing. Colonel Donop and some 2,000 Hessians crossed the Delaware on October 22, moved inland, surrounded Mercer, and demanded its immediate surrender. Inside were Col. Christopher Greene and most of his 1st Rhode Island Regiment, as well as Col. Israel Angell's 2nd Rhode Island Regiment, about 500 men in total. The Americans, of course, had no intention of capitulating so easily, even with the threat of no quarter. The fort had been strengthened and ammunition was plentiful. Three attempts to carry the works failed; some 400 Hessians were killed and wounded in the assaults, against 14 dead and 27 injured for the Americans. Among the fallen was the fatally injured Donop, who lingered for three days before dying on October 25. Aware that he was mortally wounded, Donop is said to have confided to another Hessian officer, "It is finishing a noble career early; but I die the victim of my ambition, and of the avarice of my sovereign." To Howe's dismay, Washington maintained his grip on the Delaware River.[11]

Unable to seize the fort on the Delaware's eastern bank, an angry Howe refocused his attention on Fort Mifflin. The poorly supplied 400-man American garrison in that post, commanded by Maj. Simeon Thayer, already had suffered

10 Reed, *Campaign*, 264; Jackson, *British Army*, 61; *Narrative*, 28-29.

11 Chastellux, *Travels*, 160.

through miserable conditions and a fitful artillery fire from British batteries and Royal Navy ships. Now Howe ordered a heavy and sustained bombardment, which began on November 10 and continued for five days. Unable to remain inside the battered fort, and having suffered some 250 killed and wounded, the exhausted Americans abandoned Mifflin on the night of November 15 and escaped by boat to Fort Mercer. The British occupied Fort Mifflin the next day. With Mifflin in enemy hands, Christopher Greene was unable to maintain his position at Mercer and had no choice but to abandon that position as well; he issued the necessary orders on November 19. General Howe had finally gained control of the Delaware River, and with it access to the Philadelphia docks for his brother's supply ships.[12]

* * *

For the next month, the campaign continued with minor actions rather than significant events like the fall of the river forts. Having done all he could that season, Washington moved his army into winter quarters at Valley Forge on December 19. He had neither prevented the fall of the capital nor managed to wrest it back, but his primary strategy all along was to keep his command intact, defeat Howe if possible, and make sure the Continental Army lived to fight another day. In this he was successful, and his army and officers were now battle-tested veterans. With the assistance of French infantry and naval forces, the Americans would go on to win the war four long years later on the Virginia Peninsula at Yorktown.

The war took what many consider its decisive turn that October when General Burgoyne's army, marching south into New York from Canada, was trapped and forced to surrender by Horatio Gates's northern army at Saratoga. That news, coupled with the fighting at Germantown, convinced the French that the American cause was not only viable but winnable, and they entered an alliance that provided significant military aid to the colonists.

Howe justified his failure to attempt to support Burgoyne by pointing out the strategic importance and psychological impact of capturing Philadelphia. The inordinate time it took to do so, much of which was due to the circuitous route Howe had chosen in order to accomplish it, guaranteed there would be no concentration with Burgoyne that summer or fall. The important American supply

12 McGuire, *Campaign*, vol. 2, 219.

centers at Reading, Lancaster, and York remained intact. Worst of all for the British, the promised uprising by Pennsylvania Loyalists never came to fruition.

After all the effort and bloodshed, Howe concluded he could not win the war as it was being waged and tendered his resignation soon after Germantown, with the explanation that his policies were not receiving sufficient support to warrant his remaining in command. London finally accepted Howe's resignation the following April. He returned to England and was replaced by Lt. Gen. Sir Henry Clinton.

The focus of British policy shifted thereafter to the Southern colonies, which required that Philadelphia be abandoned in the early summer of 1778. Clinton marched his army across New Jersey, and eventually back to New York City. The march included the bitterly contested but inconclusive combat at Monmouth on June 28, where Washington's refreshed and retrained army stood toe-to-toe against the finest soldiers the Crown could field.

The dream of American independence was on its way to becoming reality.

Epilogue

Germantown Considered

"Our cause is just, our men are becoming more warlike, the blood already spilt will raise a spirit of obstinacy & revenge which will supply the place in some measure of discipline."[1]

— Charles Carroll, October 12, 1777

The Battle of Brandywine on September 11, 1777 was the largest battle of both the Philadelphia Campaign and the Revolutionary War and garners most of the attention from historians and readers. Germantown, however, fought three weeks later on October 4, stands out in its own right. It was one of the larger engagements of the Revolution and like Brandywine ended in a sharp tactical American defeat. More importantly, it was the first time George Washington launched an assault against the main British army in North America. He nearly won.

1 Smith, et al., eds., *Letters*, vol. 8, 113.

Contemporary American Views

Many of the Americans who recorded their opinions of the battle remained optimistic about the colonial cause even though some found fault with how the battle was managed.

Nathanael Greene, who commanded one of Washington's assault columns, was blamed for not doing enough at Germantown. Officers involved in the Conway Cabal, including Thomas Mifflin, attacked Greene in an effort to undermine him, and by doing so elevate Horatio Gates. "General Mifflin and his creatures have been endeavouring too wound my reputation," was how Greene put the conspiracy in a letter to Alexander McDougall, one of his brigade commanders during the battle, on January 25, 1778. "There has been some insinuation to my prejudice respecting the Germantown battle," he alleged. "You had the best opportunity to see the greatest part of my conduct that day, and to know my reasons more fully than anyone. . . . I wish to know wither I shewed a want of activity in carrying the troops into action, a want of judgment in the disposition, or a want of spirit in the action or retreat," he asked. "If you think me blameable in any instances, be so good to point them out." McDougall replied, offering his full support for his commander. "I did not see the least indication of your want of activity or spirit in carrying on the Troops that day but the contrary," he asserted. "Those of your and Genl Stephens Divisions marched so brisk or ran to the charge that they were some minutes out of sight of my Brigade, although we formed and marched immediately behind your division." The allegation continued to nag at Greene, who five years later pleaded his case with Light Horse Harry Lee: "At Germaintown, I was evidently degraced, altho I think if ever I merited any thing it was for my exertions on that day." Conversely, any lethargy on Greene's part passed unnoticed by his enemies. Lieutenant Henry Stirke of the 10th Regiment of Foot's light company attested to Greene's success when he wrote, "the 1st battln of Light Infantry was entirely Surrounded, their Wigwams, & provision Waggon in possession of the Enemy."[2]

Another of Greene's brigade commanders, George Weedon, found reason to be optimistic in the wake of the defeat. "[T]the British Army is by these Engagements diminishing fast," he observed, while "ours are reinforcing . . . we

2 Dennis M. Conrad, Roger N. Parks, and Martha J. King, eds., *The Papers of General Nathanael Greene, 3 December 1781-6 April 1782*, 13 vols. (Chapel Hill, NC, 1998), vol. 10, 379; Showman, McCarthy, and Cobb, eds., *Papers*, vol. 2, 260-261, 283; Stirke, "Journal," 172.

shall be stronger than the first day we opened the Campaign." Weedon was philosophical about the loss of the battle. "The chance of war [is] so uncertain, that when victory was in our hands, we had not Grace to keep it, Indeed the misfortunes of that Day was owing to the most horrid Fogg I ever saw," he complained. "That with the smoak together rendered it impossible to Distinguish our men from the Enemy at a greater Distance than sixty yards, and many favourable advantages were lost, from not being certain who were friends & who Foes, And From the Different Divisions and Brigades not being able by that means, to Co-operate with each other." So much had hinged on the battle's outcome, and the rebels were as close to victory as they had ever been. "[T]he Grand cause was in my opinion in one Quarter of an hour of being finally settled that Day, to the eternal honor of America," Weedon asserted. "They [the British] confess themselves had we Continued the attack fifteen minutes longer, a general retreat over the Schuylkill would have taken place, to Chester in Delaware where their shipping lay, it was ordered by Genl Howe just as we gave way."[3]

Colonel Charles Webb, the commander of the 2nd Connecticut Regiment, also part of Greene's column, remained confident. "Our men are not dejected nor disheartened," he explained, and "vengeance burns in every breast, and we shall undoubtedly very soon be at them again." At least two officers from Stephen's division recorded their thoughts on the battle. Lieutenant Colonel William Heth of the 3rd Virginia had nothing good to say about Stephen, but cheerfully echoed the optimism coursing through the army. "Tho we gave away a complete victory, we have learned this valuable truth: [we can] beat them by vigorous exertion, and that we are far superior [in] point of swiftness. We are in high spirits," he confirmed. "Every action [gives] our troops fresh vigor and a greater opinion of their own strength. Another bout or two must make their [the British's] situation very disagreeable." Captain John Marshall of the 15th Virginia expressed similar thoughts later in life: "Had his [Washington's] troops possessed the advantages given by experience, had every division performed precisely the part allotted to it; there is yet much reason to believe that his most sanguine hopes would have been realized."[4]

3 Letter, George Weedon to John Page, 4 October 1777; Letter, George Weedon to John Page, 8 October 1777.

4 "Contemporary Account," 331; Commager and Morris, eds., *Spirit of Seventy-six*, 629; Marshall, *Life of Washington*, vol. 3, 179.

Pennsylvanian Anthony Wayne, who marched in John Sullivan's column, had faced his own difficulties following Paoli, but had nothing but praise for Washington. "You are now in my Humble Opinion in as good if not a better Situation than you were before this Action," he explained. "[Y]our Men are convinced that the Enemy may be drove, and Altho' we fell back yet our people have gained Confidence—and have Raised some Doubts in the Minds of the Enemy which will facilitate their total Defeat the Next Tryal ... which I wish to see brought to Issue the soonest Possible. Upon the Whole," he wrote, "it was a Glorious day." Wayne concluded with a word of caution: "I don't yet despair; if our Worthy General will but follow his own good Judgement, without listening too much to some Counsel." Wayne, in his unique way, was warning Washington not to depend upon artilleryman Henry Knox as much as he had before the fatal hour at Cliveden.[5]

"Our army is in higher spirits than ever . . . being convinced from the first officer to the soldier, that our quitting the field must be ascribed to other causes than the force of the enemy: for even they acknowledged that we fled from victory," wrote a defiant Maj. Henry Miller of the 1st Pennsylvania, part of Wayne's division. "We hope to meet them soon again, and, with the assistance of Providence, to restore to our suffering citizens their possessions and homes." Miller went on to describe the confusion many of the Americans seem to have experienced during the battle. The British had time to rally during the attack on Cliveden, he explained, which "prevented a complete victory, and obliged us to leave the ground to a conquered foe, with the artillery, &c., which had first fallen into our hands: they having stabbed their horses." Once the enemy rallied, Miller continued, the British advanced "in force upon them that, owing to the mist they mistook part of our men for the Enemy, which made them think the Enemy was on their flanks when in fact they were only in front."[6]

Pennsylvania militia commander John Armstrong referenced the hand of God when writing to Horatio Gates five days after the battle: "The triumphing Tories again shook at the center, the drooping spirits of the Whigs a little relieved—thus God supports our otherwise sinking spirits." Like many others, Armstrong blamed the fog for the defeat. "So that a victory, a glorious victory fought for and eight tenths won, was shamefully but mysteriously lost, for to this moment no one man

5 Chase and Lengel, eds., *Papers*, vol. 11, 389; Stille, *Anthony Wayne*, 96-97; Letter, Anthony Wayne to Horatio Gates, 21 November 1777.

6 "Memoir of Miller," 427.

can or at least will give any good reason for the flight," he explained. "The conjectures are these: The morning was foggy and so far unfavourable. It's said ours took the manuvres of part of our own people for large reinforcements of the enemy and thereby took fright at themselves or at one another."[7]

Light Horse Harry Lee of the light dragoons wrote extensively on the battle as his life progressed. Victory, or as he described it, "[t]his precious fruit is only to be plucked by the cooperating skill and courage of the whole body. Unfortunate as was the issue of the battle at Germantown," he elaborated, "it manifested the unsubdued, though broken spirit, of the American army; and taught the enemy to expect renewal of combat, whenever adequacy of force or fitness of opportunity should authorize repetition of battle." The sharp combat at Germantown, Lee concluded, "gave, too, animation to the country at large, exciting in congress, and in the people, invigorated zeal in the great cause in which they were engaged."[8]

As proud as Lee was, he was not averse to leveling criticism. Ultimately, he penned in his postwar memoir, the defeat "must be ascribed to deeper causes: to the yet imperfect discipline of the American army; to the broken spirit of the troops, who, from day to day, and month to month, had been subjected to the most trying and strength-wasting privations, through the improvidence of the tribe of generals; and to the complication of the plan of assault: a complication said to have been unavoidable."[9] Lee summarized his feelings in a letter to Patrick Henry on October 8, 1777. "The morning was so foggy, which with the state of the air keeping down the smoke of the cannon &c, effectually prevented our people from knowing their success, occasioned delay," he concluded, "and gave the enemy time to rally and return to the charge."[10]

Major Benjamin Tallmadge, also of the light dragoons, blamed the loss of the battle on the decision to assault Cliveden: "The situation of our troops was uncomfortable, their ardor abated, and the enemy obtained time to rally." Lieutenant Samuel Shaw of Proctor's Artillery felt the same way. The time just before the assault on the Chew house "was the critical moment; had things gone on in the same train five minutes longer, we, perhaps, at this time should have been in

7 Letter, John Armstrong to Horatio Gates, October 9, 1777.

8 Lee, *Memoirs*, vol. 1, 29.

9 Ibid.

10 James Curtis Ballagh, ed., *The Letters of Richard Henry Lee, 1762-1778*, 2 vols. (New York, 1911), vol. 1, 325.

quiet possession of Philadelphia."[11] Shaw also blamed divine intervention for the loss. "I know of no other reasons which can be assigned for our leaving the ground, unless we conclude that it was not the will of Heaven we should succeed," he wrote in his journal. "This, and this only," he continued,

> seems to be a consolation for the loss of victory, even after it was in our grasp, and is at the same time so comfortable a persuasion that I shall always cherish it. . . . For my own part, I am so fully convinced of the justice of the cause in which we are contending, and that Providence, in its own good time, will succeed and bless it, that, were I to see twelve of the United States overrun by our cruel invaders, I should still believe the thirteenth would not only save itself, but also work the deliverance of the others. This, however, is not the case. From the bravery, and, I may add, the discipline, of our troops, much may be expected. In the late engagement they did their duty, maintaining the action upwards of two hours and a half, teaching themselves and the world this useful truth, founded on experience, that *British troops* are proof against neither a surprise nor a vigorous attack.[12]

Except for Washington, who had the final say in the matter, Henry Knox contributed more to the American defeat than any other individual. He never acknowledged his role in the decision to assault Cliveden; his writings focus on other aspects of the fighting at Georgetown. "This is the first attack made during the war by the American troops on the main body of the enemy; and had it not been [for] the unlucky circumstance of the fog," he asserted, "Philadelphia would probably have been in our hands. Our men are in the highest spirits, and ardently desire another trial." He continued, "I know of no ill consequences that can follow the late action; on the contrary, we have gained considerable experience, and our army have a certain proof that the British troops are vulnerable." Like others, Knox referenced his faith in the army's future. "Our troops are in prodigious Spirits at being able to drive nearly the whole collective of the enemy so far—God who orders all things for the best gave us not the final Victory [perhaps] he will next time." Knox also blamed the fog in a letter to Artemas Ward three days after the battle. "In this unusual fog it was impossible to know how to support, or what part to push," he claimed truthfully. "At this instant, the enemy again rallied and obliged part of our troops to retire; and after a smart resistance, the retreat of the line became general." Knox never commented on the role he played in convincing

11 Tallmadge, *Memoir*, 23; Shaw, *Journals*, 41.

12 Shaw, *Journals*, 41.

Washington to stop the general assault and focus on taking the Chew house. "With the enemies taking possession of some stone buildings in German Town is to be ascribed the loss of the victory which we had been in possession of for above two hours," was how Knox presented the matter to his wife on October 6, 1777.[13]

Commissary of Musters Joseph Ward, one of Washington's staff officers, also referenced faith: "Altho' we may have let golden opportunities pass unimproved, and Howe might perhaps have been routed in a fortnight after his landing, yet we must hold fast the good doctrine, *That Providence overrules all things for the best end.* I very much apprehend that the *toryfied City of Philadelphia, and this lethargic State*, wants more scourging to open their eyes to see and their *hearts to feel the Curse of British power* and to realize the worth of Freedom." Ward remained confident of the army's long-term prospects. "Although we did not . . . complete our design, yet it reflects honor upon the General and the Army, and I am confident that great advantages will arise to our Country," he wrote. "The spirit of the Army is higher . . . and firmer than before; our Troops find that the boasted discipline skill and courage of the Enemy, will all give way, when charged *home* with that spirit and valour which Americans can exert." Ward added, "the enemy had too much time to recover from their surprize and disorder, and our troops were exposed to get into disorder and to other fatal accidents."[14]

Charles Cotesworth Pinckney, who had attached himself to Washington's staff, also attributed "the loss . . . principally to the thickness of the Fog," which he thought did not allow the men "to see immediately when the enemy retreated; by which means our Soldiers continued firing & expending their ammunition when the Enemy were gone." Many of the men showed Pinckney their cartouche boxes "without a single Cartridge in them; & I knew before they went into action, that each man was supplied with 60 rounds of Cartridge."[15]

Adjutant general Timothy Pickering had been in the middle of the decision as to whether the army should stop to assault the Chew house. He later wrote extensively about Germantown and criticized nearly every aspect of the battle. "[O]ur stop here [Cliveden] gave the enemy time to recollect themselves and get reinforced, and eventually to oblige us to retreat," he complained to his journal,

13 Drake, *Correspondence*, 52-53; Letter, Henry Knox to Lucy Knox, October 6, 1777.

14 Letter, Joseph Ward to John Adams, 9 October 1777, *Papers of John Adams*, Robert J. Taylor, et al., eds., 18 vols. (Cambridge, MA, 1983), vol. 5, 304; Letter, Joseph Ward to James Bowdoin, 12 November 1777, 410.

15 Letter, Charles Cotesworth Pinckney to Henry Johnson, November 14, 1820, 204.

"for this period was all suspense, and the brigades not well collected and formed in the mean time. Indeed, this would have been, perhaps, impracticable, for the troops were greatly broken and scattered, great numbers having left their corps to help off the wounded, others being broken by other means, or by carelessness; for officers and men got much separated from each other, neither (in numerous instances) knowing where to find their own."[16]

"During this time [the attack on Cliveden] there was a cessation of firing, but soon the enemy advanced, and our troops gave way on all sides, and retired with precipitation," he lamented. "This retreat surprised every body (all supposing victory was nearly secured in our favor); but I think the facts before mentioned will tolerably well account for that event." Pickering placed most of the blame on the fog, powder smoke, and lack of a breeze of any kind. The air moved, he continued,

> very little, but what there was bringing the smoke and fog in our faces . . . and the body of smoke from the firing, absolutely prevented our seeing the enemy till they had advanced close upon us. This also prevented the two wings, and even the different brigades of the same wing, from seeing each other and cooperating in the best manner; nay, I am persuaded they sometimes fired on each other, particularly at Chew's house, where the left wing supposed the cannon-balls fired by the right at the house came from the enemy. In a word, our disaster was imputed chiefly to the fog and the smoke, which, from the stillness of the air, remained a long time, hanging low and undissipated. But, on the other hand, it must be remembered, that the fog blinded the enemy as well as ourselves, though it certainly injured us most.[17]

Pickering added that several other factors contributed to the defeat. Germantown "abounded with small enclosures, strongly fenced with rails. These, in some instances, were attempted to be pulled down, and in others the troops mounted over them. If a fence is to be thrown down," he continued, "the best way is for the whole rank to press it two or three times backwards and forwards, and then, seizing the under rails, to lift the posts out of the ground and throw the whole down together; but if the fence be strongly set, the best way is to get over it." Apparently this issue had been discussed by the American officers. "Some, indeed, suggest it as better to make openings in it here and there, that the troops may march through in columns, and then form again in line; but I cannot agree with them. If a

16 Pickering, *Pickering*, vol. 1, 168.

17 Ibid., 169-170.

battalion of brigade marches up regularly to a fence, they may get over in a tenth part of the time that it would take them to go through in columns and form again, especially if the troops are not very expert at maneuvering. In such grounds the officers ought to be on foot, otherwise they will of necessity be separated from, and many times fall behind, their men."[18]

"This battle taught me the absurdity of helping off wounded men during the heat of the action," Pickering warned. "By doing it you save a few mangled bodies, but most probably lose a victory. By such numbers going off with the wounded, the ranks are thinned and broken, their arms dropped and lost, and few of them ever return to the charge." Helping wounded comrades off the field, he added, "furnishes the timorous with an admirable pretext for deserting their duty. Frequently from two to five and six men were seen helping off one wounded man; whose death, too, from the badness of his wounds, was probably inevitable and not far off. By these losses, added to the killed and wounded, your ranks must be so broken and your strength so greatly reduced," he concluded, "that it can never be a matter of surprise if victory declares against you."[19]

To prevent the practice, Pickering suggested, "it ought . . . to be an established rule, that where a man falls, there he should lie, unless his own strength and the assistance of the drummers and fifers could remove him from the field. This maxim, to some, may appear destitute of humanity; but the contrary practice is certainly the greatest evil. Rout and ruin are the most probable consequences. Nor is there much tenderness in hoisting a man with a broken limb into a wagon, and then driving over rough ways, where every jar tortures his inmost soul; and, if no limb be broken, he will probably get off the ground alone." Pickering found but one exception to this rule. "The only case which can warrant . . . bringing off wounded men during the action is when you maintain the fight retreating. Another capital defect, in many instances, in this action was, the separation of the officers and their men; by which means to rally and form them again, when broken, was a thing impracticable."[20]

Disagreements arose in the years following the battle as to whether the British were surprised by the attack that morning. Pickering had no doubt about the

18 Ibid., 170-171.

19 Ibid., 170.

20 Ibid.

answer and offered his analysis in an 1826 letter to historian Jared Sparks. "The term here applied to these advanced corps of the enemy," he began,

> that they were *'forced* from their ground,' shows that they were *in arms*, and *resisted* the assailants; and the previous brush with the picket, a guard always posted in advance on purpose to give notice of an enemy's approach, roused 'the light infantry and other troops,' who had time enough to take their arms and form for action. They retreated, of necessity, before the greatly superior force of the whole right wing of our army. But the 'leaving of their baggage' authorizes the inference that they had no knowledge of the march of the American army, until the firing in the engagement with the picket guard gave the alarm. If then these advanced corps of the enemy were not, in the strict sense of the word *surprised*, that is, 'caught napping,' unprepared for action, much less could the main body, posted in the centre of Germantown, two miles farther off, have been *surprised*. This distance gave them ample time to prepare for action, in any manner which the attack of their enemy should require.[21]

Major General William Heath, who served in the northern theater, thought the battle did Washington proud, and stunned the enemy as well. Although "this attempt was not crowned with victory," Heath believed that "it caused the British to have a more reverential opinion of Gen. Washington, whom they now found dared to attack their whole army, even in a chosen position of their own." As he did throughout the war, Washington himself chose not to highlight in public the mistakes made by his high ranking officers; he instead focused on the positive aspects of the battle. Germantown, he began, "has serv'd to convince our people that when they make an Attack, they can confuse and Rout even the Flower of the British Army with the greatest Ease and that they are not that Invincible Body of Men which many suppose them to be. Upon the whole," the commander continued, "it may be said the day was rather unfortunate, than injurious. We sustained no material loss of Men and brought off all our Artillery, except One piece which was dismounted; The Enemy are nothing the better by the event, and our Troops, who are not in the least dispirited by it, have gained what All young Troops gain by being in Actions."[22]

Washington provided additional thoughts on the battle in his subsequent report to John Hancock, but did not mention the mistakes made at Cliveden. "The

21 Letter, Timothy Pickering to Jared Sparks, August 23, 1826, 426.

22 Chernow, *Washington*, 311; Chase and Lengel, eds., *Papers*, vol. 11, 394, 447.

Morning was extremely foggy, which prevented our improving the advantages we gained so well, as we should otherwise have done," he began. "This circumstance,"

> by concealing from us the true situation of the Enemy, obliged us to act with more caution and less expedition than we could have wished, and gave the Enemy time to recover from the effects of our first impression; and what was still more unfortunate, it served to keep our different parties in ignorance of each Others movements, and hindered their acting in concert. It also occasioned them to mistake One another for the Enemy, which, I believe, more than any thing else contributed to the misfortune which ensued. In the midst of the most promising appearances—when every thing gave the most flattering hopes of victory, the Troops began suddenly to retreat; and intirely left the Field in spite of every effort that could be made to rally them.[23]

Washington elaborated further on his misfortune in a letter to his brother on October 18. "After we had driven the Enemy a Mile or two, after they were in the utmost confusion, and flying before us in most places, after we were upon the point (as it appeared to every body) of grasping a compleat Victory, our own Troops took fright & fled with precipitation and disorder. How to act for this I know not," he confessed, "unless, as I before observd, the Fog represented their own Friends to them for a Reinforcement of the Enemy as we attacked in different Quarters at the same time, & were about closing the Wings of our Army when this happened." Washington also blamed the wasting of ammunition. "One thing indeed contributed not a little to our Misfortune, and that was want of Ammunition on the right wing [Sullivan's command], which began the Ingagement, and in the course of two hours and 40 Minutes which it lasted, had (many of them) expended the 40 Rounds which they took into the Field."[24]

The Marquis de Chastellux, who arrived in America in 1780, spoke with veterans of the battle and toured the field. He then opined that two mistakes had been made: "Losing time in ranging in line of battle General Sullivan's column, instead of marching directly to the camp of the enemy," and "wasting time in attacking the stone house." As the French officer saw it, the first error "will appear very pardonable to those who have seen the American troops such as they then were; they had no instruction and were so ill disciplined that they could neither

23 Chase and Lengel, eds., *Papers*, vol. 11, 394.

24 Ibid., 551.

preserve good order in marching in a column, nor deploy when circumstances required it." The second mistake, Chastellux continued

> may be justified by the hope they always had of getting possession of the stone house, the importance of which was measured by obstinacy of the enemy in defending it. It is certain that two better measures might have been adopted: the first, to pursue the march without worrying about the musketry fire, which could always have been sufficiently slackened by detaching a few men to fire at the windows; and the second, that of leaving the village on the left, to enter it again three hundred paces further on, where it would then have been sufficient to take possession of another house opposite the one occupied by the enemy: even though this house were not quite so high as the other, the fire from it would have been sufficient to contain the English and ensure a retreat in case of necessity.[25]

Numerous politicians commented on the battle and campaign. Maryland congressman Charles Carroll remained as optimistic as many of Washington's officers. "Our cause is just, our men are becoming more warlike, the blood already spilt will raise a spirit of obstinacy & revenge which will supply the place in some measure of discipline. We have many resources, if we have sense enough to [use] them; then let us hope we shall make use of them, and that we shall conquer in the end." Connecticut congressman Eliphet Dyer insisted that before the fog—which he labeled "this Unfortunate mistake"—"[s]natched [victory] out of our hands the prospect was full, of our Army in a very few hours again entering Philadelphia but once more disappointed." John Adams firmly believed that the heavy attack at Germantown helped negotiations with the French and wrote precisely that to fellow congressman James Lovell. "General Gates was the ablest negotiator you ever had in Europe; and next to him, General Washington's attack upon the enemy at Germantown. I do not know, indeed, whether this last affair had not more influence upon the European mind than that of Saratoga," he posited. "Although the attempt was unsuccessful, the military gentlemen in Europe considered it as the most decisive proof that America would finally succeed."[26]

John's cousin Samuel Adams was less inclined to blame meteorological conditions than he was to place the onus for the loss on "a miserable Set of General Officers." Unlike Pickering, Adams did not blame the rank and file for any aspect

25 Chastellux, *Travels*, 140-141.

26 Smith, et al., eds., *Letters*, vol. 8, 76, 113; Francis Wharton, ed., *Revolutionary Diplomatic Correspondence of the United States*, 6 vols. (Washington, DC, 1889), vol. 2, 664.

of the defeat: "That our Men are brave, Brandy Wine & German-town can witness. Let us then give them officers worthy of them, and Heaven will prosper our righteous Cause." North Carolina congressman Thomas Burke had aimed his barbs at the army's leadership after Brandywine, and he was just as critical of the high-ranking officers in the wake of Germantown as he was the men in the ranks. "Upon the whole it appears that our miscarriage sprung from the same source, want of abilities in our Superior officers, and want of order and discipline, in our army," he wrote Gov. Richard Caswell of North Carolina. "This, Sir, is an Evil of the most dangerous tendency, & to remedy it has long been the object of my thoughts and endeavours." Thomas Jefferson succinctly described his thoughts on Washington to Walter Jones, a Virginia politician, in 1814: "Certainly no General ever planned his battles more judiciously. But if deranged during the course of the action, if any member of his plan was dislocated by sudden circumstances, he was slow in readjustment. The consequence was, that he often failed in the field."[27]

The British View

There was plenty of blame to go around—even within the victorious army. William Howe had made no effort to put his Germantown camp in a defensive posture in the days leading up to the battle. The matter of his deployment interested Parliament, before which he testified on the matter. "I beg leave to inform the Committee, that my first position at German-Town was taken to cover Philadelphia, during the operations carrying on against Mud-Island [Fort Mifflin], and was therefore more extended than it otherwise would have been," he explained. "It is true, however, that I did not expect the enemy would have dared to approach after so recent a defeat as that at Brandywine. In this Idea I did not direct any redoubts to be raised for the security of the camp or out-posts," Howe continued, "nor did I ever encourage the construction of them at the head of the line when in force, because works of that kind are apt to induce an opinion of inferiority, and my wish was, to support by every means the acknowledged superiority of the King's troops over the enemy, which I considered more peculiarly essential, where strength was not to be estimated by numbers, since the

27 Letter, Samuel Adams to Richard Henry Lee, 1 January 1778, *The Writings of Samuel Adams*, Harry Alonzo Cushing, ed., 4 vols. (New York, 1904), vol. 4, 1-2; Letter, Thomas Burke to Richard Caswell, 4 November 1777, *State Records of North Carolina*, Walter Clark, ed., 26 vols. (Raleigh, 1895), vol. 11, 668; Thomas Jefferson, *Writings*, Merrill D. Peterson, ed. (New York, 1984), 1318.

A surviving example of the Germantown medal Osborne had made for his men.

Yale University Art Gallery

enemy in that respect, by calling in the force of the country upon any emergency, must have superior." Howe concluded, "I confess also it was for the above reasons I did not change my position, after making the detachments before mentioned, choosing rather to trust to the well-tried vigiliance of the troops, and the activity of the patroles (though I had intimation that an attack might be made) than to give the army unnecessary fatigue, by making more cautionary preparations."[28]

It is not unreasonable to believe many British were embarrassed about being surprised by a ragtag American army they had defeated just three weeks earlier. American Col. Walter Stewart received a report from a civilian named Lucy Leonard who "heard the [British] officers say at dinner, twas the severest blow they had yet met with, twas plan'd with Judgement, executed with Spirit and they cant tell why we left it unless for want of Ammunition."[29]

28 *Narrative*, 27-28.

29 Letter, Walter Stewart to General Gates, October 12, 1777, 400. Jonathan Miller, Washington's deputy quartermaster general, also reported on the Leonard account thusly: "In my presence several British Officers who had returned from the Action of the 4th Instant Confessed that they had never met with so severe a Drubbing since the Battle of Bunkers Hill,

The Americans' halt at Cliveden was a gift for Howe. "The enemy was held up a long time by this fortunate decision," confessed Ensign Wilhelm Freyenhagen of the Hessian von Donop Regiment. "This gave the army time to get organized, meet all the attacks and send the necessary reinforcements there. General Washington, in spite of his overwhelming numbers, was beaten back." Captain von Muenchhausen of Howe's staff confirmed that "this maneuver [into the Chew house] by Colonel Musgrave was extremely helpful to our corps. This eased the situation [the collapse of the front]."[30]

A Tory civilian living in New York complained about the battles Howe was waging and dared to ask, "What are the Advantages gained by our victories? None. The Rebellion is more established, more general than ever. The Rebels have been made Soldiers by our lessons: they even attack the King's troops in battle-array, as was the case at *German-Town*. The minds of the people are more and more alienated," continued the Loyalist, "from the slowness of relief, or from being left at the mercy of the Rebels after having shewn their loyalty. There never was, even in the *army*, such general murmuring; such general complaints in every department. As to the military manoeuvres, there has been such a concentration of blunders, as no drill Serjeant would have been guilty of."[31]

While many British seemed reluctant to comment openly on the battle, the Hessians had no such apprehension. Even Friedrich von Muenchhausen, Howe's aide, voiced as much. "Everyone admits that Washington's attack was very well planned," he confessed. "He knew our exact positions through his very good spies. He was also aware that all regiments stood in one line in our camp, which by now was not quite as large, several detachments having been sent off. He was further aware that we could not send any regiments to places where he might attack without breaking our line." Jaeger officer Lt. Heinrich von Feilitzsch openly praised the American attack. "If the rebels had only moved forward and had not delayed, our oncoming regiments would not have had a chance to ready their arms; the plan of the rebels was very good," he concluded, "but its execution had flaws." The Anspach jaeger even criticized the British high command. "At our army, everything was in confusion, a few battalions of Hessians which were located

that the Attack was made with great Judgement & Supported with equal Bravery." Chase and Lengel, eds., *Papers*, vol. 11, 419.

30 "Journal of Freyenhagen," 68; Von Muenchhausen, *At Howe's Side*, 38.

31 *Historical Anecdotes Civil and Military: in a Series of Letters, Written from America, in the years 1777 and 1778, to different Persons in England* (London, 1779), 30.

behind the Jagers, did not even take up their weapons, they had been completely forgotten, under these circumstances, a bold enemy could do anything. It was previously known, that the enemy wanted to attack, the army had been informed," he chastised, "and still, those at headquarters were so lax—I don't know what to think of that!"[32]

Captain Johann Ewald, who was critical of British decision-making throughout the war, praised Lt. Col. Thomas Musgrave's defense of Cliveden, but bashed Howe's generalship. "This example of a single brave and intelligent man, through whom the entire English army was saved, shows what courage and decision in war can do," asserted the German. "For had the English army been defeated here, enclosed within the angle of two rivers with a large city of rebellious-minded inhabitants in the rear, all honor truly would have been lost, though it would have been destroyed solely through the negligence of the Commanding General." Few commented on the overall meaning of the battle as did Ewald, but many praised Musgrave. Sir George Osborne commanded the grenadier company of the Brigade of Guards during the campaign and became colonel of 40th Regiment of Foot (Musgrave's regiment) in 1786. Osborne was so proud of how the regiment performed at Germantown that he personally paid for a commemorative medal to be struck (bronze for the enlisted men and silver for the officers). It was one of the earliest examples of a British army decoration for valor, and predated the Victoria Cross.[33]

Contemporary Loyalist Newspapers

Several papers reprinted letters from officers about the fighting, and at least one provided its own report on the battle. The *Gaine's Mercury*, a Tory newspaper published in New York City, filed a report on November 10. "The rebels attempted, with all their force, in six columns, to penetrate on the outposts of our army . . . where they were so warmly received that they did not make the least impression for the space of two hours; at length being overpowered with numbers, and risking to be stranded if longer opposition was made, our two battalions thought it expedient to retire. These columns imagining victory was about to declare in their favor, two of them came into the village, while the third filed off

32 Von Muenchhausen, *At Howe's Side*, 39; Von Feilitzsch, *Journal*, 101.

33 Ewald, *Diary*, 96; McGuire, *Campaign*, vol. 2, 124.

obliquely to our left . . . but the rebels did not think proper to maintain that ground, retiring precipitately upon the approach of this small corps; and although we pursued for nine miles, till three in the afternoon, we were never able to come up with any considerable body."[34]

The View of History

Educator and military historian Donald Brownlow, one of the earliest writers to complete a documented history of the battle, outlined nine reasons for the American defeat. The plan of attack was too complicated, especially when considering the many fences and enclosures around Germantown that impeded the movement of formations. The morning fog, coupled with battle smoke, made communication between the various columns difficult (Casimir Pulaski's cavalry seems to have failed in that task). The Continental Army was not the professional force it became after Valley Forge, while its opponent was one of the best field armies in the world. The Chew house diversion played a prominent role, but Brownlow did not believe it was the most important one. He also claimed the British were superior in numbers (though this author does not agree with that assessment). In Brownlow's view, "the significant factor was the comparatively inexperienced officers and men facing the continual changes and problems with which they had little if any knowledge of how to cope with them." Brownlow did not analyze Washington's leadership at Germantown, but one of the more recent and better documented histories of the campaign by historian Thomas McGuire did exactly that. "Washington's attack at Germantown had been a surprise in many ways, and showed the possibilities of military success," argued McGuire. "Though it was a defeat for the Americans, it raised morale significantly in the Continental Army. The British had won the battle more by default than design, thanks to the heroic actions of Musgrave and a few others."[35]

Most histories of the battle are critical of Washington. English author and popular historian Christopher Hibbert was unimpressed by his attack, concluding that "even on a clear day Washington's intricate plan would have been difficult for inexperienced troops to execute." An early historian of the campaign named John Reed found Washington wanting. He "had never at any time, during the course of

34 Moore, ed., *Diary*, 504-506.

35 Brownlow, *Germantown*, 66-67; McGuire, *Campaign*, vol. 2, 124.

the fight, had central command of it, a weakness that hurt his chances." Though critical of Washington, Reed also believed the Continental Army was on the upswing: "The Americans had fought the British army to a standstill for more than five hours, and had come near to defeating it, and they knew it. For half a day the poorly-equipped American army had kept the issue in doubt. Only fog, the error in judgment in assaulting the Chew House, and Stephen's drunkenness had really defeated it. The near victory (although admittedly an American defeat), when coupled with Gates' defeat of Burgoyne, had loud repercussions in Europe." Professor and military historian Charles Royster thought Washington's mistakes would not have been forgiven so easily had he fought for the British. "Few generals could make errors like these and have them overlooked," he concluded. "The British general who opposed Washington got no such consideration in New York or in London. But unlike the comments on Howe in England," Royster added, "the criticism of Washington was private, not published or spoken formally."[36]

John Jackson, the author of several works on the Delaware River fighting, summarized his thoughts on the battle: "Contributing to the failure of Washington's strategy at Germantown was the inaccurate judgement of the distance each column was to travel, unfamiliarity with the roughness of the terrain, and American intelligence that failed to pinpoint the location and strength of the various British units." Alfred Lambdin, who wrote one of the first histories of the battle in 1877, would have agreed with Jackson. "To move an army in four detachments on such wide lines, over such a country and among such obstacles as were encountered at Germantown, without the means of constant communication, which should keep every part subject to the General's instant direction," insisted Lambdin, "was an enterprise that, according to our modern ideas, would not appear promising."[37]

Like Washington, William Howe has not passed into history unscathed. American military historian and professor Ira Gruber was critical of the British commander's leadership. "As Howe had not fortified his camp," concluded Gruber in his study *The Howe Brothers and the American Revolution*, "the rebel attack on October 4 might well have succeeded had not chance and a stubborn British officer interfered." Bicentennial writer John Pancake likely would have agreed with

36 Christopher Hibbert, *Redcoats and Rebels* (New York, 1990), 160; Reed, *Campaign*, 218, 236-237; Charles Royster, *A Revolutionary People at War: The Continental Army & American Character, 1775-1783* (Chapel Hill, NC, 1979), 179.

37 Jackson, *Delaware Bay*, 15; Lambdin, "Battle of Germantown," 398.

Gruber as to Howe's faults. "Though they had been surprised and driven, the redcoats did not panic. Their commanders formed them for a counterattack and delivered it with coolness and precision. The American army had developed neither the skill of command nor the steadiness under fire that could bring them to victory in the open field against an opponent nearly equal in strength to their own," Pancake wrote. "The Continentals could be counted on to win only when they had a clear tactical superiority of either numbers or position."[38]

Several historians explained the importance of the battle to the coming French alliance. Most students of the war attribute the alliance with France to Burgoyne's surrender at Saratoga—and they would be right. Historian Mark Urban argued, however, that Horatio Gates's victory wasn't possible without Washington's campaign for Philadelphia. "Howe's gamble, his hope for a decisive battle in front of Philadelphia, had failed spectacularly," concluded Urban. "Not only had he contributed to the surrender of 5,000 redcoats at Saratoga by taking himself off to Pennsylvania, but he failed to cripple Washington's corps of the Continental Army, a reality brought home by the battle of Germantown." Others, such as professor Harry Tinkcom, believed the fierceness of the fighting at Germantown, coupled with the British defeat at Saratoga, helped lead to the alliance. "But the determination with which the Americans attacked, and their conviction that they had been on the verge of winning," Tinkcom summarized, "did much for their morale and impressed the French government, which was contemplating an American alliance." In his book *A Leap in the Dark*, author John Ferling concluded that "Washington's bold stroke captured the imagination of the French government, and the American public, which heard only Washington's and Congress's disingenuous accounts of the fray, looked upon the engagement as a moral, and even an actual, victory."[39]

Final Analysis

In the weeks leading up to the battle, William Howe detached units to garrison various posts in his rear, which weakened that part of the army assembled at Germantown. When the American attack came, the defending force was but a

38 Gruber, *Howe Brothers*, 248; Pancake, *1777*, 197.

39 Mark Urban, *Fusiliers: The Sage of a British Redcoat Regiment in the American Revolution* (New York, 2007), 130; Weigley, ed., *Philadelphia*, 136-137; John Ferling, *A Leap in the Dark: The Struggle to Create the American Republic* (Oxford, 2003), 199-200.

shadow of that which had fought at Brandywine. Some of the army's elite units, especially the light infantry and grenadiers, were worn down and had suffered substantial casualties. Despite their weakened condition, Howe did not erect significant field fortifications to protect the Germantown camp.

The British high command was warned of the impending attack and had at least two hours to prepare to receive it. Unfortunately for the men on the front line, not all the units at Germantown were told that the enemy was approaching in the dark, including the outposts that would be hit first. The mental and physical fatigue brought about by months of campaigning had worn down the British leadership by October 4, 1777.

Once the engagement began, the light infantry experienced a complete breakdown of discipline and were overwhelmed by superior numbers and, at least early in the fighting, by better tactical management. Their conduct disgusted Howe, but the superior discipline within the British ranks proved decisive in the end, despite the shortcomings of Howe and the tactical surprise achieved by Washington.

Thomas Musgrave's decision to save his regiment by moving into Cliveden, rather than surrendering on the spot or fleeing with the rest of the British, proved fatal to Washington's attack. As they had done throughout the campaign, the Hessian jaegers performed admirably. Once the rally began, Generals Grant, Grey, and Agnew moved their brigades forward and pushed the Americans out of Germantown. Although he did not arrive in time to provide material assistance, Charles Cornwallis organized a relief force from the Philadelphia garrison and dashed toward the sounds of fighting.

Ten months earlier, George Washington had planned a surprise attack on Trenton. Three columns were supposed to cross the Delaware River at night, and then come together for an attack on the Hessian garrison. Only one column fulfilled its mission. The other two, composed of militia, never made it. Washington's audacious plan was successful even though it fell apart. Whatever he had learned from Trenton, by the time Brandywine was behind him, Washington firmly believed his army could undertake a much more complicated task. His command had spent the months before Germantown rebuilding itself and was semi-professional at best; much of it was still composed of mostly raw militia. Two of the four columns, which were slated to use four different roads in order to approach Germantown prior to the assault, were composed of militia. Perhaps the most surprising achievement that day was that all four columns arrived at their assigned destinations. Despite poor communication and the lackluster performance of Pulaski's horsemen, who failed to maintain contact between the four columns, they also arrived almost simultaneously.

John Sullivan's column performed well. He redeemed his reputation after the fiascos at Staten Island and Brandywine by arriving on time, opening the fighting with his assault on the British picket post at Mount Airy, and driving into the northern outskirts of Germantown before fog, confusion, and diminishing ammunition slowed him down. Sullivan's Maryland men proved their fighting qualities after their pitiful performance along the Brandywine. Anthony Wayne had performed admirably in a rear guard fight at Brandywine, but had been surprised and humiliated at Paoli. His Pennsylvanians were eager for revenge and proved themselves by driving through the British formations alongside the Marylanders. The same factors that slowed their Maryland counterparts after pushing into Germantown also stopped the advancing Pennsylvanians.

Although Nathanael Greene's column arrived slightly late, it drove south and southwest, overwhelmed the British light infantry units, and drove into the eastern fringes of Germantown. Once Greene's men overran the main British light infantry camp, a series of factors doomed the performance of the Virginians. The fog and battle smoke made communication and alignment between brigades and regiments impossible, large gaps in the formation opened, and confusion reigned. Adam Stephen issued orders to his own division, as well as to units under Peter Muhlenberg's command, and lost control of his troops. It was later determined that Stephen was intoxicated during the battle. The inexperience of many of Greene's officers, coupled with a limited line of sight on unfamiliar terrain, doomed their initial success.

Lord Stirling, commanding the army's reserve division, had a limited role. While his New Jersey brigade assaulted Cliveden, he played no part in that decision. Despite being in a supporting role at Cliveden, the North Carolinians lost their promising commander, Francis Nash. Stirling's men did what was asked of them, but did not distinguish themselves.

Most historians claim William Smallwood's militia column played little or no role at all in the battle, but contemporary documents, casualties, and pension records paint a different picture. Smallwood arrived with his men where he was ordered to be, and he engaged elements of the British Brigade of Guards and the Queen's Rangers. The Maryland and New Jersey militia may not have distinguished themselves, but they made a long and difficult night march, organized for battle, drove in the enemy pickets, and exchanged fire with their counterparts until the threat of a flank assault collapsed their line and sent the men rearward.

Of the four columns, John Armstrong's Pennsylvania militia turned in the least impressive performance. They made the night march, arrived as ordered on Ridge Road, and engaged the Hessian jaegers. After the early minutes of the fighting, however, their conduct for the rest of the day was worse than lackluster. Their effort to cross Wissahickon Creek was half-hearted at best, and no serious, organized attempt was made to punch through the jaegers in order to support Sullivan's right flank. Von Wurmb's jaegers admitted that maintaining their position was never in doubt. The show of force by James Irvine's militia brigade near Philadelphia was intended to prevent reinforcements from being sent to Germantown. The mission failed utterly and Cornwallis wasted no time rushing to his commander's aid.

Regardless of the performance and ability of the four columns, the responsibility for the defeat rested with George Washington. Once the American columns arrived and the British line was collapsing, the pivot point of the battle rested on the decision made at Cliveden to surround and assault Musgrave's men barricaded inside the Chew house. Washington's senior staff members, including Henry Knox, were not blessed with military training or genius. Rather than make his own intuitive decision, Washington held an impromptu council of war on the field. Knox insisted that the troops inside the house had to be neutralized before the drive south into Germantown could continue. It was a tactically flawed decision that tied up many hundreds of men and commands that otherwise would have pressed the attack and kept the British off balance. Washington's decision turned the initiative over to the enemy. Men like Timothy Pickering argued against the move, but Washington ordered the assault to stop while Lord Stirling's reserve division deployed to eliminate Musgrave's position. A much better tactic would have been to leave an exhausted regiment or two behind to keep Musgrave inside the house while the balance of the available men continued the attack. Stirling's fresh units may well have proven decisive in overwhelming the British camps deeper in Germantown. Instead, the men under Wayne and Sullivan at the front heard firing in their rear, believed they had been flanked, and reversed course. During the chaotic withdrawal, Americans fired into one another. The time wasted around Cliveden and the withdrawal of the two divisions in the middle of the American assault gave the British the time they needed to regroup and push back Hazen's exhausted and ammunition-starved division west of the Germantown Road, and to rout elements of Muhlenberg's command to the east of it.

The well-trained, veteran British troops pushed back the confused and inexperienced Continentals, regained the lost ground, freed Musgrave's men from Cliveden, and drove the Americans off the field. The rank-and-file Americans did their duty and performed heroically. Once again, choices made at the highest levels of command failed them. Just as poor intelligence had doomed the Americans at Brandywine, poor tactical decisions did the same at Germantown. Ultimately, George Washington failed the Continental Army; the army did not fail him.

Appendix A

Order of Battle

The Battle of Germantown

Continental Forces

Gen. George Washington, Commander in Chief

Right Wing: Maj. Gen. John Sullivan

3rd Pennsylvania Brigade: Brig. Gen. Thomas Conway
3rd Pennsylvania Regiment: Col. Thomas Craig
6th Pennsylvania Regiment: Lt. Col. Josiah Harmar
9th Pennsylvania Regiment: Maj. Francis Nichols
12th Pennsylvania Regiment: Col. William Cooke
Spencer's Additional Continental Regiment: Col. Oliver Spencer

3rd Division: Col. Moses Hazen[1]

1st Maryland Brigade: Col. John Stone[2](w)
1st Maryland Regiment: Col. John Stone
3rd Maryland Regiment: Lt. Col. Nathaniel Ramsey
7th Maryland Regiment: Col. John Gunby
Delaware Regiment: Col. David Hall (w)
5th Maryland Regiment (2 companies): Capt. Jesse Cosden

1 John Sullivan was tapped to command the right wing of the army, which left Moses Hazen as the highest-ranking officer with the Maryland division. He presumably commanded the division during the battle.

2 The brigade's regular commander, Brig. Gen. William Smallwood, had been detached to command the Maryland militia earlier in the campaign, and John Stone led it at Brandywine. He almost certainly remained in command of the brigade at Germantown.

2nd Maryland Brigade: Col. Thomas Price[3]
2nd Maryland Regiment: Col. Thomas Price
4th Maryland Regiment: Col. Josias Hall
6th Maryland Regiment: Lt. Col. Benjamin Ford
German Regiment: Col. Henry Arendt
2nd Canadian Regiment (Congress' Own) (2 battalions):
Col. Moses Hazen/commander unknown

4th Division: Brig. Gen. Anthony Wayne

1st Pennsylvania Brigade: Col. Thomas Hartley
1st Pennsylvania Regiment: Col. James Chambers
2nd Pennsylvania Regiment: Maj. William Williams (c)
7th Pennsylvania Regiment: Maj. Samuel Hay
10th Pennsylvania Regiment: Lt. Col. Adam Hubley
Hartley's Additional Continental Regiment: Lt. Col. Morgan Connor

2nd Pennsylvania Brigade: Col. Richard Humpton
4th Pennsylvania Regiment: Lt. Col. William Butler
5th Pennsylvania Regiment: Col. Francis Johnston
8th Pennsylvania Regiment: Col. Daniel Brodhead
11th Pennsylvania Regiment: Maj. Francis Mentges

Left Wing: Maj. Gen. Nathanael Greene

Connecticut Brigade: Brig. Gen. Alexander McDougall
2nd Connecticut Regiment: Col. Charles Webb
4th Connecticut Regiment: Col. John Durkee
5th Connecticut Regiment: Lt. Col. Matthew Mead[4]
7th Connecticut Regiment: Col. Henan Swift

3 With Moses Hazen in command of the division at Germantown, Thomas Price, as the next highest-ranking officer, would have led the brigade.

4 Col. Phillip Bradley was escorting a 100-man detachment of the brigade from the Hudson Highlands and would not join the army until after the battle. Jackson, *Fort Mifflin*, 29.

1st Division: Brig. Gen. Peter Muhlenberg[5]

1st Virginia Brigade: Col. William Russell[6]
1st Virginia Regiment: Col. James Hendricks
5th Virginia Regiment: Col. Josiah Parker
9th Virginia Regiment: Col. George Matthews (c)
13th Virginia Regiment: Col. William Russell

2nd Virginia Brigade: Brig. Gen. George Weedon
2nd Virginia Regiment: Col. Alexander Spottswood
6th Virginia Regiment: Lt. Col. Charles Simms
10th Virginia Regiment: Col. Edward Stevens
14th Virginia Regiment: Col. Charles Lewis
Pennsylvania State Regiment: Col. Walter Stewart

2nd Division: Maj. Gen. Adam Stephen

3rd Virginia Brigade: Col. Alexander McClanachan[7]
3rd Virginia Regiment: Col. Thomas Marshall
7th Virginia Regiment: Col. Alexander McClanachan
11th Virginia Regiment: Col. Christian Fehiger
15th Virginia Regiment: Col. David Mason

4th Virginia Brigade: Brig. Gen. Charles Scott
4th Virginia Regiment: Col. Robert Lawson
8th Virginia Regiment: Col. Abraham Bowman
12th Virginia Regiment: Col. James Wood
Grayson's Additional Continental Regiment: Col. William Grayson
Patton's Additional Continental Regiment: Col. John Patton

5 Nathanael Greene was in command of the left wing of the army, which left Peter Muhlenberg as the highest-ranking officer in the Virginia division. He presumably commanded the division during the battle.

6 With Peter Muhlenberg in command of the division at Germantown, William Russell, as the highest-ranking officer remaining, would have led the brigade.

7 Brig. Gen. William Woodford had been wounded at Brandywine and had not yet recovered in time to fight at Germantown. Alexander McClanachan was the highest-ranking remaining officer and led the brigade.

Corps de Reserve:
Maj. Gen. William Alexander (Lord Stirling)

New Jersey Brigade: Brig. Gen. William Maxwell
1st New Jersey Regiment: Col. Mathias Ogden
2nd New Jersey Regiment: Lt. Col. William De Hart
3rd New Jersey Regiment: Col. Elias Dayton
4th New Jersey Regiment: Lt. Col. David Rhea

North Carolina Brigade: Brig. Gen. Francis Nash (mw)
1st North Carolina Regiment: Col. Thomas Clark
2nd North Carolina Regiment: Col. Alexander Martin
3rd North Carolina Regiment: Col. Jethro Sumner
4th North Carolina Regiment: Lt. Col. James Thackston[8]
5th North Carolina Regiment: Col. Edward Buncombe (w & c)
6th North Carolina Regiment: Lt. Col. William Taylor
7th North Carolina Regiment: Col. James Hogun
8th North Carolina Regiment: Lt. Col. Samuel Lockhart
9th North Carolina Regiment: Col. John Williams

Smallwood's Militia Column:
Brig. Gen. William Smallwood

Maryland Militia: Col. Mordecai Gist[9]
Baltimore Battalion: Col. Darby Lux
Prince George Battalion: Col. Luke Marbury (c)
Montgomery Battalion: Col. John Murdock
Frederick Battalion: Col. Baker Johnson
Ann Arundel Battalion: Col. Thomas Dorsey
Queen Anne Battalion: commander unknown
Caroline Battalion: commander unknown
Kent Battalion: commander unknown

8 Col. Thomas Polk, the 4th North Carolina's regular commander, was overseeing the army's baggage train and guarding the hospital facility in Bethlehem, Pennsylvania.

9 Since Col. Gist was serving as Smallwood's deputy commander of the Maryland Militia, it is logical that he commanded the Maryland militia during the battle because Smallwood was responsible for both the Maryland and New Jersey militia in this column.

New Jersey Militia: Brig. Gen. David Forman
Forman's Additional Continental Regiment: Lt. Col. Thomas Henderson
1st Somerset Battalion (detachment): Cpt. Jacob Eyck
2nd Somerset Battalion (detachment): Col. Abraham Quick
2nd Hunterdon Battalion (detachment): commander unknown
3rd Hunterdon Battalion (detachment): commander unknown
4th Hunterdon Battalion (detachment): commander unknown
1st Monmouth Battalion: commander unknown
Middlesex Batttalion: commander unknown

Armstrong's Militia Column: Maj. Gen. John Armstrong

1st Pennsylvania Militia Brigade: Brig. Gen. James Potter[10]
Philadelphia County Regiment: Col. John Moor
Philadelphia County Regiment: Col. Benjamin McVeagh
Bucks County Regiment: Maj. John Folwell
Lancaster County Regiment: Col. James Watson
Berks County Regiment: Col. Daniel Hunter
York County Regiment: Lt. Col. John Ewing
Cumberland County Regiment: Col. James Dunlap
Philadelphia Light Horse: commander unknown
Philadelphia County Artillery: Col. Jehu Eyre[11]

Light Dragoons Brigade: Brig. Gen. Casimir Pulaski

1st Continental Light Dragoons: Col. Theodorick Bland
2nd Continental Light Dragoons: Col. Elisha Sheldon
3rd Continental Light Dragoons: Lt. Col. Francis Byrd
4th Continental Light Dragoons: Lt. Col. Anthony White
Corps of North Carolina Light Dragoons: commander unknown

10 Potter's brigade was accompanied by four light field pieces.

11 Two companies of the battalion were present at Germantown. The other companies were defending the Delaware River fortifications.

Artillery Brigade:
Brig. Gen. Henry Knox[12]

Proctor's Continental Artillery Regiment: Col. Thomas Proctor
Lamb's Continental Artillery Regiment (detached companies):
New York Battery: Capt. Sebastian Bauman
New Jersey Battery: Capt. John Dougherty
Continental Battery: Capt. James Lee
Continental Battery: Capt. Andrew Porter
Crane's Continental Artillery Regiment (detached companies):
Continental Battery: Capt. Thomas Randall (w & c)
New Jersey Battery: Capt. Thomas Clark
Pennsylvania Battery: Capt.-Lt. Gibbs Jones

Independent Detachment: 2nd Pennsylvania Militia Brigade:
Brig. Gen. James Irvine[13]

Philadelphia County Regiment: Lt. Col. Jonathan Smith
Chester County Regiment: Col. Evan Evans
Lancaster County Regiment: Col. Phillip Greenwalt
Lancaster County Regiment: Col. Alexander Lowrey
Northampton County Regiment: Lt. Col. Stephen Balliet
Berks County Regiment: Col. Daniel Udree

12 The artillery brigade did not operate as an independent command. The companies of the three regiments were distributed among various brigades of the army, and some remained as a general reserve under Henry Knox's direct control. However, the records do not indicate which specific batteries were assigned to which brigade or division at Germantown.

13 This brigade was not present with the army at Germantown. However, primary accounts indicate that American troops were operating on the south side of the Schuylkill River in order to serve as a distraction to the British garrison in Philadelphia. It is likely, therefore, that it was these troops who conducted the operation south of the Schuylkill.

Crown Forces

Gen. William Howe, Commander in Chief

Germantown Garrison

Picket Outposts:

Light Infantry Brigade:[14]
1st Battalion: Lt. Col. Robert Abercrombie
2nd Battalion: Maj. John Maitland

40th Regiment of Foot: Lt. Col. Thomas Musgrave
Queen's Rangers: Maj. James Wemys[15]

Right Wing: Maj. Gen. James Grant

1st Brigade:
4th Regiment of Foot (King's Own): Lt. Col. James Ogilive
28th Regiment of Foot: Lt. Col. Robert Prescott
49th Regiment of Foot: Lt. Col. Henry Calder

2nd Brigade:
5th Regiment of Foot (Shiners): Lt. Col. William Walcott (mw)
27th Regiment of Foot (Enniskillings): Lt. Col. John Maxwell
55th Regiment of Foot: Maj. Cornelius Cuyler

Guards: Brig. Gen. Edward Matthew
1st Battalion: Lt. Col. Henry Trelawny
2nd Battalion: Lt. Col. George Ogilvie

16th Light Dragoons (Queen's Own), 1 squadron

14 The 1st Light Infantry Battalion was composed of the following Regiments of Foot's light companies: 4th, 5th, 7th, 10th, 15th, 17th, 22nd, 23rd, 27th, 28th, 33rd, 35th, and 38th. The 2nd Light Infantry Battalion was composed of the following Regiments of Foot's light companies: 37th, 40th, 42nd, 43rd, 44th, 45th, 46th, 49th, 52nd, 54th, 55th, 57th, 63rd, 64th, and two companies from the 71st.

15 Maj. Wemys had been wounded at Brandywine, and it is unclear whether he remained in command at Germantown.

Left Wing: Lt. Gen. Wilhelm von Knyphausen

3rd British Brigade: Maj. Gen. Charles Grey
15th Regiment of Foot: Lt. Col. John Bird (k)
17th Regiment of Foot: Lt. Col. Charles Mawhood
44th Regiment of Foot: Maj. Henry Hope

4th Brigade: Brig. Gen. James Agnew (k)
33rd Regiment of Foot: Lt. Col. James Webster
37th Regiment of Foot: Maj. James Cousseau
46th Regiment of Foot: Lt. Col. Enoch Mankham
64th Regiment of Foot: unknown commander[16]

Hessian Jaegers:[17] Lt. Col. Ludwig von Wurmb

Hessian Brigade: Maj. Gen. Johann von Stirn (w)
Leib Regiment: Col. Friedrich von Wurmb
Von Donop Regiment: Lt. Col. Philip Heymell
Von Minnigerode Grenadier Battalion:
Lt. Col. Ludwig von Minnegerode

Philadelphia Garrison: Lt. Gen. Charles Cornwallis

British Grenadier Brigade:[18]
1st Battalion: Maj. Edward Mitchell[19]
2nd Battalion: Lt. Col. Henry Monckton

Hessian Grenadier Brigade: Col. Carl von Donop
Von Linsingen Battalion: Lt. Col. Christian von Linsing

16 Major Robert McLeroth had been severely wounded at Brandywine and it is unclear who held the field command of the regiment at Germantown.

17 Includes the Anspach-Bayreuth jaegers.

18 The 1st British Grenadier Battalion was composed of the following Regiments of Foot's grenadier companies: 4th, 5th, 7th, 10th, 15th, 17th, 22nd, 23rd, 27th, 28th, 33rd, 35th, and 38th. The 2nd Grenadier Battalion consisted of the following grenadier companies: two Royal Marine companies, and the following from Regiments of Foot—37th, 40th, 42nd, 43rd, 44th, 45th, 46th, 49th, 52nd, 54th, 55th, 57th, 63rd, 64th, and 71st.

19 Lt. Col. William Meadows had been severely wounded at Brandywine.

Lengerke Battalion: Lt. Col. George Lengerke

23rd Regiment of Foot (Royal Welch Fusiliers): Lt. Col. Benjamin Bernard[20]

16th Light Dragoons (Queen's Own), 2 squadrons

Artillery: Brig. Gen. Samuel Cleaveland[21]
2nd Battalion, New Jersey Volunteers: commander unknown[22]

Chester, PA Garrison:

10th Regiment of Foot (Springers):[23] Maj. John Vatass
42nd Regiment of Foot (Royal Highlanders):[24] Lt. Col. Thomas Stirling
71st Highlanders:[25] Lt. Col. Archibald Campbell

Wilmington, DE Garrison:

Von Mirbach Regiment:[26] Lt. Col. Justus von Schieck
Combined Regiment von Loos:[27] Col. Johann von Loos

20 This regiment was detached from the 1st British Brigade on October 3, 1777 to guard the Middle Ferry in Philadelphia.

21 While the army's heavy artillery was almost certainly with Gen. Cleaveland in Philadelphia at this point preparing to besiege Fort Mifflin, the various battalion pieces were still with their respective units in the field.

22 This Loyalist battalion was attached to the Royal Artillery during the campaign and presumably was stationed with the heavy artillery preparing for the bombardment of Fort Mifflin.

23 This regiment had been detached from the 2nd British Brigade on September 29, 1777 and was on duty at Chester, Pennsylvania.

24 This Regiment had been detached from the 3rd British Brigade on September 29 and was on duty at Chester.

25 The 71st Highlanders consisted of three battalions at Brandywine, but was consolidated into two battalions prior to being sent to Wilmington, Delaware.

26 The Von Mirbach Regiment had been detached from the army following the Battle of Brandywine and was on garrison duty at Wilmington.

27 The Combined Regiment von Loos was detached from the army after the Battle of Brandywine and was on garrison duty at Wilmington. The unit was composed of the remnants of the regiments that had been decimated at the Battle of Trenton on December 26, 1776.

Appendix B

The Court Martial of Adam Stephen

After the Battle of Germantown, four senior officers of the Continental Army faced court martials for their actions in the campaign.

Major General John Sullivan was charged with incompetency at Staten Island and Brandywine, but was acquitted and continued to lead independent operations for the rest of the war.

Brigadier General Anthony Wayne was charged with negligence at Paoli but was cleared of that charge by the court. He also continued in high command.

Brigadier General William Maxwell was charged with drunkenness at Brandywine and at the Battle of the Clouds. While Maxwell never held independent command again, he was acquitted of the charge.

The fourth officer, Maj. Gen. Adam Stephen, was charged with drunkenness at Germantown. General Washington issued the general order for an inquiry into the charges:

> The Court of enquiry, of which Genl Greene is president, is to sit . . . at the president's quarters, to enquire into the conduct of Major General Stephen, on the march from the Clove to Schuylkill-falls—in the action of the 11th of September last on the Brandywine—and more especially in the action of the 4th instant at and about Germantown, on which occasions he is charged with 'Acting unlike an officer'—Also into the charge against him, for 'Drunkenness, or drinking so much, as to act frequently in a manner, unworthy the character of an officer.'"[1]

The court of inquiry met on October 26 and determined there was enough evidence against Stephen to hold a full court martial hearing:

1 Chase and Lengel, eds., *Papers*, vol. 11, 605-606. "Acting unlike an officer" can be interpreted to mean not being with his own troops in the battle and interfering with other officers' commands.

The Court of enquiry having fully examined into the Charges exhibited against Major Genl Stephens, for Unofficer like behavour on the march from the Clove; In the actions at Brandywine and Germantown; Also for drunkenness. Beg leave to report the substance of the Evidences, as follows:

To the first charge there are several unquestionable Evidences of their being great confusion upon the march from the Clove to the Delaware, that General Stephen frequently contradicted by verbal orders his own written ones. He issued in orders that the first Brigade which got ready to march in the morning should march in front; this produced some altercation and great confusion. On this March the Genl was often seen intoxicated, which was generally supposed the cause of the confusion and disorder which pr[e]vailed. At Howels Ferry the General was seen in open view of all the soldiers very drunk taking snuff out of the Boxes of strumpets.

To these positive Evidences the General produced many positive ones of good repute, who say they were with the Troops on that march and neither saw the confusion aforementioned or the General in the least intoxicated with Liquor, although they saw him at the very places where he was said to be drunk. Most of his Family and several others who frequented his Table declare they have not seen the General intoxicated this Campaign.

The Evidences produced in support of the second Charge against the General in the Action of Brandywine and those he brought in justification of himself, all serve to prove the General did not pay that general attention to his Division which might be expected from an officer of his Command.

The Evidences produced in support of the third Charge respecting the Generals conduct in the Action of Germantown and those which the General brought in justification, all serve to prove that the General was not with his Division during the Action. The Evidences also prove their stand might have been made on the retreat at White Marsh Church, and that it was necessary to cover straglers which were coming in. General Stephens was the oldest Officer on the Ground to whom application was made by General Scott and others to have the Troops formed and to post some Artillery to check the Advances of the Enemy; But the General went off under pretence to reconoitre ordering off the Artillery at the same Time and left his Division behind; for want of this necessary Disposition tis supposed many Stragglers fell into the Enemys Hands.

The General produced many Evidences to prove he did not shrink from danger in the actions at Brandywine and Germantown, and that he always appeared cool and delivered his orders with deliberation and firmness becoming the dignity of an Officer and shew no uncommon fear of personal Danger.[2]

On November 3, 1777, just one month after Germantown, Stephen arrived at Maj. Gen. John Sullivan's headquarters for trial. The next two weeks were consumed with testimony, and the judgment of the court was announced on November 20, 1777, when Washington issued the following general order:

A General Court Martial of which Major General Sullivan was president, was held on the 3rd instant, and on divers other days, to the 17th instant inclusively, for the trial of Major General Stephen, charged with—"1st Unofficerlike behavior on the march from the Clove—2nd Unofficerlike behavior in the actions at Brandywine and Germantown—3rd. Drunkenness."

The Court declared their opinion and sentence as follows: "The Court having considered the charges against Major General Stephen, are of opinion, that he is guilty of unofficerlike behavior, in the retreat from Germantown, owing to inattention, or want of judgement; and that he has been frequently intoxicated since in the service, to the prejudice of good order and military discipline; contrary to the 5th article of the 18th Section of the articles of war—Therefore sentence him to be dismissed [from] the service—

The Court finds him not guilty of any other crimes he was charged with, and therefore acquit him, as to all others, except the two before mentioned."

The Commander in Chief approves the sentence.[3]

Adam Stephen was removed from the army and spent the rest of his life defending his actions, beginning with several letters over the next few months. Five days after the decision, Stephen wrote to Virginian Richard Henry Lee, a member of the Second Continental Congress who had authored the "Lee Resolution" in June 1776, calling for the colonies to separate from England. "You will See my dismission from the Continental Service," began Stephen,. "I do not sink in my own Esteem by it," he continued,

& when the proceedings of the Court are Seen I am firmly persuaded that I shall rise in the Esteem of my friends—I will have them published as soon as possible, & let the World Judge—It will appear that The greatest [unclear] could not prove me once drunk since I

2 Showman, McCarthy, and Cobb, eds., *Papers*, vol. 2, 188-189.

3 Frank E. Grizzard, Jr., and David R. Hoth, eds., *The Papers of George Washington: Revolutionary War Series*, 23 vols. (Charlottesville, VA, 2002), vol. 12, 327-328.

entered the Service—And it will appear that my Attention & Judgement in the Retreat from German Town [unclear] Saved a great part of the Army; after behaving wth bravery & Judgement in the Action . . .

You will please observe the Court has avoided calling that they had considered the Evidence—It will appear to the Considerate & Inquisitive that they have paid but little regard to the Evidence.

It was an unprecedented Court ordering an inquisition into my Conduct Since I Entered the Service—I would tell my view—freely & [unclear] to be in the way, & to do my self Justice shall be obliged to Expose the worship & [unclear] of a great many officers of Rank.[4]

Lee had been a supporter of Stephen since the French and Indian War, and Stephen surely hoped Lee's influence in Congress could get him reinstated. No reply from Lee has been found. Two weeks later, on December 6, Stephen appealed directly to the Second Continental Congress. Henry Laurens, whose son John served on Washington's staff, received the letter, which read as follows:

It has been my misfortune to become the Object of hatred of a Person of high Rank [Washington], for no other reason that I know, but for delivering my Sentiments on the Measures pursu'd this Campaign, with that Candour & Boldness which becomes an old officer of Experience, who had the Interest of America at heart.

By his Orders I have been tryd, after Serving thirteen Campaigns with reputation; for unofficerlike Behaviour on the march from the Clove to Sculkill, unofficerlike behavior in the Action of Brandywine, & unofficerlike behavior more particularly in the Battle of Germantown--& for Drunkeness.

It will appear by the proceedings of the Court that my Conduct in both Actions merited Applause instead of Censure; & by the testimony of My Aide de Camp and other Gentlemen more Conversant with me, that I have not been drunk since I enterd the Service of the States; & that I was Sober at the very hour & place where some mistaken people Swore I was drunk.

It will appear that I acted like an Officer of attention & Judgement on the retreat from german town and I have reason to believe that all the officers of Experience & Judgment

4 Letter, Adam Stephen to Richard Henry Lee, 25 November 1777, Lee Family Papers, Special Collections, University of Virginia Library, Charlottesville, VA.

on the Court were of that Opinion—The majority of the Court were officers of one or two Campaigns Standing: There were four Lt Colonels which is unprecedented in any Service.

Your Excellency will be pleasd to Observe that the General descends to No particular Charge, but that of Drunkenness; that instead of a Court Martial it was a Court of Inquisition, unparalleled in any Army to the Westward of Asia.

Without doubt the General did not Consider how dangerous it was to himself to Establish such a Precedent.

I have only to [unclear] the Honable The Congress of the United States, that although I am justly disgusted with the Malevolence of Certain Persons yet I am zealously Attachd to the American Cause & when to vindicate my Own Character I publish My Case to the World, I may be naturally led to Expose the Weakness & partiality of Some Commanders—yet I hope to be Acquitted of Any Intention of hurting the Interests of America—None of her Officers are willing to go further lengths to Save her.[5]

Stephen appealed to other powerful leaders in Virginia, including Robert Carter Nicholas, former treasurer of the colony in a December 15, 1777 letter:

If my Conduct has been such as to Sink me in my own Esteem, or in that of any person of Integrity & honour I would not have wrote you—I am Conscious that Since I enterd the Service I have Served the United States, as faithfully and Effectually as any officer in it of whatever rank or denomination; and as I intend to publish my Case as soon as I get it ready, the Public may Judge whether the Army of my Self, sustaind the greatest dishonor by my dismission—There had been a great Many faux pas Committed this Campaign—But I need to Convince the public that they are not with justice to be Charged on me, & that had my Sentiments been adopted, Matters in all probability would have been in a way more favourable for America.[6]

Stephen was right about one thing: There indeed "had been a great Many faux pas Committed this Campaign," especially at Germantown, but no other senior officer was court martialed for the October 4 battle. Captain John Marshall, who served in the 15th Virginia of Col. Alexander McClanachan's brigade in Stephen's division, thought the

5 Letter, Adam Stephen to Henry Laurens, December 6, 1777, Papers of the Continental Congress, National Archives, Washington, D.C., accessed on www.fold3.com.

6 Letter, Adam Stephen to Robert Carter Nicholas, December 15, 1777, Gratz Collection, Historical Society of Pennsylvania, Philadelphia.

matter important enough to observe that "no inquiries appear to have been made into the conduct of other general officers."[7]

One stunning example of a general whose questionable conduct did not lead to a formal inquiry was Thomas Conway, who would go on to lead the movement to remove Washington from command of the army during the Valley Forge encampment. "Genl Conway was charged with cowardice at the battle of German Town, and that a gentleman of rank and reputation, desir'd to be called upon as an evidence," confided John Laurens to his father on January 3, 1778. "It is notorious that he disobey'd his orders, and that he was for a considerable time separated from his brigade. The Gen'l [Washington], however, thinking that a public investigation of this matter set on foot by him, might be attribut'd to motives of personal resentment, suffer'd it to pass over."[8]

Washington and Stephen had a long history and had served together during the French and Indian War, but in an army known for widespread drinking, Washington allowed the inquiry and court martial against Stephen to grind ahead. Perhaps Washington, by dismissing a major general for actions many junior officers surely also committed, sought to use Stephen as an example to the rest of the army. "Genl. Stevens is dismissed with several inferior Officers by sentence of Court martial *approved* by Genl. Washington," wrote congressman James Lovell, "which looks a little like firmness and rising Discipline. Cowardice, Theft & Drunkeness must take warning." Massachusetts congressman Samuel Adams questioned the entire affair in a scathing letter to Richard Henry Lee wondering how the army came to lose Germantown, yet charged and dismissed only a single high-ranking officer in connection with the defeat. "We may avoid Factions and yet rid our Army of idle cowardly or drunken officers. HOW was Victory snatchd out of our Hands at German Town!" he demanded. "Was not this owing to the same Cause? And Why was only one General officer dischargd? Was it because there were just Grounds to suspect only one? Is there not Reason to fear that our Commander in Chief may one day suffer in his own Character by Means of these worthless Creatures? May he not suffer under the Reputation of an unfortunate Commander, than which I think he cannot suffer a greater Evil."[9]

Adam Stephen was one of only two general officers cashiered from the service during the entire war (the other being Charles Lee after the Battle of Monmouth). The court drew a distinction between Stephen's "want of judgement" and the allegation of drunkenness. The court found that he was "frequently intoxicated since in the service," but not *specifically* drunk at Germantown. The charge of failing to rally his troops is especially vague,

7 Marshall, *Life*, vol. 3, 184.

8 William G. Simms, ed., *The Army Correspondence of Colonel John Laurens in the Years 1777-8, Now First Printed from Original Letters Addressed to his Father, Henry Laurens, President of Congress, with a Memoir* (New York, 1867), 102-103.

9 Smith, et al., eds., *Letters*, vol. 8, 339; Letter, Samuel Adams to Richard Henry Lee, 1 January 1778.

considering the entire army was retreating in a disorderly manner. Why were other high ranking officers not brought up on the same charge? The court took care to reference Stephen's conduct over the four-month period from July through October 1777, meaning his overall behavior was the primary issue, not just his actions at Germantown. The court was unable to prove that Stephen was drunk at Germantown, but his excessive drinking during his service, it concluded, contributed "to the prejudice of good order and military discipline."[10]

It is interesting to note that Charles Lee, the only other general removed during the Revolution, also had a strained relationship with Washington and was eventully accused of avoiding his responsibilities and failing to rally his command. Lee and Stephen (as well as Timothy Pickering, the commander's own adjutant general) criticized Washington for relying on the wrong men for counsel—a charge that seems credible given the manner in which the ad hoc council of war in front of Cliveden took place. Both Stephen and Lee believed that young and ambitious officers misstated the facts against them during court proceedings in order to impress Washington. It is important to note, however, that initially Lee was only temporarily suspended from the service. It was his subsequent contemptuous letter to Congress concerning his commanding officer that tipped the scales and resulted in his dismissal. Stephen penned a similarly scathing letter to Congress, but it was delivered after he had been removed from the army. Only Congress had the power to reinstate either officer. By writing that letter, Stephen forfeited any chance he may have had for a fair hearing from Congress.[11]

The entire army was worn down after months of campaigning, and marched all night to arrive at Germantown at dawn and attack a veteran enemy. Stephen, like every other officer and man in the ranks, was exhausted even before the battle began. Evidence exists that some officers fell asleep on their horses. Washington issued rum to stimulate the men, and it was not unusual for American officers to be seen on occasion sipping from flasks before and during a battle.

Stephen's dismissal left his division leaderless. The Marquis de Lafayette was given command of Stephen's Virginians after he returned to the army on December 4, 1777 following the recovery of his Brandywine wound. Washington knew he needed to find a suitable command for the young talented Frenchman. Perhaps Stephen's actions on the field at Germantown offered Washington that opportunity.[12]

10 Ward, *Stephen*, 200-201.

11 Ibid., 202-203. For a recent and definitive examination of the Washington-Lee controversy, see Christian McBurney, *George Washington's Nemesis: The Outrageous Treason and Unfair Court-Martial of Major General Charles Lee during the Revolutionary War* (Savas Beatie, 2019).

12 Jackson, *British Army*, 44.

Appendix C

The Chew House after the War

Today, it is impossible to get any true sense of the landscape and obstacles encountered by the armies in 1777. The wide vistas battlefield enthusiasts enjoy at Antietam or Gettysburg no longer exist at Germantown. Contemporary houses present during the battle remain, but their large, sprawling properties have been swallowed by urban blight. Thankfully, the property with the most open space still in existence is the one that played the most important role in the battle: Cliveden.

When it looked as if the British fleet would sail up the Delaware River at the end of July 1777, members of the Continental Congress panicked and passed a resolution that recommended "to make prisoners such of the late crown & proprietary officers and other persons in and near this city as are disaffected or may be dangerous to the publick liberty and send them back into the country, there to be confined or enlarged upon parole as their characters & behavior may require." Two of the most prominent people subsequently arrested were Gov. John Penn, grandson of the founder of Pennsylvania, William Penn, and Chief Justice Benjamin Chew, a prominent Philadelphia lawyer and Quaker who owned the large stone home bearing his name in the village of Germantown. Chew, a brilliant legal scholar and jurist, had opposed many of the British actions before the Revolution, but had adamantly opposed independence, and as a Quaker was thoroughly against the war.[1]

As a result, Chew was not present during the battle because he was under "house arrest" near Trenton, New Jersey. He would have escaped his fate had he signed a loyalty oath to the colonial government. Instead, Chew and his servants lived at the home of a friend. While he was in exile, battle raged on the grounds of his country estate. As noted earlier, the house and grounds sustained significant damage. The picturesque cherry trees

1 Hazard, ed., *Pennsylvania Archives*, Series 1, vol. 5, 469.

lining the entrance were stripped of their bark and leaves, and dozens of fresh graves dotted the once-manicured yard around the house.[2]

Chew's prospects of returning to his estate were bleak. "I had, by the late Act, ten days allowed me after my return into this state to take the Test, under penalty of confiscation of my whole estate, and of being dealt with in every other respect as an enemy of the United States," he explained in a letter to an unknown recipient on July 15, 1778. "However great my sins may have been," Chew continued,

> I am now in a state of resignation with respect to temporal emoluments at least. The little property that is left me to subsist my family for some time to come, but taxes and the monstrous prices of every necessary of life, even with the strictest economy, afford a very gloomy prospect. A thousand reasons incline me to quit this city. I am looking out for a good farm in a healthy situation with tolerable house to accommodate so numerous a family as mine, and shall think myself happy if such a one can be found to lease or purchase. I would retire to Cliveden for a time if it was habitable. At present it is an absolute wreck, and materials are not to be had to keep out the weather.[3]

Because of ongoing friction with members of the Continental government, Chew decided it was best to sell his beloved country home. The property changed hands in 1779 when Chew sold it to Philadelphia merchant Blair McClenachan for $8,000. McClenachan owned the property for eight years before falling into financial troubles. Chew reacquired the property in 1797 for $25,000, and conducted additional repairs on the house.[4]

It took some time for Chew to regain his prominence in Philadelphia's social circles. He became close with several revolutionaries, including George Washington and John Adams, and although he did not attend the Constitutional Convention, he was extensively consulted because of his brilliant legal mind and background. Washington attended the wedding of one of Chew's daughters in May 1787, a social event that made it clear he was back among good graces. Chew died at his home at age 88 on January 20, 1810, and is buried in St. Peter's Churchyard in Philadelphia.

Cliveden remained in the family for the next five generations. During the next 150 years, "the estate dwindled from its sprawling acreage to its present six acres of park land." The Marquis de Lafayette visited the home in 1825 during his tour of the United States, and President William Howard Taft did so on the 135th anniversary of the battle in 1912. In

2 Martin, *Campaign*, 110-111.

3 Burton Alva Konkle, *Benjamin Chew, 1722-1810: Head of the Pennsylvania Judiciary System under Colony and Commonwealth* (Philadelphia, 1932), 191.

4 Martin, *Campaign*, 111; Cotter, Roberts, and Parrington, *Buried Past*, 349.

1972, the National Trust for Historic Preservation acquired the property, which still contains many Chew family furnishings.[5]

* * *

John Eager Howard, a major in the 4th Maryland Regiment, marched into battle on October 4 with Sullivan's Maryland Line, whose attack west of the Germantown Road surged past Cliveden before eventually falling back across the same ground later that morning. Howard was promoted to lieutenant colonel on March 11, 1778 and eventually served in the Southern colonies with distinction. The Confederation Congress awarded him a silver medal for his bravery at the Battle of Cowpens on January 17, 1781, and eight months later he was wounded by a bayonet at Eutaw Springs. Maj. Gen. Nathanael Greene, under whom he served in the Carolinas, boasted that "Colonel Howard is as good an officer as the world afforded, and deserves a statue of gold, no less than the Roman or Grecian heroes." Howard's lengthy account of the fighting at Germantown, penned in 1827, remains an invaluable primary source on the battle.[6]

Howard's connection to the estate resumed ten years after the battle when he married Peggy Chew on May 23, 1787—the same wedding Washington attended while serving as president of the Constitutional Convention. Howard visited his in-laws at the estate in 1797 after the Chew family reacquired Cliveden. He went on to become governor of Maryland, served as a United States senator, and was offered (but declined) the position of secretary of war in 1795. Much of Baltimore was built on land once owned by Howard.[7]

Battlefield Markers

Unfortunately, very little of the Germantown battlefield has been preserved. Most of what remains are small plots surrounding historic structures associated with the fighting. In 1906, a Battle of Germantown monument was erected in Vernon Park. The only other markers associated with the battle are twelve bronze tablets put up throughout the area in 1929 at the following locations: the 1768 Johnson House on the west side of Germantown Road south of Tulpehocken Street; the Wyck House; the grounds of the former Germantown High School; Market Square at the intersection of Church Lane and Wister Street; the intersection of Church Lane and Limekiln Pike; the intersection of Limekiln Pike and Haines Street; the intersection of Germantown Road and Mount Pleasant Avenue; the 1719 Church of the Brethren; the grounds of Cliveden; and the grounds of Upsala, across Germantown Road from Cliveden.

5 Cotter, Roberts, and Parrington, *Buried Past*, 348; Martin, *Campaign*, 111.

6 www.nps.gov/cowp/learn/historyculture/johneagerhoward.htm.

7 McGuire, *Germantown*, 93.

The 1906 Battle of Germantown Monument located in Vernon Park in Germantown. *Photo by author*

Bibliography

Manuscripts

American Philosophical Society, Philadelphia, PA

John Andre to his mother, letter, September 28, 1777, postscript dated October 8
James Hutchinson Papers
Narrative letter, probably by Lt. William Keough, adjutant of the 44th Regiment of Foot, dated September 28, 1777
William Scott "Memorandum on the Battle of Germantown"

Author's Collection

Letter, John Hang to unknown recipient, March 17, 1789 (scanned copy from private family collection)

Canadian Archives, Ottawa, Canada

Gilbert Purdy diary, Item MG23-B14

Chicago Historical Society, Chicago, IL

George Weedon letters

William L. Clements Library, University of Michigan, Ann Arbor, MI

Loftus Cliffe Papers
Germain Papers

Harlan Crow Library, Dallas, TX

Heinrich Von Feilitzsch, Journal of several Campaigns in America by Heinrich Earl Philipp von Feilitzsch Prussian Lieutenant of the Ansbach Feldjager. Manuscript journal

David Library of the American Revolution, Washington Crossing, PA

Sol Feinstone Collection
Horatio Gates Papers
William Irvine Papers within the Draper Manuscripts
William Livingston Papers
Parker Family Papers

Delaware Historical Society, Wilmington, DE

William Dansey letters

Duke University Library, Durham, NC

Ephraim Kirby Papers

Durham University, England

Grey Papers, Lord Cantelupe Diary

First City Troop Archives, Philadelphia, PA

Capt. J. H. C. Smith, "History of the 1st City Troop," based largely on the recollections of Trooper John Donaldson

Historical Society of Pennsylvania, Philadelphia, PA

Dreer Collection
Gratz Collection
John H. Hawkins Journal 1779-1782 [sic]. MS Am. 0765
Penn Family Papers
Robert Proud memoranda and letter copies, 1770-1811
Anthony Wayne Papers

Library of Congress, Washington, DC

Richard Fitzpatrick Papers
Peter Force Papers
George Washington Papers online

Maryland Historical Society, Baltimore, MD

Bayard Papers
Papers of Captain William Beatty of the Maryland Line
Mordecai Gist Papers
Letter, William Smallwood to Governor Johnson, September 23, 1777

Massachusetts Historical Society, Boston, MA

William Livingston Family Collection
Timothy Pickering Papers

Morristown National Historical Park, Morristown, NJ

Hessian Documents of the American Revolution

National Archives and Records Administration, Washington, DC

Papers of the Continental Congress (also available through www.fold3.com)
Ltrs Sent, J. Howell, Comm. Accounts, RG93
Revolutionary War Pension and Bounty-Land-Warrant Application Files (M804) [RWPF], Record Group 15, Records of the Veterans Administration

National Archives of Scotland, Edinburgh

James Grant Papers

National Library of Scotland, Edinburgh

Stuart Steven Papers

New York Historical Society, New York, NY

Gilder Lehrman Collection
John Miller Journal, Joseph Reed Papers

New York Public Library, New York, NY

Thomas Addis Emmet Collection

North Carolina Department of Archives and History, Raleigh, NC

Governor's Papers

Pennypacker Mills Archives, Schwenksville, PA

Letter, James Pennepacker to unknown recipient, 1 November 1874
Oral history recorded through Abraham Pennypacker on October 14, 1907
Waldie's Select Circulating Library, Furnishing the Best Popular Literature, Novels, Tales, Travels, Memoirs, Biography, &c. (1838 dated copy)

Public Records Office, London

Judge Advocate General Office: Court Martial Proceedings and Board of General Officers' Minutes, War Office. WO71/84/342-383

University of Delaware, Newark, DE

Nathanael Greene Papers

University of Virginia Library, Charlottesville, VA

Lee Family Papers, Special Collections

Virginia Historical Society, Richmond, VA

David Griffith Letters
Martin Pickett Letters

Windsor Castle, England

Archibald Robertson, manuscript map of "The Battle of Germantown." RCIN 734029.d.
King's Map Collection

Printed Original Sources

Anburey, Thomas. *Travels Through the Interior Parts of America.* North Charleston, SC: Createspace, 2017.

Anderson, Enoch. "Personal Recollections of Captain Enoch Anderson, an officer of the Delaware Regiments in the Revolutionary War." Henry Hobart, ed. *Historical and Biographical Papers of the Historical Society of Delaware*, vol. 2, No. 16 (1896), 3-61.

Andre, John. *Major Andre's Journal: Operations of the British Under Lieutenant Generals Sir William Howe and Sir Henry Clinton. June 1777 to November 1778. Recorded by Major John Andre, Adjutant General.* Tarrytown, NY; William Abbatt, 1930.

The Annual Register: or, a View of the History, Politics, and Literature, for the year 1777, 4th ed. London: J. Dodsley, 1777.

Ballagh, James Curtis, ed. *The Letters of Richard Henry Lee*, vol. 1, *1762-1778.* New York: The Macmillan Company, 1911.

Beatty, William. "Journal of Capt. William Beatty, 1776-1781." *Maryland Historical Magazine*, vol. 3, (1906), 104-119.

Biddle, Charles. *Autobiography of Charles Biddle, Vice-President of the Supreme Executive Council of Pennsylvania, 1745-1821.* Philadelphia, PA: E. Claxton, 1883.

Blaine, Ephraim. *"My Last Shift Betwixt Us & Death": The Ephraim Blaine Letterbook 1777-1778.* Joseph Lee Boyle, ed. Berwyn Heights, MD: Heritage Books, 2001.

Boudinot, Elias. *"Their Distress is almost intolerable:": The Elias Boudinot Letterbook 1777-1778.* Joseph Lee Boyle, ed. Westminster, MD: Heritage Books, 2008.

Browne, William H. *Archives of Maryland, Vol. 16, Journal and Correspondence of Safety/State Council 1777-1778.* Baltimore: Maryland Historical Society, 1897.

Burgoyne, Marie E., and Bruce E. Burgoyne, eds. *Journal of the Hesse-Cassel Jaeger Corps and Hans Konze's List of Jaeger Officers.* Westminster, MD: Heritage Books, Inc., 2008.

Burnett, Edmund C., ed., *Letters of Members of the Continental Congress, v*ol. 2. Washington, DC: Carnegie Institution of Washington, 1923.

Butterfield, L. H., ed. *Letters of Benjamin Rush.* Princeton, NJ: Princeton Univ. Press, 1951.

Carter, Dr. Henry Yates. Unpublished diary quote in Robert J. Hunter, "The Origin of the Philadelphia General Hospital." *The Pennsylvania Magazine of History and Biography*, vol. 57. (Philadelphia: The Pennsylvania Historical and Museum Commission, 1933), 32-57.

Chase, Philander D., and Frank E. Grizzard, Jr., eds. *The Papers of George Washington*, Revolutionary War Series, vols. 6 and 11. Charlottesville/London: Univ. Press of Virginia, 1994, 2001.

Chastellux, Marquis de. *Travels in North America in the Years 1780, 1781 and 1782 by the Marquis de Chastellux.* Trans. Howard C. Rice. Chapel Hill, NC: The Univ. of North Carolina Press, 1963.

Clark, Joseph. "Diary of Joseph Clark." *Proceedings of the New Jersey Historical Society* (1855), 93-116.

Clark, Walter, ed. *State Records of North Carolina*, vol. 11. Winston, NC: M.I. & J.C. Stewart, 1895.

Commager, Henry Steele, and Richard B. Morris, eds. *The Spirit of Seventy-six: The Story of the American Revolution as Told by its Participants.* Edison, NJ: Castle Books, 1967.

Conrad, Dennis M., Roger N. Parks, and Martha J. King, eds., *The Papers of General Nathanael Greene, vol. 10, 3 December 1781-6 April 1782.* Chapel Hill, NC: The Univ. of North Carolina Press, 1998.

"Contemporary Account of the Battle of Germantown." *Pennsylvania Magazine of History and Biography*, vol. 11. (Philadelphia: Historical Society of Pennsylvania, 1887), 330-332.

Continental Journal & Weekly Advertiser, November 21, 1777.

"Correspondence Between Hon. Henry Laurens and His Son John, 1777-80." *The South Carolina Historical and Genealogical Magazine.* vol. 6, no. 1. (January 1905), 3-12.

Cresswell, Nicholas. *The Journal of Nicholas Cresswell, 1774-1777.* New York: The Dial Press, 1928.

Cushing, Harry Alonzo, ed. *The Writings of Samuel Adams*, vol. 4. New York: G.P. Putnam's Sons, 1904.

Dann, John C., ed. *The Revolution Remembered: Eyewitness Accounts of the War for Independence.* Chicago: The Univ. of Chicago Press, 1980.

David, Ebenezer. *A Rhode Island Chaplain in the Revolution: Letters of Ebenezer David to Nicholas Brown 1775-1778.* Jeannette D. Black and William Greene Roelker, eds. Providence, RI: The Rhode Island Society of the Cincinnati, 1949.

Delaware Archives: Revolutionary War. Wilmington, DE: Charles Story Co., 1919.

de Pontgibaud, Chevalier. *A French Volunteer of the War of Independence.* Robert G. Douglas, ed. New York: D. Appleton and Company, 1898, 65.

Dohla, Johann Conrad. *A Hessian Diary of the American Revolution.* Bruce E. Burgoyne, trans. & ed. Norman, OK: Univ. of Oklahoma Press, 1990.

Drake, Francis S. *Life and Correspondence of Henry Knox, Major-General in the American Revolutionary Army.* Boston: Samuel G. Drake, 1873.

Drinker, Elizabeth. *The Diary of Elizabeth Drinker, vol. 1: 1758-1795.* Elaine Forman Crane, ed. Boston: Northeastern Univ. Press, 1991.

Ewald, Johann. *Diary of the American War: A Hessian Journal: Captain Johann Ewald.* Joseph P. Tustin, ed. and trans. New Haven, CT: Yale Univ. Press, 1979.

Ewing, George. "Journal of George Ewing, a Revolutionary Soldier, of Greenwich, New Jersey." *American Monthly Magazine*, vol. 38 (1911), 5-8, 50-53.

"Extract of a Letter from an English Officer serving with the Hessians in America, dated Philadelphia, Oct. 10, 1777," *London Chronicle*, Jan. 3-6, 1778. *Pennsylvania Magazine of History and Biography*, vol. 11. Philadelphia: Historical Society of Pennsylvania, 1887: 112-114.

Fisher, Daniel. "Extracts from the Diary of Daniel Fisher, 1755," *Pennsylvania Magazine of History and Biography*, vol. 17. Philadelphia: The Historical Society of Pennsylvania, 1893: 263-278.

Fisher, Sarah Logan. "A Diary of Trifling Occurrences." Nicholas B. Wainwright, ed. *Pennsylvania Magazine of History and Biography*, vol. 82. Philadelphia: The Historical Society of Pennsylvania, 1958: 411-465.

Fitzpatrick, John C., ed. *The Writings of George Washington from the Original Manuscript Sources 1745-1799.* Washington, DC: Government Printing Office, 1931-1933.

Ford, Worthington Chauncey, ed., *Journals of the Continental Congress 1774-1789.* Washington, D.C.: Government Printing Office, 1907.

Fortescue, John, ed. *The Correspondence of King George The Third: From 1760 to December 1783: Printed from the Original Papers in the Royal Archives at Windsor Castle.* London: Macmillan and Co., 1928.

Frazer, Persifor. *General Persifor Frazer: A Memoir Compiled Principally from His Own Papers by His Great-Grandson.* Philadelphia, n.p., 1907.

Freyenhagen, Wilhelm Johann Ernst. "The Journal of Ensign/Lt. Wilhelm Johann Ernst Freyenhagen Jr., 1776-78; Part 2: 1777-1778." Henry J. Retzer, trans., Donald M. Londahl-Smidt, ed. *The Hessians: Journal of the Johannes Schwalm Historical Association*, vol. 14. (2011).

Galloway, Joseph. *Letters to a Nobleman on the Conduct of the War in the Middle Colonies.* London: J. Wilkie, 1779.

Graydon, Alexander. *Memoirs of a Life, Chiefly Passed in Pennsylvania, within the Last Sixty Years.* Edinburgh: William Blackwood, 1822.

Greenman, Jeremiah. *Diary of a Common Soldier in the American Revolution 1775-1783.* Robert Bray and Paul Bushnell, eds. DeKalb, IL: Northern Illinois Univ. Press, 1978.

Grizzard, Frank, ed. *The Papers of George Washington, Revolutionary War Series.* Charlottesville and London: Univ. Press of Virginia, 1998.

Grizzard, Frank and David R. Hoth, eds., *The Papers of George Washington, Revolutionary War Series.* Charlottesville and London: Univ. Press of Virginia, 2002.

Hagist, Don N., comp. *British Soldiers American War: Voices of the American Revolution.* Yardley, PA: Westholme Publishing, 2012.

Hammond, Otis G., ed. *Letters and Papers of Major-General John Sullivan: Continental Army.* Concord, NH: New Hampshire Historical Society, 1930.

Harcourt, Edward W., ed. *The Harcourt Papers*, vol. 11. Oxford: James Parker and Co., n.d.

Hazard, Samuel, et. al., eds. *Pennsylvania Archives: Selected and Arranged from Original Documents in the Office of the Secretary of the Commonwealth.* Series 1. Harrisburg and Philadelphia, 1853.

Hazard, Samuel, ed. *The Register of Pennsylvania, Devoted to the Preservation of Facts and Documents, And Every Other Kind of Useful Information—Respecting the State of Pennsylvania, vol. 1, January to July 1828.* Philadelphia: W.F. Geddes, 1828.

Heinrichs, Johann. "Extracts From the Letter-Book of Captain Johann Heinrichs of the Hessian jaeger Corps, 1778-1780." *The Pennsylvania Magazine of History and Biography*, vol. 22. Julius F. Sachse, trans. Philadelphia: The Historical Society of Pennsylvania, 1898: 137-170.

Heyl, John K. "Trout Hall and Its Owner James Allen: Excerpts from Diary of James Allen." *Proceedings of the Lehigh County Historical Society*, vol. 24. Allentown, PA, 1862: 81-82.

Hill, Baylor. *A Gentleman of Fortune: The Diary of Baylor Hill, First Continental Light Dragoons, 1777-1781.* John T. Hayes, ed. Ft. Lauderdale, FL: Saddlebag Press, 1995.

Hiltzheimer, Jacob. *Extracts from the Diary of Jacob Hiltzheimer, of Philadelphia, 1765-1798.* Jacob Cox Parson, ed. Philadelphia: n.p., 1893.

Historical Anecdotes, Civil and Military: in a Series of Letters, Written from America, in the Years 1777 and 1778, to Different Persons in England; Containing Observations on the General Management of the War, and on the Conduct of our Principal Commander, in the Revolted Colonies, During that Perios. London: Printed for J. Bew, 1779.

Holmes, Asher. "Letter Concerning the Battle at Germantown, 1777." *Proceedings of the New Jersey Historical Society: A Magazine of History, Biography and Notes on Families*, vol. 7, no. 1. Newark, NJ: New Jersey Historical Society, January 1922: 34-35.

Howard, John. "Col. John Eager Howard's Account of the Battle of Germantown writing to Timothy Pickering in 1827." *Maryland Historical Magazine*, vol. 4. Baltimore: Maryland Historical Society, 1909: 314-320.

Hunter, Martin. *The Journal of Gen. Sir Martin Hunter and Some Letters of his Wife, Lady Hunter.* A. Hunter, ed. Edinburgh: Edinburgh Press, 1894.

Idzerda, Stanley J., et. al., eds. *Lafayette in the Age of the American Revolution: Selected Letters and Papers.* Ithaca, NY: Cornell Univ. Press, 1977.

Inman, George. "George Inman's Narrative of the American Revolution." *The Pennsylvania Magazine of History and Biography*, vol. 7. Philadelphia: Historical Society of Pennsylvania, 1883: 237-248.

———, ed. "List of Officers Killed Since the Commencement of the War 19th April 1775, Regiments Etc. and Officers of Marines Serving on Shore." *Pennsylvania Magazine of History and Biography*, vol. 27. Philadelphia: Historical Society of Pennsylvania, 1903: 176-205.

Jarvis, Stephen. *Stephen Jarvis: The King's Loyal Horseman, His Narrative 1775-1783.* John T. Hayes, ed. Fort Lauderdale, FL: Saddlebag Press, 1996.

Jefferson, Thomas. *Writings.* Merrill D. Peterson, ed. New York: Library of America, 1984.

Jordan, John W., ed. "Bethlehem During the Revolution: Extracts from the Diaries in the Moravian Archives at Bethlehem, Pennsylvania." *The Pennsylvania Magazine of History and Biography*, vol. 12. Philadelphia: The Historical Society of Pennsylvania, 1888: 385-406.

———, ed. "Bethlehem During the Revolution: Extracts from the Diaries in the Moravian Archives at Bethlehem, Pennsylvania." *The Pennsylvania Magazine of History and Biography*, vol. 13. Philadelphia: The Historical Society of Pennsylvania, 1889, 71-89.

Kalm, Peter. *Travels into North America*, vol. 2. Warrington: William Eyres, 1770.

Kemble, Stephen. *Journals of Lieut.-Col. Stephen Kemble, 1773-1789.* New York: New York Historical Society, 1883.

Lafayette, Marquise de. *Memoirs, Correspondence and Manuscripts of General Lafayette Published by his Family.* New York: Saunders and Otley Anne Street, 1837.

Lee, Henry. *Memoirs of the War in the Southern Department of the United States.* Philadelphia: Bradford and Inskeep, 1812.

Lee, Richard Henry. *The Letters of Richard Henry Lee*, vol. 1 *1762-1778.* New York: The Macmillan Company, 1911.

Lesser, Charles H., ed. *The Sinews of Independence: Monthly Strength Reports of the Continental Army.* Chicago: The Univ. of Chicago Press, 1976.

Linn, John B., and William H. Egle, eds. *Pennsylvania Archives.* Series 2. Harrisburg, PA, 1880.

Marshall, Christopher. *Passages from the Diary of Christopher Marshall, Kept in Philadelphia and Lancaster During the American Revolution.* William Duane, ed. Philadelphia: Hazard & Mitchell, 1839-1849.

Marshall, John. *The Life of George Washington, Commander in Chief of the American Forces, During the War Which Established the Independence of His Country, and First President of the United States*: Philadelphia: C.P. Wayne, 1804.

Martin, Joseph Plumb. *Private Yankee Doodle: Being a Narrative of Some of the Adventures, Dangers and Sufferings of a Revolutionary Soldier.* George E. Scheer, ed. Eastern National, 1962.

Massey, Samuel. "Journal of Captain Samuel Massey 1776-1778." John F. Reed, ed. *Bulletin of the Historical Society of Montgomery Countiry Pennsylvanvia*, vol. 20, no. 3. (Fall 1976), 205-251.

McDonald, Hugh. *A Teen-ager in the Revolution: Being the Recollections of a High-Spirited Boy Who Left his Tory Family at the Age of Fourteen and Joined the Continental Army*. Harrisburg, PA: Eastern Acorn Press, 1966.

McMichael, James. "Diary of Lieutenant James McMichael, of the Pennsylvania Line, 1776-1778." William P. McMichael, ed. *The Pennsylvania Magazine of History and Biography*, vol. 16. Philadelphia: The Historical Society of Pennsylvania, 1892: 129-159.

"Memoirs of Brigadier-General John Lacey, of Pennsylvania." *The Pennsylvania Magazine of History and Biography*, vol. 26. Philadelphia: The Historical Society of Pennsylvania, 1902: 101-111.

Miller, Lillian B., Sidney Hart, and Toby A. Appel, eds. *The Selected Papers of Charles Willson Peale and His Family, vol. 1, Charles Willson Peale: Artist in Revolutionary America, 1735-1791*. New Haven, CT: Yale Univ. Press, 1983.

Mitchell, S. Weir, ed. "Historical Notes of Dr. Benjamin Rush, 1777." *The Pennsylvania Magazine of History & Biography*, vol. 27. (Philadelphia: Historical Society of Pennsylvania, 1903), 129-150.

Monroe, James. *The Autobiography of James Monroe*. Stuart Gerry Brown, ed. Syracuse, NY: Syracuse Univ. Press, 1959.

Montgomery, Thomas Lynch, ed. *Pennsylvania Archives*, Series 5. Harrisburg, PA, 1906.

Montresor, John. "The Montresor Journals." G. D. Delaplaine, ed. *Collections of the New York Historical Society for the Year 1881* (1882).

Moore, Frank, ed. *Diary of the American Revolution: From Newspapers and Original Documents*, vol. 1. New York: C. Scribner, 1860.

Mordecai, Jacob. "Addenda to Watson's Annals of Philadelphia." *Pennsylvania Magazine of History and Biography*, vol. 98 Philadelphia: Historical Society of Pennsylvania, 1974, 131-70.

Morton, Robert. "The Diary of Robert Morton." *The Pennsylvania Magazine of History and Biography,* vol. 1 Philadelphia: The Historical Society of Pennsylvania, 1877, 1-39.

Muhlenberg, Henry Melchior. *The Journals of Henry Melchior Muhlenberg*. Trans. by Theodore G. Tappert and John W. Doberstein. Philadelphia: The Muhlenberg Press, 1958.

Nagle, Jacob. *The Nagle Journal: A Diary of the Life of Jacob Nagle, Sailor, from the year 1775 to 1841*. John C. Dann, ed. New York: Weidenfeld and Nicolson, 1988.

The Narrative of Lieut. Gen. Sir William Howe, in a Committee of the House of Commons, on the 29th of April, 1779, Relative to His Conduct, During His Late Command of the King's Troops in North America: to Which are Added, Some Observations Upon a Pamphlet, Entitled, Letter to a Nobleman. London: H. Bladwin, 1780.

New Jersey Gazette, January 7, 1778.

New York Packet, October 23, 1777.

New York Royal American Gazette, November 6, 1777.

North Carolina Gazette, October 31, 1777.

Paine, Thomas. "Military Operations near Philadelphia in the Campaign of 1777-8." *The Pennsylvania Magazine of History and Biography*, vol. 2. Philadelphia: The Historical Society of Pennsylvania, 1878, 283-296.

Paullin, Charles Oscar, ed. *Out-Letters of the Continental Marine Committee and Board of Admiralty: August, 1776-September, 1780*, vol. 1. New York: DeVinne Press, 1914.

Peebles, John. *John Peebles' American War: The Diary of a Scottish Grenadier, 1776-1782.* Ira D. Gruber, ed. Mechanicsburg, PA: Stackpole Books, 1998.

Pickering, Octavius. *The Life of Timothy Pickering.* Boston: Little, Brown and Company, 1867.

"Pickering, Timothy to Jared Sparks, August 23, 1826." *The North American Review*, vol. 23. Boston, 1826, 414-440.

Pickering, Timothy. "Col. Timothy Pickering's Account of the Battles of Brandywine and Germantown." *The Historical Magazine And Notes and Queries Concerning the Antiquities, History and Biography of America*, vol. 7. New York, 1863, 219-220.

"Pinckney, Charles Cotesworth, to Henry Johnson, November 14, 1820." *The Historical Magazine, Notes and Queries, Concerning the Antiquities, History and Biography of America*, vol. 10. Morrisania, NY, 202-204.

Public Papers of George Clinton, First Governor of New York, 1777-1795—1801-1804, vol. 2. New York: Wynkoop Hallenbeck Crawford Co., 1900.

Reed, William B. *Life and Correspondence of Joseph Reed, Military Secretary of Washington, at Cambridge; Adjutant-General of the Continental Army; Member of the Congress of the United States; and President of the Executive Council of the State of Pennsylvania*, vol. 1. Philadelphia: Lindsay and Blakiston, 1847.

Remembrancer; or, Impartial Repository of Public Events for the Year 1777. London: J. Almon, 1778.

"Revolutionary Service of Captain John Markland." *The Pennsylvania Magazine of History and Biography*, vol. 9. Philadelphia: The Historical Society of Pennsylvania, 1885, 102-111.

Robertson, Archibald. *Archibald Robertson, Lt. Gen. Royal Engineers: His Diaries and Sketches in America, 1762-1780.* Harry M. Lydenberg, ed. New York: New York Public Library, 1930.

Ryan, Dennis P., ed. *A Salute to Courage: The American Revolution as Seen Through Wartime Writings of Officers of the Continental Army and Navy.* New York: Columbia Univ. Press, 1979.

Shaw, Samuel. *The Journals of Major Samuel Shaw: The First American Consul at Canton.* Josiah Quincy, ed. Boston: William Crosby & H.P. Nichols, 1847.

Showman, Richard K., Robert M. McCarthy, and Margaret Cobb, eds. *The Papers of General Nathanael Greene*, vol. 2, January 1, 1777 - October 16, 1778. Chapel Hill, NC: Univ. of North Carolina Press, 1980.

Simcoe, John. *Simcoe's Military Journal: A History of the Operations of a Partisan Corps, Called the Queen's Rangers, Commanded by Lieut. Col. J. G. Simcoe, During the War of the American Revolution.* New York: Bartlett & Wellford, 1844.

Simms, William G., ed. *The Army Correspondence of Colonel John Laurens in the Years 1777-8 Now First Printed from Original Letters Addressed to his Father, Henry Laurens, President of Congress with a Memoir.* New York: The Bradford Club, 1867.

Smallwood, William to unknown recipient, letter, October 9, 1777. *The Pennsylvania Magazine of History and Biography*, vol. 1. Philadelphia: Historical Society of Pennsylvania, 1877, 401-402.

Smith, George. *A Universal Military Dictionary.* London: J. Millan, 1779.

Smith, Paul H., et. al., eds. *Letters of Delegates to Congress.* Washington, DC: Library of Congress, 1981.

Smith, Samuel. "The Papers of General Samuel Smith." *The Historical Magazine and Notes and Queries, Concerning the Antiquities, History and Biography of America*, vol. 7, 2nd series, no. 2 Morrisania, NY, February 1870, 81-92.

Stevens, Elisha. *Fragments of Memoranda Written by him in the War of the Revolution.* Meriden, CT: H. W. Lines, 1893.

Stewart, Walter to Gen. Gates, letter, October 12, 1777. *The Pennsylvania Magazine of History and Biography*, vol. 1. Philadelphia: The Historical Society of Pennsylvania, 1877, 400-401.

Stille, Charles J. *Major-General Anthony Wayne and the Pennsylvania Line in the Continental Army.* Philadelphia: J.B. Lippincott, 1893.

Stirke, Henry. "A British Officer's Revolutionary War Journal, 1776-1778." S. Sydney Bradford, ed. *Maryland Historical Magazine*, vol. 56. (1961), 150-175.

Stirn, Johann Daniel. "Diary Installment from Major General Johann Daniel Stirn." Henry Retzer and Donald Londahl-Smidt, eds. *Journal of the Johannes Schwalm Historical Association*, vol. 6, no. 2. (1998), 6-7.

Stockdale, John, ed. *The Parliamentary Register; or, History of the Proceedings and Debates of the House of Commons: Containing an Account of the most interesting Speeches and Motions; accurate Copies of the most remarkable Letters and Papers; of the most material Evidence, Petitions, &c laid before and offered to the House, During the Fifth Session of the Fourteenth Parliament of Great Britain*, vol. 10. London: Wilson and Co., 1802, 20-415.

Sullivan, Thomas. *From Redcoat to Rebel: The Thomas Sullivan Journal.* Joseph Lee Boyle, ed. Bowie, MD: Heritage Books, Inc., 1997.

Syrett, Harold C., ed. *The Papers of Alexander Hamilton.* New York: Columbia Univ. Press, 1961.

Talbot, Charles. "Letters of Charles Moile Talbot to Charles Talbot." Mrs. J. B. Friend and Elizabeth V. Gaines, eds. *The William and Mary Quarterly*, vol. 11. Williamsburg, VA, 1931, 315-318.

Talbot, Silas. *An Historical Sketch to the End of the Revolutionary War, of the Life of Silas Talbot, Esq. of the State of Rhode-Island, Lately Commander of the United States Frigate, the Constitution, and of an American Squadron in the West-Indies.* New York: G & R Waite, 1803.

Tallmadge, Benjamin. *Memoir of Col. Benjamin Tallmadge.* New York: Thomas Holman, 1858.

Taylor, Robert J., et. al., eds. *Papers of John Adams*, vol. 5. Cambridge, MA, 1983.

Tilghman, Tench. *Memoir of Lieut. Col. Tench Tilghman, Secretary and Aid to Washington, Together with an Appendix, Containing Revolutionary Journals and Letters, Hitherto Unpublished.* Albany, NY: J. Munsell, 1876.

Von Baurmeister, Carl. "Letters of Major Baurmeister During the Philadelphia Campaign, 1777-1778." *The Pennsylvania Magazine of History and Biography*, vol. 59. Philadelphia: The Historical Society of Pennsylvania, 1935, 392-409.

"Von Cochenhausen, Johann Ludwig, to Gen. Friedrich von Jungkenn, letter, October 9, 1777." Henry Retzer and Donald Londahl-Smidt, eds. *Journal of the Johannes Schwalm Historical Association*, vol. 6, no. 2 (1998), 1-6.

Von Donop, Carl. "Letters from a Hessian Mercenary (Colonel von Donop to the Prince of Prussia)." Hans Huth, ed. *The Pennsylvania Magazine of History and Biography*, vol. 62. Philadelphia: The Historical Society of Pennsylvania, 1938, 488-501.

Von Muenchhausen, Friedrich. *At General Howe's Side: 1776-1778: The Diary of General William Howe's aide de camp, Captain Friedrich von Muenchhausen.* Ernst Kipping, trans., and Samuel Steele Smith, ed. Monmouth Beach, NJ: Philip Freneau Press, 1974.

"Von Wurmb, Ludwig, to Gen. Friedrich von Jungkenn, letter, October 14, 1777." *Journal of the Johannes Schwalm Historical Association*, vol. 6, no. 2 (1998), 7-12.

Wallace, James, to Michael Wallace, letter, October 12, 1777. Horace Edwin Hayden, *Virginia Genealogies: A Genealogy of the Glassell Family of Scotland and Virginia, Also of the Families of Ball, Brown, Bryan, Conway, Daniel, Ewell, Holladay, Lewis, Littlepage, Moncure, Peyton, Robinson, Scott, Taylor, Wallace, and Others, of Virginia and Maryland.* Wilkes-Barre, PA: E.B. Yordy, 1891: 707-708.

Ward, Joseph, to James Bowdoin, letter, November 12, 1777. "The Bowdoin and Trumbull Papers." *Collections of the Massachusetts Historical Society*, 6th series, vol. 9. Boston: The Massachusetts Historical Society, 1897: 409-414.

Watson, John F. *Annals of Philadelphia and Pennsylvania, in the Olden Time; Being a Collection of Memoirs, Anecdotes, and Incidents of the City and its Inhabitants*, vol. 2. Philadelphia, PA: Parry and McMillan, 1855.

Watson,Winslow C., ed. *Men and Times of the Revolution; or, Memoirs of Elkannah Watson, Including Journals of Travels in Europe and America, From 1777 to 1842, with his Correspondence with Public Men and Reminiscences and Incidents of the Revolution.* New York: Dana and Company, 1856.

Watts, Henry Miller, ed. "A Memoir of General Henry Miller." *The Pennsylvania Magazine of History and Biography*, vol. 12. Philadelphia: The Historical Society of Pennsylvania, 1888: 425-431.

Wharton, Francis, ed. *Revolutionary Diplomatic Correspondence of the United States*, vol. 2. Washington, DC: Government Printing Office, 1889.

Whinyates, F.A., ed. *The Services of Lieut.-Colonel Francis Downman, R.A. in France, North America, and the West Indies, Between the Years 1758 and 1784.* Woolwich: Royal Artillery Institution, 1898.

Wilkin, Walter Harold. *Some British Soldiers in America.* London: Hugh Rees, Ltd., 1914.

Wilson, James Grant. "A Memorial of Colonel John Bayard." *Proceedings of the New Jersey Historical Society*, 2nd Series, vol. 5. Newark: The Daily Advertiser Officer, 1879: 141-160.

Wister, Sally. *Sally Wister's Journal: A True Narrative Being a Quaker Maiden's Account of her Experiences with Officers of the Continental Army, 1777-1778.* Albert Cook Myers, ed. Philadelphia, PA: Ferris & Leach, 1902.

Wortley, Mrs. E. Stuart, ed. *A Prime Minister and His Son: From the Correspondence of the Third Earl of Bute and Lt. General The Honourable Sir Charles Stuart, K.B.* London: John Murray, 1925.

Secondary Sources

Anderson, Fred. *Crucible of War: The Seven Years' War and the Fate of Empire in British North America, 1754-1766.* New York: Vintage Books, 2000.

Anderson, Isaac. "Historical Sketch of Charlestown Township." *Potter's American Monthly: Illustrated Magazine of History, Literature, Science and Art*, vols. 4-5 (1875), 26-31.

Anderson, Troyer Steele. *The Command of the Howe Brothers During the American Revolution.* New York and London: Oxford Univ. Press, 1936.

Bancroft, George. *History of the United States, From the Discovery of the American Continent.* Boston: Little, Brown, & Co., 1866.

Baule, Steven M. and Stephen Gilbert, *British Army Officers Who Served in the American Revolution 1775-1783.* Westminster, MD: Heritage Books, 2008.

Beattie, Daniel J. "The Adaptation of the British Army to Wilderness Warfare, 1755-1763." *Adapting to Conditions: War and Society in the Eighteenth Century*. Maarten Ultee, ed. Birmingham, AL: Univ. of Alabama Press, 1986.

Bertolet, Benjamin. "The Continental Army at Camp Pottsgrove." *Historical Sketches: A Collection of Papers Prepared for the Historical Society of Montgomery County Pennsylvania*, vol. 3. (1905), 9-43.

Bining, Arthur Cecil. *Pennsylvania Iron Manufacture in the Eighteenth Century*. Harrisburg, PA: Pennsylvania Historical Commission, 1938.

Bobrick, Benson. *Angel in the Whirlwind*. New York: Penguin Books, 1997.

Botta, Charles. *History of the War of the Independence of the United States of America*. George Alexander Otis, trans. Cooperstown, NY: H & E Phinney, 1845.

Bowler, R. Arthur. *Logistics and the Failure of the British Army in America 1775-1783*. Princeton, New Jersey: Princeton Univ. Press, 1975.

Brecht, Samuel Kriebel, ed., *The Genealogical Record of the Schwenkfelder Families*, vol. 2. Pennsburg, PA: Rand McNally & Co., 1923.

Brooks, Noah. *Henry Knox: A Soldier of the Revolution*. New York: G.P. Putnam's Sons, 1900.

Brownlow, Donald Grey. *A Documentary History of the Battle of Germantown*. Germantown, PA: The Germantown Historical Society, 1955

————. *A Documentary History of the Paoli "Massacre."* West Chester, PA: Horace F. Temple, Inc., 1952.

Chadwick, Bruce. *The First American Army: The Untold Story of George Washington and the Men Behind America's First Fight for Freedom*. Naperville, IL: Sourcebooks, Inc., 2005.

Chambers, Thomas A. *Memories of War: Visiting Battlegrounds and Bonefields in the Early American Republic*. Ithaca, NY: Cornell Univ. Press, 2012.

Chernow, Ron. *Washington: A Life*. New York: Penguin Press, 2010.

Cotter, John L., Daniel G. Roberts, and Michael Parrington. *The Buried Past: An Archaeological History of Philadelphia*. Philadelphia: Univ. of Pennsylvania Press, 1993.

Cox, Caroline. *A Proper Sense of Honor: Service and Sacrifice in George Washington's Army*. Chapel Hill, NC: The Univ. of North Carolina Press, 2004.

Curtis, Edward E. *The British Army in the American Revolution*. Gansevoort, NY: Corner House Historical Publications, 1998.

Dorwart, Jeffery M. *Fort Mifflin of Philadelphia: An Illustrated History*. Philadelphia: Univ. of Pennsylvania Press, 1998.

Edgar, Gregory T. *The Philadelphia Campaign*. Bowie, MD: Heritage Books, Inc., 1998.

Ferling, John. *A Leap in the Dark: The Struggle to Create the American Republic.* Oxford: Oxford Univ. Press, 2003.

————. *Struggle for a Continent: The Wars of Early America.* Arlington Heights, IL: Harlan Davidson, Inc., 1993.

Fischer, David Hackett. *Washington's Crossing.* Oxford: Oxford Univ. Press, 2004.

Flexner, James Thomas. *Washington: The Indispensable Man.* Bostin: Little, Brown and Company, 1969.

Ford, Worthington Chauncey. *British Officers Serving in the American Revolution, 1774-1783.* Brooklyn: Historical Print Club, 1897.

————. "Defences of Philadelphia in 1777." *The Pennsylvania Magazine of History and Biography*, vol. 18. Philadelphia: The Historical Society of Pennsylvania, 1894: 1-19.

Frantz, John B., and William Pencak, eds. *Beyond Philadelphia: The American Revolution in the Pennsylvania Hinterland.* University Park, PA: The Pennsylvania State Univ. Press, 1998.

Futhey, J. Smith, and Gilbert Cope. *History of Chester County Pennsylvania.* Philadelphia: Louis H. Everts, 1881.

Gillett, Mary C. *The Army Medical Department 1775-1818.* Honolulu, HI: Univ. Press of the Pacific, 2002.

Gordon, William. *The History of the Rise, Progress, and Establishment of the Independence of the United States of America: Including an Account of the Late War, and of the Thirteen Colonies, from Their Origin to that Period.* New York: Samuel Campbell, 1801.

Graham, Dan. "French Creek Continental Powder Works and Gun Manufactory Chester County, Pennsylvania." *The Local Historian* (Fall 2011), 1-7.

Gruber, Ira D. *The Howe Brothers & the American Revolution.* New York: Antheneum, 1972.

Hagist, Don N. *The Revolution's Last Men: The Soldiers Behind the Photographs.* Yardley, PA: Westholme, 2015.

Haller, Stephen E. *William Washington: Cavalryman of the Revolution.* Bowie, MD: Heritage Books, Inc., 2001.

Harris, Michael C. *Brandywine: A Military History of the Battle that Lost Philadelphia but Saved America, September 11, 1777.* El Dorado Hills, CA: Savas Beatie, 2014.

Hay, Denys. "The Denouement of General Howe's Campaign of 1777." *English Historical Review*, vol. 74. (1964), 498-512.

Heitman, Francis B. *Historical Register of Officers of the Continental Army During the War of the Revolution.* Baltimore: Clearfield Company, Inc., 2003.

Heston, Alfred M. "Red Bank: Defence of Fort Mercer." Paper read before the Monmouth County, (New Jersey) Historical Association July 26, 1900.

Heyl, Francis. *The Battle of Germantown.* Philadelphia: The City Historical Society of Philadelphia, 1908.

Hibbert, Christopher. *Redcoats and Rebels.* New York: W.W. Norton & Company, 1990.

Jackson, John W. *The Delaware Bay and River Defenses of Philadelphia 1775-1777.* Philadelphia: Philadelphia Maritime Museum, 1977.

————. *Fort Mifflin: Valiant Defender of the Delaware.* Norristown, PA: James & Sons, 1986.

————. *The Pennsylvania Navy, 1775-1781: The Defense of the Delaware.* New Brunswick, NJ: Rutgers Univ. Press, 1974.

————. *With the British Army in Philadelphia.* San Rafael, CA: Presidio Press, 1979.

Katcher, Philip R. N. *Encyclopedia of British, Provincial, and German Army Units 1775-1783.* Harrisburg, PA: Stackpole Books, 1973.

Ketchum, Richard M. *Saratoga: Turning Point of America's Revolutionary War.* New York: Henry Holt and Company, 1997.

Kidder, William L. *Crossroads of the Revolution: Trenton 1774-1783.* Lawrence Township, NJ: Knox Press, 2017.

Knouff, Gregory T. *The Soldiers' Revolution: Pennsylvanians in Arms and the Forging of Early American Identity.* Univ. Park, PA: Pennsylvania State Univ. Press, 2004.

Konkle, Burton Alva. *Benjamin Chew 1722-1810: Head of the Pennsylvania Judiciary System under Colony and Commonwealth.* Philadelphia: University of Pennsylvania Press, 1932.

Lambdin, Alfred C. "Battle of Germantown." *The Pennsylvania Magazine of History and Biography*, vol. 1. Philadelphia: The Historical Society of Pennsylvania, 1877: 368-403.

Leach, Douglas Edward. *Roots of Conflict: British Armed Forces and Colonial Americans, 1677-1763.* Chapel Hill, NC: The Univ. of North Carolina Press, 1986.

Lefkowitz, Arthur S. *George Washington's Indispensable Men: The 32 Aides-de-Camp Who Helped Win American Independence.* Mechanicsburg, PA: Stackpole Books, 2003.

————. *The Long Retreat: The Calamitous American Defense of New Jersey 1776.* New Brunswick: Rutgers Univ. Press, 1999.

Lender, Mark Edward and Garry Wheeler Stone. *Fatal Sunday: George Washington, the Monmouth Campaign, and the Politics of Battle.* Norman, OK: Univ. of Oklahoma Press, 2016.

Lengel, Edward. *General George Washington: A Military Life.* NY: Random House, 2005.

————. *Inventing George Washington: America's Founder, in Myth & Memory.* New York: Harper, 2011.

Lossing, Benjamin J. *The Pictorial Field-Book of the American Revolution.* New York: Harper and Brothers, 1852.

Lowell, Edward J. *The Hessians and the Other German Auxiliaries of Great Britain in the Revolutionary War.* Gansevoort, NY: Corner House Historical Publications, 1997.

Luzader, John F. *Saratoga: A Military History of the Decisive Campaign of the American Revolution.* El Dorado Hills: Savas Beatie, 2008.

Mackesy, Piers. *The War for America: 1775-1783.* Lincoln: Univ. of Nebraska Press, 1964.

Mahon, John K. "Anglo-American Methods of Indian Warfare, 1676-1794." LW524: Student Reading Package, APUS Faculty, Fall 2009. Charles Town, WV: National Archive Publishing Company, 2009.

Mahon, Lord. *History of England from the Peace of Utrecht to the Peace of Versailles: 1713-1783*, vol. 6. London: J. Murray, 1858.

Martin, David G. *The Philadelphia Campaign: June 1777-July 1778.* Conshohocken, PA: Combined Books, Inc., 1993.

Martin, James Kirby, and Mark Edward Lender. *"A Respectable Army": The Military Origins of the Republic, 1763-1789.* West Sussex, United Kingdom: Wiley-Blackwell, 2015.

Mayer, Holly A. *Belonging to the Army: Camp Followers and Community during the American Revolution.* Columbia, SC: Univ. of South Carolina Press, 1996.

McGuire, Thomas J. *Battle of Paoli.* Mechanicsburg, PA: Stackpole Books, 2000.

————. *The Philadelphia Campaign: Brandywine and the Fall of Philadelphia.* Mechanicsburg, PA: Stackpole Books, 2007.

————. *The Philadelphia Campaign: Germantown and the Roads to Valley Forge.* Mechanicsburg, PA: Stackpole Books, 2007.

————. *The Surprise of Germantown October 4th, 1777.* Gettysburg, PA: Thomas Publications, 1994.

Miller, John C. *Triumph of Freedom 1775-1783.* Boston: Little, Brown, 1948.

Myers, Richmond E. *Northampton County in the American Revolution.* Easton, PA: Northampton County Historical Society, 1976.

Nagy, John A. *Rebellion in the Ranks: Mutinies of the American Revolution.* Yardley, PA: Westholme Publishing, 2008.

————. *Spies in the Continental Capital: Espionage Across Pennsylvania During the American Revolution.* Yardley, PA: Westholme Publishing, 2011.

Neff, Jacob. *The Army and Navy of America: Containing a View of the Heroic Adventures, Battles, Naval Engagements, Remarkable Incidents, and Glorious Achievements in the Cause of Freedom.* Philadelphia: J.H. Pearsol & Co., 1845.

Newland, Samuel J. *The Pennsylvania Militia: The Early Years, 1669-1792.* Annville, PA: Commonwealth of Pennsylvania, Department of Military and Veterans Affairs, 1997.

O'Donnell, Patrick K. *Washington's Immortals: The Untold Story of an Elite Regiment Who Changed the Course of the Revolution*. New York: Atlantic Monthly Press, 2016.

Ousterhout, Anne M. *The Most Learned Woman in America: A Life of Elizabeth Graeme Fergusson*. Univ. Park, PA: Penn State Univ. Press, 2004.

Pancake, John S. *1777: The Year of the Hangman*. Tuscaloosa, AL: U. of Alabama Press, 1977.

"A Partial List of Pennsylvania Troops Killed, Wounded, and Captured at the Battle of Germantown." *The Pennsylvania Magazine of History and Biography*, vol. 40. Philadelphia: The Historical Society of Pennsylvania, 1916, 241-243.

Peckham, Howard. *The Colonial War: 1689-1762*. Chicago: Univ. of Chicago Press, 1964.

———, ed. *The Toll of Independence: Engagements & Battle Casualties of the American Revolution*. Chicago: The Univ. of Chicago Press, 1974.

Pennypacker, Samuel Whitaker. *Annals of Phoenixville and its Vicinity: From the Settlement to the Year 1871, Giving the Origin and Growth of the Borough, with Information Concerning the Adjacent Townships of Chester and Montgomery Counties and the Valley of the Schuylkill*. Philadelphia: Bavis & Pennypacker, 1872.

———. *Pennypacker's Mills in Story and Song: With the Incident of the Settlement, The French and Indian War, and the Encampment of Washington's Army September 26th to October 8th, 1777, Before and after the Battle of Germantown*. Norritstown, PA: Historical Soc. of Montgomery Co, 1902.

Phillips, Edward B. Essay in *150th Anniversary of The Battle of Germantown: October 1st to 4th, 1927*. Germantown, PA: Fleu & Fetterolf, 1927.

Rankin, Hugh F. *The North Carolina Continentals*. Chapel Hill, NC: The Univ. of North Carolina Press, 1971.

Reed, John F. *Campaign to Valley Forge: July 1, 1777-December 19, 1777*. Phila: Pioneer Press, 1965.

Resch, John, and Walter Sargent, eds. *War & Society in the American Revolution: Mobilization and Home Fronts*. DeKalb, IL: Northern Illinois Univ. Press, 2007.

Risch, Erna. *Supplying Washington's Army*. Washington, DC: Center of Military History, 1981.

Rosswurm, Steven. *Arms, Country, and Class: The Philadelphia Militia and the "Lower Sort" during the American Revolution*. New Brunswick, NJ: Rutgers Univ. Press, 1989.

Royster, Charles. *A Revolutionary People at War: The Continental Army & American Character, 1775-1783*. Chapel Hill: The Univ. of North Carolina Press, 1979.

Russell, Peter E. "Redcoats in the Wilderness: British Officers and Irregular Warfare in Europe and America, 1740-1760." LW524: Student Reading Package, APUS Faculty, Fall 2009. Charles Town, WV: National Archive Publishing Company, 2009.

Scharf, J. Thomas. *The Chronicles of Baltimore; Being a Complete History of "Baltimore Town" and Baltimore City from the Earliest Period to the Present Time.* Baltimore: Turnbull Brothers, 1874.

Scheer, George F., and Hugh F. Rankin. *Rebels & Redcoats: The American Revolution Through the Eyes of Those Who Fought and Lived It.* New York: Da Capo Press, 1957.

Smith, Robert F. *Manufacturing Independence: Industrial Innovation in the American Revolution.* Yardley, PA: Westholme Publishing, 2016.

Smith, Samuel S. *Fight for the Delaware 1777.* Monmouth, NJ: Philip Freneau Press, 1970.

Spring, Matthew H. *With Zeal and With Bayonets Only: The British Army on Campaign in North America, 1775-1783.* Norman, OK: Univ. of Oklahoma Press, 2008.

Steele, Ian K. *Warpaths: Invasions of North America.* New York: Oxford Univ. Press, 1994.

Sullivan, Aaron. *The Disaffected: Britain's Occupation of Philadelphia During the American Revolution.* Philadelphia: Univ. of Pennsylvania Press, 2019.

Trevelyan, George Otto. *The American Revolution*, vol. 4. New York: Longmans, Green, and Company, 1912.

Trussell, John B. B. *The Pennsylvania Line.* Harrisburg, PA: Commonwealth of Pennsylvania, Historical and Museum Commission, 1993.

Urban, Mark. *Fusiliers: The Saga of a British Redcoat Regiment in the American Revolution.* New York: Walker and Company, 2007.

Ward, Christopher. *The War of the Revolution.* 2 vols. New York: Macmillan Company, 1952.

Ward, Harry M. *General William Maxwell and the New Jersey Continentals.* Westport, CT: Praeger, 1997.

————. *Major General Adam Stephen and the Cause of American Liberty.* Charlottesville, VA: Univ. of Virginia Press, 1989.

Ward, Townsend. "The Germantown Road and Its Associations." *The Pennsylvania Magazine of History and Biography*, vol. 5. Philadelphia: Historical Society of Pennsylvania, 1881, 241-258.

Weaver, Ethan Allen, ed. *Annual Proceedings, Pennsylvania Society of Sons of the Revolution, 1907-1908.* Philadelphia: Pennsylvania Society of Sons of the Revolution, 1908.

Weigley, Russell F., ed. *Philadelphia: A 300-Year History.* New York: Barra Foundation, 1982.

Wood, W. J. *Battles of the Revolutionary War: 1775-1781.* Cambridge, MA: Da Capo Press, 1990.

Wright, Robert K., Jr. *The Continental Army.* Washington, DC: Government Printing Office, 1983.

Index

About the Author

Michael C. Harris is a graduate of the University of Mary Washington and the American Military University. He has worked for the National Park Service in Fredericksburg, Virginia, Fort Mott State Park in New Jersey, and the Pennsylvania Historical and Museum Commission at Brandywine Battlefield. Mike conducts tours and staff rides of many east coast battlefields and enjoys speaking with audiences about all things military, and especially about the American Revolution and Civil War. Mike is certified in secondary education and currently teaches in the Philadelphia region. He lives in Pennsylvania with his wife Michelle and son Nathanael.

His first book, *Brandywine: A Military History of the Battle that Lost Philadelphia but Saved America, September 11, 1777*, was awarded the American Revolution Round Table of Richmond Book Award (2015) and was a Finalist for the Army Historical Foundation Distinguished Book Award.